Breaking Barriers

The Unfinished Story of Women Lawyers and Judges in Massachusetts

PATTI B. SARIS
MARGOT BOTSFORD
BARBARA F. BERENSON
EDITORS

MCLE
LEGAL
HERITAGE
Series

Printed in the United States of America

This publication should be cited: *Breaking Barriers: The Unfinished Story of Women Lawyers and Judges in Massachusetts* (MCLE, Inc. 2012)

Library of Congress Card Number: 2012938660

ISBN: 1-57589-719-9

Massachusetts Continuing Legal Education, Inc.
Ten Winter Place, Boston, MA 02108-4751
800-966-6253 | Fax 617-482-9498 | www.mcle.org

Contents

Acknowledgments

Breaking Barriers: The Unfinished Story of Women Lawyers and Judges in Massachusetts is part of Massachusetts Continuing Legal Education's (MCLE | New England) Legal Heritage Series. Its proceeds will benefit MCLE | New England's Pro Bono Scholarship Fund and its publication would not have been possible without the work of many dedicated volunteers.

First and foremost, MCLE extends its sincere appreciation and thanks to the book's coeditors: the Honorable Patti B. Saris, the Honorable Margot Botsford, and Barbara F. Berenson. We thank them for the many hours they have spent brainstorming the book's content, reaching out to and working with contributors, and reviewing and writing content. This expansive publication would not have been possible without their long-term commitment and dedication.

Second, we express special thanks to the book's large roster of contributors. These talented lawyers, judges, and academics have shared their vast knowledge and personal stories to create a wide-ranging and heartfelt presentation of the women in Massachusetts' legal community from 1882 to the present. While there are many more worthwhile women in the legal profession than could possibly be chronicled within the confines of a one-volume publication, we hope that we have presented a well-rounded account.

Thanks also go to Elizabeth A. Brown and Therese M. Rohrbeck for their considerable efforts in preparing and conducting many of the interviews that appear in this book. We also express our gratitude to Julia Huston for her extensive assistance in the development of Chapter 5, to Meredith L. Ainbinder for her work in soliciting and gathering the quotes from women lawyers in private practice appearing in Chapter 5, to Maura S. Doyle for compiling the data on women admitted to the bar in the 1940s and 1950s, and to David J. Seipp for his guidance and assistance particularly with respect to Boston University's role in the history of Massachusetts women lawyers.

Additionally, we extend our appreciation to the American Bar Association's Senior Lawyers Division and Commission on Women in the Profession for permitting us to adapt their Oral History Project interviews of the Honorable Ruth I. Abrams, Tamar Frankel, and the Honorable Rya W. Zobel for this book. Similarly, we thank the John F. Kennedy Presidential Museum and Library for permitting us to adapt portions of the transcript of their forum with the Honorable Margaret H. Marshall and Stefanie T. Silverman for permitting us to use portions of her interview with the Honorable Raya S. Dreben, which she conducted for a course on American Jewish women while a student at Brandeis University.

We also acknowledge the following Boston-area courts and institutions that permitted us to use images from their archives and media collections: U.S. District Court for the District of Massachusetts, Massachusetts Supreme Judicial Court, Massachusetts Appeals Court, Boston College Law School, Boston Public Library Print Department, Boston University School of Law, Harvard Law School and the Arthur and Elizabeth Schlesinger Library on the History of Women in America at Radcliffe, New England Law | Boston, Northeastern University School of Law, and Suffolk University Law School.

Moreover, we are grateful to the following individuals who provided assistance during various stages of the book's development: Joyce Hurley, Joan Kenney, Tina LaFranchi, Marie C. Losco, Dove Neal, Sarah Allison Thornton, and Pauline Quirion.

A number of undergraduate students and law students also provided valuable research and writing assistance: Courtney Caruso, Meghan Gowan, Melissa Nasson, Joanna Ray, Maureen Sarna, Michelle Brady Sisco, Haylee Trahan-Liptak, and the following University of Massachusetts Boston students under the direction of J. Shoshanna Ehrlich: Stephanie A. Bonvissuto, Farrah Bruny, Georgia L. Buckley, Stefanie M. Carey, Andrea Chiarenza, Gretchen L. Coffey, Maria Dixon, Katora E. Gaines, Sheena Goldhagen, Cheyanne Aura Gracia, Dominique Marie Jaeger, Alexandra B. Janis, Marie-Krantz Elisabeth Mars, Gaelen James McGrail, Nathan Miller-Foster, Genti Rapi, Amanda Shea, Debora Clementino Silva, Christina Rose Spinelli, Julie Hyeeun Yu, and Sarah Adragna (teaching assistant).

Finally, we would like to acknowledge the work of MCLE staff and graphic designer Susan Theil in preparing this book for publication.

On behalf of John M. (Jack) Reilly, Publisher; Maryanne G. Jensen, Editor-in-Chief; and the MCLE Board of Trustees, our appreciation extends to all whose talent and hard work helped create this book.

ALEXIS J. LEBLANC, Publications Attorney
SALVATORE RICCIARDONE, Director of Philanthropy and Special Projects

JUNE 30, 2012

About the Editors

Hon. Patti B. Saris is a judge of the U.S. District Court for the District of Massachusetts. She also serves as chairperson of the U.S. Sentencing Commission. Previously, she was an associate justice of the Massachusetts Superior Court and a U.S. magistrate judge. She is a graduate of Harvard Law School and Radcliffe College.

Hon. Margot Botsford is an associate justice of the Massachusetts Supreme Judicial Court. Previously, she was an associate justice of the Massachusetts Superior Court, an assistant attorney general in the Office of the Massachusetts Attorney General, and an assistant district attorney for Middlesex County. She is a graduate of Harvard Kennedy School of Government, Northeastern University School of Law, and Barnard College.

Barbara Fischbein Berenson is a senior attorney at the Massachusetts Supreme Judicial Court. Previously, she was an assistant attorney general in the Office of the Massachusetts Attorney General, assistant district attorney for Middlesex County, and an associate at Hill & Barlow. She is a graduate of Harvard Law School, Harvard Kennedy School of Government, and Harvard College.

About the Contributors

Hon. Ruth I. Abrams is a retired associate justice of the Massachusetts Supreme Judicial Court.

Libby S. Adler is a professor of law at Northeastern University School of Law.

Meredith L. Ainbinder is a partner with Sunstein Kann Murphy & Timbers LLP.

Essence McGill Arzu is a partner with Foley Hoag LLP.

Navjeet K. Bal is of counsel with Nixon Peabody LLP.

Jane Taubner Barney is a senior client advisor at TFC Financial Management.

Elizabeth Bartholet is the Morris Wasserstein Public Interest Professor of Law at Harvard Law School.

Janice Bassil is a partner with Carney & Bassil, P.C.

Mary L. Bonauto is civil rights project director at Gay & Lesbian Advocates & Defenders.

Jacquelynne J. Bowman is the executive director of Greater Boston Legal Services.

Elizabeth A. Brown is an adjunct professor in the department of law, taxation, and financial planning at Bentley University.

Margaret A. Burnham is a professor of law at Northeastern University School of Law.

Andrea J. Cabral is the Suffolk County Sheriff.

Marisa A. Campagna is a sole practitioner in Boston.

Hon. Denise Jefferson Casper is a judge of the U.S. District Court for the District of Massachusetts.

Ronald Chester is a professor of law at New England Law | Boston.

Mary Beth Basile Chopas is an adjunct assistant professor at the University of North Carolina School of Law at Chapel Hill.

Martha Coakley is the attorney general of Massachusetts.

Mary M. Connolly is a retired executive director of the Volunteer Lawyers Project of the Boston Bar Association.

Miriam Conrad is the federal public defender for the Districts of Massachusetts, New Hampshire, and Rhode Island.

Hon. Judith A. Cowin is a retired associate justice of the Massachusetts Supreme Judicial Court.

Cynthia Stone Creem is a partner with Stone, Stone & Creem and a Massachusetts state senator.

Susan L. Crockin is the principal at the Crockin Law & Policy Group LLC.

Cheryl M. Cronin is a partner with Cronin & Leonard.

Gene D. Dahmen is senior counsel with Verrill Dana LLP.

Kate Nace Day is a professor of law at Suffolk University Law School.

Hon. Barbara A. Dortch-Okara is an associate justice of the Massachusetts Superior Court.

Virginia Drachman is chair of the department of history and the Arthur and Lenore Professor of American History at Tufts University.

Hon. Raya S. Dreben is a retired associate justice of the Massachusetts Appeals Court.

Hon. Fernande R.V. Duffly is an associate justice of the Massachusetts Supreme Judicial Court.

J. Shoshanna Ehrlich is chair of the women's studies department and an associate professor at the University of Massachusetts at Boston.

Elaine M. Epstein is a partner with Todd & Weld LLP.

Susan M. Finegan is a litigation partner with Mintz Levin Cohn Ferris Glovsky and Popeo, P.C.

Ruth Ellen Fitch is president and chief executive officer of the Dimock Center.

Tamar Frankel is a professor of law at Boston University School of Law.

Marion R. Fremont-Smith is an adjunct lecturer and senior research fellow at the Hauser Center for Nonprofit Organizations at Harvard University.

Christine C. Gannon is an associate with Ross Silverman LLP.

Hon. Nancy Gertner is professor of practice at Harvard Law School and a retired judge of the U.S. District Court for the District of Massachusetts.

Karen F. Green is a partner with Wilmer Cutler Pickering Hale & Dorr LLP.

Eileen M. Hagerty is a partner with Kotin, Crabtree & Strong LLP.

Vickie L. Henry is a senior staff attorney at Gay & Lesbian Advocates & Defenders.

Kay H. Hodge is a partner with Stoneman, Chandler & Miller LLP.

Julia Huston is a partner with Foley Hoag LLP.

Hon. Barbara M. Hyland is an associate justice of the Massachusetts Probate and Family Court.

Hon. Leila R. Kern is a retired associate justice of the Massachusetts Superior Court.

Renée M. Landers is a professor of law at Suffolk University Law School.

Kristen Lasker is a sole practitioner in Cambridge.

Hon. Barbara A. Lenk is an associate justice of the Massachusetts Supreme Judicial Court.

Stephanie S. Lovell is senior vice president and general counsel with Blue Cross Blue Shield of Massachusetts.

Joan A. Lukey is a partner with Ropes & Gray LLP.

Erik Lund is senior counsel with Posternak Blankstein & Lund LLP.

Sandra E. Lundy is a senior attorney at the Massachusetts Supreme Judicial Court and deputy advisor to the Trial Court Access to Justice Initiative.

Hon. Sandra L. Lynch is chief judge of the U.S. Court of Appeals for the First Circuit.

Hon. Diana L. Maldonado is first justice of the Chelsea District Court.

Hon. Margaret H. Marshall is senior counsel with Choate Hall & Stewart LLP and a retired chief justice of the Massachusetts Supreme Judicial Court.

Jennifer J. Mather is a litigation associate with Mintz Levin Cohn Ferris Glovsky and Popeo, P.C.

S. Beville May is an attorney in Pennsylvania who consults with companies to prevent and resolve lawsuits.

Sarah McClean is a sole practitioner in Boston.

Martha L. Minow is dean of the faculty and the Jeremiah Smith, Jr., Professor of Law at Harvard Law School.

Wendy J. Murphy is an impact litigator who specializes in the representation of women and children domestic violence victims and teaches at New England Law | Boston.

Camille A. Nelson is dean and professor of law at Suffolk University Law School.

Maureen A. O'Rourke is dean and professor of law at Boston University School of Law.

Carmen M. Ortiz is the U.S. attorney for the District of Massachusetts.

Stephanie Page is retired from the public defender division of the Committee for Public Counsel Services.

Regina M. Pisa is a partner and chairman with Goodwin Procter LLP.

Krista Green Pratt is associate general counsel at Biogen Idec.

Glendora McIlwain Putnam is a retired attorney in Boston.

Maria E. Recalde is a shareholder with Sheehan Phinney Bass + Green PA.

Alice E. Richmond is a founding partner with Richmond & Associates.

Lauren Stiller Rikleen is executive-in-residence at the Carroll School of Management Center for Work and Family at Boston College.

Alan Rogers is a professor in the department of history at Boston College.

Rebecca Rogers is a sole practitioner in Boston.

Therese M. Rohrbeck is a clinical fellow at the Transactional Law Clinics at Harvard Law School.

Carol Rose is executive director of the American Civil Liberties Union of Massachusetts.

Mary K. Ryan is a partner with Nutter McClennen & Fish LLP.

Jamie Ann Sabino is the Violence Against Women Act S.T.O.P grant coordinator for the Administrative Office of the Massachusetts Trial Court.

Elizabeth D. Scheibel is a retired district attorney for the Northwestern District of Massachusetts.

Sandra Shapiro is of counsel with Foley Hoag LLP.

Nancy S. Shilepsky is a partner with Shilepsky Hartley Robb Casey Michon LLP.

Wendy Sibbison is a sole practitioner in Greenfield.

Emily A. Spieler is dean and the Edwin W. Hadley Professor of Law at Northeastern University School of Law.

Carol Steiker is the Henry J. Friendly Professor of Law at Harvard Law School.

Carolyn Stafford Stein is assistant director for alumni advising at the Bernard Koteen Office of Public Advising at Harvard Law School.

Evelynne L. Swagerty is assistant counsel with Bank of America.

Haylee Trahan-Liptak is a law student at Boston College Law School.

Vivian Tseng is vice president and general counsel at Welch's Foods, Inc.

Susan H. Vickers is in-house counsel at PeopleGIS, Inc.

Gina Walcott is the executive director of the Fair Housing Center of Greater Boston.

Sarah E. Wald is chief of staff and senior advisor in the dean's office at the Harvard Kennedy School of Government.

Mary E. Weber is a partner with Ropes & Gray LLP.

Kathy B. Weinman is a partner with Collora LLP.

Sarah R. Wunsch is a staff attorney at the American Civil Liberties Union of Massachusetts.

Valerie A. Yarashus is a principal of Meehan, Boyle, Black & Bogdanow, P.C.

Hon. Rya W. Zobel is a judge of the U.S. District Court for the District of Massachusetts.

Introduction

Ten years ago, Justice Rudolph Kass edited *Legal Chowder: Lawyering and Judging in Massachusetts,* which was published by Massachusetts Continuing Legal Education. Like chowder, the book was an eclectic mix; its ingredients were lawyers, judges, cases, buildings, law schools and anything else that reflected the institution of law in Massachusetts. However, as Justice Kass acknowledged, he did not include the many great lawyers and judges working at the time of the book's publication: "We decided not to include any of them because of the risk of giving unintended offense to someone we failed to include." As a result, the blossoming and increasingly robust role of women in the Massachusetts legal community was an important ingredient absent from the chowder.

This book focuses on that missing ingredient. It begins with a chapter on the history of the pioneering women who were the first to be admitted to the bar, starting with Lelia J. Robinson in 1882. It then presents, discusses, and reflects the voices of women lawyers who have been practicing over the past fifty years and of those who are practicing today in the private sector and in public interest, women in legal academia who are teaching at or are deans of Massachusetts law schools, and leaders in the many bar associations in this state. We include the stories of many women judges at the state and federal level through personal reflections, interviews, and third-hand accounts. A separate chapter highlights the special challenges of women lawyers and judges of color. There are, as well, pieces discussing some of the dramatic developments in our law in the areas of sexual assault, reproduction, domestic violence, marriage and divorce, and gender discrimination in the workplace—areas that profoundly affect the lives of Massachusetts women, and in which Massachusetts women lawyers and judges have played leading roles.

A book of this sort necessarily comes with several caveats. We apologize in advance that this book is necessarily under-inclusive: we simply could not discuss or feature many women who have been vibrant, significant contributors to both bench and bar. (We have much envied Justice Kass's elegant solution of not including current practitioners.) We have called upon many lawyers, judges, and scholars to write articles and reflections, and nearly every one we asked generously agreed to do so. However, we emphasize that their views are not necessarily our own. We also recognize that this book is limited by its focus on what has been achieved to date by lawyers in Massachusetts; it is descriptive rather than prescriptive. Finally we emphasize that what we present here is an unfinished story, and that the next generation of women lawyers will leave their unique footprints.

A thank you to Massachusetts Continuing Legal Education, particularly to Salvatore Ricciardone and Alexis LeBlanc for their help in editing and organizing all the materials presented here, and to John M. Reilly for his stewardship. He and the board of MCLE saw the need for this book and provided all the key support.

PATTI B. SARIS

MARGOT BOTSFORD

BARBARA F. BERENSON

CHAPTER 1

Achieving Citizenship: From Bar Admission to Jury Service

From the Pioneers to the New Women

VIRGINIA G. DRACHMAN

In 1888, Lelia J. Robinson, the first woman admitted to the Massachusetts bar, offered women advice on how to succeed in the legal profession. "Do not take sex into the practice. Don't be 'lady lawyers.' Simply be lawyers, and recognize no distinction—no existence of any distinction between yourselves and the other members of the bar.... You can take this stand and yet in no wise cease to be ladies—true ladies in every sense of the word." Mary Anne Greene, Robinson's friend and "sister in law," and the second woman admitted to practice law in the Commonwealth, took a different tack. While Robinson made the argument for gender equality, Greene highlighted the importance of gender difference, claiming that women's unique sympathies gave them a special place in the legal profession. Greene envisioned law as an ideal "field for women" because "just as many women would prefer to consult a woman physician because they could talk freely and be more sure of sympathy, so they would, for the same reasons, consult a woman lawyer."

Despite their accomplishments as pioneer women lawyers in Massachusetts, neither Robinson nor Greene could forget that she was a woman in a male-dominated profession. Indeed, the nineteenth-century woman lawyer straddled two worlds. As a woman, her place was at home, the caretaker of the family. As a lawyer, her place was in the office and the courtroom, the protector of justice. As a woman, she was expected to be modest, sentimental, and caring. As a lawyer, she needed to be assertive and rational. The challenge was not unique to Robinson and Greene. Rather, one nineteenth-century woman lawyer identified this conflict between gender and professional identity as the burden of "double consciousness" that confronted every "woman who wishes to be a lawyer." This dilemma of double consciousness endured long after Robinson and the women of her generation had overcome the institutional obstacles necessary to practice law in Massachusetts.

The history of women lawyers in Massachusetts begins with Lelia J. Robinson, the first woman to graduate from Boston University School of Law, in 1881, and the first woman admitted to the Massachusetts bar, in 1882. Mary Greene followed Robinson, graduating

▲ Virginia G. Drachman is the Arthur and Lenore Stern Professor of American History at Tufts University. Her teaching and research interests focus on women in modern American history. She has a PhD in history from SUNY Buffalo.

IMAGE COURTESY OF VIRGINIA G. DRACHMAN/ TUFTS UNIVERSITY

"From The Pioneers to the New Women" was adapted by the author from her book, *Sisters in Law: Women Lawyers in Modern American History* (Harvard University Press 1998). For full supporting sources for the information cited here, see that publication's notes beginning at p. 273 therein.

second in her law school class at Boston University in 1888, and gaining admission to the bar of Suffolk County that year, ranking first among approximately forty applicants. By 1890, eight women were studying law at Boston University and several others were reading law in offices. Numbers tell only part of the story: behind the growth of women lawyers in Massachusetts is a more complicated history. On the one hand, it is a story of women's struggles to break barriers and overcome gender discrimination as they strived to make it in the legal profession. At the same time, it is a personal story of women trying to blaze professional paths without sacrificing their traditional domestic responsibilities. Finally, the history of the first half-century of women lawyers in Massachusetts reveals the origins and development of the dilemma of double consciousness, a struggle that persists today.

> "[B]ut it remained for the United States to inaugurate the era of the woman lawyer of today. And this was so short a time ago—for the woman lawyer in the abstract has not yet attained her majority—that the novelty of her very existence has scarcely begun to wear off, and the newspapers publish and republish little floating items about women lawyers along with those of the latest sea-serpent, the popular idea seeming to be that the one is about as real as the other.
>
> Lelia J. Robinson

As the first woman lawyer in Massachusetts, Lelia Robinson encountered both obstacles and opportunities. The elite law schools in the Northeast—Harvard, Columbia, Yale, and the University of Pennsylvania—were all closed to women. In contrast, law schools in the western part of the country were more hospitable to women. The University of Iowa and Washington University in St. Louis opened their doors to women in 1868, the newly founded law school at the University of Michigan opened to women in 1870, and Ada Kepley graduated from Union College of Law (Northwestern) in 1870 to become the first woman to earn a law degree in the country. As the trend toward coeducation in law schools spread in the West, Boston University bucked the tide in the East. When it opened its doors in 1872 to both men and women, it gave women access to the first law school in the country that required an admission exam before entry as well as a three-year course of instruction.

Robinson enrolled at Boston University School of Law in 1878 and graduated fourth in her class. Despite her superior record, she confronted obstacles daily as she negotiated the delicate task of being the only woman among 150 male classmates. "I knew none of the students, and the dean, to whom I introduced myself, did not give me any introductions to students or professors." Left to make her own way, Robinson sat up front in her classes, unaware of the tradition of alphabetical seating. She shunned the demure behavior expected of a proper lady of her day, resolved to be friendly and outgoing with her male classmates, and ultimately won them over. "I was not permitted to realize or remember the fact that I was the only woman in a large school of men," Robinson recalled proudly. "I was simply a student like the rest."

After graduating with honors from Boston University School of Law, the first female graduate of the school was denied admission to the state bar because she was a woman. In response, Robinson sued to establish the right of a woman to practice law, and while she lost in court, she nevertheless secured her victory when Massachusetts adopted a statute specifically permitting women to practice law on the same terms as men. In 1882, Robinson became the first women lawyer admitted to practice in the state, crossing, as she put it, "the grand Rubicon which made me a full fledged attorney." Robinson's admission was an important victory in the history of the pioneer generation of women lawyers in

First Woman Lawyers By State[1]

Year	Name	State
1869	Arabella Babb Mansfield	Iowa
1870	Lemma Barkeloo	Missouri
1871	Sarah Killgore Wertman	Michigan
1872	Georgianna Snow Carlton, Phoebe W. Couzins	Utah
1872	Clara Hapgood Nash	Maine
1872	Charlotte E. Ray	District of Columbia
1873	Alta M. Hulett	Illinois
1873	Nettie Cronise Lutes	Ohio
1875	Elizabeth Jane Eaglesfield	Indiana
1878	Martha Angle Dorsett	Minnesota
1878	Clara S. Foltz	California
1878	Tabitha A. Holton	North Carolina
1879	Rhoda L. Goodell	Wisconsin
1880	Jennie Mitchell Kellog	Kansas
1882	Ada Bittenbender	Nebraska
1882	Mary Hall	Connecticut
1882	**Lelia J. Robinson**	**Massachusetts**
1886	Caroline Burnham Kilgore	Pennsylvania
1886	Mary Leonard	Oregon
1886	Katherine Stoneman	New York
1888	Almeda Hitchcock	Hawaii
1890	Ella Knowles Haskell	Montana
1892	Henrietta Pettijohn Buck	New Mexico
1892	Sarah Herring Sorin	Arizona
1893	Laura M. Tiden	Nevada
1895	Sophonisba Breckinridge	Kentucky
1895	Mary Philbrook	New Jersey
1895	Helen Louise Young	Idaho
1896	Agnes Westbrook Morrison	West Virginia
1898	Louise Rebecca Pinnell	Florida
1898	Betty Runnells	Louisiana
1899	Grace R. Herbard	Wyoming
1902	Jessie LaFountain Bigwood	Vermont
1902	Etta H. Maddox	Maryland
1905	Helen Hamilton	North Dakota
1907	Marion S. Griffin	Tennessee
1908	Maude McLure Kelly	Alabama
1910	Hortense Sparks Ward	Texas
1911	Blanche Coleman	South Dakota
1913	Rebecca Jane Hurn	Washington
1913	Mary F. Lathrop	Colorado
1913	Kathryn Clyde Sturdevant	Oklahoma
1914	Lucy Greaves	Mississippi
1917	Stella Akin	Georgia
1917	Agnes Winifred McLaughlin	New Hampshire
1918	James Perry	South Carolina
1919	Isabel Klein	Arkansas
1920	Ada Sawyer	Rhode Island
1923	Evangelyn Barsky, Sybil Ward	Delaware
1923	Elizabeth N. Tompkins	Virginia
1934	Mildred Hermann	Alaska

The first woman lawyer in Massachusetts

Lelia J. Robinson

1850–1891, admitted 1882

Lelia J. Robinson

IMAGE SOURCE: *LEGAL CHOWDER: LAWYERING AND JUDGING IN MASSACHUSETTS* (MCLE, Inc. 2001)

When Lelia J. Robinson wagered a friend that she could read sixty pages of Blackstone's *Commentaries on the Law,* she had no intention of pursuing legal studies.[2] Yet Robinson found law so interesting she read the entire book, and soon enrolled at Boston University School of Law. Initially, Robinson was interested only in reversing her ignorance of the law and had no plan to practice. But she changed her mind by her final year of school and decided to take the unprecedented step of opening her own legal practice in Massachusetts.

As the first woman to apply for admission to the Massachusetts bar in 1881, Robinson's application was sent to the Supreme Judicial Court for approval. The court promptly rejected the petition, ruling that under the current law only men could be admitted. Although the decision was against her, Robinson told the *Boston Globe* that the ruling followed the wording of the law and that she believed a change in the statute was needed for women to gain bar admission. Representative John Hopkins of Millbury introduced such a bill, which passed without opposition. Robinson became the first woman lawyer in Massachusetts when she was admitted to the bar in 1882.

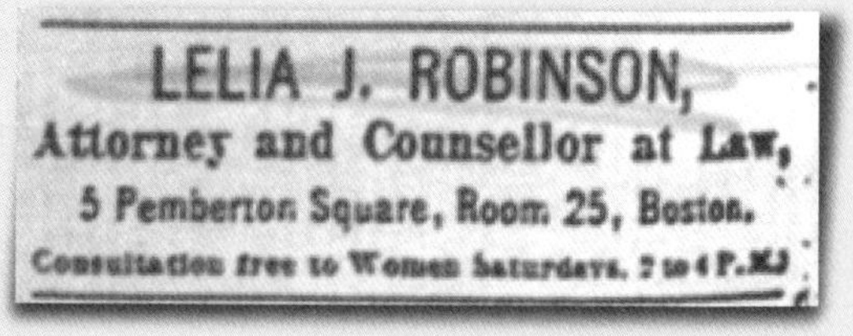

LELIA J. ROBINSON,
Attorney and Counsellor at Law,
5 Pemberton Square, Room 25, Boston.
Consultation free to Women Saturdays, 2 to 4 P.M.

An advertisement for Lelia Robinson's practice.

IMAGE SOURCE: *WOMEN'S JOURNAL*, BOSTON, AUG. 24, 1889

Although she had overcome the initial hurdle, Robinson continued to face opposition in the male-dominated legal field. Law offices in Boston refused to hire a female lawyer, so Robinson opened her own office. In court she felt tremendous public pressure, believing any mistake would reflect poorly on her gender's abilities in the public sphere. Robinson often avoided court by finding another attorney to take her place in public appearances, although she did briefly appear in Probate Court in January 1884.

That same year Robinson moved to the Washington Territory, where she believed there were better opportunities for women. In stark contrast to Massachusetts, women in Washington Territory were gaining the rights of both suffrage and jury service. While she had been turned away at Boston firms, Robinson was welcomed into Struve, Haines & McMicken, the oldest law firm in Seattle. Robinson expanded her skills under the tutelage of a local judge and was appointed to defend a client in her first trial, *Territory v. Ah Mon*. Robinson successfully defended Ah

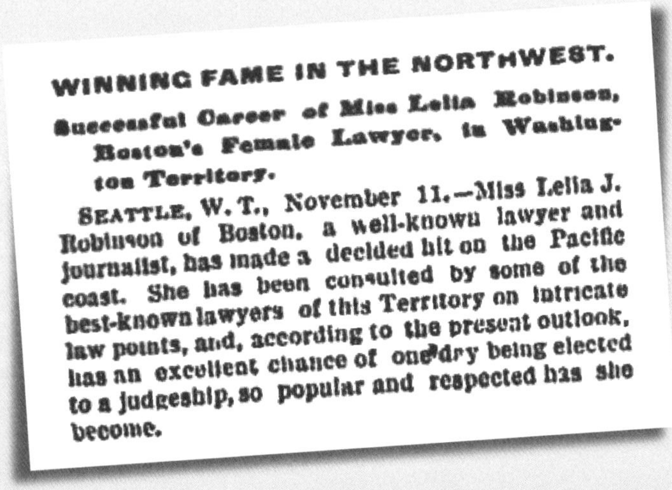

WINNING FAME IN THE NORTHWEST.

Successful Career of Miss Lelia Robinson, Boston's Female Lawyer, in Washington Territory.

SEATTLE, W. T., November 11.—Miss Lelia J. Robinson of Boston, a well-known lawyer and journalist, has made a decided hit on the Pacific coast. She has been consulted by some of the best-known lawyers of this Territory on intricate law points, and, according to the present outlook, has an excellent chance of one day being elected to a judgeship, so popular and respected has she become.

An article on Robinson in the November 12, 1884 edition of the Boston Daily Globe.

IMAGE SOURCE: *BOSTON GLOBE* ONLINE ARCHIVES

The biographies of pioneering women lawyers in this chapter were prepared by Haylee Trahan-Liptak, the editors, and MCLE.

Mon, who was acquitted of transporting Chinese individuals into the United States from British Columbia. Robinson's court appearance in Seattle was the first time in the United States that a female lawyer argued before a jury composed of both men and women.

When Robinson returned to Massachusetts in 1888 she noted in her yearly letter to the Equity Club, a national correspondence group of women lawyers and law students, how the legal landscape in Massachusetts had changed while she was away. Her years of experience combined with the more accepting legal climate led her to begin attending court regularly and helped her increase her base of clients.

While best known as a lawyer, Robinson also enjoyed success as a writer. Her three books all strove to make legal matters more understandable for the general public, especially women. *Law Made Easy* was written during her first few years of practice in Boston and was published after she left for the Washington Territory. *Law of Husband and Wife* and *Women Jurors* followed after her return from Seattle. Originally, Robinson wrote to the Equity Club that she believed women could remain in private practice while taking breaks from work for things such as writing and family. After returning to practice in 1888, however, she gained a different perspective and began to insist that women work tirelessly to legitimize their work on behalf of their gender as a whole. She wrote in an 1888 letter to the Equity Club that a woman "may be the more successful lecturer for her legal training, doubtless, but the world will say that she lectures because she cannot succeed in practice. And so of any other path, aside from that of the law itself, which she may choose."

Throughout her legal career, Robinson served as an advocate for women in the workplace. Robinson and fellow lawyer Mary Greene founded the Pentagon Club and Portia Club to support other pioneering women. The Pentagon Club was dedicated to women in professional life, including doctors, lawyers, and other professionals, while the Portia Club exclusively supported female lawyers. Robinson was also elected president of the Second Nationalists Club, a group that condemned discrimination and criticized class competition. Despite these other endeavors, Robinson was always conscious of how she represented female lawyers to the public. Throughout her life, she ensured that she set a functioning and respected precedent for women in Massachusetts. Robinson passed away in August 1891.

Lelia J. Robinson's Case

In 1881, the statute governing admission to practice law in Massachusetts stated: "A citizen of this State...may...petition the Supreme Judicial or Superior Court to be examined for admission as an attorney." 1876 Mass. Acts c. 197. The court's opinion in *Lelia J. Robinson's Case,* 131 Mass. 376 (1881) thus focused on the meaning of the word "citizen," specifically whether the term included women.

Although the court recognized that the word "citizen" in "its most common and most comprehensive sense" included women, the court, in an opinion written by Chief Justice Horace Gray, nevertheless concluded that "[A] woman is not, by virtue of her citizenship, vested by the Constitution of the United States, or by the Constitution of the Commonwealth, with any absolute right, independent of legislation, to take part in the government, either as a voter or as an officer, or to be admitted to practice as an attorney."

The court continued, "Our duty is limited to declaring the law as it is" and any change would be a "question for the legislative and not for the judicial department of government."

Chapter 139 of the Acts of 1882 was approved by the legislature on April 10, 1882. It provided: "The provisions of law relating to qualification and admission to practice of attorneys at law shall apply to women."

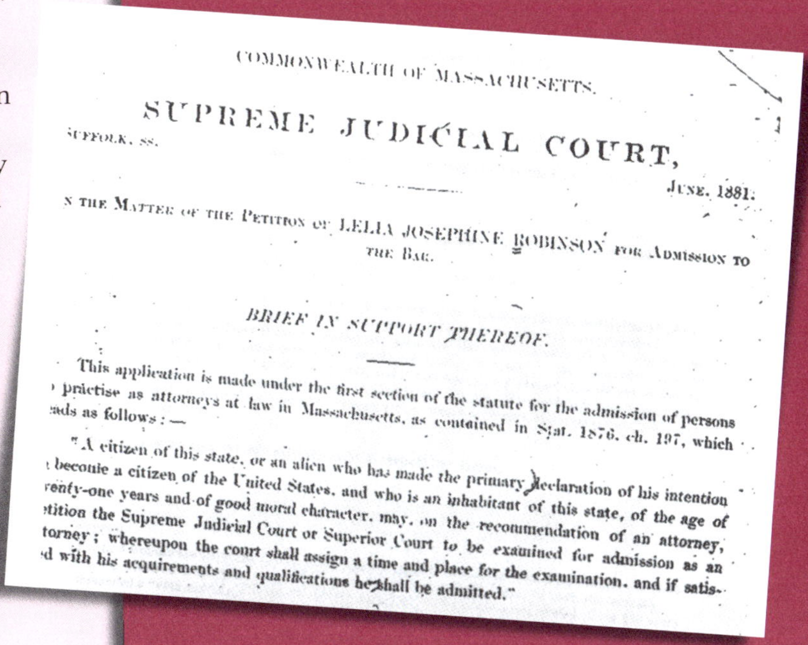

COMMONWEALTH OF MASSACHUSETTS.

SUPREME JUDICIAL COURT,

SUFFOLK, SS.

JUNE, 1881.

N THE MATTER OF THE PETITION OF LELIA JOSEPHINE ROBINSON FOR ADMISSION TO THE BAR.

BRIEF IN SUPPORT THEREOF.

This application is made under the first section of the statute for the admission of persons practise as attorneys at law in Massachusetts, as contained in Stat. 1876, ch. 197, which ads as follows:—

"A citizen of this state, or an alien who has made the primary declaration of his intention become a citizen of the United States, and who is an inhabitant of this state, of the age of enty-one years and of good moral character, may, on the recommendation of an attorney, tition the Supreme Judicial Court or Superior Court to be examined for admission as an torney; whereupon the court shall assign a time and place for the examination, and if satis-d with his acquirements and qualifications he shall be admitted."

Massachusetts, but she quickly realized that it was only the first step. No one in Boston would hire the first woman lawyer in the state, so she opened her own office. She tried to build a practice for three and a half years, but "business came in very slowly...and consisted mostly of small and rather hopeless claims for collection." Robinson finally faced the hard truth that she could not make it as a woman lawyer in Boston and turned her sights to the West, where she had heard that views on women were more liberal than they were in the Northeast.

Lured by the promise of more open attitudes toward women, Robinson moved to Seattle where she found open doors that were shut tight in Boston. A male judge befriended her and encouraged her to do courtroom work, something she had dreaded back in Boston. To help her get started, he appointed her as counsel for a prisoner. "With fear and trembling," Robinson defended her client before a judge and jury, and learned firsthand that she "could do the work" she had deemed the sole domain of her male colleagues in Boston. Quickly, she established a lucrative law practice that combined office and courtroom work, but after barely a year, she gave it all up and went back to Boston in 1888 to be near her family.

Robinson returned home a more confident and experienced lawyer. She opened an office at 5 Pemberton Square, near the newly completed Suffolk County Courthouse, and built a modest practice. Robinson was also delighted to find a small group of women lawyers who had gained admission to practice in Massachusetts while she was away. "These ladies have helped to accustom our good old conservative Boston to the thought of women in the legal profession." Among this group of women lawyers were Mary Greene and Anna Christy Fall, both of whom had managed to establish successful careers. Greene found encouragement and opportunity from prominent Boston attorney Alfred Hemenway, who opened his office to her, enabling her to "learn what I could of office work," while lending his prestige to the cause of women lawyers in Massachusetts. Anna Christy Fall, another honors student at Boston University School of Law, was admitted to the bar in 1891. In search of community among this group of local women lawyers, Robinson organized the Portia Club, and invited Greene, Fall, and the several women law students at Boston University to meet monthly at a downtown hotel for dinner and conversation. Robinson and Greene also joined the Equity Club, a correspondence club for women lawyers around the country.

Robinson's and Greene's letters to their "sisters in law" in the Equity Club make clear that these two pioneer women lawyers of Massachusetts struggled with the dilemma of double consciousness that challenged all women lawyers of their day.

Double consciousness touched every aspect of nineteenth-century women lawyers' professional lives: the type of practice they chose; their relationship to social reform; whether they worked in an office or ventured into the courtroom; and if they went to court, how they should dress.

In this era, when women belonged at home, women lawyers debated their proper place in the profession. Some, like Robinson, believed that a woman lawyer was more suited to the office than the courtroom. The office was a private work place, like the home, and demanded the skills familiar to a housewife—detail, organization, efficiency, and compromise. In contrast, the courtroom resembled a saloon, with its spittoons and the presence of thieves, murderers, and prostitutes. Here, in the public eye, male lawyers engaged in legal combat,

The second woman admitted to the Massachusetts bar

Mary Anne Greene

1857–1936

The purpose of this Manual is to present in a clear, simple, and, if possible, entertaining way, those principles of law governing the business world and domestic life which most men understand in some degree, or think they do, but which most women do not understand, and wish they did.

So begins *The Woman's Manual of Law,* a book by Mary Anne Greene dedicated to teaching American women about their limited legal rights and instructing them in laws governing their expanding careers.[3] The manual, along with Greene's numerous other publications, reflected her experience as a pioneering woman lawyer. Greene enrolled at Boston University School of Law in 1885 at age twenty-eight after realizing that she was "woefully ignorant of the very first principles of our Common Law," and that other women shared the same unawareness. Greene graduated second in her class, becoming BU Law's third female graduate. The following year, Greene became the second female member of the Massachusetts bar, joining her close friend Lelia Robinson.

Mary Anne Greene

IMAGE SOURCE: FRANCES E. WILLARD & MARY A. LIVERMORE, EDS., *A WOMAN OF THE CENTURY* 339 (MOULTON 1893)

Together, Robinson and Greene founded the Portia Club, an informal monthly dinner club for women lawyers and law students in Massachusetts. The club provided a much-needed space for women to socialize and discuss their experiences in the legal field. Greene also joined the Equity Club, comparing motivations and experiences through annual letters exchanged with other female attorneys across the country.

Greene returned to her home state of Rhode Island two years later and started a practice that dealt with estate management and conveyancing law. In addition to her law practice, Greene was a teacher, prolific writer, and public speaker, primarily on subjects relating to the legal rights of women. As one of the few women in the field, she forged a path of firsts, including her lectures on business law for women at Lasell Seminary in Auburndale, Massachusetts, from 1889 to 1906, and her 1890 publication in the *American Law Review* of her article, "Privileged Communication in Suits between Husband and Wife." *The Woman's Manual of Law* followed in 1902. Greene believed her mission was to educate women to use the rights they possessed, leaving it to others to demand new legal rights. In 1920 Greene moved to Pasadena, California; passing away there in 1936 at age seventy-nine.

> A woman lawyer ought to go into court. Her beneficial influence is needed there quite as much as in the law schools and offices, and the less agreeable the moral atmosphere the more is her presence needed.

Mary Anne Greene in an 1889 letter to the Equity Club

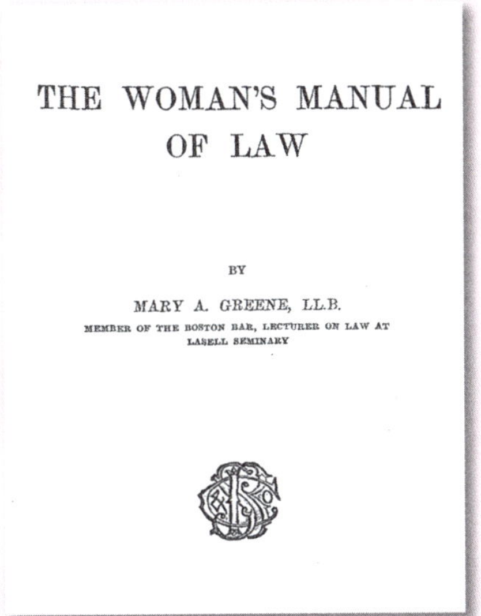

THE WOMAN'S MANUAL OF LAW

BY

MARY A. GREENE, LL.B.

MEMBER OF THE BOSTON BAR, LECTURER ON LAW AT LASELL SEMINARY

The title page of Greene's book.

IMAGE SOURCE: GOOGLE BOOKS

flaunting their manly qualities—combativeness, competitiveness, and hard-hearted objectivity. "I very emphatically chose office practice," explained Robinson, who often referred her litigation cases to male lawyers to avoid the hostile atmosphere of the courtroom. Greene disagreed, arguing not only that a woman lawyer belonged in the courtroom, but that "the less agreeable the moral atmosphere" of the courtroom, "the more is her presence needed."

Despite the larger and more difficult challenges Robinson had confronted as she fought to overcome barriers against women lawyers in Massachusetts, her query [regarding wearing hats in court] was no frivolous matter.

Despite their differing views on women in the courtroom, both Robinson and Greene occasionally went to court, where they confronted another challenge of double consciousness, namely, the perplexing problem of the hat. Robinson raised the issue with the Equity Club members in 1888 when she had to take a case to court for the first time. "Shall the woman attorney wear her hat when arguing a case or making a motion in court, or shall she remove it?" Robinson wanted to know. Despite the larger and more difficult challenges Robinson had confronted as she fought to overcome barriers against women lawyers in Massachusetts, her query was no frivolous matter of fashion. Social etiquette of the day required that respectable women wear hats in public, but professional, male standards demanded that lawyers remove their hats in the courtroom. Seeking a solution to the quandary she faced whenever she entered a courtroom, Robinson discovered that there was little consensus among nineteenth-century women lawyers on the matter.

A woman lawyer in Chicago explained that she always removed her hat in court. "Some seem to think that a bonnet is absolutely necessary on a woman's head to redeem her from the curse deserved for lifting up her voice on the rostrum…but I object on principle." A women lawyer in Milwaukee took a more open view, insisting on "the inalienable right of each lady to follow her 'own sweet will.'" In Boston, Robinson and Greene, as well as "the ladies who are at present studying law" all preferred to wear a hat in court. Greene observed, "The matter seems to be settled in Massachusetts in the affirmative."

Even as Robinson and Greene resolved the dilemma of the hat for themselves, double consciousness permeated their personal lives, confronting them with the more enduring tension between marriage and career. Again, Robinson put her finger on the problem. In 1889, as she published a book on family law, *The Law of Husband and Wife*, and contemplated her own marriage, Robinson turned once more to the women lawyers of the Equity Club for advice. "Is it practicable for a woman to successfully fulfill the duties of wife, mother and lawyer at the same time? Especially a young married woman?" In an era before the availability of reliable methods of birth control, Robinson understood all too well that she would never be free to build her professional career until the arrangements of her personal life were well in order. For some women, the answer to Robinson's question was simple: women had to choose between career and marriage. Greene, for one, remained single, and devoted her time to her career. Still, even as a single woman, she found that household responsibilities intruded on her work. Explaining that she had to "sandwich law and housekeeping together," Greene lamented that she could not "practice just as a man does."

Robinson took a different path. In 1890, she married Eli Sawtelle, a piano dealer, who was supportive of his new wife's career. Robinson's decision to marry Sawtelle reflected the understanding among nineteenth-century women lawyers that the key to managing career and marriage was finding the right man. Women lawyers need not fear marriage, explained one woman lawyer in Chicago, "but it makes all the difference in the world who one marries." Sawtelle's wedding gift to his new wife was a "fine roll-top desk" for her office, and he willingly took time out of their honeymoon trip so that she could be admitted to the U.S. Supreme Court in Washington, D.C. Anna Christy Fall married a lawyer and went into practice with him. With her husband's support, Fall took cases to court. In November 1891, she became the first woman to try a jury case in the Commonwealth, winning her case against "one of the ablest and most noted lawyers of Massachusetts." A mother of two young children early in her practice, Fall did not let motherhood hinder her courtroom career, even when she was nursing. Instead, her sister or a domestic servant brought the baby to court at a scheduled feeding time. The judge, in the face of Boston's conservative reputation, usually granted a recess at Fall's request, and she quickly retreated into the witness room to nurse before resuming her position before the bench.

[Lelia] Robinson's decision to marry Sawtelle reflected the understanding among nineteenth-century women lawyers that the key to managing career and marriage was finding the right man.

Although the prevailing view in the late nineteenth century was that women must choose between marriage and career, Robinson and Fall were testimony to the fact that for the pioneer generation of women lawyers, marriage to a supportive husband could encourage and nourish a woman lawyer's public career. At the same time, even the happiest married women lawyers were not unaffected by the expectations of domesticity and sacrifice that defined the parameters of proper womanhood in their day. While Robinson's husband barely complained when "every pair of socks is in need of mending," Robinson would "sit down the same instant, usually, and have a pair ready in about three minutes." Still, she felt that even that may not have been enough. "I think I haven't neglected my husband, but am not quite certain even of that," she confessed privately to another women lawyer.

In 1890, the year of her marriage, Robinson published an essay in the law journal *Green Bag* entitled "Women Lawyers in the United States." Although she was well aware of the obstacles that women lawyers faced as they headed toward the twentieth century, her essay was a celebration of women lawyers' accomplishments in the late nineteenth century and concluded with the optimistic claim that women would continue to enter the law in increasing numbers. Unfortunately Robinson never witnessed any of her projected progress; she tragically died a year later from an overdose of medication while vacationing at her husband's family homestead in Amherst, New Hampshire.

Nevertheless, Massachusetts' first woman lawyer left an important legacy that extended beyond the professional barriers she broke in Massachusetts. Keenly aware of the dilemma of double consciousness, Robinson identified and challenged other women lawyers around the country to grapple with some of its thorniest issues, from courtroom etiquette to the dilemma of marriage and career. These challenges endured well into the twentieth century, challenging a younger generation of women, the new women lawyers of the early twentieth century, to find solutions in the midst of an era of optimism and progress.

The growth in the number of new women lawyers in the early twentieth century rested in part on Portia Law School, the first all-women's law school in the country. Founded in 1908 by Arthur Winfield MacLean, a graduate of Boston University School of Law, Portia was a part-time school, like Suffolk Law School and the YMCA Law School (Northeastern), that provided part-time legal education to working women, mostly the daughters of Irish, Italian, and Jewish immigrants. In 1914, six years after it opened with just two students, Portia Law

Portia in Pictures

Portia Law School began quite simply as a tutorial offered by attorney Arthur Winfield MacLean to assist two women in preparing for the 1908 Massachusetts bar examination. From this small beginning, however, the school grew—in 1919 it was granted authority by the state to award the LL.B. degree to women, and in the decade that followed it would regularly enroll more than 400 students per year.

Portia was named after the heroine in Shakespeare's Merchant of Venice, *who disguises herself as a young lawyer. It is believed that MacLean's wife, Bertha Robinson MacLean, came up with the name. Bertha herself earned a degree from Portia and also served the school during various time periods as an administrator and professor.*

IMAGE COURTESY OF NEW ENGLAND LAW | BOSTON, LAW LIBRARY ARCHIVES

The school's openness is exemplified by this 1920 invitation for the recipient and one female friend to attend the "opening lecture of the thirteenth year, on the subject of contracts."

IMAGE COURTESY OF NEW ENGLAND LAW | BOSTON, LAW LIBRARY ARCHIVES

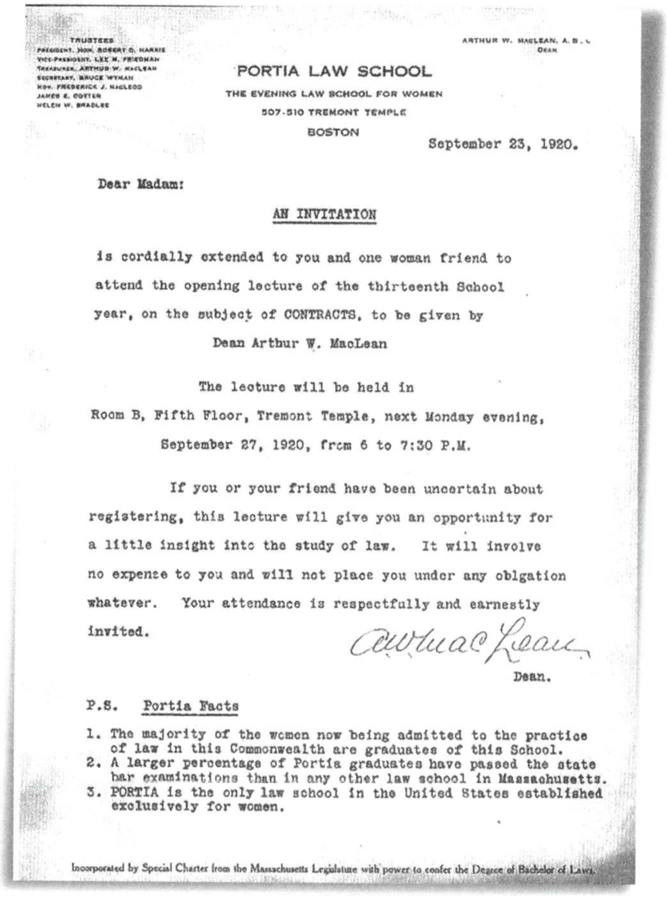

TRUSTEES
PRESIDENT, HON. ROBERT O. HARRIS
VICE-PRESIDENT, LEE M. FRIEDMAN
TREASURER, ARTHUR W. MACLEAN
SECRETARY, BRUCE WYMAN
HON. FREDERICK J. MACLEOD
JAMES E. COTTER
HELEN W. BRADLEE

ARTHUR W. MACLEAN, A.B., L
DEAN

PORTIA LAW SCHOOL
THE EVENING LAW SCHOOL FOR WOMEN
507-510 TREMONT TEMPLE
BOSTON

September 23, 1920.

Dear Madam:

AN INVITATION

is cordially extended to you and one woman friend to attend the opening lecture of the thirteenth School year, on the subject of CONTRACTS, to be given by Dean Arthur W. MacLean

The lecture will be held in Room B, Fifth Floor, Tremont Temple, next Monday evening, September 27, 1920, from 6 to 7:30 P.M.

If you or your friend have been uncertain about registering, this lecture will give you an opportunity for a little insight into the study of law. It will involve no expense to you and will not place you under any obligation whatever. Your attendance is respectfully and earnestly invited.

A.W. MacLean
Dean.

P.S. Portia Facts

1. The majority of the women now being admitted to the practice of law in this Commonwealth are graduates of this School.
2. A larger percentage of Portia graduates have passed the state bar examinations than in any other law school in Massachusetts.
3. PORTIA is the only law school in the United States established exclusively for women.

Incorporated by Special Charter from the Massachusetts Legislature with power to confer the Degree of Bachelor of Laws.

MacLean, a self-made man and entrepreneur, believed it was important to society to educate women in the law. In 1919, he emphatically told the Boston Sunday Advertiser *that women made the best law students: "It isn't a theory, it's a fact. Five or six of the Suffolk Law School professors deliver the same courses of lectures to the women of our school and our women students rate higher than the men who take the course at Suffolk...." He is pictured here with students in 1938. MacLean served Portia as dean until his death in 1943.*

IMAGE COURTESY OF BOSTON PUBLIC LIBRARY PRINT DEPARTMENT

Portia began admitting men in 1938. In 1969 it was renamed New England School of Law. In 2008, the school celebrated its centennial and was again renamed: New England Law | Boston. Shown here is the Portia seal and the school's present-day shield with the year 1908 serving as a reminder of its beginnings as Portia Law School.

IMAGES COURTESY OF NEW ENGLAND LAW | BOSTON

The Portia Law School Class of 1928, pictured in their first year: 1924. Many of Portia's students were the children and grandchildren of immigrants from Ireland, Italy, and eastern Europe who worked during the day and attended classes at night. Although at first many students did not finish high school before enrolling, by 1929 more than 80 percent held a high school diploma, and by 1931 a high school diploma or its equivalent became a prerequisite for enrollment.

IMAGE COURTESY OF NEW ENGLAND LAW | BOSTON, LAW LIBRARY ARCHIVES

While Portia's first classes were taught in MacLean's home in Roxbury and office in Boston, the school eventually found a long-lasting home at 45 Mount Vernon Street in Beacon Hill in 1921. Once home to such prominent women as Julia Ward Howe, Louisa May Alcott, and Elizabeth Palmer Peabody, Beacon Hill was the ideal location for a women's law school. When the school moved into its new quarters, its student population had risen to 200. As time passed, the school outgrew its home at Mount Vernon Street and relocated first to Newbury Street and finally to its current location on Stuart Street. At top, students congregate in front of the school in 1941. At bottom, 45 Mount Vernon Street as it looks today.

PHOTO BY MCLE | NEW ENGLAND

The information presented here on Portia is derived from the work of Professor Ronald Chester in Unequal Access: Women Lawyers in a Changing America *(Bergin & Garvey 1985) and "A Women's Law School in Boston: Portia Law School 1908-1938" (2011) (unpublished manuscript on file with author and prepared for this book when its working title was* Athena's Daughters: The Unfinished Story of Women Lawyers and Judges in Massachusetts*).*

School boasted an enrollment of forty women, more than the total number of women who had graduated from Boston University since 1872. In 1920 alone, there were over 170 women enrolled. By 1929, nearly 30 percent of all women law students in the country were enrolled at Portia. Measured by enrollment, it seemed that Portia had become almost overnight the most popular law school for women in the country. Moreover, even as Portia grew under the shadow of the more prestigious law schools in Boston, its graduates thrived. They performed impressively on the state bar exam, scoring higher than the men who had graduated from Northeastern or Suffolk law schools throughout the 1920s. Nevertheless, not all aspiring women lawyers in Boston were content to attend Portia Law School, even if it was the only all-women's law school in the country.

For a brief moment in 1915, women in Boston had three law schools to choose from: Portia, Boston University, and the Cambridge Law School for Women. In stark contrast to Portia, which attracted immigrant and working-class women, Cambridge Law School for Women was an exclusive institution geared to educationally privileged women. A full-time day school with a strict admission requirement of a bachelor's degree from a four-year college, the school deliberately modeled itself after Harvard, which continued to reject women. Well-known lawyer and Harvard law professor Joseph Henry Beale arranged for several Harvard law school faculty members to offer lectures separately to nine women, including his daughter, who made up the first-year class. Despite its lofty goals, Cambridge Law School for Women was a short-lived venture, closing the following year after few women applied. While Cambridge Law School appealed to the elite few, it was Portia Law School that played a major role in accelerating the integration of a generation of women into the legal profession in the early decades of the twentieth century.

It was precisely in this era, when hundreds of women graduated from Portia, that a younger generation of women entered the legal profession, confident that they would not have to face the double consciousness that plagued the pioneer generation of women lawyers. Few women captured the optimism of this era of new women lawyers better than Massachusetts lawyer Jeanette Phillips Gibbs. A graduate of Smith College, Gibbs followed in the footsteps of her father and grandfather, both of whom were prominent lawyers in Massachusetts, earning her LL.B. in 1917 at Boston University School of Law. She was a member of the state bars of both Massachusetts and New York, though she never practiced law. Instead she wrote novels, including her 1926 book *Portia Marries*. Its main character, Jane Thorndike, embodied all the qualities of the successful new woman in law. Jane was a bright, independent woman who measured up to the most rigorous standards in the legal profession. She built a thriving office practice and fell in love with Tommy, her former college boyfriend. Jane and Tommy married and built a companionate marriage that made room for Jane's legal career. The couple endured ups and downs over the years, as Tommy tired of all the sacrifices he made so that Jane could build her practice while raising their son. The book ends happily, as Tommy comes to understand that he loves Jane precisely because she is not a traditional wife and mother.

To many observers in the early decades of the twentieth century, the fictionalized Jane Thorndike was a reality. Everywhere one turned, one could find examples of successful women lawyers. There was much that this younger generation of women lawyers had to be

Created because of Harvard Law School's refusal to admit women

Cambridge Law School for Women

1915–1917

From its early days, Harvard Law School was recognized for excellence in legal education.[4] By 1900, the case-law method pioneered at Harvard had revolutionized legal education, and its standards for admission required either an undergraduate degree or passage of a rigorous entrance exam. But both Harvard Law School and Harvard College continued to admit only men, even as neighboring schools, such as Boston University, extended admission to women. Harvard's sister school, Radcliffe College, offered an excellent undergraduate education but lacked a law program. When Radcliffe student Elizabeth Beale, daughter of Harvard Law professor Joseph Henry Beale, took an interest in law, Professor Beale suggested to the Harvard Corporation that a non-degree-granting law school be created at Radcliffe. The Radcliffe students, however, told Beale they did not want a separate school; they wanted admission to Harvard Law and a law degree upon graduation.

Beale, along with her Radcliffe College classmate, Greta C. Coleman, and thirteen other "seven sisters" school students, circulated a petition in 1914 asking for admission to Harvard Law School. The petition claimed women were in a unique position to promote social causes and contribute to the public good through law. The petition also emphasized the petitioners' elite backgrounds as "seven sisters" school students, stating that it was "highly desirable" that "properly qualified women" become lawyers.[5]

Despite the petition's arguments, the Harvard Corporation rejected the idea in February 1915. The Corporation articulated three major reasons for its rejection: "(1) the law school already had sufficient students, (2) co-education would not help the school and might harm it, and (3) if anything should be done to educate women in the law, Radcliffe, not Harvard Law School should do it."[6]

With few options remaining, Professor Beale decided to open a small private law school to educate women. The new Cambridge Law School for Women mirrored Harvard's legal education but promised only a diploma, not a law degree. Although Radcliffe allowed Professor Beale to teach classes on its campus, both Radcliffe and Harvard disassociated themselves with the endeavor, stressing that Cambridge Law School was a private school and not affiliated with Harvard in any way. Teachers were usually young with strong academic credentials, and many also taught at Harvard. Like Harvard Law, entering students were required to be college graduates.

Cambridge Law School for Women was open only two academic years, from 1915 to 1917. Some scholars have suggested the school closed due to Elizabeth Beale's marriage and loss of interest, but this explanation is uncorroborated. While Elizabeth Beale did marry, she continued her study of law at George Washington University, suggesting the school did not close solely from her lack of interest. The school faced declining admission as it admitted only a select group of women, did not broadly advertise, and did not offer degrees. America's entry into World War I further reduced the applicant and faculty pool, forcing Cambridge Law School to close.

Cambridge Law School for Women reopened temporarily from 1920 to 1921. However, the same problems continued to plague the school, and soon it closed for good.

LAW SCHOOL FOR WOMEN.

Cambridge to Have First Institution of the Kind in America.

Special to The New York Times.

CAMBRIDGE, Sept. 26.—The first graduate law school in America devoted exclusively to women will be opened here this Fall with Professor Joseph H. Beale of the Harvard Law School in charge. The new school is to be called the Cambridge Law School for Women, and the lectures will be delivered in classrooms provided by Radcliffe College.

The organization is the result of an attempt of a group of Radcliffe seniors, headed by Miss Elizabeth C. Beale, the professor's daughter, to persuade President Lowell and the Board of Overseers to admit them into the Harvard Law School. The Harvard authorities were solidly against this proposition, and Miss Beale then prevailed on her father to organize the new school.

Professor Beale will lecture on torts, criminal law, and principles of legal liability. His assistants will include Gustavus H. Robinson, Chester A. McLain, and Whitney H. Shepardson. Harvard modes of teaching and case books will be used in the new school.

An article from the New York Times *announcing the new school. Although Beale agreed to open only on a trial basis, the press treated the opening as that of a permanent institution.*

IMAGE SOURCE: *N.Y. TIMES*, SEPT. 27, 1915

By 1920, there were 1,738 women lawyers in the country, every state bar was open to women, and most law schools admitted women.

optimistic about. They did not struggle for decades to gain admission to the bar as had Lelia Robinson and the pioneer women lawyers of the nineteenth century. By 1920, there were 1,738 women lawyers in the country, every state bar was open to women, and most law schools admitted women. By 1930 the number of women lawyers nationwide had almost doubled, rising to 3,385.

Women in Massachusetts benefited from this era of progress. In 1905, there were enough women lawyers in the state to organize a separate, all-women's professional organization: the Massachusetts Association of Women Lawyers. In 1916, the Bar Association of the City of Boston admitted women. By 1920, the year women won the vote nationwide, Massachusetts ranked fifth among all states where women lawyers practiced, and by 1939 Massachusetts was third, behind only New York and Washington, D.C. Most women lawyers in the state practiced in Boston, the fourth most populous city for women lawyers in 1920 and the third, after Washington, D.C. and New York, in 1939. The growing numbers of women lawyers reveal the important advances women made in the legal profession in Massachusetts in the half-century from the 1880s through the 1930s.

While the late nineteenth century was an era of struggle for Robinson and other pioneer women lawyers, the 1930s, according to Massachusetts lawyer Emma Fall Schofield, was "the golden age of opportunity for women." Schofield had much to be optimistic about. The daughter of lawyers Anna Christy Fall and George Fall, Schofield followed her parents' professional path. She graduated from Boston University School of Law in 1908, married, had two children, and built a remarkable legal career. She was the first woman in Massachusetts to serve both as a commissioner on the Massachusetts Industrial Accident Board and as assistant attorney general. In addition, she was the first woman probation officer in the western part of the state, a dean of women at the Northeastern University Evening Law School, and a professor of constitutional law at Portia Law School. Schofield also balanced her legal career with marriage and motherhood. If Jane Thorndike was the fictional symbol of the ideal new woman lawyer of the day, Emma Schofield stood as proof that the image could be a reality.

In 1920, Boston lawyer Dorothy Hobson echoed Schofield's optimism, predicting that women's newly-won right to vote would increase their professional opportunities even further. The impressive accomplishments of individual women throughout Massachusetts seemed to reinforce Schofield's and Hobson's buoyant confidence in the future of women in the legal profession. In 1923, Portia Law School graduate Ellen L. Buckley became the first assistant U.S. attorney in New England; in 1927, Margaret M. McChesney, another Portia graduate, became the first woman lawyer to appear before the full bench of the Massachusetts Supreme Judicial Court. Schofield herself, along with Sadie Lipner Shulman, both BU Law graduates became Massachusetts' first female judges when they were appointed to the Malden and Dorchester District Courts in 1930. In 1934, Ethel E. Mackiernan, a Portia graduate, was appointed to the Nantucket District Court, becoming the first woman to serve as presiding justice of a court in Massachusetts. Meanwhile, Portia graduate Blanche Braxton stood as proof that an African-American woman could also succeed in the law in this era of opportunity. In 1923, Braxton became the first African-American women lawyer in Massachusetts, and a decade later she became the first African-American woman to practice law in the U.S. District Court in Massachusetts.

Despite the impressive accomplishments of individual women lawyers, most women never came close to achieving the professional status and autonomy of women like Schofield. Instead, a nationwide pattern of gender discrimination existed in the legal profession, stretching from large cities like New York and Chicago, to southern cities like Baltimore and Atlanta, to cities in the west like Omaha and Tacoma. The administrator at DePaul University College of Law in Chicago attested to the pervasiveness of this gender discrimination. "Out of hundreds of requests for law clerks...I have never received one request for a young woman, nor have I been able to place one unless through influence, as the daughter of a lawyer." African-American women lawyers fared even worse as race combined with gender to create even more resistance. By 1930, the U.S. Census listed only four African-American women lawyers practicing in the District of Columbia, three in New York State, and none in Massachusetts.

Women lawyers in Massachusetts did not escape this national pattern of gender discrimination in the legal profession. As early as 1912, Boston attorney Alice Parker Lesser exposed the hard reality behind women lawyers' expressions of optimism. In an interview with the *Saturday Evening Traveller*, she confessed: "I realize that for years I and other women lawyers have lied when we said that we were on an equal basis with men in our profession. It is not so, and I am going to tell the real truth about the situation now. The field of law is no better today for girls than it was 20 years ago when they entered it." Women had more opportunities than ever before to study law, Lesser acknowledged, but they still lacked the opportunity to practice it. "Of course, she has all the book learning any lawyer can have...but practice of law tells another tale." The title of the article in the *Saturday Evening Traveller*, "Girl Lawyer Has Small Chance for Success," summed up Lesser's gloomy picture.

Women had more opportunities than ever before to study law, but they still lacked the opportunity to practice it.

Other women lawyers in Massachusetts agreed with Lesser's pessimistic view, expressing caution, if not despair, about the lack of professional opportunities available to the new women lawyers of the day. Portia graduate Edith Batchelder explained that law was an "interesting" vocation for women, but it was "not necessarily profitable." The usually optimistic Dorothy Hobson admitted that "it is much more difficult for women to get connected with good firms than for men." The highly trained Marjorie Hurd, who earned both a bachelor of arts and a master of arts in economics from Radcliffe College, attended the Cambridge Law School for Women, and then graduated from Portia Law School, took an even dimmer view. Law "is overwhelmingly a man's profession and in the give and take of casual and formal association a woman is at a disadvantage," she explained. There is "very little chance for women."

Such expressions of pessimism were not misguided. In 1931, Catherine Murdock failed the oral portion of the Massachusetts bar exam when her examiner told her that "women belong in the kitchen, not in the bar." Finally admitted in 1932, Murdock found that no law firms would admit women, so she joined two other Portia graduates, Elizabeth Curry and Helen Mowles, and opened Curry, Mowles and Murdock, Boston's first all-women's law firm. Ignoring the warnings about competing with men, they opened their office at 6 Beacon Street, decorated it with white curtains and a picture of the Supreme Judicial Court with Justice Olive Wendell Holmes, and set out to practice law. "We're just going to be ourselves.

We know law and will go about it quietly, not looking for any favors because we are women and giving the very best advice we can." Yet, despite their claims, it was impossible for Boston to ignore the gendered composition of Curry, Mowles and Murdock. Writing about the three women lawyers at the firm, a reporter for the *Boston Traveler* explained that the "girls plan to cook their own lunch. They know just as much about the culinary art as the most modern homemaker and just between ourselves, they think law is much more simple than making an angel food cake!"

Other women lawyers seeking work in Boston had to settle for then gender-appropriate office positions where they assisted male lawyers. Dorothy Hobson was a secretary and Edith Batchelder was an office manager. With the help of Harvard professor Joseph Beale, the eminently qualified Marjorie Hurd worked briefly as a law clerk at Hale and Dorr, but left to become Beale's secretary, because "he wanted me." For a salary of fifteen dollars for a three-day workweek, Hurd became the invisible assistant behind Beale's *Treatise on the Conflict of Laws,* "looking up cases, writing the simpler chapters, revising, etc."

In addition to the challenge of finding work, women lawyers also discovered that, unlike the fictional Jane Thorndike, it was very difficult to find a husband who would encourage their careers. Even the happily married Schofield warned young women lawyers to be careful when they looked for a mate and to choose "a cooperative husband" for a marriage partner. "A girl must be very sure that her husband is sympathetic with her ideals and what she hopes to attain and will be willing to let her do the things she wants to do." Few new women lawyers were as fortunate as Schofield, who managed to balance marriage and motherhood with her thriving career. Instead, most discovered how difficult this was to achieve. Summing up the new realism, one new woman lawyer lamented: "Marriage is too much of a compromise; it lops off a woman's life as an individual. Yet, the renunciation too is a lopping off. We choose between the frying-pan and the fire—both very uncomfortable." Another wrote simply: "Give it up!!"

Boston attorney Lucy Tunis followed this advice. Though she was a successful lawyer, she abandoned her active career for her husband. In an article entitled "I Gave Up My Law Books For a Cook Book," she admitted to the readers of *American Magazine* in 1927 that she had failed in her attempt to balance marriage and career. Instead, when Tunis faced a choice between her professional needs and those of her husband, she willingly abandoned her law practice in Boston to move with her husband to New York City. "And what was I to get in return?" she asked rhetorically. Her sacrifice, Tunis reassured her readers, brought its own rich reward of domestic fulfillment in the sanctuary of her home. "I would find happiness in

Catherine Murdock Dewey

on taking the oral portion of the bar exam

As told to Elizabeth A. Brown, December 23, 2009:

> *One of [the bar examiners] wanted to know why I wanted to become a lawyer, and I said, "Well, it's something I had on my mind for many years." Then he said, "Well, I'll tell you something. Women belong in the kitchen. They don't belong in the bar."*
>
> *I said, "Well, I'm still coming back," and I did go back the next year and he was still there, and he said, "Oh, you did come back." He said, "Most of them don't come back again."...I don't think he liked any woman on the bar. He didn't want them there. They didn't belong in the bar. They belonged in the kitchen. He told that to me. I said, "I can do the kitchen, too."*

Catherine Murdock Dewey was one of fourteen women who passed the Massachusetts bar in 1932 (that year the exam had just a 31 percent passage rate overall).[7] She continued to practice law until age eighty. She died in 2010 at age 101.

the home that I knew I could create, the home that was to be an inspiration for my husband." If Tunis was disappointed about the sacrifice of her career, she hid it from her readers behind her enthusiastic embrace of women's traditional domestic role. "I would gain satisfaction in being perfect at one job at least, in conquering the problem of housework that had baffled me, and in striving to make the husband I loved happy." Despite the optimistic belief among the new women lawyers of the era that they could have it all, most women lawyers in the early decades of the twentieth century faced the same wrenching choice between marriage and career as this one-time Boston woman lawyer.

Despite the persistent obstacles, by the end of the 1930s several issues were clear. Women lawyers were practicing in every state and had established themselves as permanent members of the legal profession. Nationwide, they worked in a wide range of situations including solo practice, law firms, business offices, government agencies, and courts. These accomplishments fueled the optimism of the new women lawyers of the early twentieth century. In Boston, women could be especially optimistic about the opportunity to study law, because Portia Law School and Boston University School of Law played a crucial role in building a new generation of women lawyers for the twentieth century. In 1939 alone, thirty-one women attended BU Law, while forty-nine women attended Portia, second only to New York University School of Law, where fifty-five women were enrolled. Together, the eighty women law students in Boston represented more than half (54 percent) of all the women lawyers in the country in 1939. A decade later, as more law schools around the country began to admit women, the number of women studying law in Boston fell to fifty-two. Despite the drop, more than a third of all women law students in the country studied in Boston in 1949, and Massachusetts ranked fourth in the nation among all states where women practiced law in 1949.

[M]ore than a third of all women law students in the country studied in Boston in 1949, and Massachusetts ranked fourth in the nation among all states where women practiced law in 1949.

During World War II, women made some long-sought inroads into the legal profession, finding employment opportunities in government agencies and large law firms that had long resisted hiring women. In New York City, Cadwalader became the first major Wall Street law firm to promote a woman to partner. In Washington, D.C., Justice William Douglas hired the first female clerk to the Supreme Court, and the Federal Bar Association elected its first woman president. Meanwhile, in Boston, Portia graduate Catherine E. Falvey became the youngest elected member of the Massachusetts House of Representatives in 1940; joined the armed forces in 1942, where she became a major; and went on to become the only female department head on the American legal staff during the Nuremberg trials. Still, patterns of discrimination persisted alongside progress. Long a city where women could gain access to legal education, the "good old conservative Boston" that Robinson described in 1888 remained resistant to women in its best law firms and closed tightly to them at the very top throughout the first half of the twentieth century. In fact, no woman became a partner in a major law firm in Boston until the 1970s.

The persistent discrimination against women lawyers in Massachusetts leaves little doubt: despite the barriers Robinson and the women of her generation broke to enter the legal profession in the Commonwealth, becoming a lawyer was just the first step in the struggle for women to rise to the top of the legal profession in Massachusetts. In addition, in the early decades of the twentieth century, as new women lawyers made additional professional inroads in Massachusetts, they still faced the thorny challenge of double consciousness. Robinson's queries about wearing a hat in court and how to balance marriage and career continued to challenge women lawyers in Massachusetts, though sometimes in different forms, throughout the second half of the twentieth century. It would be up to women lawyers in the latter part of the twentieth century once again to tackle the enduring dilemma of balancing their gender and professional identity.

Biographies of the Pioneers

Anna Christy Fall

1855–1930, admitted 1891

First woman to argue before a jury in Massachusetts

Anna Christy Fall pushed to increase legal rights for all women.[8] Born in Chelsea, Massachusetts, in 1855, Fall worked as a typesetter before enrolling at Boston University to study journalism. At BU, she met her husband, George Howard Fall, who established his own legal practice. Fall was integral in her husband's practice, working in his office and sitting beside him in court to assist him as his hearing worsened. Through her work, Fall developed her own strong interest in the law and, while raising three small children, enrolled in Boston University School of Law in 1889. She took the December 1890 Massachusetts bar exam and was admitted in January 1891. Fall graduated magna cum laude from BU Law in June 1891 and began practicing with her husband under the firm name Fall & Fall. The couple practiced together for forty years.

Many early women lawyers delegated courtroom matters to their husbands, but Fall chose to become an active trial lawyer. In November 1891, only five months after her graduation, she became the first woman in Massachusetts to argue a case before a jury, winning $700 for her client.

In addition to her practice, Fall took an active role in the women's suffrage movement. Speaking alongside prominent suffragist Lucy Stone, Fall advocated around the state for equal rights for women. She also sought to change discriminatory laws. Her book, *The Tragedy of a Widow's Third,* published in 1898, was distributed to every member of the Massachusetts House and Senate and was a key force in helping pass the 1902 legislation that eliminated the practice of the "widow's third." She also advocated for equal guardianship rights for mothers, which became law in 1902. Fall lectured, wrote, and practiced law until her death in 1930.

Anna Christy Fall

IMAGE COURTESY OF THE SCHLESINGER LIBRARY, RADCLIFFE INSTITUTE, HARVARD UNIVERSITY

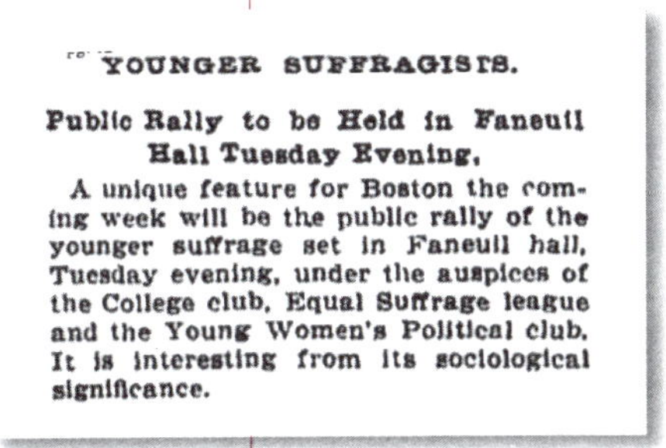

YOUNGER SUFFRAGISTS.

Public Rally to be Held in Faneuil Hall Tuesday Evening.

A unique feature for Boston the coming week will be the public rally of the younger suffrage set in Faneuil hall, Tuesday evening, under the auspices of the College club, Equal Suffrage league and the Young Women's Political club. It is interesting from its sociological significance.

Boston Daily Globe, *April 15, 1901*

IMAGE SOURCE: *BOSTON GLOBE* ONLINE ARCHIVES

The widow's third: when a husband died without a will, his wife received only one-third of his estate. By contrast, when a wife died, her husband received her entire estate.

IMAGE SOURCE: ANNA CHRISTY FALL, *THE TRAGEDY OF A WIDOW'S THIRD* 11 (IRVING P. FOX 1898)

Teresa A. Crowley

1874–1930, admitted 1899

Lawyer and advocate for women's suffrage

Born in Wakefield, Massachusetts, in 1874, Teresa A. (O'Leary) Crowley developed a passion for the law when she was exposed to research and study while growing up alongside her brother.[9] Crowley did not attend law school, but read law in the Boston Public Library while working as a secretary at a law firm. She suspended her education to marry prominent Boston attorney John E. Crowley, and together they raised three children. Crowley eventually resumed her legal studies and, despite never studying at a law school, passed the Massachusetts bar exam in 1899. Of the fifty-six who passed, she was the only woman.

▲

Teresa A. Crowley

IMAGE COURTESY OF THE SCHLESINGER LIBRARY, RADCLIFFE INSTITUTE, HARVARD UNIVERSITY

> My own personal interest in the suffrage cause is very closely tied up with my interest in good government. I believe the cause of civics and of suffrage for women go hand in hand.
>
> "Suffragist at Sixteen," *Boston Daily Globe*, Aug. 22, 1909

While working as a legal secretary, Crowley developed an increased awareness of the inequality faced by women. Crowley recalled to a reporter: "I soon found from contact with actual life that I could do nearly everything a man does except vote." Association with women active in the suffragist movement led Crowley to distribute suffragist literature in her office and attend local rallies and debates. At one such rally the scheduled speaker fell ill and Crowley was called to the podium in her place. After delivering an eloquent speech, Crowley was soon called upon to speak at debates around Massachusetts and was hailed as one of the best spokeswomen for women's suffrage.

Crowley believed that law and suffrage went hand in hand, leading her to pursue the cause as chair of the legislative committee of the Massachusetts Woman Suffrage Association. As chair she became a fixture at the State House as she lobbied for support, calling on the spirit of justice and freedom in Massachusetts' history to encompass women. Crowley and other suffragists

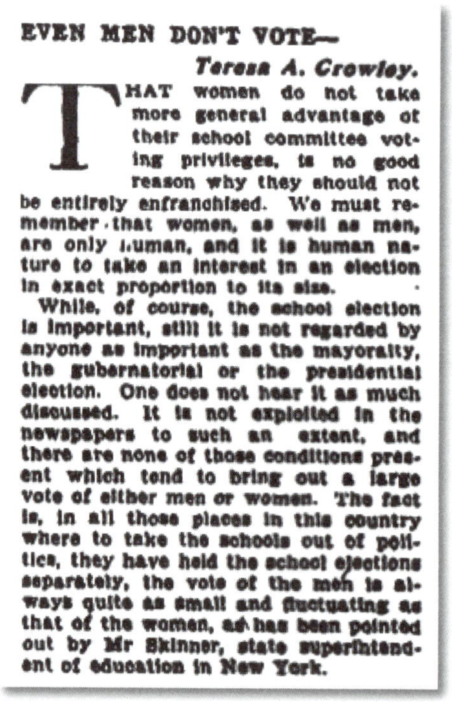

EVEN MEN DON'T VOTE—

Teresa A. Crowley.

THAT women do not take more general advantage of their school committee voting privileges, is no good reason why they should not be entirely enfranchised. We must remember that women, as well as men, are only human, and it is human nature to take an interest in an election in exact proportion to its size.

While, of course, the school election is important, still it is not regarded by anyone as important as the mayoralty, the gubernatorial or the presidential election. One does not hear it as much discussed. It is not exploited in the newspapers to such an extent, and there are none of those conditions present which tend to bring out a large vote of either men or women. The fact is, in all those places in this country where to take the schools out of politics, they have held the school elections separately, the vote of the men is always quite as small and fluctuating as that of the women, as has been pointed out by Mr Skinner, state superintendent of education in New York.

◀

In an opinion column in the August 22, 1909, edition of the Boston Daily Globe, *Crowley argued that women's low turnout for school committee elections was "no good reason why they should not be entirely enfranchised."*

IMAGE SOURCE: *BOSTON GLOBE* ONLINE ARCHIVES

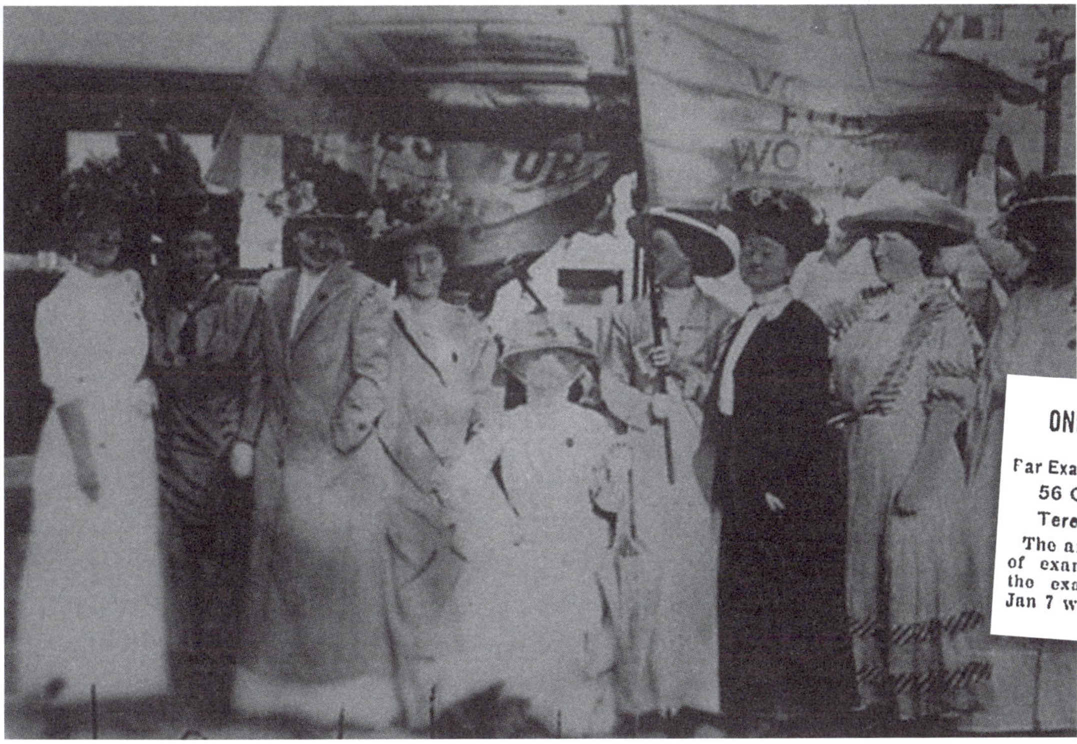

Suffragists at an open air meeting in Dedham, Massachusetts in 1909. Crowley is second from the left.

IMAGE COURTESY OF THE SCHLESINGER LIBRARY, RADCLIFFE INSTITUTE, HARVARD UNIVERSITY

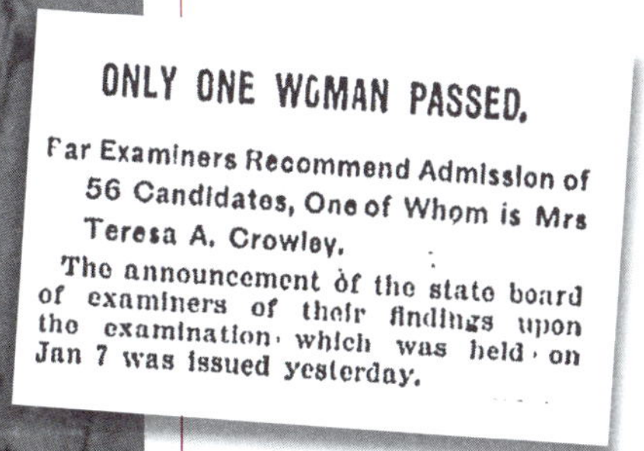

ONLY ONE WOMAN PASSED.

Far Examiners Recommend Admission of 56 Candidates, One of Whom is Mrs Teresa A. Crowley.

The announcement of the state board of examiners of their findings upon the examination, which was held on Jan 7 was issued yesterday.

A Boston Daily Globe *headline from January 31, 1899.*

IMAGE SOURCE: *BOSTON GLOBE* ONLINE ARCHIVES

campaigned against candidates who opposed their efforts, including Levi H. Greenwood, the president of the state senate. Greenwood fell victim to their efforts when Crowley revealed how his actual voting record differed from his campaign promises. Crowley used the same tactic to defeat Massachusetts U.S. Senator John W. Weeks, who also opposed suffrage. Weeks' defeat paved the way for the passage of the Nineteenth Amendment in the next Congress.

Crowley died in 1930 at age fifty-five.

Emma Fall Schofield

1885–1980, admitted 1908

First woman judge in Massachusetts (with Sadie Lipner Shulman)

Emma Fall Schofield built upon the accomplishments of her mother, Anna Christy Fall, and others in the women's rights movement to become one of the first two female judges in Massachusetts. Schofield, born in Malden, Massachusetts, earned her bachelor of arts from Boston University in 1906 and her bachelor of laws from BU Law just two years later. Following graduation, she studied law at the Sorbonne and Paris Law School for one year before joining her parents' firm, Fall & Fall.

In a time when only around fifty women actively practiced law in Massachusetts (most reading law in the confines of a relative's office), Schofield's legal endeavors were groundbreaking. Schofield founded the Malden Women's Equal Suffrage League and campaigned for suffrage across the state. In 1922, at age thirty-seven, she was appointed by Governor Channing Cox as commissioner of the Massachusetts Industrial Accident Board, a quasi-judicial position she held for five years. Then, only seven years after women obtained the right to vote, Schofield was named the first woman assistant attorney general in Massachusetts in 1927.

In 1930, Governor Frank Allen simultaneously appointed Schofield to the Malden District Court and Sadie Lipner Shulman to the Dorchester District Court. Schofield would serve in that position for twenty-seven years until her retirement in 1957. During her years on the bench, she taught classes at Portia Law School and the Chandler School of Boston while lecturing to the general public on topics including everyday law for women and wit and wisdom of the bench and bar.

Throughout her life, Schofield worked to assist probationers and juvenile delinquents. In addition to her law degree, Schofield received a degree in 1911 from the Boston School of Social Workers. She was the first female probation officer in the Springfield District

Emma Fall Schofield

IMAGE COURTESY OF THE SCHLESINGER LIBRARY, RADCLIFFE INSTITUTE, HARVARD UNIVERSITY; SIGNATURE IMAGE SOURCE: *THE STORY OF MASSACHUSETTS* (THE AMERICAN HISTORICAL SOCIETY 1938)

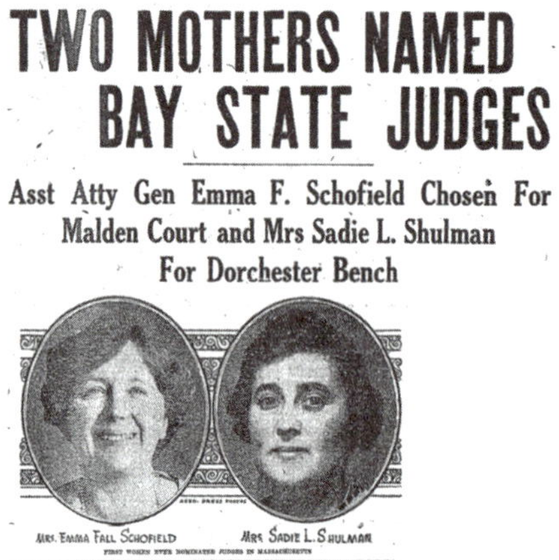

TWO MOTHERS NAMED BAY STATE JUDGES

Asst Atty Gen Emma F. Schofield Chosen For Malden Court and Mrs Sadie L. Shulman For Dorchester Bench

MRS. EMMA FALL SCHOFIELD MRS. SADIE L. SHULMAN

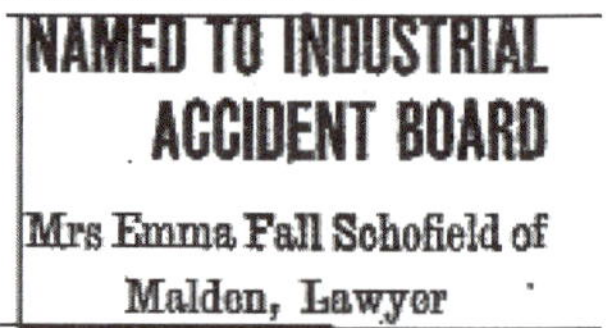

NAMED TO INDUSTRIAL ACCIDENT BOARD

Mrs Emma Fall Schofield of Malden, Lawyer

WOMEN HERE PLEAD TO SERVE ON JURIES

Mrs Schofield Leads Group at Legislative Hearing

Two of Sex Speak In Opposition to Bill Before Legislature

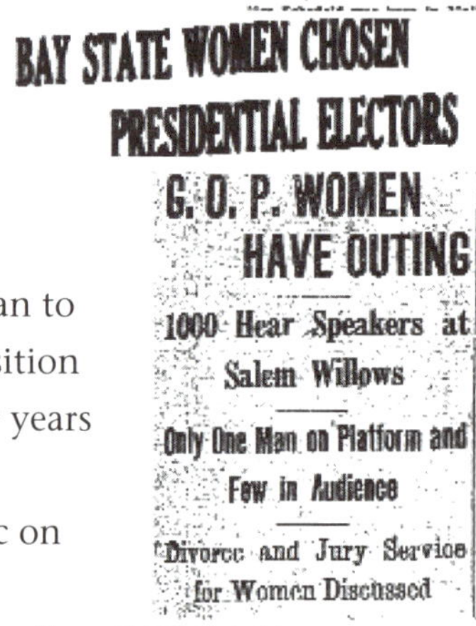

BAY STATE WOMEN CHOSEN PRESIDENTIAL ELECTORS

G. O. P. WOMEN HAVE OUTING

1000 Hear Speakers at Salem Willows

Only One Man on Platform and Few in Audience

Divorce and Jury Service for Women Discussed

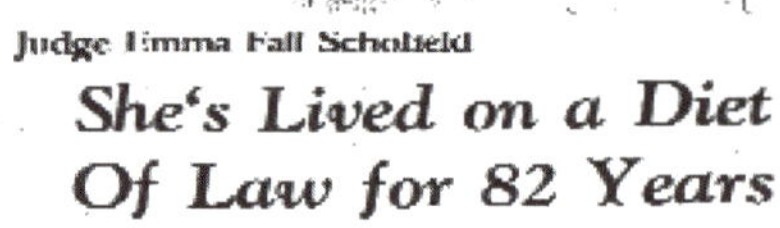

Judge Emma Fall Schofield

She's Lived on a Diet Of Law for 82 Years

Newspaper articles from Schofield's career spanned many years.

IMAGE SOURCES: *BOSTON GLOBE* ONLINE ARCHIVES[10]

Court. Later in her career, Schofield studied the prevention of juvenile delinquency around the country, citing a lack of moral training and discipline as its chief cause.

Among her many accomplishments, Schofield was president of the Professional Women's Club of Boston, the Women Graduates' Club of Boston University, the Woman's Republican Club of Malden, and the Business and Professional Women's Republican Club of Massachusetts. In addition to being a member of the American Bar Association, she was the first woman elected to its local council in Massachusetts. In the last decade of her life, Schofield authored three books about her parents and childhood, including *Anna Christy Fall, My Remarkable Mother.*

Sadie Lipner Shulman

1891–1998, admitted 1912

First woman judge in Massachusetts (with Emma Fall Schofield)

Sadie Lipner Shulman was inspired to become a lawyer when she met her uncle, a lawyer in Poland, as a child.[11] Although she lived in a country where women were not yet able to vote, she pursued her dream and became one of the most legally accomplished women of her time.

Shulman was born in New York City in 1891. Her family moved to Boston, where she graduated from Roxbury High School and then enrolled in Boston University School of Law in 1908. At age seventeen Shulman was the youngest member of her class, and when she graduated at age twenty, she did not meet the age requirements for admission to the Massachusetts bar. She was admitted a year later, in 1912. By 1913 she had been named chief counsel for the Boston Civic Service. She married Charles Shulman, a prominent Boston attorney, and in 1918 they established the firm Shulman and Shulman. The couple had one son.

During her early legal career, Shulman focused on trial practice, specializing in domestic issues such as adoption and divorce. In 1926 she was appointed assistant corporation counsel for the City of Boston; she was the first woman to hold the position.

By 1930 Governor Frank Allen decided it was time for women to be

Shulman and Schofield being administered the oath of office as Massachusetts' first women judges by Governor Frank Allen in 1930.

IMAGE COURTESY OF BOSTON PUBLIC LIBRARY PRINT DEPARTMENT

represented in the judicial branch in Massachusetts. Recognizing her accomplishments and ability, the governor named Shulman special justice to the Dorchester District Court (while simultaneously appointing Emma Fall Schofield special justice to the Malden District Court). The appointments made her and Schofield the state's first woman judges, and made Shulman the first Jewish woman judge in the state. In one notable case, Shulman sentenced a juvenile who had killed a pedestrian while driving a stolen car to go view the victim's body at the funeral home. She observed, "I believe that if there is anything you can show a person in reality that will help them or prevent them from repeating a wrong, then it should be done."

Beauty and brains are here entwined,
A charming person—a brilliant mind,
An enviable reputation—none can begrudge
And with this all—an Honorable Judge.

Massachusetts Association of Women Lawyers, tribute poem presented at April 6, 1954 luncheon honoring past presidents.

Shulman served on the court until 1973, when a Constitutional amendment was passed by the voters instituting a mandatory retirement age of seventy for Massachusetts' judges.

In addition to her judicial accomplishments, Shulman was president of the Massachusetts Association of Women Lawyers, founded and served as the first president of the Business and Professional Women's Republican Club of Massachusetts, served as a Republican presidential elector, and was the first female president of the Boston University School of Law Alumni Association. Shulman died at age 107.

Jennie Loitman Barron

1891–1969, admitted 1914

First woman associate justice of the Massachusetts Superior Court

When Jennie Loitman Barron was born in the West End of Boston in 1891, female lawyers around the country were beginning to discuss the limits family life imposed on professional careers.[12] Many women believed that a legal career and motherhood were incompatible, yet in 1959, Barron, then an associate justice of the Massachusetts Superior Court, was named American Mother of the Year.

Barron's parents were Russian-Jewish immigrants and her childhood home often hosted recent immigrants transitioning into the new culture. Along with her three sisters, Barron received an education denied to many girls: she graduated from Girls' High School in 1907 at age sixteen. She then enrolled in Boston University, where she began campaigning for women's suffrage, a campaign that led to her founding of the BU Equal Suffrage League and took her beyond the college realm to speak on street corners, at parades, and at lunches. When women were finally given the right to vote, Barron

Jennie Loitman Barron, circa 1959

IMAGE COURTESY OF THE SCHLESINGER LIBRARY, RADCLIFFE INSTITUTE, HARVARD UNIVERSITY

▲

Barron receiving the American Mother of the Year Award from the American Mothers Committee in 1959.

IMAGE COURTESY OF THE SCHLESINGER LIBRARY, RADCLIFFE INSTITUTE, HARVARD UNIVERSITY

used her platform to encourage them to exercise their new ability. She financed her education by teaching Americanization classes and working in the Women's Educational and Industrial Union's law department.

> "Justice to women, and even to the community, demands that women should be eligible to sit as jurors, for if women are like men, they surely should serve; and if women are unlike men, then their point of view, different from that of the men, should be represented on our juries.
>
> League of Women Voters, Jury Service for Women, Washington, D.C., 1924

Self-described as having the "gift of gab," Barron graduated from Boston University School of Law in 1914, but soon found that "[n]o one would hire a woman, let alone a woman lawyer." Barron opened her own private practice, and four years later she married her childhood sweetheart, Samuel Barron Jr., a lawyer and banker. Together they began a law firm under the name Baron & Barron. The couple had three daughters while Barron continued to practice, developing an emphasis on the values of motherhood and family in her work. She campaigned to "put a mother on the Boston School Committee," winning a seat for herself in 1926.

Barron served as president of the Massachusetts Association of Women Lawyers from 1918 to 1919, successfully campaigning for women to become notaries. She advocated for jury service for women, writing a pamphlet on the subject in 1924 that was published by the Committee on the Legal Status of Women of the National League of Women Voters (LWV). In the same year she served as a LWV delegate to the National Commission on Uniform Laws, where she addressed the need to improve marriage and divorce laws while creating more equitable guardianship laws.

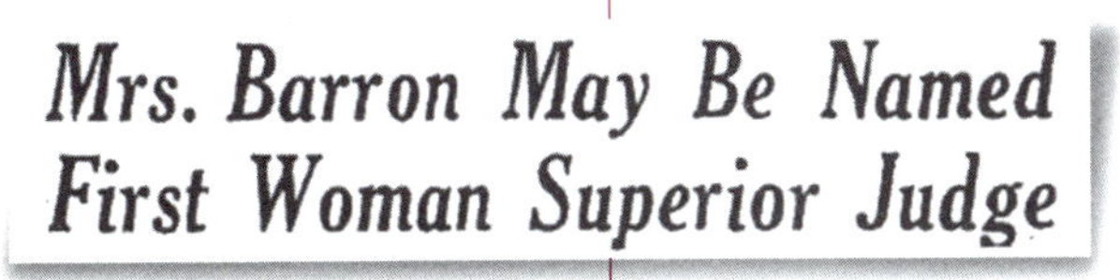

Mrs. Barron May Be Named First Woman Superior Judge

▲

Boston Daily Globe, *January 20, 1959*

IMAGE SOURCE: *BOSTON GLOBE* ONLINE ARCHIVES

In 1933 Barron was appointed assistant to Massachusetts Attorney General Joseph E. Warner. In this capacity she became the first woman to present evidence before a grand jury in Massachusetts and the first to prosecute a major criminal case in the state. At the time, Barron declared there was "no reason in the world why women should not make as successful lawyers as men."

Barron's first judicial appointment came in 1934 as special justice of the Western Norfolk District Court, a part-time position. Just three years later, she was appointed as a full-time judge of the Boston Municipal Court. In that position she became an authority on juvenile delinquency and often called her court a "clinic," where she emphasized rehabilitation for defendants, stressing that judges should also be "social engineers." The honor of Mother of the Year, bestowed on her in 1959, was a nod both to her ability to juggle motherhood and a career, as well as to her accomplishments as a caring and effective judge. In the same year, Barron was appointed associate justice of the Massachusetts Superior Court, the first woman to hold the position.

> "There's no reason in the world why women should not make as successful lawyers as men. They are just as apt to possess the sound judgment, discretion, intuition and the willingness to work very hard which are the most necessary attributes of a successful lawyer.
>
> "What My Job Has Taught Me," *Boston Daily Globe,* Aug. 21, 1925

While she paved the way for many future women in law, Barron told the *Boston Daily Globe* that she also learned a great deal from her job. For her, the biggest satisfaction in a legal career was the ability to help people. She credited her position with teaching tolerance and a faith in humankind.

Greta C. Coleman

1891–1952, admitted 1918

Advocate for women on juries

Greta C. Coleman was no stranger to advocating for women's rights when, in 1915, she petitioned for admission to the male-only Harvard Law School.[13] Coleman was the niece of well-known suffragist Zara du Pont and had campaigned for suffrage throughout her college years at Radcliffe. She spent her college summers campaigning for women's suffrage in Ohio by delivering speeches on street corners and making telephone calls. During the school year, she continued to promote the cause as a prominent debater for the College Equal Suffrage Association.

As a junior at Radcliffe, Coleman developed a profound interest in legal reform and was determined to receive a high-caliber, elite legal education that would support her work toward further activism. Although Portia Law School and Boston University School of Law admitted women, Harvard remained exclusively male, leading Coleman and a group of like-minded women to petition Harvard Law for admission. The petition was unsuccessful, but the effort ultimately led to the creation of the Cambridge Law School for Women. Coleman attended for a year before transferring to the University of Chicago Law School, from which she graduated with honors.

Coleman's Radcliffe graduation portrait

IMAGE COURTESY OF THE SCHLESINGER LIBRARY, RADCLIFFE INSTITUTE, HARVARD UNIVERSITY

Coleman was admitted to the Massachusetts bar in 1918. She joined the well-known Boston firm Dunbar, Nutter & McClennen, but left the firm four years later. Her short term at Dunbar, Nutter & McClennen reflected the legal climate women faced during the World War I era. Positions typically dominated by men were opened to women while men were away at war. The end of the conflict brought men back to their former positions and women were left

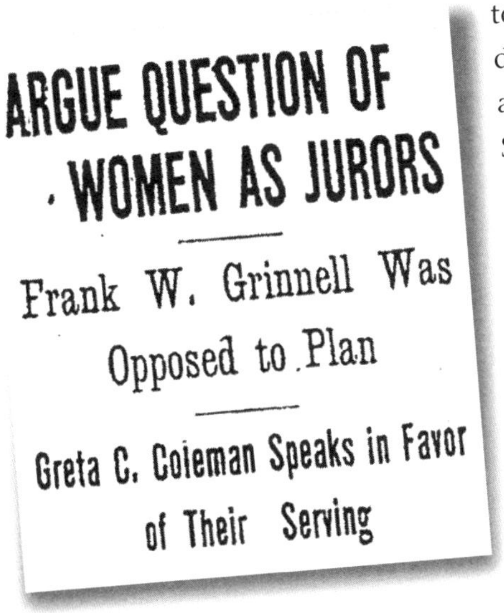

ARGUE QUESTION OF WOMEN AS JURORS

Frank W. Grinnell Was Opposed to Plan

Greta C. Coleman Speaks in Favor of Their Serving

▲

A Boston Daily Globe *headline from January 22, 1927.*

IMAGE SOURCE: *BOSTON GLOBE* ONLINE ARCHIVES

to scramble once again for admission to the male-dominated world. Coleman opened her own practice and became a staff member at the Boston Legal Aid Society.

Coleman joined the faculty at Portia Law School, as well as at the Cambridge Law School for Women when it briefly reopened in 1920. She also taught a private course on the practical aspects of law for young male lawyers who had received training primarily in legal theory. Coleman continued advocating for women's rights as the chair of the Committee on the Legal Status of Women for the Massachusetts League of Women Voters. As chair she campaigned for female jury service, arguing that extending service to women would implement the historic principal of jury service: that service was open to *all voters who were eligible.* In answer to the common objection that criminal cases with unpleasant evidence were too disturbing to women, Coleman stated that such cases made a female's point of view even more necessary.

Coleman was the first female member of the Council of the Boston Bar Association. In 1944 she was appointed by Governor Leverett Saltonstall to serve on a recess commission of the legislature to study and report on abolishing the defenses of contributory and imputed negligence in cases of children under age seven.

Elizabeth Marston

1893–1993, admitted 1918

The inspiration for Wonder Woman

Children and adults have adored superheroes for decades, but few know that a woman lawyer inspired the creation of Wonder Woman.[14] When William Moulton Marston, a psychologist, decided to create a new superhero, his wife Elizabeth urged him to make the superhero a woman. She reportedly said, "We have enough male superheroes already. Let's have a female superhero!" William agreed and modeled his new superhero after his wife.

Wonder Woman, a strong and wise warrior, bore marked similarities to Elizabeth Marston. Marston received a B.A. in psychology from Mount Holyoke College in 1915 and continued her studies at Boston University School of Law. When she asked her parents for BU's $100 tuition fee, Marston was told she belonged at home, not in the public sphere, so she sold cookbooks to raise the money. She was one of three women in BU Law's 1918 graduating class.

After she was admitted to the Massachusetts bar Marston joined her husband in Harvard's psychology labs. Together they worked to develop the polygraph lie detector test while William earned a Ph.D. and Elizabeth a master's degree. Their work inspired the magic Lasso of Truth.

Marston worked tirelessly to support her family and further her career. She lectured on law, ethics, and psychology at New York University and American University; served as an editor of *Encyclopedia Britannica*; and indexed the documents of the first fourteen Congresses. During the Great Depression, Marston kept her family fed as assistant to the chief executive of Metropolitan Life Insurance. When her husband created Wonder Woman in 1941, Marston's strength and resilience in the male-dominated public realm made her the perfect model for the wise and caring crusading superhero. Wonder Woman made her debut in All Star Comics in December 1941, published under William Marston's pen name Charles Moulton, and to this day remains one of the most popular comic-book characters.

Wonder Woman

IMAGE COURTESY OF MOULTON "PETE" MARSTON

Marston and her husband on a summer vacation in 1916.

IMAGE COURTESY OF MOULTON "PETE" MARSTON

Inez C. Fields

1896–1978, admitted 1924

First African-American woman to graduate from Boston University School of Law

Inez C. Fields

IMAGE SOURCE: *1921 YEARBOOK OF THE BOSTON UNIVERSITY LAW SCHOOL*, p.30

Inez C. Fields was born in Hampton, Virginia, in 1896.[15] As an African American in Virginia, Fields had difficulty gaining a proper education in the public schools. Seeking better educational opportunities, Fields and her family moved to Massachusetts, where she graduated from Cambridge High School in 1918. Still excluded from Virginia law schools due to her race, Fields enrolled at Boston University School of Law. Although the school had admitted women and African-American students for several years, Fields became the first African-American woman to graduate from the school in 1922.

Two years later, in 1924, Fields became the second African-American woman admitted to the bar in Massachusetts. (The first African-American woman, Blanche E. Braxton, had been admitted in 1923.) She returned to Virginia, where she became that state's third African-American woman admitted to the bar in 1928. She joined her father, George Washington Fields, in his practice. She died in 1978.

Clara Burrill Bruce

1880–1947, admitted 1926

First African American to serve as editor-in-chief of a law review

Clara Burrill Bruce was born in Washington, D.C., in 1880. She first attended Howard University and then transferred to Radcliffe College, where she majored in economics.[16] She left Radcliffe to marry Roscoe Bruce, son of U.S. Senator Blanche Bruce and a graduate of Harvard University. The couple then moved to Alabama, where Roscoe worked with his mentor, Booker T. Washington, as director of academic affairs at Tuskegee Institute. After several years they moved again, to Washington,

Clara Burrill Bruce, pictured with her fellow law review members.

IMAGE SOURCE: BU LAW INTERACTIVE HISTORY TIMELINE, HTTP://WWW.BU.EDU/ LAW/TIMELINE/

Continued Discrimination

The Bruces' children—Roscoe Jr., Clara Jr., and Burrill—were educated at the same colleges their parents attended, yet discrimination penetrated the walls of their prestigious schools.

In 1922, Harvard and Radcliffe allowed only white students to live in the dorms. The Bruces were enraged. They took the matter to the newspapers, igniting a firestorm of debate and gaining the support of both President Franklin D. Roosevelt and W.E.B. DuBois. One year later, Harvard's board of trustees overturned the policy.

D.C., so Roscoe could serve as "Assistant Superintendent in Charge of Colored Schools." Roscoe insisted on modifying the curriculum of the schools, an initiative scorned by area residents, and the Bruces faced economic and political difficulties.

Meanwhile, Clara Bruce's own interest in liberal issues and politics grew, and by 1915 she was writing political essays. She decided to pursue her interest in law apart from her husband and moved to Cambridge with her three children while Roscoe stayed behind in West Virginia. In 1923, when Bruce's daughter, Clara Jr., entered Radcliffe College, Bruce herself enrolled at Boston University School of Law. One of the oldest students in her class, Bruce developed a reputation for her intelligence and dedication to legal studies. In her second year she was elected to the law review, and one year later she was elected editor-in-chief, the first African-American student in the United States to hold such a position. While on the law review, Bruce published four articles, including "Circumstantial Evidence," "Bills and Notes," and "Workman's Compensation."

Bruce graduated from BU Law with honors in 1926 and was chosen as the graduation-day class speaker. She was admitted to the Massachusetts bar that same year, the third African-American woman admitted in Massachusetts. Bruce then moved back to Washington, D.C. Later, she and her husband relocated to New York and together they managed a Harlem apartment complex owned by John D. Rockefeller. Bruce volunteered with the New York League of Women Voters and edited the *Dunbar News*. In 1938 she was nominated for the New York State Assembly. Bruce's younger son also became a lawyer after entering Harvard Law School in 1934.

Bruce also served as executive secretary of the National Council of Negro Women, organizing meetings and speaking at events for the group. The council's mission was to speak for African-American women who were underrepresented in society, drawing on the testimony and support of those who had surpassed discrimination to attain higher education. Bruce died in 1947.

25 Firsts: Massachusetts Women Lawyers and Judges

	First	Who	When
1	Lawyer in Massachusetts	Lelia J. Robinson	1882
2	First woman to argue before a jury in Massachusetts	Anna Christy Fall	1891
3	Assistant U.S. attorney	Ellen L. Buckley	1923
4	Judges in Massachusetts (District Court)	Hon. Emma Fall Schofield Hon. Sadie Lipner Shulman	1930
5	All-woman law firm	Curry, Mowles and Murdock	1932
6	Presiding justice of a Massachusetts court (Nantucket District Court)	Ethel E. Mackiernan	1934
7	Dean of a Massachusetts law school (Portia Law School)	Margaret H. Bauer	1952
8	Partner of a large Boston law firm (Palmer & Dodge)	Virginia H. Aldrich	1969
9	Chief justice of a Massachusetts state court (Land Court)	Hon. Marilyn M. Sullivan	1973
10	Associate justice, Supreme Judicial Court	Hon. Ruth I. Abrams	1978
11	Judge, U.S. District Court for the District of Massachusetts	Hon. Rya W. Zobel	1979
12	U.S. magistrate judge (in Massachusetts)	Hon. Joyce London Alexander	1979
13	President, Massachusetts Bar Association	Alice E. Richmond	1986
14	President, Boston Bar Association	Gene D. Dahmen	1987
15	President, Massachusetts Continuing Legal Education	Mary E. Weber	1990
16	District attorney	Elizabeth D. Scheibel	1993
17	Judge, First Circuit	Hon. Sandra L. Lynch	1995
18	Managing partner of one of Boston's largest law firms (Goodwin Procter & Hoar LLP)	Regina M. Pisa	1998
19	Chief justice, Supreme Judicial Court	Hon. Margaret H. Marshall	1999
20	Elected to statewide office (Massachusetts state treasurer)	Shannon O'Brien	1999
21	Sheriff	Andrea Cabral	2002
22	Massachusetts attorney general	Martha Coakley	2006
23	Bar counsel, Office of the Bar Counsel	Constance V. Vecchione	2007
24	U.S. attorney for the district of Massachusetts	Carmen M. Ortiz	2009
25	Massachusetts state auditor	Suzanne M. Bump	2011

The Letters of the Equity Club

VIRGINIA G. DRACHMAN

I felt convinced that here was a field for women, that just as many women would prefer to consult a woman physician because they could talk freely and be more sure of sympathy, so they would, for the same reasons consult a woman lawyer.

—Mary A. Greene, Massachusetts, 1887

Mary A. Greene…is a woman whom I shall be most glad to welcome into the ranks of the profession, for when there are two of us we can march on with a firmer and stronger tread.

—Lelia J. Robinson, Massachusetts, 1888

On the evening of October 6, 1886, seven women lawyers and law students at the University of Michigan in Ann Arbor met at the home of law student Letitia Burlingame for an all-women's dinner. By the end of the evening, this small group of women had formed the Equity Club. Though local at its founding, the Equity Club quickly developed into a correspondence club for women lawyers and law students throughout America and in other countries as well. It was the first national organization of women lawyers in American history.

The founders of the Equity Club made their organization as inclusive as possible, hoping to build a broad professional community for women lawyers. All women lawyers and law students, as well as nonpracticing women lawyers, were welcome to join. Over the course of the four years of the Equity Club's life, a total of thirty-two women participated. Membership varied by year; while only fourteen women joined in 1887, twenty-two participated in 1888. Altogether the members of the Equity Club wrote sixty letters. They sent their letters to the corresponding secretary, who was responsible for collecting the letters and preparing them for circulation among the members.

While the Equity Club brought together women because of their common professional interests, its all-female membership made it a safe place for women lawyers to discuss their private lives as well. Protected by the confidentiality of the club, its members opened their hearts to each other about intimate, personal concerns including health, marriage, and sexuality.

Finally, the Equity Club provided a vehicle by which its members identified matters of professional importance for women lawyers in the late nineteenth century. Through their debates over issues such as court versus office practice, charity versus paying clients,

"The Letters of the Equity Club" was adapted by MCLE with permission from Virginia G. Drachman, *Women Lawyers and the Origins of Professional Identity in America: The Letters of the Equity Club, 1887-1890* (Univ. of Mich. Press 1993).

professional versus political work, and marriage versus career, the women lawyers of the Equity Club not only identified their own professional concerns; they laid the groundwork for the professional agenda for women lawyers in the twentieth century. From this point of view, the Equity Club left an enduring legacy for women who followed them.

On Family and Marriage

> *I am now wife and mother, yet I do not regret the study of law; for I consider it an important step in the direction of confirming the theory, that true woman can think and act for herself independently, yet modestly; at the same time adorning the virtues of womanhood.*
>
> —Leona T. Lounsbury, Nebraska, 1887

> *A woman may justifiably abandon her legal practice, as she may her dressmaking, or her dishwashing, or any other employment of her single life, if she marries and such employment proves incompatible with the new duties which she has assumed, because they are woman's highest duties and must be paramount; but the happiest thing, surely, for the woman lawyer who marries is to marry into law rather than out of it. Was there ever a more delightful romance than that of husband and wife, who, having studied together in college and law school, graduated to start...in practice together?*
>
> —Lelia J. Robinson, Massachusetts, 1888

On Femininity

> *Do not take sex into the practice. Don't be "lady lawyers." Simply be lawyers, and recognize no distinction—no existence of any distinction between yourselves and the other members of the bar. This will be your surest way to that forgetfulness of self which will give your mind freedom to achieve success. Let no one regard you as a curiosity or a rara avis. Compel recognition of your ability and respect for your industry from all. You can take this stand and yet in no wise cease to be ladies—true ladies in every sense of the word.*
>
> —Lelia J. Robinson, Massachusetts, 1887

> *Every step that woman takes interests me. If backward, she arouses my fear for her safety; if aside, she has my sympathy in her sorrow; if forward, she inspires in me hopes for better times, when man and woman will venerate truth and justice more than they now do custom.*
>
> —Ce Dora Lieuellen, Indiana, 1888

> *While women have achieved many victories, there is a greater victory yet to be achieved. Woman is doubly enslaved while man is but singly enslaved. There is a bondage which is tightening every day about the limbs of the producers of this country which must enslave woman though she stood man's equal. If woman would rise man must rise also.*
>
> —Marion Todd, Michigan, 1888

On Practice

When I wrote you before it was with a hampered pen, for one thing I wanted to say that now women had proven themselves entirely capable of studying law, it was all essential for them to prove themselves capable of practicing law, and that it was the duty of every woman who had been admitted to the bar to get into active practice as quickly as possible, and to stay there, working her way, rapidly or slowly, as other lawyers work theirs.

—Lelia J. Robinson, Massachusetts, 1888

Woman's place in the practice of the law, as elsewhere, is not such much to bring to it wisdom and justice, as the purifying—graces,—lifting the profession to higher and nobler purposes than the selfish aggrandisement that now characterizes so much litigation.

—Sara K. Wertman, Ohio, 1888

Surely there is need of woman's presence in the criminal courts during the judicial investigation of crimes closely affecting woman's welfare. What more fitting than that a woman, trained in legal reasoning, a member of the local bar, should be there to study the needs and rights of members of her own sex in law.

—Margaret L. Wilcox, Wisconsin, 1888

On Court

I have found in experience that the public, from whom business must come if at all, judges a woman lawyer as it does a man, largely by his success or non-success in court, and if one is never seen or heard there, one's abilities are matter of serious doubt.

—Lelia J. Robinson, Massachusetts, 1888

On the Equity Club

I learned a great deal from the last Equity Club letters. I had not thought that women were peculiarly needed in the law, as I thought they were in medicine. I did not think that it was an odd thing for a woman to want to study law, or that few women had done it, or that it had ever been hard work, or that it would make things easier for some one else. I knew nothing, as a matter of fact, about women in the law.

—Jessie E. Wright, Massachusetts, 1888

Hats in Court

Shall the woman attorney wear her hat when arguing a case or making a motion in court or shall she remove it?

—Lelia J. Robinson, 1888

The issue of double consciousness found its way into many aspects of women's lives. Lelia Robinson's question regarding hat etiquette was more about a woman's role in professional life than a query about fashion. By wearing her hat in court a woman differentiated herself from her male counterpart, who invariably removed his hat indoors. Femininity, however, required that women wear their hats when in public. The debate that arose demonstrated differing opinions both on how women should present themselves in the public arena as well as the role women would play in professional life.

Robinson started the discussion by explaining why she had chosen to wear a hat in court:

> *[M]y chief idea was to feel as much at ease as I could, I determined to wear a small hat which sat back from the face, knowing that if I should uncover my head there would be an added sense of unaccustomedness besides that which the place and the business must create.*
>
> —Lelia J. Robinson, Massachusetts, 1888

Several Equity Club members echoed Robinson's sentiments. For them, it simply came down to how they could feel most comfortable when entering a foreign atmosphere.

> *[T]he matter settled itself naturally. Having been accustomed to wearing my bonnet from morning till night in lecture hall, library, and court-room during my student days, nothing would have made me feel more conspicuous and awkward than to remove it upon trial of a case at the bar.*
>
> —Mary A. Greene 1889

> *If one should choose to lay aside her bonnet in the courtroom…whether one should plead with the bonnet on…I maintain that it is the inalienable right of each lady to follow her "own sweet will." Her keen intuition will guide her aright.*
>
> —Margaret L. Wilcox, Illinois, 1889

For others, it was a matter of principle; the answer was an absolute "no."

> *[S]ome seem to think that a bonnet is absolutely necessary on a woman's head to redeem her from the curse deserved for lifting up her voice on the rostrum. Of course, the bonnet of to-day doesn't cover much of a woman's head, but I object on principle as much as though it were a hood or sun-bonnet.*
>
> —Catharine G. Waugh, Illinois, 1888

Finish the Fight: The Struggle for Women's Jury Service in Massachusetts

ALAN ROGERS

The celebration following the 1920 ratification of the Nineteenth Amendment to the U.S. Constitution was short lived. Although the suffrage movement had included jury service among the rights it sought for women, as late as 1943 only twelve states permitted women to serve on juries on the same basis as men. Fifteen other states allowed women to volunteer for jury service, but less than 1 percent of eligible women signed up. In Massachusetts, Chief Justice Arthur P. Rugg of the Supreme Judicial Court advised the legislature in 1921 that the word "person" in the state's jury statute excluded women, an interpretation that blocked for three decades women's achievement of full political rights. After numerous legislative skirmishes and court battles, Massachusetts women finally were made eligible for jury service in 1950. However, because the jury selection law offered women easy exemptions and because the court permitted discriminatory practices, it was not until a groundbreaking 1979 decision by the Supreme Judicial Court that women jurors achieved equality.

Before 1920, women's suffrage advocates quietly folded the argument for jury service into their broader arguments for the vote. Suffragists either insisted generally that women were entitled to full and equal participation in the constitutional community or highlighted women's presumed moral virtue—seen as a beneficial difference from men. A suffragist told the National Council of Women that the "feminine heart, the maternal influence, are needed in the courtroom as well as in the home." Boston's Jennie Loitman Barron, however, downplayed women's uniqueness. Following enactment of the Nineteenth Amendment, she emphasized women's professional experience and educational accomplishments and concluded that mixed juries would bring "a deeper understanding and a broader general experience than could be expected from a jury from either sex alone."

The Massachusetts women and men who resisted extending jury service to women after 1920 drew on arguments left over from the suffrage debate. They saw jury service as a threat to the sanctity of the home and to feminine character, arguments that revealed the depth of cultural opposition to changes in the social construction of womanhood. Political, ethnic, religious, and class fissures also fragmented and frustrated women's effort to win jury service. For this reason, the struggle to make women full and equal participants in the judicial system was protracted and contentious.

Alan Rogers is a professor of history at Boston College. His research and teaching focuses on the U.S. Constitution and American legal history.

IMAGE COURTESY OF ALAN ROGERS

"Finish the Fight" was adapted by the author from his article in *Massachusetts Historical Review*, vol. 2 (2000). For complete sources and supporting materials, see the footnotes accompanying that article.

In March 1921, the Massachusetts House asked the Supreme Judicial Court for an advisory opinion, a move meant to test the court's reading of the Nineteenth Amendment. Chief Justice Arthur P. Rugg, who presided over the Supreme Judicial Court from 1911 to 1938, already had prepared an answer. According to the common law, Rugg wrote, a "jury" meant "a jury of twelve men" and the Nineteenth Amendment giving women the right to vote did not change this fact, nor did it restrict a state's right to limit jury service to men. Rugg noted that while the word "person" in the existing Massachusetts statute seems broad enough to include women, according to the rule of statutory construction, reenactment of an existing statute "does not affect its meaning or enlarge its scope in the absence of definite indication of a legislative purpose to that end." For these reasons, Rugg concluded, neither the U.S. Constitution, the Massachusetts constitution, nor the existing jury statute opened the way for women to serve as jurors. The legislature must enact a new law specifically making women eligible for jury service.

Over the next decade, advocates of women's jury service testified at numerous hearings held before legislative committees and they crowded into the State House gallery whenever a jury eligibility bill came to a vote. But success eluded them. A formidable coalition of politicians, lawyers—led by the Massachusetts Bar Association's Frank Grinnell—and women who championed the importance of family and home blocked every effort to change the jury law. A sharp division within the pro–jury-service ranks also weakened their campaign. The moderate League of Women Voters was committed to achieving specific reforms, including jury service, while the radical National Woman's Party eschewed incremental reforms and raised the banner for an equal rights amendment. Opponents of women's rights easily exploited the difference between one-step-at-a-time and all-or-nothing.

Grinnell, who sometimes concealed his identity under a pseudonym, orchestrated the opposition. He wrote a widely circulated leaflet attacking politically active women and used his influential positions as editor of *Massachusetts Law Quarterly* and as spokesperson for the Massachusetts Bar Association to decry any change in the jury statute. Writing as "a Member of the Bar" in a flyer distributed by the Women's Legislative Council and reprinted in the *Quarterly* in 1923, Grinnell conceded that women might make good jurors, but he argued that any positive results would be outweighed by the disruption to home life caused by a woman's presence in a courtroom and by the destruction of her femininity that would inevitably follow. A woman should not be forced by law to have "the iron enter her soul" simply to satisfy the demand of a few for equality.

Grinnell predicted other negative consequences. If women pushed for "blanket equality," he warned, it would alienate the legislature and end any chance of beneficial legislation protecting women. He also argued that whatever the legislature decided about jury service for women, nothing should be done until experts thoroughly studied the present system. If women jurors "were suddenly injected into the law…the whole problem of studying and implementing needed improvements would be made more difficult."

In the autumn of 1923, a special Commission on Jury Service, which included two women newly elected to public office, heard testimony from proponents and opponents of female jurors. The commission divided sharply. A majority of four—State Senator Walter Shuebruk and Representatives Merle Graves, Sylvia Donaldson, and Edith Haynes—voted in

[W]omen were too delicate, too easily tainted by the process, and "happily" too different from men to be effective jurors.

favor of voluntary jury service for women. But Shuebruk, Graves, and Haynes wanted compulsory jury service and embraced voluntarism only as a lesser evil than no jury service for women whatsoever. The commission's three male lawyers opposed any kind of jury service for women, arguing that women were too delicate, too easily tainted by the process, and "happily" too different from men to be effective jurors.

In their argument for compulsory female jury service, Shuebruk, Graves, and Haynes contended that women have the right and duty to serve on juries on the same basis as men. Jury service and voting have been linked since colonial times and "it is not fair play to establish some new political distinction between male and female citizens." They claimed that the Supreme Judicial Court wrongly interpreted the law on this point and that the commission's majority also wrongly proposed voluntary jury service. Whether men or women want to be jurors is not the point, they said; jury service is an obligation of citizenship that women could capably fulfill. They urged the legislature to have "faith in the stamina and moral fiber of the best womanhood in the Commonwealth" and make women eligible for jury service on the same basis as men without delay.

The commission's lack of unanimity, Grinnell's high-profile opposition, and Rugg's negative advisory opinion meant that women had little or no chance of winning a vote on jury service in the legislature. Still, they tried. In 1924, the League of Women Voters petitioned the House for compulsory female jury service. Two hundred determined women packed a sweltering Judiciary Committee hearing to demand justice. To "laughter and applause," Jennie Loitman Barron, a young Boston lawyer and chair of the League's Committee on the Legal Status of Women, dismissed the question of whether women were the same as men or different. "[I]f women are like men," Barron told the Judiciary Committee, "they surely should serve; and if women are unlike men, then their point of view, different from that of men, should be represented on our juries." The League's effort was crushed. The Judiciary Committee rejected the bill—the House voted 147 to eighteen against compulsory jury service and the Senate voted down voluntary jury service for women twenty-two to fifteen.

Undaunted, the League launched an educational campaign led by prominent women attorneys. Barron, who in 1959 would become the first woman judge on the Massachusetts Superior Court, put the issue in context. First, she reminded opponents of female jury service that nearly 20 percent of adult women worked for pay outside the home, and that the ease or difficulty with which they could perform jury service was no different than male wage earners. Second, many women's "children" were adults who "would not miss mother's care more than usual." Third, those women who had sole responsibility for the care of small children might be excused "for cause" like men with professional responsibilities. Finally, Barron argued, many women regularly left the household to work, volunteer, or attend a club meeting without "grace and charm departing from the American home; family life has not been destroyed...children have not gone, in greater numbers than before, breakfastless to school."

The struggle continued without success through the 1920s and 1930s. The 1925 defeat of a female jury bill sent women pouring out of the Senate gallery to surround the opposition leader, Senator James Moran, who insisted that only a handful of women wanted jury service. In 1930 the Massachusetts Women's Council again brought the issue before the House, but with Representative Sylvia Donaldson leading the opposition, the bill went to an easy defeat.

The following year, the League of Women Voters regrouped and turned to the Supreme Judicial Court, making use of an otherwise minor criminal case. In *Commonwealth v. Welosky*, 276 Mass. 398 (1931), Chelsea resident Genevieve Welosky was charged with violating the unpopular Volstead Act. During a hot Fourth of July weekend in 1930, police raided Welosky's tenement and discovered "all the apparatus to make whiskey." Welosky was arrested, indicted, and tried for "keeping…intoxicating liquor with intent unlawfully to sell" it. Before her trial began, she challenged the constitutionality of excluding women from the jury pool. Superior Court Judge George Hayes rejected the motion, the defense recorded its objection, and the court found her guilty. The Supreme Judicial Court heard Welosky's appeal in the summer of 1931.

District Attorney William J. Foley appeared for the Commonwealth. He rehearsed the arguments against women jurors, beginning with the fact that ten years ago the Supreme Judicial Court heard the same questions and decided unanimously against allowing women jurors. Jury service is not a right, he insisted, but a duty for which the state has the constitutional right to prescribe qualifications.

Attorney Edward Shanley's argument for Welosky was peppered throughout with acerbic criticism of the court's earlier advisory opinion. That opinion, he argued, had no bearing on the question now before the court, because the rule of stare decisis did not apply to an advisory opinion. Therefore, Shanley asserted, the question remained as to the legality of the jury pool from which the court selected Welosky's trial jury. He contended that a jury must be drawn from the "whole body of qualified voters, composed of both men and women."

The League of Women Voters' amicus brief equaled Shanley's in power and authority, but it was less contentious and more historical. Greta Coleman's argument sought to trap the Supreme Judicial Court within its own conservative jurisprudential paradigm. She established that every other excluded group had become eligible to act as jurors whenever legislation or constitutional amendment expanded the electorate. For 136 years, jurors had been chosen from the entire electorate without any corresponding change in the wording of the jury statute. Therefore, Coleman concluded, women became eligible jurors with the ratification of the Nineteenth Amendment.

Greta Coleman's argument sought to trap the Supreme Judicial Court within its own conservative jurisprudential paradigm.

In its 1921 advisory opinion, the court had stated that the legislature's reenactment of the jury statute could not be interpreted to include women. Lawmakers, according to the court, must specifically include women. Coleman turned the court's argument on its head: because of the historic automatic inclusion process, the burden actually lay on the legislature to exclude women. In view of the "notorious character" of the Nineteenth Amendment, the legislature must have known when they renewed the jury statute that women—like all other previously excluded groups—automatically would be eligible jurors.

Chief Justice Rugg remained unmoved by Welosky's arguments. On September 9, 1931, he again dashed women's hope for jury service. As used in the Massachusetts jury statute, "person" was defined by gender. Therefore, only men who entered the electorate were persons eligible to become jurors. "These concurring enlargements of those liable to jury service," Rugg held, "were simply an extension to larger numbers of the same classification of persons," namely men. When the Nineteenth Amendment created a new legal class of women voters, it effected a "radical, drastic and unprecedented" innovation that pertained only to the right to vote. It was "unthinkable" and "inconceivable" that the legislators who drafted or reenacted the jury statute had any intent to include women in the meaning of the word "person." If the legislature intended to make a change in the legal capacities of women, it must do so explicitly. Since it had not, the "true construction" of the jury statute remained that "women are not eligible to jury service."

Highlighting two U.S. Supreme Court decisions, Rugg also rejected Welosky's constitutional argument. In dictum, the Court noted in *Strauder v. West Virginia*, 100 U.S. 303 (1880), that a state could confine jury eligibility to men, and in *In re Lockwood*, 154 U.S. 116 (1984), it ruled that states could confine the word "person" in the Fourteenth Amendment to men alone. Therefore, concluded Rugg, no conflict existed between the Supreme Judicial Court's interpretation of the jury statute and the Fourteenth Amendment.

Less than six months after Rugg's death in 1938, newly elected representative Leslie B. Cutler took up the fight for women's jury service, pumping new life into the flagging effort. She introduced a bill permitting women to serve as jurors on the same basis as men. It is "a shame to keep women out of the jury box with the pretense of sheltering them," the forty-nine-year-old Needham resident declared. "There is no place unfit for a pure women to go if she can do good." The Judiciary Committee rejected Cutler's bill, and after a very brief debate the House voted down her measure, eighty-seven to fifteen.

Cutler reintroduced the bill in 1941 with the backing of a bipartisan women's coalition and, as a result, the procedural votes in committee and on the House floor drew more closely together. However, deep and powerful cultural imperatives still fueled men's opposition to women's autonomy and to their entrance into the male sphere of the courtroom.

▲

A satirical cartoon on the argument that women were too sentimental to serve on juries by Kenneth Russell Chamberlain, published in 1915 by Puck Publishing Corporation.

IMAGE SOURCE: LIBRARY OF CONGRESS PRINTS & PHOTOGRAPHS ONLINE CATALOG

On April Fool's Day, Representative Edmond Donlan, a Boston Democrat, introduced two amendments to Cutler's bill. The first required women to file with the Election Commission a physician's certificate stating that "they have examined such woman and have found that [jury] service would not impair her physical condition or health." Donlan's second amendment proclaimed, "No married woman shall be permitted to serve as a juror unless she has the written consent of her husband." The first resolution went down by a slim margin, but the House voted in favor of a "husband's right." As amended, the House mercifully killed the bill by a vote of 111 to ninety-five.

By the time the House met again, in 1943, the nation was at war. Millions of women took jobs outside the home for the first time; millions more performed volunteer work, donated blood, served on local rationing boards, and sold defense bonds. Nearly 350,000 women enlisted in the Armed Services. Advocates of jury service for women did not hesitate to point out how irrelevant the Victorian prescriptions for women's behavior had become. Cutler asked, "Are we going to tell our women who have been serving as nurses on Bataan and Corregidor, who have been ferrying planes for the Army, who have been taking men's places in war industries, that they are incapable of being jurors?"

"Are we going to tell our women who have been serving as nurses on Bataan and Corregidor, who have been ferrying planes for the Army, who have been taking men's places in war industries, that they are incapable of being jurors?" –Representative Leslie B. Cutler

Following another legislative defeat in 1946, Cutler's nonpartisan coalition decided to "ascertain the will of people." Approved by the House and Senate, the question went before Massachusetts voters: "Shall the General Court enact legislation requiring jury service for women with such reservations as it may prescribe?" As president of the Non-Partisan Committee for Jury Service for Women, Cutler led a campaign aimed primarily at women voters. Cutler reminded her audiences of women's wartime accomplishments and pointed out how "ridiculously inconsistent" it was that Massachusetts had women defendants and plaintiffs, women lawyers, and women judges, but no women jurors.

In the midst of a Republican sweep of state offices, Massachusetts voters supported the ballot measure by nearly a two-to-one margin. "Women have waited a long time for this morning, but it's a glorious morning today," Cutler stated cheerfully. Delighted as she was, the veteran legislator knew the road to victory still had to run through the male-dominated legislature. In fact, the voters' mandate for women jurors encountered years of frustrating male intransigence.

When the legislature convened in 1949, Cutler occupied a Senate seat, only the second woman to serve in the Massachusetts upper house. With the backing of the League of Women Voters, Cutler introduced a bill making women eligible for jury service. She and her allies turned back two early attempts to derail the bill, but they could not block the majority from adding damaging amendments allowing a woman to choose to have her name omitted from the jury list and to be excused from rape and child-abuse cases "if she would likely to be embarrassed." Cutler reluctantly accepted the bill as the best she could get. Following a brief debate, the House concurred with the Senate's bill. Hailing the measure as "another step in the emancipation of women," Governor Paul A. Dever signed the bill on May 26, 1949. When the act became effective on July 1, 1950, Massachusetts became the thirty-ninth state to make women eligible for jury service, one of twenty-eight states that allowed women an exemption based on gender, and the only state to include a specific provision designed to protect women from potentially embarrassing testimony.

In the summer of 1951, the first women were selected for jury service. The Suffolk County grand jury included a fifty-year-old female machinist, born in England, who immigrated to the United States in 1915, and the venire for the Suffolk County criminal court included a married woman, born in Boston of Irish-American parents, who worked as a night supervisor at Western Union. Both expressed their willingness and happiness to be among the "pioneer women to do jury duty in Massachusetts."

[E]very jury need not mirror the community, but a trial jury should be as near an approximation of the ideal cross-section of the community as random selection allows.

The judicial system slowly integrated women jurors, but their occasional inclusion on juries did not mean equal treatment. Persistent Victorian courtroom etiquette perpetuated a dual standard and reinforced a picture of women as "vulnerable," "sentimental," "bewildered," "stubborn," and "silly." Other, more serious forms of gender discrimination also persisted. For twenty-five years jury commissioners deliberately underrepresented women, and attorneys used peremptory challenges to systematically eliminate those few women included in jury pools in order to create all-male panels. In 1975 the Supreme Judicial Court ended the practice of underrepresenting women in jury pools, and in *Taylor v. Louisiana*, 419 U.S. 522 (1975), the U.S. Supreme Court ruled that excluding women violated the "fair-cross-section requirement" embedded in the Sixth Amendment.

Three years later, a handful of women legislators in the Massachusetts House sought to chase the double standard of sexual morality from the courtroom by amending the "embarrassment section" of the jury law to include men. The proposed law used gender-neutral language: "no person" shall be required to serve as a juror in any prosecutions for rape or child abuse if it appears to the trial judge that "such person would be likely to be embarrassed" by the testimony or the deliberative discussion. The law passed easily and went into effect on January 1, 1979, thirty years after the jury eligibility statute brought women into the jury box for the first time.

Later that same year, the Supreme Judicial Court handed down an innovative decision that created a new standard for the use of peremptory challenges in Massachusetts courts. Relying on Article 12 of the Massachusetts Declaration of Rights, Justice Paul J. Liacos ruled that every jury need not mirror the community, but a trial jury should be as near an approximation of the ideal cross-section of the community as random selection allows. For this reason, Liacos wrote in *Commonwealth v. Soares,* allowing members of discrete groups to be excluded by peremptory challenges "would leave the right to a jury drawn from a representative cross section of the community wholly susceptible to nullification." The *Soares* ruling drove expressions of crude gender bias from the courtroom.

Thirty years after the passage of the Nineteenth Amendment, Massachusetts women won the right to serve on juries. Still, for another quarter of a century the legislature and the courts permitted discriminatory treatment, giving free reign to the full panoply of negative stereotypes of women. After seventy-four years, women finally finished the fight and won the right to serve on juries on the same basis as men.

The Quiet Decades: 1940 to 1960

The period between 1940 and 1960, the prelude to the second wave of the women's movement, was largely a time of stagnation for women in the law. In 1940, there were 4,447 women lawyers, constituting just 2.4 percent of the profession.[17] By 1960, the number had increased only slightly to 7,543, or 3.3 percent.[18] In Massachusetts, just ten women were admitted to the bar in 1941. The number of females admitted stayed largely the same through 1959, when twelve women were admitted.

A primary obstacle for aspiring women lawyers during this period of stasis was law school admissions.[19] In 1951, one year after it became the last Massachusetts law school to admit women, Harvard Law School admitted nineteen women; in 1965, the number was only twenty-two. Similarly, in 1965, only 4 percent of Suffolk University Law School students were women.[20] Yet, the number of female applicants had increased dramatically during those years.

A 1943 U.S. Employment Service poster encouraging women to work.

IMAGE SOURCE: LIBRARY OF CONGRESS PRINTS & PHOTOGRAPHS ONLINE CATALOG

Those women who did graduate from law school frequently had difficulty finding legal work. World War II provided job opportunities for women, as large numbers of men were serving in the armed forces. Strong, capable Rosie the Riveter symbolized the women who contributed mightily to the war effort. But the benefits to women's economic advancement were temporary. During the war, the U.S. government encouraged women to "do their duty" and fill the many jobs critical to wartime production. When World War II ended, women were explicitly or implicitly given the message that their services were no longer needed. Returning veterans needed jobs, and there was a fear that excess numbers of workers might trigger a postwar depression. One woman noted: "When the war came and this downtown firm called me, it was because I was a woman. In other words, their young men were all being drafted, and they wanted a woman. They weren't just calling for a lawyer; they were calling for a woman. Someone they wouldn't have to keep."[21]

When retired U.S. Supreme Court Justice Sandra Day O'Connor graduated third in her class at Stanford Law School in 1953, she received no legal job offers; she was offered a

"The Quiet Decades" was prepared by Melissa Nasson, intern to the Honorable Patti Saris; MCLE; and the editors.

Women Lawyers Admitted in Massachusetts: 1940 to 1960

In 1941, women comprised 2 percent of those who passed the August administration of the Massachusetts bar examination. By the December 1959 examination that percentage remained stagnant at 2.2 percent (with the exception of a brief jump during the war years). From 1941 to 1959 a total of 5,503 men were admitted to the Massachusetts bar and just 266 women.

Date(s) of Bar Examination	Total who sat	Total who passed	Women passed/ admitted	% Women passed of total who sat	% Women passed of total who passed
August 1941	501	162	10	2%	6.2%
February 1942	457	128	13	2.8%	10.2%
July 1942	359	133	**26**	7.2%	19.5%
December 1942	244	126	25	**10.2%**	**19.8%**
December 1943	150	76	13	8.7%	17.1%
June 1944	117	48	7	6%	14.6%
December 1944	119	37	3	2.5%	8.1%
June 1945	125	47	5	4%	10.6%
December 1945	172	71	8	4.7%	11.3%
June 1946	373	106	4	1.1%	3.8%
December 1946	365	96	7	2%	4.3%
July 1947	389	158	5	1.3%	3.2%
December 1947	452	233	6	1.3%	2.6%
July 1948	596	197	6	1%	3.0%
December 1948	575	229	9	1.6%	4.0%
July 1949	550	223	8	1.5%	3.6%
December 1950	557	282	11	2.0%	4.0%
July 1951	742	334	5	0.7%	1.5%
December 1951	535	160	3	0.6%	1.9%
July 1952	671	267	6	0.9%	2.2%
December 1952	462	151	3	0.6%	2.0%
July 1953	614	303	12	2.0%	4.0%
December 1953	371	93	5	1.3%	5.4%
July 1954	634	285	13	2.1%	1.6%
1955 (no data)*	**1,049**	**427**	11	1.0%	2.6%
December 1956	295	137	8	2.7%	5.8%
1957 (no data)*	**1,049**	**427**	11	1.0%	2.6%
1958 (no data)*	**1,049**	**427**	11	1.0%	2.6%
July 1959	484	239	5	1.0%	2.1%
December 1959	317	167	7	2.2%	4.2%

* The numbers for the years with no data were calculated based on an average of the statistics for the four years (1951, 1952, 1593, and 1959) in which two examinations were administered.

** This chart was adapted from data and extensive research provided by Maura S. Doyle, Clerk of the Supreme Judicial Court for the County of Suffolk.

position as a legal secretary at the firm of Gibson Dunn.[22] Only eighteen women lawyers worked at Wall Street firms in 1956.[23]

A 1958 U.S. government publication advised women lawyers to concentrate on "real estate and domestic relations work, women's and juvenile legal problems, probate work and patent law."[24] Many women lawyers became self-employed or worked for federal, state, or local governments. In 1950, 41.1 percent of women lawyers were self-employed and 27.7 percent were government workers.[25] In 1960, these numbers remained unchanged.[26]

Women's presence in academia was also very limited. Although a small number of women were hired as law school faculty in the 1950s, their courses were limited to family law, trusts and estates, and legal research and writing.[27] Female attorneys also struggled to enter professional associations. In 1951, women comprised only 2 percent of the American Bar Association's membership.[28]

But by the early 1960s, change was in the air. In 1961, President John F. Kennedy created the President's Commission on the Status of Women. Two years later, Betty Friedan published *The Feminine Mystique,* generally credited with sparking the second wave of the women's movement. Women's extensive participation in the civil rights struggles of the late 1950s and early 1960s led to an increased awareness of the lack of women's rights and to a commitment to social and legal activism. The stage was set for the extraordinary changes of the next decades.

1963's The Feminine Mystique

PHOTO BY MCLE | NEW ENGLAND

NOTES

1 In some cases the first woman lawyer was admitted while the state was still a territory. This list was compiled by MCLE via a search of state bar association, women's bar association, and historical commission websites.

2 The information presented on Lelia J. Robinson is derived from: "Ms. Lelia Robinson," *Boston Daily Globe*, Aug. 19, 1881; "Second Nationalist Club," *Boston Daily Globe*, Dec. 12, 1889; "Winning Fame in the Northwest," *Boston Daily Globe*, Nov. 12, 1884; "Women as Lawyer's Hearing," *Boston Daily Globe*, Feb. 15, 1882; "Women at the Bar," *Boston Daily Globe*, Mar. 12, 1882; "Women Before the Bar," *Boston Daily Globe*, Sept. 21, 1890; Sarah Killingsworth, *Women's Legal History Biography Project*, Stanford Univ., *available at* http://www.stanford.edu/library/womenslegalhistory/papers/RobinsonL-Killingsworth.pdf.

[3] The information presented on Mary Anne Green is derived from: Mary A. Greene, *The Woman's Manual of Law* (Silver, Burdett & Co. 1902); Frances E. Willard & Mary A. Livermore, eds., *A Woman of the Century, Fourteen-Hundred Seventy Biographical Sketches Accompanied by Portraits of Leading American Women*, 283–84 (Moulton 1893).

[4] The information presented on Cambridge Law School for Women is derived from: Nina A. Kohn, "Cambridge Law School for Women: The Evolution and Legacy of the Nation's First Graduate Law School Exclusively for Women," 12 *Mich. J. Gender & L.* 119 (2005).

[5] Nina A. Kohn, "Cambridge Law School for Women," 12 *Mich. J. Gender & L.* at 125.

[6] Nina A. Kohn, "Cambridge Law School for Women," 12 *Mich. J. Gender & L.* at 132–33.

[7] "Top Women of Law," *Mass. Lawyers Weekly*, Nov. 15, 2010; Gloria Negri, "Catherine Dewey, 101," *Boston Globe*, Aug. 21, 2010.

[8] The information presented on Anna Christy Fall is derived from: Frances E. Willard & Mary A. Livermore, eds., *A Woman of the Century, Fourteen-Hundred Seventy Biographical Sketches Accompanied by Portraits of Leading American Women*, 283–84 (Moulton 1893).

[9] The information presented on Teresa A. Crowley is derived from: "Only One Woman Passed," *Boston Daily Globe*, July 31, 1899; "Even Men Don't Vote," *Boston Daily Globe*, Aug. 22, 1909; Letter from Ms. Barton Jenks to Teresa Crowley, June 1942 (Schlesinger Library, Radcliffe Institute, Harvard Univ.); Letter from Curan Crowley Tiffany, Oct. 1943 (Schlesinger Library, Radcliffe Institute, Harvard Univ.).

[10] From top to bottom: *Boston Daily Globe*, Dec. 11, 1930, at 1; *Boston Daily Globe*, Sept. 14, 1922, at 12; *Boston Daily Globe*, Feb. 10, 1927, at 7; *Boston Daily Globe*, Aug. 26, 1925, at 1; *Boston Globe*, Feb. 12, 1967, at A34.

[11] The information presented on Sadie Lipner Shulman is derived from:: John R. Vile, ed., *Great American Judges: An Encyclopedia* (ABC-CLIO, Inc. 2003); "First Woman Judges Named in Baystate," *Boston Daily Globe*, Dec. 11, 1930; *Bostonia*, Summer 1960; "Panel Recognizes Astral Advances in Women in Law," *BU Bridge*, Apr. 19, 2002; "World News About Women," *The Women's Journal*, Jan. 1931; "Sadie Lipner Shulman," *Woman's Lawyers Journal*, Aug. 1932, at 23; "Jewess Named Justice by Massachusetts Governor." *Jewish Telegraphic Agency*, Dec. 12, 1930.

[12] The information presented on Jennie Loitman Barron is derived from:"What My Job Has Taught Me," *Boston Daily Globe*, Aug. 21, 1925; "Mrs. Barron May Be Named Superior Court Judge," *Boston Daily Globe*, Jan. 20, 1929; "In Favor of Juries," *Boston Daily Globe*, Feb. 10, 1927; "Jennie Barron, Mass' First Woman Judge," *Boston University Alumni Today*, Nov.–Dec. 1990.

[13] The information presented on Greta C. Coleman is derived from: "Appealing to New Citizens," *Boston Daily Globe*, July 4, 1915, at 41; "Argue Questions of Women as Jurors," *Boston Daily Globe*, Jan. 22, 1927, at 19; Nina A. Kohn, "Cambridge Law School for Women: The Evolution of the Nation's First Graduate Law School Exclusively for Women," 12 *Mich. J. Gender & L.* 119 (2005).

[14] The information presented on Elizabeth Marston is derived from: "Wonder Woman: a MoHo?" *The Mount Holyoke News*, Mar. 10, 2006, *available at* http://themhnews.org/2006/03/features/wonder-woman-a-moho; Marguerite Lamb, "Who Was Wonder Woman 1?," *Bostonia*, Fall 2001, *available at* http://www.bu.edu/bostonia/fall01/woman; Phone Interview with Moulton "Pete" Marston (Apr. 20, 2012).

[15] The information presented on Inez C. Fields is derived from: J. Clay Smith, Jr., *Emancipation: The Making of the Black Lawyer 1844–1944*, 111, 232, 237 (Univ. Of Pennsylvania Press 1993) (citing Feb. 22, 1991 letter of Richard J. Rouse, Clerk of the Supreme Judicial Court for Suffolk County, verifying Fields' admission date as Apr. 15, 1924).

[16] The information presented on Clara Burrill Bruce is derived from: Lawrence Otis Graham, *The Senator and the Socialite* (HarperCollins 2006); J. Clay Smith, Jr., *Emancipation: The Making of the Black Lawyer 1844–1944*, 111 (Univ. Of Pennsylvania Press 1993) (citing Mar. 20, 1991 letter of Richard J. Rouse, Clerk of the Supreme Judicial Court for Suffolk County, verifying Bruce's admission date as Oct. 27, 1926).

[17] Cynthia Fuchs Epstein, *Women in Law* 4 (University of Illinois Press 1993) (citing U.S. Bureau of the Census, *Census of Population, 1960*, vol. 1, table 202, pp. 528–33).

[18] Cynthia Fuchs Epstein, *Women in Law* at 4.

[19] See *infra*, Chapter 2.

[20] See *infra*, Chapter 2.

[21] Cynthia Fuchs Epstein, *Women in Law* at 4.

[22] Joan Buskupic, *Sandra Day O'Connor: How the First Woman on the Supreme Court Became Its Most Influential Justice* 28 (HarperCollins 2005).

[23] Joan Buskupic, *Sandra Day O'Connor: How the First Woman on the Supreme Court Became Its Most Influential Justice* at 176.

[24] Cynthia Fuchs Epstein, *Women in Law* at 81 (quoting Verna Elizabeth Griffin, *Employment Opportunities for Women in Legal Work* (Washington D.C.: U.S. Department of Labor, U.S. Government Printing Office, 1958)).

[25] Cynthia Fuchs Epstein, *Women in Law* at 97 (quoting U.S. Department of Commerce, Bureau of the Census, Census of Population 1950).

[26] Cynthia Fuchs Epstein, *Women in Law* at 97 (quoting Table 21, U.S. Bureau of Census *Subject Reports: Occupational Characteristics*, Final Report PC(2)–7A, 1963, p.277).

[27] Cynthia Fuchs Epstein, *Women in Law* at 97 (quoting Table 21, U.S. Bureau of Census *Subject Reports: Occupational Characteristics*, Final Report PC(2)–7A, 1963, p.233).

[28] Cynthia Fuchs Epstein, Women in Law at 97 (quoting Table 21, U.S. Bureau of Census *Subject Reports: Occupational Characteristics*, Final Report PC(2)–7A, 1963, p.250).

Challenging the Status Quo

Employment

Rebecca Rogers

Introduction

From 1940 to the start of the twenty-first century women's representation in the United States workforce nearly doubled.[1] Those demographic changes in the American workforce prompted a number of legal protections that at first protected women entering a predominantly male workforce from the blatant gender discrimination that was once commonplace. Later they allowed even greater numbers of women to fully participate in the workforce through limits on more subtle forms of discrimination like sexual harassment or restrictive pregnancy and maternity leave policies.

Percentage of United States Workforce Represented by Women, 1940–2000

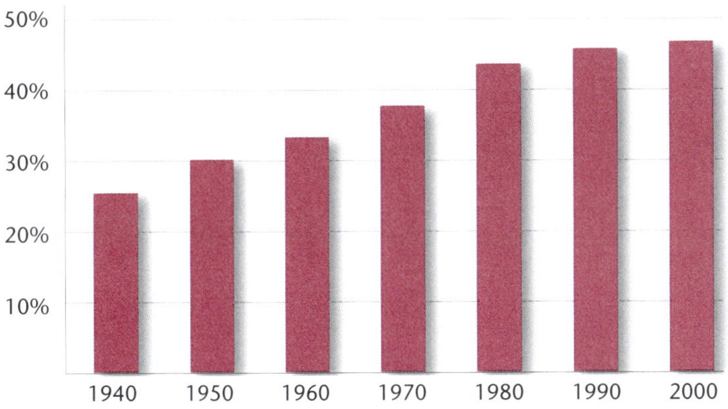

The current legal protections from gender-based employment discrimination are made up of a patchwork of state and federal statutes covering a variety of subjects. In Massachusetts, legislation addressing workplace gender equality began in the 1940s with the Massachusetts Equal Pay Act, G.L. c. 149, § 105A, in 1945. More and stronger workplace protections were added through the 1960s and 1970s.

Today, the two primary statutes that prevent gender discrimination in employment for workers in Massachusetts are the Massachusetts Fair Employment Practices Act, G.L. c. 151B, § 4, and Title VII of the Civil Rights Act of 1964, 42 U.S.C. § 2000e. Chapter 151B did not initially include protection from gender discrimination. As originally passed in 1946, it declared "[t]he right to work without discrimination because of race, color, religious creed, national origin or ancestry...to be a right and privilege of the inhabitants of the commonwealth."[2] Protection from discrimination based on gender was added much later, in 1965.[3] Title VII, too, as initially conceived, did not include protection from sex discrimination. The provision regarding discrimination based on "sex" was added during the debate on the bill, as opponents of the bill hoped that including something they regarded as so absurd as protection from gender discrimination would ensure defeat of the bill. The attempt failed, and Title VII was passed in 1964 and included the amendment adding protection from sex discrimination.[4]

Rebecca Rogers is a lawyer working in Boston. She previously clerked for Justices Martha Sosman and Margot Botsford of the Massachusetts Supreme Judicial Court.

IMAGE COURTESY OF CARRIE-ANN KERWIN

President John F. Kennedy signing the Equal Pay Act in the oval office on June 10, 1963.

IMAGE SOURCE: JOHN F. KENNEDY PRESIDENTIAL LIBRARY AND MUSEUM, BOSTON; CECIL STOUGHTON, WHITE HOUSE PHOTOGRAPHS

In addition to Title VII and G.L. c. 151B, the Massachusetts Equal Pay Act, G.L. c. 149, § 105A, requires equal pay for equal or comparable work. Enacted in 1945, it was the first state statute in the United States to require equal pay for work of "like or comparable character." The Federal Equal Pay Act, 29 U.S.C. § 206, enacted in 1963, provides similar protection.

Finally, one of the most significant statutory protections affecting women in the workplace has been the creation of certain rights for pregnant employees and parents under the Family and Medical Leave Act (FMLA), 29 U.S.C. § 2601 et seq., and the Massachusetts Maternity Leave Act (MMLA), G.L. c. 149, § 105D. Enacted in 1993, the FMLA provides twelve weeks of unpaid leave to eligible employees for pregnancy or the birth or adoption of a child, for care of ill family members, or for the employee's own serious health condition. However, coverage is limited by a waiting period of at least one year, and to employees working at sites with fifty or more employees. The MMLA, enacted in 1972, provides only eight weeks of unpaid leave for the sole purpose of giving birth or adopting a child. The MMLA is narrower than the FMLA in that it is applicable to a smaller set of family circumstances (excluding foster care, for example, as well as illness related to pregnancy itself) and provides a shorter leave period (eight weeks rather than the twelve provided under the federal statute), but it is much broader as to the category of eligible employees covered, reaching all employees working for employers with six or more employees, and with a much shorter probationary period of no more than six months.

Pregnancy Discrimination

Pregnancy and parenthood do not present the same obstacle to a woman's ability to work that they once did. In 1975, only 47 percent of women with children under eighteen worked. By 2009 that figure had increased to almost 72 percent.[5] As the number of pregnant workers increased, courts and legislatures were pressured to eliminate employment policies that prevented pregnant women from working or limited the circumstances under which they could work.

While protection from gender discrimination was included in both G.L. c. 151B and Title VII, it was not initially clear that discrimination based on gender encompassed discrimination based on pregnancy. Today, employment discrimination based on pregnancy has been held unlawful under G.L. c. 151B, see *School Committee of Brockton v. Massachusetts Commission Against Discrimination,* 377 Mass. 392, 393 (1979). Through the Pregnancy Act, a 1978 amendment to Title VII, it is unlawful under federal statute as well. Although the legal protections for pregnant employees facing discrimination are now well established, the route that the courts and legislatures took to reach this point was a long and winding one.

At the federal level, a pair of cases from the U.S. Supreme Court, the first in 1974 and the second in 1976, held that discrimination based on pregnancy was not gender discrimination. In *Geduldig v. Aiello,* 417 U.S. 484 (1974), the Court held that the Equal Protection Clause was not violated by a state employee insurance program that provided disability insurance for all long-term disabilities with the sole exception of disabilities resulting from pregnancy.[6] The Court's reasoning was based primarily on the idea that under the policy, "[t]here is no risk from which men are protected and women are not [and] there is no risk from which women are protected and men are not."[7]

Shortly after that decision, in *General Electric v. Gilbert,* 429 U.S. 125 (1976), the Court used the same reasoning to hold that Title VII, too, did not prohibit an employer's disability plan that, like the state-sponsored program at issue in *Geduldig,* offered compensation for all periods of long-term disability with the sole exception of pregnancy-related disabilities.[8] The decision in *Gilbert* was not unanimous. In his dissenting opinion, Justice Brennan, joined by Justice Marshall, cited General Electric's long history of open gender discrimination in its treatment of its workers. He pointed out, for example, that when General Electric's disability program was originally conceived in 1926, it "offered no benefit plan to its female employees because 'women did not recognize the responsibilities of life, for they probably were hoping to get married soon and leave the company.'"[9] Justice Stevens, too, dissented, with the straightforward observation that the policy placed "the risk of absence caused by pregnancy in a class by itself" and that "[b]y definition, such a rule discriminates on account of sex; for it is the capacity to become pregnant which primarily differentiates the female from the male."[10]

Shortly thereafter, Massachusetts courts addressed the same issues in a series of cases testing whether leave policies that discriminated on the basis of pregnancy constituted sex discrimination in violation of G.L. c. 151B, § 4. The first of these cases came in 1978, in *Massachusetts Electric Co. v. Massachusetts Commission Against Discrimination,* 375 Mass. 160 (1978). At issue in *Massachusetts Electric* was a leave policy nearly identical to the one considered in *Gilbert.* It provided temporary disability benefits for all types of disabilities with the exception of those disabilities resulting from pregnancy, excessive use of drugs or alcohol, or a failure to follow the company's safety rules.[11]

The court's opinion, written by Justice Abrams, stated plainly that "any classification which relies on pregnancy as the determinative criterion is a distinction based on sex." It concluded that "[t]he exclusion of pregnancy-related disabilities, a sex-based distinction, from a comprehensive disability plan constitutes discrimination."[13]

The court dismissed the argument that, in light of the Supreme Court's decision in *Gilbert* and the similarity between Title VII and G.L. c. 151B, the exclusion of

State high court rules in bias case

Disability pay for pregnancy ills ordered

The Boston Globe, *May 5, 1978*

IMAGE SOURCE: *BOSTON GLOBE* ONLINE ARCHIVES

The *Massachusetts Electric* Complainants

Beverly Harris, an employee of Massachusetts Electric and a member of Local 337 of the Brotherhood of Utility Workers, suffered a miscarriage on May 8, 1973, when she was approximately four and one-half months pregnant. In connection with the miscarriage she was hospitalized for five days. Harris returned to work after an absence of five weeks; her doctor stated that during that time she was unable to resume active employment. Prior to her return to work, Harris was notified by her supervisor that because her absence was pregnancy-related she was ineligible for temporary disability benefits. Accordingly, she never received any benefits to compensate her for the period during which she was absent from work.

Glenna Lehtonen, a company employee and a member of Local 337, suffered a miscarriage on December 18, 1973, when she was approximately two months pregnant. She was absent from work for three days, her physician having advised her to remain home during this period. Prior to her return, Lehtonen was informed by her supervisor that she was ineligible for disability benefits since her absence was pregnancy-related. She never received disability benefits for the period during which she was absent from work due to the miscarriage.

Rita Moore, a company employee and a member of Local 12007 of the United Steel Workers of America, suffered pregnancy complications at the end of January, 1974, when she was approximately seven weeks pregnant. Her physician advised her to remain at home until February 12, 1974. On February 12, Moore's doctor advised her that she could return to work on a part-time basis. However, she was advised by her supervisor that there was no part-time work available for her. On March 12, 1974, Moore returned to work full time. Prior to her return, she had been informed by her supervisor that she was not eligible for temporary disability benefits because her absence was pregnancy-related.[12]

pregnancy from a leave policy should not be considered discriminatory under G.L. c. 151B. The depth of the court's disagreement with the Supreme Court is striking. Not only did the court decline to follow the Supreme Court's decision interpreting a nearly identical federal statute, but the decision quoted directly from both dissenting opinions in *Gilbert,* and Justice Brennan's dissenting opinion in *Geduldig.*[14]

The Supreme Judicial Court was not alone in its reaction to the decision in *Gilbert.* Ultimately, the reaction to *Gilbert* was so overwhelmingly negative that Congress soon began the process of amending Title VII through passage of the Pregnancy Discrimination Act, which essentially reversed the holding in *Gilbert* and explicitly included within Title VII a prohibition on discrimination based on pregnancy.

A number of similar cases arose in the years following the Supreme Judicial Court's decision in *Massachusetts Electric,* as employers struggled to adapt their policies for employee leave and pregnancy. A large number of these cases were brought by teachers against the school committees that employed them. During the 1960s and 1970s, public school teachers were mostly female. In 1960 women made up 71 percent of all public school teachers. Although that percentage declined slowly over the following decades, the majority of teachers remained female: in 1965, 68 percent of public school teachers were women; it was 67 percent in 1970, 66 percent in 1975, and 66 percent in 1980.[15] Yet even with an overwhelmingly female workforce, many cities and towns had begun the 1960s with policies that required a teacher to resign for a period of time during and after her pregnancy. For example, in Malden, the policy, as of 1968, required teachers to resign at the end of their fourth month of pregnancy, and teachers were not eligible for reinstatement until six months after the birth of the child.[16] Similarly, in 1962, the City of Lynn required a pregnant teacher to resign at least four months before her expected delivery and did not allow her to return to work until seven months after delivery.[17]

In 1974, the Supreme Court held that similar mandatory resignation policies in the public schools in Cleveland, Ohio, and Chesterfield County, Virginia, were unconstitutional violations of the Due Process Clause of the Fourteenth Amendment because of the heavy burdens they placed on teachers who chose to bear children.[18] However, as school districts adapted their policies to allow teachers to continue working through pregnancy, they struggled to incorporate pregnancy-related absences into their existing structure of sick leave and temporary disability policies. Many school districts adopted voluntary maternity leave policies but continued to prevent teachers from using sick leave for periods of pregnancy-related illness or disability.

In 1979, in *School Committee of Brockton v. Massachusetts Commission Against Discrimination,* 377 Mass. 392 (1979), the Supreme Judicial Court held that one such policy in Brockton, which excluded pregnancy-related disability or illness from its sick leave policy, violated G.L. c. 151B, § 4. Similarly, in *School Committee of Braintree v. Massachusetts Commission Against Discrimination,* 377 Mass. 424 (1979), employees in the Braintree and Needham public school systems successfully challenged the provisions of their contracts that prevented them from using accrued sick leave for pregnancy-related disabilities occurring at the outset of maternity leave because the provisions violated G.L. c. 151B.

While the issue of pregnancy discrimination in employment is now well settled, courts, legislatures, employees, and employers still struggle with the subject of maternity leave. In *Global NAPs, Inc. v. Awiszus,* 457 Mass. 489 (2010), the Supreme Judicial Court, in a 4-3 opinion, concluded that the MMLA offered no protection for an employee fired by her employer when she attempted to return to work after taking several additional weeks of maternity leave offered by her employer because those weeks extended beyond the minimum eight weeks required by the MMLA. When the employee attempted to return to work at the end of the extended leave, the employer told her that she no longer had a job. The majority determined that the employer's promise of maternity leave was not covered by the MMLA. Because the employer did not meet the more stringent requirements of the FMLA, she was not entitled to twelve weeks of leave under federal law. The court's decision prompted some calls for an increase in the length of leave required by the MMLA, from eight weeks to twelve.[19] However, as in the earliest cases regarding pregnancy-related employment protection, businesses balk at the cost of providing any additional protection.[20]

Sexual Harassment

For many women sexual harassment is a major impediment to full and equal participation in the workforce. Although estimates of its frequency vary, between one-third and one-half of all working women have probably experienced sexual harassment in the workplace.[21] Women are not the only victims of sexual harassment in the workplace, nor are men the only perpetrators. Nonetheless, although the number of sexual harassment claims brought by men has been steadily increasing, the vast majority are still brought by women.[22]

[B]etween one-third and one-half of all working women have probably experienced sexual harassment in the workplace.

For many years women who experienced sexual harassment at work had little if any legal recourse. The term itself was not coined until the 1970s, and most instances of sexual harassment remained unreported. According to one 1982 study, less than 5 percent of women who experienced sexual harassment reported the incident or took legal action.[23]

Today the primary legal protection from sexual harassment in the workplace comes from G.L. c. 151B and Title VII. Early sexual harassment cases were "quid pro quo" cases. In these lawsuits, women charged that sexual favors had been demanded in exchange for employment benefits. Thus, they were subjected to an impossible choice: giving in to sexual demands to get ahead at work, or refusing sexual advances and losing out on workplace opportunities. These earliest sexual harassment cases were brought under Title VII and were dismissed as courts refused to apply Title VII protection to behavior that could, however rarely, be directed at both men and women.[24]

The first case to recognize a cause of action for quid pro quo sexual harassment under Title VII was decided in 1976, although it was later reversed on other grounds.[25] A cause of action based on a hostile work environment was first recognized in 1986 in *Meritor Savings Bank, FSB v. Vinson,* 477 U.S. 57 (1986). The first hostile work environment claim to be recognized under Massachusetts law was *College-Town, Division of Interco, Inc. v. Massachusetts Commission Against Discrimination,* 400 Mass. 156 (1987).

In *Meritor Savings Bank v. Vinson,* the Supreme Court recognized that sexual harassment claims could be brought under Title VII's requirement that an employer not "discriminate against any individual with respect to his compensation, terms, conditions, or privileges of employment because of such individual's race, color, religion, sex, or national origin." The Court observed that "[s]exual harassment which creates a hostile or offensive environment for members of one sex is every bit the arbitrary barrier to sexual equality at the workplace that racial harassment is to racial equality."[26]

On the issue of employer liability, however, the Court was less clear, distinguishing between quid pro quo cases and hostile work environment cases. In quid pro quo cases, a plaintiff's submission to or rejection of sexual advances is the basis for an employment decision. Hostile work environment claims arise out of unwelcome sexual conduct that creates a hostile, humiliating, or offensive work environment. In the case of quid pro quo harassment, it was well settled that the employer was liable for the harassing behavior of its employee. To determine whether an employer could be sued for the hostile work environment created by its employees, the Court endorsed the use of agency principles, and held that liability would probably not be imputed to the employer unless some kind of notice was provided to the employer.[27] The Court was deeply divided on the issue of how liability might extend to the employer. In a concurring opinion joined by three other justices, Justice Marshall dismissed the notice requirement for employer liability in hostile work environment claims that was suggested in the majority opinion. Relying on the rules regarding employer liability as developed in other applications of Title VII, he argued that an employer's liability should extend to any sexual harassment conducted by a supervisor of an employee that leads to a hostile work environment.[28]

The year after *Meritor* was decided, Massachusetts had its first opportunity to address the application of G.L. c. 151B to sexual harassment claims in *College-Town, Division of Interco, Inc. v. MCAD*. At the time *College-Town* was decided, G.L. c. 151B, like Title VII, did not include an explicit provision addressing sexual harassment.[29] *College-Town,* like *Meritor,* dealt with a claim of hostile work environment.

The plaintiff in *College-Town,* Loretta Rizzi, had recently been hired by the company. Shortly after she began work, her supervisor, Chester Broad, began making sexually suggestive comments to her—for example, at one time saying, "You have a sexy walk. I like the way you walk," and another time providing a performance evaluation in which he said, "You handled it very well. Do you know the best way you handled it? I like the way your tits stood out in the red shirt."[30]

Four months after she began working there, after her supervisor asked her, "Are you a good f---?," Rizzi complained to the director of manufacturing about Broad's behavior. The company's response was to direct someone from the personnel department to speak to Broad about the accusations, which he denied, and then to convene a meeting that included Broad, all of the women in his department except Rizzi, and a representative from the personnel department. When a number of the employees at the meeting expressed support for Broad, the company apparently concluded that the issue was resolved and took no further action.

The *College-Town* Case

S. Beville May

Sexually Hostile Work Environments Outlawed in Massachusetts

I remember writing. And rewriting. And then rewriting again. I remember visiting all manner of Harvard libraries and researching the economic, sociological, physical, and psychological impacts of sexual harassment on working women and men for our Brandeis brief for the Supreme Court. A Brandeis brief, first employed by legal giant Louis Brandeis, for whom it is named, marshals a host of nonlegal arguments in favor of a legal conclusion—a daunting undertaking for two young attorneys.

I also remember collapsing on a beach in the Dominican Republic once our brief in *Meritor Savings Bank, FSB v. Vinson* was filed. Brandeis briefs for the U.S. Supreme Court are not for the fainthearted! Then Alison Bell and I did it all over again for the Supreme Judicial Court in *College-Town, Division of Interco, Inc. v. MCAD*—the first case concerning a sexually hostile work environment to be considered by the Massachusetts high court.

It was 1986. There was only one woman on the U.S. Supreme Court, and Justice Ruth I. Abrams was the lone woman on the Massachusetts Supreme Judicial Court. While it may seem dated by today's standards, there was real concern at the time whether male-dominated courts could appreciate the toll that sexual harassment takes on working women. More importantly, would the courts find that sexual harassment violated Title VII of the Civil Rights Act of 1964 and Chapter 151B of the Massachusetts General Laws? Neither statute specifically mentioned sexual harassment in its strictures against sex discrimination, although guidelines for both laws provided persuasive arguments that sexual harassment should be considered a form of sex discrimination.

▲ Beville May works with companies to prevent lawsuits. She is a mediator, a licensed investigator, and a member of Intellenet, an international organization of investigators. She is a past president of the Women's Bar Association of Massachusetts who now lives in Pennsylvania.

IMAGE COURTESY OF S. BEVILLE MAY

The Women's Bar Association of Massachusetts (WBA) demonstrated a strong presence in both cases by signing on as "friends of the court" (amici curiae) in the briefs Alison and I filed in the *Meritor* and *College-Town* cases. The Massachusetts Civil Liberties Union also joined in on the *College-Town* case, which had been won below by the Massachusetts Commission Against Discrimination. Women's bar associations from three other states joined the WBA in *Meritor.* Coalitions had formed across the nation to argue one of the most important legal issues of the day for working women.

We were so intent on framing the issue as a "women's" issue for the high courts that we gave only a nod to the fact that working men as well as women are sexually harassed on the job. Indeed, the most statistically reliable random sample study available at the time reported that 15 percent of working men in the federal workforce had experienced sexual harassment on the job, but this statistic did not make it into our *College-Town* brief.

Sexual harassment was of special concern to women's bar associations and women judges, we argued to the Supreme Judicial Court, because of the following:

> [W]omen attorneys and other professional women in historically male-dominated professions such as medicine, engineering, science, law enforcement, and the military, are more likely to be harassed, and are

> likely to be subject to more severe forms of harassment, than are women in "traditionally female" careers.

We defined sexual harassment as a continuum of conduct ranging from rape and sexual assault to suggestive looks or leering. We related that one out of every 100 women in the workplace had—at that time—been raped or sexually assaulted on the job. We also pointed out that 0.3 percent of male workers had also been raped or sexually assaulted at work.

By the time *College-Town* came before the Supreme Judicial Court, *Meritor* had already been decided by the U.S. Supreme Court, so we had some excellent and persuasive precedent in our hip pocket. We hoped that the Massachusetts high court would be inclined to follow and find that sexual harassment was a form of sex discrimination under state law. Left undecided in *Meritor* was under what circumstances an employer would be responsible for the acts of its employees. After all, a corporate entity was hardly the "person" usually engaging in harassment. This issue was laid squarely at the steps of the Supreme Judicial Court.

As a practical matter, it mattered little if the Supreme Judicial Court agreed that sexual harassment was a form of sex discrimination if it did not find that employers were responsible for sexual harassment by their supervisory employees. If that were the case, women (and men) would be left with a right but without a remedy, as supervisors were likely to be unable to satisfy any monetary award that a plaintiff might win.

Fortunately, the case books were replete with findings that employers are liable for the acts of their supervisors in cases involving harassment based on race, religion, or national origin. Our citations of legal authority for this proposition ran on for a full page. Only two cases held that an employer was required to be notified of the sexual harassment before it would be held responsible. These two cases, we argued, were simply wrong.

We took comfort in a cogent concurring opinion by Justice Thurgood Marshall in the *Meritor* case, and we cited it to the Supreme Judicial Court:

> [I]t is precisely because the supervisor is understood to be clothed with the employer's authority that he is able to impose unwelcome sexual conduct on subordinates. There is therefore no justification for a special rule, to be applied *only* in "hostile environment" cases, that sexual harassment does not create employer liability until the employee suffering the discrimination notifies other supervisors.

When the decision came down, it was a resounding win for the Massachusetts Commission Against Discrimination, the Women's Bar Association of Massachusetts, and the Massachusetts Civil Liberties Union—and for working women and men throughout the Commonwealth. Not only did the court find that sexual harassment violated Massachusetts law, it also found that companies would be held responsible for sexual harassment by their supervisory employees.

And making the victory sweeter still was the fact that the Supreme Judicial Court kindly acknowledged our Brandeis brief in a footnote to the opinion. Whew! I guess those Brandeis briefs are worth the effort after all.

The company also decided that in order to relieve tension in the workplace caused by Rizzi's accusations and her subsequent lawsuit, she would be transferred to another office.[31] Rizzi declined the suggestion that she move offices, and shortly thereafter she was fired for refusing the transfer.

As in *Meritor,* the court in *College-Town* unanimously agreed that sexual harassment was prohibited by workplace antidiscrimination laws. Sexual harassment, according to the court, falls under G.L. c. 151B's prohibition on discrimination in the "terms, conditions or privileges of employment."[32] Also as in *Meritor,* the court was closely divided on the issue of employer liability for hostile work environment claims. Unlike *Meritor,* however, the Supreme Judicial Court majority concluded that G.L. c. 151B did extend liability to employers for the hostile work environment created by a supervisor's sexual harassment of an employee under his supervision. Citing *Massachusetts Electric Co. v. MCAD,* 375 Mass. 160 (1978), for the proposition that interpretation of G.L. c. 151B need not follow interpretation of Title VII, the court concluded that an employer is liable for the sexual harassment of subordinates and no additional notice requirements needed to be satisfied in the case of claims involving a hostile work environment.[33]

While *Meritor* affirmed a plaintiff's ability to bring a sexual harassment case based on hostile work environment, successful cases were rare. In 1987, Catherine A. Broderick filed a hostile work environment claim against the U.S. Securities and Exchange Commission in the U.S. District Court for the District of Columbia. While the U.S. Supreme Court had decided that a hostile work environment claim could violate Title VII, this would be the first case in which a federal trial judge would have to determine whether a hostile work environment had indeed occurred. In *Broderick v. Ruder,* 685 F. Supp. 1269 (D.D.C. 1988), the plaintiff herself was subjected to few unwanted sexual comments; she charged instead that managers' sexual affairs with their secretaries created a hostile work environment for both women and men in the SEC's regional office, since the implicit message was that a worker had to sleep with the boss to get ahead. On Friday, May 13th, 1988, Broderick won. The case, reported on the front page of *The Washington Post,* catapulted sexual harassment issues into the public consciousness from the United States to Canada, and as far away as Japan, where that nation's first sexual harassment case was wending its way through the Japanese court system.

It was not until the early 1990s that large numbers of sexual harassment cases based on a hostile work environment were brought. This increase was due in part to the passage of the Civil Rights Act of 1991, which allowed plaintiffs to recover both punitive damages and damages for emotional distress in Title VII cases. The increase in the number of cases was also due to increased visibility of sexual harassment claims following the nomination of Clarence Thomas as associate justice of the U.S. Supreme Court. During Thomas's confirmation hearings, television news networks showed hour after hour of his former employee Anita Hill describing in vivid detail her story of Thomas sexually harassing her, followed by the responses of incredulous senators questioning her story. As controversial and divisive as the hearings were, they did more to raise the profile of sexual harassment in the workplace than any other single event.

The hearings occurred within one month of the passage of the amendment to Title VII modifying its damages provisions, and the combination of these factors resulted in a dramatic increase in the number of sexual harassment claims during the 1990s. The increase continued throughout the decade: in 1992, 10,532 charges of sexual harassment were filed with the EEOC. By 1995 that figure had grown nearly 50 percent, to 15,549. The number of claims remained steady through 2001, after which the number decreased somewhat. In 2009, the most recent year for which figures are available, the EEOC reported 12,696 claims of sexual harassment. Although the overall number of sexual harassment claims has dropped slightly since the 1990s, sexual harassment claims remain one of the most litigated areas of discrimination law.

[S]exual harassment claims remain one of the most litigated areas of discrimination law.

Today, the protections from sexual harassment under G.L. c. 151B are stronger than they were in 1987. General Laws c. 151B was amended in 1996 to include a provision requiring employers to adopt a policy against sexual harassment and distribute it annually to employees, as well as an internal process for filing sexual harassment complaints. G.L. c. 151B, § 3A. The protection under federal law has increased somewhat from the limits suggested in *Meritor,* but it remains less than what is available under state law. In the area of protection from gender discrimination in the workplace, Massachusetts remains in the forefront.

REFLECTION

Marisa A. Campagna

When I went into the practice of law in 1988, I decided to focus on the rights of women in the workplace. Work is a critical aspect of many women's lives, and the barriers to full equality in the workplace were formidable.

I'd like to think I have made some difference. In this regard, I have won several jury verdicts on behalf of women police officers who were subjected to blatantly discriminatory conduct by supervisory personnel and other officers who were seeking to drive them out of the force. Of course, these things still happen today, but one of the most promising changes I have seen is that men are much more willing to speak up when they hear sexist comments being directed at a female colleague. They get it that it's not all right to call someone a bitch or a whore—and that such comments have no place in an acceptable work culture.

Timeline of Key Developments

Year	Development
1945	Massachusetts Equal Pay Act, G.L. c. 149, § 105A, requires equal pay for like or comparable work.
1963	Equal Pay Act, 29 U.S.C. § 206, requires equal pay for equal work under similar conditions.
1964	Civil Rights Act of 1964, including protection from gender discrimination in employment in Title VII.
1965	Protection from gender discrimination in employment added to Massachusetts Fair Employment Practices Act, G.L. c. 151B, § 4.
1972	Massachusetts Maternity Leave Act, G.L. c. 149, § 105D, provides eight weeks of unpaid leave for the birth or adoption of a child.
1974	*Cleveland Board of Education v. LaFleur,* 414 U.S. 632, holds that mandatory resignation policies for pregnant employees violate the Due Process Clause of the Fourteenth Amendment. *Black v. School Committee of Malden,* 365 Mass. 197, holds that a policy requiring teachers to resign at the end of the fourth month of their pregnancy and deeming them ineligible for reinstatement until six months after the child's birth is unconstitutional.
1976	*General Electric v. Gilbert,* 429 U.S. 125, holds that excluding pregnancy from long-term disability program is not gender discrimination prohibited by Title VII. *Williams v. Saxbe,* 413 F. Supp. 654 (D.D.C.), recognizes quid pro quo sexual harassment claim brought under Title VII.
1978	*Massachusetts Electric Co. v. Massachusetts Commission Against Discrimination,* 375 Mass. 160, holds that excluding pregnancy from company's long-term disability program is gender discrimination prohibited by G.L. c. 151B. Pregnancy Act amends Title VII to prohibit discrimination based on pregnancy.
1979	*School Committee of Braintree v. Massachusetts Commission Against Discrimination,* 377 Mass. 424, holds that an employer's denial of permission to use accrued sick leave for pregnancy-related disabilities is unlawful sex discrimination.
1986	*Meritor Savings Bank v. Vinson,* 477 U.S. 57, recognizes hostile work environment sexual harassment claims brought under Title VII.
1987	*College-Town, Division of Interco, Inc. v. Massachusetts Commission Against Discrimination,* 400 Mass. 156, holds that sexual harassment is prohibited by G.L. c. 151B, and that an employer may be liable for the sexually harassing behavior of its employees. Catherine Broderick wins first sexually hostile work environment claim in the United States.
1991	Civil Rights Act of 1991 expands available damages in Title VII cases. Confirmation hearings for Supreme Court nominee Clarence Thomas publicize workplace sexual harassment. *Automobile Workers v. Johnson Controls, Inc.,* 499 U.S. 187, holds that a policy that excludes only fertile women from certain jobs due to potential reproductive risks violates Title VII.
1993	Family and Medical Leave Act, 29 U.S.C. § 2601 et seq., provides twelve weeks of unpaid leave for pregnancy or birth or adoption of a child.
1996	Massachusetts Fair Employment Practices Act amended to require employers to adopt policies against sexual harassment, G.L. c. 151B, § 3A.
1998	*Faragher v. City of Boca Raton,* 524 U.S. 775, holds that an employer may be held liable under Title VII for the acts of a supervisory employee whose sexual harassment of subordinates creates a sexually hostile work environment.
2001	*Cuddyer v. The Stop & Shop Supermarket Co.,* 434 Mass. 521, holds that the continuing violation doctrine is applicable to an employee's hostile work environment claim and thus the claim is not barred by the six-month statute of limitations set forth in G.L. c. 151B for claims filed with the Massachusetts Commission Against Discrimination.
2005	*Modern Continental/Obayashi v. Massachusetts Commission Against Discrimination,* 445 Mass. 96, holds that an employer may be held liable for failing to respond reasonably to acts of sexual harassment of which it is aware or reasonably should be aware even if the harasser is not its agent or employee.

REFLECTION

Nancy S. Shilepsky

Three Cases and More

During my career, I have had the honor of participating in many cases which have increased legal protections for women in the workplace. Some were high profile; some helped specific women lead economically secure lives; and some impacted the law. I have been asked to reflect on three of these cases but what I have to say goes beyond them—and beyond me.

***Bowman v. Heller*, 420 Mass. 517 (1995)**

I was privileged to "inherit" this case from the Hon. Nancy Gertner (Ret.) when she took the bench. *Bowman* involved workplace sexual harassment, and drew public attention as a supposed clash between political correctness and the First Amendment. That description blurred the line between workplaces (where speech is highly regulated) and public forums. We managed to get our point across in the public forum, and this is not an argument we hear anymore, at least not regarding workplace speech.

Name Withheld

I was asked by Monica Halas of Greater Boston Legal Services to help Natasha Thomas in a matter that was pending at the Massachusetts Commission Against Discrimination (MCAD). I was so compelled by the facts, and shocked by the pattern of discriminatory treatment of mostly female, immigrant workers, that I asked if I could be Natasha's cocounsel. Soon, Shirley Cruz joined our team. In addition to obtaining remedial relief for our clients (through a confidential, post-probable cause conciliation and settlement at the MCAD), we met with the MCAD commissioners so as to make them aware of broader, industry-wide issues, including national origin-specific humiliating treatment of the sort found actionable in *Trustees of Health and Hospitals of the City of Boston, Inc. v. MCAD*, 449 Mass. 675 (2007).

***Stonehill College v. MCAD*, 441 Mass. 549 (2004)**

The MCAD is an administrative enforcement agency with a broad statutory mandate to eradicate discrimination. For a time, however, employers could undermine the Commonwealth's administrative enforcement scheme by requiring the MCAD to "re-litigate" its administrative enforcement decisions before a jury. In *Stonehill*, the Supreme Judicial Court reestablished the breadth of the MCAD's administrative enforcement powers by holding that jury trial rights do not attach to MCAD administrative enforcement actions. Consistent with *Stonehill*, in *Joule v. Simmons*, 459 Mass. 88 (2011), the court upheld the administrative enforcement powers of the MCAD, irrespective of an arbitration agreement between employer and employee.

Continued ▶

▲ Nancy S. Shilepsky

IMAGE COURTESY OF NANCY S. SHILEPSKY

What all these cases have in common, in addition to their impact on women's lives and the law, is the involvement of women working together to eradicate discrimination and increase economic access and opportunities for all. Since *Stonehill*, Anne Josephson and I have cofacilitated what became known as the Amicus Group. The Amicus Group has enlisted primarily women (e.g., Anne, Nina Kimball and Patricia Washienko) to draft and file amicus briefs on behalf of not-for-profit and community organizations in discrimination cases, providing a voice for working women and men in cases such as those named above. Much has been done; much is still to be done. None of us can do it alone.

NOTES

1 *See Statistical Abstract of the United States: 1961,* Table 268; Statistical Abstract of the United States: 2004–2005, Tables 569, 571.

2 1946 Mass. Acts c. 368, § 1.

3 *See* 1965 Mass. Acts c. 397, §§ 4–6.

4 *See* Susan Estrich, "Sex at Work," 43 *Stan. L. Rev.* 813, 819 (1990–91).

5 *Women in the Labor Force: A Databook,* U.S. Department of Labor, 2010, p. 1 & Tables 6, 7.

6 *Geduldig v. Aiello,* 417 U.S. at 494.

7 *Geduldig v. Aiello,* 417 U.S. at 496–97.

8 *General Elec. v. Gilbert,* 429 U.S. at 140.

9 *General Elec. v. Gilbert,* 429 U.S. at 149 n.1 (Brennan, J., dissenting).

10 *General Elec. v. Gilbert,* 429 U.S. at 161–62 (Stevens, J., dissenting).

11 *Massachusetts Elec. Co. v. MCAD,* 375 Mass. at 162.

12 *Massachusetts Elec. Co. v. MCAD,* 375 Mass. at 162–63.

13 *Massachusetts Elec. Co. v. MCAD,* 375 Mass. at 167, 168.

14 *Massachusetts Elec. Co. v. MCAD,* 375 Mass. at 170–71.

15 *American Education 1870–1991: A Statistical Handbook,* Table 14 (1993).

16 *See Black v. School Comm. of Malden,* 365 Mass. 197, 199 (1974).

17 *Lynn Teachers Union, Local 1037 v. MCAD,* 406 Mass. 515, 517 (1990) (the teacher did not bring suit until an issue with seniority came up years later).

[18] *Cleveland Bd. of Educ. v. LaFleur,* 414 U.S. 632, 650 (1974).

[19] *See* Editorial, "SJC Ruling Shows the Need for Increased Maternal Leave," *Boston Globe,* Aug. 12, 2010.

[20] *See* Megan Woolhouse & Katie Johnston Chase, "Maternity Leave Quandary," *Boston Globe,* Aug. 12, 2012.

[21] *See* B. Glenn George, "The Back Door: Legitimizing Sexual Harassment Claims," 73 *B.U. L. Rev.* 1, 2 n.3 (1993); Joanna L. Grossman, "The Culture of Compliance: Final Triumph of Form Over Substance in Sexual Harassment Law," 26 *Harv. Women's L.J.* 3, 5–6 (2003).

[22] *See Sexual Harassment Charges EEOC & FEPAs Combined: FY 1992–FY 1996, available at* http://www.eeoc.gov/eeoc/statistics/enforcement/sexual_harassment-a.cfm (in 1992, 91 percent of sexual harassment claims were brought by women); *Sexual Harassment Charges EEOC & FEPAs Combined: FY 1997–FY 2009, available at* http://www.eeoc.gov/eeoc/statistics/enforcement/sexual_harassment.cfm (in 2009, 84 percent of sexual harassment claims were brought by women).

[23] *See* Tangri, Burt & Johnson, "Sexual Harassment at Work: Three Explanatory Models," 38 *J. Soc. Issues* 33, 47 (1982).

[24] *See* Susan Estrich, "Sex at Work," 43 *Stan. L. Rev.* 813, 819 (1990–91).

[25] *See Williams v. Saxbe,* 413 F. Supp. 654 (D.D.C. 1976), *rev'd sub nom. Williams v. Bell,* 587 F.2d 1240 (D.C. Cir. 1978).

[26] *Meritor Sav. Bank v. Vinson,* 477 U.S. at 67.

[27] *Meritor Sav. Bank v. Vinson,* 477 U.S. at 69–71.

[28] *Meritor Sav. Bank v. Vinson,* 477 U.S. at 78 (Marshall, J., dissenting).

[29] That has since changed. In 1996, G.L. c. 151B was amended to include Section 3A, which requires employers to adopt and disseminate policies against sexual harassment, including a process to manage internal complaints.

[30] *College-Town, Div. of Interco, Inc. v. MCAD,* 400 Mass. at 158.

[31] *College-Town, Div. of Interco, Inc. v. MCAD,* 400 Mass. at 160.

[32] *College-Town, Div. of Interco, Inc. v. MCAD,* 400 Mass. at 162.

[33] *College-Town, Div. of Interco, Inc. v. MCAD,* 400 Mass. at 164–66.

CHAPTER 2

Educating Women Lawyers: Students, Professors, and Deans

The History of Women in Law Schools

MARY BETH BASILE CHOPAS

REFLECTIONS AND INTERVIEWS

As recently as 1960, men dominated the legal profession nationwide. Women comprised only about 4 percent of lawyers in the United States and were a distinct minority in the law-school classroom.[1] Some law schools in Massachusetts followed this trend. Harvard Law School did not open its doors to women law students until 1950, and the number of women remained a nominal percentage of each class for the first couple of decades of coeducation. Boston College Law School admitted women in 1941, about a decade earlier than Harvard, but the student body there was nearly all male until 1970. Other Boston-area law schools had healthier numbers of women early on. New England School of Law—by far the most supportive of women lawyers since it originated as the all-female Portia Law School in 1908—consistently had equal or greater percentages of women than men. Boston University School of Law, which was open to both women and men from its inception in 1872 and was the sixth law school in the United States to admit women, even had a Girls' Student Council beginning in the 1920s and chapters of several legal sororities.

When did Massachusetts' law schools open to women?

Law School	Founded	Women Admitted
Boston University School of Law	1872	1872
New England Law | Boston *Originally Portia Law School*	1908	1908
Western New England University School of Law *Originally Springfield Division of Northeastern University*	1919 Full-time law program: 1973	1919
Northeastern University School of Law *Originally Boston YMCA Law School*	1898	1922
Suffolk University Law School	1906	1937
Boston College Law School	1929	1941
Harvard Law School	1817	1950
University of Massachusetts School of Law *Originally Southern New England School of Law*	1981	1981
Massachusetts School of Law at Andover	1988	1988

▲ Mary Beth Basile Chopas is an adjunct assistant professor of law at UNC School of Law. She is a graduate of Boston College Law School and Dartmouth College.

IMAGE COURTESY OF UNC SCHOOL OF LAW, PHOTO BY ROBERT CAMPBELL

The number of women at Boston University School of Law rose steadily but did not approach equality until 1980, when approximately 40 percent of the graduating class was women. As early as the 1970s, when men far outnumbered women at most law schools, Northeastern University School of Law recruited and admitted women students at a much higher rate than national law-school averages. The Honorable Margot Botsford, associate justice of the Massachusetts Supreme Judicial Court and a 1973 graduate of Northeastern, recalls a dynamic group of women who comprised a significant percentage of her law-school class. Suffolk University Law School, founded in 1906 by Gleason Archer as an evening school for men, formally barred women until the graduation of Archer's daughter in 1937. Since Marian Archer MacDonald was such an impressive student, other women were allowed to enroll. However, by 1965 only 4 percent of Suffolk Law students were women. That number jumped to 35 percent by 1980, and today Suffolk has close to 50 percent women. Massachusetts law schools outside the Boston area have all been coeducational since their foundings: Western New England University School of Law in 1919 (full-time law program: 1973), University of Massachusetts School of Law in 1981, and Massachusetts School of Law at Andover in 1988.[2]

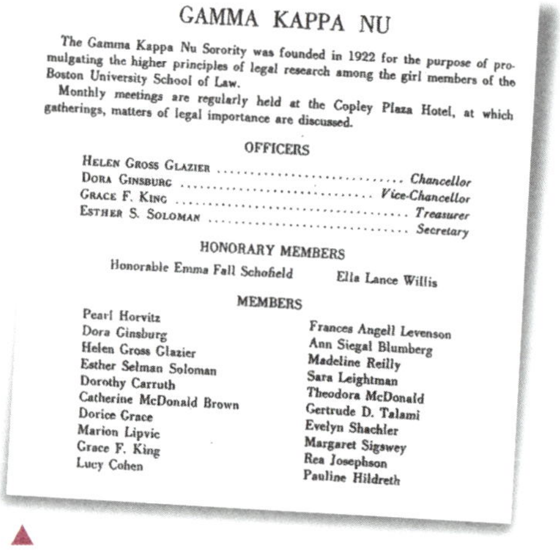

GAMMA KAPPA NU

The Gamma Kappa Nu Sorority was founded in 1922 for the purpose of promulgating the higher principles of legal research among the girl members of the Boston University School of Law.

Monthly meetings are regularly held at the Copley Plaza Hotel, at which gatherings, matters of legal importance are discussed.

OFFICERS

Helen Gross Glazier .... *Chancellor*
Dora Ginsburg .... *Vice-Chancellor*
Grace F. King .... *Treasurer*
Esther S. Soloman .... *Secretary*

HONORARY MEMBERS

Honorable Emma Fall Schofield   Ella Lance Willis

MEMBERS

Pearl Horvitz
Dora Ginsburg
Helen Gross Glazier
Esther Selman Soloman
Dorothy Carruth
Catherine McDonald Brown
Dorice Grace
Marion Lipvic
Grace F. King
Lucy Cohen
Frances Angell Levenson
Ann Siegal Blumberg
Madeline Reilly
Sara Leightman
Theodora McDonald
Gertrude D. Talami
Evelyn Shachler
Margaret Sigswey
Rea Josephson
Pauline Hildreth

The Gamma Kappa Nu Sorority was founded at BU in 1922.

IMAGE COURTESY OF PROFESSOR DAVID J. SEIPP

BU Law's 1924 Girls' Council.

IMAGE COURTESY OF PROFESSOR DAVID J. SEIPP

The early days of coeducation were challenging. Alumnae of Harvard and Boston University who graduated in the 1960s and early 1970s remember "Ladies' Days," when professors designated certain days on which they called only called on female students to respond to questions.[3] Professors chose legal topics on Ladies' Days that were considered female in nature, such as rape, or discussed cases and hypothetical scenarios whose subjects were domestic topics such as knitting, sewing, or, even more embarrassing, woolen underwear. The brave women who were students in that era report that male classmates were often hostile and that professors discriminated against them because they were women. The prevalent sexist attitude was that women took the places of men who could actually use a legal education to support their families. The male-dominated culture contributed to women having low self-esteem as they worked hard to prove they deserved a place in their law-school class. Some people justified this culture by saying that it prepared women for the discrimination they would inevitably face in the real world, and that on the whole, conditions were more equal in the legal academy than in practice.

Nationally during the 1970s, women were organizing for change in admissions and hiring policies at institutions of higher learning, relying on recent legislation as weapons to bring about equality in education. In January 1970, the Women's Equity Action League

Professor W. Barton Leach sits amongst his male students on Ladies' Day in 1965.

IMAGE SOURCE: *HARVARD LAW SCHOOL YEARBOOK* 1965, p.11

(WEAL), a spin-off of the National Organization for Women, filed a class-action lawsuit against all universities and colleges for the enforcement of Executive Order 11375, which was issued in 1968 and prohibited employment discrimination based on sex. WEAL's advocacy efforts focused on equal opportunities for women in education and employment; its complaint made claims of sex discrimination in several areas, including faculty hiring. WEAL worked through its state divisions, including Massachusetts, to press the federal government to investigate discriminatory hiring practices at universities.[4]

During this period there were initiatives specifically aimed at law schools. At its annual meeting in 1970, the Association of American Law Schools adopted an amendment to its articles of association that prohibited sex discrimination in admissions, employment, and placement by its member schools.[5] In April 1971, the Professional Women's Caucus brought a class-action sex discrimination suit against American law schools, prompting investigations by the U.S. Department of Health, Education and Welfare. The first such investigation was conducted at Harvard University. Not only did the federal government bind educational institutions to a hiring policy of nondiscrimination on the basis of sex, race, color, national origin, and religion, but it obligated schools to institute affirmative action programs to rectify inequalities in employment practices.[6]

Harvard's Women's Law Association in 1972.

IMAGE SOURCE: *HARVARD LAW SCHOOL YEARBOOK* 1972, p.205

In 1972, Congress extended Title VII of the Civil Rights Act of 1964, prohibiting discrimination in employment practices based on race, sex, and other factors, to protect employees at universities.[7] Also in 1972, Congress amended the Higher Education Act with the passage of Title IX prohibiting sex discrimination in employment and admissions policies and practices of all institutions of higher learning receiving federal aid.[8] In response, affirmative action guidelines were put in place in universities and the search for qualified women was underway. However, the results of this legislation were not immediately evident in student bodies and at all levels of faculty.[9] At Harvard Law School, students took the initiative to bring about change more quickly. In December 1972, two third-year female students, on behalf of the Women's Law Association, made a Title IX complaint against Harvard, alleging past and continuing discriminatory practices in admissions, student recruitment, faculty hiring, and administrative hiring, citing the basis of faculty hiring as the "old boy network."[10] Harvard Law Dean Al Sacks called the charges "groundless," explaining that the percentage of women available for faculty positions was "much below the percentage of women in the general population."[11]

After Executive Order 11375 was issued and law schools began enforcing it, women started appearing in significant numbers on law-school faculties. However, the increase in women faculty was not proportional to the steady increase in women law students. The Boston-area law schools responded gingerly to the national legislation with respect to the hiring of women law professors for full-time positions. Although there had been a number of women on the law-school faculties for several decades in part-time teaching and research positions, few women held tenure-track positions, and still fewer were tenured. Among the pioneer women law professors in Massachusetts are the following: Diane Lund, who taught at Northeastern and who, in 1972, was appointed as an assistant professor at Harvard, where she taught trusts, fiduciary responsibility, family law, and the legal status of women; Martha Field, who began teaching at Harvard in 1978 after teaching at Penn, and whose research interests are federal courts, constitutional law, and family law; Elizabeth Bartholet, who was the first woman to rise through the ranks at Harvard from assistant professor in 1977 to tenured professor in 1983, and who developed a clinical course in public interest litigation, directs the Child Advocacy Program, and teaches civil rights and family law; Mary Ann Glendon, whose areas of expertise are property and comparative law, and who was the first woman professor at Boston College Law School beginning in 1968, was tenured there in 1973, and joined Harvard's faculty more than ten years later; Tamar Frankel, who has expertise in corporations and trusts, and who has taught at Boston University since 1968 and visited at Harvard; and Zipporah Wiseman, whose fields are commercial law and feminist legal theory, and who taught at Northeastern from 1974 until 1990.[12]

▲

Zipporah Wiseman pictured in Harvard Law's 1986 yearbook as a visiting professor from Northeastern.

IMAGE SOURCE: *HARVARD LAW SCHOOL YEARBOOK* 1986, p.63

Perhaps the most controversial appointment of a woman law professor in Massachusetts was that of Clare Dalton at Harvard Law School. Professor Dalton, a critical legal studies scholar and expert in contracts, became an assistant professor at Harvard in 1981. When Dalton was being considered for tenure in 1987, she was four votes short of the two-thirds vote of the faculty needed for tenure. Although her scholarship had received high ratings from an outside review committee, there was feeling among the Harvard faculty that her book on nineteenth-century British law, which was under agreement with the Oxford

University Press, and her article on contracts published in the *Yale Law Journal* did not meet Harvard's standards. When Dalton was denied tenure, she filed sex discrimination complaints with state and federal agencies, believing that her denial was based on her challenge to the status quo. She also engaged the American Association of University Professors and the American Association of Law Schools to investigate the tenure process. Dalton's suit against Harvard Law School claiming sex discrimination resulted in a $260,000 settlement in 1993. The money from the settlement was contributed to a joint Northeastern-Harvard domestic violence institute, of which Dalton is the founder.[13]

Clare Dalton joined the Northeastern University School of Law faculty in 1988.

IMAGE COURTESY OF NORTHEASTERN UNIVERSITY SCHOOL OF LAW, PHOTO BY DAVID LEIFER

Between 1970 and 1980 there were remarkable changes in the composition of the legal profession across the United States. At the beginning of the decade, women comprised 9 percent of the nation's law students and 5 percent of its lawyers; by the end of the decade they accounted for approximately 33 percent of all law students and 11 to 12 percent of all lawyers.[14] Ten years later, in 1990, women comprised approximately 24 percent of lawyers nationwide.[15] Most recent statistics from the American Bar Association Commission on Women in the Profession cite the percentage of lawyers in the United States who are women as 31 percent, while the percentage of law degrees awarded to women in 2009 was 45 percent. How does Massachusetts measure up to the national trend? In recent years women outnumbered men at some Massachusetts law schools. For example, Boston University School of Law had 53 percent women students in 2002, and Northeastern had more than 50 percent women students in 2009.[16] However, most law schools in Massachusetts today have fewer than 50 percent women law students. It is unclear whether this phenomenon is driven by the factor of fewer women applicants or fewer acceptances of female students. As for

Margaret H. Bauer

Margaret H. Bauer, a 1937 graduate of Portia Law School, was appointed dean of the school in 1953 and served until her resignation in 1962. Her appointment made her the first woman dean of any law school in Massachusetts.

Margaret Bauer as dean pictured in academic regalia.

IMAGE COURTESY OF BOSTON PUBLIC LIBRARY PRINT DEPARTMENT

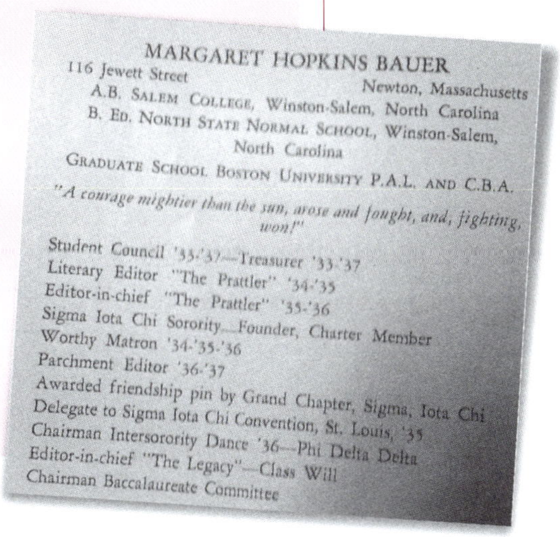

MARGARET HOPKINS BAUER

116 Jewett Street Newton, Massachusetts

A.B. Salem College, Winston-Salem, North Carolina

B. Ed. North State Normal School, Winston-Salem, North Carolina

Graduate School Boston University P.A.L. and C.B.A.

"A courage mightier than the sun, arose and fought, and, fighting, won!"

Student Council '33-'37—Treasurer '33-'37
Literary Editor "The Prattler" '34-'35
Editor-in-chief "The Prattler" '35-'36
Sigma Iota Chi Sorority—Founder, Charter Member
Worthy Matron '34-'35-'36
Parchment Editor '36-'37
Awarded friendship pin by Grand Chapter, Sigma, Iota Chi
Delegate to Sigma Iota Chi Convention, St. Louis, '35
Chairman Intersorority Dance '36—Phi Delta Delta
Editor-in-chief "The Legacy"—Class Will
Chairman Baccalaureate Committee

Margaret Bauer's student profile in the Portia Law yearbook.

IMAGE COURTESY OF NEW ENGLAND LAW | BOSTON, LAW LIBRARY ARCHIVES

Joan E. Mahoney

Joan E. Mahoney became the first woman dean of a Massachusetts law school since Portia's Margaret Bauer upon her appointment as dean of Western New England College School of Law in 1994. She served as dean until 1996. Mahoney then served as dean of Wayne State University's law school from 1998 to 2003, making her the first woman law school dean in Michigan. She is now retired.

Joan E. Mahoney

IMAGE COURTESY OF WAYNE STATE UNIVERSITY

professors, the percentages of women at Massachusetts law schools range from as low as 18 percent to as high as 54 percent at Northeastern. According to the 2007–2008 Association of American Law Schools Statistical Report on Law Faculty, approximately 37 percent of law teachers reported in the directory are women. So there is certainly much more progress needed in order to achieve gender balance on this level.

The final frontier in reaching equality of the sexes in law schools lies in deanships. Nationally women comprise 19.8 percent of law-school deans.[17] While Margaret Bauer was named dean of Portia Law School (now New England Law | Boston) in 1953, it would be over forty years before a Massachusetts law school would name another woman dean. In 1994, Joan E. Mahoney was named dean of Western New England College School of Law (now Western New England University School of Law) and in 2002, Emily A. Spieler became dean of Northeastern University School of Law. Spieler has brought a rich practice background to the position; as an attorney, she specialized in legal problems of women workers. Spieler was an early member of the Women's Law Collective, a feminist legal practice based in Cambridge, and a special assistant attorney general for the Massachusetts Department of Health's Lead Poisoning Prevention Division. Her areas of expertise are employment law and social insurance programs. In 2003 Harvard Law School had its first female dean in Elena Kagan, a former aide in President Clinton's administration who served as deputy director of the Domestic Policy Council from 1997 to 1999. When appointed dean, Kagan was teaching administrative law at Harvard. She served as dean until 2009, when she was appointed solicitor general in the Obama Administration. She is now an associate justice on the U.S. Supreme Court. In addition to Dean Spieler at Northeastern, four other Massachusetts law schools currently are headed by women. In 2009, Martha Minow, the Jeremiah Smith, Jr. Professor of Law, became Kagan's successor. Minow taught at Harvard since 1981. She is an expert in human rights, and in particular legal and educational issues pertaining to women, children, and persons with disabilities. Her teaching interests are civil procedure, constitutional law, family law, and education law. Since 2006, Maureen A. O'Rourke has served as dean of Boston University School of Law, where she has taught in the areas of intellectual property, commercial law, and computers and the law since 1993. Finally, Camille A. Nelson became Suffolk University Law School's first woman dean in 2010 and Mary Lu Bilek became University of Massachusetts School of Law's first woman dean in 2012.

Women have certainly come a long way in the academy from the days when there were only a token few per law-school class, to today, when women comprise nearly half of the student body at some Massachusetts law schools. What remains to be seen is whether this achieved gender equality in the student body will ever translate to equality in the bar, bench, and faculty and administration in law schools.

Reflections, Interviews, and Biographies

Boston College Law School

An Argument for Women at BC Law

Believing that Boston College Law School should become coeducational, the school's dean, Father William J. Kenealy, wrote a memorandum on December 12, 1940, to the president of Boston College advocating why women should be admitted:

(1) women need an institution to study law [under] Catholic "auspices";
(2) there have been a "huge number of inquiries" from women seeking admission to study under Catholic auspices;
(3) finances have decreased since institution of the military draft;
(4) other Catholic law schools admit women;
(5) since women are admitted at the School of Social Work, the graduate school, and the "Intown" school, they should also be admitted to the law school.

Ruth-Arlene W. Howe

Ruth-Arlene W. Howe has been at Boston College Law School since 1970, first as a student and then ascending to the position of professor emerita. Teaching a variety of courses in family law, elder law, legal interviewing and counseling, and professional responsibility, she is the first and only African-American woman to achieve tenure and the rank of full professor at Boston College Law School.

Ruth-Arlene W. Howe

IMAGE COURTESY OF BOSTON COLLEGE LAW SCHOOL

Photos of students during BC Law School's early years of coeducation.

IMAGES COURTESY OF BOSTON COLLEGE LAW SCHOOL

Father Kenealy received no response from the president. Accordingly, he submitted a second memorandum on March 4, 1941, in which he started:

(1) in the experience of faculty who have taught at law schools with women, the presence of women fosters competition since only the most serious and intelligent women attend;

(2) "women alumnae are extremely loyal";

(3) finances as they are would force closure of the law school and result in extreme hardship on the faculty—women make this possibility more remote;

(4) closure of the law school would "have a profoundly harmful effect upon the good name and progress of the University as a whole";

(5) women should not be denied the ability to "champion Canon Law."[18]

The school's first woman student would graduate in 1945, the second in 1948, and the third in 1949.

Mary Ann Glendon

Mary Ann Glendon is the Learned Hand Professor of Law at Harvard Law School, where she teaches and writes on bioethics, comparative constitutional law, property, and human rights in international law. In 1968, Glendon became Boston College Law School's first woman faculty member. She received tenure there in 1973. She joined Harvard's faculty as a tenured professor in 1986.

Glendon became the first woman president of the Roman Catholic Church's Pontifical Academy of Social Sciences when Pope John Paul II appointed her in 2004. She served as U.S. Ambassador to the Vatican from February 2008 to January 2009.

Mary Ann Glendon pictured in 1979 as a visiting professor at Harvard Law School.

IMAGE SOURCE: *HARVARD LAW SCHOOL YEARBOOK* 1975, p.51

Boston University School of Law

Tamar Frankel

Professor, Boston University School of Law

Born in Tel Aviv, Israel, Tamar Frankel first came to the United States as a visiting scholar at Harvard Law School. She has taught at Boston University School of Law since 1968. She was the school's first woman appointed to a tenure-track position and the first woman to receive tenure.

Frankel is a leading expert in the areas of mutual funds, securitization, financial system regulation, fiduciary law, and corporate governance. She also has been in private practice in Boston; Washington, D.C.; and Israel. In 1998, Frankel was instrumental in the establishment and corporate structure of the Internet Corporation for Names and Numbers (ICANN). ICANN is a nonprofit organization dedicated to keeping the Internet secure and stable by promoting competition and developing policy on the Internet's unique identifiers.

Frankel served as an attorney in the legal department of the Israeli Air Force, an assistant attorney general for Israel's Ministry of Justice, and the legal advisor of the State of Israel Bonds Organization in Europe. She received her LL.M. from Harvard Law School in 1964 and her S.J.D. from Harvard Law School in 1972.

Legal Education

What was your legal education like in Israel?

I enrolled in law school during the British rule under a mandate, in 1943. The school accepted candidates directly from high school. This "college" that I went to was so far away from anything closely resembling a college in the United States. Yet it was the only school in Israel that awarded a "certificate to practice law." There was no university that you could graduate from with that certificate. The alternative was England, to which I couldn't, and wouldn't, go. So, this Jerusalem Law Classes was a night school. The classes were held between I think it was 5:00 and 9:00 in a building called the Evelina De Rothschild, which had a big hall. My education consisted of going to and listening to these lectures. There was no discussion whatsoever; there were no seminars. There were just lectures and you took notes. The other part of the education was self-motivated. Nearby were the courts. And I kibbitzed. I sat and listened to cross-examinations, to arguments for hours, and learned an awful lot in this way. Then after two years of listening to classes, you took examinations of three hours. You took one in the morning and one in the afternoon, four days a week for three weeks. Two years later, you had eight such exams and one year, the fifth, you had to

Tamar Frankel

IMAGE COURTESY OF TAMAR FRANKEL

The questions and answers presented here were adapted for this book from the American Bar Association's Women Trailblazers in the Law "Oral History of Tamar Frankel" (Renee M. Jones, interviewer) with the permission of the American Bar Association and with review by Tamar Frankel.

ıcpecial Students

KENNETH MONTAGUE GEORGE
B.A., LL.B. London
195 Charlotte St., Georgetown, British Columbia
DAVID ANTHONY GORDON
B.A. '60, LL.B. '62, U. of Natal
78 Vause Rd., Durban, Natal, Rep. of South Africa
PETER ROSS GRAHAM
B.A. '60, LL.B. '63, U. of Sydney
4 Lagonda Ve., Killara, N.S.W., Australia

FRANCISCO G. de GUZMAN
B.A. '56, LL.B. '55, Manuel L. Quozun U.
Magsaysay St., Cuyapo, Nuera Ecija, Philippines
Sutherland Club
BARRETT KINGSBURY HAWKS
BB.A. '60, LL.B. '63, Emory U.
812 Thomaston St., Barnesville, Ga.
TAMAR HED-HOFMAN
Jerusalem Law Classes & Hebrew U.
24 Rothschild Blvd., Tel Aviv, Israel

JAMES AUGUSTUS HENDERSON
B.A. Princeton '59, LL.B. Harvard '62
8 Wright St., Cambridge, Mass.
JESUS R. HERRERA VILLAMEDIANA
Bachelor's, Liceo Alcazar '54, LL.B. U. dic Zulia-Ven '62
3A Av. Los Palos Grandes, Edif. El Morichal, Caracas, Venezuela
Maguire, I.L.C.
GIDEON HOLIN
M. Jur. Hebrew U. '60, M.C.L. U. of Mich. '63
50 Weitzmann, Givatayim, Israel
LUIZ BUARQUE DE HOLLANDA
Tax Law, U. Da Guanabara '61
Rua Jardim Botanico 622, Rio de Janeiro, Brazil
NIELS EILSCHOU HOLM
Artium Metropolitanskolen '55, Cand. Juris U. of Copenhagen '60
15 Radim, Shims Alli, Copenhagen, Denmark
FRANCISCO CAMACHO JIMENEZ
Bachelor, National Preparatory '49, Lic. en Derecho, National U. '56
Canareas 1105-B, Mexico City, D.F., Mexico

KENNETH FRANCIS JOYCE
B.A. '58, LL.B. '61 Boston C.
229 Neponset Valley Parkway, Hyde Park, Mass.
GEN KAJITANI
LL.B. Tokyo U. '57, M.C.L. U. of Mich. '63
2-512, Matsubara-Cho, Setagaya-Ku, Tokyo, Japan
GEORGE KALINSKI
B.A. '57, LL.B. '59, Wayne St. U.
11042 Aletta, Culver City, Calif.
S. T. More

NADARAJA KASIRAJA
LL.B. U. of Ceylon '56, LL.M. Stanford '63
24A Alfred Place, Colombo, Ceylon
Morgan-Brown, I.L.C.
DAVID J. KAYNER
B.S. U. of Ill. '60, J.D. U. of Mich. '63
4800 Chicago Beach Dr., Chicago, Ill.
MUHAMMAD H. M. KIDWAI
B.A. '47, LL.B. '48, M.A. '48 Lucknow U., India
"Al Kaiser", 2/50 Drigh Rd. Colony, Karachi, Pakistan Marshall, I.L.C.

Tamar Frankel's 1964 Harvard Law Yearbook photo; notably she is the only woman of eighteen students pictured on the page.

IMAGE SOURCE: *HARVARD LAW SCHOOL YEARBOOK* 1964, p.57

take five more, if I remember correctly—the last.

In order to get a certificate to practice law: you had also to be an apprentice (clerk), which means to work in a law firm for two years. And then you didn't have to be in class: so what happened to me was I became an apprentice at my father's office, and he taught me really well. And because the War of Independence occurred in 1948, I finished my exams, my last exams, in Tel Aviv. We couldn't reach Jerusalem, by that time as it was under a siege. And the mandatory British government gave me a diploma, but refused to give me a certificate because I was not yet twenty-three years old, and that was the minimum age for practicing law. At that time I was so upset, you wouldn't believe. But then as a result of it, I got one of the first certificates in the State of Israel. That is the story.

And were there a lot of other women in your law class, or was it mostly men?

There was one, and there were thirteen women altogether in a group of probably about 200 students. So we were a very small group. The one that I remember, Rennana Goodman was her name, was in that group. But we didn't congregate this way—by gender. I was the only woman in my group, but I felt comfortable. It didn't really matter, it wasn't so important.

Early Career

Can we start from when you finished Jerusalem law classes, I think it was 1948? What was your first position after you finished your studies?

My first position was at the Air Force, which was nothing like the Air Force we think about today. It was a very small group of people, and they needed a legal advisor. I had no real experience, but I knew the commanders and was part of the group. So we started with me, and if I'm not mistaken, I already said that one of my first objectives was to find a really good international advisor who had experience, and I did.

But in the meantime we did have legal issues, and one of the legal issues that I did deal with, was the foreigners that came to help. They were good pilots but did not wish to have any recognition of their being in Israel because they may have lost their own citizenship. And there were other issues of this sort. But I stayed in the legal department for a while. I did establish a library...

A law library?
A law library, and then fortuitously met someone from the Ministry of Justice. The Ministry of Justice at that time was composed of twelve people, and they were established in a small suite of offices near Tel Aviv, in a place called Keria which was adjacent to Tel Aviv, and composed of the minister and his secretary, and the director general, and the attorney general. Then there were two people who dealt with legislation, and a group that began to establish the prosecution.

When did you leave the Ministry of Justice?
The Ministry of Justice moved to Jerusalem. I was married at the time, and although my husband was in the army, our home was Tel Aviv. So I went and worked with my father.

And then your first child, Anat, was born in 1951?
That's right.

And how did motherhood impact your life and your career?
My father died when I was pregnant, and that created a very heavy burden.

When she was born did you stay home for a while, or did you go right back to work?
I stayed home for about two months, and there were the demands of the office—so I started going to the office. But again, the office wasn't that far, so I could come home at noontime also, and there was a break always at work. So I saw quite a bit of her, and we "got acquainted."

Did you feel that it was manageable to be a working mother in your early career?
Yes. It was also not an unusual situation. In other words, whatever the mother did, she was entitled to free time. That's the model I had. So instead of free time, I worked, I had responsibilities. But nonetheless, there were two other lawyers in the office, so it didn't shut down work altogether. But I had to learn, and I did. So the answer was, the feeling of guilt that I saw here in America kind of didn't exist in Israel. Sometimes I wanted to be home more than I wanted to be at work, of course, but it was not accompanied by a devastating feeling that I was ruining my daughter's life or mine or anybody else's.

You went to Paris in 1962. What were your duties as a legal advisor [for the State of Israel Bonds Organization]?
Well, it was a mixture of legal advice, but much of it was also sales. Not that I went to sell, but mainly what I told you before, the difficulties were foreign currency, and at that time

Europeans did not allow sale of obligations in dollars. It required negotiations. Sometimes there were issues, such as who was entitled to a certain bond when somebody died. And I wanted to see a death certificate, and so on.

So sort of securities work and investment banking work?
That's right. That is what it was.

Moving to the United States and Attending Harvard

How did you end up in the U.S. at Harvard?
Well, I went back to Israel. Then suddenly I lost my anchor, if you will. I was everywhere and nowhere, and then I got this invitation. The one thing I learned when I was in Europe was that I wanted to be in a university. When I was in Europe, I also went to England from time to time. And I sat one day in the evening alone in Oxford, and I thought that this is where I wanted to be, in a university. I always loved the studying and the writing. So when I came back to Israel and got this invitation for a nine-month visit, to come as a visiting scholar to Harvard Law School, I decided to take it.

...I had a room, a very prestigious room, adjacent to Professor Paul Freund in the first floor in the library. And it was then that I met my husband. It took about two months for me to realize two things. First, that I may well stay here, and the second one was a very clear recognition that I knew nothing. I understand nothing, and that whatever experience I had, is not enough.

So you felt like you needed to continue your education?
I needed to study. I enrolled in the LL.M. program and continued to receive the money that the school gave me and took some absolutely superb classes. The legal process I took with Hart, he was still alive. And Louis Loss, I took two courses with him. I took Chinese law at the time. It was wonderful.

[S]ome faculty members did not want a woman, and did not know what to expect and were fearful of disruption of the culture of the group.

Teaching at Boston University School of Law

Could you describe a little bit more about how you were first approached by BU and what your first experiences were there?
It is interesting that I don't remember exactly how I was approached. I know that the dean and a group of faculty members wanted a woman, and that was a bone of contention because some faculty members did not want a woman, and did not know what to expect and were fearful of disruption of the culture of the group.

Had they had women on the faculty of BU before you were hired?
No. Never.

▲

Boston University School of Law's 1969 faculty. Tamar Frankel is at the far right.

PHOTO BY MCLE | NEW ENGLAND, IMAGE ON DISPLAY AT BOSTON UNIVERSITY SCHOOL OF LAW

What about adjuncts?

I don't think there were any adjuncts. I don't know, but I doubt it. The assumption, or at least the concern, was that there would be some disruption of the cohesive group. Group members were very, very good teachers. The decision was not only to hire a woman but also to hire people who were scholars who wrote, and I at a very early stage wrote. I also had an S.J.D., or at least at that time I was a candidate. I finished all the requirements. I think there was only one who had a degree of that level on the BU faculty, but not from Harvard. I think from Columbia, which was very good.

Now, who approached me I don't remember, but what I do remember was my conversation with the dean, and it shows you what happens to someone who comes from another country. He asked me how much I charge, or how much I would expect to be paid, and I had no idea because in Israel there was a list, and someone who started got paid X, and then with seniority and change of status got paid Y and Z. So I said, "Whatever is acceptable." And so I thought I was being paid the right amount. Then about five years later, I had tenure—after three years I got tenure. I published, and then after five years I met with someone who was just accepted at another school, a woman, and she said to me, "I'm getting paid X Dollars. Do you think it is okay?" And I was shocked because she was getting paid about $5,000 more than I.

After you had tenure?

After I had tenure, I think after I got my S.J.D. She did not have any of that. But I asked her, "Why, do you have a different amount?" And she said, "Well, we negotiated." And that's the first time I realized I didn't have a mentor. That was the first time I realized, all of a sudden, I simply did not negotiate.

You just accepted what you were offered?

He suggested, and I said okay. I thought that was what everybody else got when he started or she started. In Israel there was no negotiation, there was no bargaining.

So did you go to the dean at that point?

I did not. I did not go to the dean, I just said, "It serves you (me!) right! You didn't ask, so don't come complaining now." In 1979 I went to Harvard, I visited there. At that time I had published four volumes, *The Regulation of Money Managers*, and the publisher was Little Brown. I came to the president of Boston University, and I gave him the volumes. He of course was very pleased. When I came back from Harvard, he asked, and I heard that later, I don't remember from whom, "Why is Frankel being paid so little?" There was really no answer to that, especially in light of what I'd done in the meantime. And so all of a sudden, I think within one or two years, my salary was increased by 30% and you know I wasn't ecstatic. It did not matter that much.

...When I came to BU, or even before that, I kind of had to make a decision as to whether I'm going to combine my knowledge of Israeli law with American law and teach and write in these two areas of comparative law. I decided I'm not going to do that, I'm going to be an American lawyer, and [teach] variable annuities and mutual funds. When I started teaching the first class I did teach, among others, was...international business transactions, because I took that course at Harvard and I knew a little bit about it, so I could teach that and I had a feel for it. But very soon thereafter I taught trusts and estates and "bread and butter" American courses.

You started off as assistant professor?

Yes. There was one more thing of which I had no idea, and that was the value of tenure. In Israel the security of staying in one place was very high. If you started in one place, you could stay there for a long time. The competition was not as fierce, so I didn't really understand why everybody was talking about tenure. And I was surprised, I think I got a contract for one year, and I said, "Fine."

So it was a contract?

It was a tenure track, and I was appointed as such, but I had no idea about that and didn't really care very much. So then I got a contract for another year, and then the third year, if I'm not mistaken, I got tenure.

What was interesting, and years later, I heard that there was one member of the faculty who was tremendously against my being appointed. And he said at that time, "I don't know her, and it's not personal, but I don't want a woman." I was told at that meeting when the tenure was decided, he stood up and he said, "I want to make the motion, because I was wrong."

I take my hat off to my colleagues at that time. They had no idea what a professional woman was. They took their model from their wives, and some of the wives, who may have been very demanding in terms of, if not hand kissing, then standing up when they came into the room. I don't know what they thought they were getting into. I was not interested in any of that. The other thing that they did, which funnily enough, I didn't care about, was to put me in the basement of the library.

I take my hat off to my colleagues at that time. They had no idea what a professional woman was.

Your faculty office?
My faculty office was as far from the faculty as could be, and I was delighted with it because I could take all the books and not have to return them to their place. I could keep them and work from them the next day.

What was the atmosphere of BU Law like when you started? What was the relationship among the faculty, and between students and faculty?
The students did not expect and did not demand what the students demand today. There was little coddling. Some of the teachers still used the most rigorous Socratic Method. To the extent that one teacher, who called on someone who was not prepared, demanded that the student leave the room, until that student or another student turned around and said, "I'm paying my fees, and I'm staying." And then the teacher had to leave, but he couldn't leave forever, so commanding students who were unprepared to leave the classroom stopped.

At the same time, the teachers were very gifted teachers. They really were on top of their subject matter. So they taught very, very well, and students realized that. However, they didn't write much.

Were there other scholars on the faculty?
No. When I came, I think there was no one, or maybe beginning to be. And then they hired a very large number of teachers who were writing. There developed a split. There were about twelve who ruled the roost, and there were the rest of us.

The scholars who ruled the roost?
No. The teachers who were there first ruled the roost, and the scholars were the second-class citizens.

So were you under pressure as a woman on the faculty? Did you feel singled out at all?
I was older than most beginners. And I am by nature, I think, a loner, not in the sense that I'm not social or sociable, but in the sense that I was a loner at Harvard too when the students were much younger than I was. Sure I was in fact separate, but did I want to mingle and be one of the boys? Absolutely not. I didn't want to make a name for myself, except that I wanted to write. Personally, I didn't want anyone to know who I was, what I was. It was nobody's business.

You wanted to be inconspicuous?
Correct.

You preferred that, and that's how you were treated, so it was a good fit?
Precisely. It was a good fit in that respect, and my colleagues felt comfortable. The one thing I did do, to a great extent, is present a model of a professional woman to the women students. For example, they didn't know how to dress. They didn't know how to decide what to wear. I didn't say a word, but I showed. I wore a suit which nobody did, and they began to wear suits. Maybe for other reasons too, but at least I showed them that.

I also showed them how to behave. What I also showed them is that it is possible to have a husband, a child, and a profession. That these are not mutually exclusive, because I invited students home. Not only the women; I invited everybody home. I had a very large home in Brookline where 100 students could fit, and then they saw a little boy three years old walking with his cookies, and saying, "Try it, I tried it in the kitchen and it tastes good!" And then afterwards I brought him to school and he would go with his roller-skates in the corridors of the school. So here was a model, and I baked my own cookies. I don't know that I did it on purpose even, but it was a model without preaching, and it turned out to be quite effective.

> "I was born in Israel, where a prime minister, judges, and lawyers were women—feminine and strong. I came to an America where the women's roles were far more limited, and to a culture that took me years to understand. Yet this culture was, and still is, very generous. It allowed me to ignore the environment and what other people thought or said about me as an academic and as a woman. I could close the door and follow my hunger for inquiring, for learning, for writing, and for perfection, knowing that it will never be reached. Other women pressed for recognition and equality. I am the beneficiary of their efforts, for which I am thankful.
>
> Tamar Frankel, March 2011

I don't know if I told you, but I got a letter from a judge, a woman judge a few years ago, maybe two years ago. She said to me, "I was a student at the time when people thought that if you are a lawyer, you can't have children and you can't have a husband, and you helped us believe that is all possible. I have four children, I was a prosecutor, I'm now a judge for ten years, and I have of course a husband and so on, so thank you." That came out of the blue, I didn't remember the student. I did not have personal relationships with many students. With a few I did. My coauthor of *Regulation of Money Managers* was a former student of mine, a woman.

What were some of the challenges of being a professor and having a young child?
Funnily enough, I don't know that there are challenges because there's one thing I don't have that women I think were inculcated here, and that's the sense of guilt. I had a sense of guilt, which I think every woman does, every mother does. But my guilt is not linked to the fact that I was, quote, "working." [M]y mother didn't work, but she felt she was entitled two or three times a week to go to the hairdresser, to have coffee klatch with a friend, if she wanted to. And so when I was eighteen months old, I went to a group; there was an older woman who took care of a group of young children for a few hours. My daughter did the same; I did the same thing, and she remembers going to the group to this very day. There was no feeling of rejection on the one hand, and no feeling of guilt on the other hand. And you sometimes have to be more flexible. When I saw in the child a need, I was there and found a way to resolve the issue. It's true that in the U.S. I did not go to work in a law firm,

but I know a friend, Brooksley Born, and she was the first woman in a firm that insisted when she had children on being a part-time partner.

So do you feel that being an academic gave you the flexibility that you needed to be there for your son when he needed you?
Yes, that's right. I had long hours, maybe longer than women in a law firm, but my hours were more flexible and night was one of them. It's true, I remember I once cut down on sleep and then I stood in front of the class and the class kind of was moving a little bit one way or another, and I said to myself, "Hold, hold." And then I decided to sleep some more.

So you were sleep-deprived.
I was sleep-deprived, and sometimes the drive to write came not because somebody demanded, but because I wanted to finish what I was doing. I did not even want to finish it. I wanted to *do* it. There was another thing. I wanted to do what I was doing, not necessarily finish it. As a matter of fact I have kind of an empty feeling when I finish a book or even an article.

Did you ever feel that corporate law was a field that was more challenging for women academics?
No, that is another thing that surprised me. I am not interested in family law; it has nothing to do with me as a woman. I'm interested in the financial system, without necessarily practicing. But I'm interested in that branch of the law as an academic because I can watch, I can watch people. For example, yesterday I was on a panel and there was a paper given about the personality of CEOs. That interests me because it has to do with power, it has to do with impact on society, and it has to do also with how you can change it. So if you see something wrong and something right, how you can strengthen it.

I guess my question is, did you find it was more difficult to be accepted in that field as a woman?
Oh, oh. I would guess that the answer is yes, except that I didn't try. What I did is write. That is the power of the written word. The people who read my treatise did not care if I was a woman or not. What they did care about is that what I wrote helped them in their job. And so I found that a lot of the problems that a woman would have—for example, if she were a partner or an associate—didn't happen to me.

Maureen A. O'Rourke

Dean and Professor, Michaels Faculty Research Scholar, Boston University School of Law

Maureen A. O'Rourke

IMAGE COURTESY OF BOSTON UNIVERSITY SCHOOL OF LAW

Maureen O'Rourke began her legal career as an attorney for the IBM Corporation, where she handled a variety of issues pertaining to software licensing. In 1993, she joined the faculty of Boston University School of Law. She was named the school's dean in 2006, becoming the first woman to hold this position at the law school. Her primary academic interests focus on the intersection of intellectual property law and other fields, such as contract and antitrust law, particularly in the context of software and technology.

O'Rourke was one of the first to consider comprehensively the status of hyperlinking on the Internet under copyright law and the viability of a trespass claim for access to and use of a website. She is a prolific author, having coauthored one of the leading copyright casebooks in the United States and published numerous articles. Prior to becoming dean, O'Rourke taught courses in commercial law and intellectual property law and served as faculty supervisor for the student-run *Journal of Science and Technology Law*.

O'Rourke attended Marist College, graduating summa cum laude in accounting and computer science in 1985. She attended Yale Law School and received her J.D. in 1990.

After college you started your career as an accountant for IBM. Why did you decide to go to law school and not attend business school?

It was the mid to late eighties, the heyday of Rudy Giuliani in New York putting the mob behind bars. And the movie *The Untouchables*, where Al Capone is captured and sent to prison for tax evasion charges, had just come out. I felt my accounting background would open a lot of career opportunities in the legal field, whether it was working on the corporate side in business or commercial law or working as a prosecutor.

What did you enjoy about Yale Law School?

I enjoyed the atmosphere. It was, in some ways, divorced from the real world practice of law and provided an intellectual forum for people to talk about ideas and theories and ways of thinking about the law. Having worked for a couple of years, I certainly had the real-world perspective, so it was an opportunity to reimmerse myself in an environment that encouraged thinking about the bigger theories that influenced the practice of the law. I also had terrific professors.

While you were at Yale, did you experience any gender bias that you can remember?

Not that I can remember, no. It is possible, but it is also possible I wouldn't have perceived it in that way. So, I can't give you any incidents that I thought were gender biased in any way at Yale.

The questions and answers presented here are excerpted from an interview with Dean O'Rourke by Therese Rohrbeck for this book in November 2010.

Do you remember the classroom ratio that you experienced? Was it pretty even?
I never really thought about it. I recall that there may have been more men than women, but it wouldn't have been by a large margin. And it may have just depended on course selection.

How long did you stay with IBM as an attorney?
Three years.

And then what did you move on to after?
I moved on to teaching at BU.

How did you get your job as dean of Boston University School of Law?
I joined the faculty in 1993 and I got tenure in 1998. It is a tradition here that the most recently tenured professor becomes one of the associate deans. When our dean stepped down in 2004, I was asked to serve as interim dean. It was also at a time when BU had an interim president and interim provost. As interim dean, I had a lot of rebuilding to do, especially in the development and alumni relations area. We also didn't have a communications and marketing function, so that unit had to be created. At that point, I decided to apply for the job as dean because I had put so much work into rebuilding that I hoped to be the one to benefit from those efforts.

Do you feel like you've been able to use your legal skills in this current job or do you use different types of skills?
The job requires a number of different skills, including diplomacy, budget management, and strategic thinking. The legal skills can certainly provide the background for carrying out many responsibilities. I still teach, which is great. The legal skills can be helpful when I'm talking to alumni about their jobs because it's important to understand their profession. Certainly, when employment issues come up, having some background knowledge helps a fair amount.

What makes this job such a great fit for you?
It lets me do a lot of different things. I can move from dealing with faculty to dealing with staff to working with the students to meeting the alumni all in the same day, and I enjoy that aspect of it. It is something different every day. I guess it fits, to a certain extent, my personality. I can connect reasonably well with most people and I think that is a helpful quality to have in this job. You have to be organized. I don't know if I am an expert at it, but people keep me organized.

What do you like best about your job?
It depends on what day you ask the question because, on any given day, the answer would vary. I love that I am still able to teach and I am very fond of our students. I would say the best part is the students and the alumni. I wouldn't have the same opportunities to meet the alumni if I weren't dean. Also, I've tried to create a very collegial community among the faculty, the students, and all the school's constituencies. That has been a very rewarding part of the job, working to change the culture of an institution.

I don't think of myself as a woman dean. I just think of myself as the dean.

When you first took your position as dean or even now, do you feel like a woman dean or do you feel just like the dean?
I am the first woman to serve as dean of BU Law, so that distinction will come up periodically and I think it means something to people. I don't think of myself as a woman dean. I just think of myself as the dean.

Do you feel like being a woman affects your job?
Personality affects the way that you do the job, but how much of it is gender-driven is hard to say. When faced with a conflict, I am probably more likely than a man to sit down and say, "Can we work this out? Let's figure out a compromise," than I am to just command [a course of action]. So, my leadership style may be a bit more flexible and inclusive than a man's. There are things that I've learned over the years that are more "women specific." When I first started at BU, Fran Miller was my "shepherd," a senior faculty member assigned to help a junior faculty member acclimate to the school. I left her a voice message once and she played it back for me. I did the "woman thing" of making every sentence sound like a question. My voice went up at the end of every sentence, whether declarative or not. So, she got me Deborah Tannen's book [*You Just Don't Understand*] about how women communicate. So, I've worked on that over the years and have become very conscious of that now. I hear it with our own students. You always want to tell them that it makes them sound like they are unsure of themselves if they turn everything into a question. I also think that it is a "woman thing" to apologize even if something is not your fault. So, I've tried to work on that and not be so apologetic for something that actually is not my fault.

How do you balance work and family?
You just do, I guess, is the answer to that. In some ways I think it is easier now because you don't have to physically be here [at the office] as much. You can have the iPhone or the Blackberry with you and be accessible. So, it is really a conscious choice. I will very rarely cancel family plans because something comes up at work. I won't do it. I don't know if I would have that same freedom at a law firm, but I have it here. So, you just make a point of it. At the end of the day, I am not going to miss the time that I didn't spend here. I will miss the time I didn't spend with the people who value me as me, not as the dean.

Do you have children? Did you ever take time off from your career?
We don't have children. I got married at thirty-four and we decided not to have children, but that decision didn't have anything to do with my career.

Do you have any thoughts about how to balance work and family?
Part of it is you need to be willing to ask for help, whether that is from another family member or a friend. You can't try to do it all on your own. You have to be able to ask for help when you need it.

Who or what do you attribute your success to in the legal profession?
I think whatever success I have begins with my mom. My parents were both middle-class, but there was never any question that their children would go to college. There was never

Massachusetts' First Female Law School Deans

1953	Margaret H. Bauer	Portia Law School
1994	Joan E. Mahoney	Western New England College School of Law
2002	Emily A. Spieler	Northeastern University School of Law
2003	(Hon.) Elena Kagan	Harvard Law School
2006	Maureen A. O'Rourke	Boston University School of Law
2010	Camille A. Nelson	Suffolk University Law School
2012	Mary Lu Bilek	University of Massachusetts School of Law

any question that we could be whatever we wanted to be. What was most important was your character. It wouldn't have mattered if I were a bank teller or dean of a law school, as long as I tried my best to be a good person. So, she has made a huge difference.

At Yale, Abe Goldstein, who is now deceased, hired me as his research assistant. I didn't talk to him all that much about career, but he was very smart and very supportive and he helped me out as a reference and with things like that.

Mike Harper was the chair of the appointments committee at BU, and Mike picked out my resume when other people wouldn't. I had excellent grades, but for teaching you were supposed to have clerked for a judge, been on law review, and worked for a firm. I didn't have any of those things. So, he called me up and he said, "Well—" You have to know him. He harrumphed a bit and then said, "Well, we'll interview you anyway." I was glad to get the interview, but then I thought, "How am I going to make up for these omissions?" When I got here for the interview, another member of the faculty, Jack Beermann, said to me, "Just tell everybody you want to teach commercial law because that is what we are looking for." So, I did. That is how I got the job to teach commercial law. When I started working here, Rob Merges, who is now at Berkeley, was in the office next to me. He came in one day, gave me an article, and said, "I think this is wrong, but I don't have time to write about it. Why don't you check it out?" And my scholarly career was born.

Then, finally, Fran Miller, who I mentioned before. When it came to anything—teaching, dealing with the students, dealing with the other faculty members—Fran was tremendously helpful.

Do you consider all of these people in your life mentors?
On the mentor front, certainly Fran. I think Fran and my mom would be the main ones. People come in and out of your life, and sometimes you know and sometimes you don't that they've just given you a helping hand or a little push on your way and that is where others fit in. The women law deans are a good resource because I can call them for advice. Within Boston, there is the New England deans group. We get together a couple times a year and that is helpful.

In your opinion, what are some boundaries that women face in legal education, if you think there even are boundaries?
I can't prove it, but I think you can still be underestimated sometimes just based on gender. Sometimes based on clothing. Sometimes just based on general appearance, weight,

I think women probably still get underestimated quite a bit. However, when it happens, you just have to turn it to your advantage. I'd rather be underestimated than overestimated.

attractiveness. I think that definitely still happens. I think that women in firms still have a hard time having children and working. I do think that remains a barrier. They still have to work with an older generation that may not give women the same professional respect as men. So, I think women probably still get underestimated quite a bit. However, when it happens, you just have to turn it to your advantage. I'd rather be underestimated than overestimated.

What has been the greatest challenge in your career and how did you deal with it?
It was the adjustment from the practice of law at IBM to academia because I didn't understand what the expectations were in academia. I had this vague notion that one had to write. But I didn't quite understand what that meant and I'd gotten used to task-oriented work. You've got to get that software license agreement done. You've got to release the product. You've got to proof the press release. Then you get here and we are sitting around thinking deep thoughts and not much is happening on the surface. So, it was a culture shock. I didn't quite get it at first. It took time for me to adjust to the freedom to think critically about legal issues and the opportunity to contribute to important debates through scholarly work. I also had to overcome the intimidation that I felt from being surrounded by faculty colleagues with incredible intellectual fire power; some of whom literally wrote the book on important areas of law. The teaching wasn't easy when I started. I taught computers and the law, and I remember thinking then that I was getting more attitude from the students because I was a woman than I otherwise would have experienced in that class. I still think I'm probably right about that.

Because of the subject matter you were teaching and the fact that you were a woman?
Yes, because of the subject matter, because I was a woman, and because I was young. I was twenty-nine, but I looked younger. The first semester of teaching was a miserable experience. It was just a tough adjustment because the students showed a lack of confidence in me. I just thought, "Wow, I would have never talked to the professor that way." Things got better the next semester when I taught commercial law because we moved at a much faster pace and it was clear, unlike computer law, which was much more amorphous. Also the people here gave me a lot of teaching advice, which I learned to filter, because you can't be somebody that you are not. So that helped, but it was definitely a big challenge, the transition from corporate law to academia.

What about the law are you passionate about?
I will break it down in three ways. One is legal education. I love thinking about it, thinking about what is going to happen in the next five to ten to twenty years. That is very important to me. The second thing is the importance of the Constitution and fidelity to it. I am not a constitutional law scholar by any means. As a student, I found con law frustrating because it seemed extremely result-oriented to me, but now I worry that our students today are not getting enough civics in high school and that they don't understand the value of the foundational documents of this country. They don't understand the value of the rule of law in the U.S., that it is something special, and that we should cherish it.

Then the last thing is I'm a business lawyer and I love secured transactions. It sounds ridiculous to say someone is passionate about secured transactions, but I just think the Uniform Commercial Code was a monumental legislative achievement. It is an amazing thing that the American Law Institute and the National Conference of Commissioners on Uniform State Laws did and I have tremendous admiration for it. So, I just love to teach it.

It would be those three things: legal education, the whole framework that the law gives to our society, and my particular niche of secured transactions, which, as I try to tell the students, is "real law" and very important.

What advice would you offer other young women starting their law careers?

Be who you are and don't worry about what other people think of you and what somebody else's idea of success is. It is easy, especially for women, to get caught up in the race to achieve. This is one of the conversations I have had with my friends here. It is very easy to get caught up in the feeling that because of your past achievements, it is necessary to constantly pursue the next level of success that society values. That means I have to keep going for that next higher job whether it makes any sense for me or will make me happy. My advice is to avoid that trap. Do what will make you happy and don't worry about how somebody else is going to perceive it.

Harvard Law School

Elizabeth Bartholet

Professor, Harvard Law School

In 1983, Elizabeth Bartholet became the third woman to attain tenure at Harvard Law School; she was the first woman to rise from an assistant professorship to a tenured position. She is presently the Morris Wasserstein Public Interest Professor of Law and faculty director of the Child Advocacy Program at Harvard Law School, where she teaches civil rights and family law, specializing in child welfare, adoption, and reproductive technology. Before joining the Harvard faculty in 1977, she practiced civil rights and public interest work, first with the NAACP Legal Defense Fund, and later as founder and director of the Legal Action Center, a nonprofit organization in New York City focused on criminal justice and substance abuse issues.

Bartholet graduated magna cum laude from Harvard Law School in 1965 and served as the only woman on the *Harvard Law Review* from 1963 to 1965. She received her B.A. cum laude in English literature from Radcliffe College in 1962.

Why did you decide to go to law school?
I always wanted to do some form of public-interest, social-change work and was interested in civil rights work, other forms of public interest work. And after thinking about a couple of different possible directions, I decided law would be a good tool for that kind of work. There was nobody in my family in law—I had one uncle who had been a lawyer but he ended up teaching English literature on the university level—so there was nobody in my family who was encouraging me to go to law school. Indeed, when I decided to go to law school everybody in my family as well as my [now former] husband's family opposed it. This decision really came out of just thinking how I would get myself positioned to try to do social-change work.

Why would you say you received so much opposition?
It was definitely not the thing for a woman to do then—very few women were going to law school at the time. Even though I went to Radcliffe College, where we were in many ways being educated to do something professional, we were also still part of an era where most people thought mainly that you should get married, you should have babies, and you shouldn't get in the way of your husband's career. So the opposition to my going had to do with the idea that you could ruin your husband's career by being there, being in his way. I mean, now it seems rather shocking to women, but then it was a pretty common attitude.

The questions and answers presented here are excerpted from an interview with Professor Bartholet by Therese Rohrbeck for this book in November 2010.

What did you enjoy about Harvard Law School?

I enjoyed the first year, which was learning to play this new game. I was on law review and enjoyed the training we got there, which was a very good discipline in writing, and I enjoyed the camaraderie of the buddies on the law review who were quite welcoming, given that I was the only woman in my two years on the law review. I probably knew that law review was going to help position me to do some good things in a world that was still very discriminatory against women.

Elizabeth Bartholet

IMAGE COURTESY OF HARVARD LAW SCHOOL

Did you experience any gender bias when you were at Harvard Law School that you can remember?

It was a very male place that was enormously uncomfortable with the presence of women. People didn't know what to do with us, so yes there was a lot of sex bias at that time. I didn't have the professors who did the "ladies day" event—when the professor only called on women on a certain day, seating them up in the front row. But I had two professors who only gave me hypotheticals that had to do with knitting and sewing, which triggered laughter in the class. But given the era, I'm not sure any of us women were that bothered by this kind of thing. We were in a world which had only just passed the federal Civil Rights Act in '64. So during the whole period we were at law school there was overt discrimination against women in all sorts of jobs in the outside world. There was the kind of attitude that I faced discouraging me from even coming to law school. Compared to all of that, the law school, despite the fact that it made a joke of women being here, was a meritocracy. This was a place where if you studied, you could do well. You would in the end be graded on the merits. You could get onto law review by grades. You could emerge from law school with a Harvard degree and a law review credential based on the merits. That was a lot less discriminatory than the world in which we were living at the time. So I don't think many of us experienced the obvious and ongoing sex bias as a major problem. Women now would be outraged if they were treated the way we were, but then it didn't seem that big a deal, given both the way the world was outside and what we were getting from the law school in terms of a work credential.

Do you think that you have some sort of innate quality in yourself, whether it's drive or ambition, that led you to be able to succeed in this environment where all your professors were male and you were coming against that pressure of perhaps taking the position of a man or being in a man's profession? How did you push that aside and focus so that you could succeed and get the grades needed and not have that affect your self-esteem?

Sometimes I have thought that maybe the fact that the pressure on me, if anything, was not to do too well, maybe it was relaxing as compared to the guys who came here with pressure on them to succeed. I mean, nobody was looking at me and saying you've got to make law review, if anything just the opposite. But in addition, I obviously had some strong inner drive that made me decide to come despite the opposition to my coming and made me want to do well. Also I think the very fact of being a woman at Harvard Law School at the time made us all feel somewhat special. You weren't anonymous. You felt like, wow, you're really doing something just by virtue of being here. I can't look back and say, oh, you know, this was a dreadful environment and I should feel proud of myself that I survived it. It took a certain amount of drive for any of us at the time to decide we wanted to come here. Once the school accepted us, it was probably just the same drive that got you here that meant you were going to try to do well. I was very surprised to do well, actually. I didn't have any expectation that I would first year. It was all brand new to me.

Did you know when you were at Harvard Law School how you were going to use your legal education?
I was pretty sure the whole time that I wanted to use it in some kind of social-change policy work. The pressure was very strong to think about going to a commercial law firm. I did do that after my second year and did not enjoy the work particularly. And that reaffirmed me in not spending more time in that world, despite the pressure here. I was always quite confident that what interested me in going to law school was using it as a vehicle to get into social-change work and I stuck to that. There was, by the way, at the time no support for that. So if I look back and think of the things that were not helpful here I know that I would not think of the sex bias as much as I would think of the fact that there was no OPIA [Office of Public Interest Advising]. No support for public interest except to the degree that there were a handful of us, maybe more than that, that thought that this kind of work was what we wanted to do.

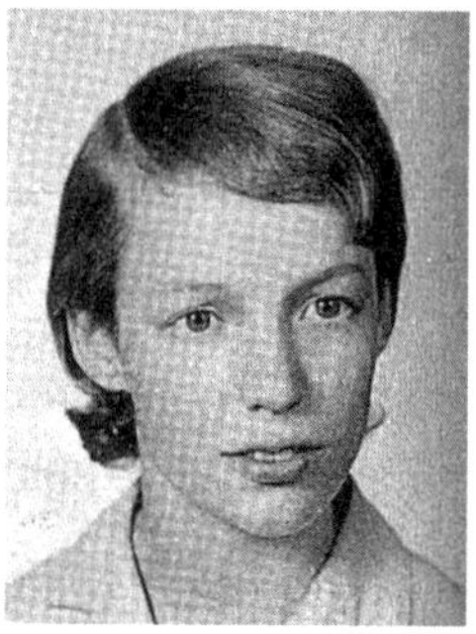

▲

Elizabeth Bartholet's Harvard Law School graduation photo.

IMAGE SOURCE: *HARVARD LAW SCHOOL YEARBOOK* 1965, p.90

For public-interest work, how were you able to find your opportunities early in your career?
If you're going to do public-interest work, you're going to need to think of yourself as an entrepreneur in terms of your own career and you need to think about building it and networking early on, something I never paid enough attention to at law school. I often tell students that it's important to work at organizations for people or with people who are going to be good advisors for future jobs and who are really decent people who are not going to simply use you but will help you get the next job. I also think a lot of times students interested in public interest don't realize that it's just as grade- and credential-oriented and probably more so than the private commercial world because a lot of these jobs are very hard to get. So the NAACP Legal Defense Fund always kept a fifty-fifty, black-white ratio on its staff and it had very little turnover and probably less turnover among the white lawyers. It was hard to get a job there. And grades often aren't enough because people like to know what somebody they know and trust thought of you when you worked for them.

When did you become interested in civil rights and in child welfare issues?
Two different answers. Civil rights I would say in my teens. I went for high school in the fifties to a private boarding school, all girls, and all white, just as was true of the private elementary school that I went to in New York City. I know a few of us went to the headmaster of this private boarding school and asked, "When is this school going to admit black girls?" I was aware of what was going on in the civil rights world around me in the fifties and interested in it. How I developed that interest I don't know. My family was quite conservative, Republican, but somehow, maybe because of what was in the air—or maybe because I was the third child—they're supposed to be more rebellious—I developed this

Martha Field

IMAGE COURTESY OF HARVARD LAW SCHOOL

Martha Field

Martha Field is the Langdell Professor of Law at Harvard Law School. She is a noted scholar of constitutional law, family law, bioethics issues such as the rights of the mentally challenged, and the civil justice system in Central America. After having taught at the University of Pennsylvania as the only woman faculty member for several years, Field began at Harvard Law School in 1978. In 1979, she became only the second woman, after international law scholar Elizabeth Owens in 1972, to receive tenure at Harvard Law. Field earned her B.A. from Radcliffe College in Chinese history in 1965. She earned her J.D. from the University of Chicago Law School in 1968 and clerked for U.S. Supreme Court Justice Abe Fortas.

interest in civil rights. So that was true through the sixties and was part of what I thought I might do afterward when I wanted to come to law school.

At the Legal Defense Fund, I did a variety of civil rights work. I did antideath-penalty work. I had amazingly interesting clients like Muhammad Ali and Bobby Seale and some other Black Panther leaders and I just had a very interesting mix of work, including some major employment discrimination cases. I then started a public interest law firm called the Legal Action Center, which still exists, and there I decided our focus should be on fighting discrimination suffered by ex-offenders and ex-addicts.

It wasn't until 1985 that I got interested in issues having to do with children and youth and that was entirely through the experience in my personal life of adopting two children. I have one child by birth from this early marriage and then, as a single parent long divorced from my husband, I adopted in 1985 and then 1987, two kids who were born in Peru. I was not in search of a new career, but I got very interested in the issues surrounding adoption and reproduction, as I felt that the policies surrounding these practices were crazy and didn't serve the interest of children or women at all well. Eventually I got interested in all the issues surrounding children and youth particularly in the area of maltreatment, adoption, and foster care. So I became involved in these issues simply because the accident of life threw me into adoption, and then what always interested me as a professional was trying to change public policy for the better.

You founded and became the faculty director of the Child Advocacy Program in the fall of 2004. Why did you decide to create this program?

Increasingly from 1985 to 2004 I was focusing my professional work on this area, and I became increasingly convinced that children were among the most underserved groups. For all we talk about best interest of the child, actually there is a lot of policy that is quite hostile to children's interest and very adult-oriented, and I just saw this as an important area that not only was underserved in terms of law and policy, but also in terms of law schools at the top of the hierarchy in terms of prestige. Harvard and other high-ranking schools had paid almost no attention to children's issues. Among the signs of how badly children's issues are valued are that the lawyers who work for children tend to be the least-well-paid, the courts that specialize in children's issues are the lowest in the hierarchy. And if you looked around the country at the time we founded the CAP program here, the only child advocacy programs of any size and significance were at the less-well-known law schools. So one of the reasons I wanted to start the Child Advocacy Program here at Harvard was that I thought it would be a statement that might have some influence on other law schools. Another reason is that I felt I'd be able to have more influence on both students in terms of what their future career interests might be and on policy if I was faculty director of this program, not just Professor Bartholet teaching in this area.

Why is this job such a great fit for you?
Well, I'm an activist by inclination so I am not a totally natural fit with the academic community. I think I'm more oriented than most of my colleagues to having law make a difference and to trying to make a difference in terms of my own career and not just by trying to educate students to be smarter, better lawyers, which doesn't interest me. What interests me is getting more students to care about social justice issues and to use their careers to actually promote social justice. That's not an easy thing to do. You can't just go into a classroom and say, "Well, here we are teaching civil procedure but I'd like you all to go and be social activists." I think this program is a really good vehicle for making large numbers of Harvard students care more about the issues involving children and youth and helping them think about putting future career energy into this world. In our CAP art of social change course we now have 110 enrolled students. I think that's pretty amazing at a school that used to have no courses with "child" in the name of the course.

What do you like best about your job?
...One of the things I like best about it is the freedom to define the nature of your job. That is true not only with respect to any specific course you're teaching, but also you decide what you're doing with all the hours of the week other than the five hours you teach. Very few jobs provide that luxury of choice. Indeed, mostly the only people with the luxury to define and redefine their job that law professors have are people with large inherited incomes.

Do you feel like child advocacy is particularly a women's issue?
If you look at our classes, a disproportionate number of the people taking CAP courses are women. I would like to change that, and someday we should count to see whether each year we are getting significantly more men. I think it's really important to get more men into this field. If you look at the people who serve children in general, it's women. So you look at parenting and most parenting is done by women, not by men. You look at elementary school teachers and they're mostly women. And preschool teachers and social workers and on and on. This is a problem because in general the world undervalues the jobs that are done by women. If we want children and youth to be treated better, we need to get the people whose jobs it is to serve children and youth to be thought of better and to be paid better, treated better in a variety of ways, and one of the ways to do that is to integrate the workforce. I think for that reason among others we need more men in this field.

▲

Elizabeth Bartholet (second row, center) with fellow members of the law review. She was the only female member during her two years on the law review.

IMAGE SOURCE: *HARVARD LAW SCHOOL YEARBOOK* 1965, p.185

How do you balance work and family?

I think it's a really major issue how one does this. When I teach two of the courses I teach, family law and employment discrimination, I always tell students the major problem for women, and to some degree men, is work-family conflict. Part of the problem for women is that, although by law in 1964 we theoretically opened up the work world and said no discrimination based on sex, and that has helped deal with the major forms of overt discrimination, we did nothing significant and still haven't done anything significant to change the nature of the work world so that it is compatible with family. Much of the work world is still designed for men who have a wife at home taking care of the children and the family and all that goes with that. This is particularly hard for people going into the kinds of jobs that many law students go into, which are longer than the normal nine-to-five Monday through Friday work week. I would say an inflexible nine-to-five Monday through Friday work week is very incompatible with parenting. Longer than that is overwhelmingly incompatible, and the law world has done almost nothing to change. What it has done seems to me to be minimal Band-Aid "family-friendly" programs that really just tell women that they will have reduced opportunity for partnership if they work a pretty rigid nine-to-five Monday through Friday week. Well, in my view, that's not adequately family-friendly. I think the work world is similarly bad for men in that I think most men would actually, if given the chance, enjoy participating more actively in parenting and family.

Do you have any advice for how to balance work and family life?
My main advice is that work-family conflict is better than not having the conflict by giving up having the family, which is what many women who make it to high career levels do. That's the first piece of advice. Don't give up having the family. I suppose, secondly, I would urge students when they get out there in the world to work on changing employer policies to make them more family-friendly. I think the current situation is very hard. Women are put under a lot of pressure to put off parenting so that they can make it to partner or tenure before they have family, and I think that is a pretty cruel pressure because it results in infertility for a lot of them. So I do think it's worth looking before you choose a career direction and at least considering choosing one that's going to both provide work that you actually care about and feel good about and think is socially worthwhile and is going to be compatible with having a family and putting time into that family.

What do you or whom do you contribute your success to in the legal profession?
I think the popular answer is mentors, and I did not feel in my life conscious of mentors playing that major a role for me. I think I was probably pushed in the direction of being ambitious and making it in a competitive world which was a man's world by having a tough childhood. By having in my childhood a family shattered by divorce, a mother who was economically and otherwise sort of initially destroyed by the divorce. I think seeing that probably had an impact on me pushing me in the direction of never wanting to be that vulnerable.

Do you feel like in your life you had a role model?
No. I am not conscious of having any major significant role models. As a very young child I think, to some degree my brothers functioned as parent substitutes and to some degree were

Lani Guinier

Lani Guinier is the Bennett Boskey Professor of Law at Harvard Law School where she devotes her teaching and research to issues of race, gender, and democratic decision making, as well as the responsibilities of public lawyers and access to higher education. In 1998, she became the first woman of color to be appointed to a tenured professorship at Harvard Law. Prior to teaching at Harvard, Guinier taught at the University of Pennsylvania. A graduate of Smith College in 1971 and Yale Law School in 1974, she also worked in the civil rights division at the U.S. Department of Justice and headed the voting rights project at the NAACP Legal Defense Fund in the 1980s.

Lani Guinier

IMAGE COURTESY OF HARVARD LAW SCHOOL

Vice-Dean Livingston Hall greeting Harvard Law's first women students in 1950.

IMAGE COURTESY OF HISTORICAL & SPECIAL COLLECTIONS, HARVARD LAW SCHOOL LIBRARY

my role models. That may have contributed to me feeling that the way to make it was to break into this man's world, and model myself on them.

What has been your greatest challenge in your career? And how did you deal with it?
I've definitely experienced all sorts of challenging things, including fighting for tenure at Harvard Law School and dealing with secondary infertility long after the birth of my first child. But dealing with infertility led me in the end to adoption and to two children that I can't imagine my life without. So I don't look back on that as some tragedy. Life is all about how you deal with what happens. I often said when I got back from Peru after these two adoptions, the most challenging thing in my life had been the three months in Peru for each of the adoptions. And yet I'm really glad I spent a total of six months in Peru back then because it gave me a chance to get to know the country and have a different feeling about the country that my two kids come from, and provided us all important lifelong friends in Peru. Bottom line, I don't think it makes sense to dwell on things that at the time can seem tragic or overwhelmingly difficult.

You became an assistant professor of law in 1977. How has the legal academic community changed for women in the last thirty-four years?
Well it certainly looks very different. When I was first here as an assistant professor there were almost no women on the faculty. I arrived hearing that this, that, and the other woman had been driven out or had not gotten tenure. Certainly teaching was different then because students weren't used to women professors. And so now, women are all around. We have a woman president of Harvard University as well as our second woman dean at the law school. All that's pretty extraordinary and has helped changed Harvard from being as overwhelmingly male an institution as it seemed when I first got here. And they've taken a lot of those males off the walls and put up portraits of women.

What has been your favorite contribution as a scholar and advocate?
It's hard to say my favorite. Certainly one of my favorites as a scholar was this book that I wrote called *Family Bonds* in which, since it was a post-tenure book, I was free to do what I wanted and free from a tenure committee audience. I combined a story of my personal experience with adoption with my views on the related child welfare and reproductive

Harvard's "New Look"

The *Harvard Law School Record* included the following poem by an anonymous poet, "Omar," on the occasion of the announcement that women would be admitted to the school in 1950.[19]

They got the job, and then the vote,
Invaded bars, and then the bar;
There seems a matriarchal note,
So strong appears their rising star;

We'll mourn the harried profs' morale,
As classes just are not the same,
For no one questions a gal,
And no one reasons like a dame;
Despite the drawbacks to this dare,
Two years of staring at these walls,

(With sour judges pictured there)
Of trudging through depressing halls,
Of reading law, dull legal books,
Have made me sigh for long blonde curls,
For sweet young things with lots of looks,
And so I say "Bring on the girls!"

policies. In terms of my academic career, it was one of my most creative and personally satisfying pieces of work.

What about the law are you passionate about?
I really don't find the law itself particularly interesting. It's more as a tool of social oppression or social change that it interests me. So I think the actual practice of law is often quite dull and detail-oriented and yet, when I was involved in litigation using law to change things I would find myself fascinated with, for example, how the transit authority in New York organizes its training and promotion. Not because that's at all intrinsically interesting but because I could use the nature of that system to force the transit authority to hire ex-addicts who were on methadone and needed employment if they were to have a chance at rehabilitation. I see law as potentially a method for social change and I think social change is interesting. I'm not sure the law itself is intrinsically interesting, and I can hardly make my way through Supreme Court opinions anymore because the surface reasoning seems so often completely fake. What's interesting is how the law can be used either for good or ill.

What do you wish you would have known when you were a young lawyer?
If I go back to being a student, I wish I had known more about how important it is to get to know the people around you as students. I was too oriented toward the apparent merits, not realizing enough that so much has to do with who's running what. If you take advantage of all the opportunities at school to get to know the people around you and later in life to get to know people, you have a real head start in thinking about how to change things.

What advice would you offer other young women starting their law careers?
I would tell them to focus on what they really want out of life and what they want out of a career, what they're going to find satisfying in the way of work. They need to recognize that work is going to be a huge part of their lives if they're going to take work seriously, and they don't want to be spending it doing stuff that isn't intrinsically interesting and worthwhile. I also would advise them not to worry overly about whether they are going to face discrimination. I think discrimination, even unconscious discrimination or what is called the glass ceiling, is really not that significant. What's significant is the work-family conflict and that's what they need to be thinking about—how to position themselves to do the kind of work they will find worthwhile while at the same time having the chance to enjoy family. Sex bias exists, but I don't think it has to get in their way. What is potentially going to get in their way is how to meld work and family in a satisfying way.

Martha L. Minow

Dean and Professor, Harvard Law School

There are few aspects of American society undergoing more change in my lifetime than women's place in the professions. When I was a child, a riddle that truly stumped people asked how it could come to pass that when an injured young person, delivered to the hospital by his father, there met an aghast surgeon, who said, "But I cannot operate on my own child!" Neither I nor those I knew immediately realized that the surgeon was the child's mother. We knew no women doctors or clergy or CEOs of major companies. But I did know one woman lawyer: my cousin, also named Martha. That she became a lawyer after getting a divorce simply added to her anomalous status and challenges toughing out tragedy, although she seemed thoroughly engaged by her work.

Coming from a family one generation removed from immigrants, I knew women working long hours for pay—and women as smart and capable as any man. Coming also from a family of three daughters and no sons, perhaps my sisters and I were freed from some of the gendered assumptions of our youth. In any case, our parents always made clear that we could do and become anything. My father brought to the dinner table questions from his law practice and roles in government; my mother sought our views about her work with abused children, immigrant children, and civic organizations. Engaging their children in the civil rights and antiwar debates of the 1960s, my parents propelled their children with a sense of service and justice.

As my older sister decided to pursue law, my course was to find something else. I chose educational reform, and yet barely months into my graduate studies, I learned that lawyers were central to the school desegregation, school finance, and free speech issues of the 1970s. So off to law school I went, planning to pursue educational reform. At Yale Law School, I did work on school reform, as well as child advocacy, and thought these would continue to be my focus. Along the way, faculty members encouraged me to be a law clerk. I worked for Chief Judge David Bazelon and Justice Thurgood Marshall. A change in administration altered my plan to work for the Department of Justice and, in 1981, I entered law teaching with the thought that later I would return to politics.

From the start, I loved the chance to create my own courses on children and the law and law and education, as well as civil procedure, family law, nonprofit organizations, and later constitutional law and international criminal justice. I found that from the base of a law school, I could pursue education reform and child advocacy even as I was drawn into reforming legal education.

In all of this I faced remnants of bias against women while also benefiting from emerging efforts to rectify it. My university had nominated me for a Rhodes Scholarship before they were awarded to women. I was asked how I would combine a career with raising children; I replied that my father had. The following year, the selection committee picked its first woman recipient. My law school class was about 25 percent women. Few women were on any law faculties across the country, but as I graduated, a number of schools recruited me. This reflected the recognition of the need for change on the part of many faculties.

Martha L. Minow

IMAGE COURTESY OF HARVARD LAW SCHOOL

Martha Minow speaking with students.

IMAGE COURTESY OF MARTHA L. MINOW, PHOTO BY TONY RINALDO

As the third woman joining the Harvard Law School faculty, I had what I have learned was a common experience when any two female colleagues talked: a male colleague would ask whether we women were engaged in a conspiracy. I don't think I ever imagined a woman dean or president of the institution. As the second female dean at my school, working for a woman president of the university, I celebrate changes that were both slow and sudden. I was one of three women out of thirty-five Supreme Court law clerks working for all-male justices; now there are three women on the Court—including Justice Ruth Bader Ginsburg, who litigated the landmark gender discrimination cases; Justice Sonia Sotomayor, my classmate; and Justice Elena Kagan, my student. Women judges, managing partners of law firms, ministers and rabbis, physicians and scientists, heads of agencies, and candidates for high elected office make it almost difficult to imagine what was mysterious in the riddle about the female surgeon.

What I have learned is that change—real and substantial change—is possible. These changes came from direct advocacy in courts and in institutions around the country, from the imaginations of authors and screenwriters crafting narratives that held out possibilities before they became fact, and from the courageous lives of women and men inventing different ways to organize their work, families, and ways of being. I study struggles for racial justice and efforts for gender equality, disability rights, minority language rights, religious freedom, and other efforts for an inclusive and just society, and despite deep disappointments and frustrations in each of these arenas, my own life's course suggests the promise of change through law.

Northeastern University School of Law

Libby S. Adler

Professor, Northeastern University School of Law

When I started law school at Northeastern University School of Law in the fall of 1991, several of my teachers were grieving the death, just a few months earlier, of their much-loved friend and colleague, Professor Mary Joe Frug of the New England School of Law. Some were working on their contributions to the memorial volume of the *New England Law Review.* Mary Joe was, as members of the Boston-area legal academic community know, murdered in broad daylight while walking not far from her home on a lovely, residential street in Cambridge. The crime remains unsolved.

Notoriously, Mary Joe strode the halls of her law school in high heels, fishnet stockings, and short leather skirts. Her professorial attire recalled that of another profession, and true to her particular brand of feminism, it rendered her a powerful presence. Mary Joe was a postmodern, pro-sex feminist, struggling mightily against that version of feminism according to which women are understood principally as victims. Indeed, for Mary Joe, the very categories of "men" and "women" were part of the problem. As she famously wrote, "only when the word 'woman' cannot be coherently understood, will oppression by sex be fatally undermined."

Responding to my academic inclinations and my interest in gender and sexuality, one of my law professors urged me to read Mary Joe's book *Postmodern Legal Feminism,* which includes an essay assessing a standard contracts casebook from a postmodern feminist perspective. The book was formative for me. It introduced me to a deeper level of analysis, in which one can glimpse how the law *makes us* into men and women as we understand those terms, rather than merely regulates us as people who fall naturally into those categories.

Libby Adler teaching a class.

IMAGE COURTESY OF NORTHEASTERN UNIVERSITY SCHOOL OF LAW, PHOTO BY DAVID LEIFER

After graduating from law school, I spent a few years working as a policy lawyer and regulatory drafter for the state child support agency under Governor William Weld and Commissioner of Revenue Mitchell Adams. Many of the women attorneys at the agency were feminists dedicated ideologically to child support enforcement on the grounds that it required men to shoulder some of the burden of poverty that fell disproportionately on women and children. Many of the men who worked at the agency were associated with the Log Cabin Republicans, a gay group that had supported Weld due to his fiscally conservative but socially liberal leanings. Ideologically, they were dedicated to child support enforcement because it recouped public assistance expenditures. The overlap and dissonance between these two constituencies formed a complex map, from which I began to tease out certain distributional politics associated with (but not inherently tied to) gender and sexuality.

I also became interested in the relationship between federal and state law, especially with regard to family. My time at the child support agency included the year following the enactment of the 1996 federal welfare reform act signed into law by President Bill Clinton. It was, ostensibly, the age of bloc grants, and states were supposed to assume responsibility for the allocation of federal disbursements, yet I spent much of my day as a state regulator trying to figure out end-runs around new, rigid federal rules in order to achieve state policy objectives. This problem provided me with the proposal for my LL.M. application to Harvard Law School. I wrote an LL.M. thesis under the supervision of Professor Jerry Frug, Mary Joe's widower, which eventually became my first academic article, "Federalism and Family." I also deepened my analyses of gender, family, federalism, administrative law, and other areas that have been the hub of my research and teaching.

That paper and another helped me to secure a faculty position at my first institutional love, Northeastern, where for more than a decade I have taught constitutional law, administrative law, family law, and a seminar on sexuality, gender, and the law. My scholarly work has migrated a bit to the limits of gay rights (and occasionally women's rights and transgender rights), especially the limits of relying on equality argumentation to achieve concrete distributional goals that would actually improve the living conditions of the most marginalized among us. Some of what I write now is "queer," which entails a critical posture toward identity-based claims, and therefore owes a debt to the postmodern feminism of Mary Joe.

A few years into my job at Northeastern, I received the supreme honor of being invited by some of Mary Joe's friends to join as a coeditor of her casebook, *Women and the Law*. She had been assembling such a book when she died. Her husband gathered what she had done and published her work posthumously, preferring that it be released unfinished rather than be lost. Three of her close surviving friends, Professors Martha Minow, Judith Greenberg, and Dorothy Roberts (the first two of whom hail from the Boston-area legal academic community) took over to produce the second and third editions.

When it was time to begin work on the fourth edition, however, they felt that to really honor Mary Joe, and to keep the book growing as she would have continued growing, they should bring in a couple of younger editors. To that end, they called on Professor Lisa Crooms of Howard University to add a global and human rights perspective, and me, to "queer it up." We did our best to live up to the toughness of the law professor in heels and fishnets, and to assure her friends that her legacy would carry on.

Margaret A. Burnham

Professor, Northeastern University School of Law

Margaret Burnham has been a professor at Northeastern University School of Law since 2002. She was appointed an associate justice of the Boston Municipal Court in 1977; her appointment made her the first African-American woman to serve in the Massachusetts judiciary. Her legal career began as a public defender.

The First Session of the Suffolk Superior Court, Criminal, on the seventh floor of the old New Courthouse, was, in the days before dockets went electronic, an awesome place—at least in the eyes of a kid lawyer. In 1973 I had to appear often in the session, usually on bail appeals on behalf of clients of the Roxbury Defenders Committee.

The port of entry to the busiest trial court in the state, cases ranked "serious" were graduated from the county's lower courts to the First Session. The session judge dispatched cases ready for trial to other judges and handled motions and our bail appeals. A prosecutor controlled the session list, which was posted each day. The cavernous, ill-lit, and crowded courtroom was an uneasy crossroads for neighborhoods that were geographically adjacent but racially distant, families on opposite sides of a crime, public defenders and prosecutors, and policemen and the subpoenaed witnesses dodging them. The bar marked a de jure separation between the elect, lawyers all, and the public. It divided, de facto, women from men and blacks from whites. Behind the bar were about twenty wooden graffiti-dressed benches where mothers and girlfriends of all races waited, a somber pall resting on their anxious shoulders. Against the left wall of the courtroom were two or three church-pew-length pine benches, lined up behind each other, on which perched (or slouched) the defendants, often handcuffed to one another, sometimes chained at the feet, eyes down-turned, and waiting, silently, for the prosecutor to bellow out their names. Over these men hovered court officers whose dock keys, hooked to their belts, clanked with their every move. The all-male benches were the most integrated space in the room; unlike their family members seated in racial clusters in the back of the courtroom, the defendants on display could not choose their seatmates. From time to time a woman defendant would appear on the bench, but because of the configuration of the lockup and perhaps the preferences of the court officers, she was usually by herself.

Margaret Burnham

IMAGE COURTESY OF NORTHEASTERN UNIVERSITY SCHOOL OF LAW. PHOTO BY DAVID LEIFER

Along the right wall, a box built for jurors held the room's most comfortable chairs, in which were seated, seemingly haphazardly, but, to the practiced eye, roughly in order of their renown, the town's famous criminal lawyers—Joseph Balliro, Alan Chapman, Reuben Dawkins, Alfred Farese, William Homans, Robert Stanziani—all aligned within the sightline and earshot of the prosecutor running the session. The prosecutors worked from an oversized desk and behind them were two smaller defense tables, one of which was assigned to us, the public defenders. Back then the official proceedings were all captured by a shorthand stenographer on a steno pad. What with the court officers' keys, the steady buzz around the desks, and the negotiations among the lawyers, it was somewhat noisy as courtrooms go, and

Margaret Burnham being administered the oath of office as an associate justice of Boston Municipal Court by Governor Michael Dukakis in 1977.

IMAGE COURTESY OF MARGARET BURNHAM

every so often the judge would gavel down the volume or the court officer would boom out, "Quiet back there!," aiming his voice back at the women and their children, although they were not the most offending. The session was the ultimate male preserve, governed by moves, rules, delays, and attitudes, not unlike a basketball court or a trading floor.

If you did not know what you were doing, or doing there, the First Session could scare a recently barred lawyer away from the high-minded ideals that had sustained your resolve to learn about things (of utterly no significance to you personally, but bar-worthy) like the UCC and adverse possession, just so you could one day be a decent criminal lawyer. One new to the session had the sense that secret codes, known only to certain of the men in front of the bar, controlled the courtroom. Sheer luck determined when one's case would be called, unless you were in the jury box, and there were never any women there. One could wait for hours in the session, where no newspapers were allowed and no one yet had an iPhone. You could spend the time preparing for your case, over and over again, but if you prepared, it was a guarantee your case would not get called. (Leave the file you needed in the Roxbury office; that would get you to the top of the list.) Most often, it was a "just missed" situation: "Sorry, your case was just called, come back later." Or, "Sorry, your client isn't in the dock today, come back later." If you got to the session too early, the prosecutor on your case would not be there yet; if you got there an hour later, he would be on trial in another courtroom. It seemed, though it cannot possibly be true, that public defender cases were the last ones called. It could take three or four days to clear up a single matter in the session, unless you could get the right man's attention at the right moment.

Bit by bit, the session revealed a few of its secrets. Get in before 9:15, line up to put a word in the ear of the unfriendly prosecutor calling the list ("My mother called me from the *Titanic*; I must be on the first call"), and never wait until 12:45 to try to have your case called. Smile. A lot. Remember if the Red Sox lost again. Tightrope walk the bar, navigating between the female family members who look like your real relatives on one side, and your brothers of the bar on the other. You cannot appear to befriend the women, for then the men on the other side will not take you seriously, and you cannot seem too distant (read: "white"), for then the women will dismiss you as a sellout "court lawyer." If the court officers tell you your client isn't in the dock, go back there and take a look. The lockup cages could each hold about ten men, and one had to slowly inspect each of them, peering in at every man without attracting undue attention. Ignore the whistles, construction-site stares, and pleas for help, and discern which of these aggressive, attractive young men, a predominant number of whom are black, is your client.

Unlike the virtually all-white and all-male Superior Court bench, the Roxbury District Court jurists, included African-American men and, indeed, that court's presiding judge, was a proud product of Roxbury's black community. This judge had, it was well-understood, authored a Roxbury-specific rule book on bail, which book was unwritten and unascertainable, and which was one reason we public defenders found ourselves so often in the First Session. If Roxbury's presiding judge—who ran that court's First Session—disapproved of the arguments offered on your behalf by a wet-behind-the-ears public defender, a defendant's bail could reach the heavens—an injustice that, if you, the assigned counsel, could master its ways, you stood a good chance of correcting in the First Session, where two very decent men—Judge Reuben Lurie and Judge Thomas Dwyer—frequently presided. With the stars properly aligned—prosecutor, police officer, defendant, and you all before the judge at the same time—you had a better than 50 percent chance of a bail reduction. Even if you obtained that reduction, however, if your client could not make the new bail immediately, the Roxbury judge would sometimes reapply his rule book when your client reappeared before him, in which case you would high-tail it, indignantly (did you miss the law school class about lower courts reversing upper court judgments?) and perhaps by now futilely (but it was the principle of the thing) back to the First Session.

Eventually, you find your place comfortably in front of the bar in the First Session. Eventually, there are more women. Eventually, you sit in the jury box and wait for your case to be called. But you try to remember when the bar was a tightrope and you tried not to fall off. You try not to forget the anguishing ride on the Orange Line from Dudley downtown, the tension and electricity of the old First Session.

Diane Theis Lund

Professor, Northeastern University School of Law

By Eric Lund

Diane Lund (1938–1995)—lawyer, equal rights advocate, law school professor, member of the first Judicial Nominating Commission, first woman chair of the Board of Bar Overseers, writer and editor, wife and mother, role model and mentor—was a forerunner for women during a critical period when women were gaining acceptance into the legal profession and into law school faculties. Her life and career is notable not only for her own achievements but for its intersections with the careers of other women in the legal profession who were important in the increasingly influential role of women in the law. I write about her not only as a lawyer, which I am, but as her husband, which I was from our time together in law school until her untimely death, thirty-five years later.

Diane Theis Lund

IMAGE COURTESY OF ERIC LUND

The obstacles she had to overcome began in Harvard Law School, when we married in June 1960, following her second year there[20], and she began interviewing during the fall hiring season. Her class ranking at that time was twelfth out of a class of some 500. As I had grown up in Maine and we were giving some thought to returning there, she interviewed with Portland law firms. The best (and only) Portland offer she received was from its leading law firm, which, noting her typing skills, offered her a position as a secretary, together with a promise that she would be given the opportunity to do some legal research and, after some years, perhaps be considered for an associate's position.[21]

Boston's establishment law firms, by contrast, all offered Diane a position as an associate—but when she later reported to them that she had become pregnant, all but one—Herrick, Smith, Donald, Farley and Ketchum—withdrew their offers. Herrick, Smith modified its offer to what was, for the times, an unheard-of proposition: if Diane would come to work full time three months after the birth of her child, and be trained for a year in the area of trusts and estates, the firm would thereafter accommodate her working for them on a part-time, 60 percent schedule until her children (two more were to come) were in school. She accepted and began work in late September 1961.

The arrangement turned out well for the firm because, in gratitude, Diane would bring work home to do in late evening hours in order to make up for time lost on account of her part-time status. In effect, the firm had hired an accomplished full-time lawyer for two-thirds pay. The arrival of her third child, however, was too much, even for Herrick, Smith, and in the year in which her classmates were considered for partnership, she was neither considered nor given any explanation other than that the firm felt, given her family status, she could not be relied upon.

Being left behind by her peers didn't sit well, and she decided to consider opportunities in the public sector, outside the private law firm context. She soon found one through a lawyer and friend, Allan Rodgers, who had recently become head of the Massachusetts Law Reform Institute, a nonprofit public-interest law firm whose charge was to represent the interests of poor people. There, in 1969, she joined forces with another woman lawyer, Regina Healy, and the two of them accomplished extraordinary changes to the inequities that then faced women in Massachusetts across a broad spectrum of opportunities that were being denied them.

Regie, born and bred in poverty in Lowell, had been the director of a neighborhood antipoverty agency in East Baltimore, but, having seen what lawyers could accomplish for her agency, had returned to Boston to go to law school. Along the way she became a member of Mayor Kevin White's Commission on the Status of Women, whose conclusions linked poverty to the inadequate education women, discriminated against in the public schools, were receiving. Paternalistic laws that assumed women should be trained for marriage and taken care of by their husbands served to exclude women from vocational education despite the ever-increasing number of women heads of families without men to support them. One of Diane's and Regie's signal achievements was the drafting, proposed by MLRI, and enacted by the legislature, of Chapter 622 of the Acts of 1971[22], which prohibited exclusion on account of sex from any course of study in the public

Diane Lund in 1973 as an assistant professor at Harvard.

IMAGE COURTESY OF ERIC LUND

schools. As a result, for the first time, women became trained in, and began to be employed in, the trades—plumbing, auto repair, bricklaying, electrical skills, etc.—and began to be able to command a wage that supported their families.

Diane and Regie were likewise instrumental in, or responsible for, the Maternity Leave Act, which required employers to grant eight weeks of maternity leave and to restore women to the positions of seniority they had held before their leave (previously, it had been customary simply to fire women who became pregnant and had to leave work to give birth), and the Bail Reform Act, the effect of which was to preclude judges from jailing welfare mothers until they disclosed the identity of the fathers of their children. They were instrumental in the passage of other pieces of social legislation, as well.

Northeastern University School of Law invited Diane to become the first woman member of its faculty in 1971. She accepted, and within weeks her classes began to be monitored by members of the Appointments Committee of Harvard Law School, whose failure to hire women had become a cause célèbre, not only among its students, but with the federal government. Harvard had sought to appease both by hiring Rutgers Law School Professor Ruth Bader Ginsburg in September 1971 to teach as a visiting professor, with the promise of a likely tenured appointment.

Northeastern University School of Law invited Diane to become the first woman member of its faculty in 1971.

Tenure, however, failed to materialize by the end of her first semester at Harvard, as one of its distinguished faculty members blocked it, opining that, in his opinion, Ginsburg's performance didn't meet Harvard's standard of excellence. Harvard's dean sought to assure her that the faculty was likely to change its mind at the end of the academic year, but Ginsburg, having been offered tenure at Columbia, accepted the offer and left Harvard.

Harvard turned to Diane, who was, in truth, reluctant to leave Northeastern, where she had already made an important impact, both in the faculty's willingness to accept a woman and among a student body that, even then, included more women than virtually any other law school in the country. In the end, urged on by friends and colleagues who believed she would be able to influence the future for many women besides herself, she felt she had to accept the offer. But not before imposing conditions on her acceptance.

Her conditions, which Harvard accepted with alacrity, were that her appointment to a tenure-track position as assistant professor would be on a two-thirds time basis so that she could have time with her children, then eleven, nine, and seven years old. She began at Harvard in the fall of 1972, and it soon became apparent that, as in the private sector, a less than full-time appointment of a woman was illusory. She was immediately appointed to both the admissions committee and the faculty appointments committee, dual responsibilities previously never given to any single faculty member. For those and a number of other reasons, both personal and professional, she was stretched thin, but she took both responsibilities as integral to what she was doing at Harvard. During the next seven years the number of women in the 500-strong Harvard class increased from thirty-eight to 138.[23] During the same period, faculty teaching positions were offered to Mary Ann Glendon, Raya Dreben, and Elizabeth Bartholet.[24]

Diane, meanwhile, taught courses in fiduciary responsibilities, employment discrimination, women and the law, professional responsibilities, and family law. Her collaborative approach—that people should think, reason, and work together to solve community issues—was unique in the Harvard context of the confrontational Socratic method, and she gained a loyal following there, as she had at Northeastern. What was lacking at Harvard, however, was an active participation in the greater community outside of the insular environment of Harvard, and she needed that facet in her life.

When Governor Michael Dukakis took office in January 1975, his Executive Order No. 1 created an unheard-of nonpolitical entity called the Judicial Nominating Commission, consisting of eleven members, both lawyers and nonlawyers, whose task it was to recommend three qualified candidates for each judicial vacancy, a slate from which the governor would choose one. He asked Diane to be one of the first members of the commission, and she accepted. The opportunity resonated with every aspect of her views concerning public service, the rights of the public, and the interests of women to be considered for office on a level playing field with men. The JNC had neither rules nor guidelines to follow, and Diane and the JNC's chair worked nights and weekends to create them, and then, with the rest of the commission, to implement them. She was a pivotal force in the creation of an institution that lasts to this day, and has served the legal profession well.

▲

Regina "Regie" Healy, now of Healy, Fiske, Richmond & Matthew.

IMAGE COURTESY OF HEALY, FISKE, RICHMOND & MATTHEW

Choosing to leave the tenure track at Harvard, she returned to private practice (although continuing on at Harvard as a lecturer on family law and professional responsibilities) and partnered with Regina Healy in a domestic relations practice in which their cases advanced the interests of women and children in domestic crises. She was frequently appointed by the Probate Court to represent and advocate for the best interests of children whose parents were divorcing, then a novel role for a lawyer.

In 1978 the Supreme Judicial court appointed her to fill a vacancy on the Board of Bar Overseers. By September 1982 she had served two terms as its vice chair, the first woman to do so, and according to custom and practice, should have been appointed its chair for the following year, but instead the Supreme Judicial Court reappointed the current chair, a man, for a second year. While she would do nothing publicly to embarrass either the Supreme Judicial Court or the chair, someone for whom she had a great deal of respect, she made it clear, privately, to the chief justice, that this sexist treatment of her had to be remedied. The following fall, her term was extended for an additional year and she was appointed as the first woman chair of the Board of Bar Overseers.

In the spring of 1984, at Governor Dukakis' suggestion, Diane applied for appointment to fill a vacancy on the Appeals Court. Ironically, hers was not one of the three names sent to the governor by the JNC, one of the few major disappointments in her professional career.

The following year, however, she accepted another, different kind of challenge when she became a member of the Bowdoin College Board of Overseers at a time when Bowdoin was in the throes of transition from an all-male to a co-ed institution. In that capacity, for the next ten years, she was instrumental in causing Bowdoin to establish and build a children's center, arguing that such a center, which would provide day care for young children, was critical to the college's being able to attract qualified women to its faculty, as, indeed, it proved to be; and she undertook personally to review and revise and catalogue the deeds of gift establishing Bowdoin's endowed funds to eliminate discriminatory clauses and to bring Bowdoin's accounting practices into the twenty-first century.

We set about establishing other roots in Maine, buying and renovating an eighteenth-century farmhouse on the Kennebec River, a half-hour's drive from Bowdoin, where we and Regina Healy and her husband (yet another lawyer) founded the *Maine Lawyers Review,* a biweekly newspaper containing feature articles and reports and commentary on cases of interest to the Maine bar. Diane was still hard at work right up to the time of her untimely death, from cancer, in May 1995.

Emily A. Spieler

Dean and Professor, Northeastern University School of Law

Emily Spieler graduated from Harvard-Radcliffe College in 1969 and has been a member of the Massachusetts bar since 1974, after graduating from Yale Law School. Early in her career she practiced law in Boston, specializing in the legal problems of women workers. She was an early member of the Cambridge-based Women's Law Collective.

▲

Emily Spieler

IMAGE COURTESY OF NORTHEASTERN UNIVERSITY SCHOOL OF LAW, PHOTO BY DAVID LEIFER

Spieler is dean and Edwin W. Hadley Professor of Law at Northeastern University School of Law, having held the position of dean since 2002. She is the law school's first woman dean. She is an expert in labor and employment law and social insurance programs. During the winter of 2008–2009, she served on President Barack Obama's transition team for the Department of Labor.

Prior to beginning her academic career, Spieler practiced labor and employment law in Boston and West Virginia. She held several senior state government positions in West Virginia. She joined the faculty of the West Virginia University College of Law in 1990, where she taught courses in labor, health, and employment law, social policy, negotiation skills, and appellate advocacy. She returned to Boston in 2002 to assume her position as dean.

Why did you decide to go to law school?

This isn't an "I always wanted to be a lawyer" story. Actually, there were no lawyers in my family, and I wasn't sure what I was going to do after college. I was working for the City of New York in the Housing and Development Administration, and I found that people simply wouldn't take me seriously. I was often asked, "Well, where did you go to law school?" because of the kind of work that I was doing. Frankly, I decided that it was pretty clear that in order to be taken seriously, I was going to have to have a degree. It seemed that a law

The questions and answers presented here are excerpted from an interview with Dean Spieler by Therese Rohrbeck for this book in December 2010.

degree would be the most useful one. I suspect that it was difficult to be taken seriously because I was a young woman, combined with the lack of degree.

What did you enjoy most about law school?
...The intellectual challenge of thinking about how rules are made in a society and then enforced, and how this relates—or doesn't—to the creation of a peaceful and just world.

Can you remember if you experienced any sort of gender bias when you were a student at Yale Law School? Was it a woman-friendly place?
I can't imagine that any law school was woman-friendly at that time! There were probably twenty-five to thirty women in my class. The whole class was around 170 to 180 students. There was only one woman professor—she later became the chief justice of the Connecticut Supreme Court.... It was clear that there was not an expectation that there would be women there. So, there were a variety of things that happened that were clearly gender related, but it was also at the beginning of the women's movement.... There were remarkable second- and third-year women students who had formed a women's law caucus at the school. The year [1970] that I was a first-year student, in particular, the third-year students were real leaders. One of them was Nancy Gertner. There were several others of similar powerful personalities and intellect in the group; they recruited the first-year women to become part of that group and encouraged us to think about issues they had begun. One of these was the case that came to be called *Women v. Connecticut*: a pre–*Roe v. Wade* challenge to the abortion statutes in Connecticut.

One symbolic example.... The only bathroom for women in the law school was down in the basement. You had to go through this dark passageway to get to this small bathroom. It is really very different now. On the other hand, as I said, there were impressive women students. And remember this was a time of a lot of political turbulence, as well as the time of growth of the women's movement. There was a Black Panther trial going on in New Haven, in addition to a lot of organizing around the Vietnam War. During my first year, there was an all-students meeting with the dean about some issue—I actually can't even remember what it was—but the most impressive person who spoke at that meeting...was a woman who was a part of this third-year group.

It was clear that there were powerful women who were able to act in a very powerful way even in that environment.

I was 100 percent convinced that I would never go into legal academic teaching, which just goes to show that you rarely know what will happen in your life.

Did you know when you were at Yale Law School how you were going to use your legal education?
I would say no. I knew I was interested in social justice issues. I worked in legal services while I was there, and I decided I did not want to do that after graduation because I did not like the income limitations for the clients. I was interested in being able to work with working people as well as the extremely poor. I was definitely not interested in going into a corporate law firm at all, and I never interviewed for any of those positions. I was 100 percent convinced that I would never go into legal academic teaching, which just goes to show that you rarely know what will happen in your life.

So, what did you think your first move would be after you graduated from law school?
What it was: I joined the Women's Law Collective, one of the law collectives that was in existence in Boston at the time. My interest in the issues facing women, particularly women at work, had solidified, and I was interested in working in an environment in which people were passionate about social change.

What was the Women's Law Collective?
At that time, there was a lot of experimentation with forms in all of the different professions. It was at the same time as the growth of free clinics and collectives in the health-care world.... The law collectives were groups of people—lawyers and others—who were dedicated to principles of social justice and who didn't believe in traditional hierarchical structures. The Women's Law Collective obviously was focused on women's issues. We did a lot of family law, but my personal interest was in employment issues and what happened to women at work. That was one of the reasons I didn't want to be in legal services, because often you couldn't represent people who were working because they were over the income guidelines.

Was the Women's Law Collective considered a feminist legal practice?
I suppose, although, I think at that time we probably wouldn't have stated it that way. At that time there was a strong view of feminism as being a middle-class, white women's movement.... I'm sure had you pressed any of us at the time, we would have said, yes, of course we were feminist....

Where did your love or your passion for women's issues and gender equality come from?
I'm not really sure.... For me, it has always been an issue that is also tied up with issues of class and issues of race. I suspect that a lot of this came from my mother. I grew up in a household that believed in labor unions, that believed in equality for people and social justice, and then I came of age in an era when the women's movement was very strong. I think that probably I am a product of all of those things.

How did you get your job as dean of Northeastern University School of Law?
I knew Northeastern and I also knew its reputation in terms of being progressive, having a commitment to social justice issues, and also being committed to experiential education—a philosophy that people learn by doing. I had administrative experience in state government as well as practice experience, and I was a tenured professor. I wrote a letter to the search committee suggesting that I might be a good match because of my commitment to the issues and commitment to experiential learning. So, I had a lot of consonance with the mission of the school. Frankly, I would never have applied for a deanship at another law school. Although there is a whole world of people who apply to a number of law schools, hoping to be selected as a dean, for me it was very much about an interest in this school and what this school was about and could do. And I hit it off with the committee. When I went into the search, I thought there was a very small chance that I would be viewed as a serious candidate for a couple of different reasons. One is that generally people like to see experience in higher

The Northeastern University School of Law class of 1926; one of the earliest classes with women students. Nine women are pictured, making up just over 6 percent of the class—including the class secretary and an executive committee member.

IMAGE COURTESY OF NORTHEASTERN UNIVERSITY LIBRARIES, ARCHIVES AND SPECIAL COLLECTIONS DEPARTMENT

education administration—as an associate dean, for example. I had just never had any general interest in higher education administration. The other reason was that I was in West Virginia, which tends to be viewed in the Northeast as a kind of third-world country. It's a prejudice, a stereotyping prejudice. I was quite surprised, actually, that I became a serious candidate.

Why is being dean such a great fit for you?

I think the reason it is a great fit here is that I'm committed to the mission of the school in a serious way and have always been. It's not just that this is an institution that hired me and therefore I am a mouthpiece for it.... This is a school that represents what I believe and tries to educate lawyers the way I believe lawyers should be educated. That is important, I think, because it is a hard job: you really need to care about the institution, particularly at Northeastern, which is more complex and in some ways much more difficult to manage than a more traditional law school. I think good deans ultimately have to have a varied set of strengths, and often people who come up out of the professoriate and just go into academic administration don't understand the set of skills that you need. You need political skills. You need to be able to manage lots of different constituencies with different views about what the institution should be. I held a couple of senior public sector jobs in West Virginia. When people ask me what was the best training for this job, I say those political jobs were the best training for this job. Understanding how politics works and how to be persuasive to people who may not agree entirely with what you believe is incredibly important.

What would you say is the hardest part of your job?

I think that what is hardest about being a dean, and this is true in all schools, is that the different constituencies really view who you are and what you should be doing very differently. For example—the university administration has one set of expectations, and they expect you to manage your school—and to raise funds. This is true of deans of all colleges, not just law schools. Faculties, however, are self-governing, and tenured faculty members have a huge amount of autonomy. The notion that a dean can simply tell a tenured faculty member what to do is actually preposterous. There is a tension between what the central administration often expects and the capacity of the person who heads a college to persuade the faculty to embrace these expectations. So, on the one hand you are managing the people up, and on the other hand, you really have to be an organizer and a leader for the people on the faculty who don't have to do what you are asking them to do. There are other constituencies, as well, with different views of the school—graduates, students, lawyers who employ our students and graduates.

One example of the challenges with students is this: You can spend three years having a conversation with the student body about something important to the school, reach closure, and implement a decision. The next group of first-year students arrives and says, "Have you ever talked about this?" There is absolutely no institutional memory in the student body. They are in a constant state of demanding replays—it's like *Groundhog Day*. That is awkward because after a while you want to say, "Look, I don't want to talk about this anymore. We've been talking about it. We've talked about it for five years. Five years of students were deeply involved in this conversation. I'm done with this conversation." But they are not. For them it is entirely new.

When you first took your position as dean, or even today, do you feel like you are a woman dean or just the dean?

...I have tended in my life to downplay gender as the central issue. I've come to wonder recently, actually, whether that is a protective kind of approach for myself, that I decided a long time ago that I was going to make it on my own merit and not rely on or blame gender. When I was in state government—and this was a long time ago in the eighties in West Virginia—the governor brought in a leadership trainer, and he went around and interviewed the thirty people in leadership positions. He reported back to the governor...that he thought the four women were stronger by and large than the men. The governor told me about this, and I said to him, "Well, of course that is true. Until you are willing to appoint women who are just as mediocre as the mediocre men you appoint, then there isn't real equality." Women almost always have to prove themselves on the merits, but then—and I think now—men get

Until you are willing to appoint women who are just as mediocre as the mediocre men you appoint, then there isn't real equality.

positions in a variety of ways that have not historically been open to women. I think this is still true, and it's true for minorities as well.

So, until recently, I never thought of myself as a woman dean although I was the first woman dean in Boston [since Portia Law School's Margaret Bauer in 1953], and I did point this out early in my tenure. I remember in my original welcome ceremony, I said something about the fact that I thought it was fitting for Northeastern to have the first woman dean in the current era, particularly because of the history of this law school and the fact that lots of women came to Northeastern in the seventies because other law schools were not very friendly to women at that time. The Northeastern president said to me afterward, "I never really thought about it. I hired you on merit." And I think that was in fact true. Recently, I think I've thought more about it, because we have not yet achieved diversity in the ranks of college deans at Northeastern University. There are quite a few deans of colleges at Northeastern, and I was the first woman dean and the only woman from the time I arrived in 2002 [until a woman was hired in fall 2011 to head the health sciences college].

I really try to feel like a dean, not like a woman dean. That is certainly my goal. But there is a moment every year when the women deans of law schools go off alone at a national meeting to have a dinner. The rules of this dinner are that nothing that is said there goes outside; we go around the room and talk about the thing that was hardest for us in the course of the year and the best success in the course of the year. People tell very intimate stories about their positions and many of them, I think, reflect a situation in which there was gender bias. I think that however women choose to deal with it, it is an issue that you have to navigate.

Do you feel like being a woman affects the way you do your job?
Well, that kind of goes back to the question of feminism. To some extent, I think women have a tendency to do certain things that men have a tendency not to do...but I think it is on a spectrum. It's not all women do this and all men do that. I have a tendency to intervene in conversations in a different way than my male colleagues—but since I am the only woman it is hard to know whether that is about gender or just about me. I think when I came there were some expectations about how a woman would—or should—function that I am not sure I met. I felt that to be very gendered.

Let's see if we can speak a little bit about family and work. Did you take time off from your career to raise children?
We were in southern West Virginia when we had kids. Before I got pregnant, I had cobbled together a set of projects that I was working on. Some of them I let slide, and some of them I continued. I actually shared office space with someone through that period, and I cocounseled on some pretty complex cases. I wasn't working full time in the sense that people think of full-time work in urban environments, but I was certainly working hard. I had never worked at a traditional law firm. So, it wasn't as if I had had this highly structured career and then I went to a highly unstructured situation.

But you continued to work all throughout?

Yes, but not work in the sense that I get up in the morning, find child care, drop my kid off at day care, put hose on, and go out the door. It was much more a— You know, I have a case coming up. I had neighbors who took in our kids on a regular basis. My husband was a full-time practicing physician in the coalfields at that time. But I would sometimes call him and say, "You have to come home. I have to leave." It was a rural existence, for one thing. So,...those words don't mean the same thing in that situation. You have kids and they affect every corner of your life, and if they don't, there is something wrong with the way that you are relating to your children. But I had flexibility that doesn't exist for many people in urban areas.

How did you balance work and family?

Poorly. I have a really hard time when I have an important task not being obsessive about how well I do it. I have to think it is an important task, but if I think it is an important task, I am incapable of doing it part way. I actually think having kids makes your life whole, even someone like me who has not got the kind of patience that makes you a perfect parent.... For me having children is an aspect of life that I wouldn't have given up in the world.

Could I have had a more linear career and been more successful? I have no idea. Was it children or a variety of other things that made me make decisions that didn't look like a more traditional career? Again, I don't think it was the children. I think, although, there were times— The only time I remember turning something down that I would have liked to have done, I think has as much to do with my husband as it had to do with the kids. I gave up my position in state government, went to Morgantown to join my husband who had moved there, and joined the law faculty at West Virginia University. Then a couple of years later the governor called and asked me to come back for his second term as his chief of staff. I really did want to do that job, and I think I could have made a difference for the state in that job. But I concluded that I wasn't going to do it because we had settled the kids, and my husband loved his job. I had a tenure-track position at the law school, I wasn't willing to commute, and I didn't think we should move back to southern West Virginia just for this opportunity. I think for all of us, that was a hard decision. But that is the only time I can remember making a decision that was controlled by having a family.

Do you have any advice on how to balance work and family?

You have to have a partner who is fully engaged, and then it is just a matter of negotiation. Young women ask me, "How did you do this and have a family, too?" And I think, well, for one thing I didn't have a linear career. I think the kind of opportunities that I had partly had to do with the fact that my husband and I were both willing to live on very little money and were mutually supportive. So, we had a lot of flexibility in what we could choose to do. I also think that it can't be one person being flexible and the other one being focused on career. It has to be a joint enterprise. I see too many families who are young where that is not true, and I think that is what really, really makes it hard. Then, the question becomes how much are you willing to make compromises? Do you have a single vision of who you want to be as a family or whether you are able to juggle things? I think it is possible to do that, but my guess is that it is a whole lot harder to do if you have a spouse who thinks that his career is primary.

What or whom do you attribute your success to in the legal profession?
You know actually, I recently had an interesting conversation with a group of women, including Nancy Gertner, about this. Did we have mentors? And we concluded no. I think—I've actually thought a lot about this recently because I am clearly in the stage of my life where I feel as if I should be mentoring young people. So, in part, I think we were really the late sixties, early seventies generation and very much into doing it on our own. We had a hard time accepting mentorship, I think. And there were not that many women who were people you would look to, anyway. Occasionally, I came across someone, but it was infrequent.

I think that you are a whole lot more powerful as a human being when you have collaborators—and collaborators who will tell you when you are wrong.

I would say my success is more about collaborations I have had with people over time where there has been a genuine give and take, where we've learned from each other and learned from each other's mistakes and been supportive of each other. I think that you are a whole lot more powerful as a human being when you have collaborators—and collaborators who will tell you when you are wrong.

There was recently a symposium honoring Professor Clare Dalton. It was called "Challenging Boundaries in Legal Education." What would you say are some boundaries women face in legal education?
This is increasingly no longer true, but it was clear to me when I entered teaching—and the vast majority of the people on the faculty were men—that there really was a different standard, a different way that women candidates for positions were discussed. I remember losing my temper more than once.... I'll tell you an anecdote about my prior institution. Once, there were five of us on the committee that was supposed to interview people and pick finalists for faculty positions, and then bring the finalists in for review by the rest of the faculty. For the first time, this hiring committee had a majority of women on it. The two men displayed a lot of gendered behavior and were not very self-aware. At one point, the three women on the committee did not want to interview a particular person but the two men did. I thought this was simply a disagreement among colleagues, but one of the men on the committee said, "I don't know what it is with you people." It was clear that he saw us as a bloc, when actually the three of us were simply expressing our individual views. It was a preposterous moment, a telling moment because it told me that he looked at us and what he saw was three women and two men, not five individuals in the room. I actually stopped the meeting. I said, "Wait a minute. What exactly is it that is going through your mind that made you say that?" It was a kind of interesting conversation because he was just nonplussed. He couldn't even rerun it and see that it was inappropriate. I suspect this is an experience that people of color have too often.

That was probably 1995. It was not that long ago. I think times are changing, but they are not changed.

How has the legal academic community changed for women in the last twenty years?
It has changed tremendously, but there are still huge issues. On one hand, half of entering law students now are women, many law faculties have lots of women on them, and there are lots of women deans. A friend of mine at one of the law schools in Washington says that when the group of women deans started to get together for dinner, there were about ten of them. It was really like a support group. Now, it is a big room with multiple tables. Women aren't half of deans, but just in Boston you can see the difference: I was the first woman dean in Boston and now BU, Harvard, and Suffolk also have women deans, and it is simply not a big issue. Women are in all fields, not just women's fields. On the other hand, I think there are still barriers. People still tend to think of business law or tax law as male fields. You still see way more women doing family law than you see men. And there are far fewer women who are partners in large law firms or judges on major courts than men. Even legal services organizations around the country still tend to be headed by men. There is a complicated thing that happens to women as they make compromises about how to live their lives. Or they confront compromise differently in the way they live their lives than men seem to do. But nevertheless, in the legal academy, there has been a huge shift numerically, and that changes the culture. This notion of critical mass is a real one. I think that although there is still a lot to be done, we are definitely at a critical mass place now.

What has been your favorite contribution as a scholar and an advocate? What are you most proud of having accomplished?
There are different paths in my life and there are different pieces of my answer to that. For example, for this law school, I think that I have, with a lot of help from a lot of other people, been part of a process of bringing the law school forward to think about who we want to be in 2020 instead of who we were in 1970—sort of a shift to the future, I think, that has been very important. If I were ten years older and I was looking back at my life and asking did I have impact anywhere, I would point to issues of how injured workers are treated. I think I have played a role in making sure that people maintain some focus on what happens to the injured worker as opposed to what is the cost to the employer, or how does the insurance work. Because of the role I've played, there are people who are willing to talk about fairness to workers as the centerpiece of what the issue is. I hope the result is that there will be a better system for injured workers. I like to think I've had a real impact on that national conversation.

What do you wish you would have known when you were a young lawyer?
I think I wish I would have known how powerful it would have been to have mentors. On the other hand, I think that I did some things as a young lawyer that would have been regarded as nuts by someone more experienced, but which worked—sometimes really well. So, I think that it can be constraining to have someone who has experience as well as liberating. But I do believe that, on balance, I would have benefited tremendously by starting out with people who had more practice experience. I don't think this was entirely about gender. I think it was really about the times that we were living and the notion that we could just wing it.

What advice would you offer other young women starting their law career?
I give everybody the same advice. If you are going to have a life partner, it needs to be someone who is in it with you, not in the legal practice with you, but in life with you as a real partner. That is one. The second thing I always tell people is to take risks. People are much more anxious now, I think, than we were. Most of the good things that have happened to me in the course of my life happened because of risk taking. I think my ability to take risks, quite frankly, was helped by the nature of my relationship with my husband. These two things are really very intertwined. When I go out and talk to our graduates, the people who are the most excited about their lives, their work lives, but also their lives in general, they are people who have made decisions to do things that might not have been the safest. There is a lot of financial anxiety now because of the amount of loans that people have. And I think that really changes the landscape. But there are opportunities that come along, and people really need to be willing to take them on. The other piece of advice is that you should find people you trust who you can talk to, whether they are collaborators or mentors who can help you think things through. That it is just hugely valuable. I have been watching my son, who is not a lawyer, navigate some difficult times. He is a journalist which is a pretty scary field to be in these days. He has several people to whom he goes to for advice when things become difficult, and I think it has really been helpful to him. I think that young people—but especially young women—really benefit from that kind of mentoring and counseling.

Suffolk University Law School

Kate Nace Day

Professor, Suffolk University Law School

Law often proceeds in formal spaces filled with art, carpets, and ceremonial gestures where language moves between people, much as it does in conversation. Law, though, imposes a structure on its dialogue, an exchange of questions and answers that mirrors the form of legal reasoning and the internal dialogue seen throughout appellate cases. In courtrooms and classrooms, the language of law defines a geography where arguments and strategies about hierarchies, authority, and legal categories often displace concerns with justice and caring, social context, and ethical dilemmas.

Stories told in law's language are potent artifacts of "thinking like a lawyer," our traditional methodology of translating the messy details of human stories—bodies and emotions, lived realities, and moral doubts—into apparently neutral and universal stories of written texts, precedent, and authority. Law's stories are highly structural, almost architectural—foundations deep in the marl, thick walls, and shadow boxes. The relationship of women lawyers to law is complex and personal, perhaps edgy. Some women use law's own language to challenge the very foundations of law by theorizing "up" from the sometimes messy details of women's lives. Other women—not wanting to be defined by gender or to be overlooked or undervalued for being a woman—resist those who view law as a tool, a means to an end, rather than a profession, a calling.

Each woman lawyer is her own story—in time, place, character, and life—and hers is the only voice that has the right to tell it. One must listen. She may tell her story as solitary, singular acts, gestures, and details of her achievements and daily emotions—as creative as those of Massachusetts' own women poets—Emily Dickinson, Elizabeth Bishop, and Anne Sexton. Yet, the resonances of language—the talk of conscience, the talk of power—make sidesteps, taking on the form of other stories, taking on direction, movement, development, change. This is our history we are hearing—women's challenges to the nation and the states that take us beyond personal disappointments and lessons. While events in our lives happen in time and sequence, in history our significance finds its own order, its own thread—forward and back, changing with respect to each other in open talk about law's language. There is discovery and the promise of revelation in charged meeting points of individual human memories—talk of the young and old, past and present, living and dead.

Kate Nace Day

IMAGE COURTESY OF KATE NACE DAY

In 1405, over six centuries ago, Christine de Pizan wrote that girls and women must be taught to write so that women's sense of our own history might survive. Women's history is now recorded in claims of rights—the claim to literacy, education, and critical thought; to refuse to be demeaned; to advocate against the injustices of confining women to the private sphere without rights while simultaneously excluding them from the public sphere of full citizens, paid workers, and professionals; to physical health, reproductive freedom, and—at the end of the last century—to life without violent sexual inequalities. From one country, state, or culture, the particulars of the social and political contexts may vary, but within these

The first woman graduate of Suffolk University Law School: Marian Archer MacDonald's 1937 graduation photo.

IMAGE COURTESY OF MOAKLEY ARCHIVE AND INSTITUTE AT SUFFOLK UNIVERSITY (SU-0359)

Marian Archer MacDonald was the only woman in her 1937 graduating class. She is pictured in the center of the photo, above her father, Dean Gleason L. Archer. Her admission to the school was considered to be a "trial run." Her success convinced her father to open the school to women upon her graduation.

IMAGE COURTESY OF MOAKLEY ARCHIVE AND INSTITUTE AT SUFFOLK UNIVERSITY (SU 0401)

particulars there is no doubt that women lawyers are writing an enduring record of our humanity. We are part of a story beyond law's language and spaces, one that begins with one woman and ends with another's truth in the world. We walk on broad paths, stones worn warm and smooth by women who have gone before, each of us privileged, knowing that the last word is always given to one who speaks for victims.

Camille A. Nelson

Dean and Professor, Suffolk University Law School

I have been asked to write this reflection piece as "the first woman" and "the first person of color" to be appointed as dean of Suffolk University Law School. I am, however, confronted by my unease with both monikers. This unease leads me in a few directions. First, I humbly admit and am grateful for the fact that, in some small way, history has been made; a history that might be celebrated by some and criticized by others. Second, I am left to ponder the ways in which this does and does not matter in my personal life or in the lives of others, beyond the walls and halls of Suffolk University Law School. Third, I must look inward and assess the ways in which my having been appointed into this position might mean that I have some insight or wisdom at navigating what remains, as James Brown sang, "a man's world," and I would add that, insofar as the legal profession and the legal academy are concerned, a white man's world. So the question is, "What does that say about the ways in which women in such positions 'of power' manage our multiple identities, be that gender, sexuality, class, race, or disability, etc.?"

Let me start with why this occasion might be celebrated. Presumably my appointment signals racial and gender progress, or at least inclusion that bespeaks a level of professional evolution and/or adjustment. And in reality, at least a reality, it is a momentous occasion, both on a personal level for me, my family, the communities to which I belong, and for the law school, and university. As such I too am delighted, encouraged, and appreciative of this amazing opportunity. I am deeply humbled.

However, in another way it also behooves me to consider the ways in which my appointment does not really matter, or might actually make my life or the lives of other women and people of color more challenging, or at least subject to greater scrutiny. Taking the latter point first, it is not lost on me that I am seen not just as the dean now, but as the black woman dean. So my identity becomes embedded in this title in a way that does not flow with a white male dean. You do not typically hear people whispering, "That's the dean!" or asking, "Is that the dean?" when the dean's very race, gender, and age I might add, are interpreted as archetypically or quintessentially befitting of the title or "power position" that he occupies. My race, gender, and assumed age are not, yet, normatively imbued with such power, or associated with the title of dean.

Like other women in similar positions, we are engaged on an additional level. In our positions, the added lens of identity creates an extra evaluative framework. Our decisions have implications that resonate in myriad ways based on who we are and what we are assumed to be attempting to

Camille A. Nelson

IMAGE COURTESY OF SUFFOLK UNIVERSITY LAW SCHOOL

achieve, that is, gender equality for one. For instance, I have appointed three new women to be associate deans and one man, to complement the three men who were already in those positions. I know that was perceived as risky, or perhaps risqué, by some and radical by others. But the question is why? For generations we have taken for granted that multiple slates of men could be appointed, yet the omission of women from positions of power was itself cast as the norm.

Suffolk University Law School's first woman professor, Catherine Judge, teaching a class. Judge was a 1957 graduate of the school, a time when women comprised only 4 percent of the student body. Hired as a professor in 1966, she was awarded tenure in 1970.

IMAGE COURTESY OF MOAKLEY ARCHIVE AND INSTITUTE AT SUFFOLK UNIVERSITY (SU-0656)

Yes, I confess to being specifically concerned with gender and racial equality, but I am concerned with equality, justice, and inclusion generally. However, I am equally, if not more, concerned with excellence and ensuring that we have the best team possible—the difference being that I saw excellence in areas and in people who have traditionally been overlooked for such opportunities. I think there is excellence all around us if we open our eyes to the inclusive possibilities. So when I stated that I have "to consider the ways in which my appointment, and decisions, might make the lives of other women and people of color more challenging or at least subject to greater scrutiny," I was partially referring to our new team. We have a little bit more to prove, given the novelty of the entire situation.

The irrelevance of my appointment is most evident by the fact that, outside of the law school and university, when not in "dean mode," I am alternatively invisible and/or treated with the same level of societal ambivalence, and occasional disdain, as any black woman is treated. For instance, hailing a cab in certain locales is still challenging both before and after deaning—no noticeable change—and people still occasionally refuse to put change in my hands. No need to dwell on these noticeable slights, except to mention that they still happen. They do not care what I do for a living, nor should they—we should be more concerned about the content of our character. It is for this reason that I do not write "Dean" before or after my name on a name-tag I am to wear. To the extent that some people are suddenly inclined to treat me better or respond more favorably because of the "dean" title is telling and troubling. It is an unfortunate reality, revealing our biases, and leads me to wonder how my mother, sister, friends, or strangers, without such a position or title, would be treated, versus how they too ought to be treated.

Perhaps more poignant, I have been struck by how difficult it is for some people, men and women alike, to fathom women in positions that are perceived as powerful—as a society we have a bit of a crisis of gendered expectations. I concede, however, that there is a chicken-and-egg dynamic, as this might be a function of our relative numerical and statistical invisibility in such positions, which, cycling back, might again relate to our limited gendered expectations.

To my mind this is related to a perceptual challenge that we must tackle—that is the management of identity. There have been several occasions since I started this position that I have been in a group and have been introduced as the dean, only to have the person to whom I was introduced shake the hands of the man standing next to me and say, "Great to meet you, Dean!" Of course, the correction of that mistake is inevitably awkward and a little embarrassing, as much as the moments when men and women ask, "What kind of dean are you—are you the dean of deans?" My response is usually, "Well I hadn't ever framed it that way, but yes."

So you might appreciate why it is sometimes just easier not to write Dean on your name tag. I don't want to make anyone feel uncomfortable and have to then manage their embarrassment or their faux pas—that, too, is added work. I want to emphasize, however, that these moments of confusion are not nasty, hostile, or adversarial, and indeed we often laugh about it after the fact together as a group. Rather, they are just moments of revelation—moments when we display our gendered or raced expectations of what someone in a certain position is supposed to look like and who they are expected to be. But this is the plight of progress, is it not? Perhaps these are instances of coalition-building—teaching moments that might expand our horizons. Again, that might represent progress. But the question is why, in 2011, are we surprised that a woman of color would be dean of an American law school? Our shock is all the more insightful given that women have represented approximately half of law school graduates across North America and have been well represented in law schools for some time now. This leads me finally to the systemic matters.

Jeanne Hession was the first woman at Suffolk Law elected class president. Future Congressman John Joseph Moakley ran her 1955 campaign.

IMAGE COURTESY OF MOAKLEY ARCHIVE AND INSTITUTE AT SUFFOLK UNIVERSITY (SU-0394)

I want to briefly speak to the structural matters—that is the James Brown song again. I must acknowledge first that even if I say or do nothing beyond the status quo, the fact that I am occupying this office is perceived, and encountered, as a significant change. Why is that? People come to embody structures, and structures are accepted and concretized by people. Therefore, to the extent that there has previously been only white men in the dean's office reveals a structure that is itself now very much in a state of transformation. To the extent that our identities matter, they are significant as they contribute to and shape our experiences—our experiences in turn shape our perspectives. But we nonetheless have to frame those perspectives in ways that resonate with others who have not had those experiences and who may not appreciate their significance. I am alluding to the essential management of one's identity in such situations and in large institutions. I am highlighting the negotiation of ourselves that I think of as being endemic to the experiences of women, people of color, and LGBT people.

This negotiation smacks of what W.E.B. Du Bois referred to as double consciousness.[25] Du Bois wrote, "It is a peculiar sensation, this double-consciousness, this sense of always looking at one's self through the eyes of others, of measuring one's soul by the tape of a world that looks on in amused contempt and pity."[26]

▲

The 1974 Suffolk Law Review *members are pictured outside the Massachusetts State House. Notably, there are five women among the forty-seven members.*

IMAGE COURTESY OF MOAKLEY ARCHIVE AND INSTITUTE AT SUFFOLK UNIVERSITY LAW SCHOOL (SU-0437)

Extrapolating from this concept of double consciousness, Professor Mari Matsuda refers to this "outsider-inside"[27] phenomenon as "multiple-consciousness,"[28] what Professor Lani Guinier describes as "the bifurcated thinking that allows one to shift back and forth between one's personal consciousness, and the white male perspective that dominates the status quo."[29]

According to Mari Matsuda, "multiple-consciousness allows us to operate within mainstream discourse [and I would add institutions] and within the details of our own special knowledge."[30] So when I think about the question I posed at the outset, "...[W]hat does that say about the ways in which women in such positions negotiate their identities, be that gender, sexuality, class, race or disability?" I say that part of the answer is related to the continued existence of largely homogenous structures—that it is essential that we negotiate our identities with skill and that we are critically conscious of our role in transforming institutions, even if only by our presence. Further, we must approach this reality in a way that allows us to be simultaneously authentic and true to ourselves, and institutionally effective. This is, admittedly, an added load. However, as women, and people of color, we appreciate the burden of representational firsts.[31]

Which is to say that I am aware that my success, or failure, will be a litmus test of sorts. In a nutshell, that is the power and the possibility of being "the first" (opening doors)—but that is also the pitfall (doors being closed to women and or people of color). When those more typically and traditionally found in these positions "of power" either succeed or fail, their success is not representational, vis-à-vis identitarian factors like race or gender. Specifically, in paving the way, I wish to smooth the road, not render it more bumpy or impassable for those coming after me. There were many that came before me and smoothed the road for me, and I would be remiss in not acknowledging and thanking them. I am very grateful to those human rights and civil rights trailblazers, those who we know and those who we do not.

Specifically, in paving the way, I wish to smooth the road, not render it more bumpy or impassable for those coming after me.

Ultimately, however, the test of success will necessarily be determined by how many coalitions are formed and how much work is done together to ensure institutional successes and personal success. I want everyone in our school to succeed. I know one thing for sure—success is not a solitary endeavor. No one is an island, and any success I have had and will continue to have is dependent upon the existence of positive community and effective coalitions.

This is the work and the challenge, but also the beauty and potential of any real diversity—coalition building and teamwork in the true sense of the words. The possibility of us, as women, occupying these "positions of power" is truly awesome. I am honored and moved by this appointment. It is an occasion that brought tears to my father's eyes and awe to my daughter's face. It is an occasion for which I have prayed daily to do only good with the power and privilege that have been bestowed upon me. Yet it is an occasion that I realize is beyond me. I am the first to admit that my success, our success, will be and must be a group, institutional, and community effort.

In this way I know that it's really not about me. It is about us.

NOTES

1 In 1960 there were 7,543 female lawyers in the United States and 205,515 male lawyers; thus women comprised approximately 4 percent of lawyers nationwide. Virginia G. Drachman, *Sisters in Law: Women Lawyers in Modern American History* 253, Table 2 (1998) (citing 18th Census, vol. 1, pt. 1, 1–522).

2 The information in this paragraph on each Massachusetts law school was obtained from the following sources: David L. Robbins, *A History of Suffolk University*, 1906–1996 97 (1996); Todd F. Simon, *Boston College Law School: After Fifty Years, An Informal History 1929–1979* 19 (1980); "Celebration 45: Waiting for the HLS Door to Open," *Harvard Law Bulletin*, Spring 1999, *available at* http://www.law.harvard.edu/news/bulletin/backissues.php; http://www.bu.edu/law/about/history.html; http://www.law.wne.edu; http://www.law.umassd.edu; and http://www.mslaw.edu; http://www.nesl.edu/centennial; http://www.northeastern.edu/law.

3 See Judith Richards Hope, *Pinstripes & Pearls: The Women of the Harvard Law School Class of '64 Who Forged an Old-Girl Network and Paved the Way for Future Generations* 96–103 (2003).

4 3 C.F.R. § 684; Donna Fossum, "Law and the Sexual Integration of Institutions: The Case of American Law Schools," 7 *ALSA F.* 222, 238 (1983) (citation omitted).

5 *See* Herma Hill Kay, "UC's Women Law Faculty," 36 *U.C. Davis L. Rev.* 331, 371 (2003).

6 Fossum, "Law and the Sexual Integration of Institutions: The Case of American Law Schools," 7 *ALSA F.* at 238.

7 *See* Kay, "The Future of Women Law Professors," 77 *Iowa L. Rev.* 5, 12 & n.39 (1991) (citing Pub. L. No. 92-261, § 3, 86 Stat. 103–04 (1972)).

8 Fossum, "Law and the Sexual Integration of Institutions: The Case of American Law Schools," 7 *ALSA F.* at 224, 245 n.12 (citing 20 U.S.C. §§ 1681–1686 (Supp. II 1972)).

9 *See* Fossum, "Law and the Sexual Integration of Institutions: The Case of American Law Schools," 7 *ALSA F.* at 241, 242 fig. 3, 243, where Fossum attributes increased numbers of women students to market conditions, i.e., the need of schools to enroll a certain number of students per year, rather than to legislation. Shifts in the number of men and women occurred during times of war, such as when draft deferments for men law students ended in 1968.

10 Letter from Rosalind Avnet Lazarus & Alice Walker Ballard, WLA, to J. Stanley Pottinger, Director, Office of Civil Rights, HEW (Dec. 18, 1972), reprinted in 1973 *Harvard Law School Yearbook*, at 21.

11 David J. Cocke, "Sacks Terms WLA Charge of Male Bias 'Groundless,'" *Harv. L. Rec.*, Jan. 26, 1973, at 1.

12 For more detailed information on these women and others, see Mary Elizabeth Basile, "False Starts: Harvard Law School's Efforts Toward Integrating Women into the Faculty, 1928–1981," 28 *Harv. J.L. & Gender* 143 (2005).

13 Eleanor Kerlow, *Poisoned Ivy: How Egos, Ideology, and Power Politics Almost Ruined Harvard Law School* 51–52, 306-07 (1994).

14 Fossum, "Law and the Sexual Integration of Institutions: The Case of American Law Schools," 7 *ALSA F.* at 243.

15 The 1990 U.S. Census reported 182,745 female lawyers and 564,332 male lawyers, http://censtats.gov/cgi-bin/eeo/eeojobs.pl (occupation code 178).

16 Women's Law Association, *The Herstory of Women at BUSL* 2 (2002); Emily A. Spieler, "Breaking Down Barriers," *Northeastern L. Mag.*, Winter 2009.

17 Jeri Zeder, "Are We There Yet?," *Northeastern L. Mag.*, Winter 2009, at 8.

18 Excerpted from Karen Fikes, "Women of Boston College Law School, a Progression and Social History" *BC Law eBrief*, Winter 2005, *available at* http://bc.edu/schools/law/alumni/ebrief/features/spring05.html.

19 Karen Berger Morello, *The Invisible Bar, The Woman Lawyer in America: 1638 to the Present* 102–03 (Beacon Press 1986).

20 That she chose to adopt my name as hers when we married was more than the Harvard Law School yearbook could cope with. When its 1961 edition came out, she was not included in the yearbook's graduating class.

21 A classmate of Diane's, who had received an appointment to interview with Skadden Arps in New York on December 24, arrived there to find its Christmas party in full swing, and that she was part of the all-male lawyers' entertainment for the occasion. Two years earlier, Ruth Bader Ginsburg, a member of the law review at both Harvard and Columbia, had received no job offers from New York law firms. Her status, she later said, as "a woman, a Jew and a mother, to boot" was "a bit much" for prospective employers.

22 This was the first legislation of its kind in the United States, and preceded by a year Congressional passage of Title IX, which had the same effect in federally assisted education programs.

23 The class of 1979 included 138 women, but 211 had been offered admission.

24 Each has her own story. Glendon, who then had a young family, was advised that the faculty hadn't really gotten to know her, given her family responsibilities. She returned to Boston College only to be invited again to Harvard, where she is now tenured, some years later. Dreben (now a retired associate justice of the Appeals Court) recalls that on the rare occasions when she and Diane ventured into the faculty dining room for lunch, all conversation at the other tables would stop, as if the men felt they couldn't share their conversation with women. Bartholet, who had forged a distinguished career in a public-interest law firm she had founded, was first denied tenure, but refused to accept the decision. A year later in 1983, she received tenure.

25 W.E.B. Du Bois, *The Souls of Black Folk* (Penguin Books 1996) (1903).

26 Du Bois, *The Souls of Black Folk* at 5.

27 *See generally* Lani Guinier, "Introduction of Professor Mari Matsuda," 3 *Temp. Pol. & Civ. Rts. L. Rev.* 3, 6 (1993–1994).

28 *See generally* Mari J. Matsuda, "When the First Quail Calls: Multiple Consciousness as Jurisprudential Method," 11 *Women's Rts. L. Rep.* 7 (1989).

29 Guinier, "Introduction of Professor Mari Matsuda," 3 *Temp. Pol. & Civ. Rts. L. Rev.* at 6.

30 Guinier, "Introduction of Professor Mari Matsuda," 3 *Temp. Pol. & Civ. Rts. L. Rev.* at 6.

31 Camille A. Nelson, "Racial Paradox and Eclipse: Obama as Balm for What Ails Us," 86 *Denv. U.L. Rev.* 743, 783 n.1 (2009).

Challenging the Status Quo

Divorce

Sandra E. Lundy

Background

From the time of the Pilgrims through the mid-nineteenth century, divorce was rare, and marriage, for women, was a "life sentence" of legal subservience and dependency.[1] Under the common-law doctrine of coverture, a married woman had no separate legal identity. She could not enter into contracts or buy property in her own name, and any wages she earned belonged to her husband. She was subject to her husband's discipline. Legally, she was considered not responsible for her own actions, even criminal actions.

Beginning in the latter half of the nineteenth century, married women's property acts[2] and liberalized divorce laws began to ease the lot of married women, somewhat. But the doctrine of coverture retained its hold. As late as 1960, for instance, no state recognized the crime of marital rape.[3] The late 1960s and early 1970s marked the beginning of a revolution in family law, and with it the situation of women, both married and single. The cultural forces that were transforming so much of American life—the civil rights movement, the women's movement, emerging constitutional norms of privacy and equality, the influx of women into the workforce in general and the legal profession in particular, and the Pill, to name a few—were transforming ideas, and laws, about marriage.

Coverture was a doctrine premised on notions of strict hierarchies and divisions of labor between men and women, based on the supposed God-given or innate differences between the sexes. Not surprisingly, the coverture doctrine was devised by male jurists and lawmakers and, until the very last years of its centuries-old lifespan, enforced by judiciaries that were entirely male. For example, it was not until 1955 that Beatrice Hancock Mullaney became the first female judge of the Massachusetts Probate and Family Court.[4]

By the late 1960s, due in part to the influence of books such as Betty Friedan's *The Feminine Mystique* (1963) and Simone de Beauvoir's *The Second Sex* (1949; first English translation 1953), the traditional view of marriage came under widespread criticism, displaced by the view of an ideal marriage as a mutual agreement of love and support between partners of equal status. And with such fundamental changes in ideas about marriage came fundamental changes in ideas and laws about divorce.

In 1960, the legal barriers to divorce still remained formidable in Massachusetts. Judges and lawyers operated on the assumption that, despite one spouse filing for divorce, there was still a chance the marriage could be saved, and they directed their efforts accordingly. When attempts at reconciliation failed, the spouse initiating the divorce had to prove in court that the marriage was at an end because her spouse was at "fault," a legal term defined in the Massachusetts divorce statute as "adultery, impotency, utter desertion," "gross and confirmed habits of intoxication," "cruel and abusive treatment," and similar offenses. If both the

▲ Sandra E. Lundy is a senior attorney at the Massachusetts Supreme Judicial Court and the deputy advisor to the Trial Court Access to Justice Initiative. Previously, she was a sole practitioner concentrating in family law. She received her J.D. from Yale Law School and her Ph.D. in literature from Columbia University.

IMAGE COURTESY OF SANDRA E. LUNDY

Beatrice Hancock Mullaney received her law degree from Boston University in 1928, and proceeded to practice law in Fall River and serve as an assistant attorney general in the late 1940s. During this time she became active in politics, and possessing a natural inclination toward civic affairs, became Massachusetts' first woman Probate and Family Court judge in 1955. She passed away in 1990 at age eighty-four.

IMAGE COURTESY OF MCLE | NEW ENGLAND

husband and wife demonstrated "fault" in the other spouse during the divorce litigation, then under the legal doctrine of recrimination the divorce was denied.[5] A party in a divorce action who was judged to be at fault was penalized by having to wait longer than his ex-spouse for the divorce to become final. Even where a wife was found not at fault in a divorce, judges typically refused to permit a divorced woman to resume her maiden name if she had children.[6]

By far the greatest disability incurred by divorced women fifty years ago, however, was economic. An "innocent" woman who obtained a divorce in 1960 might be awarded alimony in addition to child support, but both were awarded at the judge's discretion and were often inadequate to a woman's actual needs as head of the household and to her realistic prospects for postdivorce employment. Enforcement of alimony awards was lax at best.

Employment prospects, for most women, were not encouraging. In 1960, only 30.5 percent of married women worked outside the home, generally in jobs paying far less than those held by their husbands.[7] For a divorced woman, supporting herself after divorce usually meant retraining or retooling to reenter a hostile work environment, while still, of course, retaining primary care-taking responsibility for the children.

The Honorable Beverly W. Boorstein, retired associate justice of the Probate and Family Court, was one of only two women who graduated from Boston University School of Law in 1964.[8] She has been involved as an attorney and a judge in family law matters since 1968. Judge Boorstein recalled the circumstances of women seeking divorce in the 1960s and 1970s (at least the great majority of women who did not have the foresight to create property trusts before marriage) as "very vulnerable." Judges issued "minimal orders" for postmarital support, even where children were involved, said Judge Boorstein. "I could never understand," she added, "how judges could object to a man's breach of fiduciary duties to a business partner but not to his family."

Not surprisingly, a woman's standard of living, and that of her children, often declined precipitously after divorce, while that of her ex-husband rose. The authors of the *Gender Bias Study of the Court System in Massachusetts* found that "[t]he decline in women's standard of living after a divorce is one of the major reasons that female-headed households are now the fastest-growing segment of the poverty population."[9]

Economic Reforms

In the fall of 2011, the Massachusetts legislature enacted a statute that for the first time specifies guidelines for the duration and limits of alimony, an area of family law that generally allowed for broad judicial discretion and that resulted in vastly different alimony awards in similar circumstances. Because of the lack of specificity under the old law, alimony had been one of the least predictable and, consequently, most hotly contested areas of divorce. The new alimony scheme reflects not just a desire for less costly and more predictable divorce litigation, but, as is often the case with changes in family law, evolving notions about the marriage relationship. In Massachusetts, such changes, legislative and social, have been particularly apparent since the 1970s.

In the 1970s, reformers sought ways to equalize the economic effects of divorce between ex-spouses and to reflect the increasingly popular egalitarian view of marriage. In Massachusetts, three reforms in particular sought to improve the lot of divorced women and their children. First, the legislature amended the divorce statute (G.L. c. 208) to permit no-fault divorce and eliminate the defense of recrimination. In theory, at least, divorce became easier to obtain, as well as less humiliating. Under the old laws, a couple wishing amicably to terminate their marriage often had to exercise considerable liberties with the truth to assert convincing fault grounds, a reality that led to widespread cynicism about the process and disrespect for the divorce laws.[10] With no-fault divorce, a husband or a wife may get divorced simply by attesting in court that the marriage had "irretrievably" broken down in the eyes of one or both spouses. No-fault divorce is undoubtedly one reason that in less than fifty years the rate of divorce in Massachusetts more than doubled, from 1.1 per 1,000 of population in 1960 to 2.3 per 1,000 of population in 2007.[11]

Governor Deval Patrick signing the Alimony Reform Act of 2011 as legislators and advocates look on.

IMAGE COURTESY OF GOV. DEVAL PATRICK'S OFFICE, PHOTO BY MATTHEW BENNETT

Second, "[t]he increasing incidence of divorce in American life made it easier for legislatures to accept that the parties' economic and non-economic contributions to a marriage could justify re-ordering of property interests, regardless of who held legal title to the property. Put in its simplest terms, lawmakers realized that to treat both partners fairly when a marriage ended, property distribution should be governed by more than just title ownership."[12] Thus, in 1974, the Massachusetts legislature amended Chapter 208 by, among other things, adding Section 34, which allows a judge to assign to a divorced spouse "all or part of the estate of the other" in addition to or in lieu of alimony. The law was passed with little debate, and in fact its appearance came as a surprise to many family law practitioners.[13]

It is difficult to overstate the impact that this provision for "equitable distribution of property" had on the laws of divorce and on the position of divorced women. According to Attorney Arlene Bernstein, Section 34 "changed the whole picture" of divorce. Prior to 1974, assets acquired during the marriage—homes, cars, artwork, pensions, and the like—were awarded to the person who held title to the assets. Most often that person was the husband, the family breadwinner. Thus, the husband might leave the marriage while holding on to the marital home, the car, the investment accounts, and the pensions accounts, while the wife had few if any assets with which to begin anew and acquire future assets. Under the principles of equitable distribution, staying at home and foregoing career opportunities to take care of the children was considered as much a contribution to the wealth of the family as earning a salary and making monetary investments, and was recognized accordingly when the marital property was divided. Judges, said Bernstein, "became very conscious of the non-monetary contributions of women to marriage." As lawyers argued vigorously for the inclusion of assets such as pensions, unvested income, inheritances, and other property into the category of marital property subject to division upon divorce, the practice of family law itself became, according to Bernstein, "more intellectual," "more sophisticated," and increasingly more expensive.

Equitable distribution was designed in theory to equalize the position of the parties postdivorce. However, some attorneys and scholars contend that equitable division has also had negative consequences for the divorcing couple, especially the wife.[14] In particular, as the notion of marriage as a partnership replaced the notion of marriage as a lifetime commitment, alimony, once a resource, however inadequate, for many divorced women seeking to carve out a new life, became increasingly disfavored in court judgments and settlement agreements; and now, as noted above, the statutory scheme of alimony also has become in many ways more restrictive. Empirical studies have confirmed that alimony awards have become less frequent and of shorter duration since the 1960s, even for marriages that lasted more than twenty years and where women have been out of the workforce for decades.[15] Another negative consequence of no-fault divorce on many families is the pressure to sell the marital home, often the family's most valuable asset, in order to give both parties liquid assets with which to start their new lives. Judge Boorstein has observed that prior to the enactment of Section 34, divorcing women, who generally were homemakers, sought the family home and some support in divorce. After the advent of Section 34, many women, who by and large are still the primary caretakers of children, have been forced to return to the workplace after a significant number of years out of the workforce, often reentering in menial jobs. These women now must eke their way without the security and stability of owning the family home. Still, in the opinion of, among others, Attorney Shirley Bayle, who has been practicing law in Massachusetts since 1954, the addition of Section 34 to the divorce statute made it economically feasible for many more women to get divorced than previously.[16]

The third important change in Massachusetts family law, and the family law of other states, was sparked by the federal government. If enforcement of alimony orders was lax fifty years ago, enforcement of child support orders was, in the words of the authors of the *Gender Bias Study,* a "disgrace."[17] In 1975, in response to the large percentage of women and children who fell into poverty as a result of divorce, Congress enacted a child support enforcement program, established as Title IV-D of the Social Security Act. Title IV-D required states to establish child support enforcement programs that included mechanisms for locating absent parents, establishing paternity, setting parameters for child support awards, and collecting on delinquent payments. Title IV-D has been significantly expanded over the years to toughen enforcement and collection standards within states and across state borders. In Massachusetts, the Probate and Family Court has established a stringent set of guidelines for calculating child support designed to eliminate arbitrary and unequal awards of child support. The Massachusetts Child Support Guidelines were first enacted in 1986 and have been regularly updated and refined. The Department of Revenue, the state's designated child support enforcement entity, enforces child support orders with strong wage assignment measures that have become the model for federal standards. Today, the tools at the disposal of state and federal government for collecting delinquent child support are vast and powerful: wage assignments, liens on interests in property and workers' compensation benefits, and the suspension of driver's licenses for delinquent parents, to name just a few. Shaming is another effective technique. In Massachusetts, the Department of Revenue's "Ten Most Wanted" posters and child support tip line have led to the collection of about $4.5 million in delinquent child support payments over the past seventeen years.[18]

Custody

The advent of no-fault divorce and the idea of marriage as partnership also drove changes in custody awards. In *Doe v. Doe,* 16 Mass. App. Ct. 499 (1983), for instance, the Appeals Court held that a parent's lifestyle (in this case, being homosexual) was not in itself a basis for "severing the natural bond between a parent and a child." Doctrines such as the "tender years presumption," under which custody of children under six years of age was automatically awarded to the mother absent some extraordinary circumstance, gave way to the current thinking that custody

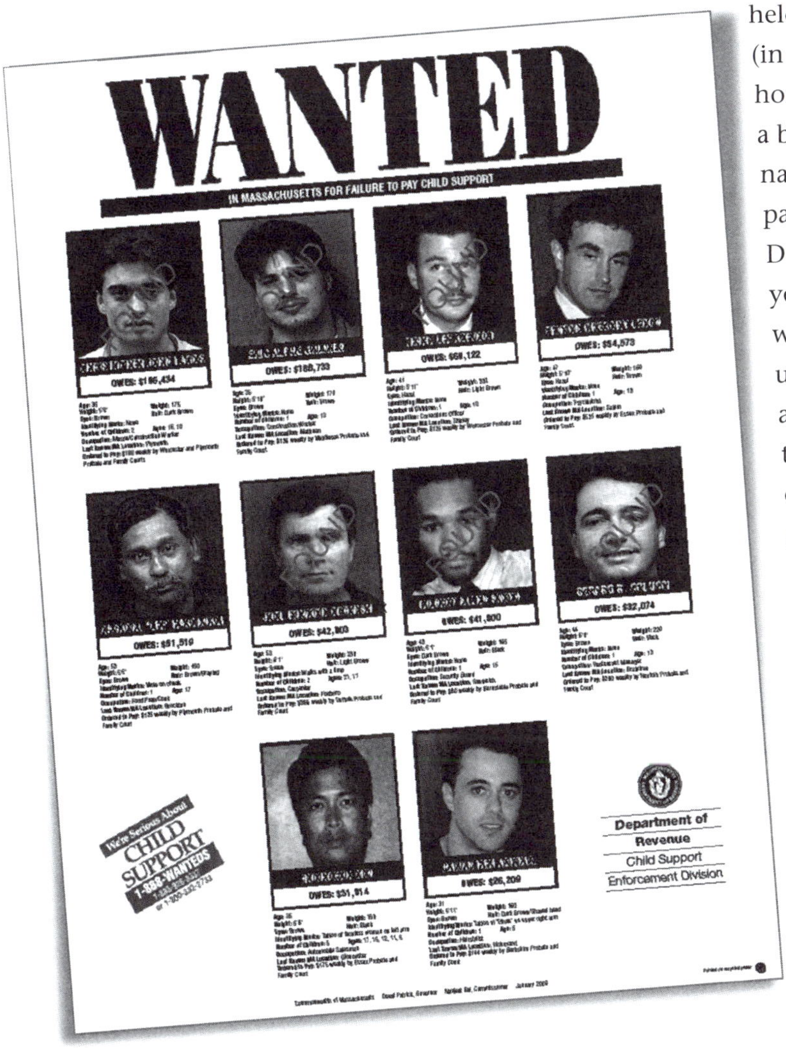

A Massachusetts Department of Revenue poster publicizing persons delinquent in their child support payments.

IMAGE SOURCE: MASSACHUSETTS DEPARTMENT OF REVENUE

determinations should be guided by "the best interests of the child." Attorney Arlene Bernstein well remembers when granting divorced fathers physical custody of minor children of any age "wouldn't have been heard of." Judge Boorstein agrees. Men who sought and obtained custody when she began practicing family law in the mid-1960s succeeded only because "something was wrong" in the divorced wife's circumstances. Whatever else one can say about the best interests standard, it put to rest the assumption that divorcing wives are virtually assured of getting custody of the children. Probate and Family Court judges are now required by law, when making custody decisions, to hold the rights of the parents equal, "in the absence of misconduct" such as domestic violence. As a result, says Bernstein, over the last twenty to thirty years men have gained "custody equality" with women. Judge Boorstein, recalling her perspective from the bench, observed that as custody matters became more contentious, custody determinations became far more difficult to adjudicate. In determining a child's best interests, a judge had to try to divine whether one of the parents had an ulterior motive for the request, such as a desire to avoid significant child support payments, or had plans to move out of state.

But the best interests of the child standard has also opened up a welcome creativity and flexibility in child custody matters. Shared parenting arrangements, in which the divorced parents spend approximately equal time with the children, are increasingly common, and the language of "visitation" has largely given way to discussions of "parenting time." Even though women still are most often the primary caretakers, if the other parent has shown himself or herself to be a dedicated parent, judges give significant attention to keeping that parental bond strong.

The Role of Women in Divorce Practice

What role did women in the legal profession play, if any, in these sweeping changes in family law over the past fifty years? It may not be mere coincidence that the growing numbers of women in the legal profession has coincided with a period of tremendous reform and energy in the area of domestic relations law. In that regard, certain facts are worth noting. First, the number of women judges in the Probate and Family Court has increased phenomenally since Judge Beatrice Hancock Mullaney took the bench in 1955, then the lone representative of her gender. As of this writing, twenty-five of forty-eight current Probate and Family Court judges are women. The chief justice of the Probate and Family Court is the Honorable Paula M. Carey, the second woman to hold this position. Second, women attorneys, who were all but nonexistent in the most prestigious family law firms and law-firm departments just thirty years ago, are now partners and managing partners, as well as bar leaders, influential family law scholars, and policy makers. Women have become influential at every level of family law practice, policy, and theory at a time of tremendous changes in family law.

Hon. Paula M. Carey

IMAGE COURTESY OF MCLE | NEW ENGLAND

Conclusion

Like the American family itself, divorce continues to both reflect and shape larger social and cultural phenomena. Whatever the future of divorce law in Massachusetts, it is certain that the growing influence of women in public life will continue to exert significant influence on this everyday phenomenon of modern American family life.

Three Women Pioneers in Massachusetts Family Law

As a student at Boston University Law School in the early 1960s, Beverly W. Boorstein remembers attending a lecture by the venerable Dean Erwin Griswold of Harvard Law School. His topic? That admitting women to law school was "a waste of an education." (Boorstein went on to become a judge.) At around the same time, Arlene Bernstein, interviewing with a large law firm in Baltimore after graduating from Harvard Law School, was told that "we've not only never hired a woman, we've never even interviewed one." (She got the job.) During the course of a long jury trial early in her career, Shirley D. Bayle, a 1955 graduate of Harvard Law School, was repeatedly addressed by the judge, along with her colleagues, as "gentlemen." (The judge later apologized for his habitual phrasing.) As one of the few women courtroom lawyers of her day, Bayle felt that every time she was before a judge or a jury, "the weight of all womanhood was upon me."

Whatever difficulties women attorneys currently face, and these are not to be minimized, the days when a woman attorney was an anomaly are long gone, thanks in large part to the many women pioneers who, through intellect, skill, and force of will, forced a hostile system to bend.

They gravitated to law because they liked the challenges or problem solving and accomplishment, and they gravitated to family law because, as Judge Boorstein said, "it tests our values," and "it is where people live." In addition to professional expertise, they developed survival strategies—a close circle of female colleagues, a great sense of humor, networking, and exchanging information at the Massachusetts Association of Women Lawyers, the Women's Bar Association of Massachusetts, and other bar groups.

The women pioneers I interviewed have seen family law practice go from a sleepy, rather imprecise area of the legal profession beholden largely to the judge's exercise of "judicial discretion" to an intellectually engaging specialty with clear standards and complex issues involving everything from child development to tax law. This is not the only change they've witnessed. To them, the growing number of women lawyers and judges is cause for celebration. But there are also some concerns: women attorneys on the whole seem less collegial today. The influx of women into the profession has had some interesting effects on male lawyers as well, notes Judge Boorstein. The same men who used to look at her like she was a creature with three heads when she began practicing law now talk with immense pride about their daughters who are lawyers, partners, and judges.

Challenging the Status Quo
Nonmarital Children

Sandra E. Lundy

Today, nearly 35 percent of children born in Massachusetts are born to parents who are not married.[19] No longer considered "children of no one,"[20] these nonmarital children[21] are legally "entitled to the same rights and protections of law as all other children."[22] The tectonic shift in societal attitudes toward marriage, sex, and family life that has taken place since the 1960s set the stage for normalizing the legal status of nonmarital children. The hard work of translating evolving social norms into concrete legal protections, however, fell primarily to a dedicated group of Massachusetts women lawyers and judges.

Paternity and Child Support: The Old Regime

For much of the twentieth century in Massachusetts, a child's legal status, and the child's security, derived from the martial status of his or her mother, and the legal and social status of a woman who had a child out of wedlock was precarious. As late as the mid-1980s, in fact, a woman who had a child out of wedlock had scant legal recourse if the father refused to acknowledge paternity or to pay child support. The Probate and Family Court did not have jurisdiction over paternity cases, as it does now. Any woman wishing to obtain child support from the putative father had to swear out a criminal complaint in the District Court for paternity and criminal nonsupport.[23] Typically, these actions were initiated by the Department of Public Welfare on behalf of women receiving public assistance through Title IV-A of the Social Security Act, Aid to Families with Dependent Children (AFDC), who were required to assign their claims to the Department as a condition of receiving benefits. The defendant, the putative father, had a right to a jury trial, and he could not be forced to testify against himself. The Commonwealth was required to prove its case beyond a reasonable doubt. While the Commonwealth was precluded from introducing blood-testing evidence, which at that time could prove a 99 percent or better probability of paternity, the defendant could produce such test results to exclude his paternity.[24]

▲ Sandra E. Lundy is a senior attorney at the Massachusetts Supreme Judicial Court and the deputy advisor to the Trial Court Access to Justice Initiative. Previously, she was a sole practitioner concentrating in family law. She received her J.D. from Yale Law School and her Ph.D. in literature from Columbia University.

IMAGE COURTESY OF SANDRA E. LUNDY

Even after 1986, when paternity actions were decriminalized with the enactment of Chapter 209C, as discussed below, "the process of establishing paternity was often humiliating and very burdensome for women," says Pauline Quirion, a leading legal advocate for the rights of nonmarital children since the early 1980s. "To establish paternity until about the early Nineties, you needed testimony from a genetic marker testing expert as well as testimony from the mother that the parties had sex with each other whenever the father contested paternity. Children, themselves, were part of the trial and it was not uncommon for the judge to take a view of the child and the father for resemblance. Even if the genetic marker results came back with over 99 percent probability of paternity, mothers were cross-examined about their sexual partners and sometimes degraded by opposing counsel. Although Chapter 209C prohibits eliciting testimony about sexual partners outside the probable period of conception, judges would permit questions on this topic. In one case I tried years ago, the judge allowed an attorney to ask my client over my objection about a child she had ten years earlier and gave up for adoption while in high school. The question had nothing to do with the case and brought her to tears. In other cases, opposing counsel and, on occasion, a judge, would make negative comments about my female clients having children with more than one man. Putative fathers with children by more than one woman, including extramarital partners, however, were rarely criticized. There was gender bias and double standard for men and women."[25]

In the rare instances when mothers won nonsupport cases, the amount of the award varied widely from judge to judge. Marilyn Ray Smith, another pioneering Massachusetts attorney in paternity cases, and chief legal counsel to the Department of Revenue from 1987 to 2010, recalls that some judges always awarded a woman an amount equal to $1 over the amount that qualified her for public assistance to provide an "incentive" for her to find a job; others awarded support in an amount $1 under the public benefits threshold so the woman could continue to receive assistance. Others had their own preferred formulas. Massachusetts judges often applied an "ability to pay" standard, which was based on the father's claimed expenses (which almost always equaled or exceeded his alleged income) rather than, as now, verifiable income. As a result, child support awards in general were low, no matter how much money the biological father made.[26]

In the rare instances when mothers won nonsupport cases, the amount of the award varied widely from judge to judge.

The popular term "absent father" captured society's and the law's prevailing attitude toward the biological father in these cases. In Massachusetts and elsewhere in the nation, unmarried men who acknowledged paternity or were legally adjudicated to be fathers were, at most, expected to provide money to support their children, and perhaps to play some peripheral part in their lives. Little was done, however, to enable or encourage their active participation in the lives of their children.

New Federal Mandates

It is not difficult to imagine that the ineffective legal scheme for establishing paternity and support, coupled with the rise in out-of-wedlock births, cast many women and children into poverty and dependence on the welfare rolls. By the 1970s, policy makers were beginning to argue for a shift away from the "government assistance model" of protecting poor children and their families and more toward a "parental responsibility model."[27] The Family Support Act of 1974 (FSA) mandated that states receiving AFDC funds establish a child support enforcement agency to meet new federal standards for child support enforcement. The Child Support Enforcement Amendments of 1984 further strengthened the FSA by requiring states to establish advisory child support guidelines and stronger child support collection mechanisms, such as wage withholding, tax liens, and deductions from income tax refunds.[28] Other and even tougher federal child support legislation followed, including laws requiring states to adopt mandatory child support guidelines and honor child enforcement orders from other states.[29]

The Massachusetts Response: Women Attorneys and Their Allies

Governor Michael Dukakis, who began his second term as governor in 1983, made it clear to the officials in his administration that he would move aggressively to implement the new federal regime. In 1984, he appointed a thirty-two-member Commission on Child Support to examine child support enforcement and collection in the Commonwealth and make recommendations to establish child support guidelines, which federal law required states to have in place by October 1, 1987. Catherine Dunham, director of Governor Dukakis's Office of Human Resources, chaired the commission. Professor Ruth-Arlene W. Howe, of Boston College Law School, and Attorney Mark Haskell were other key members of the commission.[30]

The Child Support Enforcement Amendments of 1984 stated that state child support guidelines could be imposed by statute, judicial rule, or administrative action. Attorney Marilyn Ray Smith, who headed the child support guidelines subcommittee, recalls that one of most hotly contested issues on the subcommittee was whether child support guidelines should be created by legislation or by judicial authority. Believing that issues of child support should be protected from politicking, Marilyn Ray Smith pushed hard for judicial authority over setting the new guidelines. Her subcommittee, and then the commission as a whole, agreed to her proposal. The legislature, in a bill that became known as Chapter 310, approved judicial control over the guidelines. On May 1, 1987, Chief Administrative Justice Arthur M. Mason approved interim mandatory child support guidelines.[31]

Believing that issues of child support should be protected from politicking, Marilyn Ray Smith pushed hard for judicial authority over setting the new guidelines.

Chapter 310 did more than assign authority for promulgating child support guidelines; it effected an omnibus overhaul of the Massachusetts child support scheme that would become of enormous importance to nonmarital children and their parents. The law inserted G.L. c. 119A into the statute books. That law established the Massachusetts Department of Revenue as the state agency responsible for enforcing uniform and effective child support enforcement in compliance with federal and state laws. General Laws c. 209C, the paternity statute, was also inserted by Chapter 310. Attorney Nicki Famiglietti, of Greater Boston Legal Services, was the lead draftsperson for Chapter 209C, which, among other things, established concurrent jurisdiction in the Probate and Family Court over paternity cases. Attorney Famiglietti later became the attorney in charge of litigation and appellate strategy for the Department of Revenue of Chapter 209C cases.

Women attorneys and advocates were instrumental in shepherding Chapter 310 through the legislature. Attorney Dianne Wilkerson, then assistant legal counsel for Governor Dukakis, was the point person in the governor's legal office for the legislation. Senator Patricia McGovern, head of the Senate Ways and Means Committee, and Representative Susan Schur, of Newton, were key players in ensuring the passage of Chapter 310.

Advocates knew, however, that even with new legislation on the books, robust judicial enforcement of child support orders and the new paternity law were critical to ensuring that nonmarital children and their families received the full protection of the law. Attorney Smith credits Probate and Family Court judges Mary C. Fitzpatrick and Sheila E. McGovern in particular for setting the tone for effective judicial enforcement of the new statutes.[32]

Chapter 209C marked a sea change in the legal establishment of paternity in Massachusetts. Simply put, Chapter 209C made proving paternity both legally and emotionally less difficult for mothers and putative fathers. Jury trials were eliminated. The burden of proof was reduced from "beyond a reasonable doubt" to "clear and convincing evidence." Genetic marker tests became admissible as proof of paternity. The process of establishing custody and visitation as well as support was clarified. And perhaps as important, it became possible for mothers and fathers to enter into a voluntary acknowledgment of paternity outside of the courtroom. As of 1994, parties in Massachusetts can sign a voluntary acknowledgment of paternity in the hospital or the city or town clerk's office as part of the birth registration process, bypassing the courts entirely. Marilyn Ray Smith explains the significance of these developments: "Under the old law, many unmarried fathers and mothers wanted the father's name on the child's birth certificate. But having the father sign the birth certificate created only a presumption of paternity—court action was still necessary to establish paternity.... In 1998, the law changed again, giving the paternity acknowledgment the same legal force and effect as a court adjudication of paternity, and entitled to full faith and credit."[33] As a result of streamlined processes for establishing paternity, in the decade from 1994 to 2004 alone, almost 150,000 Massachusetts children had their paternity acknowledged voluntarily.[34]

The Department of Revenue was among the first Massachusetts agencies to recognize that the establishment of paternity itself, and subsequent orders of child support, offer only an imperfect measure of security for a child. The Department makes a number of services available to assist unwed fathers in maintaining active involvement in the lives of their children.[35] Within the judiciary, Chief Justice of the Probate and Family Court Paula M. Carey has led the judicial effort in Massachusetts to involve both parents in the social as well as legal aspects of the lives of nonmarital children. Chief Justice Carey led a taskforce convened by the chief justice for administration and management for the trial court, whose mission was to undertake the first comprehensive reassessment of the child support guidelines in twenty years.[36] Her taskforce's majority report, issued in October 2008, recommended sweeping changes in the way child support was conceptualized and assessed, most of which were incorporated into the 2009 revisions of the child support guidelines. Under the new guidelines, among many other changes, the terms "custody" and "visitation" were replaced by considerations of "parenting time," and the terms "obligee" and "obligor" were replaced, respectively, by "payee" and "payor." These were more than cosmetic changes; they were meant to both reflect and encourage shared parenting in nonmarital and divorced families. Other similarly-targeted changes include a broader assessment of income from both parents in the calculation of child support.

In another innovation spearheaded by Chief Justice Carey, a taskforce chaired by Judge Elizabeth LaStaiti developed a model parenting plan to educate parents about the developmental needs of children for contact with both parents.[37] She has made paternity forms available online and established a pilot project in the Hampshire Division of the Probate and Family Court that provides "support for child-focused parenting and caregiving" solutions in paternity and other child-related actions.[38] Unmarried fathers and mothers, many of whom appear in court without legal representation, may also use the Probate and Family Court's recently revamped website to access a variety of self-help resources. These innovations reflect Chief Justice Carey's express mission to ensure "equal access to a fair, equitable and efficient forum to resolve family and probate legal matters and to assist and protect all individuals, families and children in an impartial and respectful manner."[39]

Conclusion

The past fifty years have seen enormous progress in securing the rights of nonmarital children in Massachusetts, progress attributable in large part to the determination of women lawyers, judges, elected officials, and advocates and their allies. There remains, however, much work to do. Cases to disestablish paternity continue to be brought, and won, in Massachusetts. The rights of nonmarital children to contact with and support from "de facto" parents with no biological, adoptive, or other legal tie to the child offers fertile ground for examining the evolving notion of who, and what, constitutes a "family." Questions about whether and to what extent children have constitutional rights of their own will have to be answered. And no doubt both federal and Massachusetts laws on child support, public assistance to low-income families, and programs to encourage parental responsibility will evolve in response to changing social circumstances. One safe predication is that the women's legal community in Massachusetts will continue to be at the center of new developments.

NOTES

1 Nancy F. Cott, *Public Vows: A History of Marriage and the Nation* 55 (2000).

2 Massachusetts first passed its married women's property law in 1854.

3 *See* Elizabeth M. Schneider, "Domestic Violence Law Reform in the Twenty-First Century: Looking Back and Looking Forward," 42 *Family L.Q.* 353, 353 (2008).

4 *See* http://www.mcle.org/about/fund-biography.cfm?fund=mullaney.

5 *See* Monroe L. Inker, Robert F. McGrath & Stephen R. Katz, "Abolition of Recrimination as a Defense in Divorce Cases," *Boston Bar J.*, May 1974, at 9.

6 *See* "The ABCs of Massachusetts Divorce Practice and Procedure: Revised," *Boston Bar J.*, Sept. 1973, at 17 (woman's petition to resume her married name after divorce is "usually granted when there are no children, usually not when there are children").

7 Charles P. Kindregan, Jr., & Monroe L. Inker, "A Quarter Century of Allocating Spousal Property Interests: The Massachusetts Experience," 33 *Suffolk U. L. Rev.* 11, 15 n.24 (1999).

8 Interview with Hon. Beverly W. Boorstein (Nov. 10, 2010).

9 Supreme Judicial Court, *Gender Bias Study of the Massachusetts Court System* 19 (1989).

10 *See* Nancy F. Cott, *Public Vows: A History of Marriage and the Nation* at 195–96.

11 Figures for 1960 are from *Vital Statistics for the United States 1960*, U.S. Department of Health, Education and Welfare, *available at* http://www.cdc.gov/nchs/data/vsus/mgdv60_3.pdf at Table 3B. For 2007 figures, see Division of Vital Statistics, National Center for Health Statistics, Centers for Disease Control, at http://www.cdc.gov/nchs/data/nvss/divorce_rates_90_95_99-10.pdf. *See also* Pam Belluck, "To Avoid Divorce, Move to Massachusetts," *N.Y. Times,* Nov. 14, 2004.

12 Charles P. Kindregan, Jr., & Monroe L. Inker, "A Quarter Century of Allocating Spousal Property Interests: The Massachusetts Experience," 33 *Suffolk U. L. Rev.* at 15.

13 According to Attorney Shirley Bayle, Section 34 was the brainchild of a Massachusetts professor who almost single-handedly made it his mission to see the measure passed in the legislature. Interview with Shirley D. Bayle (Nov. 22, 2010).

14 The no-fault/property distribution divorce regime has been harshly criticized by some scholars, most notably Lenore Weitzman, as causing more harm than good for women. See, e.g., Lenore J. Weitzman's controversial study, *The Divorce Revolution: The Unexpected Social and Economic Consequences for Women and Children in America* (1985). These critics argue that as a result of modern divorce laws, women are being whip-sawed between contradictory sets of cultural expectations that have worsened their economic circumstances and contributed to the "feminization of poverty." In particular, women are still widely expected to be "good mothers" by staying home with their young children, or at least assuming the primary care-taking role for children. But women now are also presumed to have the skills and aptitudes to quickly reenter the workforce, no matter how radically the workforce may have changed in their absence. These assumptions have led to drastic reductions in the awards, amount, and duration of alimony, as judges often overestimate a woman's postdivorce earning capacity. The authors of the *Gender Bias Study* relied heavily on Weitzman's work in drawing conclusions about the affect of divorce on women and children. Although Weitzman's methods and conclusions have come under heavy criticism, many commentators agree with her basic conclusion that women and children are significantly economically disadvantaged by divorce. *See, e.g.,* Pamela Laufer-Ukeles, "Selective Recognition of Gender Difference in the Law: Reevaluating the Caretaking Role," 31 *Harv. J. of L. & Gender* 1 (2008).

15 *See* J. Thomas Oldham, "Changes in the Economic Consequences of Divorces, 1958–2008," 42 *Fam. L.Q.* 419, 431–32 (2008).

16 Interview with Shirley D. Bayle (Nov. 22, 2010).

17 Supreme Judicial Court, *Gender Bias Study of the Massachusetts Court System* at 45.

18 "DOR Presents New Poster of Ten Most Wanted For Failure to Pay Child Support," Department of Revenue Press Release (Feb. 5, 2009).

19 Figures for 2009. Communications between the Registry of Vital Records and Statistics to Christina Paradiso, Esq., September 14, 2010, as appearing in Brief for Amicus Curiae Legal Assistance Corporation of Central Massachusetts, p. 8, in *Smith v. McDonald,* SJC No. 10670 (2010). The percentage of nonmarital births in Massachusetts is significantly lower than the national average of 40.6 percent (2008 figures). *See* National Vital Statistics System, *National Vital Statistics Report,* Vol. 59, No. 1 (Dec. 2010) at 1; Rob Stein & Donna St. George, "Number of Unwed Mothers Has Risen Sharply in U.S.," *The Washington Post,* May 14, 2009.

20 *See, e.g., Town of Plymouth v. Hey,* 285 Mass. 357, 359 (1934) (maternal next-of-kin not responsible for child born out of wedlock because that child is the child of no one. As the court said, citing earlier cases, "'By the common law a bastard is nullius filius. He can be the heir of no one, nor have heirs, except of his own body. He has no ancestors from whom any inheritable blood can be derived. The common law on this subject is in force in Massachusetts, except as it has been changed by the statutes.... '[T]here seems to be no maxim of [the common] law less questionable, than that a bastard is filius nullius,' it being there held that the mother of an illegitimate child does not inherit his estate.'") (citations omitted).

21 The description of children born to unmarried parents has changed significantly since the nineteenth century, when such children were commonly referred to as "bastards." The term "nonmarital child" is now the preferred characterization of such children. *See Smith v. McDonald,* 438 Mass. 540, 544 n.6 (2010).

[22] G.L. c. 209C, § 1; *see also L.W.K. v. E.R.C.*, 438 Mass. 428, 437–38 (2000) ("The protection of minor children, most especially those who may be stigmatized by their 'illegitimate' status...has been a hallmark of legislative action [in Massachusetts] and of the jurisprudence of [the Supreme Judicial Court].").

[23] On the other hand, a putative father seeking paternity adjudications could bring an equity action in the Probate and Family Court.

[24] For an excellent article discussing the history of paternity establishment in Massachusetts, see Marilyn Ray Smith, "Paternity Establishment in Massachusetts: A Quiet Revolution," *Family Mediation Q.*, Spring 2005, at 11.

[25] E-mail communication with Pauline Quirion (Nov. 1, 2010).

[26] Interview with Marilyn Ray Smith (Jan. 18, 2011). Attorney Quirion offered similar observations: "Support orders were notoriously low, no matter how wealthy the father was. Defendants often could resolve their cases by agreeing to pay $25 per week as support or a lump sum—say $2,500 (equal to less than $3 per week for eighteen years) with no further obligation to ever support the child again." E-mail from Pauline Quirion (Nov. 1, 2010).

[27] For a succinct account of these developments, see Laura W. Morgan, "Child Support Fifty Years Later," 42 *Fam. L.Q.* 365 (2008).

[28] Laura W. Morgan, "Child Support Fifty Years Later," 42 *Fam. L.Q.* at 367–68.

[29] Laura W. Morgan, "Child Support Fifty Years Later," 42 *Fam. L.Q.* at 368–69. In connection with child support enforcement legislation passed in 1996 as part of President Clinton's efforts to "end welfare as we know it," the "federal government stated that sharpened tools of enforcement are extremely important, given certain demographic realities of the late 1990s. These facts include: 14.5 million children under the age of eighteen lived in a female-headed family, almost triple the number in 1960; 65% of absent fathers contributed no child support or alimony; and only 5.5% of absent fathers contributed as much as $5,000 per year, while 91% of married fathers contributed earnings of at least $5,000 to the total family income." Laura W. Morgan, "Child Support Fifty Years Later," 42 *Fam. L.Q.* at 368–69.

[30] Interview with Marilyn Ray Smith (Jan. 18, 2011).

[31] Interview with Marilyn Ray Smith (Jan. 18, 2011).

[32] Interview with Marilyn Ray Smith (Jan. 18, 2011).

[33] Marilyn Ray Smith, "Paternity Establishment in Massachusetts: A Quiet Revolution," *Family Mediation Q.* at 12.

[34] Marilyn Ray Smith, "Paternity Establishment in Massachusetts: A Quiet Revolution," *Family Mediation Q.* at 13.

[35] See, for example, the information and services offered on the Department of Revenue's Child Support Enforcement webpage, which can be accessed through the Commonwealth's general portal, http://www/mass.gov.

[36] Probate and Family Court Chief Justice Sean Dunphy originally chaired the taskforce. Chief Justice Carey was appointed as Chief Justice Dunphy's successor on October 1, 2007; she took over as taskforce chair upon her appointment as chief justice. Other members of the twelve-member taskforce were Attorneys Marilynne Ryan, Marilyn Ray Smith, Fern Frolin, Christina Paradiso, and Gayle Stone-Turesky. The report of the taskforce is available online at http://www.mass.gov/courts/childsupport/task-force-report.pdf.

[37] *Available at* http://www.mass.gov/courts/courtsandjudges/courts/probateandfamilycourt/parentingplan.pdf.

[38] Probate and Family Court Standing Order 1–10, *available at* http://www.mass.gov/courts/courtsandjudges/courts/probateandfamilycourt/standing-order1-10.pdf.

[39] Probate and Family Court Mission Statement, *available at* http://www.mass.gov/courts/courtsandjudges/courts/probateandfamilycourt/index.html.

CHAPTER 3

Invisibility, Isolation and Resilience: Women Lawyers of Color

REFLECTIONS

Reflections of additional women lawyers of color are featured in other chapters.

The Inchoate Journey of Leadership and Service of Women Lawyers of Color in Massachusetts

RENÉE M. LANDERS[1]

> *[H]er progress slowed, probably because of her race and sex, and her continued success in private practice began to wane.*[2]

When Jacqueline Guild finished Portia Law School in 1933, she may have been the first woman in Massachusetts to follow her father to the bar and to practice with him. Guild, an African-American woman, apparently was a successful lawyer during her more than decade-long association with her father in Cambridge, but historian J. Clay Smith, Jr., relates that her "progress slowed" thereafter, "probably because of her race and sex."[3]

Reflecting in 1994 on a career that began in 1949, African-American lawyer Glendora McIlwain Putnam wrote: "Getting started was very difficult. I think being a woman was the biggest barrier. I never got beyond that barrier to test the race barrier but from what black men were facing I suspect I would have fared no better."[4] However substantial the barriers interposed to impede white women in entering and succeeding in the legal profession, these accounts indicate that women of color[5] must overcome the "double impairment"[6] of race and gender to achieve success in the legal profession.

In the American Bar Association's Multicultural Women Attorneys Network report, *The Burdens of Both, The Privileges of Neither,* published in 1994, women of color reported that "the combination of being an attorney of color and a woman is a double negative in the legal marketplace, regardless of the type of practice or geographic region involved."[7] The experiences of women lawyers of color in Massachusetts mirror these reports. The 1989 *Report of the Gender Bias Study of the Court System in Massachusetts* concluded that minority women, including women attorneys, "bear a double burden which cannot be ignored."[8] A few years later, the report of the Commission to Study Racial and Ethnic Bias in the Courts endorsed the conclusions of the *Gender Bias Study* that minority women were more likely

Renée M. Landers is a professor of law and faculty director of the health and biomedical law concentration at Suffolk University Law School. She was the first woman of color and first legal academic to serve as president of the Boston Bar Association. She has written on eliminating racial and ethnic disparities in health care and increasing diversity in the legal profession.

IMAGE COURTESY OF RENÉE M. LANDERS

"Firsts" for Women Lawyers of Color in Massachusetts

Year	First	Woman
1923	African-American woman lawyer admitted in Massachusetts	Blanche E. Braxton
1925	African-American woman on a law review (*BU Law Review*) and first African-American editor-in-chief of a law review	Clara Burrill Bruce
1933	African-American woman to follow her father into the practice of law in Massachusetts	Jacqueline Guild
1944	(One of the first) African-American women to apply to Harvard Law School	Pauli Murray
1962	African-American woman named assistant attorney general in Massachusetts	Glendora McIlwain Putnam
1977	African-American woman appointed to any Massachusetts court (Boston Municipal Court)	Hon. Margaret Burnham
1979	African-American woman U.S. District Court magistrate judge	Hon. Joyce London Alexander
1980	African-American woman appointed to Massachusetts District Court	Hon. Marie O. Jackson-Thompson
1981	African American to achieve tenured and full professor status at Boston College Law School	Ruth-Arlene Howe
1988	Latina appointed to any Massachusetts court (Massachusetts District Court)	Hon. Maria Lopez
1989	African-American woman appointed to Massachusetts Superior Court	Hon. Barbara A. Dortch-Okara
	Law firm founded by African-American women	Burnham, Hines and Dilday
1990	African-American woman appointed to Massachusetts Juvenile Court	June C. Miles
1991	African-American woman partner at a large Boston law firm (Palmer & Dodge, now Edwards Wildman Palmer LLP)	Ruth Ellen Fitch
1993	African American appointed to Massachusetts Probate and Family Court	Hon. Judith Nelson Dilday
	African-American woman elected to Massachusetts Senate	Diane Wilkerson
	Latina to serve in the Federal Public Defender's Office of Massachusetts	Hon. Diana L. Maldonado
	Latina appointed to the Massachusetts Superior Court	Hon. Maria Lopez
1994	Asian American to serve as president of the Massachusetts Bar Association	Kay H. Hodge
1996	African-American woman to lead any court in Massachusetts (chief magistrate, U.S. District Court)	Hon. Joyce London Alexander
	African-American woman to lead a lawyers' assistance program in the U.S.	Gina Y. Walcott
1998	African American and first woman to serve as chief justice for administration and management of the Trial Court of Massachusetts	Hon. Barbara A. Dortch-Okara
	African-American woman appointed to a tenured professorship at Harvard Law School	Lani Guinier
1999	Haitian American to hold elected office in Massachusetts (Massachusetts House of Representatives)	Marie St. Fleur
2000	Latina appointed to the Massachusetts Probate and Family Court, and person of color to be appointed as a first justice of the Probate and Family Court	Hon. Angela M. Ordoñez
2002	African-American woman sheriff	Andrea J. Cabral
2003	African-American woman to serve as president of the Boston Bar Association	Renée M. Landers
2008	Asian-American commissioner of the Massachusetts Department of Revenue	Navjeet Bal
2009	Latina and first woman U.S. attorney in Massachusetts	Carmen M. Ortiz
	Latina to serve as a first justice in the Massachusetts District Court	Hon. Diana L. Maldonado
2010	African-American woman on the U.S. Court of Appeals for the First Circuit	Hon. O. Rogeriee Thompson
	African-American woman on the U.S. District Court for the District of Massachusetts	Hon. Denise Jefferson Casper
	African-American woman to serve as dean of Suffolk University Law School	Camille A. Nelson
2011	Asian American appointed to the Massachusetts Supreme Judicial Court	Hon. Fernande R.V. Duffly

than any other group of attorneys to endure inappropriate interactions with judges and court employees in Massachusetts courthouses.[9]

The history of African-American women becoming lawyers in Massachusetts begins in the early 1920s, seventy-nine years after the first African-American was admitted to practice in the state and forty years after the first white woman was admitted.[10] Harry Dow became the first Chinese-American admitted to the Massachusetts bar in 1929.[11] Sui G. Woo was the first Chinese-American student admitted to Portia Law School in 1931; she graduated in 1935.[12] Thus, the history of African-American women at the bar in Massachusetts begins earlier than for other women of color. Hispanic women lawyers do not appear on the federal Census for Massachusetts until 1980, and Asian or Pacific Islander female lawyers appear only beginning with the 1990 Census.[13] While the numbers of women lawyers of color have been small and their time at the bar short relative to male lawyers, the impact of women of color on the Massachusetts legal community, legal institutions, and the law has been significant. Nevertheless, race and gender remain barriers to the full incorporation of women of color in all areas and at all levels of the legal profession. In some ways the journey is not only unfinished, it has just begun.

The history of women of color in the legal profession in Massachusetts is a story of individual achievement and collective action. While certain key individuals—"firsts" in several categories—understandably capture the attention of historians because these milestones break barriers to advancement, the quotidian work of ordinary women who sacrificed to study law and then endured indignities and insults to work in a profession that did not want their participation and that did not accept them has opened a path that today presents fewer obstacles for women lawyers of color.

Most accounts recognize Blanche E. Braxton, a graduate of Portia Law School admitted to the Massachusetts bar in 1923, as the first African-American woman lawyer in Massachusetts.[14] Ten years later, she became the first African-American woman to practice before the U.S. District Court in Massachusetts.[15] Little else is known of her career. Inez C. Fields, a 1922 graduate of Boston University School of Law, was admitted to the Massachusetts bar in 1924.[16] Upon her graduation she began working for an East Watertown attorney, Mary F. Downey.[17] A Boston lawyer, Joseph H. Samuel, also employed Fields and

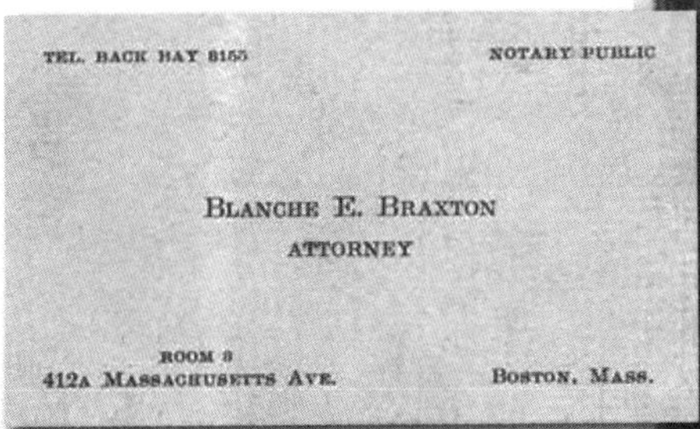
TEL. BACK BAY 8155 NOTARY PUBLIC

BLANCHE E. BRAXTON
ATTORNEY

ROOM 8
412A MASSACHUSETTS AVE. BOSTON, MASS.

Blanche E. Braxton's Portia graduation photo and her business card.

IMAGE COURTESY OF NEW ENGLAND LAW | BOSTON, LAW LIBRARY ARCHIVES helped her prepare for the bar examination. An African-American attorney who had practiced since 1903, George Latimer, recommended her to the bar examiners. Fields associated with William H. Lewis, an African-American lawyer who had served as assistant attorney general of the United States under President William H. Taft. She returned to her home state of Virginia in 1928 to practice with her father, becoming the third woman admitted in that state. Her father died in 1932, and she practiced alone for the remainder of her career. She died in 1978.[18]

In 1926, Clara Burrill Bruce was admitted to practice in Massachusetts. She had graduated from Boston University School of Law, where she was editor-in-chief of the *Boston University Law Review,* the first black woman to serve on a law review and the first black editor-in-chief in the history of legal education.[19] Following graduation, she returned to Washington, DC, to manage her husband's real estate business. Her son, Burrill Kelso Bruce, became a lawyer in 1936.

Boston University School of Law and Portia Law School [played a key early role] in educating women, particularly women of color, for the legal profession.

These stories of the earliest African-American women to enter the legal profession in Massachusetts illustrate several factors that contributed to the success of women of color in the legal profession. First, their careers demonstrate the key early role played by Boston University School of Law and Portia Law School in educating women, particularly women of color, for the legal profession.[20] Boston University admitted women as early as 1872, but the first woman to complete the program and seek admission to the bar, Lelia J. Robinson, entered the school in 1878.[21] Founded in 1908 as an evening bar preparation course, Portia Law School became coeducational in 1938, the year after Suffolk University Law School began to admit women. Northeastern University School of Law began to admit women in 1922, Boston College Law School in 1941, and Harvard Law in 1950. In 1915, a group of Radcliffe College seniors, having been unsuccessful in petitioning Harvard Law School to admit women, persuaded a Harvard law professor to create a special law school called the Cambridge Law School for Women. Admissions criteria included the requirement that applicants be graduates of four-year colleges; the school existed for only two years because this elitist (for the time) admissions requirement made it difficult to enroll sufficient numbers of students to make the school viable.[22] In 1914, six years after it opened, more women were enrolled as law students at Portia than had graduated during the entire time women could study law at Boston University. By 1929, approximately 30 percent of all women law students enrolled in the country were enrolled at Portia.[23] While African-American and Chinese-American students did not always experience a warm embrace and smooth sailing, Portia did provide a portal characterized by "emerging racial tolerance" through which they could gain entry into the legal profession.[24]

Second, this early history indicates that the opportunity to attend law school part-time in an evening program, or to attend some years after college, was necessary for the early women entrants into the profession. Many of the early women of color who attended law school enrolled in Portia Law School because a college education was not a prerequisite and because it was an evening program, which permitted women to attend law school after working during the day. Clara Burrill Bruce went to law school twenty years after graduating from Radcliffe College.[25]

While institutions like Boston University and Portia Law School could provide the academic credentials necessary for women of color to enter the legal profession, the educational opportunity did not translate into professional opportunity in Massachusetts or elsewhere in the country. The number of women of color in the legal profession still remained small. The 1930 U.S. Census reported only thirty-eight African-American male attorneys in Massachusetts when the black population of the Commonwealth was over 52,000—representing one black lawyer for 1,378 black residents.[26] More favorable ratios provided more expansive opportunities for black lawyers in states such as Illinois and New York.[27] For Massachusetts, the Census that year listed one male lawyer of a race other than white or African American.[28] The numbers fluctuated up and down. In 1940, the Census listed only twenty-six "negro" lawyers and no lawyers of another race other than white.[29] But that same year, the Census listed one "negro" female lawyer in Massachusetts. In 1950, there was still only one woman of color listed, but by 1960 there were four, and in 1970 there were five.[30] The big leap in numbers of women of color was reflected in the 1980 Census, when there were eighty-two black women; twelve American Indian, Eskimo, or Aleuts; and twenty-six Spanish Origin women lawyers counted.[31] It is no surprise that the big change was in 1980, when the advances of the civil rights movement and affirmative action programs had begun to bear fruit in developing a widening pipeline of women of color.

By the 2000 Census, the numbers for women lawyers were showing some of the up-and-down fluctuations that were indicative of the early part of the twentieth century for African-American men, though the male numbers fluctuated in relation to a much larger base. While the numbers of Hispanic women lawyers grew by a few, the number of Asian or Pacific Islander female lawyers more than doubled, but the number of black female lawyers declined by 45 percent. This number may have been depressed by the ability of Census respondents to identify more than one race, but even adding the women lawyers who identified themselves as "black & white" and the respondents who identified as having two or more races, the number still declined.[32] *All* women of color account for less than 2.5 percent of the lawyers in Massachusetts, according to the 2000 Census—with women of all races representing 32.1 percent of all lawyers. Males of color represent 2.2 percent of lawyers in the 2000 Census. As of the 2010 Census, blacks represented approximately 6.6 percent of the Massachusetts population, Latinos approximately 9.6 percent, and Asian Americans approximately 5.3 percent. The gaps between representation in the population and representation in the legal profession are not yet bridged. By 2050, the U.S. Census Bureau estimates that non-Hispanic whites will constitute 50 percent or less of the population.[33]

[W]omen of color account for less than 2.5 percent of the lawyers in Massachusetts, according to the 2000 Census—with women of all races representing 32.1 percent of all lawyers.

A striking chasm also separates women of color from full representation "in the 'higher ranks' of law firm managing and equity partners, general counsels, state or federal appellate judges, and tenured law professors."[34] For example, the National Association for Legal Career Professionals (NALP) reported that, for 2009, minority women represented 1.31 percent of partners in Boston-area law firms (1.88 percent nationally),[35] with all women lagging generally, representing only 20.36 percent of partners.[36] The *Boston Globe* reported in December 2008 that 10.2 percent of Massachusetts judges are people of color and 31.7 percent are women.[37] The first African-American woman appointed to the Massachusetts

U.S. Census Data for Massachusetts Women Lawyers by Race, 1950–2000[41]

Year	Hispanic	White	Black	American Indian, Eskimo or Aleut	Asian or Pacific Islander	Other Race	Non–Hispanic: Black and White	Non–Hispanic: Asian and White	Non–Hispanic: Two or more races	Total Lawyers: Female	Total Lawyers: Female and Male
1950	–	375	1	–	–	–	–	–	–	376	7,146
1960	–	362	4	–	–	–	–	–	–	366	7,761
1970	–	560	5	–	–	–	–	–	–	565	8,984
1980	26	2,486	82	12	–	–	–	–	–	2,597	16,463
1990	163	7,186	328	7	112	7	–	–	–	7,803	25,466
2000	170	8,815	180	20	235	–	30	20	45	9,515	29,649

Superior Court, Barbara Dortch-Okara, was appointed in 1989. She then became the first woman and African-American to serve as chief justice for administration and management of the trial courts.[38] One South Asian–American woman, Fernande R.V. Duffly, has served as a justice of the Massachusetts Appeals Court and in 2011 was appointed to the Supreme Judicial Court.[39] Several Latina/Hispanic women have served as justices of the state's trial courts, and Carmen Ortiz was appointed the first woman and first Latina U.S. attorney for Massachusetts in 2009.

Hon. Joyce London Alexander

IMAGE COURTESY OF U.S. DISTRICT COURT FOR THE DISTRICT OF MASSACHUSETTS

Joyce London Alexander became the first African-American woman federal magistrate judge, and one of the youngest of any race or gender, when she was appointed in 1979 as a magistrate judge for the District of Massachusetts. From 1996 to 1999 she was the chief magistrate judge of the district. She was an influential leader in many organizations, including chairing the Judicial Council of the National Bar Association.[40] In 2010, Denise Jefferson Casper became the first African-American woman to serve on the federal District Court in Massachusetts, and Rhode Island attorney O. Rogeriee Thompson became the first African American and the second woman to serve on the U.S. Court of Appeals for the First Circuit.

Law school faculties similarly lack diversity. Nationally, while 37.3 percent of law faculty members were women in 2008–2009, only about 6.2 percent of all law faculty members were women of color.[42] For example, it was not until 1998 that Harvard Law School appointed a woman of color to its tenured faculty when Lani Guinier moved to Harvard from the University of Pennsylvania.[43] Currently, the deans of four of the six Boston law schools are women, including Camille A. Nelson of Suffolk University Law School, who is the first woman and person of color to serve as dean of that institution.

Fueled by the changing demographics of law school graduates, nearly half of associates in private law firms are now women and 15 percent are attorneys of color.[44] NALP data indicate that in 2005, 81 percent of female associates of color had left their law firms within five years of being hired.[45] The recent ABA study, *Visible Invisibility,* stated that "[m]any women of color left firms to work in settings (especially corporations) that were lucrative, where they thought others' decisions about their careers would be less idiosyncratic, based more on merit, and where they had more flexibility to balance personal life, family, and work."[46] In addition to corporations, women and lawyers of color can be found disproportionately in public interest and government jobs.[47] Women are twice as likely as men to take public interest jobs. Women outnumber men at least two to one in government, civil legal services, public defender offices, nonprofits or education, and public interest positions, which are some of the lowest-earning fields in the legal profession.[48] This gender gap creates interesting questions about how the profession values these positions where nearly one-quarter of lawyers work and whether the salary gap is creating a "pink collar" ghetto for the women and, especially, the women lawyers of color who disproportionately work in these fields.[49] At an earlier time, these public interest and government positions were the only fields open to women lawyers and to women of color, so the public service and public interest spheres gave women lawyers like Glendora Putnam the opportunity to build careers in the law.[50]

The recent focus in the work of the American Bar Association[51] and other organizations on women lawyers of color recognizes the "double impairment" that burdens their careers. The separate gender and racial/ethnic bias studies conducted in Massachusetts reflected an initial failure to focus in a systematic way on the "intersection" of race and gender. Just as men and women are not "unitary categories," women of different racial and ethnic backgrounds have different professional and life experiences.[52]

While African-American women have been longer at the bar in Massachusetts, beginning later in the twentieth century, as the population of Massachusetts has become more diverse, women lawyers of other races began to make their mark in the legal profession and in the community, accumulating their share of "firsts" along the way. Notable milestones include the election of Kay H. Hodge, an Asian American, as president of the Massachusetts Bar Association from 1994 to 1995. She has gone on to leadership positions in the American Bar Association, having served as president of the National Conference of Bar Presidents from 2007 to 2008, as a member of the ABA's House of Delegates, and on the Board of Governors. She was a leader on the gender bias and racial and ethnic bias studies in Massachusetts and has continued to focus her work on improving access to legal services and the courts for disadvantaged populations.

[A]s the population of Massachusetts has become more diverse, women lawyers of other races began to make their mark in the legal profession and in the community....

Like Kay Hodge, other Asian-American and South-Asian women lawyers have distinguished themselves as partners in law firms. Hemmie Chang is a partner at Ropes & Gray. After becoming a partner at Goodwin Procter, Rebecca Lee became general counsel to the Boston Redevelopment Authority, and has returned to private practice as a partner at Edwards Wildman Palmer. Along the way she served as a president of the Asian American Lawyers Association of Massachusetts (AALM). Audrey Wang has been a partner in two firms, Hill & Barlow and DLA Piper, and is now in an in-house position at Harvard University. Vivien Tseng is general counsel of Welch's Foods. Navjeet Bal was a partner at Nutter McClennen, served as the first Asian-American commissioner of revenue in Massachusetts from 2008 to 2011, and has now returned to private practice at Nixon Peabody. More recently, the numbers of Asian-American women among the members of the judiciary have been increasing.

As with Asian-American women lawyers, the numbers of Hispanic or Latina women lawyers have grown with the rapidly expanding population of Hispanic Americans in Massachusetts. Maria Lopez made history when she was appointed the first Hispanic-American judge on both the District Court in 1988 and the Superior Court in 1993. Diana L. Maldonado, after serving as a law clerk to Massachusetts Appeals Court Judge

Frederick L. Brown, became the first Latina to work in the Federal Public Defender's Office in Massachusetts in 1993, the second Latina appointed to the judiciary in 1999, and is now the first Latina to serve as a first justice of the District Court Department, having been appointed to that position in 2009. Angela Ordoñez is the first Hispanic and Hispanic lesbian to serve as a justice of the Probate and Family Court. Jennifer Braceras served a term on the U.S. Civil Rights Commission and Maria Recalde has distinguished herself in private practice, now as a partner at Sheehan Phinney Bass + Green. Perhaps the most prominent achievement by a Latina is that of Carmen Ortiz, who in 2009 became the first woman and first Hispanic to serve as a U.S. attorney in Boston. Even with these achievements, the gap remains between the representation of Hispanic Americans in the overall population and in leadership positions in the legal profession.

It bears mention that from time to time the Census figures have shown the presence of several Native American, Eskimo, or Aleut female lawyers in Massachusetts. Most recently, in the 2000 Census, twenty were counted.[53] On a national level there has never been a federal judge of Native American descent, a circumstance that the National Native American Bar Association actively advocates to change.[54]

In addition to their contributions to the Massachusetts judiciary already noted, African-American women lawyers have achieved distinction in other sectors of the legal profession as well. For example, Ruth Ellen Fitch was the first African-American woman to become a partner at a major Boston law firm when she became a partner at Palmer & Dodge (now Edwards Wildman Palmer) in 1991. She now is president and CEO of the Dimmock Community Health Center. The only two African-American women partners in major Boston firms currently are Diane Patrick (wife of Governor Deval Patrick), who is a partner at Ropes & Gray, and Essence McGill Arzu, at Foley Hoag. Dianne Wilkerson is the only African-American woman to have served in the Massachusetts Senate,[55] and Marie St. Fleur became the first Haitian American to hold elective office in Massachusetts when she was elected a state representative in 1999.[56] Andrea Cabral was sworn in on November 29, 2002, as the thirtieth sheriff in the history of Suffolk County, the first female in the Commonwealth's history to hold the position. She was appointed to the position in 2002

Margaret Burnham, Judith Nelson Dilday, and Geraldine Hines of the firm, Burnham, Hines & Dilday, pictured in 1989.

IMAGE COURTESY OF HON. JUDITH NELSON DILDAY

by former Governor Jane Swift and elected to a full term in 2004 (and most recently, in 2010).

Margaret Burnham, Geraldine Hines, and Judith Dilday earned their places in history not only as members of the judiciary, but also as founders, in 1989, of a minority women's law firm in which they were partners.[57] Many African-American women lawyers have distinguished themselves in public service, including Glendora McIlwain Putnam, mentioned at the start of this chapter. Putnam had an influential role in breaking barriers as the first African-American female assistant attorney general when Edward Brooke was the Massachusetts attorney general, as chief of the Civil Rights Division of that office, and later as a commissioner of the Massachusetts Commission Against Discrimination. Putnam's career began at the middle of the twentieth century, and all the accomplishments of women of color since that time have built on these trailblazing and visible roles that she played in the legal profession.

Another important development since Putnam earned her law degree in 1948 is the rise of affinity bar associations, which have helped nurture the careers of lawyers of color and focus attention on legal issues affecting communities of color. On the national level, some organizations were formed because African-American lawyers were denied membership in the American Bar Association.[58] Similarly, the National Association of Women Lawyers, founded in 1899, did not admit its first black members until 1943.[59] In 1909 the National Negro Business League, founded by Booker T. Washington, formed a black lawyers' auxiliary known as the National Negro Bar Association. After the interests of the business professionals and the lawyers diverged, the black lawyers formed the National Bar Association in 1926.[60]

[T]he rise of affinity bar associations [has] helped nurture the careers of lawyers of color....

The reasons animating the formation of the affinity bar associations that have emerged since the 1970s may have been different. As historian J. Clay Smith points out, one reason black lawyers were able to make significant progress in the law despite their exclusion from white bar groups was the ability to combine their talents and resources in their own bar groups to "reform American law and establish a base from which to liberate their people."[61] In addition to combining talents and resources to advocate for legal issues affecting particular communities of color that may not have been appreciated by white bar organizations, the bar organizations formed by women and lawyers of color helped lawyers establish professional networks and advocate for the advancement of lawyers of color in the profession. The Massachusetts Black Lawyers' Association (MBLA) formed in 1973. Founded in 1981, the Massachusetts Black Women Attorneys (MBWA) recently celebrated its thirtieth anniversary. The Massachusetts Association of Hispanic Attorneys (MAHA) was founded in 1985 to promote the professional growth of Hispanic attorneys and advocate for the Hispanic communities of the Commonwealth.[62] The Asian American Lawyers of Massachusetts (AALM) formed in 1984, and the South Asian Bar Association of Greater Boston (SABA GB) formed in 2004.

One activity in which most of these organizations are involved is recognizing the accomplishments of lawyers of color. For example, MAHA gives a Las Primeras—meaning "first females"—award to women who have been the first to reach some achievement. Diana Maldonado, Maria Recalde, and other Latina women mentioned in this chapter have been recipients of this award. The MBLA gives its Trailblazer Award and recognized Ruth Ellen

Fitch among the honorees in 2010. AALM gives a Founders Award annually to an Asian-American attorney "who has made significant contributions in business, academics, or the community as it relates to the law."[63] The Women's Bar Association of Massachusetts has a Women of Color Committee that each year recognizes "pioneering women of color" for their achievements.[64]

Over time, these minority or affinity bar groups have worked out a collaborative relationship with the Massachusetts Bar Association (MBA) and the Boston Bar Association (BBA).[65] The MBA and BBA have recognized the important role these affinity bar groups play in the professional development of lawyers of color and that all of the organizations can work together to develop future generations of bar leaders. In addition, the organizations can combine to advocate on shared public advocacy goals. Women of color have achieved significant leadership positions in the MBA and BBA. As mentioned previously, Kay Hodge, an Asian-American woman, has been president of the MBA, and this author has served as president of the BBA—the first woman of color and the first legal academic to lead the BBA. Gina Walcott, former executive director of Lawyers Concerned for Lawyers, is the only woman of color in the nation to have led a lawyer's assistance program; she has served also as president of the MBLA.[66]

One paradox experienced by women lawyers of color is that the "double impairment" or "double burden" of sex and race, while mostly operating a negative influence on a career path, sometimes created opportunity that otherwise would not have been possible. As sociologist Cynthia Fuchs Epstein has written,

> [h]aving one status that is considered inappropriate or unattractive to members of the group one aspires to join is a problem. Having more than one compounds the negative image, as a general rule.... Yet this rule has interesting exceptions. There are cases in which the negative statuses in some women's "status sets" tend to cancel each other. In the study of older women lawyers, interviews with some black women suggested that by hiring a black woman a law firm could fulfill two debts to society's 'current call for equality, without any great threat to the firm's continuing internal structure.'...It became clear that many of the successful black women, survivors in a discriminatory society (the odds they would be able to graduate from law school were small indeed) actually got their chance because of their "double impairment." "I'm a show woman and a show nigger, all for one salary."[67]

Epstein notes that even as these African-American women lawyers perceived some isolated and limited advantages, the advantages operated relative to white women and black men, not white males.[68] Overall, most reports indicate that African-American and Latina women lawyers must work to establish competence and to become integrated into the culture of institutions.[69]

Asian-American women lawyers face barriers of a different sort. In a presentation to the steering committee of the Diversity and Inclusion Section of the Boston Bar Association, three Asian-American lawyers noted that Asian Americans historically have not entered the legal profession, reinforcing the point made earlier that Asian Americans emerged relatively recently on the rolls of Massachusetts lawyers.[70] They noted that Asian-American lawyers suffer from the "model minority myth" based on stereotypes about academic achievement, and for that reason do not receive the mentoring and other career supports necessary for success in the law. Asian Americans can be pigeonholed as good workers but not given leadership opportunities. An Asian-American woman lawyer can be stereotyped as either deferential or, if assertive, demeaned as a "dragon lady" or "Madam Mao."[71] These comments echo the findings of recent ABA reports on diversity in the profession.[72]

How optimistic one can be about the future depends on how the legal profession responds to numerous challenges in the current environment that have an impact on opportunities for women lawyers of color. One challenge involves ensuring that women as well as men have equal opportunities for advancement in all sectors of the legal profession.[73] More-reasonable approaches to parental leave and flexible or part-time work schedules will help women of color succeed in the profession. Women of color are disproportionately single parents and primary wage-earners for their families, facts which mean that the impact of the inflexibility of the law firm environment can have a particularly negative impact on their careers.[74] The highly leveraged structure of firms means that most lawyers who enter firms early in their careers will not be promoted to partner.[75] The unrelenting pressure for billable hours restricts time for the formal and informal mentoring that can help women of color feel more integrated into the culture of the profession.[76] Ironically, the recent economic recession has led to greater use of alternatives to the billable hour, a shift that may help with this aspect of the problem. Recently released National Association of Law Placement (NALP) statistics give evidence, however, of a negative aspect of the economic downturn. In 2010, the numbers of women and minority associates declined for the first time since NALP began tracking lawyer demographics at law firms. While the numbers of law firm partners who are women of color increased slightly in 2011 to 2.04 percent, the overall representation of women continued to decline compared with 2010.[77]

Some of the *Visible Invisibility* report's most heartbreaking findings were the reports from women of color of all races that "[t]he effort to behave in ways that did not come naturally to them but that they thought would be acceptable to the white men in their firms left many women of color feeling stressed and alienated from life in the law firm."[78] Institutional cultures must evolve as different people enter the organizational mix, otherwise the new entrants will face subtle impediments to progress.[79] Finally, one objection always raised to increasing the numbers of women of color in the profession is the pipeline issue. Despite the increase in the percentage of people of color in the population, Census figures indicate that, at every level of the educational process, African Americans and Hispanics disproportionately fail to advance.[80] The profession must continue to engage in activities to support the educational attainment of young people of color if more women of color are to enter the legal profession and have the opportunity to excel. Conversely, the stereotype of Asian Americans as a high-achieving "model minority" creates its own unfair burdens.[81]

Compared to the landscape that Blanche Braxton, Inez Fields, and Glendora Putnam entered in the 1920s and the middle of the twentieth century, the opportunities available to women of color in the legal profession today seem, despite the barriers to advancement, limitless.

Compared to the landscape that Blanche Braxton, Inez Fields, and Glendora Putnam entered in the 1920s and at the middle of the twentieth century, the opportunities available to women of color in the legal profession today seem, despite the barriers to advancement, limitless. This progress merits celebration—and acknowledgement of the individual sacrifices and disappointments that have made today's successes possible. "Diversity is not a destination but a journey."[82] The legal profession exerts a leading influence on every branch of government and in the ordering of private affairs. Cultural and linguistic competence is increasingly important as business and government respond to the globalization of markets and public policy initiatives. Massachusetts and the nation are becoming more diverse in many respects, and the legal profession should reflect that demographic change.[83] Women of color have made important contributions to the development of the law for communities of color and opportunities for lawyers of every race and ethnicity. To maintain its legitimacy, the legal profession must ensure that the role of women of color at every level continues to increase.

Reflections

Ruth Ellen Fitch

Diversity and the Practice of Law

Even in 1983 when I started practicing law at Palmer & Dodge I was aware that in general there were very few women and even fewer African-American women practicing law at the big Boston firms. My husband was the first African-American associate hired by a big firm and had been in practice for fifteen years. We were married in college, so I "went through" law school with him right after college; then fifteen years later he "went through" law school with me. I had worked for several years as the director of the METCO program in Brookline as an administrator and advocate primarily for African-American children and families living in Boston attending the Brookline schools.

I worked hard, enjoyed my coworkers and the challenges of work, and in time became the first African-American woman partner at Palmer & Dodge, indeed in a big Boston law firm.

When I started my law practice, I was in a very different world dealing with very different issues. I missed my racially-integrated world and working on tough issues of race, but had confidence that lawyers of color would find their way to Boston and the big firms. I worked hard, enjoyed my coworkers and the challenges of work, and in time became the first African-American woman partner at Palmer & Dodge, indeed in a big Boston law firm.

There was a steady pipeline of women law school grads who were joining law firms as associates and marching along partnership tracks. Many firms were creatively flexible in supporting men, women, and family considerations when considering associates for partnership. But the critical number of associates of color, particularly African-American associates, did not materialize. We formed the Boston Law

Ruth Ellen Fitch

IMAGE COURTESY OF THE DIMMOCK CENTER

Firm Group and got our story out to law schools and the legal community and recruited with some success but still not in critical numbers.

I attended to my law practice; chaired the Palmer & Dodge hiring committee; and led recruiting, retention, and training efforts. Fast forward to 2003 to my retirement from Palmer & Dodge and law practice. There are still very few African-American women law partners in big law firms. That for me is a huge personal and professional disappointment. I know that efforts continue to attract that significant talent to Boston and to big law firms and I still support those efforts and talk with young African-American and other women about my law firm experiences and strategies.

I believe it is important to keep the efforts going, to raise our voices, and to support the vision that diversity will enhance the business of the practice of law. We must pay attention, take the time—and keep the faith!

Kay H. Hodge

One Size Doesn't Fit All

When I graduated from law school in 1972 and was admitted to the Massachusetts bar, computers occupied whole rooms and there were certainly no cellular telephones, Blackberries, or iPads. Most law offices had real people answering the phones and used typewriters. Some offices had typewriters that had a correction function. My first briefs to the Supreme Judicial Court had "heavy" pages weighed down with white tape and whiteout covering up original text so that new text could be inserted without having to retype the entire page. In fact, fax machines were not really in use yet. Now my life is run by technology—e-mails and cell-phone calls have me tethered to my phone, computer, and iPad.

The demographics of the bar have also changed for women but not for minorities. Women now make up nearly half of the practicing bar. However, the number of attorneys of color continues to be barely 10 percent of the practicing bar. In September 1969, when I began at Boston University School of Law, we were told that our class, which had about twenty-five women out of approximately 250 students, was the largest class of women ever. If I recollect correctly, I was one of only five or six minority students in the entire class. Those low numbers were also reflected in the demographics of the Massachusetts bar. When I was in court, I was usually the only woman and the only minority lawyer in the courtroom.

Law firms and other legal employers were grappling with the need to diversify their ranks by attracting and retaining women and attorneys of color. Many of those debates continue to this day. Early on, women were attempting to get law firms to develop what we now call family-friendly policies on paid leaves of absence for maternity and childrearing, part-time work opportunities, and partnership consideration that would not penalize a woman for taking leave or working part time. It was difficult convincing an all-male management committee about the need to implement such a policy.

Kay H. Hodge

IMAGE COURTESY OF KAY H. HODGE

My response was to say that true equality would allow women the freedom to approach their work in a way that fit their needs and lifestyle.

On the other hand, it was, and remains, my belief that one size does not fit all. My personal experience provides an example. I began practicing at a then large law firm of over 100 lawyers shortly after having my first child. Because I had readily available child-care options that provided me with considerable flexibility, I was able to work long hours. I learned that several of the male partners in the firm were using me as an example of why the firm did not need to adopt the family-friendly policies being suggested by other women at the firm. In fact, a group of women associates told me that I was the problem because I was working long hours with an infant at home. My response was to say that true equality would allow women the freedom to approach their work in a way that fit their needs and lifestyle. I did not think that others had to approach work in the way that worked for me. On the other hand, I understood the arguments of male associates and women without children that they did not think it was equitable for women with children to get the same credit for working part time that they received.

Today many law firms and legal employers offer longer leaves of absence and many more part-time work opportunities for women, as well as men, who have not only family but other reasons for them (including medical needs). What is counted for partnership consideration continues to vary widely. In some ways the balance between work and family seems to be less gender-based today than it was "back then." While childrearing continues to fall primarily on women, there are an increasing number of men who not only participate in child care but take on significant child-care responsibilities. This fact may be contributing to the growing unhappiness about the often brutal hours that are required by many firms and the continued exodus of lawyers from firms to other legal employers. The struggle to find an appropriate balance between work and family continues to this day.

As long as law firms seek to increase profits and as long as billable hours are the measure of profitability, there will inevitably be a tension between the time needed to meet billable-hour requirements and the time spent with family. Legal employers must continue their attempt to strike the appropriate balance and avoid the sex-based stereotypes that have served as artificial barriers to the progress of women in our profession. Even though the number of women has continued to rise within the profession, there are still too few women equity partners and general counsels.

Unfortunately, finding an appropriate balance between work and family is a lot more difficult than changing technology. We as a professional community should continue to find ways for attorneys to balance the needs of work and family so that women, who have continued to take the leading role in childrearing, do not have to sacrifice their career goals for the sake of having a family.

Stephanie Lovell

The Discomfort of Difference

For me the challenge of being a black, female practitioner is and always has been overcoming what I will call "the discomfort of difference." Not my discomfort. Those who know me know that I am pretty comfortable in my own skin. I am speaking of the discomfort of colleagues, clients, and others in the world.

Even today I am often the only black person in a particular business setting, though I am now rarely the only woman. In those settings, it is the expectation of difference that seems to hang in the air. I tend to see more commonality than difference between me and others, but that fact seems to come almost as a surprise to the larger group.

Stephanie Lovell

IMAGE COURTESY OF STEPHANIE LOVELL

I tend to see more commonality than difference between me and others....

I do feel pressure to be the most prepared person in the room, not to prove that I am as smart (or smarter), but simply to get everyone to exhale. To get past the anticipation of some difference between us that somehow needs to be managed. To be regarded simply as client, cocounsel, opposing counsel, or some gender- and race-neutral term on which we all can agree is nothing more than a statement of fact.

Much has changed. As a young lawyer, a partner discouraged me from arguing a matter in a particular community for fear of how I would be treated there. I doubt that would happen today. But much still needs to change.

At any one time we have a plethora of organizations, committees, and initiatives devoted to diversity issues. Their aim, I fear, is largely to take note of and manage our differences. I wonder, though, whether our energy would be better spent on what we have in common. Undeniably, it is impossible to hold a conversation while at the same time holding one's breath.

Hon. Diana L. Maldonado

Know That You Can

Throughout my life and career, I have had to struggle with overcoming my own insecurities and self-doubts. I used to think this struggle was just mine alone, until I heard a colleague announce in her address to the women at a local bar association gathering: "The first thing that we, as women, must overcome is that inner voice that tells us that we are not good enough and that we can't do it." Her words resonated with me and made me remember all the times I had almost stopped myself before I had even begun.

I was in my first year at Northeastern University School of Law and having a lot of difficulty with one of the research and writing assignments. The familiar voice of insecurity and self-doubt popped into my head and I was on the verge of quitting. Fortunately, in a single telephone conversation, my parents sensed my desperation and, without my asking,

Judge Maldonado at her 2009 swearing in as first justice of the Chelsea District Court with District Court Chief Justice Lynda M. Connolly.

IMAGE COURTESY OF CHRISTINE ALTIERI

made a day trip from the Bronx to Boston one Sunday morning to simply, as my father said, "bring me lunch." Their visit was enough to empower and inspire me to work hard to overcome my weaknesses, whether real or perceived. They believed in me and I needed to believe in myself, and by the time I graduated from Northeastern, I had achieved an appellate clerkship on the Massachusetts Appeals Court.

I would love to have never had to contend with the voice of self-doubt again, but that is not my journey. After that law school experience, however, I discovered how to make that voice my strength rather than my enemy—when it reared its ugly head, I found comfort and support in my family and friends and worked hard not to let them or myself down.

I would love to have never had to contend with the voice of self-doubt again, but that is not my journey.

The voice revealed itself again when I was applying for a District Court judgeship. I started to doubt myself and wondered whether I should apply. Fortunately, I had learned early on not to succumb to the voice. Instead, I redirected my energies. In response to "you are not good enough," I made sure I was. I worked hard to ensure that my application was flawless and strong. In response to "you can't do it," I made sure I could, and, with the assistance and encouragement of family and friends, I prepped and reprepped myself for every interview along the way. When the opportunity for first justice of the Chelsea District Court arose, the voice spoke up yet again—"you are a new mother; you have no time"—and despite my having served as acting first justice for two different courts on two prior occasions, I still questioned whether I had what it took. But once again, I silenced the voice. I did my homework: I spoke to other first justices about their experiences and investigated every aspect of the court itself. By the time of my application and appointment I was more than ready for the challenge.

Today, I am incredibly grateful that my family stopped me, years ago, from making the dreadful mistake of quitting law school. I don't know where I would be had I listened to that voice and ended my legal career back then, but I do know that I would not have had the satisfaction and honor of being the First Justice of the Chelsea District Court.

Judge Maldonado with her family.

IMAGE COURTESY OF CHRISTINE ALTIERI

As of January 28, 2012, I have been a judge for thirteen years. I am confident about my position and my work. I enjoy what I do, and I do it well. The voice of self-questioning and self-doubt has dissipated significantly, and what little remains serves only to inspire. It is a reminder of who I am and from whence I came. It helps to engender in me the humility that I believe is so vital to dispensing justice in the District Court. But mostly, it motivates me to stretch beyond my comfort zone and to encourage others to do the same.

Glendora McIlwain Putnam

Sheer Determination Brought Me Through

What inspired me to go to law school? ...I selected Boston University because it was near home and I could commute to it. In addition, it was accredited and admitted women, as Harvard did not at that time. Since I did not know whether I would stay in Massachusetts, I wanted to go to an accredited law school. There was one other black woman there who was in my class. I have forgotten her maiden name, but she became Victoria Harris, having married right after graduation....

Glendora McIlwain Putnam

IMAGE COURTESY OF GLENDORA MCILWAIN PUTNAM

I had a dismal experience at Boston University principally because they turned the law school into a warehouse. I entered in 1945 right at the end of World War II. [Soldiers returning from war] were using the GI Bill for graduate school. Boston University let them in in droves and flunked them out in droves using true/false exams. It was a very stressful time. It was nothing to be in a class of 200 students. They lost a lot of good people and passed a lot of duds. Good true/false test takers could make it; others could not. It was not an enjoyable educational experience. So, we mostly made lawyers out of ourselves. Sheer determination brought me through.

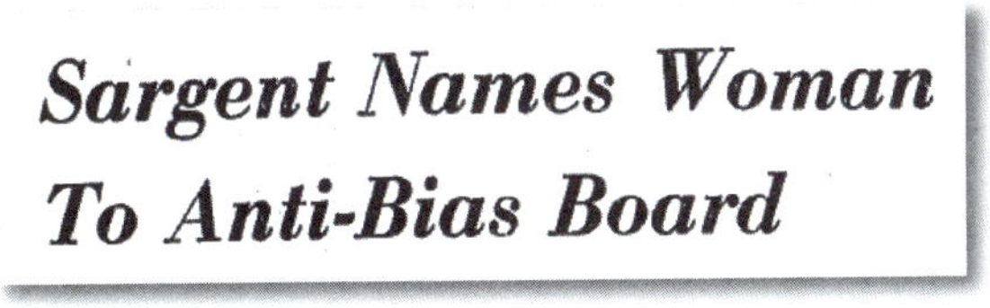
Sargent Names Woman To Anti-Bias Board

This headline appeared in the September 15, 1969 Boston Globe *article announcing Governor Francis W. Sargent's appointment of Putnam as chair of the Massachusetts Commission Against Discrimination.*

IMAGE SOURCE: *BOSTON GLOBE* ONLINE ARCHIVES

I was admitted to the bar in Massachusetts only, in 1949. Getting started was very difficult. I think being a woman was the biggest barrier. I never got beyond that barrier to test the race barrier but from what black men were facing I suspect I would have fared no better. Once they discovered I could type, they made clear that that was what women were hired to do.

My first real job was with the father of a law school classmate. I was responsible for supplementary process work, which I hated. I went to law school to help people, not to take away the jalopy some poor guy needed to get to work to earn the money to pay the bill we were trying to collect. My boss and I did not hit it off because he said I was too soft.

Reprinted, with permission, from J. Clay Smith, Jr., ed., Rebels in Law, Voices in History of Black Women Lawyers *(Univ. of Mich. Press 1998).*

Sad to say, I had no male or female lawyer role models before I went to law school. I would say that my first female role model was Constance Baker Motley, but that did not come until the mid-1950s when I began attending NAACP Legal Defense Fund Legal Institutes and the NAACP national conventions. There I found my role models in Thurgood Marshall and the attorneys from across the country working with them. They taught me so much about making the law a tool for civil rights advancement....

Now, for my tenure as an assistant attorney general of Massachusetts. Edward Brooke was the first to appoint me to that position and I was the first black woman attorney to occupy the post. Edward Brooke and I were classmates at Boston University Law School and kept up with each other. I worked in all his campaigns, two for state representative and one for secretary of state before he ran for attorney general and won. We had worked on legal redress issues for the NAACP so he knew my interest. He had a civil rights division in the attorney general's office and offered me the opportunity of my life, to work on the issues I went to law school to tackle. I did not become chief right away, but sometime into our tenure he asked me to head the division.

There had been women in other administrations, but only one in each administration. Brooke gave many women the experience during his tenure as attorney general,[84] including one other black female attorney.

Most of the work I did, I did as counsel to the Massachusetts Commission Against Discrimination. They had no attorneys at the time, so the attorney general had to represent them throughout the division. I did their litigation, drafted legislation to strengthen laws, drafted opinions, counseled hearing officers, assisted with strategy, and gave general legal advice.

Then, I was asked by the governor to chair the Commission and was charged with having to take the advice I had been giving.... In 1977 I joined the Massachusetts Housing Financing Agency as its equal opportunity officer where I could put all my experiences together to make the laws, case decisions, and regulations work. I retired from there in 1988 when I decided to spend full time completing my second term as national president of the YWCA of the USA.[85]

NOTES

1 The author is grateful to several who generously consulted with her to develop expansive lists of women lawyers of color that formed the basis for the careers and accomplishments mentioned in this chapter. In particular, Gina Y. Walcott, Ingrid Schroffner, and Diana L. Maldonado provided valuable historical context and insight. Because they shared their unique knowledge of key people and signal events, this account is more complete. Colleagues on the steering committee for the Diversity and Inclusion Section of the Boston Bar Association also provided useful information. My research assistants, Matthew L. Hartman and Liane Malcos, helped make sense of the footnotes and more recent Census data, and were careful proofreaders. Letitia Silas offered insightful comments on a draft. Of course, any errors or omissions are the responsibility of the author.

2 J. Clay Smith, Jr., *Emancipation: The Making of the Black Lawyer 1844–1944* 111 (1993) [hereinafter Smith, *Emancipation*].

3 Smith, *Emancipation* at 111.

4 Glendora McIlwain Putnam, "Sheer Determination Brought Me Through" (1994), *in* J. Clay Smith, Jr., ed., *Rebels in Law* 32 (1998).

5 See definition of the term "of color" in Commission on Women in the Profession, American Bar Association, *Visible Invisibility: Women of Color in Law Firms* 3 (2006) [hereinafter ABA, *Visible Invisibility*]:

> The phrase "of color"...is an umbrella term for persons who are Hispanic/Latina, African-American, Native American, Asian-American, and...from multiracial backgrounds.
>
> **African-American and Black** are used interchangeably to describe persons who identify themselves as having origins in the non-white racial groups of Africa.
>
> **Asian-American and Asian** refer to persons who identify themselves as having origins in East Asia (for example, Japan, China, Korea), Southeast Asia (for example, Vietnam, Philippines), or as Pacific Islanders.
>
> **Hispanic/Latina** refers to persons of Latin American descent, including but not limited to Mexico, Central America, South America, and Puerto Rico.
>
> **Native/American Indian/Alaska Native** refers to persons who identify themselves as coming from this background.

ABA, *Visible Invisibility* at 3.

6 Karen Berger Morello, *The Invisible Bar, The Woman Lawyer in America: 1638 to The Present* 143–72 (1986) (describing the "double impairment" of race and gender with which black women lawyers have to contend) [hereinafter Morello, *The Invisible Bar*]. This "double impairment" also burdens the career development of nonwhite women of other races, but perhaps affecting different races in different ways. ABA, *Visible Invisibility* at 10–11; *see also* Virginia G. Drachman, *Sisters in Law: Women Lawyers in Modern American History* 220–21 (1998) [hereinafter Drachman, *Sisters in Law*]. Drachman wrote that "African-American women suffered even deeper discrimination as race combined with sex to yield even more difficult obstacles. Although a few were able to overcome the hardships of economic struggle and racism to succeed in the legal profession, for the most part, black women who became lawyers...were part of the African-American social elite." She noted that many of the early African-American women lawyers were the wives or daughters of lawyers. She concludes, however, that "[i]n the end, no degree of social privilege could fully shelter an African American woman lawyer form the dual prejudices of racism and sexism. The paltry number of African-American women lawyers was testimony to that fact." Drachman, *Sisters in Law* at 220.

7 American Bar Association Multicultural Women Attorneys Network, *The Burdens of Both, The Privileges of Neither* 6, 9 (1994), *quoted in*, ABA, *Visible Invisibility* at 2.

8 Supreme Judicial Court, *Report of the Gender Bias Study of the Court System in Massachusetts* 153 (1989).

9 Supreme Judicial Court, *Equal Justice Commission to Study Racial and Ethnic Bias in the Courts, Final Report* 119 (1994).

10 Smith, *Emancipation* at 94, 111. In fact, Macon Bolling Allen was the first black lawyer admitted to practice in the United States when he was admitted to practice in Massachusetts and Maine in 1845. Lelia Robinson was the first woman admitted to the bar in Massachusetts in 1882. Drachman, *Sisters in Law* at 27–30; Matthew G. Berger, "Mary Hall: The Decision and the Lawyer," 79 *Connecticut B. J.* 29, 39 (2005) (citing *Lelia Robinson's Case*, 131 Mass. 376 (1881)); Douglas J. Lamar, "Lelia J. Robinson's Case and the Entry of Women

into the Legal Profession in Massachusetts," *The History of Law in Massachusetts: The Supreme Judicial Court 1692–1992* 241–74 (Russell K. Osgood, ed., 1992).

11 Thomas Gearty & Meaghan Agnew, "A Singular Career, A Shared Ethos," *Suffolk Law Alumni Magazine*, Fall 2008, at 10, 12.

12 Drachman, *Sisters in Law* at 161, 157–67 (discussing history of Portia Law School); *see also* Morello, *The Invisible Bar* at 68–70 (discussing history of Portia Law School).

13 See chart of Census data within this chapter.

14 *See, e.g.*, Smith, *Emancipation* at 111; *History of New England Law*, http://www.nesl.edu/engaged/history.cfm?pf=1&. Portia Law School became New England School of Law in 1969 and changed its name to New England Law | Boston in 2008. Peter Vickery reports that another Portia Law School graduate, Leanna S. Johnson, was admitted to the Massachusetts bar in 1922. Peter Vickery, *Black Students at Boston University School of Law 1872–1940* (unpublished manuscript 1997) (citing 24 *The Crisis* No. 1, at n.2 (1922)) [hereinafter Vickery, *Black Students*]. Charlotte E. Ray was the first African-American woman admitted to the bar in the United States when she graduated from Howard University Law School and became a member of the District of Columbia bar in 1872. Smith, *Emancipation* at 55.

15 Smith, *Emancipation* at 111; *History of New England Law*, http://www.nesl.edu/engaged/history.cfm?pf=1&.

16 Smith, *Emancipation* at 111. Inez Fields practiced in Massachusetts for a short while before returning to her home state of Virginia to join her father's practice in Hampton. *See also* Edith Spurlock Sampson, *Legal Profession Followed by Nation's Best Known Socialites* (1935), *reprinted in* Smith, *Rebels in Law* at 20 (reporting that a "Mrs. Inez Field Scott" was licensed to practice law in Virginia).

17 Vickery, *Black Students* at n.237.

18 Vickery, *Black Students* at nn.237, 238.

19 Smith, *Emancipation* at 111; Sampson, *Legal Profession Followed by Nation's Best Known Socialites* (1935), *reprinted in* Smith, *Rebels in Law* at 19 (in contrast to Smith, reporting that at that time, Bruce managed apartments in New York).

20 Smith, *Emancipation* at 113.

21 Morello, *The Invisible Bar* at 68; Drachman, *Sisters in Law* at 157–67.

22 Morello, *The Invisible Bar* at 69–70.

23 Drachman, *Sisters in Law* at 160.

24 Drachman, *Sisters in Law* at 160–61.

25 Vickery, *Black Students* at n.255.

26 Vickery, *Black Students*.

27 Vickery, *Black Students* at nn.227–28; Smith, *Emancipation* at 631. The data on which this discussion is based can be found in the Census data chart within this chapter.

28 Smith, *Emancipation* at 631.

29 Smith, *Emancipation* at 634.

30 Smith, *Rebels at Law* at 284, 285, 291.

31 Smith, *Rebels at Law* at 292.

32 See chart of Census data within this chapter.

33 U.S. Census Bureau, *U.S. Interim Projections by Age, Sex, Race, and Hispanic Origin* (2004), *available at* http://www.census.gov/ipc/www/usinterimproj.

34 Presidential Diversity Initiative, American Bar Association, *The Next Steps* 13 (2010) [hereinafter ABA, *The Next Steps*]. In the preface to its study of women of color in law firms, for example, the project cochairs wrote that

> [a]cross the board—whether we are talking about opportunities for advancement, integration into the social fabric of a law firm, or being compensated for one's efforts—the study's findings illustrate that women of color fare worse than women in general or men of

color. And, women of color are the farthest removed from the success of white men, who still tend to have the greatest levels of success regardless of where they went to school or their grades in law school.

ABA, *Visible Invisibility* at ix; *see also* The National Asian Pacific American Bar Association White Papers; *The Value of Diversity in the Workplace; The Value of Diversity in Law Firms;* and *The Path to Partnership for Asian Americans* (noting that Asian-Pacific Americans have the lowest conversion rate from associate to partner, citing studies of the New York City Bar Association and the Bar Association of San Francisco).

35 National Association for Legal Career Professionals, "Women and Minorities in Law Firms by Race and Ethnicity," *NALP Bulletin* (Jan. 2010), *available at* http://www.nalp.org/race_ethn_jan2010 [hereinafter NALP, *Women and Minorities in Law Firms*]; Press Release, National Association for Legal Career Professionals, *Law Firm Diversity Demographics Slow to Change—Minority Women Remain Particularly Scarce in Law Firm Partnership Ranks* (Oct. 10, 2008, revised Dec. 10, 2008), *available at* http://www.nalp.org/lawfirmdiversity (reports percentage for minority women partners as 1.19 percent) [hereinafter NALP, *Law Firm Diversity Demographics Slow to Change*].

36 NALP, *Women and Minorities in Law Firms.*

37 Matt Viser, "Governor Picks Fewer Minorities For Bench," *Boston Globe*, Dec. 5, 2008, at A.1.

38 *Directory of Massachusetts Trial Court Judges, available at* http://www.mass.gov/courts/courtsandjudges/judgesandjudicialofficers/dortchokarab.html. Judge Dortch-Okara was appointed to the Boston Municipal Court in 1984 and to the Superior Court in 1989. From 1998 to 2003 she served as the chief justice for administration and management. *Directory of Massachusetts Trial Court Judges, available at* http://www.mass.gov/courts/courtsandjudges/judgesandjudicialofficers/dortchokarab.html. Ruth I. Abrams became the first woman appointed to the Supreme Judicial Court in 1978. Roderick L. Ireland became the first African-American appointed to the court in 1997 and is now chief justice. Justices of the Supreme Judicial Court, *Supreme Judicial Court of Massachusetts, available at* http://www.massreports.com/justices/AllJustices.htm.

39 National Asian Pacific American Bar Association, *History of Asian Pacific American Advancement in the Legal Profession* (citing Claudette Bennett and Terrance Reeves, *The Asian and Pacific Islander Population in the United States: March 2002* (U.S. Census Bureau, May 2003) (stating that only five of the 876 authorized seats in the federal judiciary are held by Asian-Pacific Americans and that there is a lack of representation at the partner level within law firms)). The number of Asian Americans who are members of the federal judiciary has increased since that report. Asian American Bar Association of the Greater Bay Area, Asian Pacific American Federal Judges, http://www.aaba-bay.com/aaba/showpage.asp?code=current%20federal%20judges.

40 Jonathan Saltzman, "Chapter in US District Court History Ending, Alexander Broke Barriers on Bench," *Boston Globe*, Jan. 8, 2009, at B.3; New England Law | Boston, *History Project profile of Joyce London Alexander Ford, available at* http://www.nesl.edu/HistoryProject/personalities/1969-ford.html.

41 The data on this chart for the years 1950–1990 is derived from the state-by-state census data reported in J. Clay Smith, Jr., *Rebels in Law: Voices in History of Black Women Lawyers* 284–297 [Appendix C: U.S. Census: The Number of Women Lawyers by Race and Nationality in Each State/Select Territories and the Combined Total of Male Lawyers (all races), 1950–90] (1998). The 2000 U.S. Census data is from the Census 2000 EEO Data Tool, *available at* http://www.census.gov/eeo2000/.

42 Association of American Law Schools (AALS), *2008–2009 AALS Statistical Report on Law Faculty, available at* http://www.aals.org/statistics/2009dlt/gender.html.

43 Harvard Law School, Online Biography of Lani Guinier, *available at* http://www.law.harvard.edu/faculty/guinier. Her appointment followed by several years the protest of Professor Derrick Bell, now of New York University School of Law, who took two years in unpaid leaves of absence, vowing not to return until Harvard offered a tenured professorship to a minority female law professor. Victor Essien, "Visible and Invisible Barriers to the Incorporation of Faculty of Color in Predominantly White Law Schools," 34 *J. of Black Studies* 63 (2003).

44 ABA, *Visible Invisibility* at xi.

45 ABA, *Visible Invisibility* at xi.

46 ABA, *Visible Invisibility* at xii.

47 NALP, *Employment Patterns 1982–2004, available at* http://www.nalp.org/2006junemploymentpatterns.

48 Katie Dilks, "Why Is Nobody Talking about Gender Diversity in Public Interest Law?," *NALP Bulletin* (June 2010).

49 Katie Dilks, "Why Is Nobody Talking about Gender Diversity in Public Interest Law?," *NALP Bulletin* (June 2010).

50 *See, e.g.*, Morello, *The Invisible Bar* at 138–39.

51 In addition to the reports already referenced, the ABA has published two volumes of reflections from multicultural women lawyers. *Dear Sisters, Dear Daughters: Words of Wisdom from Multicultural Women Attorneys Who've Been There and Done That* (2000) and *Dear Sisters, Dear Daughters: Strategies for Success from Multicultural Women Attorneys* (2009).

52 Judith Resnik, "From the Senate Judiciary Committee to the Country Courthouse: The Relevance of Gender, Race, and Ethnicity to Adjudication," *Race, Gender, and Power in America* 200–01 (Anita Faye Hill & Emma Coleman Jordan eds., 1995) (arguing that focusing on "intersectionality" causes us to leave behind the "easy" answers of prohibiting discriminatory exclusions and calling for inclusion, but recognizing that "[m]arking intersections neither instructs us on how to negotiate them nor permits escape from evidence that conflicts of race and gender *cross* lines of race and gender").

53 See chart of Census data within this chapter.

54 Letter of Patty Ferguson-Bonhee, President Elect, and Heather Dawn Thompson, Immediate Past President, National Native American Bar Association, to President Barack Obama (Apr. 14, 2010), *available at* http://www.nativeamericanbar.org/NNABA.pdf.

55 Wilkerson resigned from the Senate in November 2008 after her indictment and arrest on federal corruption charges and pleaded guilty to eight counts of attempted extortion in 2010. Matt Viser, "Facing possible expulsion, Wilkerson quits Senate," *Boston Globe*, Nov. 20, 2008, at A.1.

56 St. Fleur resigned in 2010 to take a position with the City of Boston. Travis Anderson, "Rep. St. Fleur to take City Hall job," *Boston Globe*, Apr. 24, 2010, at B.1.

57 John H. Kennedy, "Another Barrier Broken Boston's Newest Law Firm Has Only Black Women As Partners," *Boston Globe*, Dec. 2, 1989, at 11. That same year, five white women also formed an all-woman law firm, Kern, Sosman, Hagerty, Roach & Carpenter. *See* David Abel, "Justice Sosman of the SJC dies at 56," *Boston Globe*, Mar. 12, 2008, at B.1. Margaret Burnham was the first African-American woman appointed to any court in Massachusetts when she was appointed to the Boston Municipal Court in 1977. Northeastern University School of Law webpage, biography of Professor Margaret A. Burnham, *available at* http://www.northeastern.edu/law/academics/faculty/directory/burnham.html. Geraldine Hines is now a Superior Court judge, and Judith Nelson Dilday retired in 2009 from the Probate and Family Court after becoming the first African American to serve as a judge on that court in 1993. *Directory of Massachusetts Trial Court Judges, available at* http://www.mass.gov/courts/courtsandjudges/judgesandjudicialofficers/hinesg.html; Profile of Judith Nelson Dilday, *The Long Road to Justice, available at* http://www.masshist.org/longroad/03participation/profiles/dilday.htm.

58 Smith, *Emancipation* at 541–46 (discussing the ABA's admission practices that effectively excluded most black lawyers from membership until 1943). Smith writes that "[t]he formation of black bar groups was a direct result of the exclusion of black lawyers from the national and state bar groups." Smith, *Emancipation* at 585.

59 Smith, *Emancipation* at 546, 585.

60 Smith, *Emancipation* at 552–57.

61 Smith, *Emancipation* at 585.

62 The National Hispanic Bar Association came into existence in 1975. HBNA, *HBNA Past Presidents Support Senate Confirmation, available at* http://www.hnba.com/past-presidents-support.

63 Charlotte Kim, "Toward a Greater Unity of Purpose," 25 *AALM News* 1 (Apr. 2010), *available at* http://www.aalam.org/news/042010.pdf.

64 The Women's Bar Association of Massachusetts (WBA) was created in 1978, while the Massachusetts Association of Women Lawyers (MAWL) has existed since 1905. *See* http://www.womensbar.org; http://www.mawl.org. The Massachusetts Lesbian & Gay Bar Association recently celebrated its twenty-fifth anniversary. In addition to women of color, the role of lesbian attorneys and attorneys with disabilities in the profession merit greater exploration. *See* http://www.mlgba.org/main.

[65] The MBA and BBA also have recognized accomplishments of lawyers of color, but this discussion focuses on the role of the affinity bar groups.

[66] Boston University School of Law, Office of Communications and Marketing, Apr. 11, 2008, http://www.bu.edu/law/communications/walcott-torres.html.

[67] Cynthia Fuchs Epstein, *Women in Law* 87–89 (1983) (referring to studies involving interviews with black women in 1972 and 1977–1978).

[68] Cynthia Fuchs Epstein, *Women in Law* at 87–89.

[69] *E.g.*, ABA, *Visible Invisibility* at 24–27.

[70] See above text following note 50.

[71] Joel Buenaventura, Charlotte Kim, & Ingrid Schroffner, *Presentation to Steering Committee of Boston Bar Association Section on Diversity and Inclusion*, June 25, 2009 (outline provided to author by electronic message on July 22, 2010, and on file with author).

[72] *E.g.*, ABA, *Visible Invisibility* at 10–11; ABA, *The Next Steps* at 43–48.

[73] David Leonhardt, "A Market Punishing to Mothers," *N.Y. Times*, Aug. 4, 2010, at B1, B6 (noting that "[t]aking the next step toward workplace equality probably has to start with an acknowledgment that most parents can't have it all—at least as long as part-time work, flexible schedules and long leaves do so much career damage," in a column about how the last three nominees to the U.S. Supreme Court were women who had no children).

[74] ABA, *Visible Invisibility* at 33–34.

[75] Renée M. Landers, "Plus ça change, plus c'est la meme chose: The Representation of People of Color (and Women) in Boston Law Firms," 50 *Boston B. J.* 15, 16–17 (Nov./Dec. 2006).

[76] Renée M. Landers, "Plus ça change, plus c'est la meme chose: The Representation of People of Color (and Women) in Boston Law Firms," 50 *Boston B. J.* 15, 16–17 (Nov./Dec. 2006).

[77] National Association of Law Placement, *Law Firm Diversity Wobbles: Minority Numbers Bounce Back While Women Associates Extend Two-Year Decline*, Press Release, Nov. 3, 2011, *available at* www.nalp.org/pressreleases.

[78] ABA, *Visible Invisibility* at 10–11 (describing reports of Asian-American, Native American, Latina, and African-American women of color who had to endure demeaning comments related to race and gender and who suffered from stereotypes).

[79] Renée M. Landers, "Plus ça change, plus c'est la meme chose: The Representation of People of Color (and Women) in Boston Law Firms," 50 *Boston B. J.* at 17.

[80] Renée M. Landers, "Plus ça change, plus c'est la meme chose: The Representation of People of Color (and Women) in Boston Law Firms," 50 *Boston B. J.* at 17.

[81] ABA, *Visible Invisibility* at 10–11, 24–25 (for discussion of the experience women lawyers of color have with stereotypes).

[82] ABA, *The Next Steps* at 49.

[83] *See* ABA, *The Next Steps* at 5 (setting out four rationales for creating greater diversity within the profession—the democracy, business, leadership and demographic rationales).

[84] Brooke was elected to the U.S. Senate from Massachusetts in 1966.

[85] "Retiree Putnam's Calling was Civil Rights," *Mass. Lawyers Wkly.*, Feb. 18, 1991, at 29.

Challenging the Status Quo

Domestic Violence

Susan M. Finegan
Jennifer J. Mather

Framework for Domestic Violence Reforms

Traditionally, domestic violence had not been taken seriously by the courts.[1] Domestic violence was considered a "family" matter to be "worked out" by the parties involved.[2] Victims of domestic violence were often blamed for their predicament and denied the protection of the courts.[3] Until the 1970s or 1980s, most states did not have statutes providing civil relief for survivors seeking protection from abuse, and domestic violence cases did not receive serious attention from the criminal justice community.[4]

The roots of domestic violence in the Western world can be found in traditional Roman and Christian notions of the right of men to physically and socially dominate women in their familial, social, and marital capacities.[5] The right of a man to beat his wife began with the development of marriage as an institution. The legal doctrine known as "coverture" declared a husband and wife one entity under the law, affording the husband the right of control while depriving the wife of any individual legal identity.[6] After marriage, husband and wife became one—but the one was the husband. The woman lost her separate legal status under the marriage: the husband was legally obligated to support his wife and, in return, the wife was legally obligated to obey her husband.[7] As a result, the laws pertaining to domestic violence operated within this legal framework. A man could exercise ownership over his property as he deemed appropriate, including the right to beat his wife.

The English common law contained the infamous "rule of thumb" that purported to protect wives by limiting the size of the instrument that a husband could use to chastise his wife to a "rod not thicker than his thumb."[8] The United States eventually adopted the English common law view, but by the late 1800s several states began to withdraw a husband's right to beat his wife.[9] For example, in *Commonwealth v. McAfee,* 108 Mass. 458, 461 (1871), the Supreme Judicial Court declared that "[b]eating or striking a wife

Susan M. Finegan is a litigation partner at Mintz, Levin, Cohn, Ferris, Glovsky and Popeo, P.C., currently serving as the firm's pro bono partner and chair of the Pro Bono Committee. From 2003–2006 she served as legal director of the Victim Rights Law Center.

Jennifer J. Mather is a litigation associate at Mintz, Levin, Cohn, Ferris, Glovsky and Popeo, P.C. She has represented low-income victims of domestic violence through the firm's domestic violence program.

IMAGES COURTESY OF MINTZ, LEVIN, COHN, FERRIS, GLOVSKY AND POPEO, P.C.

violently...is not one of the rights conferred on a husband by the marriage, even if the wife be drunk or insolent." While the court found that such violence was not included as part of the marriage contract, the case did not provide battered spouses with any protections from this behavior.

In the late 1960s, the battered women's movement helped bring the problem of domestic violence to the public's attention, leading to a series of legal and social reforms on the national, state, and local levels.[10] Despite efforts to increase protection for domestic violence survivors, the continued reluctance of government at all levels to intervene in family conflicts minimized the practical effect of these reforms. This hesitance stemmed from beliefs that the legal system was ill-equipped to deal with the problem and that interference would only exacerbate the violence by further angering the batterer.[11] In Massachusetts, domestic violence advocates questioned the hesitancy of law enforcement to interfere with "family" matters, and sought to hold perpetrators accountable for abusing their partners.

Around this same time, women began entering the legal profession in greater numbers, and many took it upon themselves to strengthen the Commonwealth's response to domestic violence. They challenged antiquated legal doctrines, drafted legislation to afford survivors more protection from the courts, and increased the scope of legal service organizations to include domestic violence assistance. Remarkably, many of the women effecting such change did so very early on in their careers, and their formative experiences set the stage for life-long commitments to securing legal rights and protections for victims in Massachusetts. The following piece highlights some of the substantive legal developments in domestic violence law through the lens of the women attorneys on the forefront of these initiatives. While many extraordinary women lawyers have contributed to this movement, this chapter provides a sampling of the various attorneys who continuously work for the betterment of victims in the Commonwealth.

The Abuse Prevention Act, Chapter 209A

In 1978, the Massachusetts legislature passed one of the most comprehensive and far-reaching laws on domestic violence enacted in the United States.[12] Popularly known as the Abuse Prevention Act, or "209A," the law created a civil remedy that allowed victims of domestic violence to obtain restraining orders protecting them from their abusers.[13] This legislation also provided for a unique criminal enforcement mechanism should the defendant-abuser violate the restraining order. What was truly remarkable about the law was the manner in which it was conceived by a group of Massachusetts women who were active in the battered women's movement.[14]

Members of the group of women who wrote the law, known as the Battered Women's Action Committee (BWAC), met on a weekly basis because they were frustrated in their dealings with the courts, the police, and other institutions on this issue. These institutions, notes Katherine Triantafillou, were "largely indifferent, if not hostile," to victims of domestic violence.[15] "We met to try to figure out how to do our jobs better," says Triantafillou, member of the BWAC and coauthor of the Abuse Prevention Act (Chapter 209A).[16] After

Guide to features

ARTS/FILMS	25	ECONOMY	27
BRIDGE	41	EDITORIALS	16
CLASSIFIED	44-52	HOROSCOPE	41
COMICS	42	LIVING	19
CROSSWORD	42	SPORTS	35
DEATH NOTICES	33	TV/RADIO	43

PLUS: CALENDAR

The Boston Globe

Snow shoo

THURSDAY—Clearing, near 30
FRIDAY—Sunny, 20s
HIGH TIDE — 2:17 a.m., 2:33 p.m.
FULL REPORT — PAGE 41

Vol. 215, No. 18 © 1979, Globe Newspaper Co.

Lottery number, Page 41

THURSDAY MORNING, JANUARY 18, 1979

Telephone 929-2000 Classified 929-1500 Circulation 929-2222 68 Pages — 20 Cents

Violence at home? New law offers quick relief

By Michael Kenney
Globe Staff

"There were times," Terry said, "when Al could be really nice."

Since Terry was at Quincy District Court that morning a week ago because she had sought relief from Al under Massachusetts' 6-month-old Family Abuse Prevention Law, you wondered what Al was like when he was being "really nice."

"He wouldn't beat me," Terry said quietly.

In Massachusetts, it is beginning to appear, there are many women like Terry, women who have decided they do not want to take the beatings any longer, and are using the new law to obtain protection from abusive husbands.

The Family Abuse Prevention Law has made it much easier for a woman to get court action against an abusive husband. She can get an immediate hearing before a judge and obtain a restraining order. She doesn't have to produce witnesses, and her husband doesn't have to be there. The procedure is far simpler than seeking a criminal complaint for assault, which used to be a woman's only legal recourse if her husband beat her.

Although there are no good figures available, the new law is turning up an unexpectedly large number of child abuse cases — cases in which the husband has beaten the wife and she has taken the punishment out on the child, cases in which the husband has abused his children as routinely as he has beaten his wife, and cases in which the violence between husband and wife is adversely affecting the children.

After seven rocky years with Al, it was the issue of child abuse that prompted Terry to seek a restraining order against her husband in Quincy court.

The Public Welfare Department had received an anonymous complaint that the couple's two young children were being abused and sent a protective service worker to investigate. He came on a Monday, Terry said, and on Wednesday she was in court.

"Some of the things were true," she said, "but the reason we were living on macaroni and cheese was because he was going to the racetrack. I was afraid that if I didn't get him out of the house, they'd take my children away."

According to Martha Monell, a juvenile probation officer at the Quincy court, 12 child abuse complaints have been triggered by wife-beating cases in the past six weeks alone.

Several of the state's busiest district courts — among them Lowell and Quincy — and the Suffolk Probate Court, which handles these cases in Boston, are receiving complaints and issuing temporary restraining orders against allegedly abusive husbands at the rate of one a day.

Across the state, the law is being invoked so frequently that it has sparked some controversy over whether it is as effective as it could be in actually preventing family abuse.

Judge Lawrence Shubow sponsored a day-long conference at Brookline District Court last month to discuss the lack of services available to families in court under the new law. And legal and technical problems raised by the law were among the major issues considered at a two-day conference of district court judges sponsored last week by Chief Judge Samuel Zoll.

Within the district courthouses, clerks, probation officers, and others who work with the law every day are trying to find ways to handle some of its unexpected effects.

Few complaints turn out to be a simple matter of giving speedy relief to a battered wife by ordering the abusive husband to vacate the house. In addition to the cases that have triggered child

How the abuse prevention law works

A wife — or anyone wishing to report being physically abused by a household member — files a complaint at a district court clerk's office at any hour of the day. No witnesses are necessary.

The person complaining is immediately brought before a judge for a hearing on the charge. The alleged abuser is not present nor is that person notified of the proceeding after which the judge may grant a temporary restraining order.

If the order is one that bars, for instance, a husband from the home, as is usually the case, the local police are notified. They must serve the order on the husband and they may arrest him if he violates it by returning to the home.

graduating from Suffolk Law School in 1975, Triantafillou started her own practice in her apartment in Beacon Hill. She recalls: "Many of my clients were dealing with abuse. These women had only two options. They could either divorce their husbands or file a criminal complaint. Neither were good options." Each of the women in the BWAC had dealt with hostility and indifference toward battered women.[17] Those experiences, coupled with a firm determination to do something radical, led BWAC to focus on how they could best serve the immediate needs of abuse victims.[18]

The Boston Globe, January 18, 1979, headline touting the new abuse prevention law.

IMAGE SOURCE: *BOSTON GLOBE* ONLINE ARCHIVES

Triantafillou, who was fresh out of law school with no legislative drafting experience, met with other feminist-minded friends and colleagues—including Lisa Leghorn, Rosemary Adamo, Anne Kaufman, Sue Herz, and Desiree French—in one of their apartments and brainstormed. "We decided to write the ideal law," Triantafillou recalls. "Women who were stuck in abusive relationships didn't have many options. It was a huge decision to get a divorce. We wanted to create a law that would make it easier to get protection from the state without having to make all those big decisions. We thought that a restraining order would give an abused woman breathing space to make a decision." The restraining order was conceived as a temporary vehicle that women could use in the short term to stop the violence, giving them time and space to reorganize their lives so that they could figure out their next steps.[19] The women drafters had no blueprint for drafting the legislation, since no other state had yet passed such a law.[20] And, before the Internet or email, there was no easy way to collaborate with anyone who may have been doing this work in other states. There also were hardly any domestic violence shelters where victims could seek advice from an advocacy standpoint, with Transition House in Cambridge a notable exception.

After the BWAC drafted the law, the members figured that it would never pass but they continued their feminist advocacy efforts nonetheless. Triantafillou and fellow BWAC member Lisa Leghorn, for example, attended an International Women's Conference in Texas.

As luck would have it, Triantafillou and Leghorn happened to sit in front of Massachusetts State Senator Sharon Pollard and her chief aide, Peg Ireland. Triantafillou recalls: "We got to talking, and we told them that we had drafted a law. Ireland encouraged us to meet with the Senator when we returned to Boston as we were pessimistic that anything would happen." Senator Pollard not only met with them, but also agreed to cosponsor the bill along with State Representative Barbara Gray. The bill was introduced in 1977. Ireland and Marianne Hinkle, Representative Gray's aide, worked tirelessly on the bill. "We felt like such outsiders from the system, but [the legislators] really allowed the BWAC to take the lead," Triantafillou recalls, adding: "I remember being on the floor of the Senate, advising Senator Pollard on the amendments. The really exciting thing was that it passed in one year." She recalls that the bill ultimately got stuck in one of the key committees before the final vote but, through a stroke of luck, made it to the floor in time for the vote. "After it passed, the administrators of the courts were so surprised," Triantafillou recalls. "I still remember the euphoria we felt when we saw the court form [for a restraining order application] for the first time, and feeling like, 'Oh my god, we actually did it!'"

The Abuse Prevention Act gave a battered spouse an accessible, easy vehicle to get out of an abusive situation. A plaintiff could get an immediate ex parte hearing before a judge and obtain a restraining order—without having to hire a lawyer. The victim didn't have to produce witnesses and the batterer didn't have to be notified. The procedure was far simpler than seeking a criminal complaint for assault, which, prior to the passage of the Abuse Prevention Act, was the only legal recourse other than divorce.[21]

When the statute passed, Janet Donovan was working at Transition House in Cambridge and was one of the first domestic violence advocates to be trained on the new law. She relied on Triantafillou, who advised the advocates at Transition House, for guidance. Because services for victims of abuse were scarce, Triantafillou was on call "twenty-four hours a day." Donovan recalls: "I was a fairly new volunteer at Transition House, and I remember working the evening shift on the day the 209A statute was passed.... This law was the first of its kind," she says. "For the first time, non-attorney advocates could approach the bench. In the beginning, the judges would allow us to tell the client's story.... Everyone looked at us funny because we didn't dress like lawyers." Donovan describes the enactment of 209A as "concrete systemic legal change" that had a profound effect on people's attitudes about domestic violence. "The general public is now aware that there are legal remedies for what was once a very private matter," Donovan says. "People are less likely to jump to the conclusion that it's the victim's fault."

The law, while certainly helpful, could not prevent all acts of violence. Donovan remembers a particularly haunting episode of domestic violence perpetrated on her client during this time. Although Donovan's client had obtained a restraining order, she nevertheless lost custody of her two-month-old child because the Department of Social Services (DSS) claimed that she "could not keep the baby safe." A few months later, the estranged boyfriend chased the client down several flights of stairs and out into the street, brutally murdering her with a meat cleaver and other sharp objects.[22] Luckily, this harrowing experience did not deter Donovan from making domestic-violence prevention her life's work.

She subsequently went to law school and, after working in private practice for a number of years, is now the legal advocacy program manager at Casa Myrna Vazquez, Inc., a multi-service agency for battered women and their children in Boston.

Another mentor to Donovan after the passage of 209A was Chris Butler. Butler was in her last year of law school when 209A passed. She was a summer law intern at Greater Boston Legal Services (GBLS), where she worked with staff attorney Rosemary Adamo, one of the drafters of 209A. Butler continued working at GBLS part-time during the academic year and started to work on restraining orders with her supervising attorney. Butler recalls: "When the law passed, I was one of the few people who knew what it was all about. I was going to court with advocates four or five times a week. No one knew much about it. The police didn't know much about it, the judges didn't know much about it. It was a learning process for everybody."[23]

For example, in March 1979, just months after 209A had passed, Chief Justice of the District Courts Samuel E. Zoll scheduled the first mandatory judicial training. Triantafillou and Butler both presented at the trainings. Their first audience—almost entirely male—was not friendly. "There was a lot of anger in the room. We didn't understand what was going on," Butler recalls.[24] Finally, a judge stood up and explained that he—along with many others in the room—was very upset that "household members" were able to use this law because cohabitation was illegal in Massachusetts. The judge further explained that if a cohabitating woman came before him for a restraining order, he would ask her to approach the bench. He would inform her that cohabitation was against the law. He would consider her petition for a restraining order, but he would be forced to turn her case over to the district attorney. "It was so shocking," Butler recalls. "It was the late '70s. There was so much cohabitating. We didn't think that it would be such a volatile issue."[25] Butler was concerned that other judges would adopt this approach, too. Finally, a more enlightened judge from Brookline stood up and asked the room, "Is cohabitation *really* an issue any more?" Butler recalls, however, that "the judge was met with an extraordinary hostile reception by his colleagues on the bench."

Nor was the statute itself perfect as enacted. Although the bill had initially been drafted so that victims could seek relief in the Probate and Family Court, the legislature amended the bill in committee to include the District Court as well. Thus, according to Triantafillou, some of the statutory language needed fine-tuning. The administrative offices of the District and Probate Courts commenced the amendment process soon after passage, and the advocates who drafted the original bill were included in the meetings. "We started filing amending legislation within six months. We spent the next ten years fixing the mistakes," Butler recalls.

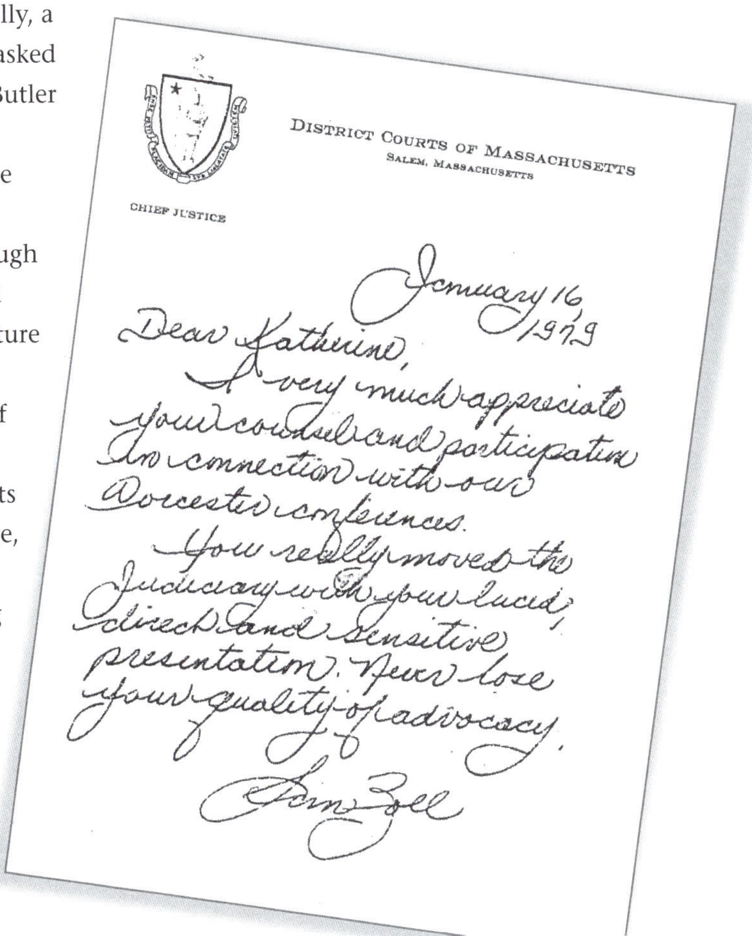

DISTRICT COURTS OF MASSACHUSETTS
SALEM, MASSACHUSETTS

CHIEF JUSTICE

January 16, 1979

Dear Katherine,
I very much appreciate your counsel and participation in connection with our Worcester conference.
You really moved the Judiciary with your lucid, direct and sensitive presentation. Never lose your quality of advocacy.

Sam Zoll

A January 16, 1979, note from District Court Chief Justice Samuel E. Zoll to Katherine Triantafillou.

IMAGE COURTESY OF KATHERINE TRIANTAFILLOU

After law school, Butler set up a part-time practice out of her apartment. "Katherine Triantafillou was a role model for me because she had set up her own practice." In 1979, Triantafillou and Butler applied together for a position at the Massachusetts Coalition of Battered Women's Service Groups (now known as Jane Doe, Inc.). The Coalition didn't want them to share the job, and Triantafillou did not want to give up her private practice, so Butler accepted the full-time position as the first statewide legal training coordinator. Butler later started her own practice sharing space with other women, and eventually joined the Women's Law Collective. The Collective became a two-attorney law firm with Maureen Monks—Butler and Monks worked together for twenty-five years, with a practice focused on family law and domestic violence. Butler now works full time in the clinical programs at Suffolk Law School, working on her own clinical course, which focuses on domestic violence, and working as the practitioner in residence in the Family Advocacy Clinic, Professor Ilene Seidman's former clinical course. When asked what has changed since 209A passed, Butler says: "As a general rule, judges are more sensitive, and people are more knowledgeable and sophisticated about the issue. People know now that domestic violence is not something that someone provoked or deserved."

In 1998, twenty years after the passing of 209A, columnist Eileen McNamara of the *Boston Globe* wrote: "There was a time, not long ago, when a man's decision to smack his wife around was considered a private matter, outside the jurisdiction of the courts. That was also a time when rape was considered a 'crime of passion.' In the 20 years, we've learned to call violence against women by its rightful name."[26] With the passage of the restraining order statute, Triantafillou says, "we accomplished what we set out to accomplish," adding that domestic violence is now considered a "crime against society" rather than a family matter. Now retired from the domestic violence movement, having stepped aside to let others take over, Triantafillou misses the "power to change things through creativity" and the "passion for the issue." But, she is quick to note: "We didn't stop domestic violence."[27]

Framingham Eight

Female attorneys in Massachusetts also played a crucial role in the movement for executive clemency for women convicted of killing their violent partners after enduring years of abuse. Evidence of "battered women's syndrome," a collection of psychological symptoms that occur as a result of repeated physical, sexual, and psychological abuse, was first admitted in Massachusetts to support a claim of self-defense at the 1989 trial of Lisa Becker Grimshaw, who was described by the prosecutor as "a cold calculated first-degree murderer."[28] Grimshaw claimed that years of torture by her ex-husband, Thomas, and a death threat by him, led her to lure him to the banks of the Connecticut River on June 5, 1985.[29] There, three of her male friends waited and pummeled him to death with baseball bats. The prosecutor called her testimony "a con job" and accused her of killing Thomas in an insurance scheme, a charge never substantiated.[30] Grimshaw was convicted and the judge sentenced her to fifteen to twenty years, essentially the maximum sentence for manslaughter.[31] Grimshaw later became one of the "Framingham Eight," the name given to eight women who fought for their freedom after they were sentenced to lengthy prison terms for killing their abusers.

In late 1990 and early 1991, governors in Ohio and Maryland fueled a nationwide clemency movement by announcing the release of several women who were imprisoned for killing their batterers.[32] The governors believed that the imprisoned women deserved clemency as a group, in part because full histories of their past abuse had not been presented at trial.[33] Governor William Weld of Massachusetts took a step in a similar direction in 1991, amending the guidelines for commutation of sentences, a form of executive clemency, to include "a history of abuse [that] significantly contributed to...the offense."[34] For the first time in Massachusetts, a history of domestic violence could be a factor in granting clemency to a convicted murderer.

In response to this change, the Framingham Eight filed petitions for commutation of their sentences on February 14, 1992.[35] Although the eight cases had different facts, they shared a common theme: since each woman had killed her batterer in order to save her own life, justice required that each be released from prison immediately.[36] Public commutation hearings were held in seven of the cases.[37] Governor Weld commuted only two of the sentences.[38] Four of the eight women later told their stories in *Defending Our Lives,* an independent film narrated by Attorney Sarah Buel. The film won an Academy Award for best short documentary in 1994.

The Framingham Eight received overwhelming support and assistance from the community of women's advocacy groups....

The Framingham Eight received overwhelming support and assistance from the community of women's advocacy groups who, among other things, recruited attorneys to represent each of the eight women in their search for sentence relief.[39] Stacy Kabat established Battered Women Fighting Back, a support group at MCI Framingham. Kabat made phone calls to various female attorneys to find out if they would participate in the clemency project at Framingham. After receiving a call from Kabat, Phyllis Goldfarb agreed to represent one of the petitioners and organized a defense team of law students at Boston College Law School. Judy McMorrow, a fellow law professor at Boston College Law School, and several law school alumnae, agreed to work with Goldfarb and the law students. Goldfarb believed that the case would provide "valuable educational lessons" to her students.[40] The attorneys working on all the Framingham Eight cases had regular meetings to discuss strategy. It was a "great collaboration," says Goldfarb. "Although we represented individual clients, we also worked cooperatively. Our collaboration was about problem solving, presenting a great model for students. It showed them that 'cause' lawyering can be a really creative activity."

Goldfarb's client, Elaine Hyde, was the first of the eight to receive a hearing. It was a complicated case because there were no prior cases from which to draw. "We had to imagine it into being, or in other words, make it up as we went along," says Goldfarb. "For our client, the process seemed therapeutic, to have her case get that much attention. The fact that people cared about her case made a difference to her.... I felt that even if we couldn't change the outcome, no matter what, we had done something positive." Hyde received a five-to-one recommendation for commutation of her sentence from the Advisory Board of Pardons and Parole. However, in light of passionate opposition from the decedent's family, Governor Weld

Phyllis Goldfarb notes that representing these clients at this stage was complicated by the fact that, in their underlying criminal trials, the lawyers representing the women may not have understood the impact that trauma has on memory. While there is "plenty of psychological awareness of what impact trauma has on memory" significantly, the lawyers at the criminal trial of these clients needed to be sensitive to that issue so they could explain inconsistencies or lapses in memory to the judge and jury. Indeed, in analyzing the underlying criminal cases of the Framingham Eight, Goldfarb states that "the things that made their stories more believable with respect to trauma made them less credible in the legal system." You cannot have a "fair" prosecution if those representing the clients don't have the "cultural awareness" to handle them. Most of the attorneys did not. One notable exception was Nancy Gertner, who did use the evidence of battering and trauma while representing Grimshaw in her criminal case.

◀ Phyllis Goldfarb

IMAGE COURTESY OF GEORGE WASHINGTON UNIVERSITY LAW SCHOOL

did not act on this recommendation. Instead, Hyde was released on parole at her first eligibility date.[41] Goldfarb kept in touch with Hyde for many years after the case. "This was my most unique experience as a lawyer and an academic," Goldfarb says. "All of these interests of mine were integrated: teaching, learning, lawyering, social justice. It was individual representation, but in a way that was a societal intervention that had the possibility of reducing suffering in the world."

One of the Framingham Eight presented challenging circumstances for the attorneys: seven of the eight women had killed a man, while the eighth, Debra Reid, had killed another woman.[42] Sandy Lundy, a junior associate at Testa Hurwitz, agreed to represent Reid, who stabbed her female partner to death and was convicted of manslaughter in 1990 and sentenced to serve up to fourteen years in prison. Reid's case was particularly difficult. "One of the challenges was advocating for her right to even be a victim of domestic violence."[43] Indeed, even the manner in which the collective team framed the other Framingham Eight cases—that domestic violence perpetrators are male—made Reid's case all the more problematic. As Goldfarb indicated, the negative impact on Reid was "the one issue that so troubled me about these cases."

Lundy stated that the transcript of the trial was "horrifying"—Reid's own counsel told jurors to "forget about this love thing" between Reid and her partner.[44] Reid's criminal trial had been "infected by homophobia," said Lundy—she did not even have the opportunity to develop a battered women's defense. Lundy says: "The word 'lesbian' was never uttered at trial, but hung over the proceeding like some ominous gray cloud." Even at the postconviction relief stage, despite the fact that Lundy and her team hired experts—such as a representative from the Network of Battered Lesbians (now known as The Network/La Red)—to help educate the parole board about same-sex domestic violence, Lundy recalls, "[t]here was an incredible amount of disbelief at the parole board. They voted 5-1 against commutation." Through it all, Lundy was so impressed at the "incredible toughness" of her client, whom she views as a "true role model."

Reid's case was also important because it resulted in trainings for police cadets, prosecutors, and court personnel on the issue of same-sex domestic violence. "People understand now that this type of domestic violence exists, there's not the sense of denial that was there before," Lundy says. Lundy also notes that "people are more sophisticated now. Then, it was hard to convince people that it wasn't just a 'cat fight.' I give the credit to Debra [Reid], who had to get up and tell this awful story to all these people, and to the advocates who work day and night on this issue." Lundy notes that important organizations, including the Gay Men's Domestic Violence Project—of which Lundy was a founding member in 1994—and The Network/La Red, now exist to provide services to victims of violence in same-sex relationships and have even more recently received federal funding to provide this important legal assistance to same-sex survivors.[45] Chris Butler agrees, stating that, now, with years of advocacy, "even though there is still homophobia in the courts as in the general population, judges have a better understanding and are more likely to treat these cases in the same way they treat intimate partner violence in all cases." Lundy's experience with Debra Reid specifically—and same-sex domestic violence generally—shaped her personal career goals, as she left Testa Hurwitz in 1994 to start her own practice focused on survivors of domestic violence as clientele, with an emphasis on same-sex domestic violence.

1978 Pages 169 to 560 No. 3

1978 REGULAR SESSION
CHAPTERS 179 to 477

SEP 06 1978

West's
MASSACHUSETTS
LEGISLATIVE
SERVICE

In this Issue

LAWS APPROVED TO JULY 17, 1978
1978 REGULAR SESSION

The cover page of the Abuse Prevention Act.

IMAGE COURTESY OF KATHERINE TRIANTAFILLOU

Sarah Buel

Attorney Sarah Buel learned about violence firsthand when she was pregnant with her son.[46] Her then-partner struck her in the face. Too ashamed to tell her friends and family, she confided in only her parish priest.[47] She left and came back twice, finally leaving for good in 1977. She fled her home in New York to Lebanon, New Hampshire, near her mother's home. Her partner pursued her, surprising her at the laundromat. "Won't someone call the police?" cried Buel to the crowd of onlookers. There were bruises on her face. Not one person came to her aid. "It's a family matter. I'm taking her home," Buel's abuser announced. They left together but, miraculously, Buel persuaded him to go back to New York alone.[48]

In 1980, Buel moved to Massachusetts and found a job as a paralegal for a legal services organization in Framingham, where she worked with elderly clients. Buel recalls that "[m]any elderly had permanent injuries." Their stories were "heartbreaking" because they had nowhere to turn. That experience opened Buel's eyes to issues of domestic violence for the elderly and people with disabilities. She then went to work for Merrimack Valley Legal Services, where she was doing utilities law and some domestic violence work on the side. Buel had no intention of sharing her own experience of abuse, but at a police training, an officer asked her, "What is it with these women? Why do they stay in these abusive relationships? A smart girl like you wouldn't stay." Buel then told him that she herself had been in an abusive relationship, and she stayed for three years. The officer responded: "If it could happen to you, it could happen to anyone." She could see the transformation in him, almost as if a light bulb had gone on. Looking back, Buel says: "I was afraid that people would think less of me, but I realized that I ought to be willing to share my story."

In 1987, Buel was accepted to Harvard Law School. Her first job out of law school was as a prosecutor in Middlesex County, but she left soon after to work in Norfolk County as its first domestic violence prosecutor. There she worked for District Attorney Bill Delahunt, a "dream boss" who provided her with the support she needed to be successful there. She also notes the mentorship of then-Middlesex prosecutor Margot Botsford.

Of all of her extensive work in this field, however, Buel's involvement in the Framingham Eight clemency project, working on several of the cases, was "one of the projects I am most proud of." Buel recalls: "None of the incarcerated women had families with any money." When two of the women, Lisa Grimshaw and Shannon Booker, were released from prison, Buel cashed in her $20,000 retirement account to give the women a fresh start—getting them jobs and setting them up in an apartment. "The more you give away, the more you get," says Buel.

The Impact of Domestic Violence on Children

Twenty years after the restraining order statute went into effect to provide respite for the abused partner, other legislative initiatives were undertaken to help alleviate the impact of battering on children. Beth Boland, the incoming president for the Women's Bar Association in 1998, had a long history of domestic violence pro bono work. As a junior associate at Mintz, Levin, Cohn, Ferris, Glovsky and Popeo, PC, she had cut her teeth representing clients at restraining order hearings. "In one of my first cases," Boland says, "I represented a client who was married to a police officer in the town where they lived. It was really tricky given that the defendant carried a weapon as part of his job, and he knew everyone in the District Court."[49] After the court granted the restraining order and the case was over, the client told Boland: "This is the first time someone has stuck up for me." So, working with the WBA in its legislative initiatives on domestic violence was a natural extension of Boland's work.[50] One key legislative initiative in the 1997–98 legislative session was the Child Custody Presumption Bill.

The [Child Custody Presumption Bill] created a rebuttable presumption that an abuser would not be granted sole or joint custody of his or her children.

The bill created a rebuttable presumption that an abuser would not be granted sole or joint custody of his or her children, a feature that its drafters perceived as vital to protecting children of abusive relationships. There is a high correlation between partner abuse and child abuse, and strong evidence that even where children "merely" witness violence in the home, they tend to suffer from the same kinds of psychological and emotional problems as the victims of direct physical abuse. The supporters of the legislation—a collaborative effort by domestic violence advocates, bar associations, governmental agencies, nonprofits, and legal services attorneys—were involved in many meetings at the State House, educating legislators and testifying at public hearings. According to then-GBLS Family Law Unit Managing Attorney Barbara Mitchell, who along with fellow GBLS attorney Pauline Quirion was involved in this effort, "[t]he legislation was on the road to being passed in 1997 when the Senate sent it to the Supreme Judicial Court for a review of its constitutionality."

Mitchell and Quirion drafted the important amicus brief for this Supreme Judicial Court case, working around the clock during the holidays to finish it in time. Quirion notes: "It was a ghost town at GBLS."[51] Characterizing the case as the most meaningful that she has worked on in her long appellate career, Quirion had a particular interest in, and specialized knowledge about, domestic violence. While previously working on a Cambridge & Somerville Legal Services (CASLS) project, Quirion wrote a white paper on the issue of the impact of domestic violence on children, and the need for a legislative presumption, which later became a law review article.[52] The decision of the court on March 11, 1998, *Opinion of the Justices to the Senate,* upheld the constitutionality of the proposed legislation. The court held that a child's interest in being free from abuse and neglect and the state's interest in promoting the welfare of its children outweigh any risk of erroneous deprivation of parental rights to a relationship with the child.

It was the first amicus brief that Quirion had worked on, and she felt "like it had made a difference in that case." She went on to author twelve more amicus briefs over the years, and worked on eight cases with published state appellate decisions. While she got involved in such work because "there was a need," she has staked out a claim for being the go-to person for domestic violence–focused appellate work in legal services. Quirion notes, however, that with domestic violence clients, "[i]t is tricky doing appellate litigation. You don't want to put the client in more danger. A lot of times you can't bring an appeal because you'll put the client in more danger by doing so. Safety is number one."

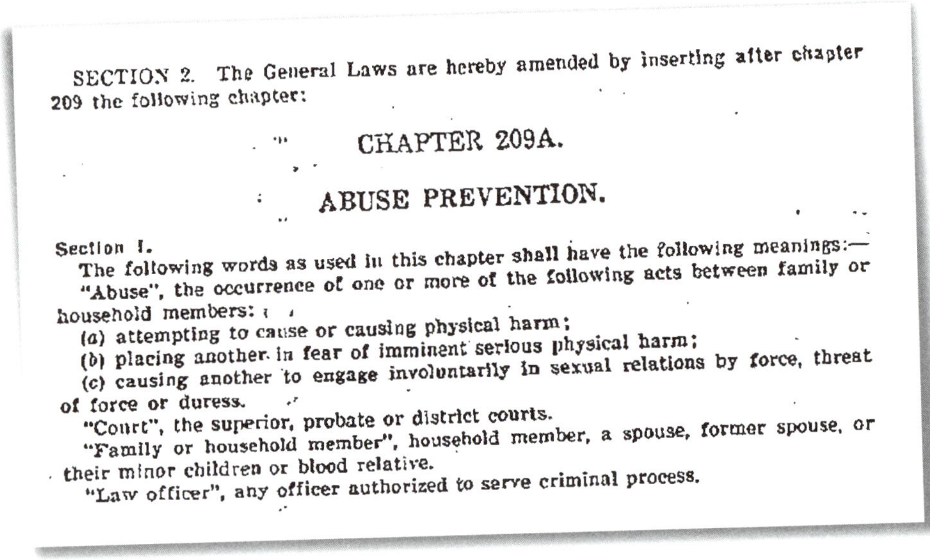

SECTION 2. The General Laws are hereby amended by inserting after chapter 209 the following chapter:

CHAPTER 209A.

ABUSE PREVENTION.

Section 1.

The following words as used in this chapter shall have the following meanings:—

"Abuse", the occurrence of one or more of the following acts between family or household members:

(a) attempting to cause or causing physical harm;

(b) placing another in fear of imminent serious physical harm;

(c) causing another to engage involuntarily in sexual relations by force, threat of force or duress.

"Court", the superior, probate or district courts.

"Family or household member", household member, a spouse, former spouse, or their minor children or blood relative.

"Law officer", any officer authorized to serve criminal process.

Section 1 of Chaper 209A.

IMAGE COURTESY OF KATHERINE TRIANTAFILLOU

Its constitutionality confirmed, the legislation passed the legislature later in 1998. The Domestic Violence Custody Presumption Bill amended a number of custody statutes to provide that "[a] probate and family court's finding, by a preponderance of the evidence, that a pattern or serious incident of abuse has occurred shall create a rebuttable presumption that it is not in the best interests of the child to be placed in sole custody, shared legal custody or shared physical custody with the abusive parent."[53] This statute codified requirements expressed by the Supreme Judicial Court in *Custody of Vaughn,* 422 Mass. 590, 599–600 (1996) (finding that in making custody decisions, courts must consider the effects of domestic violence on a child and the appropriateness of the custody award in light of that effect).

In the end, according to Mitchell, as with all legislation, "there was compromise in the language of the bill, and it was not as strong as we would have liked. Since its enactment, there have been very few [appellate] cases in which it has been discussed."[54] While it didn't necessarily have the broad-scale "impact that we had hoped for," there are certainly clients who benefited. Boland agrees. "After the legislation passed," Boland remarks, "I was representing a pro bono [domestic violence] client on a restraining order in Probate Court that also involved the custody of her children. It was one of the first cases before this court after the law went into effect." And it struck Boland, like "lightning," that "this is why we did all this. I can now argue that, under this new law, my client can get custody because she can show how her husband's abuse against her truly affects their children."[55]

Response of Other Legal Institutions

Legal Services

Legal service attorneys throughout the state had long been active in working with and advocating for domestic violence survivors. However, it was not until funding was readily available for domestic violence work that these agencies could focus their efforts in a concerted way. "Until the domestic violence crisis came to light, family law was a stepchild in legal services," says Barbara Mitchell, who in 1991 took over from Jacqui Bowman as managing attorney of the Family Law Unit at (GBLS), the largest provider of low-income legal services in Massachusetts. When Mitchell became manager of the unit, GBLS had already begun to prioritize domestic violence for several years, due in large part to Bowman and Nicki Famiglietti. When Mitchell started, the Family Law Unit had only four lawyers and three paralegals. "I was really able to grow the unit because increased funding became available in 1995, and domestic violence was a priority," Mitchell says. Bowman, who had left GBLS to work at the Massachusetts Law Reform Institute, successfully urged the state legislature to allocate funds for a four-program pilot project, the Battered Women's Legal Assistance Project, which subsequently expanded statewide. Shortly thereafter, federal funding also became available. Starting in 1999, for example, GBLS partnered for many years with Lois Kanter of Northeastern's Domestic Violence Institute, and Janet Donovan from Casa Myrna Vazquez. Together, they were effectively able to leverage federal funding from the Office of Violence Against Women of the Department of Justice to assist victims of domestic violence. This collaboration has been cited as a model among civil legal services grantees nationwide.[57] When Mitchell left GBLS in 2006 to become the executive director of Community Legal Services and Counseling Center, the Family Law Unit had twelve or thirteen attorneys working with clients, almost exclusively domestic violence survivors.

"Until the domestic violence crisis came to light, family law was a stepchild in legal services."

—Barbara Mitchell

Although she worked for many years in legal services before taking over the Family Law Unit, **Barbara Mitchell** had never previously worked on a family law case. However, she was able to get up to speed quickly, noting that her "impressive" clients were her driving force. Facing "enormous trauma," many of the clients "showed a lot of courage. The ones that stood out were the ones that were able to put their lives together." While the work was rewarding, Mitchell admits that it was also frustrating at times. She says that it was difficult when clients went back to their abusers. "You can understand it intellectually, but it was frustrating." Mitchell says that while there is a greater awareness about domestic violence than there was a few decades ago, "it needs to stay in the forefront of people's minds." She says: "We're not making the progress we should because we haven't eliminated domestic violence yet." Legislation such as 209A helps, but "the law can only go so far in changing social behavior."

Barbara Mitchell

IMAGE COURTESY OF BARBARA MITCHELL

The increase of prioritized services at GBLS is illustrative of the many other legal services agencies statewide—indeed, nationwide—that were able to expand services for domestic violence survivors during this time. Expanding legal services in this manner for this clientele has been recognized by economists as one of the primary factors in the decrease in reported incidents of domestic violence.[58] Indeed, the economists found that access to legal services is one of the primary factors contributing to a 21 percent decrease nationally in the reported incidence of domestic violence between 1993 and 1998.[59] They note that, between 1986 and 1994, the number of legal services programs serving victims of domestic violence increased by more than 254 percent, from 336 to 1,190.[60]

Law Schools

When Phyllis Goldfarb first came to teach at Boston College Law School in 1986, there were not many women on the faculty. "In 1987, in response to student requests, I offered a course on Gender and Legal Theory."[61] But there was a group of women law professors, academics, and practicing attorneys in the Boston area who met regularly as a professional support group. Mary Joe Frug, a noted feminist law professor at New England School of Law, was a catalyst for this group before her unsolved murder—an act of street violence—in 1991. "It was a very important and informative group that offered a supportive environment for women to teach and practice law in Boston," says Goldfarb. "We met regularly until Mary Joe Frug was murdered. The group never really recovered from her death."

Suffolk University Law School was the first law school to establish a domestic violence clinical program. In 1985, the Battered Women's Advocacy Program (BWAP) was formed, managed by Chris Butler. "The program was largely the result the Suffolk Women's Law Caucus reaching out to students interested in volunteering time to assist battered women and battered women's shelters." Butler recalls that Diane Margolis, a third-year law student at the time, did all the work setting up the clinic. "It was initially offered as a volunteer program for law students to be trained in order to assist plaintiffs in 209A cases," Butler recalls. "I volunteered to do intensive training and be available for students on a somewhat on-call basis; the students were volunteers as well." This was later formalized into an independent study course, known as BWAP, and was advertised to shelters and other public and private agencies. BWAP had a small office in the clinical programs office, and students staffed a crisis line to assist people by answering questions, helping with forms, and sometimes accompanying plaintiffs to court. "Within a couple of years, it became a full one-semester clinical course and Sally Landis, who ran the Prosecutors Program at Suffolk, got the law school to hire Maureen Monks as a second supervisor, and we began teaching the course together," says Butler.

The second domestic violence clinic in the area was started at Harvard.

The second domestic violence clinic in the area was started at Harvard. Sarah Buel was a driving force in getting the program off the ground when she entered Harvard Law School in 1987.[62] At Harvard, "Sarah was like Johnny Appleseed," recalls Northeastern Clinical Professor Lois Kanter, who previously worked at Harvard. Buel would go around "planting the seeds" to inspire people.[63] Along with other students, she founded the Harvard Battered Women's Advocacy Project, the Harvard Women in Prison Project, and the Harvard Children

Lois H. Kanter

IMAGE COURTESY OF NORTHEASTERN UNIVERSITY SCHOOL OF LAW, PHOTO BY DAVID LEIFER

Lois Kanter admits that she was "clueless" about the realities of domestic violence when she first began to work in the field in 1989.[55] "For example, if I negotiated a divorce agreement," she says, "there was always something that my client would have to give up, and it was often agreement to visitation. I would negotiate a deal in which my client got 95% of what she wanted, but then she would be hysterical at the idea of visitation. I would explain to her that she would have sole physical and legal custody, and I would pressure her to agree to the terms of what I thought was a good deal. I later learned that to the client, a negotiated settlement meant he was getting his way, and she had no power. And, as a practical matter, it was a way for him to get access to her, and he would use manipulation around visitation to take as much control over her life as he could."

and Family Rights Project. Buel cited her Harvard clinical supervisor Ilene Seidman as being a mentor during these formative law school years. "Ilene went to court with me twenty-three times in twenty-four months to get custody for my client [a survivor of domestic violence]. She was so supportive." In 1991, Northeastern University School of Law followed, establishing the Domestic Violence Institute. Founded by Professor Emerita Clare Dalton and directed by Kanter, the Institute has specialized in collaborating with a wide range of community agencies and institutions (both legal and nonlegal) to coordinate services to victims and to instill in its law students the value of client empowerment and working across disciplines. In addition, Boston College Law School established the Women and the Law Clinic, founded by Leslie Espinoza Garvey and later directed by other clinical faculty.

Law Firms

In February 1989, Foley, Hoag & Eliot (now Foley Hoag LLP) became the first law firm in Massachusetts—and from all accounts, the first law firm in the nation—to establish a program that offered pro bono legal services to victims of domestic violence. In late 1988, two first-year associates, Laliah Hayes and Nan Seuffert, both of whom had worked with shelters and victims of domestic violence while they were in college and law school, asked Toni Wolfman, a Foley Hoag litigation partner, to help them find a way to use their legal skills to represent victims of abuse. Coincidentally, as a member of the Supreme Judicial Court's Gender Bias Study Committee, Wolfman was hearing from trial court judges about the great need for legal representation of women seeking protection from abusive situations. In too many situations, these women were doubly victimized—not only by their abusers but also by a legal system in which counsel often assisted abusers and court personnel were unprepared to recognize and respond appropriately to potentially violent situations. As Wolfman recalls, "Because Foley Hoag took great pride in its pro bono program and had repeatedly committed itself to protecting the rights of disadvantaged and vulnerable individuals and groups, I knew that I would be able to secure institutional support for a program such as that proposed by Liah and Nan."

Over the next several months, a small group of Foley Hoag lawyers reached out to colleagues who shared their interest in representing victims of domestic violence, recruited experienced professionals to train them, and set up a system for the referral, intake, assignment, and supervision of cases. Sarah Buel, herself a survivor of abuse and at that time a Harvard Law School student who had founded the Harvard Battered Women's Advocacy Project, provided the initial training along with advocates from Greater Boston Legal Services. GBLS was the first source of referrals to Foley Hoag, and as the program grew, Foley Hoag accepted cases from many other sources. The leaders of the program, in particular then senior associates Anthony Mirenda and Claire Laporte and later legal assistant (currently pro bono managing attorney) Rebecca Cazabon, provided ongoing training and supervision and put together a handbook of relevant background materials, statutory and case law, forms, and checklists that they continually updated. Foley Hoag shared its training materials with lawyers from other firms whom they invited to participate in Foley Hoag's training sessions and encouraged other firms to establish similar programs. Foley Hoag's Abuse Prevention Project continues to engage the talents of lawyers throughout the firm and to provide a range of important services, including training, legislation, and appellate advocacy.

Later in 1989, two first-year associates—Kathy Pawlowski and Navjeet Bal—established a pro bono Domestic Violence Project at Mintz, Levin, Cohn, Ferris, Glovsky and Popeo, PC. Originally, the Project was to include not only individual representation, but also legislative initiatives. Pawlowski notes: "I'd done some restraining order work at Georgetown Law as a student. But my sense was that only assisting clients with obtaining restraining orders wouldn't take care of the larger issue of getting to safety." So, she expanded the project to include lobbying for legislative initiatives and developing a network of social service referrals for victims. Over the past two decades, the Domestic Violence Project has grown from

Toni Wolfman

IMAGE COURTESY OF TONI WOLFMAN

Toni Wolfman recalls one of Foley Hoag's Abuse Prevention Project cases, in which the husband of a client for whom the firm had obtained a restraining order commandeered her car (with her inside) when she came to pick up her children from a visit with him at his parents' home. After shooting her and pushing her out of the car onto the side of the highway, the husband stopped the car and fatally shot himself. Although the client survived, she suffered serious and permanent injuries. In addition to helping their client obtain the medical and other care that she needed and retain custody of her children against claims asserted by her in-laws and recruiting other local lawyers to represent the children in asserting claims against the husband's estate, the Foley Hoag lawyers also had to deal with the repercussions of this terrible situation on their own lives. The support of the many members of the Abuse Prevention Project was an important source of comfort.

individual representation and legislative initiatives to appellate work and nonprofit representation. Bal, now at Nixon Peabody LLP, recalls "how supportive the Pro Bono Committee and indeed the whole firm was when Kathy Pawlowski and I started the Domestic Violence Project. No one ever told us to slow down or scale back or lower our sights. Indeed, lawyers from across the firm signed up to help us. Its success belongs to the many Mintz Levin attorneys who have guided it and shaped it over the years."

In 1990, Foley Hoag, Mintz Levin, and Sullivan and Worcester joined forces with other pro bono attorneys and other domestic violence advocates to form the Domestic Violence Council....

In 1990, Foley Hoag, Mintz Levin, and Sullivan and Worcester joined forces with other pro bono attorneys and other domestic violence advocates to form the Domestic Violence Council, which met monthly to discuss issues affecting domestic violence survivors. Now known as the Domestic & Sexual Violence Council, Inc. (DSVC), it is a Massachusetts nonprofit organization that advocates for victims of domestic and sexual violence through coordination of legal services; communication and sharing of information among providers of services; training and technical assistance to providers of services; research and education relating to domestic violence and sexual assault; case monitoring; and public policy advocacy. The DSVC has participated in several important appellate cases in the areas of domestic violence and sexual assault law. The DSVC was founded by the three law firms; several legal services organizations, including Greater Boston Legal Services; and several district attorney's offices.

Beth Boland, who was an active participant in Mintz Levin's Domestic Violence Project, is now a partner at Bingham McCutchen, which is also involved in domestic violence efforts. "I'm very encouraged that the number of law firms involved in this has multiplied over time." An excellent example of this is the partnership that several firms have forged with the Middlesex District Attorney's Office, where attorneys provide free legal assistance to victims of domestic violence during the restraining order process.[66] Created in 2008, this program was designed to address a significant gap in the way that domestic violence victims are served during the restraining order process. Because a restraining order is a civil document, assistant district attorneys are unable to represent domestic violence victims during that process. Many victims are unable to afford an attorney, especially because the abuser often controls the household finances. To address this problem, the Middlesex District Attorney's office first partnered with the firm Proskauer Rose and then Cooley Manion Jones to identify victims who need legal assistance and assign a private attorney to provide representation free of charge. Other law firms working with the public-private partnership include Melick Porter and Shea, Brody Hardoon Perkins and Kesten, and Weil, Gotshal & Manges.[67] District Attorney Gerry Leone says that "restraining orders are crucial for victims of domestic violence to protect themselves, and all too often victims who cannot afford an attorney return to the abusive environment that threatens them and their loved ones. This program works to help and empower them to end that dangerous cycle."[68] In the two years the program has been in place, the program has served at least seventy victims, with 97 percent of cases resolved in favor of the victim.[69]

Justice Sydney Hanlon

After graduating from Harvard Law School in 1975, Sydney Hanlon became an assistant district attorney in Norfolk County, where she headed up the state's first Sexual Assault Unit from 1977 to 1982. In 1990, Governor Michael Dukakis appointed her to the Dorchester District Court and, in 2009, Governor Deval Patrick appointed her to the Massachusetts Appeals Court. The cases she saw at the beginning of her judicial career were horrific. "I remember one where an abuser stuck a hot fork in the arm of the victim, and she came in with an infection."[70] Around the same time she took the bench, Hanlon saw Sarah Buel speak. "I went up to her afterward and asked, 'What can the court do?'" Buel suggested having a roundtable. So Hanlon organized a roundtable with domestic violence advocates, police, prosecutors, defense attorneys, and court personnel who met regularly to discuss issues of domestic violence.

▲ Hon. Sydney Hanlon at her swearing in as an associate justice of the Appeals Court on April 29, 2009.

IMAGE COURTESY OF GOVERNOR DEVAL PATRICK'S OFFICE, PHOTO BY EUGENIA OSSI

Working at the systemic level was also a helpful "antidote" to the stress of overseeing restraining-order hearings with serious and disturbing facts. In 1992, District Court Chief Justice Samuel Zoll appointed Justice Hanlon as chair of the District Court Domestic Violence Committee.[71] This committee was also tasked with updating the Abuse Prevention Standards for the courts that had been drafted in the mid-1980s. While the committee worked extensively on drafting standards, it had a tough time getting them promulgated. Then, Supreme Judicial Court Justice Herbert Wilkins cited the draft standards in *Frizado v. Frizado,* a case challenging the constitutionality of 209A.[72] The standards were approved and promulgated soon thereafter. Hanlon also helped to organize judicial trainings for domestic violence. She was a member of a large trial court committee with representatives from every department and part of the court system. The legislature allocated $100,000 each year for several years for such training, which occurred over two days in 1994. There were presentations that demonstrated a "good" 209A hearing and a "bad" 209A hearing. There were discussion groups where court staff, along with judges, would map out what they wanted to see in their courts.

Hanlon recalls, "When I started, restraining orders weren't put on a computer database. Without access to such information, judges didn't know if the defendant had prior restraining orders with this plaintiff, or other plaintiffs. I was pleased to be asked to sit on a committee to figure out how to get restraining orders on the computers." By September 8, 1992, restraining orders had become computerized, so all old restraining orders would be pulled with a record check. If a person was arrested, the court would advance all the open restraining orders. "We couldn't do that without the registry."

In 1994, Hanlon became first justice of the Dorchester District Court and she continued to chair the Domestic Violence Committee. Hanlon notes, "Doing something to affect the system was a good antidote to seeing all the tough cases." In 1999, the U.S. Department of Justice Office on Violence Against Women selected the Dorchester Court as one of three sites in the nation for a judicial oversight demonstration initiative—the project examined the value of close judicial and probation oversight of convicted domestic violence offenders. "We doubled our probation staff. We had eight probation officers doing domestic violence cases. The rest of the money went to advocacy. We did periodic reviews with batterers." Hanlon saw much progress by the defendants, noting: "I saw a lot of progress anecdotally and the research showed that domestic violence recidivism was reduced measurably in that period."

NOTES

1 The historical context of the domestic violence movement is framed in terms of male batterer husbands and female wives as victims. However, the authors would like to note that that battering can and does occur by women against men and in same-sex relationships.

2 "Report of the Gender Bias Study of the Supreme Judicial Court," 23 *Suffolk U.L. Rev.* 575, 585 (1989).

3 "Report of the Gender Bias Study of the Supreme Judicial Court," 23 *Suffolk U.L. Rev.* at 585.

4 "Report of the Gender Bias Study of the Supreme Judicial Court," 23 *Suffolk U.L. Rev.* at 585.

5 Morgan Lee Woolley, "Marital Rape: A Unique Blend of Domestic Violence and Non-Marital Rape Issues," 18 *Hastings Women's L.J.* 269, 271 (2007).

6 *See generally* Claudia Zaher, "When a Woman's Marital Status Determined Her Legal Status: A Research Guide on the Common Law Doctrine of Coverture," 94 *Law Libr. J.* 459 (2002).

7 Caroline Dettmer, "Increased Sentencing for Repeat Offenders of Domestic Violence in Ohio: Will This End the Suffering?," 73 *U. Cin. L. Rev.* 705, 708 (2004).

8 Victoria Mikesell Mather, "The Skeleton in the Closet: The Battered Woman Syndrome, Self-Defense and Expert Testimony," 39 *Mercer L. Rev.* 545, 547–48 (1988); *see also* Katherine E. Volovski, "Crime and Punishment Law Chapter: Domestic Violence," 5 *Geo. J. Gender & L.* 175, 175 n.5 (2004) ("Prior to the twentieth century, the criminal law condoned domestic violence by granting a man the right to beat his wife, so long as the stick he used was not wider than the width of his thumb.").

9 *See, e.g., Commonwealth v. McAfee,* 108 Mass. 458 (1871); *Fulgham v. State,* 46 Ala. 143 (1871); *State v. Oliver,* 70 N.C. 453 (1874); *Gorman v. State,* 42 Tex. 221 (1875).

10 Harvard Law Review, "Developments in the Law: Legal Responses to Domestic Violence," 106 *Harv. L. Rev.* 1501, 1502 (1993).

11 Harvard Law Review, "Developments in the Law: Legal Responses to Domestic Violence," 106 *Harv. L. Rev.* at 1502.

12 Katherine Triantafillou, "Massachusetts New Legislation to Help Battered Women," *The Judge's J.*, Summer 1988, at 20.

13 "Report of the Gender Bias Study of the Supreme Judicial Court," 23 *Suffolk U.L. Rev.* at 585.

14 Katherine Triantafillou, "Massachusetts New Legislation to Help Battered Women," *The Judge's J.* at 20.

15 Katherine Triantafillou, "Massachusetts New Legislation to Help Battered Women," *The Judge's J.* at 20.

16 Interview with Katherine Triantafillou (Oct. 14, 2010).

17 Katherine Triantafillou, "Massachusetts New Legislation to Help Battered Women," *The Judge's J.* at 20.

18 Katherine Triantafillou, "Massachusetts New Legislation to Help Battered Women," *The Judge's J.* at 20.

19 Katherine Triantafillou, "Massachusetts New Legislation to Help Battered Women," *The Judge's J.* at 22.

20 Interview with Katherine Triantafillou (Oct. 14, 2010).

21 Michael Kenny, "Violence at Home? New law offers quick relief," *Boston Globe,* Jan. 18, 1979.

22 Eileen McNamara, "Still Dying in Vain," *Boston Globe,* Mar. 18, 2007.

23 Interview with Chris Butler (Nov. 9, 2010).

24 Interview with Chris Butler (Nov. 9, 2010).

25 Katherine Triantafillou, "Massachusetts New Legislation to Help Battered Women," *The Judge's J.* at 23. Apparently, the judiciary was not the first to object to such language. The statutory language "family or household members" was originally "persons cohabitating with each other." According to Triantafillou, one senator vehemently objected to this language, "threaten[ing] to kill the bill because of its ostensible encouragement of 'sin,' forc[ing] us to substitute the more vague and puzzling phrase 'household member.'" Katherine Triantafillou, "Massachusetts New Legislation to Help Battered Women," *The Judge's J.* at 23.

26 Eileen McNamara, "An Attack on Restraint," *Boston Globe,* May 20, 1998.

27 Interview wih Katherine Triantafillou (Oct. 10, 2010).

28 Stan Grossfeld, "'Safer' and in Jail: Women Who Kill Their Batterers," *Boston Globe,* Sept. 2, 1991.

29 Stan Grossfeld, "'Safer' and in Jail: Women Who Kill Their Batterers," *Boston Globe,* Sept. 2, 1991.

30 Stan Grossfeld, "'Safer' and in Jail: Women Who Kill Their Batterers," *Boston Globe,* Sept. 2, 1991.

31 Stan Grossfeld, "'Safer' and in Jail: Women Who Kill Their Batterers," *Boston Globe,* Sept. 2, 1991.

32 Phyllis Goldfarb, "Describing Without Circumscribing: Questioning the Construction of Gender in the Discourse of Intimate Violence," 64 *Geo. Wash. L. Rev.* 582, 586 (1996).

33 Phyllis Goldfarb, "Describing Without Circumscribing: Questioning the Construction of Gender in the Discourse of Intimate Violence," 64 *Geo. Wash. L. Rev.* at 586.

34 Doris S. Wong, "Board Urges Clemency for 2 in Cases Tied to Battered Women's Syndrome," *Boston Globe,* Mar. 4, 1994, at 35.

35 *See* Toni Locy, "Weld Urged to Free 8 Women," *Boston Globe,* Feb. 15, 1992, at 15, 17.

36 Phyllis Goldfarb, "Describing Without Circumscribing: Questioning the Construction of Gender in the Discourse of Intimate Violence," 64 *Geo. Wash. L. Rev.* at 587.

37 The Advisory Board of Pardons, a special seating of the Massachusetts Parole Board, is empowered to make commutation recommendations to the governor based solely on a written petition or upon a hearing of the petitioner's claims. *See* G.L. c. 127, § 154 (1992); 120 C.M.R. §§ 901.05, 901.12(5) (1993). In the cases of the Framingham Eight, the board elected to hold hearings on seven of the petitions. It deferred its involvement in one case, which was still pending on direct appeal. *See* Toni Locy, "Woman's Life Sentence Is Commuted," *Boston Globe,* Apr. 29, 1993, at 1.

38 The governor's decision to commute a sentence must also be approved by the Massachusetts Governor's Council. *See* G.L. c. 127, § 152 (1992). Governor Weld sent no other cases to the Governor's Council for approval of grants of commutation. One petitioner was released through the appellate process when a trial judge reduced her sentence to time served. *See* Doris S. Wong, "Woman Is Free in Killing of Boyfriend," *Boston Globe,* July 2, 1993, at 18. Another petitioner was released by the parole board on early parole. Three petitioners were paroled at their first eligibility date.

39 Phyllis Goldfarb, "Describing Without Circumscribing: Questioning the Construction of Gender in the Discourse of Intimate Violence," 64 *Geo. Wash. L. Rev.* at 587.

40 Interview with Phyllis Goldfarb (Oct. 22, 2010).

41 Phyllis Goldfarb, "Describing Without Circumscribing: Questioning the Construction of Gender in the Discourse of Intimate Violence," 64 *Geo. Wash. L. Rev.* at 626.

42 Phyllis Goldfarb, "Describing Without Circumscribing: Questioning the Construction of Gender in the Discourse of Intimate Violence," 64 *Geo. Wash. L. Rev.* at 587–88.

43 Interview with Sandra E. Lundy (Oct. 18, 2010).

44 Interview with Sandra E. Lundy (Oct. 18, 2010).

45 The Network/La Red was formed in 1989 when a group of formerly battered lesbians came together to address domestic violence in lesbian and bisexual women's communities in Boston. The Network/La Red has become a national resource and model for battered women's programs, batterer intervention programs, and LGBT organizations beginning to address battering in lesbian, bisexual women's, and transgender relationships.

46 Stephanie B. Goldberg, "Nobody's Victim," *ABA Journal,* July 1996, at 49–51.

47 Stephanie B. Goldberg, "Nobody's Victim," *ABA Journal,* July 1996, at 49–51.

48 Stephanie B. Goldberg, "Nobody's Victim," *ABA Journal,* July 1996, at 49–51.

49 Interview with Beth Boland (Nov. 3, 2010).

50 Her legislative work also included a number of bills to protect victims of domestic violence, including legislation requiring judges faced with a restraining order petition to be provided with a printout of the defendant's prior record of violations involving violence, and legislation requiring a defendant against whom a restraining order has been issued to immediately surrender all firearms and licenses to carry firearms. G.L. c. 209A, §§ 3B, 7.

51 Interview with Pauline Quirion (Oct. 26, 2010).

52 *See* Pauline Quirion, Judith Lennett, Kristin Lund & Chanda Tuck, "Protecting Children Exposed to Domestic Violence in Contested Custody and Visitation Legislation," 6 *B.U. Pub. Int. L.J.* 501 (1997).

53 G.L. c. 208, § 31A; G.L. c. 209, § 38; G.L. c. 209A, § 3.

54 Interview with Barbara Mitchell (Nov. 5, 2010).

55 Interview with Beth Boland (Nov. 3, 2010).

56 Interview with Barbara Mitchell (Nov. 5, 2010).

57 Domestic Violence Institute website, *available at* http://www.dvi.neu.edu.

58 Amy Farmer & Jill Tiefenthaler, *Explaining the Recent Decline in Domestic Violence* p. 3, Brennan Center for Justice (2002).

59 Amy Farmer & Jill Tiefenthaler, *Explaining the Recent Decline in Domestic Violence* p. 3, Brennan Center for Justice (2002).

60 Amy Farmer & Jill Tiefenthaler, *Explaining the Recent Decline in Domestic Violence* p. 3, Brennan Center for Justice (2002).

61 Stephanie B. Goldberg, "Nobody's Victim," *ABA Journal*, July 1996, at 52.

62 Stephanie B. Goldberg, "Nobody's Victim," *ABA Journal*, July 1996, at 52.

63 Interview with Lois H. Kanter (Oct. 15, 2010).

64 Interview with Lois H. Kanter (Oct. 15, 2010).

65 Interview with Kathy Pawlowski (Fall 2010).

66 "Fifth law firm joins Middlesex DA to help domestic violence victims," *Metro Daily News,* Nov. 22, 2010, *available at* http://www.metrowestdailynews.com/newsnow/x842513293/Fifth-law-firm-joins-Middlesex-DA-to-help-domestic-violence-victims.

67 "Fifth law firm joins Middlesex DA to help domestic violence victims," *Metro Daily News,* Nov. 22, 2010.

68 "Fifth law firm joins Middlesex DA to help domestic violence victims," *Metro Daily News,* Nov. 22, 2010.

69 "Fifth law firm joins Middlesex DA to help domestic violence victims," *Metro Daily News,* Nov. 22, 2010.

70 Interview with Hon. Sydney Hanlon (Nov. 2, 2010).

71 Hanlon also served as a member of the District Court Education Committee between 1992 and 2003, when the Dorchester District Court became part of the Boston Municipal Court Department; she later chaired the Boston Municipal Court Education Committee.

72 *See Frizado v. Frizado,* 420 Mass. 592 (1995). In *Frizado*, Richard Frizado raised constitutionally-based arguments that challenged the lawfulness of abuse prevention orders issued against him on the complaint of his former wife, asserting the facial invalidity of G.L. c. 209A. The Supreme Judicial Court found that domestic abuse proceedings under 209A were facially valid. Justice Wilkins stated: "Many of the principles that we have stated here also appear in the District Court's Draft Standards of Judicial Practice, Abuse Prevention Proceedings (December, 1994)."

CHAPTER 4

Women in Black: Judges

Women and the Judiciary in Massachusetts, Then and Now

REBECCA ROGERS
SARAH E. WALD

Introduction

For baseball players, it's making the All-Stars. For writers, it's hitting the *New York Times* bestsellers list. And for many lawyers, it's becoming a judge. In law school, we all spend three years reading, analyzing, and interpreting the words of judges. Judges are the ultimate authority figures—admired, feared, revered, cursed, but always at the center of the system of justice to which we as lawyers subscribe.

Thus, the question of whether women are fully represented as judges becomes important for the credibility and perception of the legal profession. Looking at the history of women and the judiciary raises a host of issues that not only mirror broader ones in the legal profession but also take on added weight because of the special role of judges.

The first women to be named to courts in Massachusetts were Emma Fall Schofield and Sadie Lipner Shulman, appointed in 1930 to district courts in Middlesex and Suffolk counties, respectively. This was a full forty-eight years after the first woman, Lelia J. Robinson, was admitted to the Massachusetts bar in 1882. As of January 2012, women made up 39 percent of currently sitting judges in the Massachusetts state court system and 29 percent of federal judges in the state.[1] At the time Supreme Judicial Court Chief Justice Margaret H. Marshall announced her retirement in 2010, Massachusetts was one of twenty

Rebecca Rogers is a lawyer working in Boston. She previously clerked for Justices Martha Sosman and Margot Botsford of the Massachusetts Supreme Judicial Court.

IMAGE COURTESY OF CARRIE-ANNE KERWIN

Sarah E. Wald is a lawyer and educator who is a former president of the Women's Bar Association of Massachusetts. She is currently chief of staff and senior advisor to the dean at the John F. Kennedy School of Government at Harvard, where she is also an adjunct lecturer in public policy.

IMAGE COURTESY OF SARAH E. WALD

states with a woman chief justice. This is all interesting history but worth looking at more closely from two angles: How have women gotten to the bench in Massachusetts, and why does it matter at all?

Progress: 1930–2012, What Do the Numbers Tell Us?

Looking more closely at the trends in the numbers of women on the bench in Massachusetts, several interesting themes emerge.

Progress, While Steady, Has Hardly Been Rapid

The number of women judges in state courts in Massachusetts increased only gradually at first, and for long stretches of time the number of women judges remained nearly constant. Between 1932 and 1972 there were never more than seven women judges in Massachusetts state courts at one time, and during each year between 1940 and 1972 there were between five and seven women judges.

It was not until the 1990s that Massachusetts saw its most significant increase in the number of women judges in state courts, from forty-one in 1990 to 102 in 2000.

It was not until the 1990s that Massachusetts saw its most significant increase in the number of women judges in state courts, from forty-one in 1990 to 102 in 2000. According to the 2010 *Women in Federal and State-level Judgeships* report issued by the State University of New York at Albany's Center for Women in Government and Civil Society, Massachusetts ranked second among states for the largest share of women in state-level judgeships, with 37.5 percent (following Vermont, with 40.2 percent of state-level judgeships held by women). While this number is an impressive improvement when compared to the number of women judges decades ago, it is still less than the 48 percent of women law students nationwide and the 45 percent of legal associates that are women.

Women Judges Cluster in Certain Courts

In 1930, two prominent Massachusetts attorneys became the first two women judges in the state. Emma Fall Schofield had previously been the first woman assistant attorney general in Massachusetts. Sadie Lipner Shulman had been assistant corporation counsel for the City of Boston. They were sworn in during the same ceremony: Schofield to the Malden District Court and Shulman to the Dorchester District Court.

As more women judges were appointed in Massachusetts one common pattern emerged in the distribution of judges throughout the court system. Although the first two women judges were appointed to the District Court, women judges are far more common in the Probate and Family Court and Juvenile Court (all substantive areas that could be considered more traditionally women's domains) than in the overall court system. In January 2012, twenty-three of the forty-six currently sitting Probate and Family Court judges were women. This even split is eleven percentage points higher than the statewide total.[2] This tendency of women judges to be found in the Probate and Family Court is a longstanding one in Massachusetts. The first woman to sit as a judge in the Probate and Family Court, Beatrice Hancock Mullaney, was appointed in 1955, and, in 1978, five of the fifteen women judges in Massachusetts state courts could be found in the Probate and Family Court. In part, this is another example of Massachusetts mirroring a national trend in which women judges tend to be more concentrated in courts of limited jurisdiction and most particularly in courts such as probate and family courts because such courts consider issues more closely identified with women's traditional roles.[3]

Women's presence as judges in the Juvenile Court in Massachusetts, another area in which women judges nationally tend to be concentrated, is similarly pronounced. As of January 2012, women made up nineteen of the thirty-nine currently sitting Juvenile Court judges, comprising 48.7 percent of the judges in that court, just slightly lower than the 50 percent Probate and Family Court representation, though still higher than the state overall total.[4] This concentration is of a more recent vintage, too—the first woman Juvenile Court judge, Rebekah J. Crampton Kamukala, was appointed in 1986, thirty-one years after the first woman Probate and Family Court judge.

Massachusetts Has Mirrored Federal Court Trends

In the early years, the limited progress of women judges in Massachusetts tracked the progress of women federal judges; between 1934 and 1977 only eight women were appointed to the federal bench in the entire United States.[5]

There are several ways in which the increasing numbers of women on the Massachusetts state bench and on the federal bench have mirrored each other over time, as well as some interesting ways in which the progression differs. One of the similarities is the time when the first women judges were appointed in each court system. Emma Fall Schofield and Sadie Lipner Shulman were appointed in 1930 as the first women judges in Massachusetts.[6] Only four years later, Florence E. Allen was appointed to the U.S. Court of Appeals for the Sixth Circuit, becoming the first woman appointed to a judgeship in an Article III court of general jurisdiction.[7] For President Franklin D. Roosevelt, the appointment of women to federal positions, including the appointment of Judge Allen, provided an opportunity to gain the political support of newly minted women voters.[8] In all likelihood, the appointment of

Florence Allen (1884-1966) stands waving a flag at the center of this 1912 photo in front of the women's suffrage headquarters in Cleveland, Ohio. Allen was active in the women's suffrage movement and, once women received the right to vote, was elected judge in Ohio, in 1920 to the Cuyahoga County Court of Common Pleas (making her the first woman in the country elected to a state court of general jurisdiction) and in 1922 to the Ohio Supreme Court (making her the first woman to serve on any state's highest court). Judge Allen then served on the Sixth Circuit from 1934 to 1959. Although her name was often-mentioned as a possibility for appointment to the U.S. Supreme Court, "[s]he accurately predicted a Supreme Court appointment 'will never happen to a woman while I am living.'"[9]

IMAGE SOURCE:
LIBRARY OF CONGRESS PRINTS & PHOTOGRAPHS ONLINE CATALOG

women to the bench in Massachusetts at about the same time was motivated, at least in part, by similar political concerns.

It was under the presidency of Jimmy Carter, when the first significant increase in the number of women federal judges occurred, that some interesting differences between the numbers of women judges in the two court systems emerge. During his term in office, President Carter appointed forty women to the federal judiciary (including Rya W. Zobel, the first woman federal judge in Massachusetts), a significant increase above the six women federal judges who were serving at the start of his presidency. Commentators have attributed this increase to several factors, including the passage of the 1978 Omnibus Judgeship Act, which created 152 new judicial seats, as well as President Carter's adoption of a merit selection plan for judicial appointments and an explicit outreach policy intended to increase the number of women appointees.[10] In the Massachusetts state courts, with no increase in the number of judicial positions such as occurred in the federal judiciary and no explicit outreach program in place, the number of women judges increased much more gradually. During the same period of President Carter's administration, the number of women judges in Massachusetts state courts grew only slightly, increasing from thirteen in 1977 to nineteen in 1981.

Women Judges of the U.S. District Court for the District of Massachusetts

Rya W. Zobel	1979 to present
Patti B. Saris	1993 to present
Nancy Gertner	1994 to 2011
Denise Jefferson Casper	2010 to present

"Pipeline" Issues and Efforts to Get More Women on the Bench

As these growing numbers over time show, clearly there have been strides in women entering the judiciary. But, as many commentators have noted, there is still a way to go before women are fully represented as judges. It is always tempting to ascribe lower numbers of women in legal leadership positions to the "pipeline" problem—women entered the legal profession late, they are rising now, and so, as soon as we get enough women into the pipeline, the issues of proportional representation will take care of themselves, right?

Unfortunately, things are not that simple. Though nationally, 48 percent of law students are women, as are 45 percent of law firm associates (the numbers have been close to this for some time), only 22 percent of federal judges and 26 percent of all state judges are female.[11] As one commentator noted, "With law schools and the bar readily open to women, the hurdle seems to be the selection process."[12]

In Massachusetts, of course, judges are appointed. At first glance, this might seem to bode better for women than in states where judges are elected: women traditionally have been underrepresented in electoral politics, and the prejudices of voters against women in nontraditional roles can present an additional obstacle to women judicial candidates. Though judicial appointment does not require appealing to a broad spectrum of lay voters, it is based on being recognized by peers in the profession and it is likely to help if the candidate has some ties, direct or indirect, to the elected official (the governor or the president) who is making the appointment. These are factors that may disfavor women who may have been less active in political or professional circles. As noted in a 2010 article on the rise of women in state courts, some observers believe that elective systems benefit women:

▲

The Massachusetts Appeals Court in 2009. From left to right, front row: Hon. Barbara A. Lenk, Hon. Raya S. Dreben, Hon. Frederick L. Brown, Hon. Phillip Rapoza, Hon. Charlotte Anne Perretta, Hon. Kent B. Smith, Hon. Fernande R.V. Duffly; second row: Hon. Scott L. Kafker, Hon. Janis M. Berry, Hon. Joseph A. Grasso, Jr., Hon. Elspeth B. Cypher, Hon. R. Marc Kantrowitz, Hon. James F. McHugh, Jr., Hon. Cynthia J. Cohen; third row: Hon. Ariane D. Vuono, Hon. R. Malcolm Graham, Hon. Mark V. Green, Hon. David A. Mills, Hon. Joseph A. Trainor, Hon. Gary S. Katzmann, Hon. Andrew R. Grainger; fourth row: Hon. James R. Milkey, Hon. Francis R. Fecteau, Hon. Mitchell J. Sikora, Jr., Hon. William J. Meade, Hon. Peter J. Rubin, Hon. Gabrielle R. Wolohojian, Hon. Sydney Hanlon.

"The voters recognize qualities in judicial candidates that the legal and political elites don't. The elites disqualify a candidate for not going to the right law school or being editor of the law review. The people want judges who are good listeners and thoughtful, and women are very strong with voters in these characteristics."[13]

Looking at the career paths of women who become judges shows that the route is not a straightforward one. It is interesting to note some of the trends that emerge from the stories: they are less likely to come from the private sector, and they often had a male "champion" or mentor who was more established in the profession and politics. For example, Judge Rya W. Zobel, the first woman appointed to the U.S. District Court in Massachusetts, spent her first nine years after graduation from law school as a permanent law clerk for U.S. District Court

First Women Judges on Massachusetts Courts

When	Who	Judgeship
1930	Emma Fall Schofield Sadie Lipner Shulman	District Court
1934	Jennie Loitman Barron Ethel E. Mackiernan	Boston Municipal Court Presiding Justice, District Court
1955	Beatrice Hancock Mullaney	Probate and Family Court
1959	Jennie Loitman Barron	Superior Court
1978	Charlotte Anne Perretta Ruth I. Abrams	Appeals Court Supreme Judicial Court
1979	Joyce London Alexander Rya W. Zobel	U.S. Magistrate Judge for the District of Massachusetts U.S. District Court for the District of Massachusetts
1985	Marilyn M. Sullivan	Chief Justice, Land Court
1986	Rebekah J. Crampton Kamukala	Juvenile Court
1991	Mary C. Fitzpatrick	Chief Justice, Probate and Family Court
1995	Sandra L. Lynch	U.S. Court of Appeals for the First Circuit
1998	Barbara A. Dortch-Okara Hon. Martha P. Grace	Chief Justice for Administration and Management of the Trial Court Chief Justice, Juvenile Court
1999	Suzanne V. Delvecchio Diane Horan Margaret H. Marshall	Chief Justice, Superior Court Housing Court Chief Justice, Supreme Judicial Court
2004	Lynda M. Connolly	Chief Justice, District Court
2008	Sandra L. Lynch	Chief Judge, U.S. Court of Appeals for the First Circuit

Judge George C. Sweeney. One review of the background of women named to federal appeals courts found that, compared to their male counterparts, women were more likely to have had prior judicial experience in lower courts, were less likely to have come from private practice, and had less direct, partisan political experience.[14]

In Massachusetts, the role of institutional advocate for appointing more women came initially from women lawyers' organizations.

In Massachusetts, the role of institutional advocate for appointing more women came initially from women lawyers' organizations. Both the Women's Bar Association of Massachusetts (WBA) and the Massachusetts Association of Women Lawyers (MAWL) put the appointment of women judges at the top of their priority lists starting in the late 1970s. Their advocacy—meeting with the governor, running workshops for women interested in becoming judges, compiling directories of interested women for the appointing authorities, later holding seats on the Judicial Nominating Commission—was instrumental in providing a voice and a resource on this issue. This is consistent with the advocacy and support role of other women's organizations in this area, such as the National Association of Women Judges, founded in 1979.[15] This advocacy undoubtedly was a factor in the substantial increases in the number of women judges starting around 1980. According to the American Bar Association, the proportion of women judges nationally doubled between 1980 and 1991, and in Massachusetts the number of women judges during the same period increased from seventeen to forty-four.

Do Women Judges Make a Difference?

Why should it matter whether women are fully represented as judges? Isn't justice blind? Does it make a difference—and, if so, should it matter whether a judge is a man or woman? A number of compelling reasons noted and relied upon in the past several decades suggest that the increase in the number of women judges has made and continues to make an important difference.

First, because judges hold an esteemed place in the legal profession, they can make excellent role models for both male and female lawyers. The almost half of law students who are women need to know that they can achieve in the profession, and need to see and deal professionally with women who have worked their way into leadership positions.

Men, too, need to see women in positions of authority (and the authority of a judge in a courtroom is absolute; no wise male lawyer is going to repeatedly interrupt the judge, ignore her opinion, or refuse to acknowledge her knowledge, as might be the case with a female colleague). The more familiar the sight of a woman in charge in one legal role becomes, the fewer objections may be raised when women adopt other roles in the profession. One judge noted that the presence of two women on the federal Appeals Court in Washington had a "ripple effect," resulting in more women litigators getting assigned by firms to court cases, more women law clerks hired to work for the judges on that court, and more women working in court supervisory administrative roles.[16] Some of the stories of the "chilly" reception given to early women judges by their male coworkers seem almost humorous now: one of Sixth Circuit Judge Florence Allen's male colleagues stayed in bed for several days at the thought of a woman on the bench with him, and Judge Constance Baker Motley's qualifications for the U.S. District Court in New York were listed in an introduction at a conference for new federal judges in 1968 as her having been on the boards of the YWCA and United Church Women.[17] Clearly the presence of more women in the profession has accustomed men to working with them as colleagues.

Second, the credibility of our system of justice relies on the notion that clients feel they have received a fair hearing. People who appear before the courts need to believe that no particular group is systemically favored. Having few women as judges reinforces a view that men are favored by the justice system and presents a particular picture of power in the law.[18] As noted in a March 2010 ABA study, a lack of diversity "can malign the legitimacy of not only lawyers, but the law itself."[19] Judge Constance Baker Motley, the first black woman appointed to the federal bench in the nation, summarized the argument in its most basic form: "I believe that having more women and minorities in the...judiciary...builds confidence in the government. It makes people believe that the government is fair...it says that the courts are fair."[20]

▶

These portraits hanging outside the Supreme Judicial Court chief justice's chambers at the John Adams Courthouse in Boston honor some of the first women judges on Massachusetts state courts.

PHOTO BY MCLE | NEW ENGLAND

The Massachusetts Supreme Judicial Court in 2012. From left to right, front row: Hon. Francis X. Spina, Hon. Roderick L. Ireland (chief justice), Hon. Robert J. Cordy; back row: Hon. Barbara A. Lenk, Hon. Margot Botsford, Hon. Ralph D. Gants, Hon. Fernande R.V. Duffly.

IMAGE COURTESY OF MASSACHUSETTS SUPREME JUDICIAL COURT

Third—and related to this—is that an increased presence of women judges may improve the treatment of women in court. The many state "gender bias" studies of the past two decades are filled with examples of male judges acting in demeaning ways toward women counsel or litigants. For example, the 1989 *Report of the Gender Bias Study of the Supreme Judicial Court,* resulting from a study that began in 1986, reported on a variety of common gender-biased conduct by male judges, including being more likely to address female attorneys by their first name and being more likely to ask a woman if she is an attorney. According to the study, 15 percent of attorneys reported that they had seen a male judge sexually harass a female attorney by subjecting her to inappropriate sexual comments, and 6 percent of all attorneys reported having seen a male judge touch a female attorney in an inappropriate manner.[21] As the report's executive summary stated, "[B]iased attitudes do more than hurt feelings. They affect women's ability to function in the system, and they are linked to unjust outcomes."[22]

Fourth, even if the outcome of cases is not different because of a judge's gender, the reasoning and the perspective that a woman judge may bring can influence both her colleagues and the future development of the law.[23] After some of her Supreme Court colleagues' comments at oral argument in *Safford Unified School District #1 v. Redding* seemingly minimized the emotional impact that a strip search had had on the thirteen-year-

3 Women in 320 Years: Women Clerks of the Supreme Judicial Court

- **Jean M. Kennett:** In 1984 Jean Kennett became the first woman appointed to the position of Supreme Judicial Court Clerk for the Commonwealth. She served for fifteen years until her retirement in 1999.
- **Susan Mellen:** Susan Mellen has served as Supreme Judicial Court Clerk for the Commonwealth since Jean Kennett's retirement, making her only the second woman to hold the position.
- **Maura S. Doyle:** Maura Doyle is the first woman to serve as Supreme Judicial Court Clerk for the County of Suffolk. She was appointed in 1996 and then elected to the position in 1998. She is also the first woman to have been elected to a county-wide office in Suffolk.

old girl in the case, Justice Ruth Bader Ginsburg stated to *USA Today,* "They have never been a 13-year-old girl. It's a very sensitive age for a girl. I didn't think that my colleagues, some of them, quite understood."[24]

In 1996, in *United States v. Rivera,* an all-male panel of First Circuit judges ruled that the government had not proven that the victim of a carjacking and rape had shown "serious bodily injury" within the meaning of the federal carjacking statute. Judge Sandra L. Lynch, the only female member of the First Circuit at the time (in 2008 she became the court's first woman chief judge), requested that that the court rehear the case en banc. When her request was denied, Judge Lynch wrote a stirring dissent: "It requires no leap of logic to infer that a forcible rape of an unwitting victim...involved extreme physical pain.... Congress would be appalled at this outcome."[25] Congress was, in fact, appalled. Legislation was quickly drafted and passed by Congress; afterward, U.S. Senator Edward M. Kennedy wrote to Judge Lynch, stating: "Your dissent made all the difference."[26]

U.S. Senator Edward M. Kennedy wrote to Judge Lynch, stating: "Your dissent made all the difference."

A number of empirical studies have looked at whether the presence of women on a court makes a difference in the outcome of cases. The evidence is somewhat inconclusive. Early studies of federal courts (using small pools of women) found no real difference,[27] though at least one study of state court judges found that women who identified themselves as "feminists" were twice as likely as others to rule for a woman in a hypothetical case.[28] There are indications that political ideology, rather than gender, serves as a more predictive factor in looking at rulings. A more rigorous recent analysis has shown that, for several types of cases, particularly employment discrimination and sexual harassment, there is a greater likelihood that a woman judge will rule for the plaintiffs in appellate cases.[29] It is also interesting to note that having a woman on an appellate panel significantly increases the chance that a male judge will rule for the plaintiffs in these cases.[30] One 1993 study found that the "most pro-woman" justices on their states' high courts, as defined by a "voting norm deviation" score measured by nonunanimous cases on women's issues, were Justice Rose E. Bird of California and Justice Ruth I. Abrams of Massachusetts.[31] Notably, only one male judge in all the states examined had a score that tied with a woman justice's score: Justice Paul J. Liacos of Massachusetts.[32]

Comments from several senior women judges reflect that their gender has affected their careers and roles as judges, but they are notably cautious in how much focus to put on this. As noted by Judge Patricia M. Wald, of the U.S. Court of Appeals for the D.C. Circuit,

> [b]eing a woman and being treated by society as a woman can be a vital element of a judge's experience. That experience in turn can subtly affect the lens through which she views issues and solutions. I can think of a few cases where being a woman entered into my conscience, but I can think of just as many where having worked in a factory, having been a Legal Services lawyer and having been a government official who dealt with Congress affected my perspective just as much.[33]

Or, as one state supreme court justice described it, "[t]he common denominator [for women judges]—which comes from our mutual experience of dealing as women in a formerly men's world—is this: We have all combined a gutsy opposition to accepting the status quo with a commitment to working within the status quo for change."[34]

As we see it, the goal is to make the formerly extraordinary appointment of women to the bench and, more recently, to leadership positions in the courtroom perfectly ordinary.

The 2009 and 2010 confirmation hearings for U.S. Supreme Court Justices Sonia Sotomayor and Elena Kagan reflect both how far we've come and the challenges that remain. During the 2009 confirmation hearings for Sonia Sotomayor, there was significant controversy regarding her earlier comment that she "would hope that a wise Latina woman with the richness of her experiences would more often than not reach a better conclusion than a white male who hasn't lived that life." In contrast, during her 2010 confirmation hearings, Elena Kagan steered away from any mention of gender and has, in fact, noted that it does not play a large role in her day-to-day dealings. In discussing her role as the first woman dean of Harvard Law School, she noted that gender is "not something I think about on a daily basis, and it's something that in many ways has seemed remarkably not relevant in the job."[35]

All of these perspectives belong in our courtrooms, as do women with varying heritages, experiences, lifestyles, and political opinions. The past and present generations have accomplished a great deal. As we see it, the goal is to make the formerly extraordinary appointment of women to the bench and, more recently, to leadership positions in the courtroom perfectly ordinary.

Women Judges in Massachusetts: A June 2012 Snapshot[36]

FEDERAL JUDGES

U.S. Court of Appeals for the First Circuit
Sandra L. Lynch, chief judge
O. Rogeriee Thompson

U.S. District Court for the District of Massachusetts
Denise Jefferson Casper
Patti B. Saris
Rya W. Zobel

Magistrate Judges
Jennifer C. Boal
Marianne B. Bowler
Judith G. Dein

STATE JUDGES

Supreme Judicial Court
Margot Botsford
Fernande R.V. Duffly
Barbara A. Lenk

Appeals Court
Janis M. Berry
Cynthia J. Cohen
Elspeth B. Cypher
Sydney Hanlon
Mary T. Sullivan
Ariane D. Vuono
Gabrielle R. Wolohojian

Superior Court
Carol S. Ball
Kimberly S. Budd
Elizabeth B. Donovan
Barbara A. Dortch-Okara
Renee P. Dupuis
Judith Fabricant
Elizabeth M. Fahey
E. Susan Garsh
Linda E. Giles
S. Jane Haggerty
Sandra L. Hamlin
Geraldine S. Hines
Maureen B. Hogan
Merita A. Hopkins
Bertha D. Josephson
Janet Kenton-Walker
Diane M. Kottmyer
Bonnie H. MacLeod-Mancuso
Christine M. McEvoy
Frances A. McIntyre
Tina S. Page
Regina L. Quinlan
Christine M. Roach
Barbara J. Rouse, chief justice
Mary-Lou Rup
Janet L. Sanders
Constance M. Sweeney
Kathe M. Tuttman

Probate and Family Court
Joan P. Armstrong
Theresa A. Bisenius
Amy L. Blake
Paula M. Carey, chief justice
Megan H. Christopher
Beth A. Crawford
Lucille A. DiLeo
Linda S. Fidnick
Katherine A. Field
Anne M. Geoffrion
Dorothy M. Gibson
Patricia A. Gorman
Barbara M. Hyland
Randy J. Kaplan
Leilah A. Keamy
Denise L. Meagher
Maureen H. Monks
Elaine M. Moriarty
Angela M. Ordoñez
Susan D. Ricci
Lisa A. Roberts
Catherine P. Sabaitis
Mary Anne Sahagian
Jennifer M. Ulwick
Virginia M. Ward

Land Court
Judith C. Cutler
Karyn F. Scheier, chief justice

Boston Municipal Court
Patricia E. Bernstein
Kathleen E. Coffey
Pamela M. Dashiell
Mary Ann Driscoll
Annette Forde
Shannon Frison
Sally A. Kelly
Tracy-Lee Lyons
Rosalind H. Miller
Eleanor C. Sinnott

District Court
Mary L. Amrhein
Julie J. Bernard
Heather M.S. Bradley
Martha A. Scannell Brennan
Beverly Cannone
Martine Carroll
Jacklyn M. Connly
Lynda M. Connolly, chief justice
J. Elizabeth Cremens
Patricia G. Curtin
Patricia A. Dowling
Deborah A. Dunn
Ellen Flatley
Stacey J. Fortes-White
Margaret R. Guzman
Kathryn E. Hand
Marianne C. Hinkle
Michele B. Hogan
Mary E. Hurley
Emogene Johnson Smith
Angel Kelly-Brown
Dyanne J. Klein
Rita S. Koenigs
Antoinette E.M. Leoney
Joan E. Lynch
Laurie MacLeod
Diana L. Maldonado
Janet McGuiggan
Rosemary B. Minehan
Diane E. Moriarty
Mary A. Orfanello
Patricia T. Poehler
Lynn C. Rooney
Bernadette L. Sabra
Bethzaida Sanabria-Vega
Barbara Savitt Pearson
Debra Shopteese
Sarah B. Singer
Sabita Singh
Roanne Sragow-Licht
Mary H. Sullivan
Bethzaida Vega
Maureen E. Walsh
Mary Dacey White
Therese M. Wright
Toby S. Mooney

Juvenile Court
Bettina Borders
Deborah A. S. Capuano
Leslie A. Donahue
Patricia M. Dunbar
Lois M. Eaton
Carol A. Erskine
Patricia A. Flynn
Marjory A. C. German
Dana Gershengorn
Leslie E. Harris
Mary Beth Keating
Judith A. Locke
Mary McCallum
Joan McMenemy
Amy L. Nechtem
Sally F. Padden
Judith Phillips
Mary O'Sullivan Smith
Gwendolyn R. Tyre
Kathryn A. White

Housing Court
Anne Kenney Chaplin
Dina E. Fein
Diana H. Horan
MaryLou Muirhead

Reflections and Interviews

Hon. Ruth I. Abrams

Massachusetts Supreme Judicial Court, 1977–2000
Massachusetts Superior Court, 1972–1977

Could you tell me a little bit about your family?

I was born in Boston, grew up in Newton, Mass. My father was a lawyer and my mother was a homemaker. I have one brother and one sister. All three of us are lawyers.

Did you ever go to your father's office?

Yes, we used to go on Saturdays. He took us to court when we were little; we thought the openings were quite funny.... He was in private practice under his name; when [my brother] George and I both became lawyers, we practiced under the law firm of Abrams, Abrams & Abrams. My father was the first Harvard Law-educated lawyer who had two children graduate from Harvard Law School.

So you grew up thinking it was fun to be a lawyer?

Yes.

When did you think you understood that it was unusual for a girl to be a lawyer?

A long time later. Because my father would say "women can do anything: women can do this, women can do that."

Where do you think he got that from? Did your mother have the same view?

I have no idea; I have absolutely no idea. He was way ahead of his time in many respects. My mother thought that my father was probably correct.

Justice Abrams received her undergraduate degree from Radcliffe College and then went on to Harvard Law School.

I graduated from Radcliffe in 1953 and started law school. Nineteen women were admitted and 560 men. Thirteen women graduated from Harvard in that class. Most of the faculty did not support admitting women. A "hostile environment" is what it would be called today.

The questions and answers presented here were adapted for this book from the Women Trailblazers in the Law "Oral History of Ruth I. Abrams" (Alice Richmond and Elaine M. Epstein, interviewers) with the permission of the American Bar Association and with review by Justice Abrams.

Hon. Ruth I. Abrams

IMAGE COURTESY OF MASSACHUSETTS SUPREME JUDICIAL COURT

Did they have anything at all that helped orient you or tell you what law school would be like, or even welcomed you?

No.... The dean had a dinner for women only.... It was a horrible dinner. All the dean said was that we would be lucky to get any job in law, even as a secretary. I don't think Harvard was ready to admit women even though it was 1950. [Harvard was] the last national law school to admit women.

Were you treated less than well by some of your classmates? Did some resent your being there?

You couldn't tell because they couldn't say anything. But many professors thought that women were taking the place of a man who had to support his family. Of course, many women have to support themselves and their families—that apparently scared a whole lot of people....

What did you do when you first got out of law school?

I worked with my father...and then I went over [to] the [Middlesex] DA's office. I did the appellate cases as an assistant DA.

Were there any gender issues in working in the DA's office? Did anyone treat you differently because you were a woman?

At first the police were not happy, but after a while they would rather have me than the other DAs. That was just a question of getting used to me. On that issue I think it's a question of familiarity.

How about the judges? Can you think of specific instances when they treated you differently because they didn't want you there?

Depends [on] who the judge was, but it was clear one judge didn't want me in the courtroom. He said I could not be in the courtroom without a hat and white gloves. The white hat and gloves were an excuse. Do you know how dirty the old Middlesex County courthouse was?

Women were wearing short skirts in the sixties. One of the judges had green curtains made for the jury box so that lawyers would not look at women jurors' legs.

And what did women wear in the courtroom in those days?

Dresses and skirts. Women were wearing short skirts in the sixties. One of the judges had green curtains made for the jury box so that lawyers would not look at women jurors' legs. The styles were crazy. But most women were wearing skirt suits. Basically a matching skirt, white blouse, and a jacket. Many judges objected to pant suits.

How did judges react to your being in the courtroom?

Variously. Different judges reacted very differently. [As an assistant DA] I was in the Somerville District Court on a probable cause hearing on an armed robbery. When the case was called, I stood up. The judge went crazy, absolutely crazy. He accused another assistant DA of sending a secretary to do lawyer's work. He threatened to get the DA disbarred for that and stomped off the bench. You could hear a pin drop in the courtroom. I don't know who told him I was a lawyer, the clerk, the court officer, or the DA. After a while, he came out and sat on the bench and presided, but didn't say much.

[After eight years,] I went to work with Bob Quinn. He was a classmate; he called me up and said, "How would you like to work for me?" He was just elected the attorney general...I would work in the criminal bureau....

How did you find that in relation to the DA's office?

Let me tell you I was chief of the appeals in the criminal division. Everybody in that division was paid more than I was. Absolutely everybody. So I went to see the attorney general, Bob Quinn. And I said, "That doesn't seem right," and he said, "Well, you aren't supporting a family." And I said to him, "How do you know I'm not supporting somebody?" And he said, "Well are you?" I said, "That's irrelevant, you made an assumption that isn't fair." To his credit, he corrected it to the extent he could. Not totally, but at least I wasn't the least paid.

So you were in the AG's office for how long?

1968 to 1971. Then I was staff counsel for the SJC.... [Chief Justice] Hennessey called me up and said, "The legislature is giving us this position.... We have decided we would like you to have it."

[David Nelson, an African-American judge who served with me on the Superior Court, had such a funny sense of humor.] He said to me one day, "Get in the...elevator with me and put this apron on." And I said, "What?" And he said, "Yes, do it." And then we headed down and he kept saying to people who were coming in, "We're just the cleaning help. We're just the cleaning help."

The Honorable David S. Nelson served on the Massachusetts Superior Court from 1973 to 1979. He was then appointed to the U.S. District Court for the District of Massachusetts. He was the first African American appointed to the federal court in Massachusetts.

IMAGE COURTESY OF THE U.S. DISTRICT COURT FOR THE DISTRICT OF MASSACHUSETTS

Justice Abrams explained that in 1972, while working at the Supreme Judicial Court, she received a call from Governor Francis Sargent, who invited her to interview with him for a judgeship. He asked her "a couple of questions" and then told her that he was nominating her for the Superior Court. In 1976, while serving on the Superior Court, she received a call from Governor Michael Dukakis's legal counsel informing her that she would be nominated for a vacancy at the Supreme Judicial Court.

Were you excited?

I was. I was. And I kept thinking, oh my God, I hope I can do the work. The worry every single woman lawyer I know has. Or had. They are more confident now....

In your first days and weeks on the SJC, how was it?

Terrible. I kept reading the briefs and saying, "This is horrible." Two competing interests and they were fairly close on some issues and fairly far apart on others. I would read those briefs ten, fifteen times.

Women Justices of the Massachusetts Supreme Judicial Court Since its Establishment in 1692

Justice	Years on Court
Ruth I. Abrams	1977–2000
Margaret H. Marshall	1996–2010, chief justice 1999–2010
Judith A. Cowin	1999–2011
Martha B. Sosman	2000–2007
Margot Botsford	2007 to present
Fernande R.V. Duffly	2011 to present
Barbara A. Lenk	2011 to present

So you found the work itself difficult?

Intimidating at first. Because you had to make the decision, and you had to write it....

As the years went on at the SJC, did you learn to like it more? Or less?

Yes, I did like it more.... It's not so frightening to make a decision.... You know, when you've got to make a decision, you make it. And then whatever the consequences are, you've made a decision....

Justice Abrams described the process of the justices discussing the cases in her early years on the court.

After arguments, the court has what it calls a "semble" and we go through each of the cases and everybody gives their view. Then the chief justice assigns the cases. The semble starts with one judge reciting on the case. Then it goes from the senior judge on the right, next on the left, and all the way down. And Chief Justice Hennessey used to miss me all the time. I originally thought it was because of the invisibility of women. But it wasn't that. He always missed everybody that sat in that last seat. But, for three or four years, I thought it was the invisibility of women that made him skip over me. I guess you can be too sensitive!

How many years altogether were you on the SJC?

Twenty-three. A long time.

What were the changes that you saw in the years that you were there?

Oh, it's unbelievable the number of women, the number of women in trial courts, the number of women law professors, it was just like a flood. I mean it's a slow flood, not a fast flood....

Hon. Denise Jefferson Casper

U.S. District Court for the District of Massachusetts, 2010–present

It is not often that I think about the path of my career in the law, but I recently had an extended period to do just that while going through the selection process to become a federal District Court judge. As I applied for this position and moved through the nomination and confirmation process, I necessarily had to reflect upon the professional opportunities I have had, the cases I have handled, and my experiences as an advocate in the courtroom. One of the very fortunate by-products of these reflections was that I also thought a lot about the mentors that I have had along the way, the lawyers and judges who paved the way for me and so many of my generation, and the values that my family instilled in me that led me to our great profession in the first place.

I am proud to say that I have benefited from the tutelage and guidance of a number of mentors during my career as an attorney. Some of these mentors were attorneys that I had the pleasure of working alongside in various workplaces, but a number were attorneys that I met through bar activities (activities that I undertook at the suggestion of an early mentor). Although I certainly learned a lot about lawyering from many of these mentors, I think that the most valuable lessons I learned from several of them were about working to make our profession a more noble one, making wise career choices, and maintaining a healthy work-life balance. In fact, one of my most memorable talks with a mentor, an accomplished member of the bar and a fellow working mother, came when I was a new mother of twins and was striving mightily, even with significant childcare support systems in place, to strike the right balance between the demands of work and the needs of two toddlers. She simply and wisely advised me that achieving a suitable work-life balance is a marathon, not a sprint. This conversation, which is probably a distant memory for her, made a lasting impression on me and gave me permission to feel that it was fine if my work-life balance at that time was still a work-in-progress. Having had good mentors along the way, I hope that my own efforts to mentor others have had, and will have, the same positive impact on the careers of other members of the bar.

▲ *Hon. Denise Jefferson Casper*

IMAGE COURTESY OF U.S. DISTRICT COURT FOR THE DISTRICT OF MASSACHUSETTS

As I have recently reflected on having great mentors, I have also come to recognize the benefit of having been an attorney at the bar of this Commonwealth, one that is rich with trailblazing African-American men and women, not the least of whom was Judge Reginald C. Lindsay, whose judicial seat I am very proud to accept. I have had the privilege of working

Judge Casper wrote this reflection on the eve of taking her oath of office on January 17, 2011.

Judge Casper with her sons.

IMAGE COURTESY OF DENISE JEFFERSON CASPER

with and being counseled by many of these trailblazers, but even those whom I admired from afar have inspired me with their determination to pave a new path for others, generosity of spirit, and devotion to the law.

Finally, the most personal introspection that this recent process has caused me to undertake involved the enormous influence that my family had upon my choice to become a member of the legal profession. I could not have even aspired to this profession, or my new endeavor as a judge, without the lessons that my parents taught me about hard work, respect for others, and humility. With those lessons still in my heart and mind, I look forward, proudly and humbly, to taking on my new duties.

Hon. Judith A. Cowin

Massachusetts Supreme Judicial Court, 1999–2011
Massachusetts Superior Court, 1991–1999

Supreme Judicial Court lore has it that in 1978, a major groundbreaking event occurred at the court: the first ladies' bathroom for the justices was installed. That there had not been one previously was hardly surprising. In the 286 years of the court's existence to that time, there had not been a single female justice until Governor Michael S. Dukakis ended the drought (and forced the alteration of the courthouse plumbing) by his appointment of Justice Ruth I. Abrams.

The cultural reality reflected by three centuries of male Supreme Judicial Court justices was not confined to that court. I recall my husband telling me that in his law school class of more than 500 students there were only twenty-two women. When I attended the same law school eight years later there were still twenty-two women in a class of equivalent size. Not long before, a young woman associate at a Boston law firm was told by a senior partner that she could not expect to advance in the firm because she was female. That young woman became a distinguished member of the Massachusetts judiciary. A number of years later, another woman, already a respected judge, was told that she could not enter a dining club through the entrance reserved for men. Even as more women began to appear in the law schools, they often encountered "glass ceilings" that obstructed their progress and limited the areas in which they were permitted to practice.

Shocking? Not really. The treatment of women in the legal profession reflected the general assumption and practices of the times. What is remarkable is the relative speed in

Hon. Judith A. Cowin

IMAGE COURTESY OF MASSACHUSETTS SUPREME JUDICIAL COURT

What is remarkable is the relative speed in historical terms in which the system reformed itself.

historical terms in which the system reformed itself. I graduated from law school in 1970. Forty years later, a woman is retiring after eleven years as chief justice of the Supreme Judicial Court. Of the Commonwealth's nine courts (seven trial courts and two appellate courts), women have served as chief justices of six of them. Women compete equally with men for judicial appointments; women achieve in private practice and in legal positions in government service. While there are obviously pockets of resistance, the old attitudes continue to disappear at a pace that makes ultimate equality inevitable.

This progress was plainly visible when I was appointed in 1991 to the Superior Court, the first of the two courts on which I have been privileged to sit. My appointment increased the number of women on the Superior Court bench to thirteen, hardly a controlling interest, but nonetheless a presence. To a great extent, the battle had been waged and won by others. I received support from men and women alike. I recall the statement of one of the senior members (male) of the court whom I had known previously: "You'll be surprised how all of these old judges who you thought were impatient and difficult when you were practicing law suddenly transform into the most charming and friendly colleagues imaginable." He was right.

After eight years as a Superior Court judge, I was appointed by Governor A. Paul Cellucci to a vacancy on the Supreme Judicial Court, the third woman to be so honored. It was not revolutionary. The way had been paved by Justice Abrams and by Chief Justice Margaret H. Marshall. From my perspective, my appointment, confirmation, and subsequent service on the court have taken place without particular reference to, or influence by, my gender, which is how it should be.

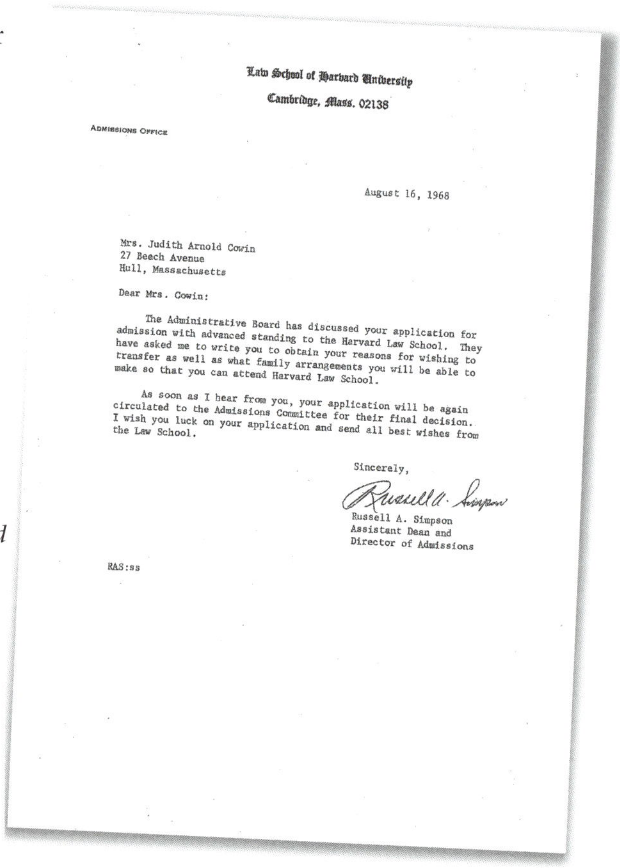

Law School of Harvard University
Cambridge, Mass. 02138

ADMISSIONS OFFICE

August 16, 1968

Mrs. Judith Arnold Cowin
27 Beech Avenue
Hull, Massachusetts

Dear Mrs. Cowin:

The Administrative Board has discussed your application for admission with advanced standing to the Harvard Law School. They have asked me to write you to obtain your reasons for wishing to transfer as well as what family arrangements you will be able to make so that you can attend Harvard Law School.

As soon as I hear from you, your application will be again circulated to the Admissions Committee for their final decision. I wish you luck on your application and send all best wishes from the Law School.

Sincerely,

Russell A. Simpson
Russell A. Simpson
Assistant Dean and
Director of Admissions

RAS:ss

"This letter was sent in response to my application to transfer to Harvard Law School after I had completed my first year at George Washington Law School. We had a two-year-old daughter at the time. Can you imagine such a letter being sent today?"
—Hon. Judith A. Cowin

IMAGE COURTESY OF HON. JUDITH A. COWIN

I have been asked to compare my experience on the two courts. In my view, the Superior Court appointment was in many respects the more difficult. The judge is almost always on stage and is often required to make decisions quickly on complicated questions that can affect the outcome of the entire case. He or she must manage schedules, jurors, lawyers, and court personnel as well as preside over trials, act on motions, and hold conferences. Decisions that displease at least one party must be made constantly, and often face-to-face with the loser. The job can be physically exhausting as well as emotionally draining. While colleagues are supportive, it is a one-person responsibility that cannot be shared.

By contrast, the Supreme Judicial Court is remote from many of these concerns. Cases come to our attention by means of paper and brief arguments by attorneys. While the work is unquestionably challenging, it can take on an abstract quality because, unlike a trial, it is removed from the people whom it directly affects. It is important to remember that a decision has a human impact; but it is also the case that a decision will influence the outcome of many proceedings, not simply the one presently before the court. It is a comfort to know that, unlike the trial court, the process is shared with six other justices.

I retired from the Supreme Judicial Court in April 2011. Two governors have given me extraordinary opportunities to participate for twenty years in a vibrant system with enlightened and experienced people committed to the common purpose to protect the law and to see to its equal application. It has been my good fortune to live at a time when women are full partners in the enterprise.

Hon. Barbara A. Dortch-Okara

Massachusetts Superior Court, 1989–present
Chief Justice for Administration and Management of the Trial Court, 1998–2003
Boston Municipal Court, 1984–1989

When I arrived in the Boston area, I was a young African-American woman from the segregated South who had the good fortune to be surrounded by teachers and community members who encouraged me to seek an education in the East. It was a turbulent time in the late 1960s when college campuses were hotbeds of protest and rebellion. Fortunately for me, my rebellion was limited to a change in my major from biology to politics, which caused me ultimately to choose a career in law.

Hon. Barbara A. Dortch-Okara

IMAGE COURTESY OF RICH MOORE, SUPERSTAR PHOTOGRAPHY

My college and law school days were a time of increasing opportunity for me personally and for African Americans in general. On the heels of the Civil Rights Movement and in the aftermath of the assassination of Dr. Martin Luther King, the enrollment of African Americans in colleges and graduate schools mushroomed with the help of scholarships and targeted recruitment efforts. There were only seven African Americans in my college freshman class. By my senior year, the number of African Americans on campus had more than doubled.

With the exception of my first year of practice with a Memphis record company, I have spent my legal career working in the public sector. When I returned to Boston to work for the City of Boston Law Department, the African-American lawyers I knew were working primarily in the public sector, with a few in private practice and an even smaller number in large downtown law firms. That handful of trailblazers in large firms was male; I can recall no African-American women in their ranks. Nevertheless, the African-American bar was well organized and vocal in its advocacy for the inclusion of black lawyers on the bench and in all aspects of the practice.

In 1984, I had the good fortune to be appointed by Governor Michael S. Dukakis to a seat on the Boston Municipal Court. Women judges and, of course, African-American women judges, were rare. At that time, there had been only two other African-American women appointed to the state court bench.[37] I was reminded of the rarity of my calling one day when I was listening to the report of a court psychiatrist who had interviewed a defendant to determine if there was a question of his competency. As the psychiatrist discussed his findings with the attorneys and me at the side bar, the defendant, who was nearby in a dock that opened up into the courtroom, began to point to me and shout, "Broad judge, broad judge, BLACK broad judge!"

Even from within the judiciary, there was puzzlement as to how female judges fit into the scheme of things.

Even from within the judiciary, there was puzzlement as to how female judges fit into the scheme of things. In the Boston Municipal Court during the 1980s there were two criminal nonjury sessions: the First Session and the Second Session. Because of the need for separate holding facilities for male and female detainees, all cases involving women were heard in the Second Session courtroom, to which the female holding dock was attached. Generally, judges rotated among the various court sessions—the First and Second Sessions, the jury sessions, and the civil sessions—on an equal basis. At a meeting of the judges, a former chief justice of the court once proudly proclaimed that only the two women judges on the court would be assigned to sit in the Second Session. He said we were doing great work with the women offenders and must continue. It was only when we met with him privately to decline the honor that it dawned upon him that he was not granting us a privilege.

Since my second appointment by Governor Dukakis in 1989, I have served happily on the Superior Court. In this court the challenges are endless, but the opportunity to resolve the most difficult conflicts in the lives of litigants has been the source of enormous satisfaction to me. While many of the criminal cases are troubling, I have always thought it was a privilege to be entrusted with the authority to bring some manner of resolution to these difficult situations.

In 1998, I was appointed by the Supreme Judicial Court to serve as Chief Justice for Administration and Management of the Trial Court. In one sentence, the job of the CJAM was to provide policy direction and operational support for the seven trial court departments. However, no single sentence could describe what the CJAM actually does. For me, the high points of my five-year tenure as CJAM were the advancement of our court technology plan through MassCourts, the professionalization of our interpreter services, and the implementation of a new job classification plan. While I was honored to serve in one of the highest leadership positions in our court system, there was so much more that remained undone. The position was and continues to be a lightning rod for the exasperation that we all feel because of the pulls and tugs of competing interests within and outside the courts.

Looking back over my career, I am amazed at the good fortune and extraordinary opportunities that have come my way through the good graces of a governor, my colleagues on the bench, and the members of the bar. With nothing but the hopes and dreams of my family of very modest means to propel me, I am still mystified as to how I landed in a position to receive the blessings bestowed on me. The single piece of advice I would give to anyone in similar circumstances today is what any of us would counsel: "Get the best education available to you." What is worrisome is that education is a far more remote possibility for African Americans today than it was when I was young. Certainly, a few of us are attaining heights that were previously unknown; nevertheless, for vast numbers of African Americans the doors of opportunity are not opening wider, but appear to be closing.

Hon. Raya S. Dreben

Massachusetts Appeals Court, 1979–2011

Family Support:

I was very fortunate because I came from a family [where] I was an only child, and where it was expected that I'd have a career.... My mother was a physician and my father was a professor and I had the feeling that I could, or they gave me the feeling that I could, do whatever I wanted. When I came out in the real world I was a bit astonished to find that there [were] all sorts of discrimination....

Harvard Law School:

I went to law school at Harvard. We were the second class of women. Out of a class of 560, there were nineteen women and we were spread out into sections. Each section had 150 people and there were four women in my section. At the time my consciousness had not been raised. So I didn't realize there was any problem. One of my classmates tells the story that she was asked by one of [our] classmates why she went to law school, and she told him, "Because I couldn't get into secretarial school." And he believed her. That's one of the things I remember. And then, after law school, I was lucky to be a clerk for Federal District Judge Bailey Aldrich...he really was a wonderful man.

Early Career: After her clerkship, Justice Dreben and her husband moved to Chicago. Her husband had been invited to teach at the University of Chicago Law School, and she spent one year as a teaching fellow while also having her first child.

[W]hen I came back to Massachusetts, I had a terrible time trying to find a job. I offered my services for nothing, to legal aid, to voluntary defenders. No one would hire me.... I'm sure it

This piece was adapted for this book from a March 2007 interview with the Honorable Raya S. Dreben at Brandeis University with permission from the interviewer, Stefanie T. Silverman (then a Brandeis student), and with review by Justice Dreben.

Hon. Raya S. Dreben. Justice Dreben's past and present law clerks presented her with a framed version of this photo in 1997.

IMAGE COURTESY OF MASSACHUSETTS APPEALS COURT

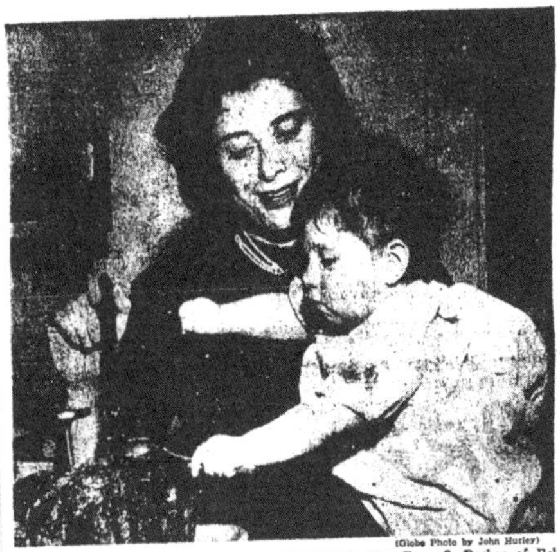

(Globe Photo by John Hurley)

NEW LAWYER—BUT STILL A HOUSEWIFE is Mrs. Raya S. Dreben of Belmont, who holds daughter Elizabeth, 13 months, while checking roast.

137 Pass, 158 Fail Bar Exam

Father of 8, Mother of 3 Among Successful Candidates

▲

Justice Dreben was featured in the Boston Daily Globe *when she passed the Massachusetts bar exam in 1957. The March 29, 1959, caption read: "NEW LAWYER—BUT STILL A HOUSEWIFE is Mrs. Raya S. Dreben of Belmont, who holds her daughter Elizabeth, 13 months, while checking roast."*

IMAGE SOURCE: *BOSTON GLOBE* ONLINE ARCHIVES

was because I was a woman and also because I wanted to work part time. They [employers] weren't ready for it. I wrote a letter to the chairman of the Board of Bar Overseers. He had written me a letter saying that I had come out first on the bar exam and he offered me a job. Somebody had died in his firm and he was afraid that the papers were messed up and he wanted someone to look through them. Because I was the lowest paid person—I was making $15 a day—this was in 1958–59—I was [also] able to work on a really interesting case. One of the partners in the firm was working on a matter, pro bono, a case involving sexually dangerous persons. The issue before the Supreme Judicial Court was whether persons who were committed civilly for a period of a year to life could be mixed with the general prison population. We claimed they could not; they weren't prisoners and were institutionalized supposedly for mental rehabilitation. We won that case.

While working at the firm described above, Justice Dreben was hired by Goulston & Storrs to assist attorney Herbert Ehrmann.

Goulston & Storrs at that time was really dreadful for women, at least for me. [Justice Dreben detoured to emphasize how different Goulston & Storrs is now, and commented that she would not have identified the firm by name except that the firm has become "one of the best places in Boston for women."] They wouldn't put my name on the door. They wouldn't put my name on the stationery. I had an argument with a partner on a legal matter, and it turned out I was right. He couldn't talk to me for three months.... [T]he men would walk by and say, "If you wore pants, you could have lunch with us."

When Ehrmann retired, Justice Dreben left Goulston & Storrs and was hired at Palmer & Dodge.

I went to Palmer & Dodge in 1964. There was another woman ahead of me. She did not become a partner for a long time, although others of her class at law school had become partners.... I could and did push and they would always say, "Oh, even if she's not a partner, you'll become a partner." And I said, "That's nonsense; you can't do that, and you wouldn't do that." It's always good to have somebody behind you to push for you; it's far more difficult to push for oneself. So I could push for her. She became the first woman partner in a major law firm in Boston. That was in 1969. And they were so proud of themselves; they were so pleased that they had done it, as if, you know, it was so natural, but it took a lot of pushing and it took her much longer [than men] to become a partner.

...[A]t Palmer & Dodge, which was really wonderful, where they put my name in the middle of the letterhead, even there, there was discrimination. First of all, when I was there, women were at the bottom of the compensation scale. Although we made much more money than we ever dreamed of making, we were on the bottom. There was a time when the probate department wanted to appoint a man as a partner but the rest of the firm was against his appointment. One of the partners, a very kind man, with three women partners sitting at the meeting, said, "But if he's not appointed, to whom will I give my clients?" We, as women, were just invisible.

▲

The Massachusetts Appeals Court in 1979, Justice Dreben's first year on the court. From left to right, front row: Hon. Frederick L. Brown, Hon. Donald R. Grant, Hon. Edmund V. Keville, Hon. Allan M. Hale (chief justice), Hon. Reuben Goodman, Hon. Christopher J. Armstrong; back row: Hon. Raya S. Dreben, Hon. John M. Greaney, Hon. Charlotte Anne Perretta, Hon. Rudolph Kass. Justice Perretta, the only other woman on the court until 1984, was the first woman appointed to the Appeals Court. She served from 1978 to 2009.

IMAGE COURTESY OF MASSACHUSETTS APPEALS COURT

While a partner at Palmer & Dodge, Justice Dreben had another opportunity to work on a case involving sexually dangerous persons. She related this incident which occurred at the Treatment Center at Bridgewater, then a facility under the Department of Mental Health located in a correctional institution under the Department of Correction.

What was really interesting was that, at first, the mental health physician in charge was very happy with me because I always pushed the mental health part rather than the prisoner part. But one day he disagreed with me and told the men (the inmates) that I was sending them down 'the river.' At the time I was also teaching at Harvard Law School. I went down to the Treatment Center at Bridgewater and I had, I think, 118 men there. I spoke to them and told them what I was doing and so on, and they asked brilliant questions. It was amazing. They were as intelligent as any of the students at Harvard, and at the end, they applauded me.... A group of them really helped me out on the case and we prepared a seventy-page statement of how horrible the conditions were. The Commonwealth folded and agreed to build a new facility and finally they did. That was rather exciting. It was the longest case that I ever had. I was teased by a Correction Department lawyer that I had to become a judge to get out of the case. It was true. I was on the matter from 1972 until I became a judge.

It was the longest case that I ever had. I was teased by a Correction Department lawyer that I had to become a judge to get out of the case.

Nomination to the Appeals Court:

I stayed at Palmer & Dodge until I came on the court. One of the partners was told that there weren't many women on the court, and someone close to the nominating commission told him that they wanted me to apply. I applied because I was asked to. I don't think I would have done it otherwise. I don't think I would have thought that I would have been appointed.

Women Judges of the Massachusetts Appeals Court Since its Establishment in 1972

Justice	Years on Court
Charlotte A. Perretta	1978–2009
Raya S. Dreben	1979–1997, recall justice 1997–2011
Edith W. Fine	1984–1995
Elizabeth A. Porada	1990–2003, recall justice 2003–2004
Barbara A. Lenk	1995–2011
Susan S. Beck	1997–2006
Fernande R.V. Duffly	2000–2011
Elspeth B. Cypher	2000 to present
Janis M. Berry	2001 to present
Cynthia J. Cohen	2001 to present
Ariane D. Vuono	2006 to present
Gabrielle R. Wolohojian	2008 to present
Sydney Hanlon	2009 to present
Mary T. Sullivan	2011 to present

We [Charlotte Perretta and I] were both nominated at the same time. I had trouble getting through the Governor's Council. There was some anti-Semitism. The Jews and the blacks were the last ones to get through. And in fact, there was also a senator...who talked about Dukakis and his "Jewdiciary."

Initial Experience on the Court:

Even when I came to the [Appeals] Court, which was in 1979, the court officers used to call me "deary," and I said, "No, no, you can't do that." And one of the judges commented when I was going down in the elevator with one of the people in the clerk's office, a male, "Oh Raya, I wish I could go alone in the elevator with you."...

The men didn't go out to lunch with us until there were three women. Once there were three women it was different. Yet, if the three of us went out to lunch, then it was a cabal.

Justice Dreben described what she considers to be her most important contributions as a judge:

We didn't fail and we showed that we were...as able as the men on the whole. I remember Sandra Day O'Connor, who also had, as you know, problems finding a job in Arizona or California. She was asked and she said, "A wise old woman and a wise old man will come out the same way in most cases." And I think that's true. I think that there are certain sensitivities, and that having diverse people, people of diverse backgrounds on courts makes a difference. There was one case where it really made a difference. One of the first cases I wrote involved the question of whether a woman as well as a man also had to support her children after a divorce. The woman had money and had remarried. We all agreed she also had the responsibility to support her children. I had inserted in my draft opinion many, many footnotes indicating the historical pattern of how women couldn't own property and so on, and I thought it was relevant.... Then one of my colleagues...made me take it all out. [Later] I wouldn't have taken it out. And what's also interesting is that today my colleague wouldn't have asked me to eliminate that material. So, it shows progress.

▲

From left to right: Hon. Elizabeth A. Porada, Hon. Fernande R.V. Duffly, and Hon. Raya S. Dreben.

IMAGE COURTESY OF MASSACHUSETTS APPEALS COURT

Hon. Fernande R.V. Duffly

Massachusetts Supreme Judicial Court, 2011–present
Massachusetts Appeals Court, 2000–2011
Massachusetts Probate and Family Court, 1992–2000

I didn't know any lawyers growing up, and it never occurred to me to become a lawyer until midway through college—when I had already considered (and abandoned) careers as an artist, junior high school teacher, professor of English literature, and print journalist. After spending a semester working at a legal aid office in a small town in Connecticut, I felt I had found the career (a bland word for what I felt—closer to a vocation, as in calling) I had been searching for my entire life. After college and before going to law school, I found jobs in other legal services organizations in Connecticut, Pennsylvania, and finally in Boston, where I worked on an SSI (Supplemental Security Income) advocacy project for the Massachusetts Law Reform Institute. Because I did not appear in court I didn't know then what I would learn soon enough: that there weren't a lot of women in the profession.

When I heard from Harvard Law School that I had been accepted for admission to the class of 1978, I hesitated, but not because women represented well under 20 percent of the class; I didn't know that at the time. I was just worried I wouldn't do well, that I'd be found out as some kind of fraud. For reasons I no longer remember, at some point I met with someone at Harvard I can no longer identify, to talk about my attending the law school. I recall that we talked about my essay, in which I mentioned my Chinese-Dutch heritage; he (I do remember it was a male) asked if I was looking for special consideration as an Asian American, because of course Asians weren't considered a minority. I can't recall what I said specifically but I am pretty sure that I didn't consider myself to be a disadvantaged minority. I remembered this conversation when I started classes, looked around, and saw that there were no Asian Americans in my section (one other half Asian American was in another section—after law school, when we worked together on a pro bono prison reform case, we used to joke that, together, we made up a whole Asian, but that one wasn't enough to start an organization). I also saw that there were many more men than women in my classes. Concerned about a potentially discriminatory admissions policy, a group of us women got together and met with an associate dean who told us that Harvard had a blind admissions policy and that the percentage of women and minorities in the class reflected the percentage of women and minorities who had applied. We developed a project, funded by Harvard, which involved our traveling to colleges and universities across the country where we talked with groups of women and minorities and encouraged them to apply; we followed up with phone calls and mentoring for women who applied and were accepted.

This is probably about the time that I became convinced that, with these kinds of efforts, it would be only a matter of time before women would overcome their secret fears of failure, apply to top academic institutions that, like Harvard, had reputations as male bastions, graduate, and develop into leaders in their chosen fields. I recall also that, before graduating, in choosing from among the law firms that came on campus to interview us, we women studied law firm profiles closely for signs of interest in hiring and promoting women and for opportunities to do pro bono work. And there were some. To be sure, there was an interview at a top Boston firm where my obviously pregnant state was commented on, and it was

Hon. Fernande R.V. Duffly

IMAGE COURTESY OF MASSACHUSETTS SUPREME JUDICIAL COURT

suggested that I would realize as soon as the baby was born that I would not want to work. But this did not happen at Warner & Stackpole, so I split my summer with them, working the other half for Nancy Gertner, whom I had admired because of her fearless advocacy for all kinds of clients.

I won't lie: becoming an associate and then a partner in the litigation department of a law firm while also having three children was not easy; and, yes, I observed and experienced what I will refer to as boorish behavior directed at women. It was a challenge navigating uncharted waters as a woman litigator in the firm, in court, and in the profession. Partners, clients, and opposing counsel seemed not quite to know what to make of us. But there were also wonderful men, and increasingly more women, who acted as mentors and role models, who hoped for my success and helped me achieve it. Looking back, this may have been a uniquely hopeful time for all of us—there were many men who believed that women as partners and judges would bring added value to the legal profession, and took concrete steps toward making this a reality for women by giving us opportunities to appear in court and meet with their clients. There were amazing women who, like Nancy (and my mentor Raya Dreben, and the many, many women I met as I entered the practice), had graduated before us and were successfully managing careers, even if they had families, while also finding the time to support and promote women.

▲

Justice Duffly at her graduation from Harvard Law School in 1978. She holds her daughter, Kate, born in November 1977.

IMAGE COURTESY OF HON. FERNANDE R.V. DUFFLY

If you had asked me thirty years ago to imagine the profession today, I would not have envisioned the place we are in, where women, people of color, and especially women of color, are not fully represented in the leadership positions within the legal profession. We are the role models and mentors now. The bright and committed young lawyers coming into the profession these days give me hope that they will work to ensure that the profession in which they will become leaders will, by then, be fully diverse.

Hon. Nancy Gertner

U.S. District Court for the District of Massachusetts, 1994–2011

What did you want to be when you grew up?

President of the United States. I remember in high school deciding that I wanted to be president. And before that I would be a senator, and since to become a senator was to become a lawyer, I would become a lawyer.

What appealed to you about being president of the United States?

I loved to speak. I love to fix things. I love politics. And I love to work with people. I also felt that I could communicate with people and that I was smart enough to try to figure out policy. It was always a dichotomy with me because on the one hand I love that public engagement but I also loved academics. I have always teetered between a public life and an academic life.

How did you decide to go to law school?

What I wanted to do was go to law school and teach law, which is something I actually have done for many years. I was not thinking of the courtroom. I wasn't thinking of litigation. In fact, just the opposite: I was thinking of academics or government. But I was hit in between the eyes by the politics of the sixties. It was very hard to go back into the library once you had represented draft dodgers or represented people who were picked up in the sweep arrests during demonstrations. I don't think I've stopped believing the mantra that if you're not part of the solution, you're part of the problem.

I don't think I've stopped believing the mantra that if you're not part of the solution, you're part of the problem.

When was your first experience of gender discrimination?

The first time was with a judge with whom I applied for a clerkship. He asked me during the interview if I would ever marry and have children. He said he didn't want to waste the clerkship on someone who was going to go marry and have children. And I didn't know what to do. Getting up and leaving seemed to be the end of one's career. Cursing didn't seem to be the appropriate thing to do. So I decided to make fun of him, but he didn't know it. I told him that I never planned to marry or have children. Now in fact, that was not far from the truth at that particular moment. I was reacting very strongly to a mother who had stayed at home, and I believed that I really was going to be a career woman and never marry and have children. About ten years later, at a party to celebrate the judge's retirement from the bench, I was asked to speak. My husband—actually, we were just living together at the time—was with me. I got up and reminded the judge that ten years ago, I promised him I would never marry and have children. Then I turned to him and got on my hands and knees and said, "Judge, I am thirty-nine and barren, release me from the pledge." And actually I got married soon thereafter.

But the worst reactions to me occurred in the courts of Massachusetts, which was very shocking and, I think, framed the kind of judge I would ultimately become. My first year I

Hon. Nancy Gertner

IMAGE COURTESY OF HARVARD UNIVERSITY

The questions and answers presented here are excerpted from an interview with Judge Gertner by Elizabeth A. Brown for this book in November 2010.

lost every case and I lost in ways that made it clear why: because I was the only woman in the courtroom and everyone felt free to make fun of me. I'd say something, and the judge would lean over and giggle to his clerk. About two years into my practice, I was with a young woman intern. I asked, "Judge, can this law student sit with me?" He looked up and said, "I thought one woman in a courtroom was bad enough." In the first year, any discretionary judgment that a judge had to make, I would lose, even continuances. I represented a black woman who was accused of failing to stop for a white police officer. It was a great case to cut your teeth on. I researched everything. I made measurements of the "crime scenes." I had briefs and memos and carefully put on our case. The judge turned to the jury and said, "Black people have rights, but no more rights than anyone else. If you find this officer guilty, you have to label an officer of the Commonwealth a miserable liar." Part of it was politics; I was representing a black person in an all-white courtroom. Part of it was what he knew he could get away with, because I was a young, powerless woman; it happened all the time. I was a partner in my own firm with two other people. In a major case against Gulf Oil, I would write to opposing counsel and he would call my male partner back. Finally my partner and I wrote the man a letter saying, "We're not going to deal with you at all until you come into the twentieth century." My own father, who was very traditional, was perplexed about the choices I was making, as was my mother. When I got into Yale Law School, my mother told me that I'd priced myself out of the male market. Not congratulations, but "Oh my, you're never going to get married."

Had she tried to discourage you from a professional career before you applied to law school?

Sure. Not direct discouragement. It was just that I wouldn't then be able to do the things she found so fulfilling. I wouldn't marry and have children. She was very frightened about that. I got that all the time. I ignored it. But I got it all the time.

Where do you think you got that strength from?

Whatever my father and mother were saying to me, they were doing different things. In other words there was a text and a subtext. The text was "don't go to law school, get married." The subtext was "you are interesting and your ideas are interesting to me. Let's debate politics until two in the morning." They would come to every event and every graduation. When my father died, I found a stack of clippings which included every time my name had been mentioned in any periodical. I knew he was doing that, so he encouraged me despite himself. My mother, too, to a lesser degree. Where did I get the courage? I think that ultimately they were supplying that to me. And then courage came from the women's movement. We had a blast. People talk about the women's movement as being humorless, but I just remember it as being so exciting.

Do you think there's still a need for the women's movement?

Without a doubt. Some people believe that the women's movement ended with giving women choices about whether to become a mother and whether to work. Those choices were not initially available when I started. I never believed that that was what we were fighting for. We were fighting to change both work and family. We were fighting so that it was not assumed that I would take care of the children when I had them nor was it assumed that the

"I was defending a prostitute. On closing argument, I wanted to say that she worked her fingers to the bone; but instead I said, 'She worked her bones off.' The jury was in stitches! I do that all the time. I guess it's a style in which you let the jury know that you're human . . . because you have no choice."

Judge Gertner retired from the U.S. District Court for the District of Massachusetts in 2011. She is now a professor of practice at Harvard Law School, and has served as a visiting professor at Yale Law School for many years. She was previously a visiting professor at Harvard Law for the 1985–86 school year. Her 1986 faculty yearbook photo and quote are shown here.

IMAGE SOURCE: *HARVARD LAW SCHOOL YEARBOOK* 1986 p.68

workplace would not be family friendly. The notion was we were going to revolutionize both. I think we failed.

And now there's a generation that believes that all one can do is make the personal choices in one's life to be at home or to be at work. Even though, as far as I'm concerned, they are often untenable choices. The workplace is not family friendly, and is squeezing women out. And you have an identity which is 2000 years old—motherhood—to easily assume. That's not a choice. And the numbers in the firms are dramatically declining. So it may be an object lesson in how fragile the changes were. You can look at Ruth Bader Ginsberg and Elena Kagan and Sonia Sotomayor and me and say we've won, but that's not remotely true. We'll win when we've changed work and family so that a woman can feel that she has the range of meaningful choices that a man has.

Do you feel like you experienced any gender discrimination on the bench?

It's not exactly gender discrimination. [Judge] Patti Saris and I talk about the meetings of our court where the judge leading the discussion was summarizing the conversation and said, "Well, Judge X said this, Judge Y said this, and Patti and Nancy said this." So it's not discrimination, but you understand your difference.

Certainly, there are awkward times with new lawyers or lawyers from outside of Boston. I remember a Southern lawyer who kept on thinking he had to shout at me, in the way that you do to someone that can't speak English. It was as if he was assuming that I had gotten my position from some political pull or something like that and couldn't be very smart. You know, but by the time I got to the bench I had done federal, state, criminal, civil, appeals, and taught at Harvard Law School. It was really hard to imagine that I was unqualified. But whenever I travel with my husband and kids and I'm in jeans, we always meet someone who only asks my husband what his business is, not mine. I can't believe I'm going through this again. But it's not discrimination in the sense that there are no meaningful adverse consequences in this stage of my career. It's atmospheric.

How do people react to you when you tell them you are a District Court judge? Do you say that, or do you make something up?

I try not to say it. But if you get into a conversation at a bank or something like that, I'll say what I do. Most of the time now people have images of women judges. Sometimes you get someone who says you don't look like a judge. And I always take that as a compliment. I really don't want to look like a judge.

You were a partner in what year of practice?

I was a partner by my second year of practice. If you create your own firm, you're always a partner. But it surely wasn't easy. When I was working for Norman Zalkind, he would send me out to get a continuance. I would even lose a motion for a continuance! I remember feeling that I was not serving my clients by trying to press the importance of being a woman lawyer. Perhaps they should have a male lawyer represent them; it was narcissistic of me to assume this role, possibly at their expense.

What helped you overcome that sense?

Winning. At the beginning, the legal world's skepticism matched my own skepticism. When I started winning, all of a sudden, I stopped being skeptical. My first year in practice, Norman Zalkind had me go into court to get a hearing on a motion to suppress postponed because he couldn't be there. I didn't know anything about the case. I took the file with me. I went before the judge and I said, "Mr. Zalkind, the lawyer in the case, requests that I get a continuance." The judge said, "No. You're going to do it." I replied: "I'm a new lawyer—I don't know anything about the case," and the judge with a twinkle in his eye and not a small amount of sarcasm said, "No, little lady, you're going to do it." So I said, "Give me two hours. Continue the case until one o'clock." I got on the phone. I read the file. And I did the motion to suppress. Until then, the only kind of trial work I did was trial work that I had scripted. You were afraid of being extemporaneous in court. You were afraid of actually listening. All of a sudden, I had to listen to the police officer. All of a sudden, I had to bend my examination to wherever he was going. I remember I didn't win the motion to suppress, but it was suddenly clear to me that I had done a really good job. At the end of my first year I finally won a motion to suppress, and then everything changed. You go into court the next time and you believe somehow you're fabulous. You have absolutely no basis for believing it the day before any more than the day after, but do. And that made an enormous difference because I could resist the kinds of comments that were being made to me. The anti-women comments no longer resonated with me.

As I have said, at the beginning, I believed those comments. My voice was higher than everybody else's. Every time I got nervous, I sounded like I would squeak. When I started to get more serious cases, I really worried whether I should subject people to my social experiment. And then over time I began to realize that in fact I should, and that it wasn't a social experiment. I actually brought to the table unique trial skills. I had a credibility with juries that oftentimes my male counterparts didn't have. I didn't know whether that was me, or the novelty of being a woman, but I started to be quite successful in front of juries.

What helped you overcome your doubts before you started winning?

Grit. I didn't feel like I could give up. You were somehow carrying the banner for all women in everything you did. We all felt that way. If you felt like crumbling in a courtroom because of something someone said, you wouldn't because you felt that if you did they would assume that all of you were weak. If you screwed up and didn't prepare, you felt that some judge was going to say, "I didn't think they were very smart either." And I had never failed before.

In fact, the first year of practice, I remember describing it like this: At Yale, it was like you're sitting behind someone who has a hat on in a movie theater and you tap the person on the shoulder and you say, "Excuse me, could you please remove your hat," and they go, "Oh, I'm so sorry. I didn't realize I had a hat on." But when I went into the Massachusetts courts, the guy in front of me had a hat on and I would say, "Excuse me, could you remove your hat," and he would say, "No, absolutely not." If you identified something gender-based when you were in law school, you were teaching people that this really wasn't something they ought to say. When I was in the courts of this Commonwealth, the gender discrimination was so pronounced and people were unapologetic about it. It was not just experiencing these kinds of things; it was experiencing these kinds of things in a world in which they were regarded as legitimate. Even in the Susan Saxe [bank robbery] case, the prosecutor would make comments about the clothes I was wearing. Once, I came in with a very loose dress; and he said: "You have no business looking pregnant representing that lesbian."

Is there anything you miss about practicing law?

Oh. I miss everything about practicing law. The first thing that I miss is knowing everything about the case when you're a lawyer. As a judge I only know what's presented, and lots of times you know there's a story going on that you're not hearing. I miss talking to juries. I love judging, but I don't pretend that I don't miss practice.

What do you love about being a judge?

It's little things and big things. The little things are to make the courtroom a humane place. As a trial lawyer, I was an outsider representing people who were also outsiders. What I love about being a judge is that I can make everyone feel welcome. That seems minor at first blush, but it is critical. It's the defendant who has a wireless transmitter that we use to interpret the proceedings for those who don't speak English. When I distributed the transmitters to his family so that they could know what was going on, I looked at their faces and realized that I had done something remarkable as far as they were concerned. I love that part of it. I'm very informal. I hate the ceremony of the courtroom. I do whatever I can to lighten the atmosphere.

It's also the ability to make the law clear. Because I was a trial lawyer, I care desperately that what I do as a judge is understandable to the people that I serve, so I write opinions that are in simple English. And I appreciate the ability to effect justice. You can't always do that in every case, but when you can it's like nothing else.

It's little things and big things. The little things are to make the courtroom a humane place.... And I appreciate the ability to effect justice. You can't always do that in every case, but when you can it's like nothing else.

How is being a judge different from what you expected?

In so many areas, the enterprise seems to be more about ducking and avoiding decisions than about making them. Discrimination law is about pleading requirements that have now become ridiculously strict, and about summary judgment standards that effectively enable a judge to substitute his or her judgment for the jury's. On the criminal side it is sentencing rules. It's a little better now that the rules have become advisory, but I dislike sentencing rules that required a judge to treat a human being like a column of figures. "I have no choice but to sentence you to 150 months," a judge would say, and then walk off the bench. Of course you have a choice. It's as if every pressure is to avoid making a decision and getting your name in the paper. It's extraordinary to me how much that matters to too many judges, the pressure of not being reversed and the pressure to avoid being criticized. Other than that, I love the job.

How have you balanced work and family?

I married well. First, I had a family at a time when my career was settled. I had a family at thirty-nine. That meant that I had the status in the community to be able to say to a judge, my son is sick, I can't appear. I'm not sure I could have done that when I was thirty. I also had a husband who loved me for everything, especially what I did for a living. It wasn't an issue about my going back to work after I had children. I mean even to raise the question is incredible to me. Of course I would. And that identity had predated the children's identity, so we had a genuine partnership and three children. He had a daughter by his first marriage, and together we had two little boys who are now not so little. That's how you combine it.

How has being a mother affected your practice? Your career? Your professional life?

It's in all sorts of little ways. I think that you get a sense of the world that everyone else is in. If your trajectory was just a career without a family, you wouldn't understand when a woman comes to you and says my baby is sick or the father says—judge this is very nice but I have to pick up the kid at daycare. You just wouldn't understand. You just have a sense of a world that is sloppy and messy and people get sick and kids intervene and you just don't have that if you didn't have a family.

Do you have hobbies?

I cook, ironically. My mother was a great cook, and I did everything I could to avoid being like her, so I didn't take up cooking until she had died. My husband and I both love to cook. I hike, bike, kayak, and swim! I also have a fancy telescope and love astronomy.

Do you have any advice for women who want to follow in your footsteps?

My career is a very odd career to follow. I feel blessed for having done what I thought was right and had this opportunity, the opportunity to be a judge. I teach at Yale Law School now and a male law student came up to me and was picking a paper topic. And he said there are some topics I don't want to try because I want to run for office and I don't want to have this on my record. And I never lived my life with the view that I was going to pull my punches now because there's something I could get later on. So one advice to lawyers, male and female, is to do what you love, and do it immediately. If you're a workaholic as I am, much of your life is spent at work. You should do what you love. And then I think that for women in particular, work is critical. The gains that we made in the seventies and eighties are fragile, very, very fragile, and you have to participate in the public and private work life. That doesn't mean pulling out the gender card; it does mean making your presence known and understanding that, beneath the surface, the old attitudes to women may still lurk.

Hon. Elena Kagan

U.S. Supreme Court, 2010–present

By Carol Steiker

Elena Kagan's ascent to the pinnacle of the legal profession—her appointment in 2010 at the age of fifty to the U.S. Supreme Court—was no surprise to anyone who knew her. As early as high school, she appeared in a high school yearbook photo clothed in a robe and holding a gavel. The child of a public-spirited lawyer and a public school teacher, Kagan grew up in New York City and attended the famously demanding Hunter College High School. She then obtained degrees from Princeton, Oxford, and Harvard Law School, where she collected many friends and admirers among her professors and peers. Her work as a writer and editor for both the *Daily Princetonian* and the *Harvard Law Review* was early evidence of Kagan's gifts of incisive thought and expression.

Justice Elena Kagan taking the Constitutional Oath on August 7, 2010, in the Supreme Court justices' conference room. Pictured are Chief Justice John G. Roberts, Jr. (administering the oath) and Jeffrey P. Minear, counselor to the chief justice (holding the Bible).

IMAGE COURTESY OF SUPREME COURT OF THE UNITED STATES; PHOTO BY STEVE PETTEWAY, COLLECTION OF THE SUPREME COURT OF THE UNITED STATES

Kagan's legal career began auspiciously and proceeded meteorically. She served as a law clerk first for Judge Abner Mikva of the U.S. Court of Appeals for the District of Columbia Circuit and then for Justice Thurgood Marshall of the U.S. Supreme Court. After working for a few years as an associate at the Washington, D.C., law firm of Williams & Connelly, Kagan joined the faculty of the University of Chicago Law School and was tenured four years later. Kagan then left academia to work in President Bill Clinton's administration in the roles of associate White House counsel, deputy assistant to the president for domestic policy, and deputy director of the Domestic Policy Council. President Clinton nominated Kagan for a seat on the U.S. Court of Appeals for the District of Columbia Circuit, but her nomination lapsed after the Republican-controlled Senate Judiciary Committee failed to schedule a confirmation hearing before the end of Clinton's second term in office.

In 1999, Kagan returned to academia, but this time to her alma mater, Harvard Law School, where only four years later she was appointed as the first woman dean in the law school's history by Harvard's then-President Lawrence Summers. Kagan's deanship was one for the ages: she achieved an unprecedented expansion of the faculty, which brought in an enormously diverse array of new talent; she presided over a hugely successful capital

Carol Steiker is the Henry J. Friendly Professor of Law and special advisor for public service at Harvard Law School.

IMAGE COURTESY OF HARVARD UNIVERSITY

The current and former women justices of the U.S. Supreme Court, from left to right: Justices Ruth Bader Ginsburg, Sandra Day O'Connor, Sonia Sotomayor, and Elena Kagan at an April 2012 panel discussion celebrating the thirtieth anniversary of O'Connor's first term on the Court. It was the first time all four justices appeared together in public

IMAGE COURTESY OF NEWSEUM, PHOTO BY MARIA BRYK

campaign as well as the construction of an enormous new law school building; and she won the hearts of the notoriously critical student body, who celebrated her with "We (heart) Elena" T-shirts.

In early 2009, Kagan broke another gender barrier when President Barack Obama appointed her to be the first female solicitor general of the United States (Justice Marshall, for whom she clerked, had been the first African-American solicitor general). Kagan's first oral argument in that role was her defense of the McCain-Feingold campaign finance reform law, which was invalidated in a five-four decision by the Supreme Court in *Citizens United v. Federal Election Commission.* Also like Justice Marshall before her, Kagan was elevated from solicitor general to the Supreme Court; she was President Obama's second appointment to the Court, nominated in May 2010 and confirmed that summer.

As a justice, Kagan's first majority opinion was issued in January 2011 in *Ransom v. FIA Card Services,* an eight-one decision on an issue of bankruptcy law. Kagan's first dissent was issued in April 2011, in a five-four decision in which Kagan wrote for all four dissenters. The case, *Arizona Christian School Tuition Organization v. Winn,* held that state taxpayers lack standing to challenge a state tax credit on that ground that it unconstitutionally subsidizes religious schools in violation of the Establishment Clause. In her dissent, Kagan argued forcefully that tax credits are as much of a government subsidy as direct payments, offering a number of provocative examples, such as the following: "Suppose a State desires to reward Jews—by, say $500 per year—for their religious devotion. Should the nature of taxpayers' concern vary if the State allows Jews to claim the aid on their tax returns, in lieu of receiving an annual stipend?"

In an admiring review of this dissent, Stanley Fish wrote in his *New York Times* "Opinionator" blog that Kagan's opinion displayed "a powerfully understated style of argument, inexorable without being aggressive, comprehensive without claiming to be so, regnant even when it is on the losing side."[39] Concluded Fish: "I look forward to more of the same." More will be forthcoming, as Kagan, the Court's youngest member as of this writing, continues her tenure in terms to come.

Hon. Barbara A. Lenk

Massachusetts Supreme Judicial Court, 2011–present
Massachusetts Appeals Court, 1995–2011
Massachusetts Superior Court, 1993–1995

All four of my grandparents separately emigrated from Poland early in the last century and Polish was my parents' first language. My father grew up in Brooklyn and made it through high school, but family needs and the Depression killed off his dream of college. He worked eighty-hour weeks running his family's small bookbindery, his hands thick with calluses from years of handling hot printers' type. My mother grew up on a hardscrabble Long Island potato farm and left home as early as she could. Equipped with an eighth-grade education, she became a live-in domestic worker for wealthy families in the city.

I grew up in Queens, blessed with parents determined that I would not earn my keep as they did. They valued family, hard work, and education, and made sure that I did, too, leaving no doubt that college was in my future. Perhaps because she had been so often stung by the treatment she had received as a maid, my mother insisted on something else, too. All persons, no matter what they did for a living or how they dressed, were to be treated with courtesy, dignity, and respect.

My parents were of modest means and did without so that I could go to the best schools they knew, a Catholic elementary school, and later, a small, all-girls Catholic high school run by an order of French nuns whose mission was to prepare the daughters of families like mine for college. When he was fifty-two and I was sixteen, my father died unexpectedly. He had been the sole support of our family and his death changed everything except my mother's resolve.

Hon. Barbara A. Lenk

IMAGE COURTESY OF MASSACHUSETTS SUPREME JUDICIAL COURT

With Social Security benefits as a base, my mother went back to manual labor as an over-sewing machine operator while I worked part time during the school year and added full-time work during the summers. The French nuns picked up where my mother left off, with written homework in every subject every night, inspiring us to believe that we could do anything. They also made it clear to us that, as educated women, we would be duty-bound to leave the world "not less and worse but greater and more beautiful" than when it was given to us. I was elected president of the school in my senior year, one of the highest honors I have ever had. With the nuns' help, I won full-tuition scholarships to Fordham University in the Bronx, to which I commuted from Queens, keeping my jobs to pay for books and clothes.

At the time, Fordham was in the early days of coeducation, having long been a college for men taught by Jesuits, and women comprised barely a sixth of my class. There were fewer still in my major subject, philosophy, and in any given class I was often the only woman. To their lasting credit, the somewhat stunned Jesuits managed to look past the clothing, hair, and gender straight through to the mind. Upon graduation, I was the first woman given the philosophy department award for excellence. With my professors' encouragement, I competed for one of the 100 nationally awarded and highly coveted Danforth Foundation fellowships, which paid all graduate school tuition, room, and board for four years. This was a huge break for me, and I was able to spend the next four years at Yale studying political philosophy. I had written half of my doctoral dissertation when I decided that the academic life was not for me. Given my growing interest in the intersection of law and political philosophy, as well as my financial responsibilities, I was grateful for the opportunity to attend Harvard Law School. While there, I finished my dissertation and defended it at the end of my 2L year, surprised and delighted to find one of my Jesuit philosophy professors in the Yale conference room beaming at me and being the first to greet me as "Doctor Lenk." During law school, perhaps because of the years at Fordham and Yale spent in the almost exclusively male academic field of philosophy, shocking as it may be now, it seemed then a breath of fresh air to be at a place where fully 25 percent of my class was female. When it came time to look for work, though, it was hardly a surprise that I would be among the first and few women at my law firm.

▲

Justice Lenk in 1998 with her family.

IMAGE COURTESY OF HON. BARBARA A. LENK

Nonetheless, pretty much from the start, I fit in comfortably at Brown Rudnick. I was given many opportunities and was carefully mentored by Donald Paulson, a wonderful lawyer of great skill and integrity. I liked my colleagues and enjoyed the challenges of practicing law and helping to manage the firm. As was true for many women then, rainmaking was not my strong suit, but I managed to sustain a wide-ranging civil litigation practice on the trial and appellate levels. I represented newspaper and other media clients on First Amendment–related matters as well as a broad-based business clientele in a number of areas including corporate, construction, employment, intellectual property, lender liability, and real estate–related disputes. In the years preceding my appointment to the Superior Court bench in 1993, I had been elected annually by the equity members of the firm to serve on the eight-person policy committee which set the firm's direction and dealt with the myriad issues involved in the management of a large multi-office law firm. I was the first and, for too long, only woman on that committee. Single at the time, I had considerable flexibility to come in early, work late, and travel at a moment's notice. The glass ceiling was not as low for me as it was for many women who were managing households.

After leaving practice, I was a Superior Court judge for several years, presiding over all manner of civil and criminal trials, both jury and jury-waived, and deciding a vast array of motions. I feel fortunate to have had this opportunity, not only because I learned so much about areas of the law in which I had not practiced, but also because I came to appreciate firsthand the complex realities of the work done in the trial courts. Trial court judges are on the frontlines of justice every day: confronting newly-emergent legal issues; dealing directly with lawyers, jurors, and litigants; sentencing people before them to prison in the presence of family members, some of whom weep for the victims and some for the prisoner. Appellate judges of necessity stand at a further remove in order to do our job of error correction and of declaring the law in ways that can function as precedent for bench and bar. Having thereafter spent almost sixteen years on the Appeals Court before my recent move to the Supreme Judicial Court, I know that I am a better appellate judge because I was first a trial court judge.

I have lived on both sides of many fences, starting with the socio-economic divide, and I know something about how difficult life can be for those with limited resources. Being one of relatively few women law firm partners with management responsibility was eye-opening, too, and taught me to see things from many vantage points. Still, though, I was unable at that time to discern how many advantages I had and simply took for granted just by having been born into an intact, white, Christian, and indubitably mainstream family. I had not yet had the experience of being a member of a minority group. That came at the age of thirty-seven, prior to my becoming a judge. Until then, I had assumed that I was straight; that assumption gave way when I met the woman who is now my spouse. Times then were considerably less hospitable for gays and lesbians and I have always been a private person. It took me longer to come out, other than to close family and friends, than I like to remember. In the end, it was having children and becoming a judge—which happened almost at the same time—that turned the tide. Both require clarity about oneself.

I have lived on both sides of many fences, starting with the socio-economic divide, and I know something about how difficult life can be for those with limited resources.

In the life-altering years that followed, we were blessed with two daughters and became a multi-racial Jewish family. In addition to knowing the joys and worries of parenthood, I came also to know something about bigotry and racism. I began to see things that before had simply escaped my notice, and I understood much more clearly the power of words and of law to shape and convey reality. Although I had long appreciated the awesome power that law has to affect lives, it came home to me in every sense when, after the decision in *Adoption of Tammy,* 416 Mass. 205 (1993), I was able to become the legally-recognized parent of our two daughters.

I now have the humbling privilege to serve on the Supreme Judicial Court, the oldest appellate court in continuing existence. Its history is replete with luminaries on whose shoulders my colleagues and I gratefully stand. We come to the work without constituencies other than those who seek justice, striving to remain faithful to our oaths, to the rule of law, and to our obligation to assure fair and equal treatment of all who come before our courts. That being said, each of the seven of us, like all judges, has had individuating life experiences that have left their mark. Mine have bridged some pretty significant divides. I hope they will enable me to see things from many perspectives as I try, in the words of the French nuns of my girlhood, to leave the world not less and worse but greater and more beautiful than when it was given to me.

▲

Hon. Sandra L. Lynch

IMAGE COURTESY OF U.S. COURT OF APPEALS FOR THE FIRST CIRCUIT

Hon. Sandra L. Lynch

U.S. Court of Appeals for the First Circuit, 1995–present (Chief Judge 2008–present)

Your father was an Army intelligence officer, so you spent your early childhood in a number of very different areas of the world. How did those experiences impact you?

Because my father was an Army intelligence officer, my family moved quite a lot. We lived in a number of states, as well as in Germany, Italy, and Taiwan. This upbringing instilled in me an enormous love of this country and its values and great gratitude that I was born a citizen of the United States. When abroad, we saw enormous poverty and inequality, in very different societies.

You went from a public high school in Dallas, Texas, to an elite, Northeastern women's college (Wellesley) during the second half of the turbulent 1960s. What was that like?

I was very fortunate in receiving a full scholarship to attend Wellesley College. The cultures, mores, and expectations at Wellesley and in Dallas were very different. In the 1960s it was evident that the promises of the Constitution, especially of equality of opportunity, had not yet been fulfilled in our society. It was a very turbulent time: there was the civil rights movement, including the Freedom Riders going to the South. There were protests against the war in Vietnam, and the women's rights movement was emerging. The climate of the times, with the emphasis on the need for change, influenced my decision to go to law school.

How did you decide to go to law school? Did your undergraduate experience at Wellesley affect your career path?

My college constitutional law class was fascinating; the courses in my major (philosophy) were rigorous, and gave training in logic, how to think through problems, and different modes of analysis. I concluded that law provided ways, ways which were accepted as legitimate, of addressing many of the social tensions and injustices in our society. There were no lawyers in my family but I was drawn by the promise of the law.

It was invaluable to have the experiences of having to face overt discrimination firsthand and to stand up and do something about it.

Ten percent of your Boston University School of Law class was composed of women, which was considered very high at the time. How were you and your female classmates treated? Is there strength in numbers?

I am very proud of BU Law School for being a leader in opening its entering class much more widely to women than other law schools did at the time. That decision was not warmly welcomed by all members of the faculty or even the student body. In my first year, a contracts professor made a derogatory comment about women, saying, "Well, class, now we know why women are not noted for their beautiful minds." I led a walkout of all of the women in the class in protest. Unfortunately, there was a similar incident during my third year in which I led a group to talk with the dean of the school about "dumb broad" jokes

The questions and answers presented here are from a written interview with Chief Judge Lynch in January 2012.

being made in class. It was invaluable to have the experiences of having to face overt discrimination firsthand and to stand up and do something about it.

After graduating from BU Law, you clerked for U.S. District Court Judge Raymond Pettine in Rhode Island, where you were that court's first woman law clerk. How was that experience and was it a smooth transition from law school?

U.S. District Judge Raymond Pettine in Rhode Island broke with convention and showed courage in hiring me as the first female law clerk in the history of that court. The clerkship was a wonderful experience. I worked with a very wise, seasoned, and respected trial judge, who gave me opportunities to take on responsibility in important matters.

Your clerkship was just one of many important "firsts" in your career. You've stated before that your generation of women is used to being first. But being a "first" can be very tough. How do you shoulder that responsibility?

In all of the positions I have held as the "first" woman, I have felt very keenly the need not only to be successful, but to excel. Anything other than success simply was not an option. Nor was it an option to in any way assist the cause of those who thought women were inferior and not up to holding the responsibilities of important positions.

Is there a case that you worked on when you were at the Massachusetts Department of Education or Foley Hoag that you are most proud of?

It is hard to single out a case. I worked on many very high-profile litigations, including the Boston school desegregation case, the Woburn toxic tort case, and reproductive freedom cases. The visibility of such cases adds additional pressure to do your best work.

How have you juggled work and family throughout your career?

My experience is that the phrase "achieving a work-life balance" was useful but was a fiction. The phrase suggests an orderly repose; the reality is things were never in balance. There were constant, unrelenting, and competing demands from all aspects of your life. You simply did the best you could. What does happen is that you do only what is essential. You postpone what you can; you know that you will enjoy the company of your

Boston Mayor Thomas Menino, Judge Lynch, and a student moot court competitor at an event by Discovering Justice, a Boston-based civic and justice education nonprofit organization.

IMAGE COURTESY OF JOHN HEYMANN PHOTOGRAPHY

friends in the future, but that you cannot hope to do everything at all points in your life.

When you were appointed to the U.S. Court of Appeals for the First Circuit, were there any particular challenges you faced being the only woman? Did you have women judges on other courts that served as your role models?

It was a tremendous honor to be appointed to the U.S. Court of Appeals for the First Circuit, a court I had long respected. There were other women who were the first women on their federal courts, notably Rya Zobel on the District of Massachusetts and Sandra Day O'Connor on the U.S. Supreme Court. I've been fortunate to know both of them and still hold them in awe for their ability to handle their roles with such grace.

How did you find the transition of moving from practicing to being a judge?

Moving from private practice as a litigator [at Foley, Hoag & Elliot] to being a Court of Appeals judge was not difficult. In private practice you must listen well to your clients and get to the essentials of their concerns and find an efficient way of resolving the problem. So, too, in being a judge: you must listen well to the arguments and come out with a resolution which goes to the heart of things in conformance with law. The collegiality of working with others at the firm was a good model for the collegiality of working with my colleagues.

Is there a case you've been involved with as a judge that you are especially proud of? Your dissent in 1996's *United States v. Rivera* is notable as it led to Congress updating the definition of "serious bodily injury" under the federal crime of carjacking to include rape.

It is particularly satisfying when I write decisions which cause a change in the law which remedies a situation of injustice.

It is particularly satisfying when I write decisions which cause a change in the law which remedies a situation of injustice. In *United States v. Rivera*, Congress updated the definition of "serious bodily injury" under the federal crime of carjacking to include rape. In immigration cases, as a result of my opinions, administrative rules were revised to bring them back into alignment with the more humane intentions of Congress. My opinions have had influence. One law review article concluded, after a several-year study, that the opinions I authored were among the opinions most frequently cited of any of the federal courts of appeals judges.

You are now chief judge of the First Circuit. Have you felt a particular drive to excel and bring a unique perspective to the position since you are the first female chief judge?

Every new position of responsibility increases the pressure to excel. Being chief judge is a very special and different role and requires some different skills. It is essential that the job be done well. The federal courts are the third branch of the federal government, and are the quiet branch. The courts are also the branch in which the people have the highest level of confidence and of which they have the highest expectations. As a matter of our democracy, it is very important that this public trust and faith be met and maintained. The courts must be, and must be seen to be, fair, impartial, unbiased, and free of partisanship in applying the law. My particular life experiences have likely enhanced, in a personal way, the importance of those requirements.

Hon. Margaret H. Marshall

Massachusetts Supreme Judicial Court, 1996–2010 (Chief Justice 1999–2010)

Why did you decide to attend law school?

I came as a graduate student to the United States to study art history at Harvard University, switching soon to complete a master's degree at the Harvard Graduate School of Education. Initially I had no intention of remaining here, but after several years it became clear that I could not return to South Africa, and I extended my stay here and ultimately became a citizen of the United States. While studying at Harvard, I became fascinated by the American form of government, with its guarantees of individual rights and equality under the law. It was so different from the perverted legal world that characterized life under apartheid in South Africa. I enrolled in Yale Law School with no expectation that I would have a career as a lawyer, but to learn more about American government. At Yale, I fell in love with the law and decided to pursue a legal career. It is a choice I have never regretted.

So with your Yale law degree, you headed back to Boston?

Yes. I joined the Boston firm of Csaplar & Bok, a relatively new firm at the time, initially as an associate in the litigation department. The work was wide-ranging and interesting, and I learned a great deal. I became a partner there, and later moved to Choate Hall & Stewart, which had a far larger litigation practice. At every step I absolutely loved the practice of law. I was fortunate to have fascinating work and superb colleagues.

You also served as president of the Boston Bar Association?

During my years in private practice, I became an involved member of the Boston Bar Association, an organization that was formed by John Adams and others in the latter part of the eighteenth century. I was honored to be elected to serve as president of the Boston Bar Association in 1991–92, the second woman to hold that position.

Then you became general counsel to Harvard University?

I accepted the invitation to become the vice president and general counsel of Harvard University (I was the first woman to hold that position) in part because my practice at Choate Hall & Stewart had begun to concentrate on intellectual property issues, and I anticipated that Harvard would be a natural fit for me. At the time I had no intention of leaving Choate, where my practice was thriving, where I was challenged every day, and where I worked with outstanding colleagues who had quickly become close friends. But Harvard was an exciting opportunity, and one from which I could not walk away. The decision was the correct one for me, and I thought I could not be happier, professionally, than I was at Harvard.

Hon. Margaret H. Marshall

IMAGE COURTESY OF MASSACHUSETTS SUPREME JUDICIAL COURT

The questions and answers presented here were adapted for this book from "A Conversation with Margaret Marshall," (Linda Greenhouse, interviewer; John F. Kennedy Presidential Museum and Library, October 4, 2011) and other public speeches, with review by Chief Justice Marshall.

You were clearly very content at Harvard. What led you to apply for a position as an associate justice of the Supreme Judicial Court?

In 1996, an opening occurred unexpectedly on the Supreme Judicial Court when Chief Justice Paul Liacos stepped down before he reached age seventy. I took what felt like an enormous risk at the time and asked to be considered to fill that vacancy. As Harvard's general counsel, my work was demanding and deeply satisfying; I had certainly not thought of leaving my position. But I also knew that opportunities for appointment to the Supreme Judicial Court, a court that I had always revered, are rare. So I decided to submit an application. Governor William Weld nominated me as an associate justice and, in 1996, I became the second woman to serve on the Supreme Judicial Court in its then three hundred and four year history.

And several years later, you were appointed chief justice of the Supreme Judicial Court, the first woman to hold that role?

Yes. A short three years later, Governor Paul Cellucci nominated me to serve as chief justice. I took the oath as chief justice in October 1999.

What was it like to serve as the first woman chief justice of the Supreme Judicial Court?

It was a great honor to serve as chief justice. The Supreme Judicial Court has a long, proud history of expanding the boundaries of human liberties. John Adams, the leading constitutional theorist during the American Revolution, was the primary author of the Massachusetts State Constitution of 1780, the oldest written constitution still in effect in the world. It was the primary model for the United States Constitution. Three years after the Massachusetts Constitution was ratified, the court concluded in 1783 that slavery was "repugnant" to the constitutional guarantees of equality and freedom contained in Article I of the Massachusetts Declaration of Rights. The case was the first anywhere in the world to rely on a written constitution to abolish slavery. And there have been many other groundbreaking decisions since then. For example, we were national leaders in decisions providing counsel for indigent defendants in criminal cases,[40] and invalidating the use of peremptory challenges based on race.[41]

You wrote the majority opinion in the 2003 *Goodridge v. Department of Public Health* case in which the Supreme Judicial Court was the first to recognize marriage for same-gender couples. You wrote that barring same-sex couples from marriage deprived them of "membership in one of our community's most rewarding and cherished institutions. That exclusion is incompatible with the

◀ *Hon. Margaret H. Marshall being sworn in as chief justice of the Supreme Judicial Court by Governor Paul Cellucci in 1999.*

IMAGE COURTESY OF GOVERNOR'S PRESS OFFICE

constitutional principles of respect for individual autonomy and equality under the law."

Justice Louis Brandeis's famous description remains apt. States, he said, have a unique ability "to remold, through experimentation, our economic practices and institutions to meet changing social and economic needs." "It is one of the happy incidents of the federal system," he continued, that "a single courageous state may, if its citizens choose, serve as a laboratory; and try novel social and economic experiments without risk to the rest of the country."[42] The Supreme Judicial Court broke ground with regard to gay marriage. But the foundation for that decision had been laid in Massachusetts over many years. For example, in Massachusetts it was by that time legal for same-sex parents to adopt children [*Adoption of Tammy*, 1993]. The state placed foster children with same-sex couples. That was not the case in some other states, where same-sex couples were not permitted to adopt children or provide homes for foster children. We, the justices of the Supreme Judicial Court, were dealing with marriage in Massachusetts only. It is also important to remember that over the course of time marital status had become closely linked to economic status, and to deny marriage to same-sex couples was to deny them and their families access to many economic benefits and obligations of marriage.

How did the court system change during your tenure as chief justice?

When I became chief justice, I embarked on a plan to reform the administration of justice by radically revamping the culture and operation of the courts. I convened a blue-ribbon commission to create a plan for change. Court leaders worked closely with judges, judicial staff, members of the legislature, the organized bar, business leaders, and others to move in the direction of reform. Together, we created the foundations of a new court culture of accountability, efficiency, transparency, and the highest quality of service. My "mantra," if I can term it that, was to make the Massachusetts courts a national model of excellence in every possible way. I am immensely proud of the many successes we achieved during my tenure.

My "mantra," if I can term it that, was to make the Massachusetts courts a national model of excellence in every possible way.

Tell us about your leadership role in the Conference of Chief Justices.

The overwhelming amount of judicial business in the United States, over 98 percent, takes place in state courts. At last count (2009) some 48 million cases are filed each year in state courts, and that excludes traffic offenses. So the performance of state courts is critical for the delivery of justice in the United States. The Conference of Chief Justices (CCJ) brings together the heads of the judicial branches in the fifty states, the District of Columbia, and several U.S. territories to work to improve the administration of justice. It serves as a "best practices" resource for every state judiciary. I was elected president of the Conference of Chief Justices in 2008, at a time when across the country states courts were facing dramatic reductions in funding and other major challenges. As president of CCJ, I worked hard to raise the national profile of CCJ, and to persuade organizations such as the American Bar Association to become advocates for better funding for state courts. Our nation's rule of law depends to a large extent on a system of independent and efficient state courts, and yet very little attention is paid to state courts nationally. That has begun to change, and I am pleased that I have been able to play some part in that shift of focus.

The composition of the Massachusetts Supreme Judicial Court during Marshall's last years as chief justice. From left to right, front row: Hon. Roderick L. Ireland, Hon. Margaret H. Marshall, Hon. Francis X. Spina; back row: Hon. Ralph D. Gants, Hon. Judith A. Cowin, Hon. Robert J. Cordy, Hon. Margot Botsford.

IMAGE COURTESY OF MASSACHUSETTS SUPREME JUDICIAL COURT

Looking back, I think I learned two lessons. The first is to take risks.... The second is to accept opportunities to excel and to lead.

As you look back over your long, varied, and fulfilling career in the law, what advice do you have for young women entering the field ?

At the beginning of my career, I had no expectation, no idea, that I would become a judge, let alone a chief justice of a great court. Looking back, I think I learned two lessons. The first is to take risks: to paraphrase the words of the amazing Yogi Berra, if there is a fork in the road, take it. The second is to accept opportunities to excel and to lead. Leaders, I have often said, are made and not born. Talent and competence are necessary. But as I made my way in the legal profession, I came to understand that leadership is less about raw ability and more about applying a set of leadership skills that can be learned by anyone. Take the time to learn those skills.

Hon. Angela M. Ordoñez

Massachusetts Probate and Family Court, 2000–present

By Hon. Barbara A. Lenk

> *"Be the opener of doors for such as come after thee."*
> —Ralph Waldo Emerson

> *"Be the change you want to see in the world."*
> —Mahatma Gandhi

> *"Pay it forward."*
> —*Pay it Forward* (Warner Brothers, 2000)

Watching the movie *And Justice for All* when she was sixteen years old "changed my life," says First Justice of the Norfolk County Probate and Family Court Angela M. Ordoñez. She knew then that she wanted to get involved in the legal world but, given her modest family circumstances, did not have any idea how to go about it. Not knowing any lawyers, she saw her opportunity when a high school English teacher mentioned in class that her husband was an attorney. Angela waited after class until she could speak with the teacher about her own interest in the law. The kind-hearted teacher offered to put her in touch with the lawyer-husband. Doubtless impressed with the teenager's pluck, the lawyer arranged for Angela to volunteer several afternoons a week at the local District Court probation department, where she worked through high school. There, she met dedicated people who not only taught her about the court system but who showed confidence in her and encouraged her to set her sights on law school. By their example, the teacher, the lawyer, and the probation department employees taught the young Judge Ordoñez an important lesson about life. "Pay it forward" became her favorite maxim: "Someone has helped me and I must help someone else." It's the code she lives by.

Anyone who has gone to a bar association dinner or similar event with Judge Ordoñez learns about that code. You also learn that you should eat first the next time. Judge Ordoñez stops at her dinner table just long enough to greet everyone and take a few bites of the first course before setting off to make the rounds of nearby tables. If she wants you to meet someone, she swings by and grabs you mid-swallow. This happens again and again between courses until she has covered the whole room. During any down time, Judge Ordoñez inputs contact data and sends follow-up e-mails on her newest electronic device. At one such dinner, I logged almost seven miles on my pedometer. You get a grace period after the event to accomplish your assigned task, but after that you can expect reminder texts and phone calls, sometimes on a daily basis.

Judge Ordoñez can work a room like few others, reaching out to connect people whenever she can. What sets her apart from so many master networkers, though, is that she does this not to advance herself but to benefit others. And she is a long-term thinker, always

Hon. Barbara A. Lenk is an associate justice of the Massachusetts Supreme Judicial Court. She previously served on the Superior Court and the Appeals Court.

mulling over how to get from point A to Z. Whether it is to further a worthy project, persuade someone to lend a hand or serve on a committee, help someone pursue a better career opportunity, or even do a little matchmaking, Judge Ordoñez strategizes, introduces, connects, encourages, nudges, pursues, and generally makes things happen. She explains this by saying that, in her job as a Probate and Family Court judge, "I frequently legally separate people. To make up for the bad karma of separating people, I find every opportunity I can to bring people together." But there is more to it than that.

Judge Ordoñez was born in 1962 to a single mother who, at the age of twenty-six, had emigrated from Bogotá, Colombia, speaking only Spanish. She worked hard to support her daughter, but it was a struggle. Seeing this, Judge Ordoñez's grandmother left all that was familiar behind in Colombia to come and help raise her granddaughter. Judge Ordoñez spoke Spanish before she spoke English, becoming bilingual by the age of four with the help of television, "one of my oldest friends." (It will come as no surprise to those who have learned high-tech tips from the iGuru that her favorite television character was Maxwell Smart, admiring what she describes as his "cool gadgets and a telephone always at the ready.") Growing up, Judge Ordoñez was quite aware that she did not have a *Father Knows Best* or *Brady Bunch* kind of life. That became more evident when she realized as an adolescent that she is gay.

Judge Ordoñez is quite clear about who she is and where she comes from. She understands how it feels to be part of a minority... and sometimes to be on the outside looking in.

Judge Ordoñez is quite clear about who she is and where she comes from. She understands how it feels to be part of a minority (actually of several) and sometimes to be on the outside looking in. She knows what a difference it makes to a child when a father takes responsibility and when he does not. She gets what it means to have few resources and appreciates the quiet heroism of those who work multiple jobs to support their kids. She brings to her work the certain knowledge that families come in many configurations and that, in all of them, it is love and commitment that matter most. She understands that the familial support she was given is not every child's experience, and that the happiness she has enjoyed for twenty-three years with her now-wife Carol is not the way of every marriage. So she pays it forward, opening doors for those who come after her. The determination to make things better for others lies at the heart of all that Judge Ordoñez does, both inside and outside the courtroom. The law has so strongly engaged her for so long largely because she sees it as being about human relationships. It can remedy wrongs, counter inequities, change lives.

Since becoming a lawyer, Judge Ordoñez has worked only in public service. After law school, she spent four years as a legal services attorney representing indigent clients, often in crisis, on a broad range of family law issues. She then became assistant register of probate in the Suffolk Probate and Family Court, where she spent seven years helping to improve the experience of those whom the court serves. In 2000, at the age of thirty-seven, she was appointed to the Probate and Family Court bench by Governor A. Paul Cellucci, becoming the first member of the Massachusetts judiciary to be both Hispanic and openly gay.

Building connections, repairing what is reparable in relationships, severing bonds that cannot be salvaged—these go to the core of the courtroom work that Judge Ordoñez has done for the past twelve years. Despite both the devastating impact of recent budget cuts on the court and the often intractable nature of the problems before her, Judge Ordoñez is not

Hon. Angela M. Ordoñez (in the second row) at a 2011 Massachusetts Bar Association Tiered Community Mentoring Program event, a program she helped initiate. Standing to Judge Ordoñez's right are U.S. Attorney Carmen Ortiz, U.S. Marshal John Gibbons, Denise Squillante (then president of the MBA), and Susan Prosnitz (then of the Rappaport Center for Law and Public Service at Suffolk University Law School).

IMAGE COURTESY OF MASSACHUSETTS BAR ASSOCIATION

deterred. She forges ahead with a sense of the possible, convinced that the cases she hears each day are of paramount importance to society as well as to the parties involved. "I love being a judge in the Probate and Family Court. I love the feeling of helping people get beyond their seemingly insurmountable differences." Because the work she does matters so much to the families affected, "there are times when no issue is too small for me to get involved in."

Having observed Judge Ordoñez during a motion session, I know this to be so. Before the morning break (by which time I had a throbbing headache), Judge Ordoñez had already heard a staggering number of cases, attending to each with nuance and care. Those who were unrepresented by counsel and those who could not speak English with fluency were given the time they needed notwithstanding the crowded courtroom. An amazingly efficient person, she somehow also manages to stay abreast of both appellate opinions and developments in pop culture, while not letting herself get behind in drafting the written findings and rulings that her work on the bench necessitates.

Outside the courtroom and in her present role as first justice, Judge Ordoñez seizes opportunities to enliven and improve the quality of life for all who work in the Norfolk courthouse. With infectious optimism and an endless supply of can-do ideas, the seemingly omnipresent Judge Ordoñez organizes and attends regular meetings of the judges, all-staff meetings, manager and bench-bar meetings; devises all manner of programs utilizing volunteers; promotes bench-bar, in-house, and community educational programs; sustains a suggestions box and an in-house newsletter; and heads up the Fun Committee (pedometer-based walking contests, Name That Tune competitions, bowling, etc.). And to make it easy for others who want to pay it forward, Judge Ordoñez initiates food pantry collections and finds good uses for donated eyeglasses and discarded sneakers.

It should go without saying that Judge Ordoñez's reach extends well beyond her own courthouse. She serves as a member of the SJC Access to Justice Commission, a subject about which Judge Ordoñez cares passionately, and has also served on the Trial Court's Gender Equality Committee, its Interpreter Committee, and its Green Energy Committee. She does not neglect the bar associations, either, having been both an attorney and judicial member of the Massachusetts and National Associations of Hispanic Attorneys, the Massachusetts Association of Women Lawyers, and the Massachusetts Gay, Lesbian, Bisexual, Transgender and Queer Bar Association. She was appointed in 2010 to be cochair of the Massachusetts Bar Association Diversity Task Force, where one of her proudest achievements was the initiation of the Tiered Community Mentoring Program. This project teams up practicing minority attorneys with diverse inner-city high school, college, and law school students to expose them to otherwise nonexistent opportunities in the legal community.

In being a person for others, Judge Ordoñez strives to be the change she wants to see in our world.

There is a remarkable consistency in all of these efforts. Whether it is giving pro se litigants without fluency in English the time they need to speak, serving on committees to promote access to justice and gender equality, or creating mentoring opportunities that will result in a more diverse bench and bar, Judge Ordoñez remembers that the law belongs to all of us. In being a person for others, Judge Ordoñez strives to be the change she wants to see in our world.

So what is it that Judge Ordoñez cannot do? Her arms, which reach out far and wide to others, are somehow not long enough to let her pat herself on the back. She honors me by letting me write on her behalf.

Hon. Patti B. Saris

U.S. District Court for the District of Massachusetts, 1993–present
Massachusetts Superior Court, 1989–1993
U.S. Magistrate Judge, District of Massachusetts, 1986–1989

When I was in college, I wanted to be a journalist. I "competed" for the *Harvard Crimson* and covered the campus during the Vietnam War and the 1972 presidential election. Little did I expect that covering the women's movement at Harvard Law School would be the journalistic experience that would change my life. Barely noticed amid all the campus turmoil, the Women's Law Association was protesting the small number of female law students at Harvard Law School. I was supposed to cover the meeting between then-Dean (later President) Derek Bok and this group, but when he found out I was from the *Crimson*, I was ejected. Hardly an auspicious beginning. When my Dad suggested that I take the LSAT—"You'd be such a good lawyer," he insisted—I at first resisted, but those women were so

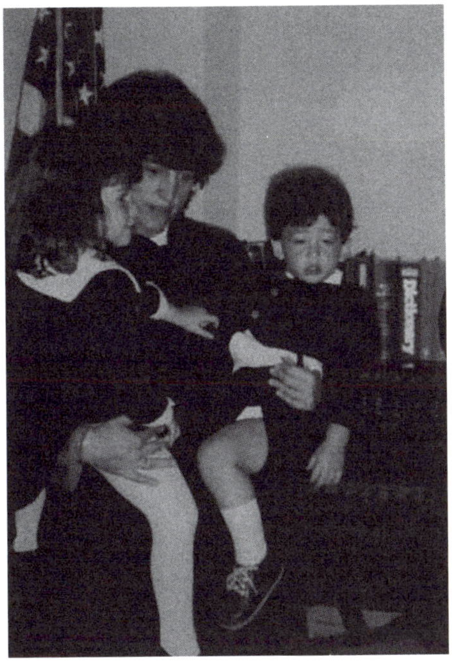

Judge Saris at her 1986 swearing-in as a U.S. magistrate judge with two (then ages two and three) of her four children.

IMAGE COURTESY OF HON. PATTI B. SARIS

terrific that I was tempted. I applied to law school and never looked back.

Law school changed the way I thought. I actually loved the 1L experience, despite the "paper chase" culture, because Harvard Law was finally ready for women in 1973. While I had no female professors, other professors (like Phil Heymann, Robert Keeton, and Larry Tribe) reached out to mentor and help me to succeed. At that age, I wanted everything—to be a trial lawyer, to get married, to have children, to become a judge. Of course, I was going to work full time and be active in the community while I raised children. No compromises.

Now as an old lady of sixty (the "new forty"), I reflect on my full-time demanding careers as a law clerk, litigator, assistant U.S. attorney for William Weld, Hill staffer for Senator Edward Kennedy, and a federal and state trial judge. I became a U.S. magistrate judge when I was thirty-six. I am now a federal District Court judge and chair of the United States Sentencing Commission in Washington, D.C. During this thirty-five year period, my husband and I also raised four children (now ages twenty-eight, twenty-seven, twenty-four, and nineteen). When I look back at the "balancing act" I performed over the past few decades, I have few regrets about my intense, rewarding career. However, my oldest daughter once said to me, "Mommy, I am so proud you are a judge; can men be judges too? But why do you always have to work so hard?" Her statement rings loud and painful even today. I missed soccer and lacrosse games and being there when the kids came home with their friends after school. My time with them at night was limited to homework and piano practice.

So when I advise my young law clerks about their futures, I say, "You have a long life. Enjoy your family while they are young. You don't have to succeed all at once, but please don't leave the profession." I am curious to see how my children and my clerks live their lives. The story of women is still evolving and I am proud to have been a part of it.

Hon. Martha B. Sosman

Supreme Judicial Court, 2000–2007
Massachusetts Superior Court, 1993–2000

By Hon. Leila R. Kern

Martha Sosman was sworn in as an associate justice of the Superior Court in 1993 and as an associate justice of the Supreme Judicial Court in 2000. She served with distinction until her untimely death on March 7, 2007.

When I was asked to reflect upon Justice Sosman in published memorials,[42] I first turned to psychiatrist and *Boston Globe* contributor Elissa Ely, who described her experience before Justice Sosman in a piece she wrote for the *Globe* in 2000.[43] Dr. Ely described the scene surrounding a case in which a psychiatric patient who had been involuntarily committed by a District Court judge was now seeking an appeal in Superior Court. First the patient, through an expert, and then the hospital, through Dr. Ely, I imagine, presented their views.

> The judge tipped her chair back and wrote in a notebook too high up to read from the [witness] stand. She made little eye contact with any witness, though seeming attentive to each; psychiatry calls this the practice of evenly hovering attention. Her expression was neutral, maybe slightly stern. Any visitor from an alternate galaxy would have recognized a captain's countenance.

Each side then summed up its case.

> Usually, this is when the judge takes the case under advisement, sometimes for weeks, and we all go home slightly deflated by our unanswered efforts. I started to pack my papers. Then the judge leaned forward and said she was prepared to render her opinion. Looking down at her notebook once or twice, but otherwise directly speaking to all of us, she spoke for 15 minutes. Her rendering was stunning. She spoke eloquently and comprehensively, addressing the case point by point with such organization I hardly recognized the points myself until she brought them to language. It was as though some mathematician had applied some pure abstract theorem to a problem in real space and time in order to make a stuck lever turn. All the time she had been looking at no one, she had been trolling for everyone's perspectives with a wide net. She got us all.... You could see the scales tipping one way then the other with each sentence. She was balancing them in front of us....

Hon. Leila R. Kern is a retired associate justice of the Massachusetts Superior Court. Justice Sosman was her colleague at the U.S. Attorney's Office and her partner in the firm of Kern, Sosman, Hagerty, Roach and Carpenter.

> A judge, listening deeply, applies the law in such a way that
> it becomes worthy of struggling to understand.

After the hearing, Dr. Ely got the court stenographer to write Martha's name down for her because the judge had "redeemed the cynicism of [the doctor's] citizen self." Those of us who were at Martha's swearing-in ceremony to the Supreme Judicial Court know that Martha had asked Dr. Ely to read her piece during the ceremony. Later her law clerks printed it out and framed it for her; it hung amidst her Red Sox memorabilia.

Martha Sosman was a judge par excellence. During her years on the bench, she was called a Jew who was anti-Catholic, after one of her decisions as a Superior Court judge involving the sale of property owned by the Roman Catholic Church, and a lesbian who nonetheless dissented in the *Goodridge* case. The only problem with both of the labels, as Martha said, was that neither was true. Small details! There was one label Martha cared about. As she said at her swearing-in ceremony to the Supreme Judicial Court, "it would not make a difference to my mother [were she alive] that I'm going on the SJC. It would make a difference to her that I'm a good judge." That made a difference to Martha as well, for whom being a good judge meant first and foremost being intellectually honest. She had no personal agenda, no axe to grind.

There was one label Martha cared about… being a good judge.

When Martha died, one of her colleagues aptly commented, "I recall how she made music whenever she [wrote], or spoke, or laughed, or moved her fingers near a piano." Martha was an accomplished pianist who practiced for hours each day. Her solo concerts were treats of both music and elegance. Many people have shared with me their memories of Martha's piano recitals. This e-mail was typical:

WE CONGRATULATE
OUR FORMER PARTNER
MARTHA B. SOSMAN
ASSOCIATE JUSTICE
SUPERIOR COURT
COMMONWEALTH OF MASSACHUSETTS

THE FIRM WILL NOW
BE KNOWN AS
KERN, HAGERTY, ROACH & CARPENTER
A PROFESSIONAL CORPORATION
24 SCHOOL STREET, BOSTON, MASSACHUSETTS 02108
(617) 720-1800
JANUARY 26, 1993

At left, Martha B. Sosman (center) enjoying a light moment with (Hon.) Leila R. Kern and Governor William Weld just before her swearing in as an associate justice of the Superior Court on January 26, 1993, at the State House. At right, a congratulatory message from Justice Sosman's former law partners that appeared in Massachusetts Lawyers Weekly.

IMAGES COURTESY OF HON. LEILA R. KERN AND EILEEN M. HAGERTY

> While Martha had her own distinctive elegance [read: quirky way of dressing], we did not think of her as a flashy dresser. Perhaps eight to ten years ago, while Martha was a Superior Court judge she gave a solo piano recital at Pickman Hall at the Longy School in Cambridge. When the moment came for her to enter, she swept on to the stage in a stunning red dress with spaghetti straps, grinning broadly, and the place just erupted. She stood there smiling, obviously enjoying the moment with her audience, then gave a wonderful performance.

This colleague and his wife marveled at a showmanship side of Martha they had not seen before. "She was so accomplished in so many ways, and so humble about it all." Little did they know, as I did, that Martha had actually designed and sewn the dress herself! I had seen this side of her years before that. Probably in 1986, Martha, who I also was used to seeing in professional garb, invited everyone in the U.S. Attorney's Office, along with others of course, to a solo piano recital. I can no longer remember if that recital was also at the Longy School or at some venue in Concord, but I will never forget what Martha looked like when she swept on to the stage. This time she was wearing a straight, form-fitting, black velvet dress with wide spaghetti straps. When Martha sat down on the tufted piano bench and began carefully adjusting the bench and her distance from the piano and so forth, it became apparent that Martha had designed the dress with slits up the sides so that the back fell away

The Supreme Judicial Court during Justice Sosman's time on the bench. From left to right, front row: Hon. Martha B. Sosman, Hon. Margaret H. Marshall, Hon. Judith A. Cowin; back row: Hon. Francis X. Spina, Hon. John M. Greaney, Hon. Roderick L. Ireland, Hon. Robert J. Cordy.

IMAGE © GEORGE PEET

as she sat and she got to show off more than just a "glimpse of stocking." In fact, if memory serves, the slit went almost to mid-thigh. Again, Martha smiled—this time demurely—before she bent her head to the very serious business of her performance. I also seem to recall Martha always had an encore prepared, knowing full well that her audience would not let her go without one.

Martha quoted Shakespeare's Romeo and Juliet in her now infamous dissent in *Goodridge*—"What's in a name? That which we call a rose, By any other name would smell as sweet." Tragically fitting is another Shakespeare quote, this from *Richard III:* "So wise so young, they say, do never live long."

Hon. Rya W. Zobel

U.S. District Court for the District of Massachusetts, 1979–present

Rya Solveig Weickert was born on December 18, 1931, in Zwickau, Germany, a town known as the birthplace of the musician Robert Schumann. After surviving the bombing of her town during World War II, the arrest of her parents by the Russians in East Germany in 1945, a stay in a displaced persons camp, and a journey with her younger brother to live with little-known relatives in the United States, she became the first woman U.S. district judge in Massachusetts in 1979. The next woman judge did not arrive for fifteen years.

Hon. Rya W. Zobel

IMAGE COURTESY OF THE U.S. DISTRICT COURT FOR THE DISTRICT OF MASSACHUSETTS

In January 1947, Judge Zobel and her brother arrived in the United States on a former troop ship called the *SS Ernie Pyle,* which was full of refugees. She remembers:

> It was a thirteen-day, stormy passage, and I was sick the whole time. Most everybody else was sick, too. But when we sailed into New York Harbor, everybody on the ship came on deck and we all saluted the Statue of Liberty. I think it is really sad that most immigrants arrive in this country by air or car now and not by ship into New York Harbor. It was an unbelievably emotional experience, to sail by the Statue of Liberty and have all of us there understand what it meant.
>
> ...
>
> That was an OK day; it was January, January 16, 1947. We docked and my uncles, aunt, and grandmother were there, waiting for us. As we drove to my grandmother's apartment, we noticed the lights. We had never seen such lights. New York was ablaze. We grew up in dim light all the time because of air raids. We also had never seen such abundance.

This piece was adapted for this book from the Women Trailblazers in the Law "Oral History of Rya W. Zobel" (Nancy D. Israel, interviewer) with the permission of the American Bar Association and with review by Judge Zobel

> The grocery stores spilled out their wares onto the street—fruits, vegetables, flowers all on the sidewalks. It was just amazing. Really wonderful. Later, my aunt, uncle, and grandmother took us out to the local drugstore for a banana split. My first banana split on my first night in this country.

In high school, Judge Zobel was sure she was going to be a chemist, but after she entered Radcliffe College in 1949, she turned to studies in the economics department and wrote her thesis on the Lowell textile mills. Her government professor suggested law school. Although she did not know any lawyers, she was intrigued by a course taught by University Professor Zachariah Chafee on habeas corpus that focused on the aftermath of the trial of William Penn. Harvard Law School admitted her in 1953. Out of 540 students in her class, there were only nineteen women (including Ruth Abrams, later on the Supreme Judicial Court).

> I knew that we were pioneers. I knew that there were several professors who didn't much care to have us there. I figured that was their prerogative and I was going to enjoy it anyhow. Some of them made nasty comments to and about the women; some called on women significantly more often than the men.
>
> ...
>
> I did the moot court, at which I was relatively successful, because every time I had to argue, I got a terrible case of laryngitis ahead of time. So by the time the argument rolled around, I sounded like Lauren Bacall. I usually won the argument.

Her generation of women lawyers was not angry at the law school.

> We were not strident because we hadn't learned to be strident yet. We were serious and we worked hard. We grumbled about some of the stuff that happened, like being called on and made to look foolish. But for the most part, we were pleased to be there.

After law school, Rya Featherston (she had married a classmate) got a job in 1956 clerking for Judge George C. Sweeney, who was then the chief of the U.S. District Court, and whom she served for nine years.

> I stayed because law firms were not hiring women as lawyers. It never occurred to me that I should go and hang out my shingle. And then eventually my children came and

> I could really do the law clerking on a more or less part-time basis. So I just did it.

Judge Sweeney's courtroom style was "brisk and decisive," a courtroom style she later emulated. After Judge Sweeney died in 1969, she went to work for a couple of years at a firm now extinct.

In 1973 Rya went to Goodwin Procter & Hoar, where she specialized in matrimonial law.

> And I found myself. I though[t] that I would be able to do a good job for my clients since I had gone through a divorce myself and had some sense of what needed to be done to make the client feel whole by the end of the process. I kept my clients informed about what was going on, explained carefully how the process would work, and then involved them in it. That seemed to make them feel better about the process, and about themselves, particularly the women, who were more often than not incredibly vulnerable.

▲ *Judge Zobel seated with the Honorable Patti B. Saris. Standing in back are Nancy McGillvray, the first woman U.S. marshal for the district of Massachusetts, and the Honorable Nancy Gertner.*

IMAGE COURTESY OF HON. PATTI B. SARIS

Goodwin Procter made her the first woman partner of the firm in 1976. During this time, she had five teenagers in the house: her three children and her two stepchildren from the marriage with Hiller Zobel (who became a Superior Court judge).

A few years later, Rya Zobel applied to the federal bench. On the Friday after Thanksgiving of 1978, the call came from Senator Kennedy saying that he would send her name to the president. When she was confirmed in March 1979, she became the thirteenth women to be appointed to the District Court in the country and the first in Massachusetts. She felt welcomed.

> I have been here now for thirty-three years and this has always been a very friendly and collegial court. It became truly collegial when Judge Tauro became the chief. But Judge Caffrey, who was the chief before him, could not have been more welcoming. He was a bit left-handed about it, but it wasn't out of meanness, it was just a lack of understanding. For example, he told me with great pride that he had ordered a vanity for my bathroom. But he meant this not in any way as a devaluation of me. It was a recognition of difference and he was trying to do the right thing. I have never felt that my colleagues ever put me down because I was a woman, not that they never put me down, but certainly not because I was a woman. I felt that they valued my opinions, and I have never had the sense that I was not

> well regarded by them or that they wouldn't let me say my piece or that they wouldn't listen. I felt very good about that, always.

Awards and honors followed. From 1986 to 1992, she served on the Harvard Board of Overseers. Later came other opportunities, like becoming the first woman director of the Federal Judicial Center (FJC) in Washington, D.C., the institution which provides training to the federal judiciary and all of its employees.

> Well, it was shortly after my marriage really came apart. I was asked to put my name in for the Court of Appeals. And then I learned about the opening for the Judicial Center directorship and I sort of agonized about the First Circuit. I was torn between the fact that this was a promotion in a way, and the knowledge that this job did not suit me. Judge Selya called me and urged me to do it, but finally, having thought about it at length, I decided I would not. Then he said, "But come and sit with us next month," and I said, "OK." We agreed on two days, and ten minutes later, three enormous boxes full of paper arrived. At that point, I just knew I had made the right decision. At the same time, I decided to apply for the Federal Judicial Center position. I thought it would be interesting to do an administrative job, yet I didn't fully realize the many other benefits from that job. The most important of these was a fantastic opportunity to get to know the federal judiciary as an institution. I traveled all around the country. The director goes to circuit conferences, gets to know the lawyers there, gets to know the cultures of different courts, goes around the country in connection with educational programs the Center runs. And I really got to know the vast majority of federal judges who were working at the time that I was at the Center. I also did a lot of foreign travel and got to know a lot of foreign judges, because one of the statutory charges to the Center is to assist foreign judiciaries. So it was from those perspectives a really terrific opportunity. And I loved doing what I was doing at the time.

She stayed at the FJC for four and a half years (1995–1999) but was eager to return home to be a trial judge, a job she loves.

> To me the difference between working as a trial judge and an appellate judge was the difference between working with

> people and working with paper. I really enjoy dealing with juries. I enjoy working with lawyers. And I enjoy being creative, or trying to be creative, in shaping a case and in trying to help people to come to a resolution, to end a dispute, to see if one can find ways which they may not have thought about that could solve a problem they have. You don't get a chance to do that as an appellate judge.

Judge Zobel loves to work with juries.

> You know, in jury cases I take great pains to bring the jury along. I will explain to them what's going on. I will explain terms to them. For example, if [there's] an objection that it's a leading question. I will explain to the jury what a leading question is. And then the next time that objection is made, the jurors shake or nod their heads. And they really love it. And they pay attention. So I explain to them why the person is asking a particular question. Or why they want to put in a particular document and why it may or may not be admissible. And they really perk up when you tell them that we will stretch every half hour. We actually do get up and stretch.

In 2002, Judge Zobel won the prestigious Margaret Brent Award for leadership in the profession and mentoring other lawyers. The proof is in the pudding. Four of her law clerks have gone on to become judges and one is the federal defender.

Does having more women on the bench make a difference?

> I think so. Has it made a difference in how the law has developed? I have no idea. I think it has made a difference in the perception of justice, certainly by women.

Her goal—

> Well, I think I would like to be known as a fair judge, as a judge who is regarded as a good judge, who is decisive but not impatient, who deals with all the litigants and lawyers as equals.

As this book goes to publication, Judge Zobel remains an active, decisive, and fair District Court judge at age eighty.

NOTES

1 Judicial statistics compiled from the Massachusetts court system Web site, http://www.mass.gov/courts; the U.S. Court of Appeals for the First Circuit Web site, http://www.ca1.uscourts.gov; and the U.S. District Court for the District of Massachusetts Web site, http://www.mad.uscourts.gov in March 2012.

2 General Laws c. 211B, § 2, authorizes fifty-one Probate and Family Court judgeships, five positions were unfilled in January 2012. Judicial statistics compiled from the Massachusetts court system Web site, http://www.mass.gov/courts. (As of June 2012, twenty-five of the forty-eight currently sitting judges, over half, were women.)

3 Lynn Hecht Schafran, "Not from Central Casting: The Amazing Rise of Women in the American Judiciary," 36 *U. Toledo L. Rev.* 953, 955 (2005).

4 General Laws c. 211B, § 2, authorizes forty-one Juvenile Court judgeships, two positions were unfilled in January 2012. Judicial statistics compiled from the Massachusetts court system Web site, http://www.mass.gov/courts.

5 Mary L. Clark, "One Man's Token is Another Woman's Breakthrough? The Appointment of the First Woman Federal Judges," 49 *Villanova L. Rev.* 487, 493 (2004).

6 Larry Berkson, "Women on the Bench: A Brief History," 65 *Judicature* 287, 290 (1982).

7 Mary L. Clark, "One Man's Token is Another Woman's Breakthrough? The Appointment of the First Woman Federal Judges," 49 *Villanova L. Rev.* at 493–94.

8 Cynthia Ellen Harrison, *On Account of Sex: The Politics of Women's Issues, 1945–1968*, 52–53 (Univ. of California Press 1988).

9 Hon. Ruth Bader Ginsburg & Laura W. Brill, "Women in the Federal Judiciary: Three Way Pavers and the Exhilarating Change President Carter Wrought," 64 *Fordham L. Rev.* 281, 283 (1995). The Supreme Court's first woman member, Sandra Day O'Connor, was appointed to the Supreme Court in 1981, fifteen years after Judge Allen's death.

10 Elaine Martin, "Women on the Federal Bench: A Comparative Profile," 65 *Judicature* 306, 308 (1982).

11 Center for Women in Government & Civil Society, State University of New York at Albany, *Women in Federal and State-level Judgeships* (Spring 2010).

12 Becky Kruse, "Luck and Politics: Judicial Selection Methods and their Effect on Women on the Bench," 16 *Wis. Women's L.J.* 67, 68 (2001).

13 Mark Curriden, "Tipping the Scales," *A.B.A. J.* (July 1, 2010).

14 Elaine Martin, "Women on the Federal Bench: A Comparative Profile," 65 *Judicature* at 310.

15 *See* Lynn C. Rossman, "Women Judges Unite," 10 *Golden Gate U. L. Rev.* 1238 (1980).

16 Hon. Patricia M. Wald, "Six Not-So-Easy Pieces: One Woman's Journey to the Bench and Beyond," 36 *U. Toledo L. Rev.* 980, 989 (2005).

17 *See* Mary L. Clark, "One Man's Token is Another Woman's Breakthrough? The Appointment of the First Woman Federal Judges," 49 *Villanova L. Rev.* at 488.

18 Anita F. Hill, "What Difference Will Women Judges Make" in Barbara Kellerman & Deborah Rhode, *Women in Leadership: The State of Play and Strategies for Change* 185 (Jossey-Bass 2007).

19 American Bar Association, *Diversity in the Legal Profession: The Next Steps* (Mar. 2010).

20 Quoted in Mary L. Clark, "One Man's Token is Another Woman's Breakthrough? The Appointment of the First Woman Federal Judges," 49 *Villanova L. Rev.* at 519.

21 *Report of the Gender Bias Study of the Supreme Judicial Court* 151 tbl.10 (Supreme Judicial Court 1989).

22 *Report of the Gender Bias Study of the Supreme Judicial Court* at 10.

23 *See* Jennifer L. Peresie, Note, "Female Judges Matter: Gender and Collegial Decisionmaking in the Federal Appellate Courts," 114 *Yale L.J* 1759, 1761 (2005); *see also* Christina l. Boyd, Lee Epstein & Andrew Martin, "Untangling the Causal Effects of Sex on Judging," 54 *Am. J. Pol. Sci.* 389 (2010).

24 Joan Biskupic, "Ginsburg: Court Needs Another Woman," *USA Today*, Oct. 5, 2009, *available at* http://www.usatoday.com/news/washington/judicial/2009-05-05-ruthginsburg_N.htm.

25 Diane Speare Trust, "Upholding the Rule of the Law: Tolerance and Compassion on the Bench" *Wellesley Magazine*, at 22 (Spring 1997).

26 Trust, "Upholding the Rule of the Law: Tolerance and Compassion on the Bench" *Wellesley Magazine*, at 22.

27 Peresie, Note, "Female Judges Matter: Gender and Collegial Decisionmaking in the Federal Appellate Courts," 114 *Yale L.J.* at 1763 n.12.

28 David W. Allen & Diane E. Wall, "Role Orientations and Women State Supreme Court Justices," 77 *Judicature* 156, 158 (1993–94).

29 Peresie, Note, "Female Judges Matter: Gender and Collegial Decisionmaking in the Federal Appellate Courts," 114 *Yale L.J.* at 1761.

30 Peresie, Note, "Female Judges Matter: Gender and Collegial Decisionmaking in the Federal Appellate Courts," 114 *Yale L.J.* at 1761.

31 Allen & Wall, "Role Orientations and Women State Supreme Court Justices," 77 *Judicature* at 161.

32 Allen & Wall, "Role Orientations and Women State Supreme Court Justices," 77 *Judicature* at 161.

33 Wald, "Six Not-So-Easy Pieces: One Woman's Journey to the Bench and Beyond," 36 *U. Toledo L. Rev.* at 989.

34 Hon. Shirley S. Abrahamson, "The Woman Has Robes: Four Questions," 14 *Golden Gate U. L. Rev.* 489, 494 (1984).

35 *See* Naomi Schoenbaum, "Post Gender Justice: What Does Being a Woman Mean to Elena Kagan," *The New Republic*, July 12, 2010, *available at* http://www.tnr.com/article/politics/76176/post-gender-justice.

36 Compiled from the Massachusetts court system Web site, http://www.mass.gov/courts; the U.S. Court of Appeals for the First Circuit Web site, http://www.ca1.uscourts.gov; and the U.S. District Court for the District of Massachusetts Web site, http://www.mad.uscourts.gov in June 2012, with confirmation from administrative personnel at each court.

37 While the number of male African-American judges was greater, the number of African-American judges was small in comparison to the total number of judges. Ten years after I was appointed to the bench there were twenty-one African-American judges out of the 328 trial court judges, or 6.4 percent. *Equal Justice, Eliminating the Barriers*, Supreme Judicial Court Commission to Study Race and Ethnic Bias in the Courts, Final Report 1994. As of June 14, 2011, there were thirty-five African-American judges out of a total of 411 state judicial positions, or 8.5 percent. The increase in women judges has been more dramatic. In 1989, there were twenty-eight women judges out of a total of 266 trial court judges, or 10.5 percent, while on June 14, 2011 there were 146 women, or 35.5 percent of the total number of state judicial positions. *Report of the Gender Bias Study*, Supreme Judicial Court, 1989; Administrative Office of the Trial Court survey for the Office of Justice Programs, June 2011.

38 *See* http://opinionator.blogs.nytimes.com/2011/04/11/a-dollar-is-a-dollar-elena-kagans-style.

39 *Pugliese* v. *Commonwealth*, 335 Mass. 441 (1957).

40 *Commonwealth* v. *Soares*, 377 Mass. 461 (1979).

41 *New State Ice Co.* v. *Liebmann*, 285 U.S. 262, 311 (1932) (Brandeis, J., dissenting).

42 Hon. Leila Kern, "In Memoriam: Justice Martha B. Sosman," 42 *New Eng. L. Rev.* 391 (2008); Hon. Judith Fabricant, ed., *Reflections of the Justices* (Supreme Judicial Court Historical Society 2009). I am grateful to the *New England Law Review* and the Supreme Judicial Court Historical Society for permission to use portions of these previously published essays.

43 Elissa Ely, "Minds That Make Their Marks, Madmen Bequeath You Their Fears, Thinkers Restore Your Hopes," *Boston Globe*, July 16, 2000, at E3.

Challenging the Status Quo

Abortion

J. Shoshanna Ehrlich

Introduction

In 1973, in the landmark case of *Roe v. Wade*, the U.S. Supreme Court held that the "right of privacy...founded in the Fourteenth Amendment's concept of personal liberty and restrictions upon state action...is broad enough to encompass a woman's decision whether or not to terminate her pregnancy."[1]

Although critics of the decision responded to *Roe* as if a permanent feature of our legal landscape had been suddenly ripped away, it is important to recognize that the criminal abortion laws invalidated by the decision had only been on the books for little more than a century. In contradistinction to this one-dimensional rendering of the history of abortion rights in this country, the reality is far more nuanced and complex, with Massachusetts playing a leading role in shaping the nation's legal approach to abortion.

J. Shoshanna Ehrlich is chair of the women's studies department and an associate professor at the University of Massachusetts Boston. She is the author of *Who Decides? The Abortion Rights of Teens* and *Family Law for Paralegals* and she is a graduate of Northeastern University School of Law.

IMAGE COURTESY OF J. SHOSHANNA EHRLICH

Massachusetts Abortion Law in the Pre-*Roe* Era

Starting with a landmark 1812 case, this section traces the shifting nature of a woman's right to abortion in Massachusetts during the nineteenth century. As we will see, critical developments in the Commonwealth would prove to have a significant impact on the nation's evolving approach to the legal status of abortion.

The Common Law Approach to Abortion

In one of the first known judicial decisions in this country on the legal status of abortion, the Massachusetts Supreme Judicial Court, in the 1812 case of *Commonwealth v. Bangs*, ruled that a criminal indictment for performing an abortion must specifically aver that the woman was "quick with child"—referring to the moment when a pregnant woman first feels fetal movement. Since the indictment in question did not include this essential element, the court held that the case against the defendant who had been charged with administering "a certain dangerous and deleterious draught or potion" to one Lucy Holman for the purpose of procuring the abortion of her "bastard child" could not be sustained.[2]

The *Bangs* decision had a significant impact on the development of the nation's abortion jurisprudence. Relying on the case as authority, courts in other states likewise retained the longstanding common law distinction between pre- and postquickening abortions. Citing Blackstone for the proposition that "[l]ife begins in contemplation of law, as soon as an infant is able to stir in the mother's womb," the eminent jurist Chief Justice Lemuel Shaw explained that it is not until this point that a fetus acquires a "separate and independent" legal existence," thus not permitting an indictment to stand which does not indicate a woman has crossed this critical threshold.[3]

Given that quickening typically does not occur until sometime between the fourteenth and sixteenth weeks of pregnancy, the judicial acceptance of this common law doctrine meant that early abortions remained legal in most states throughout much of the nineteenth century.

In addition to representing, as the *Roe* Court subsequently put it, "a confluence of earlier philosophical, theological, and civil and canon law concepts of when life begins,"[4] the quickening doctrine also had a practical significance. Notably, it was not until a woman first felt fetal movement that she could be certain that a missed period was attributable to pregnancy rather than to an obstruction of the womb. Accordingly, although certainly not reflecting contemporary feminist ideals about a woman's right to control her reproductive fate, the *Bangs* decision meant that the enforceable boundary between a lawful and an unlawful abortion would remain dependent upon a pregnant woman's intimate relationship with her own body for its effectuation.

Abortion Becomes a Statutory Crime

In 1821, Connecticut enacted the nation's first criminal abortion law. Included in an omnibus crime bill, the measure made it a crime to use "any deadly poison, or other noxious or dangerous substance" to induce an abortion. Reflecting the enduring hold of the common law, the law only applied to postquickening abortions. Following Connecticut's lead, a number of other states passed similar laws in the next two decades, although not all expressly distinguished between pre- and postquickening abortions.

Primarily intended to regulate the *practice* of abortion, which could be quite dangerous, these early laws exempted from prosecution women who had abortions. Reflective of this general purpose, these measures were typically incorporated into omnibus laws that addressed a range of criminal behaviors. Thus, for example, Connecticut's antipoisoning measure was sandwiched between a provision addressing the "intent to kill or rob" and one concerning the "secret delivery of a bastard child."[5] Reflecting the historic fact that, as historian James Mohr explains, these early laws were not grounded in a public condemnation of abortion as an immoral practice, no lawmaker during this first wave of legislative activity actually "took a political stand on abortion" or "cast a recorded vote for or against abortion as a question by itself."[6]

Breaking from this pattern, in 1845 Massachusetts became the first state in the nation to enact a law that focused exclusively on abortion as a wrongful act. Firmly repudiating the *Bangs* decision, the statute made it a crime to perform an abortion at any stage of pregnancy; in keeping, however, with the dominant legal paradigm, the aborting woman remained immune from prosecution. In a series of subsequent cases, the court read a "therapeutic" exception into the law that permitted a doctor to perform an abortion based on a "good faith and...honest belief that it [was] necessary for the life or health of the pregnant woman."[7]

Enacted in response to the sensationalized coverage of a woman's death from a botched abortion, and the subsequent trial and acquittal of the doctor, the 1845 statute reflected emerging concerns about the growing commercialization and visibility of the abortion trade. Once primarily the domain of rural midwives and other female healers, abortion had become a booming business in many urban areas, including Boston, where according to the *Boston Medical and Surgical Journal* there were "at least six practitioners openly retailing abortifacient preparations" and advertisements for products known to cure "female complaints" regularly appeared in the local press.[8] In 1847, seeking to further clamp down on the trade, Massachusetts enacted the nation's first law banning the advertising of abortion.

Other legislatures soon followed Massachusetts' lead, and by the end of the nineteenth century, most, if not all, states had enacted a statute for the specific purpose of criminalizing abortion. Again reflecting the profound influence of the Commonwealth in the shaping of the nation's abortion policy, these laws were the direct result of a vigorous antiabortion campaign that was launched in Boston by Dr. Horatio R. Storer, a prominent gynecologist. Building upon his local success, Storer mobilized "regular" physicians (meaning those with a formal medical education) across the country in an effort to eliminate the "wicked" practice of abortion, which, he argued, not only destroyed innocent lives but was a sin against women's true nature. In 1859, insisting that the scientific training of the regulars made them uniquely qualified to lead this battle, Storer persuaded the American Medical Association to rally behind the antiabortion cause.

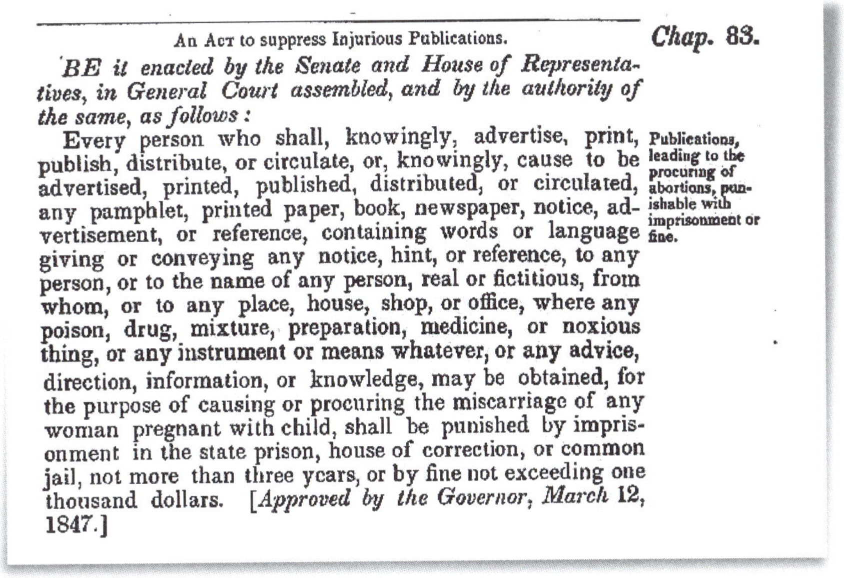

An Act to suppress Injurious Publications. **Chap. 83.**

BE it enacted by the Senate and House of Representatives, in General Court assembled, and by the authority of the same, as follows:

Every person who shall, knowingly, advertise, print, publish, distribute, or circulate, or, knowingly, cause to be advertised, printed, published, distributed, or circulated, any pamphlet, printed paper, book, newspaper, notice, advertisement, or reference, containing words or language giving or conveying any notice, hint, or reference, to any person, or to the name of any person, real or fictitious, from whom, or to any place, house, shop, or office, where any poison, drug, mixture, preparation, medicine, or noxious thing, or any instrument or means whatever, or any advice, direction, information, or knowledge, may be obtained, for the purpose of causing or procuring the miscarriage of any woman pregnant with child, shall be punished by imprisonment in the state prison, house of correction, or common jail, not more than three years, or by fine not exceeding one thousand dollars. [*Approved by the Governor, March* 12, 1847.]

Publications, leading to the procuring of abortions, punishable with imprisonment or fine.

The 1847 law banning the advertising of abortions as appearing in The Acts and Resolves Passed by the General Court of Massachusetts: 1846, 1847, 1848.

IMAGE SOURCE: STATE LIBRARY OF MASSACHUSETTS WEBSITE

Under the stalwart leadership of Storer, regular physicians across the country mobilized against abortion for a number of reasons. First, by claiming that only they possessed the knowledge and training to understand the biological truths of pregnancy, the issue gave them a way to enhance their professional status at a time when the practice of medicine was largely unregulated. Advocating an approach that would vest them with legal authority over the abortion decision, doctors sought to criminalize the practice unless a physician specifically determined that an abortion was necessary to save the life of a pregnant woman.[9]

The doctors' campaign was also infused with interlaced anxieties about the proper role of women and the changing national character. Claiming that married women who aborted were avoiding the role "for which they are physiologically constituted and for which they are designated by nature,"[10] Storer and his colleagues criticized them for being self-indulgent and foolishly believing that they were "born for higher and more noble purposes than the propagation of the species." In seeking control over the abortion decision, doctors were thus also seeking to gain control over unruly wives whose bodily transgressions challenged existing gender and marital conventions.

The aborting wife was also charged with threatening the future stability of the nation. Noting that in Massachusetts, the "increase of the population...ha[d] been wholly of those of recent foreign origin,"[11] Storer and others warned that the if respectable, middle-class Protestant women did not harness their reproductive capacity for the good of the state, the nation would soon be overrun by "aliens."[12]

In contrast to the common law approach, which depended upon a woman's reading of her own body, by the close of the nineteenth century, the power to mark the boundary between lawful and unlawful abortions had been transferred to the medical profession. Not until 1973 would doctors be divested of their legal dominion over a woman's reproductive decision making.

REFLECTION

Sarah R. Wunsch

As an attorney with the American Civil Liberties Union of Massachusetts, I have had the opportunity to work on several major cases involving the reproductive rights of minors, including *Curtis v. School Committee of Falmouth* (1995), where we helped defend a public school condom availability program, and *Planned Parenthood League of Massachusetts v. Attorney General* (1997), which challenged the two-parent consent law for minors seeking an abortion.

These cases are important because the decision to become a parent or delay becoming a parent is one of the most important personal choices anyone can make. Teens need the tools to protect themselves and their health; they should be accorded the same constitutional protection for these choices as adults. I recognize that some people worry about parental rights, but no teenager should be compelled to bear a child. And while teens should be encouraged to talk with their parents, not everyone can safely do that. I think it is really important to focus on educating teens about sex and helping them to make responsible decisions. Both of these cases involved these critical issues.

No one should take for granted the right of access to contraception and abortion. We must continue to fight for essential freedoms, including the right to protest and to make our own reproductive decisions. While law is an important tool, gains are won through taking to the streets, through committed activism. Today's generation needs to fill the streets to protect the reproductive rights of all women.

◀ Sarah R. Wunsch

IMAGE COURTESY OF SARAH R. WUNSCH, PHOTO BY MARILYN HUMPHRIES

Massachusetts Abortion Law in the Wake of *Roe*

By the time *Roe* reached the Supreme Court, a number of states had already liberalized their existing criminal laws to permit abortion in a wider range of circumstances, including, for example, in cases of rape or incest or where continuing the pregnancy posed a serious threat to the woman's mental or physical health (as distinct from life). Going well beyond these limited reforms, which, it should be noted, kept decisional control with the physician, three states (Alaska, Hawaii, and New York) boldly repealed their criminal abortion statutes.

Resisting this liberalizing trend, Massachusetts did not loosen its strict controls over abortion in the years leading up to *Roe*. Accordingly, when the Court announced its decision in 1973, the Commonwealth's mid-nineteenth-century criminal abortion law, with its narrowly crafted therapeutic exception, was still in full force and effect.

Abortion as a Constitutional Right: The *Roe* Decision

On January 22, 1973, the U.S. Supreme Court ruled that the "right of privacy...founded in the Fourteenth Amendment's concept of personal liberty...is broad enough to encompass a woman's decision whether or not to terminate a pregnancy."[13] Grounded in this reading of the Due Process Clause, the Court invalidated the challenged Texas statute that criminalized abortion, unless necessary to save a woman's life. Although recognizing the abortion right as fundamental, the Court made clear that the right was not absolute, but had to be balanced against the state's interest in protecting the health of the pregnant woman and the potentiality of life. Recognizing that pregnancy is a dynamic process, the Court held that these interests are not of sufficient magnitude throughout pregnancy to justify limiting the abortion right, but rather grow in significance as a pregnancy progresses until reaching a "compelling" point.[14]

To accommodate the tension between a woman's right to terminate her pregnancy and what it determined to be the interests of the state, the Court constructed a trimester approach to abortion. Accordingly, during the first trimester, no state interest is sufficiently compelling to justify limitation on the abortion right; in the second trimester, when its interest in protecting the health of the pregnant woman becomes compelling, a state may enact measures designed to ensure that the abortion procedure is safe; and in the third trimester, when, according to the Court, the state's interest in potential life becomes compelling, a state can prohibit abortion unless necessary to protect the life or health of the pregnant woman.

[T]he Massachusetts legislature moved quickly to encode the constitutional mandates of Roe *[v. Wade] into a new statutory scheme.*

Responding to *Roe*

With the state's criminal abortion law now clearly unconstitutional, the Massachusetts legislature moved quickly to encode the constitutional mandates of *Roe* into a new statutory scheme. In accordance with the decision's trimester framework, abortion was made legal up until the twenty-fourth week of pregnancy, and thereafter if necessary to protect the life or health of the pregnant woman.[15] In an interesting twist, the legislature did not actually repeal the existing nineteenth-century criminal statute, which makes Massachusetts one of only a handful of states in the nation to still have a law on the books, albeit an unenforceable one, that criminalizes abortion at any stage of pregnancy.[16]

Pushing back against this sweeping change, local abortion opponents sought to limit *Roe's* reach. Quickly mobilizing through newly established statewide chapters, the Massachusetts Citizens for Life (MCFL), which was founded in 1972 to fight "ballot initiatives...which sought to remove legal protection for unborn children,"[17] took aim at two particularly vulnerable groups: teens and poor women. Claiming success, within a year of *Roe* Massachusetts became one of the earliest states to impose a parental consent requirement on young women seeking to terminate a pregnancy. Several years later, the legislature approved a law banning the use of state Medicaid funds to help low-income women pay for abortion, subject to a narrow life-saving therapeutic exception. These restrictive laws were promptly challenged in court with, as we will see, mixed success.

Low-Income Women and the Right to Abortion in Massachusetts

In the wake of *Roe*, abortion opponents across the nation insisted that taxpayers should not be forced to subsidize the taking of a human life through taxpayer-funded abortions. In a powerful nod to this sentiment, in 1976 Congress approved the Hyde Amendment, which banned the use of federal Medicaid funds to help pay for abortions for financially-eligible low-income women, subject to a narrow life-saving exception.[18]

Initially, based on the recognition that an even-handed approach to funding was essential to ensure that low-income women would have the same "freedom of choice regarding abortion...as [they have]...with regard to any other medical service," Massachusetts continued to provide state Medicaid funding for abortion in accordance with the constitutional parameters of *Roe*.[19] However, responding to pressure from local antiabortion activists, in 1979 the legislature approved the Doyle-Flynn Amendment, which, like its federal counterpart, banned the use of state Medicaid funds to help pay for abortions for low-income women, subject again to a narrow life-saving exception.

The law was promptly challenged in state court by a class of Medicaid-eligible pregnant women together with an obstetrician/gynecologist whose Medicaid-authorized practice included the performance of abortion. Each of the three individual class representatives wished to end her pregnancy under non-life-threatening circumstances, but could not afford to do so without the use of Medicaid funds. The essence of the plaintiffs' claim was that the funding ban placed an impermissible burden on the exercise of a fundamental right in violation of the due process and equal protection guarantees of the Massachusetts Declaration of Rights.

In response, the defendants (all of whom were officials in the executive branch of the state government) urged the justices to follow the lead of the U.S. Supreme Court, which, in the case of *Harris v. McRae*, had upheld the validity of the nearly identical federal funding ban. Impervious to the actual impact of the ban on low-income women, the *Harris* Court held that it did not impermissibly interfere with their right to abortion. To justify this result, the Court opined that while the government may "not place obstacles in the path of a woman's exercise of her freedom of choice, it need not remove those not of its own creation."[20] Accordingly, as seen by the Court, where poverty constrains a woman's access to abortion, the fault is her own, and she has no "constitutional entitlement to the financial resources" needed in order for her to be able to exercise her rights.[21]

REFLECTION

Hon. Nancy Gertner

One of the highlights of my legal career was winning the 1981 case of *Moe v. Secretary of Administration*, which I worked on with John Reinstein, the legal director of the Massachusetts American Civil Liberties Union. *Moe* challenged the state's ban on the use of Medicaid funds to pay for abortions. The victory made abortion safe in the Commonwealth, notwithstanding the vagaries of national politics.

Some feminists urged us not to use the Massachusetts Equal Rights Amendment as the basis for our arguments. They were working towards a federal Equal Rights Amendment and feared that linking abortion and the Massachusetts ERA would doom the federal effort. But we were advocates; we believed that we needed to use all of the legal tools at our disposal. We were certainly not alone—many groups filed amicus briefs, creating a wonderful sense of unity in the prochoice community.

We based the arguments in *Moe* on not only the state ERA but also on the state's anti-discrimination law. Medicaid covered a range of medically necessary operations including male-specific operations like male sterilization. It was discrimination, we argued, to carve out medically necessary procedures that affect women from medically necessary procedures affecting men. But the court went even further, describing the right at stake as the right to privacy, described specifically as the right to be free from "nonconsensual invasion of bodily integrity." It was a stronger, more wide-ranging decision than that of the U.S. Supreme Court in *Roe v. Wade*.

This case, and the abortion effort more generally, raised a number of important questions: Can the state force women to become mothers, no matter what the cost to their life or health? And what about efforts to regulate pregnancy—to require that women have Caesarean sections, to get transfusions, or to prosecute women for their behavior during pregnancy? How far was it from such regulations to the long-standing and now discredited protective labor legislation that barred women from certain jobs, or certain industries, because of potential damage the job might do to the woman's reproductive capacity?

Although cases such as *Roe* and *Moe* were very important victories, I think that in some ways they facilitated the disintegration of the political movement for choice. We assumed the battle was over. And more troubling, the generations that followed us don't fully appreciate how vulnerable the abortion right is, and how important it is to protect the gains we have made.

And more troubling, the generations that followed us don't fully appreciate how vulnerable the abortion right is, and how important it is to protect the gains we have made.

Hon. Nancy Gertner

IMAGE COURTESY OF HON. NANCY GERTNER

Declaring that the Massachusetts Declaration of Rights "affords a greater degree of protection to the right asserted here than does the Federal Constitution as interpreted by *Harris v. McRae*,"[22] the Supreme Judicial Court soundly repudiated the pinched reasoning of the Supreme Court. Zeroing in on the discriminatory nature of the funding ban, the court made clear that *Roe* imposes a strict duty of neutrality of the state with regard to "the fundamental right of privacy."[23]

Rejecting the Supreme Court's framing of the plaintiffs' claim as one of a constitutional entitlement to a publicly funded abortion, the court recast the underlying problem as one involving the singling out of abortion for unfavorable treatment. As the court explained, once a state elects to "subsidize medically necessary services for the needy," it may not then allocate benefits in a way that "discriminatorily burdens a fundamental right."[24] In this instance, by only funding abortion upon a showing that the procedure is necessary to avert death, while funding all others medical services, including those related to childbirth and pregnancy, based solely on a showing of medical necessity, the state has unfairly weighted the choices facing a poor woman.

Adopting the dissenting views of Justice Thurgood Marshall in the *Harris* case, the court concluded: "By thus injecting coercive financial incentives favoring childbirth into a decision that is constitutionally guaranteed to be free from governmental intrusion, [this restriction] deprives the indigent woman of her freedom to choose abortion over maternity, thereby impinging on the due process liberty right recognized in *Roe v. Wade*."[25] Further repudiating the Supreme Court's view that any potential burden would be counterbalanced by the government's legitimate interest in encouraging Medicaid recipients to choose childbirth over abortion as a means of promoting its interest in potential life, the Supreme Judicial Court noted that invocation of this stated purpose "does not camouflage the simple fact that the purpose, more starkly expressed, is discouraging abortions"—a clearly unconstitutional goal.[26]

Young Women and the Right to Abortion in Massachusetts

In 1974, a pregnant Massachusetts teen whose father had previously threatened to kick her out of the house and kill her boyfriend if she became pregnant, together with several abortion providers, filed suit in federal court challenging the constitutionality of G.L. c. 112, § 12S, a newly enacted state law that required unmarried women under the age of eighteen to seek parental consent for an abortion. If parental consent was denied, the statute allowed a minor to seek authorization for an abortion from a Superior Court judge for "good cause" shown.

The case eventually made it to the U.S. Supreme Court, resulting in the landmark 1979 *Bellotti v. Baird* decision, in which the court invalidated the Massachusetts statute because it vested parents with potential veto power over their daughter's abortion decision in contravention of *Roe*.[27] In striking down the law, the Court made clear that the possibility of a court hearing did not resolve the veto problem, because once notified of their daughter's intentions, parents might prevent her from going to court, or from subsequently obtaining an abortion.

Although the Court invalidated the Massachusetts parental consent law, it went on to make clear that in light of the "peculiar vulnerability of children; their inability to make critical decisions in an informed, mature manner; and the importance of the parental role in childrearing," the constitutional rights of teens "cannot be equated with those of adults."[28] It thus concluded that states have a "special interest" in encouraging teens to consult with their parents before terminating a pregnancy, and it provided guidance to states about how they could constitutionally provide for such involvement.[29]

As set out by the court, in order to avoid the possibility of a parental veto, a minor must be given the option of going directly to court without having to first seek parental permission for an abortion.[30] Once in court, she must be given the opportunity to show that she is mature and able to consent to the abortion, or if not sufficiently mature, that an abortion is in her best interest. Lastly, the hearing and any subsequent appeals must be confidential and expeditious.

Following the decision, the Massachusetts legislature amended its parental consent law to track its requirements. Most importantly, minors could now seek judicial authorization for an abortion without the knowledge or involvement of their parents at any stage of the process.[31] The revised statute was again challenged in federal court, but finding that it met the requirements of *Bellotti*, the court refused to enjoin its enforcement and the law went into effect in 1981. With it now clear that a federal court challenge was unlikely to succeed, the Planned Parenthood League of Massachusetts, together with several other abortion providers and a pregnant teen who wished to terminate her pregnancy without parental or judicial authorization, brought an action in state court challenging the revised parental consent law on state constitutional grounds. The plaintiffs clearly had reason to hope, in light of the above-discussed *Moe* decision, that the court would likewise find that the law "impermissibly burdens a right protected by [the state's] constitutional guarantee of due process."[32]

The plaintiffs clearly had reason to hope…that the court would likewise find that the law "impermissibly burdens a right protected by [the state's] constitutional guarantee of due process."

In deciding the case of *Planned Parenthood League of Massachusetts v. Attorney General*, the Supreme Judicial Court distinctly recognized that the bypass law "delays a minor's exercise of her constitutional right to abortion," which can "increase the risk" to her, and that the court process "can be traumatic" for young women who are likely to be "fearful or anxious" about the need to secure permission from a judge for an abortion. In short, the justices agreed with the plaintiffs that the law imposed an "unquestioned limitation…on a woman's constitutional right of choice."[33]

Having accepted delay and trauma as a natural consequence of the consent law, the court focused on the question of whether this intrusion was counterbalanced by the state's interest in the "welfare of minors" and the "promotion of the interests of parents in the care and upbringing of their children." Embracing the federally constructed narrative regarding the decisional incapacity of minors, the justices concluded that mandated third-party involvement would ensure that a minor's abortion choice was "truly free and informed" or "supported by a judicial determination that it is in [her] best interests."[34] However, the court did find that the state's interest in fostering the above interests was fully served by a one-parent as distinct from a two-parent consent law, and it thus concluded that it should henceforth be "enforced as if it stated a requirement only of one-parent consent."[35]

In upholding the parental consent law (subject to only requiring the consent of one parent), the court distinguished the law from the Medicaid funding statute it had invalidated in *Moe,* claiming that it was less intrusive and the counterbalancing interests of the state were considerably stronger. However, what the court failed to recognize was that, akin to the singling out of abortion for discriminatory funding restrictions, particularly when compared to pregnancy- and childbirth-related care, the parental consent law similarly singled out abortion for less favorable treatment than pregnancy and childbirth. More specifically, Massachusetts law vests a minor who wishes to carry to term with full decisional authority over this choice, and over all pregnancy-related medical care, including childbirth.[36] In short, according to Massachusetts law, competence is contextual and fleeting—present when the decision is to become a mother, but vanishing when the decision is to avoid early maternity. So viewed, it can be argued that the invocation of the dual state interest in promoting the welfare of minors and the custodial authority of parents "does not camouflage the simple fact that the purpose, more starkly expressed, is discouraging abortions"—a clearly unconstitutional goal.[37]

Conclusion

At the moment, Massachusetts is not a battlefield state in the struggle to ensure that women retain the basic right to terminate an unwanted pregnancy. Moreover, we are among the distinct minority of states which recognizes that the abstract right of choice lacks substance if poor women are denied access to abortion services based on the cruel logic of the Supreme Court in the Medicaid funding cases. However, as this and the other articles and sidebar comments in this section make clear, the abortion right is a fragile one—and we cannot be complacent about the enduring nature of *Roe.*

Timeline of Key Developments

1965: *Griswold v. Connecticut*, 381 U.S. 479, holds that a criminal law banning the use of birth control by married couples is an unconstitutional invasion of privacy under the Due Process Clause.

1972: *Eisenstadt v. Baird*, 405 U.S. 438, extends the *Griswold* right of privacy to unmarried individuals under the Equal Protection Clause.

1973: *Roe v. Wade*, 410 U.S. 113, holds that the constitutional right of privacy is broad enough to encompass a woman's decision to terminate a pregnancy.

1974: *Doe v. Doe*, 365 Mass. 556, holds that a husband does not have a right to prevent his wife from having an abortion.

1977: *Carey v. Population Services International*, 431 U.S. 678, holds that a ban on distribution of nonprescription contraceptives to minors interferes with their right of procreative privacy.

Maher v. Roe, 432 U.S. 464, holds that the constitutional rights of low-income women are not burdened by a ban on the use of Medicaid funds for abortion, even though the costs of pregnancy and childbirth are fully subsidized.

Framingham Clinic v. Board of Selectmen of Southborough, 373 Mass. 279, holds that it is impermissible discrimination against a fundamental right for a town to selectively ban clinics that perform abortions.

1979: *Bellotti v. Baird*, 443 U.S. 622, holds that states may not give parents blanket veto authority over their daughter's abortion decision, and that parental involvement laws must therefore include an alternative consent provision.

1981: *Moe v. Secretary of Administration and Finance*, 382 Mass. 629, holds that the denial of state Medicaid funds for abortion discriminatorily burdens the exercise of a fundamental right.

1964 65 66 67 68 69 70 71 72 73 74 75 76 77 78 79 80 81 82 83 84 85 86 87 88

A Burdened Right: The Abortion Consent Law

Marisa A. Campagna
J. Shoshanna Ehrlich
Kristen Lasker
Sarah McClean
Jamie Ann Sabino

Introduction

As long-time members of the Steering Committee of the Judicial Consent for Minors Lawyer Referral Panel (Panel), which is responsible for coordinating the state-wide group of attorneys who represent minors seeking court authorization for an abortion, we welcome the opportunity to share our reflections on the state's parental consent law. Collectively, in addition to having coordinated the Panel for over twenty-five years, we have represented thousands of minors in judicial bypass hearings; served as expert witness in court challenges to parental laws in other states; given legislative testimony in opposition to these laws; trained lawyers and family planning providers around the country on how to implement these laws in the least burdensome manner possible; and published multiple law review articles and a book on the topic that draws heavily on the experience of Massachusetts teens.

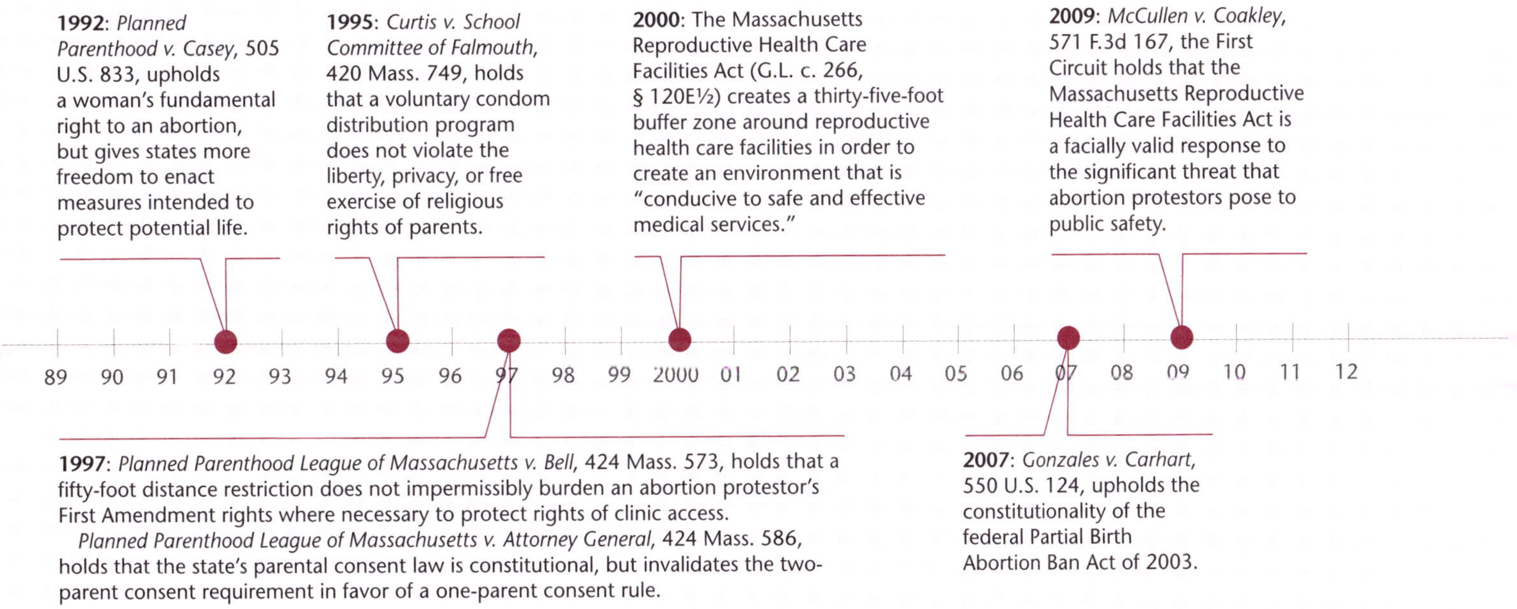

Our comments and ultimate conclusion that parental involvement laws, such as the one we have here in Massachusetts, burden young women without providing them with an offsetting benefit represent this cumulative experience.

In It From the Start: The Legal Context and the Origins of the Judicial Consent for Minors Lawyer Referral Panel

Jamie Ann Sabino

The original Massachusetts parental consent to abortion law was enacted in 1974. Under the law, if a pregnant minor wanted to terminate her pregnancy, she had to first seek the consent of both parents. If consent was denied, a young woman was entitled to seek judicial authorization for the abortion. Notably, her parents were entitled to notice of and the opportunity to participate in the hearing.

This law was immediately challenged by, among others, a pregnant teen who was afraid that if her father learned she was pregnant, he would throw her out of the house and kill her boyfriend. The case was eventually heard by U.S. Supreme Court, resulting in the landmark *Bellotti v. Baird* decision.[38] The *Bellotti* Court struck down the law on the grounds that it impermissibly burdened a young woman's choice because once informed of their daughter's wish to terminate her pregnancy, parents could potentially prevent her from going to court or from having the abortion. However, the Court made clear that a state could constitutionally provide for parental involvement in the abortion decision of their daughter if it gave her the right to go directly to court without having to first consult or notify her parents.[39] In short, to meet constitutional muster, the statute had to include a parental bypass option that guaranteed her confidentiality.[40]

> "Although it satisfies constitutional standards in large part, § 12S falls short of them in two respects: First, it permits judicial authorization for an abortion to be withheld from a minor who is found by the superior court to be mature and fully competent to make this decision independently. Second, it requires parental consultation or notification in every instance, without affording the pregnant minor an opportunity to receive an independent judicial determination that she is mature enough to consent or that an abortion would be in her best interests. Accordingly, we affirm the judgment of the District Court insofar as it invalidates this statute and enjoins its enforcement."
>
> —*Bellotti v. Baird*

Jamie Ann Sabino is the Violence Against Women Act S.T.O.P Grant Coordinator for the Administrative Office of the Trial Court of Massachusetts. Previously, she practiced family law and criminal defense with the firm of Klibaner & Sabino. She is a graduate of Wellesley College and Northeastern University School of Law.

Massachusetts then amended its parental consent law, G.L. c. 112, § 12S, in order to bring it into conformity with the *Bellotti* decision. A minor now had the right to go directly to court to seek judicial authorization for an abortion without any parental involvement requirement at any stage of the proceeding. In considering her request, a judge is required to

REFLECTION

Jamie Ann Sabino

It is important to note that most teens do involve their parents in the abortion decision. At least two-thirds of teens involve their parents in states with parental involvement laws and in states without such laws. Teens who *can* involve their parents *will*, regardless of the law. Teens who *cannot* involve their parents *will* not, regardless of the law. Indeed, we should feel compassion for those teens who cannot go to their parents, instead of making them jump through hoops and feel like criminals.

One client told me that her mother was drunk by ten in the morning, so I could pick her up at home. Another related that her mother had not asked her what courses she was taking in school for the past five years. These families might be genetically related but they are really no more than boarders in the same house.

Think of what the teen who walks into a judge's chambers has already accomplished. She has acknowledged her pregnancy, sought testing, received counseling, gotten up the nerve to call an attorney, made her way to a courthouse, walked into a clerk's office, and been willing to face a black-robed stranger with the most intimate details of her life. As one judge said, he should be able to find her mature as soon as she walks into his office.

I came to this work from the perspective of providing legal services to people who needed court-appointed lawyers. I had never been involved in any prochoice work or activities. Within a few cases, it became clear that the right to make a choice about whether or not to have a child at a particular time in one's life is a vital civil right and a critical issue for all women.

For many attorneys, representing minors seeking judicial authorization for abortion is an important part of their work and their lives. After all, how often do you get to assist in ensuring that someone's constitutional rights are protected and allow them to make critical choices in their lives that they might not be able to do without your assistance, all while handling a case with no discovery and that is over in a few days?

Within a few cases, it became clear that the right to make a choice about whether or not to have a child at a particular time in one's life is a vital civil right and a critical issue for all women.

determine whether the young woman is mature and capable of giving informed consent to the abortion; if not, the judge must determine whether the abortion is in her best interest.[41]

Before the law went into effect, representatives from the Women's Bar Association of Massachusetts, the Massachusetts Chapter of the National Lawyers Guild and the Planned Parenthood League of Massachusetts came together to figure out how it could be implemented in the least burdensome manner possible. Working together, this original group developed an integrated counseling and legal referral system that was carefully designed to ensure that the constitutional rights of teens would be protected as they negotiated the court bypass process.

Since that time, working closely with the counseling staff at the Planned Parenthood League of Massachusetts, the Panel has recruited and trained hundreds of lawyers through out the Commonwealth to represent the many young women each year who seek judicial consent for an abortion. Today, this integrated approach is a nationwide model for the delivery of services to teens who go through the bypass process.

The Lawyers' Perspective: Why These Cases Matter

Marisa A. Campagna
Kristen Lasker
Sarah McClean

The lawyers who represent minors in judicial bypass proceedings come to this work for a multitude of reasons. Some are prochoice activists. Some have had personal or family experiences with abortion that motivated them to help young women facing an unplanned pregnancy—this connection is often particularly significant for those who recall the pre-*Roe* era. For others, it may have been an affiliation with the Women's Bar Association or other groups focused on improving the status of women that brought them to this work.

Regardless of what brings us to this work, all of us who take these cases share a commitment to ensuring that our clients are able to make their own reproductive decisions. Central to this is making sure that they have access to a confidential and expeditious judicial bypass hearing.

To this end, we work closely with the counseling staff at the Planned Parenthood League of Massachusetts to ensure our clients fully understand their reproductive and legal options. We also take whatever steps are needed to minimize the burdens of the court process and to make certain that these young women are treated with the respect they are entitled to as petitioners before the court. Many of us also position ourselves to advocate for reform in this area of the law.

Working with young women who must go to court in order to exercise their right to an abortion requires us to play a different role than we are accustomed to as litigators in adversarial proceedings, or as transactional practitioners who do not otherwise deal one-to-

Marisa A. Campagna is a sole practitioner concentrating in employment discrimination and other civil rights cases. She represents plaintiffs/employees exclusively. She is a graduate of Suffolk University and Loyola University School of Law.

Kristen Lasker is a sole practitioner in Cambridge, Massachusetts, specializing in mental health and elder law. She also serves as guardian and/or conservator for myriad individuals.

IMAGE COURTESY OF KRISTEN LASKER

Sarah McClean is a Boston-based sole practitioner whose practice includes criminal defense as a bar advocate. She is a past president of the Women's Bar Association and the Women's Bar Foundation.

IMAGE COURTESY OF SARAH MCCLEAN

REFLECTION

Sarah McClean

I have probably handled well over a thousand Mary Moe petitions. The client that stands out for me, though, is the one I could not get to the courthouse. This young woman sat frozen and nearly mute in my office for hours, while I gently tried and failed to put her at ease and prepare her for the hearing. These things were clear: She was pregnant by accident. In no way was she prepared to be a mother. She did not want to have a baby and wanted to terminate the pregnancy. However, she was simply too frightened, depressed, and overwhelmed to participate in a bypass hearing. No matter what I said or did to help and reassure her—and I'd had lots of practice and success at this—she felt too helpless and hopeless to go through the process. She left my office that day without ever seeking judicial consent. I still wonder about her, and the baby she probably had. I hope they are together and all right, although I fear otherwise. To my way of thinking, a law that forces a young woman to bear a child in this way is just plain cruel.

There is a quote from the poet Khalil Gibran that sums up quite nicely why I do this work—and all of my pro bono work: "It was in my heart to help a little because I was helped much."

one with clients or ever set foot in the courthouse. Since our clients often need to get into court on unusually short notice, and without tipping anyone off as to what is going on in their lives, we need to be far more accessible and flexible than is typically required in our practices.

Because the proceedings can be so stressful and anxiety producing for our young clients, we are often called upon to provide them with emotional support in addition to legal representation. We also must help them negotiate the sometimes complex logistics demanded by the process. Their need to keep their pregnancy and abortion plans secret can make this an exceedingly complicated and delicate task. For example, we may have to help clients with no reliable access to transportation figure out how to make travel arrangements to distant courts without arousing the suspicion of their parents, or find ways around obstacles placed in the paths of our clients by non-cooperative and sometimes hostile adults in their lives, including school personnel and caseworkers from social service and juvenile justice agencies.

From the start, some judges and court personnel have appreciated how stressful it is for our young clients to appear before the court on such an intimate matter. They accordingly make every effort to demystify and streamline the process, and to treat these young women with the respect they deserve.

That being said, however, in the early days, bypass proceedings frequently ranged from the overly paternalistic to the inquisitional. Today, although some judges continue to intimidate and frighten our clients by over-emphasizing the relatively low risks of death and sterility or otherwise conveying their disapproval of abortion, the development of guidelines and a body of case law have helped to rein in objectionable practices. Judicial training and the presence of more women on the bench have also helped make these proceedings somewhat less onerous.

The Teen Perspective: Listening to the Voices of Young Women

J. Shoshanna Ehrlich

In addition to my work on the Panel and as an attorney handling Section 12S cases, my perspective on parental involvement laws is informed by in-depth interviews I conducted with young women in Massachusetts as part of a research project on the decision making process and experience of teens who do not seek parental consent for an abortion. This project grew out my frustration about the fact that the voices of young women were missing from the public debate over the wisdom of parental involvement laws.

[T]he voices of young women were missing from the public debate over the wisdom of parental involvement laws.

This frustration was intensified by the common characterization of teens who choose to abort without parental consent as rebellious young women who do not appreciate the seriousness of the abortion decision or the importance of adult guidance in this difficult matter—a characterization that simply did not square with the reality of most teens who go through the bypass process. Similarly troubling was the *Bellotti* Court's conclusion that the abortion rights of teens can be limited in favor of mandated adult involvement because they lack the ability to "make critical decisions in an informed, mature manner" that takes account of "both immediate and long-range consequences."

Most striking to me in the interviews I conducted was the seriousness with which the young women approached the decisions they were facing. Poignantly aware of both loss and connection, they spoke openly about what brought them to this moment in their lives and of their hopes for the future—a future that frequently included plans for motherhood.

They typically reasoned about both the abortion decision and the decision not to involve their parents in multi-dimensional ways that reflected the complexity of their young lives. For some the decision to abort reflected a powerful desire to protect their future. Some expressed a fear that they would resent a child who would rob them of their youth, and others, reflecting perhaps their own painful childhoods, vowed that they would not bring a child into the world until they were in a position to provide him or her with a stable life.

As far as the decision not to involve their parents, here too the young women expressed multiple reasons for why this was not possible for them. Grounded in the reality of their lives, some spoke of a history of parental abuse or neglect. Others feared irreparable harm to the relationship that they had, and a fierce desire not to damage these important connective strands. Others spoke sadly of fragile family situations that might strain to the breaking point under the weight of the disclosure. A common theme was also the lack of open communication about sexuality, which clearly made it more difficult for these teens to

Excerpted from: Who Decides? The Abortion Rights of Teens, J. Shoshanna Ehrlich (Praeger 1st ed. 2006).
All names are pseudonyms.

The abortion decision...

I don't want to say "devastation." I mean, life is wonderful—it should never be devastating—but it was really confusing.... You know, I've worked since first grade. I knew I was going to college.... I did the math in months, and if I had a child, it would be like August, which is right when I would be getting into school, starting my freshman year of college. So many things are just so important...it's just not the right time.

—Beth Smith, age seventeen

It would be awful to bring a child into a situation where a mom doesn't like him because it ruined her life...I don't want [him] to be reminded of it every time he does something bad, I've seen it happen.

—Miranda Roberts, age seventeen

It wasn't fair of me to raise a child that I couldn't take care of. I want to be able to give it a good life.

—Mary Smith, age seventeen

The decision not to involve parents...

I just didn't think it was the right time because of my dad—he was the assistant vice president at a big company—and he just got laid off because of a corporate merger, and since then, he hasn't had a job...they have a lot of financial problems...they're pretty stressed right now.

—Anna Lynne Albano, age seventeen

My mom and I have no relationship.... If I hadn't moved out, I would have thought about talking with her, but not now. I have no relationship with her.

—Amy Michaels, age seventeen

The court experience...

I think that [when] a girl under 18...finds out she's pregnant...[it's] already nerve-wracking...it's just so scary. Alone, you feel so alone.... And then you have to go to court...it was just so scary. Thank God I had my friends with me.... If I ever had to go to court on my own, I probably would have been crying every day.

—Mary Sousa, age sixteen

The whole time waiting, I was just nervous. I was thinking, what happens if they don't give me the consent? What am I going to do now? ...That's the only thing on my mind.... You know then I [would] have to go through all that I was trying to avoid.

—Miranda Roberts, age seventeen

It was just so overwhelming. I mean to have so much going on and then to have to go to a huge courthouse to sit and talk to a judge who was going to make this decision that really doesn't involve them.... I mean it was so uncomfortable...having to share something so intimate and so personal with a stranger...here I was with my big mistake and strangers saying if my decision was right or wrong.

—Beth Smith, age seventeen

imagine discussing their abortion plans with a parent. Notably, for some, this would have been their first ever real communication about sex.

Finally, as far as the court experience was concerned, none of the young women I interviewed felt that the court process had helped them to make a better decision. Rather, often experienced as a do-or-die high stakes test, they were clear that the hearing was a daunting barrier they had to successfully surmount in order to effectuate their decision not to become a mother.

Conclusion

Based on our cumulative experience with the Massachusetts parental consent law, we continue to dispute its value. It is premised on an assumption of decisional incapacity which is at odds with the richly textured nature of the decision making process exhibited by most teens we have represented over the years.

We are also keenly aware of the biased nature of the law in this state which allows a teen to make all pregnancy-related decisions, including the decision to carry to term, on her own, except when she chooses abortion. The antiabortion sentiment that underlies the segregation of abortion from other pregnancy decisions continues to fuel our resolve to try to change the law, while also working to ensure that young women receive the compassionate and effective legal representation that they are entitled to as they seek to exercise their protected (albeit burdened) right of choice.

NOTES

1 *Roe v. Wade*, 410 U.S. 113, 154 (1973).

2 *Commonwealth v. Bangs*, 9 Mass. 387, 9 Tyng 387 (1812).

3 *Commonwealth v. Parker*, 50 Mass. 263, 267, 9 Metcalf. 263 (1845).

4 *Roe v. Wade*, 410 U.S. at 134.

5 James C. Mohr, *Abortion in America, The Origins and Evolution of a National Policy, 1800–1900* 20–21, 42 (1978).

6 James C. Mohr, *Abortion in America, The Origins and Evolution of a National Policy, 1800–1900* at 42.

7 *See Kudish v. Bd. of Reg. in Med.*, 956 Mass. 98 (1969).

8 As quoted in James C. Mohr, Abortion in America, *The Origins and Evolution of a National Policy, 1800–1900* at 53. For details about the case and the legislative process, see James C. Mohr, *Abortion in America, The Origins and Evolution of a National Policy, 1800–1900* at 120–22.

9 *See* Kristen Luker, *Abortion and The Politics of Motherhood* (Univ. of California Press 1985).

10 Horatio Storer, *Why Not: A Book for Every Woman* 29 (Lee & Shepard 1868).

11 Lecture by Dr. David Humphrey Storer, father of Horatio Storer and prominent professor at Harvard Medical School, available at http://www.abortionessay.com/filesHumphreys.

12 In addition to Mohr, for further detail about the doctors' campaign, see, Kristen Luker, *Abortion and the Politics of Motherhood* (1985). Reva Siegel, "Reasoning from the Body: A Historical Perspective on Abortion Regulation and Questions of Equal Protection," 44 *Stan. L. Rev.* 261 (1992); Nicola Beisel and Tamara Kay, "Abortion, Race, and Gender in Nineteenth-Century America," 69 *American Sociological Rev.* 498 (2004).

13 *Roe v. Wade*, 410 U.S. at 154.

14 Note that the Court subsequently abandoned the trimester framework in favor of the "undue burden" standard. This new approach gives states more regulatory authority over abortion so long as any enacted laws do not impose an "undue burden" on the abortion right. *See Planned Parenthood of Southeastern California v. Casey*, 505 U.S. 833 (1992).

15 G.L. c. 112, §§ 12L, 12M.

16 *See* G.L. c. 272, § 19. For information on other statutory provisions regulating abortion in the Commonwealth, see http://www.prochoiceamerica.org/government-and-you/state-governments/state-profiles/massachusetts.html.

17 *See* http://www.masscitizensforlife.org/aboutus.html#faq2.

18 The Hyde Amendment is actually an appropriations bill that requires regular reauthorization. Accordingly, in some years, Congress has expanded the exceptions, to permit, for example, abortion in cases of rape and/or incest.

19 *Moe v. Sec'y of Admin. & Fin.*, 382 Mass. 629 (1981) (quoting introduction to Massachusetts Public Assistance Policy Manual).

20 *Harris v. McRae*, 448 U.S. 297, 316 (1980).

21 *Harris v. McRae*, 448 U.S. at 316.

22 *Moe v. Sec'y of Admin. & Fin.*, 382 Mass. at 651.

23 *Moe v. Sec'y of Admin. & Fin.*, 382 Mass. at 651.

24 *Moe v. Sec'y of Admin. & Fin.*, 382 Mass. at 652.

25 *Moe v. Sec'y of Admin. & Fin.*, 382 Mass. at 655 (quoting Justice Marshall in dissent, *Harris v. McRae*, 448 U.S. at 833).

26 *Moe v. Sec'y of Admin. & Fin.*, 382 Mass. at 654 (quoting Michael J. Perry, "The Abortion Funding Cases: A Comment on the Supreme Court's Role in American Government," 66 *Geo. L.J.* 1191, 1196 (1978)).

27 *Bellotti v. Baird*, 443 U.S. 622 (1979). This was actually the second time the case reached the Supreme Court. However, the first time, the Court remanded the case to the Supreme Judicial Court for construction of the statute under state law, and did not reach the merits of the case. *See Bellotti v. Baird*, 428 U.S. 132 (1976). For details on the complex litigation history of this case, see J. Shoshanna Ehrlich, "Journey Through the Courts: Minors Abortion and the Quest for Reproductive Fairness," 10 *Yale J. L. and Feminism* 1 (1998).

28 *Bellotti v. Baird*, 443 U.S. at 634.

29 In his concurring opinion, Justice Stevens argued this aspect of the decision was purely advisory in nature. *Bellotti v. Baird*, 443 U.S. at 656 (Stevens, J., joined by Brennan, J., Marshall, J., and Blackmun, J.). The Court, however, has since made clear that *Bellotti* establishes the applicable legal standards against which constitutionality of parental involvement laws are to be evaluated.

30 The *Bellotti* Court spoke in terms of a court alternative to parental consent; however, it noted that this was not the only permissible way to structure a bypass option. *Bellotti v. Baird*, 443 U.S. at 643 n.22.

31 G.L. c. 112, § 12S (1974), *as amended by* 1980 Mass. Acts c. 240.

32 *Moe v. Sec'y of Admin. & Fin.*, 382 Mass. at 646.

33 *Planned Parenthood League of Mass. v. Attorney Gen.*, 424 Mass. 586 (1997).

34 *Planned Parenthood League of Mass. v. Attorney Gen.*, 424 Mass. at 593–594.

35 *Planned Parenthood League of Mass. v. Attorney Gen.*, 424 Mass. at 600. In this limited regard, the Supreme Judicial Court proved more attuned to the rights of minors than the Supreme Court which had recently ruled that the availability of a bypass option cures the problems inherent in a two-parent consent requirement. *See Hodgson v. Minnesota*, 497 U.S. 417 (1990).

36 In fact, with the exception of abortion (and sterilization) a pregnant teen can consent to all of her own health care, and once the baby is born, she has complete decisional authority over her own and the baby's care. For a fuller discussion of this bias, see J. Shoshanna Ehrlich, *Who Decides? The Abortion Rights of Teens* (2006)

37 *Moe v. Sec'y of Admin. & Fin.*, 382 Mass. at 654 (quoting Michael J. Perry, "The Abortion Funding Cases: A Comment on the Supreme Court's Role in American Government," 66 *Geo. L.J.* 1191, 1196 (1978)).

38 *Bellotti v. Baird*, 443 U.S. at 651.

39 443 U.S. at 651.

40 It should be noted that the amended statute was subsequently challenged in state court, ultimately resulting in a decision that upheld the law, but recrafted it so that it only imposed a one parent, as distinct from a two parent, consent requirement.

41 In order to implement the statute, the Supreme Judicial Court issued suggested guidelines, later adopted by the Superior Court in the form of a standing order. The guidelines provide that hearings must be confidential and must be given precedence over other matters pending before the court.

42 *Bellotti v. Baird*, 443 U.S. at 634 & 640.

CHAPTER 5

Private Practice: Partners, Associates, and Corporate Counsel

Opening the Door

LAUREN STILLER RIKLEEN

For centuries, the practice of law was conducted with a comfortable consistency and was closed to women. Margaret Brent, who came to the colonies in 1638, is known to be the first woman lawyer in America.[1] Incredibly, more than 200 years passed before history recorded the names of any other women lawyers.[2]

> [The] civil law, as well as nature herself, has always recognized a wide difference in the respective spheres and destinies of man and woman.... The natural and proper timidity and delicacy which belongs to the female sex evidently unfits it for many of the occupations of civil life.... [T]he...domestic sphere... properly belongs to the domain of and functions of womanhood.
>
> The paramount destiny and mission of woman are to fulfill the noble and benign offices of wife and mother.
>
> *Bradwell v. Illinois,* 83 U.S. (16 Wall.) 130, 141 (1872) (Bradley, J. concurring)

It was not until the 1860s that women began to seek entrance into the legal profession in earnest.[3] But these intrepid women faced daunting challenges: sexual discrimination was deeply rooted in the legal system, and the profession itself posed more barriers to the entry of women than any other in the nineteenth century.[4] To gain entry, women had to file lawsuits in state and federal courts, as well as seek the passage of statutes that would specifically permit women to practice law.[5]

In Massachusetts, Lelia J. Robinson earned her place in history when she became the first woman admitted to practice law in the Commonwealth, but only after enormous struggle. Even with the impeccable credential of being fourth in her graduating class in 1881,[6] she was denied admission to the bar by the Massachusetts Supreme Judicial Court.[7] It took an act of the legislature before she was finally granted her well-earned right to practice law.[8]

Portions of "Opening the Door" were adapted by the author from her book, *Ending the Gauntlet: Removing Barriers to Women's Success in the Law* (Thompson West 2006).

Lauren Stiller Rikleen is executive-in-residence at Boston College's Carroll School of Management Center for Work and Family and founder and president of the Rikleen Institute for Strategic Leadership. She was previously an equity partner at Bowditch & Dewey LLP.

IMAGE COURTESY OF LAUREN STILLER RIKLEEN

▲

An advertisement for West Publishing Company's key number system in the 1974 volume of the Women Lawyers Journal.

IMAGE SOURCE: *WOMEN LAWYERS JOURNAL*

As a result of the brave efforts by Lelia Robinson and others like her around the country, by the turn of the twentieth century, thirty-five states and territories and the District of Columbia had opened the profession to women.[9]

But even as the profession opened its doors, a national pattern of discrimination in the early 1900s created pervasive barriers that greatly hindered opportunities for women to work.[10] One author described a professional world in which women lawyers lucky enough to be employed were limited in their choices to solo practices or office work outside the courtroom. Others found work as stenographers or law clerks.[11]

These barriers to meaningful work persisted throughout the mid-twentieth century. Women law school graduates were frequently told directly that, despite outstanding qualifications, the law firms' doors were closed to them.[12] One law professor advised a Harvard Law School admittee that she should attend secretarial school after obtaining her law degree—to guarantee landing a personal secretarial position for a senior partner at a high-prestige firm.[13]

Perhaps the most famous example of the overt discrimination women faced in their early careers is the often-told story of the first woman to serve on the U.S. Supreme Court, Sandra Day O'Connor. Upon her graduation from Stanford Law School (as number three in her graduating class), she was unable to obtain a job offer from any California law firm, except a position as stenographer.[14] Justice O'Connor's experience vividly demonstrates that informal barriers persisted long after formal prohibitions on women's entry into the profession were lifted.

By the early 1960s, women comprised approximately 3 percent of the legal profession.[15] Amazingly, more than 300 years after Margaret Brent came to America, women seeking entry into the legal profession were still pioneers.

When the American Association of Law Schools prohibited its member schools from gender discrimination in their admissions, one of the last formal legal barriers was eliminated and the floodgates to the profession opened.[16] In 1970, 8.5 percent of incoming law students and approximately 5 percent of all law firm associates were women.[17] By 2001, women constituted approximately half of the students entering law school and about 30 percent of the profession.[18]

But just as women finally overcame centuries of obstacles and began to take their place in law schools and as new lawyers, the profession itself underwent a radical transformation. To truly understand the daunting hurdles facing women in the legal profession at the dawn of the twenty-first century, it is necessary to understand the challenges facing the profession itself. In less than three decades, revolutionary changes in the practice of law resulted in working conditions that significantly impeded women's opportunities to succeed.

Through the years following World War II, law firms were generally considered stable entities with manageable growth.[19] Even the "big" law firms at that time were markedly smaller than today's behemoths; in the late 1950s, only thirty-eight firms had more than fifty lawyers. In 1985, more than 500 firms had over fifty lawyers.[20] Within twenty years, the top 100 firms ranged in size from 197 to just under 3,000 lawyers.[21] And those numbers have continued to skyrocket.

Until the early 1970s, associate attorneys in law firms were primarily men who could expect that the firms they entered were secure institutions, that they had a reasonable opportunity to succeed and be elected partner, and that, even if a billable hour requirement were articulated, it would likely be around 1,700 hours a year.[22] But the law firms women entered in large numbers in the 1980s were changing rapidly: billable hour demands grew dramatically, law firms were exploding in size and gross revenues, some law firms broke up, lateral hiring increased, and firms engaged in hiring practices that varied from the associate to partner model that had long been the hallmark of the law firm's organizational structure.[23]

For years, those concerned by the grim statistics that chronicled the small percentage of women who became law firm partners were offered the same rationale: that the disparity was due to the small number of women in law schools. According to this "pipeline" theory, once women graduated in larger numbers and began working in private practice as associate attorneys, they would emerge triumphantly as partners in ever-increasing numbers. After all, the progression of women accepted to and graduating from law school has been on a steady upward trajectory for more than two decades. Until the early 1970s, women were consistently much less than 10 percent of the entering class; by 1980, more than a third of the first-year students were women.[24] Today, that number is closer to 50 percent.

But the statistical gains during these decades tell only a small part of the story. These were years in which women faced overt discrimination in all aspects of their efforts to practice law. Many of these experiences have been fully chronicled in reports conducted by state bars or judicial task forces.[25]

Gitta M. Kurlat

The story of Gitta M. Kurlat is an unusual one for a woman lawyer who entered private practice in the mid 1960s. She found success both at a law firm and as an entrepreneur. Kurlat joined the firm of Guterman, Horvitz, Rubin and Rudman (now Rubin and Rudman LLP) in 1968 and became partner after only three years. Also in 1968, she cofounded Eikonix Corporation, a digital imaging and technology company, for which she served as director until it was sold in 1985 to Eastman Kodak. In 1986, after leaving Rubin and Rudman, Kurlat founded Kurlat Associates, a Cambridge firm specializing in business, securities, and international corporate law, and Kurlat Ventures, a venture capital company specializing in high-tech industries.

IMAGE COURTESY OF GITTA M. KURLAT

▲

An advertisement for Matthew Bender's Current Legal Forms in the 1981 volume of the Women Lawyers Journal.

IMAGE SOURCE: *WOMEN LAWYERS JOURNAL*

The simple fact is that, for more than two decades, there has been a sufficiently large pool of female law school graduates in the pipeline to warrant a proportional increase in women partners.[26] But that has not happened.

In 1987, the American Bar Association (ABA) created the Commission on Women in the Profession, recruiting as its first chair a Little Rock attorney named Hilary Rodham Clinton. The commission's first major task was to identify the barriers that were preventing women attorneys from fully participating in the profession. The ABA president who appointed the first commission members articulated the critical need to recognize and acknowledge gender differences as an important step toward achieving equality: "Clearly, the quest for gender equality must become a central objective of the legal profession if we are to be faithful to the professional ideal of opposing all forms of discrimination, and if we are to achieve full integration and equal participation of women."[27]

But years after the commission issued its first report, many of the obstacles remain in place, notwithstanding the continued attention focused on these issues. In 1983 and 2000, the *ABA Journal* polled lawyers to determine how women were progressing in the profession. Although the comparative results demonstrate progress in certain areas—particularly with respect to opportunities to obtain the first job after law school—it is startling that the data reveal that substantial ground has actually been lost.[28]

For example, in 1983, 38 percent of the women polled stated that they had to work harder than male lawyers to get the same result; by 2000, that number increased to 56.9 percent. The responses also demonstrated that, in 2000, significantly fewer women and men believed that high-level responsibilities, prospects for advancement, high salaries, and opportunities for direct client contact were equally available to men and women.[29] And, of even greater concern, fewer men and women were confident that women could realistically combine their role as lawyer with that of wife and mother successfully.[30]

Numerous studies and reports confirm the slow progress of women in obtaining partnership status—and the data are worse for women equity partners. This, in turn, affects the opportunity for women to achieve leadership roles. A 2011 survey conducted by the National Association of Women Lawyers reveals that 11 percent of the 200 largest firms in the country report no women on their governing committees, only 5 percent have women as managing partners, and women account for less than 15 percent of the equity partners.[31]

After more than two decades of observing the pipeline clog and develop leaks, it is clear that the simple mathematical progression previously anticipated is an expectation built on flawed assumptions. Instead of taking their place at the top of the profession, women are leaving in disproportionate numbers.

How are women in private practice doing nationally?

National Percentages of Women Partners and Associates at the Country's 200 Largest Firms, and Women Fortune 500 General Counsel[32]

Year	Partners	Associates	Fortune 500 General Counsel
2000	15.6	41.7	13.7
2002	16.3	42.4	14.9
2004	17.1	43.4	15.4
2006	17.9	44.3	16.6
2008	19.2	45.7	15.0
2010	19.4	45.4	18.8

And the progress of women in law firms is a harbinger for the progress of women generally. Law firms matter, as they are prominent institutions in our society. As such, the modern law firm is a critical source of power and influence. In describing lawyers as the "gatekeepers of our nation's justice system," the ABA calls for attorneys to be the "trailblazers in promoting equality."[33]

The importance of this challenge to our profession grows as the authority of lawyers extends even further into American society. Today, there are approximately one million practicing lawyers in the United States.[34] Lawyers have a seat at the table in important board meetings of major businesses and institutions, and corporations today rarely make decisions without attorneys at their side, serving as advisors and protectors. The large corporate law firm has been described as the authoritative center of the legal profession—the primary function of the legal system.[35] Writing of the elite law firms, one author observed that such firms were bound together by "their representation of America's major banks, financial institutions and corporations, the country's greatest concentrations of economic power."[36]

Large law firms also set the standard for their smaller counterparts, thereby exerting a significant influence throughout the legal community as a whole.[37] And private practice itself is currently the largest employment setting for women lawyers.[38]

Moreover, law firms serve as significant training grounds for those who become major societal figures of influence. Lawyers who have achieved critical authoritative positions in our society—such as judges, high government officials, or members of boards and commissions—often move into such positions from a partnership in a major law firm.[39] As reported by the Congressional Research Service, more than half the members of the U.S. Senate and 168 members of the House of Representatives have law degrees, and President Barack Obama is the twenty-fourth lawyer to serve as the president of the United States.

> Lawyer-dominated legislatures and bureaucracies now extend their reach into every corner of contemporary American life.... The positions that lawyers occupy throughout the corporate, financial, and commercial worlds are no less strategic. Judges increasingly seem to have the last word on the most divisive and hotly contested questions of the times.[40]

These words, written more than a decade ago by Harvard Law School Professor Mary Ann Glendon, proved prophetic in light of the pivotal role of the Supreme Court in the 2000 presidential election, as well as the role of the state judiciaries in ruling on such societal issues as whether same-sex couples have the right to marry.

Does age matter?

Percentages of Women Lawyers Under 39 and Over 40 by Firm Size in 2005[41]

Firm Size	Women Under Age 39	Women Over Age 40
Solo	32.3	63.5
2 Lawyer Firm	3.9	5.4
3 Lawyer Firm	2.0	2.6
4 Lawyer Firm	1.7	1.8
5 Lawyer Firm	2.6	2.0
6–10 Lawyer Firm	8.4	4.8
11–20 Lawyer Firm	5.5	3.2
21–50 Lawyer Firm	10.6	5.1
51 or More Lawyer Firm	33.0	11.6

The importance of lawyers to our democratic society, therefore, means that we all have a stake in this profession whose influence extends far beyond its office towers. The state of the profession in the early twenty-first century demonstrates that parity is still an elusive goal, as women lawyers face a gauntlet of challenges. The reality of these challenges was starkly depicted in a 2009 report by the Women's Bar Association (WBA) of Massachusetts, which analyzed employment patterns of women attorneys in Massachusetts.[42]

The WBA reviewed, by gender, data maintained by the Massachusetts Board of Bar Overseers, analyzing both where Massachusetts attorneys worked and the distribution of active, inactive, and retired attorneys. The report categorized employers by the following sectors: law firms (which were also sorted by size), companies, academia, government, and nonprofits.

The study provided an important look at Massachusetts women attorneys in the first decade of the twenty-first century. The WBA reported that women were overrepresented in government and nonprofit sectors relative to their representation in the profession. That is, although women were approximately a third of the active working attorneys, more than 50 percent of the total number of attorneys in the nonprofit and government sector (excluding judges) were women. Yet women appeared to be underrepresented in private practice: 69 percent of all female attorneys were in private practice, compared to 81 percent of all male attorneys.

Significantly, the WBA also reported that women comprised a disproportionate percentage of inactive attorneys. Of those lawyers who identified themselves as inactive, 57 percent were women. This striking finding means that women are leaving the active practice of law in greater numbers compared to their male colleagues.

Are women attorneys "opting out" of private practice or feeling forced out?

The WBA report raises important questions about the future of our profession. Are women attorneys "opting out" of private practice or feeling forced out? Are there policies and practices in the nonprofit and government sectors that are more favorable for women than those found in private practice? Is the preponderance of women attorneys in the nonprofit and government sector due to the fact that they may attach greater value to public service in their work? These questions make clear that much remains to be learned about the experiences that women face in our profession.

As women continue to push for equality in the profession, it is important to look to our role models and trailblazers for guidance. History matters, because lessons of the past can guide our future choices. When we look, for example, at the life of Lelia Robinson after she was finally admitted to practice law in Massachusetts, we see in her lonely path significant insights—perhaps even a road map—for how women can continue to move forward.

Notwithstanding her own personal struggles, Lelia Robinson was deeply concerned about the progress of other women lawyers. She created several networking groups, including the Portia Club, an informal network of women lawyers and law students, in which all of the Massachusetts women lawyers participated—which by 1890 numbered four. In these efforts, Lelia Robinson teaches us one of our most important lessons: that the success of each woman is enhanced by the success of others.

Lelia Robinson also chronicled the efforts and successes of other women, by locating and describing more than half of the 208 women lawyers counted in the 1890 U.S. Census.[43] Again, foreshadowing the future struggles of working mothers, Lelia Robinson learned in that census review that approximately half the women attorneys were married, but only five had children.

Lelia Robinson's account of women lawyers' lives also foreshadowed the studies that continue to help us understand where women go when they leave the profession. Even as today's media tries to portray attrition statistics as simply "opting out," Lelia Robinson taught us the first lesson about attrition: women leave the profession more often for other careers where they may find greater satisfaction and opportunity. In Lelia Robinson's chronicle, women lawyers left to teach; to become writers, legal publishers, and journalists; or to engage in social and political reform, addressing suffrage and temperance.

We must continue the work of Lelia Robinson, by chronicling the stories and struggles women face as they continue to pursue equality in the legal profession. The legal profession today is very different from the one Lelia Robinson entered in the 1880s, but inequities persist. Lelia Robinson teaches us that, together, we can ensure that we leave behind a profession that provides full and equal opportunities for our daughters.

2010: Voices of a New Generation of Women Lawyers

What experience have you found most rewarding in your practice?

I feel like I have advanced a wonderful legacy. My grandmother, the wife of a politician and judge, worked for many years as a legal secretary. She understood the law and knew how to run a practice. I have often thought that if she had been of a different generation, she would have attended law school, been a star advocate, perhaps even entered politics herself. Today, my sister and I are attorneys here in Massachusetts. We are in different areas of practice, yet we both pay tribute to our grandmother's dedication and commitment every time we solve a problem, protect someone's rights or step into a courtroom. She is proud of what we have accomplished and I hope that we can also serve as role models to attorneys in the generations that follow us.

*—**Meredith Ainbinder**, Boston College Law School 2004, intellectual property litigation*

I am a family lawyer, and my practice is about helping to create and support families. I get enormous rewards from learning about each person or family that walks through my door and helping them navigate the joys and sorrows of the legal issues facing them. In recent months, I helped a transgender client change his gender marker on his birth certificate. He had tried once before, years earlier, and been denied, hurtfully. The experience had been painful, and he was wary of trying again. Together, we successfully navigated the system and made the change. His beautiful hand written thank you note sticks in my mind, and I am thankful I was able to help. In my work, it is rewarding to see people persevere through difficult times and come out stronger.

*—**Patience Crozier**, Boston College Law School 2002, family law*

People contact lawyers when they need help. Whether working with employees of a corporation to navigate a complex government investigation or advocating on behalf of a pro bono client to secure educational services for a child, I find it tremendously gratifying to use my legal skills and expertise to assist people through difficult times.

*—**Dara Kesselheim**, University of Virginia School of Law 2004, government enforcement and compliance; major commercial litigation*

Mentoring opportunities have shaped my career. Early in my legal career, I was told that I should not rely on one mentor, but try to put together a sort of personal "board of directors" that could assist me in different aspects of my career. Those relationships, as well as the relationships I have had with students and new attorneys have been among the most fulfilling and have had a substantial impact on the course of my career, as well as my personal connection to it.

*—**Natasha Varyani**, Suffolk University Law School 2003, tax law*

What do you find the most surprising about being an attorney?

Before law school, during law school—after law school, so many people told me they would never recommend practicing law to a friend. It's only been 5 and a half years, but I still love being a lawyer. I love thinking like a lawyer to help my clients solve their problems.

*—**Allyson Kurker**, Northeastern University School of Law 2005, employment counseling and litigation*

How do you feel that being a woman affects you as an attorney?

I think I have more empathy for my clients because I am a woman. Women are sometimes criticized for being too emotional or attached but it's that attachment and emotion that my clients feel when I advocate for them. Clients know that I take their success or failure seriously and more than just as a competitive aspect of wanting to win a case.

*—**Victoria Walton**, Suffolk University Law School 2001, business litigation and real estate litigation*

Women, in general, tend to have more difficulty than men exercising power in business and personal relationships. The best advice I ever received about negotiating was from my father, who first told me that the person who is more willing to walk away has more power in a transaction or relationship. To be clear, my father was not encouraging me to live my life in a Machiavellian or manipulative manner. He was simply reminding me that I always have the inherent power to choose not to participate in something that challenges my morals or ethics or otherwise weakens me as a person. In the practice of law, just because it is possible to do something and a client is willing to pay you to do it, it is not necessarily the right or most prudent thing to do. Obviously, there can be a cost to walking away, but with 20/20 hindsight, the deal or the client that gives me a bad feeling often turns out to have been worth leaving behind.

*—**Michelle Kalas**, University of North Carolina School of Law 2004, trusts and estates, corporate, and nonprofit law*

Generations of women lawyers have worked to eliminate obstacles to success for women in the profession. What do you see as the next frontier for women lawyers?

I believe the next frontier is to foster strong networks and mentoring relationships among and between senior and more junior women lawyers in order to aid women lawyers in business development. Additionally, until work-life balance is made a priority for all attorneys—both women and men—the burden of child care will fall on women's shoulders.

*—**Kara DelTufo**, Boston College Law School 2003, labor and employment law*

"Unconscious bias." I believe that people (including lawyers) typically aspire to make good and fair decisions in promoting, hiring, and recognizing their colleagues and employees. The sad truth though is that their decisions, although well meaning, can easily be and often are influenced and overwhelmed by unfair biases that have sort of sustained and built upon years of experience coupled with the ever elusive "gut instinct." It is often difficult to pinpoint these age-old biases and "gut instinct" decisions in what otherwise comes across as a welcoming and celebratory community.

*—**Sa'adiyah Kanvel Masoud**, Boston University School of Law 2003, construction litigation, professional liability defense*

Although it sounds cliché, the next frontier for women lawyers is advancing professionally while caring for family. Women lawyers must fight to change the negative repercussions of leaving practice to care for an elderly parent or young child. It is my observation that once a female attorney gets off the partner track by taking an extended leave of absence beyond what is required by law or the firm's leave policy, she can rarely get back on track, no matter how talented she is.

*—**Laura A. Otenti**, Boston College Law School 2004, litigation*

As is the case with other professions, many women lawyers feel that they need to choose between having a career and having a family because it is impossible to do both. Whatever choice we make, we are judged by others as if the choice we made was the wrong one. I think the next frontier for women is to better support each other and the choices that we make both personally and professionally.

*—**Serena Madar**, New England Law | Boston 2002, commercial litigation, products liability defense, insurance coverage*

The next frontier for women lawyers is the formidable challenge of "work/life balance." In order to keep women in the profession, firms must adapt and value their lawyers on other bases in addition to billable hours. A female lawyer, who wants to have a family, will never be valued at the same level as her male colleague if the measure of success is billable hours. In order to reverse years of thinking, women bear the challenge of changing the overall philosophy in firms and changing how an attorney—male or female—is valued within the organization.

—Anonymous, Suffolk University Law School 2008, employment law

What has been the biggest challenge you have faced as an attorney? Or describe a challenging or difficult experience.

The biggest challenge has been coming to terms with the fact that the only avenue to obtain justice for catastrophically injured individuals and families is monetary compensation. Providing monetary settlements, no mater how substantial, to families of devastatingly injured clients never seems to be enough to bring them justice. No matter how happy the family is with the monetary compensation or how thrilled my supervisors are with the result, I am always left wishing I could do something more—they deserve more before I can call it "justice."

*—**Kimberly Dougherty**, Northeastern University School of Law 2003, pharmaceutical mass tort*

Serving as lead counsel on my first jury trial was one of the best but most challenging experiences I've had in my career to date. Although I learned quite a bit about what not to do from that experience, it was still the best feeling in the world when the jury came back with a verdict in my client's favor.

*—**Lurleen Gannon**, Boston College Law School 2002, employment and commercial litigation*

The biggest challenge is feeling as though there are never enough hours in the day to accomplish all that you've set out for yourself in that day and accepting that you are not going to be able to do it all and have it all.

—Anonymous, Boston University School of Law 2005, mergers and acquisitions

The Law Firm Experience—Decade by Decade

MARION R. FREMONT-SMITH

What was it like to practice law in Boston in the mid-sixties? In March of 1964, I was attempting to find out. I was thirty-eight years old; a 1951 graduate of Boston University School of Law; a member of the Massachusetts bar since graduating; married; and the mother of three children (ages thirteen, eleven, and five) and five stepchildren. My prior legal experience consisted of serving two and a half years as an assistant attorney general and director of the Massachusetts Division of Public Charities between 1959 and 1962. Before that I had been home with family, taught some courses in political science at Wellesley, and volunteered for a number of nonprofit and political organizations. After leaving the attorney general's office, I spent two years writing a book on government regulation of foundations, a study that was commissioned and subsequently published in 1964 by the Russell Sage Foundation.

The only basis on which I thought the firm might be interested in me was my experience in the Division of Public Charities, created under a 1954 law that gave extensive enforcement powers over charitable fiduciaries to the attorney general and his or her deputies and to which every charity in the state other than churches was required to file annual financial reports. During my time in the attorney general's office, I had revised the reporting forms, established an advisory committee of attorneys, bankers, accountants, and executives of the larger charities and businesses in the state, and, under the direction of the attorney general, increased enforcement of the state laws governing charitable trusts and corporations. My work included protecting bequests to charities in will contests. We cooperated with personnel from the Massachusetts Department of Revenue and the Internal Revenue Service in attempts to identify charities within the Commonwealth and determine whether they were in compliance with both state and federal tax rules for exempt charities.

Marion Fremont-Smith is an adjunct lecturer and senior research fellow at the Hauser Center for Nonprofit Organizations at Harvard's John F. Kennedy School of Government. She is retired from private practice at Choate, Hall & Stewart LLP.

IMAGE COURTESY OF MARION FREMONT-SMITH

In those years, the position of assistant attorney general, with a few exceptions, was a half-time job. Most of the other attorneys had private practices and were able to adjust their schedules as best suited their dual responsibilities, so long as their public duties were fulfilled. I used to say that my other job was my family. Through my position in the Office of the Attorney General, I came to know many of the local members of the bar and gained a sense of which firms might be interested in someone with my unusual background. The first firm I tried was Choate, Hall & Stewart, at that time one of the ten largest firms in the state. Fortunately for me, I was offered a position as an associate, working full-time, but with the ability to work from home as I found appropriate, given my responsibilities to the firm's attorneys and clients.

The one caveat given by the hiring partner during my first interview was to the effect that, although he did not agree with the policy, he thought it unlikely that the firm would ever take a woman partner and he felt I should be forewarned. I thanked him, inwardly thinking that I would just have to take my chances. I believed then, as now, that with more law schools admitting women than had been the case in 1948 and more women in law schools, their male classmates would have less reluctance to work with them professionally than men who had never been in coed classrooms. And once there were more women attorneys, the doors would have to open for them.

I started work on July 1, 1964. The firm was located on the top three floors at 30 State Street. On the top floor, the ninth, in front of the elevators was a wooden railing with a gate, behind which were two dark green horsehair sofas and a desk at which a receptionist sat. Behind her was a cubby for the switchboard operator, and behind that was a fairly long, narrow room with one window at the end and three desks lined up facing one of the walls. This was the "women's office." Two of the desks were occupied while the third was waiting for me. One of my office mates, Carla Herwitz, had joined the firm in 1960, having been an associate at Winthrop Stimson in New York prior to coming to Boston. Her specialty was blue sky laws. She had one child when she came to the firm, her second had been born after she arrived, and she was working part-time. The other associate had just been hired as a member of the corporate department. I was assigned to work with the tax, estate planning, and trust attorneys, where I would work as a specialist in matters involving charities, dealing with compliance with fiduciary duties, tax issues, and litigation, as well as estate planning and trust law. It did not seem to matter that the other attorneys with whom I would work were located two floors below. It was considered unsuitable for women to share offices with men, even though I was ten to fifteen years older than the younger associates with whom I might otherwise share an office.

It did not seem to matter that the other attorneys with whom I would work were located two floors below. It was considered unsuitable for women to share offices with men....

There was little, if any, opportunity in those early years for the women associates to have any contact with partners other than those with whom we worked directly. There were only two social occasions during the year in which any associates participated. The partners had their own annual Christmas lunch at the Somerset Club, the support staff had a party in the library the afternoon before the Christmas holiday, and the associates were "allowed" to have a dinner in a private room at Locke-Ober, where they could order as they wished from the menu. This was considered to be in lieu of a bonus, so that in a year in which the associates were unhappy with the firm, for whatever reason, but particularly if a favorite seventh-year lawyer was not elected partner and thus would be gone from the firm by the end of the year, the tab was likely to include some of the most expensive wines.

The other social occasion was "Field Day," an outing for the male lawyers held at a suburban country club. There was golf, tennis, bridge, a softball game, and a formal dinner, at which the newest associates presented a skit lampooning the firm. This was followed, for some of the most stalwart, by poker games that lasted well into the night. Of course, my knowledge of these social occasions during my first seven years at the firm was secondhand. It was not until 1971, when Carla and I were elected partners, that we were invited to both the Christmas lunch and Field Day, with all of the paralegals also being invited to Field Day that first year, for fear that we two might be uncomfortable.

Outside of the firm I found that there were other venues where women were not welcome. Most notable, given my area of practice, was an institution called the Lunch Club, founded many years before I started to practice, to assure that the business and professional men working in the city had a healthy lunch each working day: there was no alcohol and

The social limitations women faced when I first joined the firm began to disappear in the late sixties and early seventies.

there were always Oreo cookies on the table. The annual membership fee included lunch every weekday for ten months, with one month off at the member's option, and no service during August. Because their lunch had already been paid for, members were reluctant to eat anywhere else, so it was a very rare occasion when I might have a sandwich or even a more formal luncheon with a club member. Since the membership included not just attorneys but the whole range of business and professional men working downtown, this meant women were excluded from the place where one was most likely to meet business colleagues.

These social limitations were minor drawbacks in comparison with the great intellectual and personal pleasures I found practicing law in a field in which I was greatly interested and always challenged. The firm represented both well-established and newer charitable nonprofit organizations with interesting problems and I was also dealing with estate plans involving the then-complicated interplay of marital and charitable deductions. With very few exceptions, I found that clients were far less reluctant to work with me than were some of my colleagues in my first years at the firm. I never experienced discrimination by the partners and associates with whom I worked most closely. Rather, they were eager to introduce me to clients and, as time passed, I found I was taking on an ever-greater responsibility for client matters, as well as being consulted by a growing number of partners with questions that I was there to try to answer.

The social limitations women faced when I first joined the firm began to disappear in the late sixties and early seventies. Within a few years after I joined the firm, women associates were allowed to share offices with men. Three years later, when we moved from 30 State Street to the new forty-story building at 28 State Street, we all had separate offices. The firm's quarters were on several floors. On the top, segregated from the rest of the floor by the main entrance, was a wing in which the most senior partners were located. It was better furnished and more formal than the rest of the space and had a hushed atmosphere in which one felt like tiptoeing across the carpet if called by one of the senior men. In 1973, the firm moved to still another new building, this time across the street to 60 State Street, where our quarters included a firm lunchroom. By then, as a partner, I was in a spacious office with a view of the harbor.

Twenty-eight State Street had been the first of the many new buildings built in downtown Boston starting in the late sixties and early seventies. On their top floors, a number of the buildings had a variation of the Lunch Club, but without any yearly prepayment requirement; they were also open to males and females if they met other requirements. It was not unusual to have business or social lunch meetings in any of these venues. With moves to new larger spaces, the offices also included conference rooms, which became a common venue for lunch meetings. I do not remember any conference rooms at 30 State Street.

During these years, law firms were expanding in size, and as they grew larger, so did the number of women attorneys in their ranks. In 1971, there were thirty partners and thirty-one associates in the firm, of which possibly five or six were women (I have been unable to find records to confirm the exact numbers), and we two women partners. Roslyn Daum became the third woman partner on July 1, 1982, while working part-time with a baby at home. She had started in the firm as an associate so that her partnership track was the same as the male associates, except that she had taken leave when her daughter was born. The growth in number of women partners was thus very gradual. The next year for which we have statistics is 1988: as of March of that year, there were forty-six male partners, six female partners, and three attorneys serving as of counsel. This title was given to attorneys who were expected to stay with the firm but with no anticipation of becoming a partner.

In 1964, there had been no formal firm management structure. The senior partner ran the firm, with final say on partner shares, there were no formal departments, and unless one came to the firm with a special area of practice, the area in which one would work depended on the relationship one established with individual senior partners. There were three major fields of practice—litigation, corporate, and trust. The few tax lawyers were consulted by the litigators and business lawyers on the one hand, and the trust and estate attorneys on the other. There were two attorneys who were known not to be on a partnership track, one handling real estate and the other probate filings for wills and trusts. For some women, it was difficult to find a place in one of the major fields of practice. The difficulty was not with them; it was with the men, most particularly some of the older ones, who were unaccustomed to working with professional women and, for various reasons, were uncomfortable doing so.

Marion Fremont-Smith pictured in 1969 at Choate, Hall & Stewart's 28 State Street offices.

IMAGE COURTESY OF MARION FREMONT-SMITH

I was fortunate to be welcomed into the firm by a group of partners who valued my contributions and worked hard to assure that I succeeded. In those early years, I learned from these men the essentials for a successful and ethical practice built on service to one's clients, providing the most thorough research into the legal aspects of their situations, with specific attention to their particular needs, and all the wisdom the firm could provide to solve their problems. The sense of the firm as an institution to which you had been admitted on condition that you lived up to its high standards was very strong. It was a time when one was "up or out" after seven years. And once admitted to partnership, it was rare that a partner resigned and only in the rarest circumstances that one moved to another firm.

It was very soon after I came to the firm in July 1964 that I attracted my first client, a venerable foundation needing guidance on governance. The referral came from one of my uncles, an attorney himself who was a trustee of the foundation. I continued as counsel to this client until my retirement. Referrals from family are always good, but not a sufficient basis on which to build a successful practice. For me, starting with referrals from within the firm, I found that clients were being sent to me by members of the community with whom I had dealt during my years in the Office of the Attorney General. An important source of referrals was the trust officers in the larger banks who were administering charitable trusts. After I became a partner, the pace of growth accelerated. I was representing a wide range of nonprofit charities, including schools and colleges, hospitals, churches, museums, and a large and varied group of private foundations.

As with most of the larger Boston firms, Choate, Hall & Stewart had, almost from its founding in 1899, operated a trust office, with partners serving as individual trustees. This meant that there were a large number of beneficiaries and their families seeking estate planning advice, many of whom were committed to making substantial charitable gifts or establishing foundations. Helping them to carry out these goals was particularly satisfying and I enjoyed the chance to serve as counsel and trustee for members of several generations in a given family. There were, from time to time, both men and women clients who either explicitly or by innuendo made it known that they were not comfortable working with a woman. We acknowledged this by arranging for a man to take over their representation, a response that I believe is always appropriate. In contrast, as time went by and the women's movement grew, I found that many older women considered having a woman as their personal attorney as their contribution to the movement.

During the seventies, the pace of law practice started to accelerate; the firms became larger and took on new areas of practice such as health care, ERISA, and bankruptcy, while the real estate practice expanded. It soon became evident that a more formal structure was needed if the firm was to continue to provide the best service to its clients while continuing to be a profitable operation. The change had been gradual. The firm grew from forty-seven lawyers in 1964 to seventy-six in the early 1980s, with thirty-five partners and forty-one associates. The partners had adopted a formal governance structure, electing managing partners for fixed terms and a firm committee, half of the members of which were elected from among the younger partners and half from among the older ones. A chief operating officer (although not so designated at the time) was retained as well as a financial support staff. Soon thereafter, there was new staff to handle human resources and public relations, as well as financial officers.

Although our children might have disapproved of our accepting such "traditional" roles, I believe we were, in fact, slowly changing the climate in the firm to be more inclusive.

There were two other changes in the firm "structure" that occurred soon after Carla and I were elected partners. Carla had knowledge of and a particular gift for interior decoration, and firm management recognized the wisdom of taking advantage of this unique talent, asking her to assume responsibility for the planning and furnishing of our offices at 60 State Street. Her skill was again called on six years later when the firm moved to Exchange Place at 53 State Street. My assignment was to arrange for firm social functions, not by dint of expertise, but, I believe, because the management felt that I might have a better sense for this than any of the male partners. The format for Christmas Partners Lunch and Field Day remained unchanged, but in time there was a holiday party for the entire firm, together with spouses and guests; dinners for retiring partners; and receptions for clients and other friends of the firm when we moved to new quarters or celebrated the accomplishments of some of the firm's members. Although our children might have disapproved of our accepting such "traditional" roles, I believe we were, in fact, slowly changing the climate in the firm to be more inclusive.

During my early years at the firm, in addition to the volunteer positions I held that are described above, I was active in the greater Boston legal community. I served on the Attorney General's Committee on Ethics and Conflict of Interest, as well as on the Advisory Committees on Charities established by subsequent attorneys general. I was elected a member of the council of the Boston Bar Association, the board of the Federal Tax Institute of New England, and the Boston Tax Lawyers lunch group, in each instance the first woman to be included. There were major changes in the federal tax laws almost every year at that time and it was not unusual for me to participate as a panelist at the programs organized by the Federal Tax Institute and MCLE describing these developments.

Virginia Aldrich

One of the first women lawyers at Palmer & Dodge (now Edwards Wildman Palmer LLP), Virginia Aldrich joined the firm as an associate in 1957 upon her graduation from Georgetown Law School. Passed over for promotion year after year in favor of men who came to the firm after her, Aldrich in 1969 became the first woman to be admitted to partnership in a major Boston law firm. She opened the door for others to follow her, and, two years later, in 1971, Mary Gogan Sullivan and Raya S. Dreben joined her as the next two women partners at the firm. Aldrich retired in 1989; she passed away in 2011.

The first three women partners at Palmer and Dodge (now Edwards Wildman Palmer LLP): Virginia Aldrich (above), Mary Gogan Sullivan (right) and Raya S. Dreben (far right).

IMAGES COURTESY OF EDWARDS WILDMAN PALMER LLP

In 1971 (a banner year for me), I was elected to serve as a trustee of the Carnegie Endowment for International Peace, a foundation created by Andrew Carnegie to achieve world peace. The first woman trustee of the Endowment was Clare Booth Luce, who served in the forties; it was not until 1971 that any other women were elected. I had taught international relations at Wellesley, and serving on the board of the Endowment meant I could further my interest in that field within an organization with global interests. In 1988, I became a founding trustee of the Massachusetts Environmental Trust and soon thereafter an overseer of the Museum of Fine Arts. In each case, the mission of the organization was one to which I was dedicated, and although I did not have a great deal of time to devote as a volunteer, I tried to apply my skills to their benefit, not as legal counsel, but as what I hoped was a wise fiduciary.

As noted, Carla Herwitz and I were elected partners in 1971, effective July 1 of that year. At that time, there were no women partners in the large New York firms and just a few in Washington, D.C. We were among the first in the Boston firms, Virginia Aldrich of Palmer & Dodge having been elected a short time before we were. I was surprised by the change in status between a partner and an associate—hard to define, but definitely a distinction in the eyes not just of colleagues in the bar but also of clients, prospective clients, friends, and acquaintances. I believed that this action by the firm would help to defray any remaining animosity toward us, and that once the ground was broken, acceptance of women partners would spread throughout the bar. When by the 1980s women comprised almost one-third of the number of law students, the reluctance to hire new women associates that I had faced had all but disappeared. While serving on the hiring committee and interviewing law students on campus in the mid to late 1980s and later, I found that our firm was singled out by prospective associates as being particularly welcoming to women. The firm members were proud of this reputation and worked to make the atmosphere in the firm friendly to and supportive of women.

Indicative of the firm's support of women during my early years, including my time as an associate and during my first decade as a "new" partner, the firm had been willing to permit me and a few other women with families to work either part-time or what became labeled "flex time." The flexibility afforded by the ability to work at home and determine my office time was extremely important to me, even as the children grew older and I wanted to attend their sports events, school plays, glee club performances and the like. Neither flex time nor part time were considered feasible arrangements for litigators and for those in some aspects of corporate business practice, but it has become increasingly workable in other areas of practice, particularly with the introduction of computers and the now ubiquitous smartphones. However, changes in the nature of law practice that first appeared in the early to mid eighties signaled changes in the role of women in practice that have been discouraging for those of us who had hoped that women would continue to be encouraged to practice their profession in the larger law firms.

Most observers point to the summer of 1986 as the start of a major change in the nature of law practice. This change was signaled by an abrupt upward jump in the starting salaries for new associates.

Most observers point to the summer of 1986 as the start of a major change in the nature of law practice. This change was signaled by an abrupt upward jump in the starting salaries for new associates. The salaries for starting associates in the large firms in cities across the country have traditionally been pegged to that of the larger New York firms. During the early eighties, these firms found that they were losing their better-trained, more senior associates to the investment banking firms, which were paying considerably more than the law firms. The response from the New York firms was to increase the salaries for new associates who would be starting work in September 1986 from a projected $52,000 to $62,000. Firms in large cities across the country were initially reluctant to follow suit, but shortly thereafter the Boston firms announced that they would continue to offer the same salaries as the New York firms. This meant, of course, raises all along the scale, with the salaries of the seventh-year associates projected to be $140,000, a sum that in many firms was close to the amount that the youngest partners were reported to be earning. These larger firms were already paying higher rents in their new downtown offices, adding new support staff, and installing costly networks of computers and other electronic equipment. Substantially higher salaries for associates meant higher costs, which in turn meant pressure to increase hours billed and to bring in more clients. Critics described the changes as making the practice of law into a business rather than a profession.

During the decade of the eighties and into the nineties, it was not uncommon for the larger law firms to engage consultants who specialized in providing advice on conducting a law practice, with particular attention to the economics. Law partners, together with their consultants, went on retreats, where they learned the details of the changing nature of practice and considered how best to fit the firm into what in some respects seemed a new world. A direct result of our first retreat was the establishment of formal departments and the appointment of chairmen, as well as adoption of a firm policy requiring new associates to rotate among the departments for two years before choosing a field in which to concentrate. However, as the firm grew even larger and the class of summer associates likewise grew,

Choate, Hall & Stewart's 1971 partners' Christmas luncheon at the Somerset Club on Beacon Street in Boston. As a newly-elected partner that year, Marion Fremont-Smith was invited to the lunch for the first time.

IMAGE COURTESY OF CHOATE, HALL & STEWART LLP

formal rotation was no longer manageable. All attorneys were required to establish individual goals for hours worked, the number of billable hours recorded, and the amounts brought into the firm from their clients. In time, attorneys were required to adopt business plans. Although some guidance was provided as to how to attract new clients, the advice often was too abstract to be really helpful, particularly for the youngest associates. This pressure persists and imposes an impediment for many women.

The changes that started in the eighties were followed by an exponential growth in the number of partners in the largest firms, accompanied by the expansion of these firms through mergers or otherwise into nationwide or global entities. The time commitments for all lawyers grew substantially, as did the requirements for attracting clients. Along with these changes, I observed that the management of many of the larger law firms became more reluctant to agree to special work arrangements such as working part-time or flex-time beyond the generally agreed-on terms for maternity leaves. There was little or no flexibility for women with school-age children who wanted to spend more time with their families, and, where a special arrangement was permitted, the price that was paid was compensation proportionately far below that of full-time associates and partners. Sadly, in many instances, this required giving up the chance for a full equity partnership. The result was a marked loss of some of the brightest and most well-rounded women to positions as in-house counsel to various for-profit and nonprofit institutions, where the professional demands were not as all-consuming. This may not have been intentional discrimination, but it has created practical obstacles for women with family responsibilities that do not disappear after their children are no longer infants.

There is another external change that has posed more difficulties for women with children than was true in the years before my children had all left for college, namely the availability of child care at what was then a reasonable price. In the sixties and seventies, many of us had au pair help, namely young women coming from Europe who were able to live in our homes or come in by the day and who would stay for several years. Unfortunately, this is no longer the case. When help is available, or one relies on daycare centers, it is expensive and often difficult to arrange, if not impossible, when, as is inevitable, children are sick. I believe it would not have been possible to practice and care for my family as I did without support at home that assured me that my family was being well cared for during the times I was not there.

One of the greatest pleasures of practicing in a larger firm was the ability to work with and, more specifically, to teach, new associates. While I was in college and law school, I had considered teaching as a career and even started on that route but found that lack of a doctorate would preclude an academic career. This was all to the good, for when I started practicing I soon realized that there had been a reason why I chose to attend law school rather than seeking a graduate degree. What I had not anticipated when I started at the firm was that almost every year there would be new young lawyers eager to learn the basics of our specialties. When some of them in time became partners, we had a particular bond that was reflected years later when I was preparing to retire and was referring my clients to these attorneys with a tinge of regret but no hesitation as to the expertise and caring attention that I knew they would provide.

Before I joined the firm, while I was writing my book on regulation of foundations, I had been asked to join the board of the Foundation Center, an exempt organization that published *The Foundation Directory* and served as a clearinghouse for information on foundations. This meant joining a small group of foundation board members, business executives, academics, and public officials from across the country dedicated to improving foundation practices. The Center's focus was on increasing the amount of public disclosure of the assets and expenditures of foundations, and the members of the board represented the field before Congress. Through these associations with national organizations, starting at the end of the 1960s I had a unique chance to contribute to the development of national tax legislation regulating exempt organizations. Also before joining the firm, I had been requested to provide advice to the Treasury Department for a report issued in 1964 recommending changes in the regulation of foundations, particularly addressing the appropriate sanctions for violation of the tax-exempt provisions in the Internal Revenue Code. In 1968 and 1969, I participated in ongoing discussions with congressional staff members who were drafting what became the Tax Reform Act of 1969, and subsequently with Treasury personnel as they drafted the regulations governing the implementation of the Tax Reform Act provisions.

During and immediately following these years, two independent commissions were created within the private sector to address the future of philanthropic institutions. I served as a consultant to the Peterson Commission and was commissioned to write two papers for the Filer Commission. In later years, I testified before the Senate Finance Committee on compliance with the 1969 act and before the House Ways and Means Committee on the effectiveness of the provisions taxing the unrelated business income of exempt charities. During 1988 and 1989, I participated in the work of an advisory committee on exempt organizations established by the IRS commissioner to provide guidance as to the content of regulations relating to those sections of the Internal Revenue Code defining the term "educational" as it related to the limits on lobbying. In each instance, it was gratifying to believe that one was, albeit in a small way, influencing government policy toward the nonprofit sector.

Although in my early years at the firm the senior partners were not supportive of associates participating in bar association activities, I did join the Exempt Organization Committee of the American Bar Association Tax Section, attending meetings at my own expense. At the first meeting that I attended, in Washington, there were about fifteen men standing together having drinks, almost all of them formerly with the IRS and thus with inside knowledge of IRS policies relating to charities and other tax-exempt organizations. It was unclear whether their lack of welcome was because of my sex or the fact that I was one of a small but growing group of lawyers from around the country who were trespassing in their field. The number of members of this committee has grown substantially over the years, as has its influence in the framing of government policy toward the tax-exempt sector. By the time I was named chair of the committee, we had grown to approximately 100 members (membership continues to grow). My professional associations also included membership in the American Law Institute, to which I was elected in 1977, as well as the American College of Tax Counsel and the American College of Trust and Estate Counsel, in each case joining a small but increasing number of women specializing in these fields of the law. Happily, since the 1980s, the management of the firm has strongly supported attorneys who choose to become active in the programs of the various bar associations, reversing the policy of the original partners and those immediately following them—a policy of unknown origin.

In 1964, the partnership agreement did not have a mandatory retirement age. After witnessing a few episodes where it was clear that an elderly partner was experiencing memory loss, I came to believe that there should be a limit on one's ability to continue to practice. Such a policy was adopted by the firm in 1970, with retirement required at seventy-two, preceded by two years during which one's workload and client responsibility would be transferred to younger partners. Mandatory retirement age was reduced to seventy in 1989 at a time when many other firms and the accounting professions were setting the age at sixty-five. In our case, there were stringent prohibitions on continuing to practice after retirement. Other firms permitted retirees to retain some continuing responsibilities within the firm or in situations in which there would be no direct competition with it. In my case, having joined the firm at age thirty-eight, not the usual age of twenty-five or twenty-six, I felt disadvantaged by being deprived of the ability to continue as a partner for at least the number of years I had deferred starting to practice law, but with a caveat that this would be possible only so long as my mental and physical condition remained unchanged. I believe that being deprived of the ability to continue earning for a "normal" span of years puts women who postpone their careers at an unfair disadvantage, whether they take leave immediately after law school or at some date after having started practicing. I know this is an issue not likely to be addressed in the near future. Certainly, the current criteria adopted by the larger firms in hiring new associates or permitting them to take leave in these early years of the twenty-first century do not accommodate those who follow that alternate route in their career. Furthermore, even if the policy should change, until or unless there is a large enough group of women who followed the route I chose or a similar one, it is unlikely that the issue will be addressed.

I learned early on that any time I felt pulled in too many directions, I had to step back and try to sort out my priorities.

I have often been asked how I managed with all of the responsibilities I took on, particularly in my early professional years. All of us have personal responsibilities to other individuals or groups, whether to a spouse, children, parents, a close friend, or a cause. It is never easy to combine these responsibilities with a professional career. We need to make choices among these demands daily. I learned early on that any time I felt pulled in too many directions, I had to step back and try to sort out my priorities. I would try to do this by listing all of my responsibilities in descending order, starting with those that I thought needed immediate attention. Sometimes it would be work, at other times, family. I then forced myself to discard the responsibilities at the bottom of the list, the ones that were more easily set aside or abandoned, even if it was not really easy to do so. I found that I could then concentrate on the responsibilities that headed my list and ride out the storm as to the others.

While setting priorities, I have been fortunate to have the support of my children, stepchildren, their families, and, until his death in 2000, my late husband Paul Fremont-Smith. As I wrote in my book *Governing Nonprofit Organizations: Federal and State Law and Regulation,* published in 2004, "[h]is love, his empathy and his unwavering support of my career are behind all I have been able to accomplish." I still feel that way today.

Massachusetts Largest Law Firms: Women Attorneys and Equity Partners by the Numbers[44]

How do firms with fifty or more attorneys compare?

In 2011, at Massachusetts law firms with fifty or more attorneys, approximately 33.4% of attorneys were women and approximately 18.2% of equity partners were women.

Rank by Size	Male Attorneys	Female Attorneys	Male Equity Partners	Female Equity Partners
1	301	187	108	33
2	295	155	97	17
3	186	127	81	27
4	164	97	62	16
5	154	89	84	24
6	131	76	N/R	N/R
7	127	66	40	7
8	106	55	58	7
9	104	47	59	20
10	95	52	40	11
11	94	52	39	5
12	79	42	29	5
12	85	36	24	5
14	84	32	39	10
15	83	32	N/R	N/R
16	84	26	44	4
17	70	35	17	2
18	65	28	19	2
19	55	24	14	4
20	46	31	9	6
21	N/R	N/R	N/R	N/R
22	47	24	29	7
23	55	14	34	7
24	49	19	19	1
25	50	15	37	7
26	52	12	11	1
27	48	15	28	3
28	41	20	12	2
28	42	19	N/R	N/R
30	47	13	27	4
31	39	18	N/R	N/R
32	38	15	N/R	N/R
33	39	13	4	0
34	36	15	17	4

* N/R = number not reported by the firm

The Importance of Community Involvement and Living a Three-Dimensional Life

JULIA HUSTON

I entered law school in 1989 intending to make a difference in society and effect positive social change, and imagined that I would practice constitutional law or advocate for the rights of poor people. That path did not materialize for me, however, as by the time I graduated I had been a "starving student" for so many years that I felt I had to take the highest-paying job that I could get. I ended up practicing commercial litigation at a 100-attorney firm, which was charmingly viewed as a "large firm" in those days. What started out as a detour became my career, and I am now the chair of Foley Hoag LLP's trademark, copyright, and unfair competition practice group.

I did not know any litigators growing up, much less female ones, and had no role models for such a career path. I had never even owned a suit before! In my first few years of practice, I felt like a stranger in a strange land. Although I looked for women mentors during those early years, successful women partners with the time and interest in mentoring were few and far between. I developed strong mentoring relationships with several male partners and senior associates, and they were instrumental in guiding my career. Somehow I grew into the job without feeling like I had "sold out" my core values, and came to enjoy my day-to-day work. Now I cannot imagine doing anything else.

I realize that I am in a minority, however, as an astonishingly high percentage of lawyers are dissatisfied with their jobs. This dissatisfaction often bleeds over into lawyers' personal lives, and alcoholism, depression, and divorce are tragically commonplace in our profession. I have sometimes wondered how I managed to find happiness despite these odds, especially given the unique challenges and pressures facing women lawyers. I think it was because I was lucky enough to have wonderful mentors and to work at firms that encouraged me to be active in bar associations and other outside groups, and thereby strive to become what I think of as "three-dimensional" person.

Julia Huston is a partner in Foley Hoag LLP's intellectual property and litigation departments. She is chair of the firm's trademark, copyright and unfair competition practice group and cochair of the firm's advertising and marketing practice group.

IMAGE COURTESY OF FOLEY HOAG LLP

Living a Three-Dimensional Life

As lawyers, we are all committed to the work dimension of our existence. Our jobs require a lot of time, energy, and mental focus. We all have family lives of some sort, which I think of as a second dimension. A lot of attention must be given to the challenges of balancing work and family, but I think there is a third dimension that is often ignored. That third dimension is community involvement, which occurs most often through meaningful volunteer work.

Of all the lawyers I know, the happiest ones are those who engage in volunteer work that matters to them. It is difficult to make time to volunteer, but it is important, and the rewards can be enormous. In my case, I have been able to fulfill my desire to promote social justice by volunteering my time for the Women's Bar Association, the Boston Bar Association,

Greater Boston Legal Services, and other organizations. These opportunities have allowed me to expand my skill set, form meaningful relationships with leaders in the bar and the community at large, and experience the satisfaction of working toward a better society.

But perhaps most importantly, doing volunteer allows me to be me. I have been able to choose my commitments freely, and focus on issues that really matter to me. This is critically important, as my volunteer commitments are often very different from what I do at work every day. Using the law to advocate on behalf of people who are less fortunate than I am is compelling to me as an attorney and as a leader, and makes life more meaningful to me. It makes my life more three-dimensional.

A lot of attention must be given to the challenges of balancing work and family, but I think there is a third dimension that is often ignored. That third dimension is community involvement….

Revealing Oneself Through Volunteering

It is often difficult to make time for volunteer activities. On the one hand, once I make a commitment and prioritize it, I find that the time appears. On the other hand, every commitment comes at a cost, and I realize that not every attorney would make the same choices that I do. The fact that I did not have children until my forties allowed me to devote very substantial time to my career as an associate and new partner, and I was certainly no role model for work-life balance during those years. For example, when I was elected as president of the Women's Bar Association, I did not ask my firm for any reduction in billable hours, but instead asked for a second secretary to support my increased workload. Each attorney has to find a balance that is right for her, based on her priorities and resources, but hopefully that balance will include at least some meaningful volunteer work.

In my experience, volunteer work is a path to becoming a three-dimensional person because it allows every aspect of our personalities to be revealed. At work, we must behave in a certain way and comport ourselves in accordance with the expectations of our clients, partners, and organizations. Our clients' goals are our goals, as they should be. As volunteers, on the other hand, our focus expands to the larger community and to people less fortunate than we are, and our goals become extraordinary. The practice of law intersects with matters of the heart and, as a result, the fullness of our personalities is more readily revealed. For example, I served as president of Greater Boston Legal Services during a national economic downturn that resulted in devastating budget cuts. My fellow board members and I had to make some very difficult decisions, which required our expertise as attorneys, our leadership skills, and our compassion for other people. The opportunity for lawyers to bring these sides of our personalities together rarely occurs in our "day jobs" and the result is that we, too, are given the opportunity to become extraordinary.

The relationships I have built have informed my professional life in important ways. It is largely because of my volunteer work in bar associations that I have been able to build lasting lawyer referral networks. But more significantly, these relationships have enriched my personal life. Community involvement, by giving people more room to be themselves, allows people to get to know one another in a way that the practice of law typically does not allow. Working on behalf of others with exceptional people from many different backgrounds, firms and organizations, in whom I would always place my trust, has given me enduring personal relationships that are very valuable to me.

Julia Huston speaking as chair of the Equal Justice Coalition at the Eleventh Annual Walk to the Hill for Civil Legal Aid on January 27, 2010. The walk mobilizes private bar support for civil legal aid programs and is cosponsored by the Equal Justice Coalition, the Boston Bar Association, the Massachusetts Bar Association, and twenty-nine local and specialty bar associations.

IMAGE COURTESY OF KENNETH MARTIN/AMSTOCKPHOTO.COM

Our Shared Journey

Finally, volunteering has allowed me to connect with a wide variety of women lawyers in different practices and understand the issues that we commonly face. While each of our journeys is necessarily an individual one, there are most definitely some common themes. Volunteering outside the office, particularly on projects related to the status of women in the legal profession, has provided me with a valuable context for my own journey. It has also provided me with a rich network of colleagues and friends. It is these relationships that have sustained me through the highs and lows of my career. I am privileged to have had an opportunity to participate in the professional journeys of so many talented women attorneys and am fortunate that so many of them have chosen to participate in mine. I know that I am a better person—and a more "three-dimensional" person—because of it.

Reflections of Women Lawyers in the Private Sector

Essence McGill Arzu

Lift As You Climb

When I graduated from law school in 2000, I had been blessed with the opportunity of learning in a very diverse environment at Columbia Law School. We had a strong contingent of African-American students, a wide array of foreign students from the LL.M. program, and a number of students who had prior experiences in diverse environments. I was really excited to go out and conquer the corporate world knowing that I would have a wide variety of mentors and colleagues there to conquer it with me.

Imagine my surprise when I landed at my first law firm out of law school and was one of only two African-American attorneys. I thought that perhaps it was just my firm—I had picked a smaller New York office of a larger law firm with many foreign offices. So I reached out to my classmates, who unfortunately were facing similar numbers at their firms. I thought to myself, "What happened?" Throughout my life I have had plenty of experience being "one of only a few" or "the only one" in many environments. I was one of only a handful of students of color at almost every ballet school I ever attended. As a Russian studies concentrator, I got a strange look more than once when I walked into a class or lecture. As an avid college football fan and a manager of my college football team, people always were surprised that I knew a first down from a teacup. But in the law profession in the twenty-first century, I had expected better.

So I set off on my journey to become a corporate lawyer and developed a highly varied practice in domestic and international corporate finance, mergers and acquisitions, and nonprofit law. Being the daughter of sixties radicals, I also tried to blend this professional success with civic engagement, social justice, and personal fulfillment. In my career I have been blessed with a richness of many who, knowing the dearth of attorneys of color, especially women attorneys of color in the field, reached out to me to help me train, excel, and ascend. In particular, I give great credit to my current firm, Foley Hoag LLP, which welcomed me as a lateral seven years ago, enveloped me into the corporate practice as one of its own, and through strong advocates within (and outside)—both men and women, both of color and not—set its sights on seeing me succeed. I also credit the pioneers who set the path for me to follow—Ruth Ellen Fitch, the first African-American woman partner at Palmer & Dodge, and Diane Patrick, First Lady of the Commonwealth and partner at Ropes & Gray. Their success allowed the idea that I could be a partner to be a reachable possibility. In addition, I credit the efforts of the Boston Lawyers Group, whose advocacy and support on these issues was critical to my success in Boston. Through all these countless supporters, I made it to the promised land—partnership! And yet I am still one of only a few African-American women partners at a major law firm in Boston. I never thought I would still be a "first," but here I am and I am determined to make sure that I am not the last.

Essence McGill Arzu

IMAGE COURTESY OF FOLEY HOAG LLP

I have tried to live by a few mottos that I hope will be helpful to others in their careers:

- **Find your passion and bring your whole authentic self to the table.** When you are committed to your passions and live as your authentic self, the path, though challenging, is an enjoyable one.
- **Seek out a diverse board of directors.** Find advocates, mentors, advisors, and critics, when necessary, to be your inner circle, give you guidance, be a sounding board, be your cheerleaders, and help you on your path.
- **Dream big, but know when to take a chance.** If you don't dream big, you will never know what you can achieve, but it's also important to be strong enough to take a chance on a new and seemingly different opportunity along your path to success.
- **Lift as you climb.** As important as it is to have your own board of directors, it is just as important to serve on the board of directors to someone else and pave their way to success.

Janice Bassil

The Good Old Bad Days

Yes they were the bad old days. Judges did call you young lady and suggest that your supervisor not assign you to a sex offender case. I was a baby public defender, twenty-four years old and scared to death. It didn't occur to me for some time that I was treated badly because I was a woman. Can I tell the war stories because they are funny and sad and most of the time I thought I handled them pretty well?

I can remember waiting for a jury and the court officer asking me if I knew Nancy Gertner (and no, I never told Judge Gertner this story) and I said yes, I admired her a great deal. She had just tried the Susan Saxe murder case, the first woman lawyer to try a first-degree murder case in Suffolk County. And because the boys in charge could not stand this idea, the rumor ran through the courthouse that Nancy and her client must be in a romantic relationship. He kept asking me, do I know Nancy Gertner, what do I think of her, do I know Susan Saxe? When he apparently couldn't get the answer he wanted, he asked me why I wasn't married—now I got it. I pulled out a role of dimes—there were no cell phones then—gave him one and said, "Please call my mother and talk with her. She's needed someone to discuss this for years." He laughed, punched me lightly on the shoulder, and said "You're OK, kid," and I guess I was.

So all my study, preparation, and angst for clients came down to very little—whether I could humor and pacify a misogynistic Neanderthal who could also make not only my life miserable but those of my clients with very little effort.

In some ways, though, the bad old days left room for thoughtfulness and flexibility that doesn't exist now. Rules were not so stringent then and some of them were broken in the name of simple humanity. Another war story—I represented a young girl who became involved with a very bad man, as we liked to say. He persuaded her to commit a number of bank robberies and she was about to be sentenced. The clerk, knowing that the only judge available was a "hang 'em high" type, "suddenly" forgot and sent my client back to

Janice Bassil

IMAGE SOURCE: CARNEY & BASSIL, PC

detention until a new and better judge was available. There were many breaks I received for myself and my clients that male lawyers did not.

I do know, though, that to prove I was legitimate I had to work twice as hard as any man and be three times as prepared. I could never show fear and even though male colleagues with the same level of experience could brazen (some might say "bullsh-t") their way through a hearing, I could not do that. And none of the other women could, either. We always questioned our legitimacy. We always wondered when we would be exposed for the fake that we thought we were. But over time—over much time—that lack of confidence began to dissipate. Not only could women get good results for their clients, sometimes we could do better than our male colleagues.

I do know, though, that to prove I was legitimate I had to work twice as hard as any man and be three times as prepared.

My very best war story involves a Superior Court judge who listened, who cared, and who didn't believe in locking up everyone. I came into his court with a young man who was charged with assault with intent to murder. His father had died, and the landlord threatened to evict him and his mother if my client's mother did not have sex with him. My client arrived home one afternoon, found the landlord assaulting his mother, and shot him with bird shot with his father's rifle, causing some, but not serious, injury. I told this judge my tale of woe and he turned to me and said, "Waive your jury trial and I'll find him not guilty." He swiveled to the DA and said, "You agree with that, don't you?" As the DA tried to choke out an answer, the judge said, "How can you say no to a pretty girl?" What do you say when a judge says that? You say what I did: you say thank you.

But it was lonely at times. There were no role models. Stephanie Page and I would go up to Superior Court to watch the most respected male lawyers and realize that we couldn't do what they could. If we bore down on a witness or yelled at a judge, we were a bitch. If we tried to show some sympathy, we were seen as girls who shouldn't be in court. Men could wear the same suit every day and just change their tie. We had to look like a lawyer—whatever that meant for a female. We were told you weren't really a trial lawyer until you got drunk the night before and delivered a closing argument the next morning hungover as hell. I didn't drink—I just threw up instead each day before court from nerves. Many, many times, I was the only woman in the courtroom.

Looking back, it's been a good profession, and I have loved being a lawyer since the day I walked into the old fourth-floor Boston Municipal Court and saw the thick pall of smoke covering defendants, lawyers, police, and witnesses alike. It hasn't been easy and at times the frustration and anger at the system have been overwhelming. In a choice between a personal life and a client who was going to jail for the rest of his or her life if I didn't write the motion, find the witness, and track down the records, the client's needs came first. Maybe if I had been a man and had felt assured of my place in the world, that wouldn't have been the choice, but I have never regretted my dedication and, indeed, love of this profession.

We don't have to be tougher than the toughest male and we can bring a humanity to the courts. I see that now as a strength and not a weakness. I only hope that young female lawyers have people who look like them, talk like them, and can be the role models we all hoped for.

Elizabeth A. Brown

Charting Your Own Path

Elizabeth A. Brown

IMAGE COURTESY OF ELIZABETH A. BROWN

My story begins in the private sector but ends outside of it. I made partner at a large private firm and then walked away from it. I'd like to say that I carefully planned the path from partnership to the happier and more fulfilling life I have now, but that would be misleading. It's truer to say that after I checked off certain accomplishments, I put together a reasonably detailed vision of what I truly wanted. Actually creating that life—not ideal, but idealish—took more time.

As an associate, my biggest mistakes were believing that (1) work was a meritocracy and (2) you can succeed at anything alone. After years of excelling in school by working hard all the time, I assumed that the same formula would work in the office. So when I joined a big law firm, my assumption was that I would be evaluated based on both the quality and quantity of my work. I threw myself into my work, billing 2,000 hours annually in my first few years. For a long time, I felt I was doing well. I twisted myself into knots to do whatever the partners asked. In return, they let me argue motions and draft eloquent demand letters to opposing counsel. My work was good enough that nobody complained when I spent more time on pro bono work than other associates, year after year. Providing legal services was unusually thrilling, and I did as much nonbillable work as I could get away with. After all, for many years those clients were the only ones I could talk with directly.

It may be obvious that I had no understanding of mentors, let alone sponsors. I had heard of mentors but didn't comprehend why they were important, how to get them, or why anyone would sacrifice a potential billable hour for a casual chat. I was friendly with partners but seldom lingered in their offices after we'd finished discussing the case. Since I worked over every meal, the idea of having lunch with another human being seemed like something that would hurt my career rather than help it. My career strategy amounted to planning my vacation during the week that a case emergency was least likely to come up. I treated the partners I worked with as my clients and it would never have occurred to me to ask a client for career advice. Instead, I devoted myself to making the partners happy, usually at the expense of my own happiness. It rarely, if ever, occurred to me that happiness and accomplishment were two different things.

My personal life, or lack thereof, threw up another professional roadblock. Being single was anomalous at my law firm, especially as my associate class got more senior. I was single throughout my associate years although I usually had an inappropriate boyfriend who took up the little free time I had. That left me with nothing to talk about with my colleagues besides work. Fortunately, I listen well.

Eventually, a broken engagement led to a fascination with yoga, which in turn opened up space for introspection. This amazed me, and never one to do anything halfway, I got my yoga teaching certification in a weekend training program while working full-time. Taking the time to breathe consciously and move through difficult poses was both humbling and deeply satisfying. That was my first step toward noticing that my frantic work life and exorbitant income weren't really making me happy. The people I loved made me happy. At that time, they were mostly related to me and still living near Boston, where I grew up. So in my late thirties, still single, I moved from San Francisco to Boston.

That decision set off a chain of enormous changes. In a one-year period, I moved 3,000 miles, bought a house in the suburbs of Boston, joined a new law firm, met the love of my life, got engaged, made partner, got married, and got pregnant, in more or less that order.

I can't say much about what it was like to be pregnant as a litigation partner, but it did make me think long and hard about what path I wanted to follow after my daughter was born. Some combination of pregnancy and yoga set off instincts I could no longer suppress. I realized that I could not be the kind of mother I wanted to be while working as hard as I always had and did not return to my firm after my maternity leave.

I realized that I could not be the kind of mother I wanted to be while working as hard as I always had....

For a while, I wandered in the professional wilderness, exploring as potential options multiplied in my mind. Spending a year providing pro bono services in Family Court helped me decide that I wasn't cut out to do that full-time. I thought about joining a small law firm close to home, and about giving up law entirely. Choosing the right option wasn't simply a matter of balancing potential income and family time. Once I opened up the range of possibilities, there were more factors to consider than I'd ever anticipated. It was less like a seesaw and more like whack-a-mole. What priority should I give to intellectual challenge? To income? To helping people in need? To a flexible schedule? To maintaining the ability to impress people just by sliding a business card across the table?

Through networking—which, happily, is easy if you know what to ask, and even easier if you have ten years of experience deposing people—I started teaching business law to undergraduates. Teaching is one of the most thrilling things I've ever done and draws on a lot of my courtroom skills. After teaching for a year, and with my daughter in part-time day care, I had time to think about what else was missing from my life. I missed working with successful women and recalled that one of the most rewarding things I had done was to run an alumnae organization in San Francisco (while working full time as an associate). I started asking people if they knew of any groups that focused on professional women. Again, through networking, I found my next part-time position: as the executive director of the Boston office of Golden Seeds, an angel investor network that funds women-led businesses. I also counsel businesses on a part-time basis and serve on the boards of organizations whose work matters to me, like the ACLU.

Most importantly, my part-time work schedule leaves me ample time to be with my awe-inspiring daughter. I no longer have one eye on the smartphone when I'm with the ones I love. When I have the opportunity to help my daughter write her name or dance with her or watch her eyes as she discovers something new, I feel the joy of a life well-lived.

After so many years of intellectual grinding, I'm grateful for the current complexity of my life and my ability to integrate meaningful work and family time. I'm still in the process of tailoring what I do to better reflect who I am, and that no longer makes me nervous. If that process is lifelong, I hope practice helps. Like every other person I know who has left big law firms, however, I have no regrets whatsoever about leaving. The safety of a known path is no match for the rewards of charting your own.

Cheryl Cronin

Framing a Professional Life

Cheryl Cronin

IMAGE COURTESY OF CHERYL CRONIN

When I graduated from law school in 1980, I did not understand how important it would turn out to be that my legal career progressed in a way that made it possible for me to accommodate other choices I made in my life. If my career had developed in a more conventional way, it is very unlikely I would still be a practicing lawyer today. Always interested in politics, I was fortunate to land a job as the general counsel for the Office of Campaign & Political Finance right out of law school. In addition to permitting me to develop an expertise in the political rules of engagement, this position gave me an opportunity to learn a substantive area that formed the foundation of my private practice down the road. Experience as a government regulator often brings credibility. That happened for me, so that by the time I left state government in the late 1980s, I had the ingredients for a niche private practice in campaign finance, ethics, and other aspects of political/public law—areas that were increasingly becoming concerns of candidates, political organizations, nonprofits, and all types of business entities.

Even then, however, I did not take the more traditional route of joining a large law firm. I had just had my first child, and I was afraid that the long and often unsatisfying hours demanded of me as an associate at a large law firm would not permit me to spend the time I wanted with my young child. This conflict—between the more ambitious traditional path of a lawyer and my desire to spend time with my family—would be an integral part of all the professional choices I made throughout my career. I hung out my own shingle, as they say, and for the next ten years, worked to develop a private practice of my own. I networked incessantly, wrote many articles for a variety of publications, made presentations whenever I was asked, and found countless opportunities to expand my circles. I strongly believed that, if I represented clients effectively and was thoughtful and professional in my interactions with them, my practice would grow. Eventually, I did indeed spend several years at two large law firms. But I came full circle and returned to my belief, that from the perspective of my law practice itself, as well as the rest of my life, I preferred my own small firm environment.

Cheryl Cronin with her family in April 2010 at a Massachusetts Democratic Party event at which she was honored with the party's Eleanor Roosevelt Award.

IMAGE COURTESY OF CHERYL CRONIN

Women lawyers often abandon their careers because it is so difficult to sustain the professional demands in the face of all the other demands and priorities in their lives. It has been most important to me to frame a professional life that has also allowed me to be a full participant in the lives of my three children, as well as to indulge my other great passion—politics. My interest in politics, both in the daily strategies and tactics, as well as the important public policy debate it offers, has led me to take on significant roles in various political campaigns. This political work has been incredibly rewarding, as well as great fun, and I have viewed it as a necessary and wonderful companion to the more traditional legal work I do.

It is so important to pull away from all the expectations and think clearly about what you truly want for yourself. In the end, you have to make your own way.

Karen F. Green

Confessions of a Chinese Acrobat

Many years ago, Katherine McHugh likened her life as a lawyer to that of a Chinese acrobat—balancing glass plates on multiple long poles and seeking constantly to avoid having any of them fall.

Katherine's analogy has always struck me as a particularly apt description of my life as a "full-time" woman litigator. Particularly while our sons were children, I bent, bobbed, and stretched to maintain some balance.

I first became painfully conscious of my status as a "woman lawyer" when another lawyer sought to use it to his client's advantage. As an assistant U.S. attorney, I had filed a motion for summary judgment on behalf of the EPA and requested a hearing. Defense counsel had responded by moving for a stay of proceedings, which, upon my client's instructions, I had opposed. He later argued in a letter to the court, copied to all other counsel, that my status as a pregnant lawyer had triggered opposition to his motion and that my maternity schedule ought not to influence the court's consideration of the substantial public issues presented. Initially, I was stunned and mortified. After some discreet support from other defense counsel and a timely decision by the court, however, I realized that I just needed to develop a thicker skin.

I returned to private practice and vowed that I would keep my personal and professional lives separate by, among other things, sleeping fewer hours and avoiding conversations on topics such as parenting at work. My efforts were thwarted only after I became visibly pregnant again in 1988. A very senior partner with whom I had worked closely asked whether I had considered how I would practice law after I had a child. I responded that I planned to continue to practice in the same manner that I had practiced since my first child was born. When it became obvious that the senior partner did not know that I already had a child, I realized that I may have done too good a job of separating my personal commitments from my professional ones.

Karen F. Green

IMAGE COURTESY OF KAREN F. GREEN

Since then, the practice of law and the role of women within it have changed dramatically. Like others, I have had some amazing opportunities, in part because my status as a "woman lawyer" was viewed as an asset rather than a liability. And I have had a dizzying array of opportunities to apply my talents and training to the solution of some very complicated legal problems.

Now that our children are adults, I am balancing commitments to care for parents, family, and friends with those to serve clients and others in my larger community. Despite my best efforts, I have regrettably and occasionally let some plates slip. Nevertheless, I remain content with the choices I have made and am even more determined to keep my many plates twirling.

Eileen M. Hagerty

Fantasy V

When I look back at the firm that I helped start—Kern, Sosman, Hagerty, Roach & Carpenter, P.C.—I think especially about the early years. Beginnings are exciting, full of possibility. The end, however, was bittersweet, coming in 2008, when Chris Roach, the sole remaining partner, closed the firm to go on the bench and only two of the other four former partners, Leila Kern and I, were there to see it.

The beginning, however: The scene was the U.S. attorney's office in Boston, mid-1988. Martha Sosman was chief of the civil division; Leila, Chris, Ellen Carpenter, and I were all assistant U.S. attorneys within that division. We later said that, although the firm was Leila's idea, Martha took the first steps toward its formation by hiring the rest of us in 1987. (I remember my interview well. Martha, noting that I had a background in English literature, brought up George Eliot, whose novels we proceeded to discuss for much of the interview.) Martha, Leila, Chris, and I all hailed from litigation departments in large Boston firms. Ellen, a Vermont native, had been working as a trial attorney at the Department of Justice in D.C. Chris and I were law-school classmates but had not known each other well. The others of us had not met before.

For a while, all went well at the U.S. attorney's office. For me—and I am sure for the others, too—it was a time of challenge and growth, as we learned to handle cases independently, in a way that had not been possible at the big firms. Martha was the best chief one could wish for—always there if you wanted to consult with her, but always trusting our judgment. We grew to like and respect each other as friends and colleagues. The twelve or so assistants in the civil division got along so well that the rest of the office used to comment on how "civil" the civil division was.

Political turmoil then arose in the office, involving the U.S. attorney himself. It occupied the newspapers, distracted us from our work, and caused Leila—who had previously announced her intention of becoming a "double-digit AUSA" (i.e., a lifer)—to think about other options. One day in the fall of 1988, when Leila was speaking with her husband, Stewart Urist, about her discontent, he asked, "If you could do anything at all, what would you like to do?" To her surprise, Leila found herself answering, "I'd like to start a firm with Martha, Chris, Ellen, and Eileen." Stewart replied, "Why don't you ask them?" Leila did.

Eileen M. Hagerty

IMAGE COURTESY OF EILEEN M. HAGERTY

The partners of Kern, Sosman, Hagerty, Roach & Carpenter, P.C.: (Hon.) Martha Sosman and Eileen Hagerty, both seated, and Ellen Carpenter, (Hon.) Christine Roach, and (Hon.) Leila Kern, standing from left to right. The partners were photographed in 1990 for a feature article in the Harvard Law Bulletin's *spring issue.*

IMAGE COURTESY OF EILEEN M. HAGERTY

She spoke with each of us separately. Ellen later described the alarm she had felt when Leila walked into her office, closed the door, and began with, "Let me tell you about my fantasy!" Ellen's eyes grew large and she grasped her desk, unsure whether she wanted to hear what might follow. Once Leila explained, however, Ellen immediately said, "I'm in!" The other three of us were equally enthusiastic (well, almost—no one could match Ellen for enthusiasm), and the incident gave rise to the group's nickname, "Fantasy V." And thus the firm was born.

From the beginning, we were clear on the concept: ours would be a small, high-quality litigation practice, providing big-firm-caliber representation at small-firm prices. There was much to do to learn how to make that dream a reality, though, as none of us had any experience in running a business. Leila arranged for us to meet with Jeff Herman, a consultant she knew. For our first meeting, we were to gather over Chinese food at Jeff's office on Fort Point Channel. We all left the office together at the end of the day, causing one of our male colleagues who stepped into the elevator with us to ask, "What is this—a women's revolution?" We demurely assured him that it was not—and made a mental note not to leave the office en masse in the future, as we did not want our plan discovered prematurely. On the way to Jeff's, Martha informed us that that day, October 20, 1988, was her birthday, which we took as a good omen.

In that meeting and in the meetings that followed, Jeff helped us to identify the factors we needed to consider. We divided responsibility for investigating those topics and reporting back to the group at the next meeting. How much office space would we need and where should it be? How many employees would we have? What about furniture, computers, library, telephones? How much would each of these items cost and where would we get the money? What would we charge as our hourly rate? We would each need to come up with an initial financial contribution, but how much? We would need financing, a line of credit. Would a bank be willing to take a chance on a group of women with no track record as entrepreneurs and no portable clients? And the biggest question: where were the clients going to come from?

Martha believed, however—we all believed—that if we built it, clients would call.

In order to seek financing, we needed to develop a business plan. Martha was charged with drafting the plan, which we soon called "the novel" because of its dubious connection to reality. We didn't know whether we would get business at all, let alone in the precise ways that Martha confidently predicted in the plan. In retrospect, it seems foolhardy, starting a firm with not one assured source of business, relying only on our reputations as litigators and our connections within the Boston legal community. Martha believed, however—we all believed—that if we built it, clients would call.

At some point, we each had to decide whether to go forward with the venture. Amazingly, perhaps, all five of us opted in. For myself, I felt that I needed to follow the path that had opened before me. I had never thought seriously of starting a practice, but now that Leila had imagined our firm and brought us together, I couldn't imagine not being part of it.

With the help of our corporate attorney, Lauren Jennings, we decided that the firm would be a professional corporation. We would all be equal shareholders. We held a series of meetings at each other's homes to discuss and revise the shareholders' agreement that Lauren drafted. Leila's husband, Stewart, and my husband, Tom Alpert, cooked dinner at our respective houses. I recall that we were sitting around my dining room table when we decided on the name of the firm. Because of our commitment to equality, we agreed that it should include all five names—but what should the order be? Out of respect for Martha, our chief, there was a suggestion (probably Leila's) that Martha's name should be first. All of the rest of us (including Martha), however, felt strongly that the firm name should start with Kern, to acknowledge Leila's role in its inception. After agreeing on that, it went almost without saying that Sosman would be the next name. The other names just seemed to fall into place, and before we reached dessert, the firm-to-be had its name: Kern, Sosman, Hagerty, Roach & Carpenter, P.C. Only after reaching agreement on the name did we realize that the names were in exactly the same order as we were seated around the table (and also in descending order of age). After all of that thought and discussion, we could just as well have followed the more or less random order in which we were seated, or in which we were born! Or maybe, as with Martha's birthday, this was another omen.

After signing the shareholders' agreement we contributed our shares, which most of us borrowed from family and friends. Once we were incorporated and had funds, it was time to look for office space and furniture. "Modest yet tasteful" was our mantra. There were adventures in office hunting, such as the time when a receptionist peered at Leila and me (two conservatively-dressed attorneys) over the tops of her half-glasses and inquired too sweetly, "Now, just what business are you...*ladies*...in?" We ultimately leased an office on the sixth floor at 24 School Street in downtown Boston. The landlord agreed to build the space out for us. Leila served as our clerk of the works, conferring with the architect on the plans and paying near-daily visits to the site once construction started to make sure that it was being done right. Any errors were quickly corrected under Leila's watchful eye!

The attorney offices were nearly equal in size. We drew numbers to determine the order in which we would pick them. In addition to lawyer offices, we had a reception area with a secretarial station, a library/conference room, and a file room. We were quite proud of the curved reception counter with its wood top, and the glass-walled reception area and conference room. On the glass next to the door, the firm's name appeared in silver letters.

The typeface mirrored that of our stationery, which we had arrived at with the help of Martha's sister, Nancy Sosman, a graphic designer. We chose a letterhead that was fairly traditional, to convey that we saw ourselves as being equal to the oldest firms in the Boston legal community. With Nancy's help, we also designed our business cards and—most exciting of all—the announcement of the opening of the new firm. We began developing lists of people to whom announcements would be sent. This list was as inclusive as possible; no colleague, former colleague, neighbor, friend, or family member was omitted!

When it was time to buy office furniture, after looking at many options, we decided that a warehouse store in Somerville had the best combination of high quality and low price. We traveled together one sunny evening to the large store near Assembly Square. We had agreed in advance on a furniture budget per partner office (I believe it was $1,500 each). We had also disabused Martha, our thrifty Yankee, of the notion that she could find something perfectly suitable among the old pieces in her family's barn! At the furniture store, we learned the difference between a "full modesty" panel (the front of a desk goes all the way to the floor) and "partial modesty" (a front panel only halfway to the floor). Leila and Chris selected desks featuring the latter; Ellen and I took some ribbing for choosing the former. Martha, always the individualist, did not choose a conventional desk for her office. Instead, she found an elegant Chippendale-style table in a lustrous dark wood—cherry, perhaps—that she used as her desk.

We had decided that we would each have a computer on our desks (something that was by no means routine for attorneys at that time, and certainly not at the U.S. attorney's office), so that we could each do our own word processing. It was a good thing, we joked, that being women, we all knew how to type! With the assistance of Stewart, our computer guru, PCs were selected and installed. We reasoned that, since we would be doing our own typing, we could start with just one employee. As our first employee, we hired secretary/receptionist Kathy Cormier.

We had decided that we would each have a computer on our desks (something that was by no means routine for attorneys at that time…), so that we could each do our own word processing. It was a good thing, we joked, that being women, we all knew how to type!

We settled on the firm's opening date: September 18, 1989. Meanwhile, the U.S. attorney at the center of the earlier controversy had resigned, replaced first by Jerry O'Sullivan as interim U.S. attorney, and then by Wayne Budd. We considered whether to stay, in light of that development, but the discussion was brief. The plan now had a life of its own, and we were moving forward. To afford plenty of time to hire replacements, we gave notice to Wayne in June. He was entirely supportive. Word spread quickly throughout the office, and our colleagues began dropping by to speak with us. None of the five of us got much work done for a few days!

Three months later, KSHR&C opened its doors. There was a last-minute crisis when a telephone workers' strike threatened to prevent our acquisition of that vital element for any law office: a phone number. Somehow, Leila made it happen. Our first few days at the firm were scary (as we looked at our empty desktops) but exhilarating. We kept busy by sending out our announcements and organizing a reception to be held in October to celebrate the firm's opening. Articles about the firm appeared in the *Boston Globe, Boston Herald,* and other publications. Soon, potential clients began to call. Our first institutional client was the National Credit Union Administration (NCUA), a federal regulatory agency I had represented at the U.S. attorney's office, but that was allowed to hire private counsel in certain

A UNIQUE VENTURE
Former prosecutors open an all-women firm
5-woman law firm skirts feminism

▲ *The opening of Kern, Sosman, Hagerty, Roach & Carpenter, P.C. garnered a significant amount of attention. Above are headlines from a September 25, 1989,* Boston Globe *article and an October 1, 1989,* Boston Herald *article.*

IMAGES COURTESY OF EILEEN M. HAGERTY

circumstances. We were overjoyed when the NCUA general counsel's office called and asked whether I would be interested in representing the agency in litigation that it wanted to bring as conservator of a Rhode Island credit union. Yes, I would! That case led to a long relationship between the firm and the NCUA. During the banking crisis of the early 1990s, we went on to do similar work for the Federal Deposit Insurance Corporation and the Resolution Trust Corporation.

The party to celebrate the firm's opening was held on October 20, 1989, the one-year anniversary of our first planning meeting (and, of course, Martha's birthday). It drew scores of friends and colleagues. As an article in the *American Lawyer* described,

> [m]ore than 300 guests packed into the small office space, among them U.S. Attorney Budd, Judge [David] Nelson [for whom Chris had clerked], and a handful of senior litigators from the major firms in town. As if on cue, Sosman received a call—another client referral—in the midst of the party.

In addition to the *Globe, Herald*, and *American Lawyer* publicity, we were the subjects of articles by *Massachusetts Lawyers Weekly, New Woman*, and the *Harvard Law Bulletin*, among others. Much of the interest arose from the fact that we were an all-woman firm (or, as Sheila Albin, one of our friends in the NCUA general counsel's office, liked to say, an "all-girl band"). We were not the first law firm in the state, or in Boston, to be composed entirely of women. We may have been the largest; we're not sure. We were somewhat bemused (and amused) by the interest in us from that angle. Although I think each of us considered herself a feminist, we did not found the firm as a feminist statement, nor did the firm pursue any type of political agenda in its litigation. We were just a group of friends and colleagues who wanted to do high-quality litigation at reasonable prices in a humane atmosphere. We founded the firm at a time when it was possible for us, as a group of women lawyers, to entertain a reasonable hope of achieving that goal (as might not have been the case twenty or thirty years earlier) but when our doing so was still considered noteworthy, in a way that a similar venture by a similar group of women might not be today.

So the firm prospered and grew. Leila was our able managing partner. Martha remained our chief in many ways, the go-to person for discussion of legal issues and strategy. Chris was our marketing director. Ellen, whose background was in bankruptcy and tax law, was our treasurer. As our work expanded, we added several associates, another secretary, an office manager, and a paralegal. One associate, MaryAustin Dowd, would become a shareholder in the firm for a time; Brian Gallagher, our paralegal, worked for many years with Ellen on bankruptcy cases, staying with the firm until the end. Within a few years, we needed more space, so we moved to the eighth floor of our building. There were receptions to celebrate the firm's first anniversary and the new space.

There were life changes, too. I had all three of my children during my time at the firm, with my twins, David and Kitty, arriving in 1991 and my younger son, Andrew, in 1993. My partners generously gave me six months' paid maternity leave when the twins were born,

Eileen Hagerty's children, Katherine and David Alpert, during a visit to Kern, Sosman, Hagerty, Roach & Carpenter, P.C. when they were three months old for a party in their honor.

IMAGE COURTESY OF EILEEN M. HAGERTY

and three months' paid leave at Andrew's birth. Although only one of the other members of the firm, Leila, had children herself (and they had been born well before the formation of KSHR&C), the relationship between the all-woman firm and the liberal leave was no coincidence.

Before we started the firm, Martha had told us of her dream to become a judge. In 1992, she applied for a vacancy on the Superior Court. Not surprisingly, she was chosen for the position. Chris, Ellen, Leila, and I were all very glad for her. The firm held a party to celebrate her elevation to the bench, which occurred in 1993. We all attended her swearing-in. Some time previously, Martha had started a tradition: when something significant was about to happen in the life of the firm, slips of paper would appear on each of our desks, bearing a typed, Star Trek–like message about "Fantasy V." For example, when the firm opened, the message was "Fantasy V, prepare for liftoff!" At the swearing-in, each of us received a slip of paper on which was typed:

> THIS IS STAR FLEET COMMAND TO FANTASY V. READY TRANSPORTER ROOM TO BEAM DOWN SOSMAN. CONTINUE ON COURSE AT WARP 4. MISSION UNCHANGED.

We reconstituted the firm as Kern, Hagerty, Roach & Carpenter, P.C. A few years after Martha became a judge, I left the firm in order to pursue other opportunities, moving to Kotin, Crabtree & Strong LLP, in Boston, where I now practice special education law. The firm became Kern, Roach & Carpenter, P.C. Leila left not long afterward, first becoming in-house counsel at Sun Life of Canada and then becoming a Superior Court judge herself in 1999. We were all extremely proud when Martha was appointed to the Supreme Judicial Court in 2000. Chris and Ellen continued the firm for more than ten years after Leila's departure, as Roach & Carpenter, P.C. Ellen, who began the firm not only without clients but with few contacts in the Boston legal world, became a well-known bankruptcy attorney. She was increasingly active in the Boston Bar Association, ultimately being honored with its presidency from 2004 to 2005. She also served as a hearing officer for the Board of Bar Overseers, including a high-

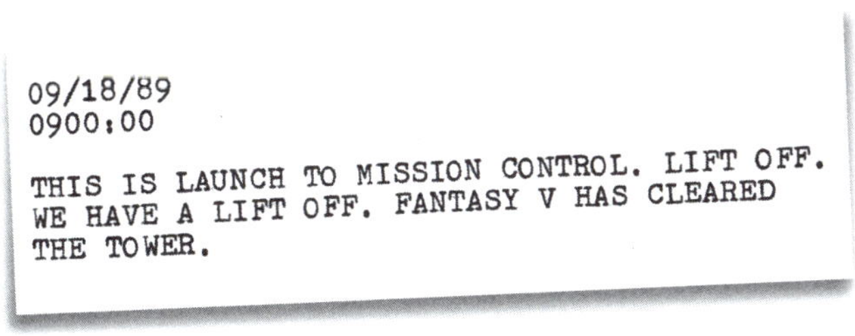
09/18/89
0900:00

THIS IS LAUNCH TO MISSION CONTROL. LIFT OFF. WE HAVE A LIFT OFF. FANTASY V HAS CLEARED THE TOWER.

A Star Trek-*style note of encouragement Martha Sosman left on the desks of her colleagues on the firm's first day.*

IMAGE COURTESY OF EILEEN M. HAGERTY

profile, time-consuming case in which she authored a more than 200-page opinion in 2005. Chris conducted a thriving litigation practice. She also kept everything going behind the scenes at the firm, enabling Ellen to perform public service with the BBA and BBO.

All of that came to a sudden end on December 10, 2006, with Ellen's death from a brain aneurysm at the age of fifty-two. Her loss was a blow to all of us and to the entire Boston legal community, but especially for Chris, who found herself running the firm alone. At Ellen's funeral, Martha looked quite unwell; at that point she had been suffering from cancer for several years. Martha died three months later, on March 10, 2007, at the age of fifty-six. Her passing was another terrible loss to us and to the Commonwealth. Chris continued the firm until early 2008, when she too became a Superior Court judge. At that point, the firm ceased to be.

September 1989 to February 2008—the firm lasted not quite nineteen years. I like to think that we did good work, had fun, ran the firm in a way that respected our clients and each other, and acquitted ourselves well. The venture was, and remained, a grand adventure. Fantasy V became reality. It has now passed into another stage, where it lives, with our two lost friends, in memory.

Stephanie Lovell

Prepare for Luck

My story is about the power of luck. Luck is sometimes ignored in this age of hypervigilant networking and thousands of books and Web sites devoted to job searching and career development. But luck is what brings me to this point, and the power of luck has given me hope when preparation and skill alone were not enough.

My job as first assistant attorney general ended on January 22, 2007, at the expiration of Attorney General Reilly's term. I had looked for another job somewhat half-heartedly. I struggled with how to repackage myself since, despite my eight years in private practice, I was then largely viewed as a government lawyer. It had been a grueling last two years and I really just longed to recharge my batteries. My plan was to take a short sabbatical and go to cooking school. I had even selected the courses I would take.

But first—three days later—I had to give an acceptance speech. I had won a Greater Boston Chamber of Commerce Pinnacle Award for Achievement in Government. My speech was supposed to be two minutes long. It was four, and in it I told a funny story about a visit I made to Boston as a child and how I refused to get out of the car. As luck would have it, a lawyer in the audience knew that Boston Medical Center's CEO, Elaine Ullian, was in the market for a general counsel. She told Elaine about the speech and suggested that Elaine and I meet. Two weeks later, we did. We had pizza in the hospital's cafeteria. I still joke that my recruitment meal cost $6.38 for both of us, with beverages.

▲ *Stephanie Lovell*

IMAGE COURTESY OF STEPHANIE LOVELL

I was more skeptical than Elaine about my making the move to Boston Medical Center (BMC). I had no background in health care, although I had represented state health-care agencies while at the attorney general's office. But in my twenty-odd years of practice, I had developed a lot of relevant skills. I had been a general counsel. I had worked for a commission that functioned much like a board of directors. I had developed the ability to handle complex, highly charged situations. I found that I could learn a variety of business models and objectives, and I could manage a large budget. I had worked closely with my attorney general, and knew how to mix legal and practical advice to a chief executive. And I knew my way around government, which was important to a hospital serving mostly Medicaid and Medicare patients. It might have been an unconventional journey, but all of the basic elements were there. And I was lucky to have the opportunity to prove that.

The philosopher Seneca wrote that "luck is what happens when preparation meets opportunity." And so it is. I could not have capitalized on the opportunity BMC presented had I not prepared for it. That meant working in a variety of settings, taking some risks and a couple of pay cuts along the way, to get a broad range of experience. But all the preparation in the world would not have led me to BMC through normal channels. I still needed a little luck. And so now I have a new motto: "Prepare for luck." And when it happens, run with it.

The philosopher Seneca wrote that "luck is what happens when preparation meets opportunity."

Joan A. Lukey

Homeward Bound

Envision this scene: It was the mid 1970s, just before Sandra Day O'Connor became the first woman justice on the U.S. Supreme Court. At age twenty-four, looking very much like a teenage Annie Hall, I walked nervously into a Suffolk trial call session (a "cattle call" as we used to say) just days after my admission to the bar. (The latter occurred, by the way, on Friday the thirteenth during a solar eclipse.) A court officer rushed over as I opened the gate, and announced in a stage whisper, "Miss, only lawyers are allowed beyond the bar." The second visit was marginally better. The judge stopped proceedings in the crowded motion session to direct a court officer to "get the young lady a chair." No harm was meant on either occasion, but it was inflicted nonetheless.

Fast forward to the 1980s, to another way-stop on the homeward journey: In a chambers conference, the judge, a stern and austere jurist of renowned intellect and equally renowned humorlessness, posed a question requiring agreement between the attorneys. Opposing counsel, a septuagenarian as kind and avuncular as any lawyer whom I had ever met, turned to me and said, "Dear, I don't think that will work because…." Before the sentence could be completed, His Honor threatened to hold that poor man in contempt for "demeaning" me with the appellation "dear." My opponent, with whom I had become quite friendly, meant no harm; and none was taken. But, someone else, oblivious to the nature of our relationship and to the signals that were being sent, assumed that there was, or should have been, a wound inflicted.

Joan A. Lukey

IMAGE COURTESY OF ROPES & GRAY LLP

Ironically, these scenarios are reflective of the same phenomenon, albeit at vastly different times in its evolutionary process. I am referring, of course, to the bane of true equality in the profession: unconscious gender stereotyping. In the first instances, the assumption was that I could not stand on my own two feet in the company of the profession's (male) titans. In the second, the assumption was that I was too rigid to understand and accept the genteel (nonmalevolent) customs of an earlier generation. Both

Joan Lukey and her daughter Heather at Lukey's 2009 installation as the first woman president of the American College of Trial Lawyers (right) and trekking in the Himalayas (above).

IMAGES COURTESY OF JOAN A. LUKEY

assumptions dictated that I was to be treated with velvet gloves, for absolutely no reason but my gender. I beg to differ, and those who know me would be far more likely to place me in the iron fist category.

Over the past three and a half decades, the legal profession has come a long way in recognizing the debilitating effect of unconscious gender stereotyping, in significant part because we have greater gender balance on the bench and in the bar. No one would think of questioning my right to come before the bar today, nor would they dare to offer me a seat. Today, the antennae of most judges, many of whom are women, would be receptive to the "vibes" between counsel, sensitive to the customs of an older generation, and aware that innocence and malevolence are very different motivators.

But we are not home yet.

My daughter has just become a member of the bar. Twenty-seven years ago, days after she was born, I sat with her in my lap marveling at the miracle that we had created; and an idle thought passed through my mind: If she were to become a lawyer a quarter century hence, would the journey for women in the profession be complete? That quarter century has now passed; and the answer is, I think, not quite.

But, if she writes her story twenty-five years hence....

Wendy J. Murphy

Mothers in Law—As if Giving BIrth Isn't Painful Enough

Many of my friends in the big firms say things are "pretty good" for women lawyers and that the number of female attorneys alone proves the point.

Of course, numbers tell us very little about true equity.

In my practice over the past twenty-five years, gendered moments have ranged from breathtakingly offensive to inspirational, as when my four-year-old daughter came to a hearing with me and watched female lawyers argue in front of a female judge. Later that day, a colleague in my office asked my daughter if she knew what Mommy's job was. Taylor replied, "Mommy goes to court" and "helps people." Prodding her a bit, my colleague then asked, "Is Mommy a lawyer?" Taylor said, "Yes, Mommy's a lawyer." When asked what Daddy did, she answered, "He goes to the office and calls people on the phone." "Is Daddy a lawyer, too?" my colleague asked, knowing he was. My daughter, giggling, replied, "Boys can't be lawyers."

Wendy J. Murphy

IMAGE COURTESY OF WENDY J. MURPHY, PHOTO BY ELISE AMENDOLA

Other incidents have made gender equity seem downright ordinary, as when my husband and I were simultaneously named "Lawyer of the Year" by *Lawyers Weekly*, and the decision makers had no idea we were married.

On too many occasions, however, it has been needlessly difficult to be female.

After spending weeks on a complex brief involving the retroactivity doctrine, I showed up to argue the issue in Superior Court wearing pants. Two senior attorneys whom I expected would critique the content of the argument instead criticized my decision to wear slacks.

Not long after that, I had a trial that went to deliberations late in the day. When the jury indicated they were close to a verdict, the judge (a woman) told us we had to stay, possibly well into the evening. When I said I had to pick up my toddlers at day care at 5:30, the judge offered to let me use the phone in her chambers (before cell phones). I smirked and said, "To call whom and to say what?" My role as caregiver was presumed less important than the trial by everyone except me.

In another case, I showed up nearly nine months pregnant, ready for trial, and the defense asked for a continuance on the grounds that my belly would provoke jurors unfairly to vote for my side. The judge ordered the trial to take place when my newborn was only two weeks old.

I brought along a sitter and asked the judge, in chambers, to allow me a fifteen-minute break in the morning because I was nursing the baby and couldn't last from nine to one without a break. He said, "We don't take breaks for that in my courtroom." Even when I offered to skip the morning feeding and had the sitter get the baby a bottle, the judge refused to start the trial unless I found another prosecutor to continue asking questions in my absence in the event the baby needed me. I eventually sent the baby home in frustration.

Eight hours later, driving back from court, my breasts were on the verge of bursting. When I tried to feed my daughter, she bounced her tiny face around like a woodpecker—in search of nipples that had long since been stretched flat.

Ten years later, a judge ordered me to appear at a hearing knowing the date was in the midst of what could have been the literal birth of my fifth child. I offered to appear prior to my due date, but he accommodated the requests of my nonpregnant male opponents and ordered the hearing to take place nine days after my due date.

When my overdue baby didn't arrive on time, I asked my doctor to deliver the baby out on a Sunday night so that I could get out of the hospital two days later and get to the courthouse the next morning. I dragged my sleepless self, a two-and-a-half-day-old infant, and two babysitters to court Wednesday morning and argued a case that easily could have been handled two weeks earlier without causing near as much distress.

Though I won the case, the needless additional burdens imposed on my client's interests, my body, and my baby were neither necessary nor fair.

As an attorney who specializes in women's rights, my experiences as a woman practitioner probably make me extra sensitive to gender disparities. But I hear similar stories from many colleagues, and most women are too nice (or fearful of repercussions) to complain. Even if women practitioners were inclined to fight for systemic change, they don't really have the power, alone, to make a real difference. We need dedicated leadership and self-critical awareness at all levels of the judiciary to ensure a sustained commitment to true equality.

Regina M. Pisa

Dare to Dream

As head of a leading national law firm, it is my role to focus on the future. Occasionally, however, when I look back and reflect, it is usually to gain some perspective on my career. What I see is a story of opportunity and luck and a few lessons learned.

My partners chose me to lead Goodwin Procter a dozen years ago, when I was forty-two years old and having a great time building a mergers and acquisitions practice. With no formal management training, I asked the obvious question—"Why me?" I was told "We are a firm in search of a moral center, and you represent that to us." I didn't fully appreciate those words then, but I do today.

When I assumed leadership of Goodwin Procter, I was the first woman in the country to chair an AmLaw 100 law firm. My partners, in true pioneer spirit, were surprised that the media made such headlines about that. For them, I was simply the right person for the job. At the time, however, they had no idea of the journey of expansion and change we would travel together.

During the next twelve years, the firm would grow from 350 lawyers in Boston to over 850 lawyers serving clients from nine locations in the United States, Europe, and Asia. We have become known within the legal industry as an innovator and change leader.

Yet, for all the accolades that have been bestowed on the firm and me, I have never thought of myself as a pioneer for achieving as a woman what I believed I could do as a person. While I am proud and humbled that so many women view me as a role model, I view myself simply as someone who was provided an opportunity and made the most of it.

Mine is an unlikely profile for someone managing one of the largest law firms in the country—institutions that are typically characterized by conservativism, or at least not generally known for their risk taking. I did not follow in a long line of family members who went to Ivy League schools. I was the first-generation child of Italian parents who were married late in life. I did not attend a fancy prep school. I attended Somerville High School, where, out of a graduating class of over 900 students, only 100 or so went on to college or postgraduate education of any kind.

So how does it happen that a kid from Somerville, a first-generation Italian immigrant, goes on to graduate from Harvard, Oxford, and Georgetown, then embarks on a legal career at one of the country's largest law firms and ends up running the place?

I would like to tell you that I was smart enough to have had some grand plan for my career, but that was not the case. There was no grand plan. I often joke that my career has been driven by "dumb luck." But the truth is that we make our own luck—through the networks we cultivate and the opportunities we create around us. Making your way to the head of the table has its own challenges, but it always starts with an opportunity. Looking back, I feel lucky to have been given that opportunity. I also feel fortunate that as a young girl I was dared to dream, and I was told over and over that there were no limits to what I could achieve in life.

To the women coming up behind me who are making their way in the profession, I offer a few pieces of advice:

Regina M. Pisa

IMAGE COURTESY OF GOODWIN PROCTER LLP

Making your way to the head of the table has its own challenges, but it always starts with an opportunity.

- **First, find out what you love to do in life and then do it with passion.** You can be good at almost anything, but you will only be great at something you truly love to do.
- **Second, whatever you choose to do, be bold and do it with courage.** Women do not take enough risks in their careers. You have to be willing to try new things, because they create the greatest opportunity.
- **Third, do not let your failures stand in your way, because you will have failures.** Periodic failure is the inevitable result of taking risks. The key is to learn how to fail faster so that you can succeed faster as well.
- **Fourth, find your own style and voice.** To be most effective—whether in law, business, or politics—you have to embrace a style and voice that is authentic and reflects who you are.
- **Fifth, don't be afraid to be compassionate.** Women have a tremendous advantage in life—we listen and we care. This makes us extraordinarily adept at managing people, which is, after all, what much of life is about. I often say that I don't manage a law firm—I manage 850 lawyers, one at a time.
- **Sixth, aggressively seek out mentors.** I am a big believer of mentors in life, especially for women. Your mentors need not be other women. Some of my greatest mentors have been men.
- **Seventh, take charge of your life.** This will mean different things to you at different points in your life. At all times, though, it means you should not wait to be offered a seat at the table—simply pull up a chair.
- **Eighth, never underestimate the power of symbols.** If they offer you the corner office, take it.
- **Finally, dare to dream.** And do not ever let anyone tell you that you cannot do something. My father came to the United States after World War II believing that all things were possible in his new home. He told me that every day as a child and I believed him.

So turn to your daughters, your sisters, your colleagues, and your friends and tell them that they can do it—they can do whatever it is they have set their sights on. Tell them that they have no boundaries. Tell them enough times and they will believe it. Dare them to dream.

Maria E. Recalde

Be Like Water

In addition to having a busy, full-time legal practice, I am an avid martial artist. Not only do I benefit from the rigorous regular exercise, but I also find my Shaolin Kung Fu practice to be an effective tool in helping me stay centered and in maintaining balance in my life. There is a philosophical principle in martial arts—to "be like water"—that I try to apply in my work and life in general. Water adapts to any form, can be still or in motion, carries tremendous power even while remaining gentle and even, and is literally always "going with the flow."

What does this mean in practice? Letting this image—to be like water—guide my work and my interactions with others helps me to be present in each moment, to see what needs to be done, to take in and not rail against the variables that cannot be changed or are outside my control, to find ways to move past obstacles, to remain calm, and at the end of the day, to let go and move on.

Twenty-five years ago as a second-year law student, contemplating job interviews with Boston law firms, I had no idea what the future might hold. I was born and raised in Managua, Nicaragua, and had originally come to the United States to get away from the political upheaval in Nicaragua and to learn English. Just a few years later—having decided to attend college and then law school in the United States—I was making the decision not to return to my home country. Everything felt uncertain. Would I be hired? Would my employer help me obtain the visa I needed to work as an attorney in the United States and then seek permanent residency? Would I pass the bar exam (knowing I only had one shot since a nonpassing grade meant having to return to Nicaragua with my student visa about to expire)?

A placement counselor at my law school had discouraged me (and others) from seeking a summer clerkship at any of the large Boston law firms because Boston was "not a hospitable city for minorities." I was determined, however, not to let one person's narrow view stand in my way. I ended up with a handful of options and ultimately decided to take a summer clerkship with Burns & Levinson in Boston. At the end of that summer, I accepted their job offer. I did pass the bar and upon my arrival in 1988, the firm proceeded to assist me in obtaining my permanent residency.

Fast-forward to 1996. I had become the youngest equity partner at Burns & Levinson and one of the first Latina partners in a large Boston firm. Fast-forward again to 2002, when I left Burns & Levinson to open up the Boston office of Sheehan Phinney Bass + Green PA, one of the largest business law firms in New Hampshire. As of this writing, I am the chair of the firm's corporate department and a member of the firm's four-person management committee. My practice, having found and followed my passion, is currently focused on the rapidly changing areas of technology and intellectual property transactions, litigation, and counseling. Looking back, I realize there was no magic involved in moving from being a scared but determined foreign student to being a successful lawyer holding a senior management position in a large law firm. But I also realize that the feeling of uncertainty about what the future holds never ceases to exist.

Maria E. Recalde

IMAGE COURTESY OF SHEEHAN PHINNEY BASS + GREEN PA

A placement counselor at my law school had discouraged me (and others) from seeking a summer clerkship at any of the large Boston law firms because Boston was "not a hospitable city for minorities."

So what factors do seem important in making one's way as a lawyer, as a woman, as a member of a minority group? Do what you love. Look for and create opportunities, especially where others see chaos. Always maintain your integrity. Look for mentors. Work hard, be responsive and reliable. Take the time to listen. Do not let failure or a discouraging word stand in your way. Believe in yourself. Trust your innate wisdom. Be grateful, kind, and compassionate. Exercise regularly. Meditate. Be mindful. Give back—you will get more than you give. Be fluid. At the end of the day, let go and move on. Be like water.

Sandra Shapiro

From Bryn Mawr to Boston

Sandra Shapiro

IMAGE COURTESY OF FOLEY HOAG LLP

In four decades at the bar, my proudest moments have been in public roles: as president of the Women's Bar Association of Massachusetts, as a contributor to the Supreme Judicial Court's Gender Bias Study of the court system in Massachusetts, as a member of the Board of Bar Overseers, and as an officer and director of Lex Mundi, the international legal network.

But looming larger in my mind as I look back over the years is the simple fact that I landed and kept a job with a major Boston law firm at a time when women were few and far between in the legal profession, except in clerical positions. I owe my good fortune to the enlightened leadership of the firm that hired me, where I practice to this day—Foley Hoag LLP (then Foley Hoag & Eliot).

I eventually became a partner at Foley Hoag—the first woman to reach that position. After my election I was warmly welcomed to my first partners' meeting and was asked whether the cigar smoke would bother me. I do not remember my reply, but I do recall that when I subsequently became the first woman on the firm's hiring committee, my goal was to share my good fortune with qualified sisters, and others, who were unlikely to smoke Double Coronas.

The institutional and social dimensions of gender had already figured prominently at two earlier moments in my career. When I first arrived in Boston fresh out of law school at the University of Pennsylvania, I would never have sought a clerkship with a federal judge in this Harvard-dominated jurisdiction if I had not also been an alumna of Bryn Mawr College. That distinction—among the happiest of my life—I shared with the wife and mother of the late Bailey Aldrich, who was at the time the chief judge of the U.S. Court of Appeals for the First Circuit. So my clerkship for Judge Aldrich was an early instance of the Bryn Mawr alumnae network at work. Another factor in my favor was Judge Aldrich's esteem for the Honorable Raya Dreben, the first woman to have clerked for him when he was still a District Court judge.

I conclude with a lunch that Foley Hoag arranged for me as part of the hiring process at the end of my judicial clerkship. I had asked to meet with some associates, so the managing partner, the late Hans F. Loeser, booked a table for five at the downtown Harvard Club, which was then on Batterymarch Street. When four male associates arrived at the appointed time with a young woman and asked for the table that had been reserved by Member Loeser, the

FOLEY, HOAG & ELIOT
10 POST OFFICE SQUARE
BOSTON, MASSACHUSETTS 02109
TELEPHONE (617) 482-1390
CABLE ADDRESS "FOLEYHOAG"

WASHINGTON OFFICE
1625 EYE STREET, N.W.
WASHINGTON, D.C. 20006

CLARENCE L. PETERSON
V. MICHAEL STRAUS

January 8, 1971

The President
Harvard Club of Boston
374 Commonwealth Avenue
Boston, Massachusetts 02215

Dear Sir:

I should like to recommend respectfully but strongly that the rule against ladies dining at the downtown facility of the Harvard Club be dropped as soon as possible. I consider the rule unwarranted, inconvenient and unwise. It is also insulting, particularly to ladies who have Harvard degrees and work professionally alongside the men in downtown offices. I venture to doubt that the rule is of any importance to a significant number of those using the downtown facility for lunch.

My reasons for recommending that this change be adopted promptly, include the fact that I feel, as I am sure you do, that if change is to come it is preferable and more dignified if it comes voluntarily rather than under the duress of unpleasantness. From the talk which I hear among downtown professionals, particularly the younger generation of Harvard graduates, I have no doubt that such unpleasant incidents will occur before long unless something is done.

Fairness, reason and practicality all call for the adoption of a rule change without delay. I recommend such action.

Very truly yours,

Hans F. Loeser

HFL/hmg.

A January 8, 1971, letter from Hans F. Loeser of Foley, Hoag & Eliot to the president of the Harvard Club of Boston after the club refused to seat Sandra Shapiro and four male Foley Hoag associates because the group included a woman.

IMAGE COURTESY OF SANDRA SHAPIRO

HARVARD CLUB OF BOSTON
374 COMMONWEALTH AVENUE
BOSTON, MASSACHUSETTS 02215
AREA CODE 617 TEL 536-1260

SECRETARY'S OFFICE

January 26, 1971

Hans F. Loeser, Esq.
Foley, Hoag & Eliot
10 Post Office Square
Boston, Massachusetts 02109

Dear Mr. Loeser:

At the request of the President, Alexander H. Bright, I am writing in response to your recent letter concerning the admission of ladies to the Downtown Dining Rooms.

There is, in fact, no prohibition against the use of these dining rooms by ladies. Upon investigation we find that there have been occasional misunderstandings in the past, but we want you to know that there is no policy against the members of the fairer sex and we would be pleased to welcome Lady Associates or ladies in the company of a member.

Very truly yours,

James M. Fitzgibbons
Secretary

The Harvard Club secretary's January 26, 1971 reply to Hans F. Loeser's letter.

IMAGE COURTESY OF SANDRA SHAPIRO

hostess refused to seat the party because it included a woman. We ended up at Dom's on the waterfront, where the food was superb and the conversation lively.

I treasure a copy of the correspondence that ensued. Hans wrote an eloquent letter of protest to the Harvard Club. The club secretary replied in part, "There have been occasional misunderstandings in the past, but we want you to know that there is no policy against the members of the fairer sex and we would be pleased to welcome Lady Associates or ladies in the company of a member." The year was 1971.

Nancy S. Shilepsky

Hearsay

Nancy S. Shilepsky

IMAGE COURTESY OF SHILEPSKY HARTLEY ROBB CASEY MICHON LLP

One of my favorite stories about my career is hearsay. Many years ago, I applied for a legal services job working with low-income senior citizens but was not hired. Sometime later, I was told that my feminism caused my potential new employer concern. Instead, I entered private practice where my feminism, and love of employment law, served me well. Realizing that male lawyers had male-friendly networks on which to rely, I helped create female-friendly networks. I joined the Monday Night Group, a loose affiliation of women lawyers in legal services and private practice; I became part of a GNO ("girls night out"), with Anne Morrill, Jean Musiker, and Ilene Robinson Sunshine; Anne Josephson and I cofounded the Amicus Group, which had primarily female roots; I started a firm with members of a new generation of up-and-coming women lawyers, Katherine Michon and Barbara Robb; and Michele Whitham and I cochaired the Women's Leadership Initiative Task Force of the Women's Bar Association. Over the years, my networks sustained me, personally and professionally. My feminism was both a life and career enhancer. The work, however, is still unfinished. Although women lawyers have made great progress, too many leave private practice or stay cabined in positions that pay less and/or have less power than those held by their male peers. I fear that one obstacle has been far more intractable than we had expected. To quote Chief Justice William Rehnquist, "the fault line between work and family" is "precisely where sex-based overgeneralization has been and remains strongest."[45] The answer, I think, is to make private practice more humane for everyone, and I hope that will happen. In the meantime, my advice to women lawyers is to support and mentor each other, and never give up. Also, live by your values. Law is a profession in which one can do well financially and at the same time do good in the world. For me, the former is not meaningful without the latter.

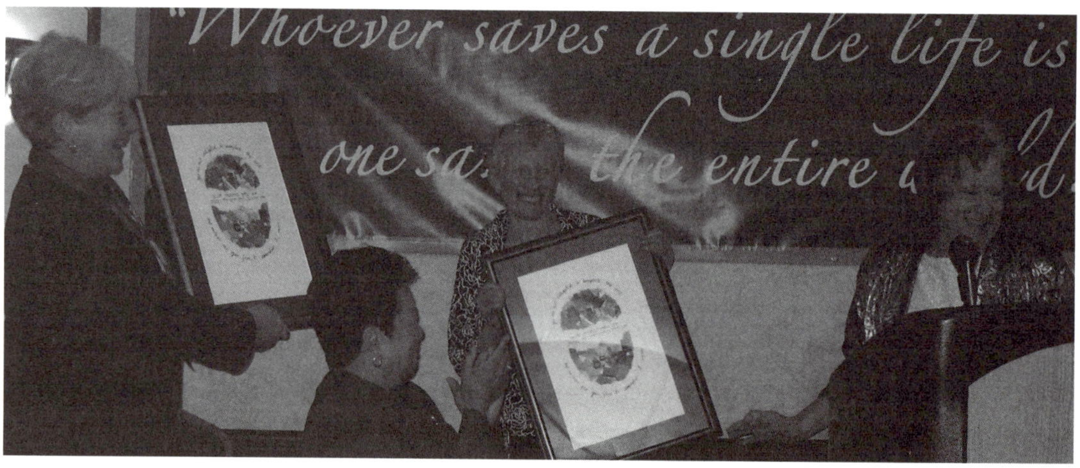

The Jewish Alliance for Law and Social Action's sixth annual meeting, February 10, 2008. From left to right: Anne Josephson, Diane Patrick (seated), Nancy Shilepsky, and Sheila Decter. Shilepsky and Josephson were honored by the Alliance for their work in founding and facilitating the Amicus Group.

IMAGE COURTESY OF NANCY S. SHILEPSKY

Wendy Sibbison

Taming the Lion, or How I Became an Appellate Lawyer

In the four years between 1977, when I graduated from law school and joined a partnership in Northampton, Massachusetts, and 1981, something bad happened: I lost my passion for the law. The piles of paper in my office, once gratifying proof of a thriving general practice, had turned into a burden that I did not want to lug. Yet at age thirty-five, starting over in another field seemed rash. After a master's degree in English and a law degree, what was next? Ornithology?

Changing focus rather than career was the prudent solution, so I set myself the task of pinpointing what I did and did not like about my practice. I liked to concentrate on a single task without interruption, and I liked big jobs that required this intense concentration. Most of all I liked conceptual, rather than factual, disputes. I had become uncomfortable with the trial lawyer's task—necessarily central to our system of justice—of selling a particular version of reality. I often found the conflicting narratives equally compelling or equally dubious. Intellectually and morally, I'm a creature of nineteenth-century American literature, where ambiguity permeates truth like the blue veins of a Roquefort. There was also the question of temperament—put me in an arena and tell me to win, and my teeth start to gnash. Controlling the beast that strained to leap out during every trial was exhausting. Trial work was not for me.

If law is an engine for change, even sluggish change, appellate litigation seemed like a chance to be a little bit bigger cog in that engine.

I concluded that appeals, of which I had worked on a grand total of two, were my destiny. Appellate practice had it all: the large piece of work requiring prolonged attention; the minimal correspondence and telephone calls; and the conceptual focus, with those ornery facts already wrangled by someone else. Every component offered pleasure: reading, researching (which in those days meant being in a library, that is, in heaven), thinking, writing, and, at the end, stepping out onto the improvisational stage of oral argument.

And there was something else, too. Like many in my generation, I had pursued law as a way to participate in social change. I went to Rutgers-Newark Law School for its progressive mission—the school's (now unconstitutional) racial, ethnic, and gender quotas had created a fresh and exciting culture. I also wanted to study with the legendary left-wing constitutional lawyer, Arthur Kinoy, who did not disappoint. If law is an engine for change, even sluggish change, appellate litigation seemed like a chance to be a little bit bigger cog in that engine.

There was a problem, though; no one in the entire state of Massachusetts thought appellate litigation should be a job. In my naiveté, I lined up interviews at large and small firms in Boston in order to discover where I might find work. The answer was, "Nowhere." At an old white-shoe firm, in a hushed conference room overlooking Boston Harbor, the hiring partner told me why. "First-year law students learn how to write a brief. We hardly need specialists to do it." I shook his hand and slunk out the mahogany door. At firm after firm, I heard the same thing, "Our litigation department does its own appeals," which was shorthand for "[o]ur associates write the brief and the partner shows up for argument." The one exception was the state public defender's office, which had a first-rate appellate division, and they weren't hiring. Well, actually, they weren't hiring *me* because of another problem: I

Wendy Sibbison

IMAGE COURTESY OF WENDY SIBBISON

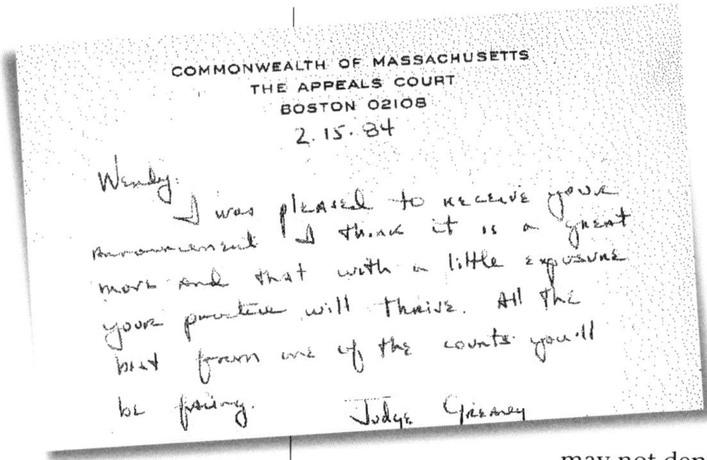
COMMONWEALTH OF MASSACHUSETTS
THE APPEALS COURT
BOSTON 02108
2.15.84

Wendy:
I was pleased to receive your announcement. I think it is a great move and that with a little exposure your practice will thrive. All the best from one of the courts you'll be facing.
Judge Greaney

▲

A February 15, 1984, note Wendy Sibbison received from the Honorable John M. Greaney of the Appeals Court.

IMAGE COURTESY OF WENDY SIBBISON

didn't know beans about either appellate litigation or criminal law. I am amazed that I didn't give up.

But I didn't give up. I kept remembering those two appeals I had worked on with my more experienced partners. In one, we reversed an armed robbery conviction where our client, a black man with a whizbang of a stutter, had supposedly spoken clearly and at length to the white victim. I remembered our client's face the day he was let out of jail and the awe I felt at what we had accomplished. In the other case, we won the first appellate ruling in the country that a judge may not deny child custody to a lesbian mother based solely on her sexual orientation. I remembered arguing that case before the Massachusetts Supreme Judicial Court in 1979, only two years out of law school: the solemnity of the judges' demeanor, the intelligence of their questions, the packed courtroom, the charged atmosphere of history being made.

So I left my firm, read some books, signed up for all the appellate trainings I could find, and got myself approved to handle criminal appeals for indigent defendants. The pay was awful—was it $19 per hour?—and my office was a walk-in closet in my apartment, but for the first time in years I was enjoying myself at work. In my spare time I wrote a book on Massachusetts divorce. Then I published and distributed the book myself. Those were lean years.

After a time, however, I started winning some significant victories and in 1986 secured a reversal of a first-degree murder conviction, which gave me some attention in the press and turned on the tap of private referrals. Then I won a few noteworthy civil appeals. I was asked to teach appellate litigation at more and more CLE functions. After several years of taking almost any appeal that passed the laugh test, I began to have the luxury to be more selective, resulting in more success, more ink, and better cases. I can't remember when I stopped worrying whether the work would dry up, but it was a long time ago.

The difficulty of building a specialized practice that, in my state, remains an outlier was worth every hardship. I have been lucky enough to crank the engine of change in several different realms of the law and to stay in my beloved western Massachusetts while maintaining a robust statewide practice. Now, on those rare occasions when I am forced to litigate some pesky facts, I glimpse with affection the beast who needed to find, and did find, a calmer arena.

Evelynne L. Swagerty

Valued for Our Individuality, Evaluated on Our Abilities

My race defines me, it is who I am—I was born and raised in a segregated southern community, educated in a totally segregated elementary and high school, and was one of four young black women to integrate my college's former officially and fully segregated living arrangements.

Fast forward to the present: I am currently a senior female in-house litigator for a large national corporation. My work as in-house counsel is very much a meritocracy where you are judged on your performance. To a certain degree, the office is color-blind, in part because the company's size often prevents face-to-face personal contact with many of the colleagues that I deal with on a daily basis, and because the corporate culture is very fast paced, performance driven, and focused on the bottom line. Here the task is to get the job done and to do it well. For the people I deal with, what is key is my performance. While there are certain diversity-related issues that do come up within the context of work (a good example is my work on the bank's initiative to retain more women and minority-owned law firms), generally, the issue of race rarely comes up. In my experience, life at work is all about the work—what do you do, how you go about doing it, and whether you were successful.

I am proud to have assumed leadership roles in numerous local organizations dedicated to providing opportunities for African Americans and women, as well as being a diverse presence in other organizations. Those who follow us should have the opportunity to experience the great benefit that I've enjoyed and that hopefully one day will be taken for granted by all: valued for our individuality, evaluated on our abilities.

Evelynne L. Swagerty

IMAGE COURTESY OF EVELYNNE L. SWAGERTY

Vivian Tseng

Skirting the Barriers by Keeping to Your True North

After graduating from law school in 1980, I stepped into the legal world the same way I grew up in American suburbia—alone. As before, I was the "only" in almost every setting: the only Asian/woman, and once I entered the corporate world, equally or more importantly, the only Democrat/nongolfer/nonsports fan.

Solitude, however, was always my friend. Or, I made it my friend by necessity. Putting aside the obvious chicken-and-egg question, I experienced the aloneness as a welcomed opportunity to turn inward, to seek companionship within myself. This experience of aloneness became the wellspring of my success in life by giving me the mindset and the skills to define that success.

I became a quick study by virtue of always walking into rooms in which no one else looked like me. The necessity of constant social reconnaissance honed my emotional intelligence and listening skills, both critical to effective lawyering. Because I was unconnected to the old boys' network, independence of thought and action became second nature. I was not tempted by the promise of social acceptance to make intellectual or other compromises so I could get along by going along. Having to make my own way, I learned

Vivian Tseng

IMAGE COURTESY OF VIVIAN TSENG

that the best option was to always address issues on the merits, to make substantive judgments as to right or wrong, good or better. And I learned that the most important person I had to get along with was myself.

With these traits, refined in the course of my career, I lived my life as a lawyer as pure intellect, seemingly without corporal form, free from ethnicity or gender. My life in law vindicated my decision as a child to favor language over math (at which I was very bad; yes, I refused to follow racial stereotypes from the very beginning) and to use that path to define my place in this improbable country whose Chinese name appropriately begins with the word "beautiful."

In the world of law, I was neither Chinese nor female, but a lawyer whose enjoyment of legal problem solving translated into skills that were consistently rewarded with professional recognition. Job offers were commensurate with law school success. Law firm mentors guided and encouraged a career development that felt merit-based. When the corporate world beckoned, I stepped into a hierarchy based on rank reminiscent of a military chain of command. An officer of the company doesn't have to be a gentleman to be given her due.

An officer of the company doesn't have to be a gentleman to be given her due.

Throughout my career, if a partner, client, or judge chose to see me first as only a Chinese woman, that initial impression fell away after I opened my mouth, after they got to know me. I always felt that I was able to travel to that plane of pure intellect—or just professionalism—fairly quickly, and after I got my audience there, we were able to stay. This was because unconnected to the allegiances of an old boys' network, I ewed to a higher and more compelling allegiance, the principle of serving the client's interest, of enhancing shareholder value, of justice.

I have followed the same path in law as I have in life, and I commend the same to you: if you base your action on the right principle, you will get the result you deserve. And if you are as smart as you need to be to have a successful legal career, you'll recognize that individual success coexists with systemic injustice. Enjoying the former without contributing to the amelioration of the latter leads to ultimate failure.

As women and people of color in the legal profession, we have a special responsibility to adhere to the following admonition: "Justice, justice shall you pursue...," (Deuteronomy 16:20) for "it is not your obligation to complete the work, but neither are you free to desist from it." (Pirkei Avoth 2:19).

Vivian Tseng is pictured in front of a collection of Welch's products; she has been in-house with Welch's, Inc. in Concord since 1986.

IMAGE COURTESY OF VIVIAN TSENG

Mary E. Weber

You Can Have it All…Almost

The last thirty-nine years (has it really been thirty-nine years?!) have been an amazing time to be a female lawyer. It is hard to imagine now that, in the sixties, even the most promising women lawyers had a hard time getting any job. Today the opportunities for women lawyers are unlimited. And women have taken full advantage of those opportunities—capitalizing on their significant skills and talents to become leaders in the legal profession: partners in fields of their own choosing, general counsel, judges, law-firm leaders, and business and nonprofit executives.

I've had the opportunity to ride the wave of these changes. Not many years before I graduated from the University of Pennsylvania Law School in 1973, most law firms consigned women to permanent associate positions, relegated them to inside offices, paid them less than men, and did not permit them to sign correspondence or meet clients. Career choices were largely limited to estate planning and state securities laws, areas considered suitable for women. Around the time I attended law school, most law firms, no doubt feeling the pressure of civil rights legislation, had recently promoted one (and usually only one) of their long-tenured women associates to partnership and hired a small handful of recent female graduates as regular associates. But the women in my law school class couldn't help but wonder: Would firms continue to hire and promote women? The future had yet to unfold.

My initial recruiting experiences and those of my peers left that picture a little cloudy. Generally, each firm would invite back only one woman from any school to the second round of interviews, presumably not to overshoot the quota for women hires. One of my female peers named Randy was summarily dismissed from an interview by a firm who had mistakenly thought from her name that she was a man. Interview topics reached broadly into areas that today would be unthinkable (and illegal), subjecting us to many personal queries including future family plans (somewhat humorous for me as I had no serious relationship at the time) and the ability to live away from our parents. I was even asked on dates by (thankfully unmarried) interviewers.

But it turned out that law firms had, in fact, progressed in their thinking, and the women in my class accumulated summer offers. And then luck played its hand for me. Incredibly, I took an interview, and then a summer job, with Ropes & Gray in Boston, a city where I'd been just once before for a day as a child. At the time, I had no compelling reason to take that interview; it was a lark because a friend said I should experience the great interviewer from Boston. Even after the summer, I turned down the firm's job offer the first time around. But fate would not be denied. My random interview led to an associate position, a partnership, and ultimately an entire career with Ropes & Gray.

Mary E. Weber

IMAGE COURTESY OF ROPES & GRAY LLP

It was lucky for me that Ropes & Gray was then and is still today a remarkable place. With a hundred-year tradition of believing in individual excellence, teamwork, collegiality, and fair play, the firm has been a progressive and welcoming place for women to forge their careers. Despite being the epitome of a "white shoe" firm, Ropes & Gray has long been staunchly convinced that outstanding legal skills are the key to both individual and firm success. This core tenet has driven Ropes & Gray ahead of its time to embrace all talented lawyers, first those who did not attend "The College" and "The Law School," followed by non-WASPs, women, African Americans, and other groups who have been historically the subject of discrimination.

Within this egalitarian culture, luck again played an important role in my becoming a corporate lawyer. Having interned at the U.S. attorney's office, I had imagined myself as a litigator. But a random summer pro-bono project kindled my interest in corporate work and led me to volunteer for the corporate group at Ropes & Gray. Imagine the context at the time: There weren't any female corporate associates or partners in Boston, let alone the country generally. Corporate law was universally regarded as a bastion of the "old boys' club," an area where women simply could not be successful. Still, Ropes & Gray welcomed me enthusiastically into the practice without even a hint of the challenges I—and the firm itself—would face. In the early years, clients had to be won over because they didn't want to work with a "girl," lawyers from other firms asked me to make copies and get coffee, and meeting participants routinely interrupted and tried to talk over me. For years, I was the only woman in the room at any meeting. The managing partner of our firm once told a client that if they wanted to choose a lawyer based on sex and not talent, they had the wrong law firm. In this regard, the firm always backed me up and supported me along with the other women in the firm.

The managing partner of our firm once told a client that if they wanted to choose a lawyer based on sex and not talent, they had the wrong law firm.

Starting with that first pro bono project, I received great opportunities to work with excellent clients and on sophisticated transactions. My decision to volunteer for the corporate group led to opportunities that I never imagined. I've been involved in exciting and broad-reaching areas of corporate law, ranging from mergers and acquisitions, public offerings and financings, to advising boards of directors, investment banks, and private equity funds, to counseling companies from start-ups to multinationals. Within our firm, I've had the chance to participate in leading the firm's strategic transformation from a one-office Boston legal practice to a nationally and now internationally renowned firm. And on the philanthropic side, I've had the ability to work with and lead some charities that are incredibly important to me—including MCLE!

Even more important than my career has been my family—my husband, who is a partner in another leading law firm, and my three children. I had not planned to continue working after the birth of my first child. It was my husband who encouraged me to continue. "You love your work," he said, "so stay at some level. You can always quit, but it will be really hard to get that job back later." What great advice! In those early days, the firm had no formal reduced-time policy. Still I worked variously three, four, and four-and-a-half days a week and flex time with the firm's support, and, in fact, made partner while working reduced time. In those days, work necessarily centered on the office because communication was based on face-to-face meetings, land-line phones, computers operated only by secretaries, and fax machines spewing long sheets of thermographic paper (no Internet, PCs, cell phones, or BlackBerries, to name a few items that have revolutionized things for working women). So my children, when young, became regular fixtures in the office, regarding visiting with other lawyers and secretaries, typing, coloring on the conference room whiteboards, and riding the elevators as great activities. There has been a lot of juggling between the needs of my family and my job, but it has all worked out.

During the course of my career, I have witnessed firsthand the deconstruction of the once palpable stigma against women lawyers. It's been a long journey for me from the time when it was a generally-held belief that a woman lawyer couldn't succeed in corporate law, and definitely not while raising three children. If I could do it, so can any other resilient and dedicated woman lawyer. But to balance this juggling act successfully is no cakewalk. For those at the beginning of their careers, I'd share a few thoughts that have been pivotal to me during my career and which I believe are keys for a woman lawyer's success.

- **Go for it!** There is nothing more important than going for it, totally and completely. Pick aspirational goals, take on the challenges, work very hard, and never get complacent. There is nothing more important to success than trying hard. I can promise you, as Wayne Gretzky once said, "You miss 100 percent of the shots you don't take." If you don't try, you definitely will not succeed. Believe in yourself and project that confidence to those around you. You will be surprised by all you can achieve.
- **Plan to succeed.** I have heard many women plan for failure—fearing that they will not be able to succeed at becoming a partner or a general counsel, to balance a career and personal life, and to be a successful lawyer, spouse, and mother. They agonize over shortchanging their husband and/or children and question whether trying to balance career and family life will be worth the effort. So often this anticipation of the worst results in unhappiness, dropping out of the workplace, or significantly scaling back on the career side. In saying this, I do not mean to suggest that women cannot make a well-informed and justified decision to leave the workforce. It may be the right decision for some women and their families. But I am suggesting that you shouldn't decide to leave before you give it a good try, and that you should not make it a self-fulfilling prophecy. Make sure not to shortchange yourself. Don't end up wondering what might have been. Believe you can do it and give your career a full chance, advancing yourself to an exciting place in your career before deciding.
- **Realize that things change.** When planning your life, remember that your career as a lawyer and a spouse/mother is very long. Things will change dramatically in your work and your family life over the years. Being the mother of a baby and being the mother of a teenager are very different jobs, and children grow up in a flash. In just a few short years, I promise that you will be negotiating to get quality time from your children and not vice versa! So many of my acquaintances who gave up good jobs to mother small children ended up searching for something else to do not that many years later. Similarly, your role as a lawyer will change materially over time. As lawyers progress through their careers, they get more control over their time and responsibilities. So try to look ten, twenty, thirty, and forty years down the road at your family and your career when making today's choices.

Mary Weber at a 2010 family wedding.

IMAGE COURTESY OF MARY E. WEBER

- **Prioritize, prioritize, and prioritize some more!** Once in a presentation to a group of women, I said, "You cannot do it all." The audience was discouraged, wanting to believe that successful women were Super Women who could do it all and that this was a skill that they too could learn. I'm smarter now—I say, "Although you cannot do everything, you can do everything that is important!" After thirty-nine years as a lawyer and thirty-one years as a mother, I can tell you that success depends upon continually deciding what is really important, prioritizing those things, and executing on those priorities. This is true for success in your family life, in your career, and, in fact, for anything you want to do.
- **Make active choices about how you spend your time.** A research study showed that prioritization is the single most important factor in achieving success. It's shocking how hard it is to decide what few items are the most important ones to accomplish in the short, medium, and long terms, and to actually execute on those items and in the time frames. But when time is in short supply and there are a lot of important things to accomplish, the only path to success—in all aspects of life—is to make hard decisions about your priorities and make sure to accomplish what is really important.
- **Pick your own path.** Don't feel compelled to make conventional choices about what is important to you. Or feel the need to accomplish those choices in conventional ways. Instead, make the choices that will work best for you and for your significant others. The press of the prevailing culture is very strong. For example, as a young mother, I felt pressured to shift my career toward types of work with more predictable hours. After all, it was accepted wisdom that any decent mother would want to get home at predictable times every day. But I really didn't like the work. Both my family and I were much happier when I returned to transactional work with its demanding hours. Instead of predictability, I focused on how I could fulfill my responsibilities in the time frames I had. I worked more flexibly, identifying when I really needed to be there, communicating clearly with my family, setting expectations, and accommodating

in various ways. For example, my children sometimes faxed in their homework so we could discuss it by phone (now, it could be Skype!). Real life does not need to emulate a television sitcom to still be successful!

- **Lean on the right partners.** You cannot do this alone. You need to partner with great mentors, coaches, and supporters. You don't need to find the one mythic mentor—you know what I mean—the one senior woman at work who singularly guides your success. There are mentors and coaches all around you—they can be men or women, old or young, lawyers or not—and you'll find them at work, at home, and in every other aspect of your life. In almost all cases, they are ready to help if you just ask them and will be pleased to share what they have learned. My most impactful mentors and coaches have included several male partners, a male associate only a few years senior to me, a client, the CEO of a charity, and our nanny! And never forget your friends. A few key friends can provide important guidance and support to advance your career.

Your most important partner, though, is your spouse. No one else is more pivotal to your success. You need to partner with someone who will actively and consistently share in the juggling and balancing that will make your career possible. And you will need to do the same. Believe me, it is a myth that both partners cannot have meaningful careers and a successful family life. Like other dual-career couples, my husband and I share a strong commitment to each other's success and that of our family, and a willingness to invest in securing that success by sharing responsibilities at home. This can be very hard. But it improves both a marriage and a family to have both partners share meaningfully in what it takes to be a successful family.

As I look back over my career, I am thankful for the experiences I've had. I do not mean to suggest that this was easy. In fact, there has been a lot of hard work and many challenges. Still, I am blessed with a career that has been stimulating, fun, and rewarding. I am blessed with a great family, including my husband and my children, who note after reading this that they are normal, well adjusted, love me, and do not wish that I had stayed at home! I would not have traded my choices for another path!

The 1989 Gender Bias Study of the Massachusetts Court System

SANDRA SHAPIRO

The 1989 *Report of the Gender Bias Study of the Supreme Judicial Court* is an historic document. It ensued from the proposal of September 30, 1985, by the Women's Bar Association (WBA) of Massachusetts to the Supreme Judicial Court to initiate a gender bias study of the court system in Massachusetts that would be similar to studies that had already begun in New Jersey, New York, and Rhode Island. In responding to the proposal, Chief Justice Edward F. Hennessey asked the WBA to confirm that other leading bar associations in the Commonwealth supported the WBA proposal; he also asked the WBA to secure funding for the study from the Massachusetts legislature. The WBA in turn sought and obtained the requisite moral support from the Massachusetts Bar Association and the Boston Bar Association and the requisite funding from the Massachusetts legislature. Senator Patricia McGovern, then chair of the Senate Ways and Means Committee, and leaders in the Massachusetts House of Representatives provided their good offices in guiding the funding request through the legislature. Thanks to their efforts, Massachusetts became the first state with a legislatively-funded gender bias study of its court system.

The cover of the 1989 Report of the Gender Bias Study of the Supreme Judicial Court.

IMAGE SOURCE: *REPORT OF THE GENDER BIAS STUDY OF THE SUPREME JUDICIAL COURT* (SUPREME JUDICIAL COURT 1989)

The study began in December 1986 with a mandate from the Supreme Judicial Court to "investigate whether gender bias exists within the Massachusetts judicial system and, if such gender bias does exist, to make appropriate remedial recommendations." The recommendations might, for example, include "proposals for the adoption of court rules, for the consideration of legislative action, for changes in administrative practices and for the development of educational programs." The Supreme Judicial Court named a thirty-eight-member committee and appointed Supreme Judicial Court Justice Ruth I. Abrams and Appeals Court Chief Justice John M. Greaney as cochairs of the study, with Supreme Judicial Court Chief Justice Hennessey as honorary chair. A status report was issued in July 1988.

The substantive work of the study was performed by four subcommittees that the committee had formed and on which sixty volunteers served. The four subcommittees were as follows:

- Subcommittee on Court Administration and Personnel;
- Subcommittee on Gender and Economics;
- Subcommittee on Gender in the Courts; and
- Subcommittee on Gender, Violence, and the Courts.

The subcommittees utilized a wide range of research methods, including group meetings, individual interviews, surveys, examination of court records, and literature reviews. A coordinating committee met regularly. Public hearings were held in Springfield, Boston, and Worcester.

Gender Bias Study 1988 Attorneys' Survey[46]

Proportion of attorneys who have ever experienced each behavior in past five years	Women	Men
Addressed by first name or terms of endearment when you expected to be addressed surname or title by counsel	59%	16%
Asked if you were an attorney by counsel	68%	14%
Received inappropriate comments about your personal appearance from counsel	30%	2%
Were subjected to inappropriate comments of a sexual or aggressive nature from counsel	12%	1%

The findings of the report concerned family law, domestic violence and sexual assault, criminal and juvenile justice, civil damages awards, gender bias in courthouse interactions, and court personnel. The report made recommendations to eliminate gender bias in the areas of education, court rules, and statutes, adding new structures and strengthening existing ones. In 1989, as the report had urged, the Supreme Judicial Court appointed a Committee for Gender Equality, chaired by Justice Abrams, to implement the recommendations of the study.

Although the gender bias study concentrated on the treatment of female lawyers, female litigants, and female witnesses *in the court system,* the study had fallout on the treatment of women within the wider legal community. To address questions about the law profession, the Boston Bar Association (BBA) commissioned a study of the role of gender in the practice of law. In the course of this study, the consulting firm of Litigation Sciences, Inc., conducted a random survey of 2,500 lawyers in the metropolitan Boston area at no cost to the BBA. According to the Honorable Sandra L. Lynch, then president of the BBA, the survey results that were released in early 1988 suggested that there was room for improvement in, among other areas, compensation, management, and "the treatment of women and the amount of respect they get." In 1988, Massachusetts and Maine were believed to be the only states that had compiled data on the role of gender in the law profession.

As we look back over the twenty-three years since the gender bias study report, the effects of its recommendations can be observed throughout the court system of the Commonwealth. Perhaps the most noteworthy, albeit indirect, result is the prominence of women on the Supreme Judicial Court itself. Justice Ruth Abrams, who cochaired the study, was the first—and at the time the only—woman on that bench. Since then, seven other distinguished women have served or are serving there, one of them, of course—the Honorable Margaret H. Marshall—as chief justice.

The 1989 gender bias study vindicated its premise that "[t]he people of the Commonwealth deserve a court system free of all bias." In emphasizing that premise, Chief Justice Hennessey concluded the study by stating, "The judicial branch is the one institution in the community that cannot afford to fail, and if human rights are to be nourished, the people must continue to have confidence in the courts."

When women, in their diverse roles, are denied credibility because of their gender, the courts are seriously impaired in their ability to deliver justice to anyone in our society.

Executive Summary, Report of the Gender Bias Study of the Supreme Judicial Court

NOTES

1 Karen Berger Morello, *The Invisible Bar: The Woman Lawyer in America, 1638 to the Present* 3 (Beacon Press 1988).

2 Morello, *The Invisible Bar* at 8. Morello reminds us of the enormously restricted society women faced: "Well into the nineteenth century married women could not vote, serve on a jury, get a professional education, hold elective office, enter into a contract, obtain custody of their own children, or control their own money, even when they had earned it. Society had become so formal...that restrictions on race, sex, and class prevented the emergence of any successors to Margaret Brent." Morello, *The Invisible Bar* at 9. The first woman admitted to the state bar was Iowa's Arabella Babb Mansfield in 1869.

3 Virginia G. Drachman, *Sisters in Law: Women Lawyers in Modern American History* 1 (Harvard University Press 1998).

4 Drachman, *Sisters in Law* at 2. "Law in the late nineteenth century was even more masculine than other male-dominated professions: it was characterized by an all-male bar, all-male judges, and the shared belief that law was the natural province of men, not women." Drachman, *Sisters in Law* at 11. Science writer Deborah Blum noted the extensive roots of such prejudice: "in the days before women were admitted to college, male scientists insisted that girls were born too fragile and emotional to even handle higher education." Deborah Blum, "Solving For XX," *Boston Sunday Globe*, Jan. 23, 2005, at E.

5 Not all efforts were successful. Most notably, in 1873, the U.S. Supreme Court denied a woman named Myrna Bradwell the right to practice law. *Bradwell v. Illinois*, 83 U.S. 130 (1973).

6 "A Lady Lawyer," *The Boston Post*, Oct. 1, 1881, at 1.

7 *Lelia J. Robinson's Case*, 131 Mass. 376 (1881).

8 1882 Mass. Acts c. 139 (approved Apr. 10, 1882).

9 Drachman, *Sisters in Law* at 12. Drachman noted that in 1879, the U.S. Congress authorized women to practice before the U.S. Supreme Court.

10 Drachman, *Sisters in Law* at 219–20. Women "knew that the meritocracy in the legal profession was not working for them and that discrimination was a central aspect of their careers in law." Drachman, *Sisters in Law* at 221. These pervasive barriers impacted the ability of women to practice in the courtroom; by 1920, only 6 percent of women lawyers specialized in trial work and criminal law. Drachman, *Sisters in Law* at 223.

11 Drachman, *Sisters in Law* at 241.

12 *See, e.g.*, Morello, *The Invisible Bar* at 136, describing a distinguished Columbia Law School graduate of 1935 who ranked second in her class being told by a Wall Street lawyer, "What a shame...with your record, we would hire you on the spot—if you were a man."

13 Morello, *The Invisible Bar* at 105.

14 Morello, *The Invisible Bar* at 194. Justice Ruth Bader Ginsberg, the second woman to serve on the Supreme Court, obtained a clerkship with a District Court judge through the assistance of a professor who overcame "the Judge's reluctance to hire a woman clerk, particularly one with a young child, by guaranteeing him a male backup as a replacement" in the event the judge could not work with her. Herma Hill Kay, "Symposium Celebration of the Tenth Anniversary of Justice Ruth Bader Ginsburg's Appointment to the Supreme Court of the United States," 104 *Colum. L. Rev.* 1, 9 (Jan. 2004).

15 Deborah L. Rhode, "The Unfinished Agenda: Women and the Legal Profession," American Bar Ass'n Comm'n on Women in the Profession, 2001, at 13.

16 Morello, *The Invisible Bar* at 86.

17 Eleanor M. Fox, "Being a Woman, Being a Lawyer and Being a Human Being—Woman and Change," 57 *Fordham L. Rev.* 955, 957 (1989).

18 Rhode, "The Unfinished Agenda: Women and the Legal Profession" at 13. Of note, the 2001 Catalyst study reported that 63 percent of the class of 2003 at the University of California at Berkeley (Boalt Hall) were women; and women comprised 53 percent and 51 percent, respectively, at Yale Law School and Harvard Law School. See "Women in Law: Making the Case," 2001 Catalyst 9.

19 Mark Galanter & Thomas Palay, *Tournament of Lawyers: The Transformation of the Big Law Firm* 20 (1991). Galanter and Palay describe the big firms, circa 1960, as "prosperous, stable, and untroubled.... It was a time of stable relations with clients, of steady but manageable growth, of comfortable assurance that an equally

bright future lay ahead—which is not to say that its inhabitants did not look back fondly to an earlier time when professionalism was unalloyed."

20 Galanter & Palay, *Tournament of Lawyers* at 46. Galanter and Palay note that not only were there more big firms, but they were growing at a much faster rate and increasing significantly in overall size.

21 "The Am Law 100," *Am. Law.*, July 2005, at 111–21.

22 Mona Harrington, *Women Lawyers: Rewriting the Rules* 17–21 (Plume Books 1995) (1993).

23 Fern S. Sussman, "The Large Law Firm Structure: An Historic Opportunity," 57 *Fordham L. Rev.* 969, 969–70 (1989).

24 American Bar Association Section of Legal Education and Admissions to the Bar, *First Year and Total J.D. Enrollment By Gender 1947–2002, available at* http://www.americanbar.org/groups/legal_education/resources/statistics.html.

25 According to the 1999 *Report of the First Circuit Gender, Race and Ethnic Bias Task Forces*, "Among attorneys, many more women than men reported that either an attorney, employee, or judge 'made an inaccurate assumption regarding their professional status.' Women were also more likely than men to report sexually suggestive comments or advances, comments about their physical appearance or clothing, demeaning or derogatory comments, and that their opinions or views were not taken seriously." *See, e.g.*, Florida Bar Association, *Report and Recommendations of the Florida Bar Special Committee for Gender Equality in the Profession* (July 1992), *available at* http://www.flabar.org.

26 American Bar Association Section of Legal Education and Admissions to the Bar, *First Year and Total J.D. Enrollment By Gender 1947–2002, available at* http://www.americanbar.org/groups/legal_education/resources/statistics.html. The U.S. Equal Employment Opportunity Commission requires law firms that employ 100 or more employees to file EEO-l reports, which compile data on the employment status of women and minorities. In 2003, the EEOC issued a comprehensive report analyzing data over a period of years and confirmed the well-stocked pipeline, noting: "In large, national law firms, the most pressing issues have probably shifted from hiring and initial access, to problems concerning the terms and conditions of employment, especially promotion to partnership." U.S. Equal Employment Opportunity Commission, *Diversity in Law Firms* (2003), *available at* http://www.eeoc.gov/stats/reports/diversitylaw/index.html.

27 Robert MacCrate, "What Women Are Teaching a Male-Dominated Profession," 57 *Fordham L. Rev.* 989, 990 (1989).

28 Hope Viner Samborn, "Higher Hurdles for Women," 86 *A.B.A. J.* 30, 30 (Sept. 2000).

29 Samborn, "Higher Hurdles for Women," 86 *A.B.A. J.* at 31–33.

30 Samborn, "Higher Hurdles for Women," 86 *A.B.A. J.* at 35.

31 The National Association of Women Lawyers and the NAWL Foundation, *Report of the Sixth Annual National Survey on Retention and Promotion of Women in Law Firms* (Oct. 2011).

32 Data compiled from ABA Commission on Women in the Profession, *A Current Glance at Women in the Law 2011, 2009, 2007, 2005, 2003* and *A Snapshot of Women in the Law 2000, available at* http://www.americanbar.org/groups/women/resources/statistics.html.

33 Laurel Bellows, *Unfinished Business: Overcoming the Sisyphus Factor* 3 (American Bar Ass'n Comm'n on the Status of Women in the Profession 1995). *See also* U.S. Equal Employment Opportunity Commission, *Diversity in Law Firms* (2003), *available at* http://www.eeoc.gov/stats/reports/diversitylaw/ index.html: "Lawyers are very often key players in designing and activating the institutional mechanisms through which property is transferred, economic exchange is planned and enforced, injuries are compensated, crime is punished, marriages are dissolved and disputes are resolved. The ideologies and incentives of the lawyers engaged in these functions directly influence the lived experience of Americans, including whether they feel fairly treated by legal institutions."

34 Ronit Dinovitzer et al., *After the JD: First Results of a National Study of Legal Careers* 19 (NALP Foundation 2004), *available at* http://www.NALPFoundation.org.

35 Harrington, *Women Lawyers: Rewriting the Rules* at 16.

36 James B. Stewart, *The Partners: Inside America's Most Powerful Law Firms* 14 (Simon & Schuster 1983). Another author observed: "As legal counsel to major corporations, the large firm participates in transactions and

disputes that have enormous consequences for society." *See Nelson, Partners with Power: The Social Transformation of the Large Law Firm* 1 (Univ. of California Press 1988).

37 Suzanne Nossel & Elizabeth Westfall, *Presumed Equal: What America's Top Women Lawyers Really Think About Their Firms* xiii (Career Press 1998).

38 American Bar Association Commission on Women in the Profession, *A Current Glance at Women in the Law* 2009 (Nov. 13, 2009).

39 Harrington, *Women Lawyers: Rewriting the Rules* at 16–17. *See also* David B. Wilkins, "From 'Separate is Inherently Unequal' to 'Diversity is Good for Business': The Rise of Market-Based Diversity Arguments and the Fate of the Black Corporate Bar," 117 *Harv. L. Rev.* 1548, 1600 (2004), noting that: "Corporate law jobs sit atop both the income and status hierarchies of the bar and serve as a gateway to prominent positions in government, business, and civil society."

40 Mary Ann Glendon, *A Nation Under Lawyers: How the Crisis in the Legal Profession Is Transforming American Society* 12–13 (Farrar, Straus & Giroux 1994).

41 Clara N. Carson, *The Lawyers Statistical Report, The U.S. Legal Profession in 2005* (American Bar Foundation 2012).

42 Data compiled From Women's Bar Association of Massachusetts, Employment Issues Committee, *Where Are We Now? A Report on the Occupational Status of Women Attorneys in Massachusetts* (2009).

43 Barbara Allen Babcock, *Making History: Lelia Robinson's Index to American Women Lawyers*, Stanford Law School, July 1998, *available at* http://www.law.stanford.edu/library/wlhbp/articles/makinghistory.htm.

44 Data compiled from *Massachusetts Lawyers Weekly*, "100 Largest Law Firms in Massachusetts" (Lawyers Weekly, Inc. 2012).

45 *Nevada Dep't of Human Res. v. Hibbs*, 538 U.S. 731, 736 (2003).

46 *Report of the Gender Bias Study of the Supreme Judicial Court* 142–43 (Supreme Judicial Court 1989).

Challenging the Status Quo

Reproductive Technology

Susan L. Crockin

Introduction

The 1978 birth of the world's first in vitro fertilization (IVF) baby in Britain caused an international uproar. Over thirty years and three million IVF births later, the 2010 Nobel Prize in Medicine was awarded to Dr. Robert Edwards, the surviving British physician who, together with Patrick Steptoe, pioneered the breakthrough technology that joined sperm and eggs outside a woman's body and inside a laboratory petri dish. That technology and those that have followed continue to reverberate in legislatures and courtrooms around the globe, as the legal arena has struggled to keep pace with these stunning medical advances. What follows is a brief overview of the short history of these historical medical achievements that have set the stage for the legal developments that have followed, as well as an overview of the central and often pivotal role the Massachusetts legal system has played in the developing law.

Since Louise Brown's birth in 1978, reproductive medicine has thrust an increasingly dazzling array of novel baby-making techniques into the public eye—from embryo cryopreservation to donor gametes and gestational surrogacy arrangements, to preimplantation genetic diagnosis (of IVF embryos—thus helping conceive children for childless families and individuals). Due to these key advancements in medicine, many infertile couples, same-sex couples, and single parents can now create children through biological and/or gestational means, which has been made possible through access to IVF technology, donor sperm, donor eggs, or both. These advances have created the possibility of previously inconceivable children, but at the same time have challenged and at times pushed past established boundaries of family law. In a small, but often widely publicized, number of cases, intended parents have created children using both donor egg and donor sperm, as well as a gestational surrogate carrier. In 1978, like most states, Massachusetts had little law—and little need for law—that applied to assisted reproductive technology (ART), the families they created, or the professionals who helped them. A single Massachusetts statute on artificial insemination (G.L. c. 46, § 4B) made it clear that a child born to a married woman using artificial insemination with donor sperm, with her husband's consent, was deemed a legitimate child of their marriage. The statute does not require written consent or medical assistance, and these children were born and recognized as legitimate under Massachusetts law without fanfare and often without the knowledge of anyone other than those involved in the actual process.

A second little-noticed—and virtually unused—statute, G.L. c. 209C, § 21, which was not designed for ART families, is found amidst the out-of-wedlock statutes which are largely intended to provide child support. Section 21 states as follows: "[i]n so far as practicable, the

Susan L. Crockin is the principal at Crockin Law & Policy Group, and an adjunct professor of law at Georgetown Law Center; she teaches reproductive technology law and has a nationwide practice representing and consulting medical ART and donor programs, institutions, adoption agencies, and individual clients. She is a graduate of Tufts University and Northeastern University School of Law.

IMAGE COURTESY OF SUSAN L. CROCKIN

provisions of this chapter applicable to establishing paternity shall apply to maternity." Under Chapter 209C, paternity can be established via DNA testing, presumed through marriage to the mother, or legally recognized through a state-issued "voluntary acknowledgment of parentage" form signed by the man claiming paternity and the mother (and by her husband denying his paternity if she is married). At the time the "maternity statute" was enacted, it was medically impossible for a woman to become pregnant or deliver a child who was not her biological child; the maternity statute saw virtually no use in Massachusetts family law.

Susan Crockin and Dr. Howard W. Jones (age 100) at a signing for their 2010 book, Legal Conceptions: The Evolving Law and Policy of Assisted Reproductive Technologies. *Dr. Jones opened the country's first IVF clinic in 1979 and was responsible for the first IVF baby born in the United States.*

IMAGES COURTESY OF SUSAN L. CROCKIN

The invention of IVF, however, by making the previously impossible possible, changed everything. These fundamental changes in the ways families can be created have given birth to a host of novel legal issues, tensions, and challenges and an emerging body of sometimes inconsistent law and policy. In the process, providers, patients, third parties, and the children they all seek to create have become part of a grand social experiment that is still unfolding today. Courts and legislatures have struggled to create workable laws and guidance, and articulate policies for both existing and future reproductive technologies and those whose lives are touched by them. Massachusetts has played, and continues to play, a critical role in this experiment.

Insurance Coverage for Infertility

In the mid-1980s, IVF was a novel, but increasingly attractive, treatment option for infertile couples who were unable to conceive with more conventional treatment. For women with blocked fallopian tubes, IVF presented an elegant solution and realistic opportunity to achieve a pregnancy. Unfortunately, at that time few medical programs offered the service and almost no health insurance policies covered the treatment. The first IVF clinic in the United States, the Jones Institute of Reproductive Medicine, opened its doors in Norfolk, Virginia, almost immediately in the wake of Louise Brown's birth. By the mid-1980s it was the "go-to" clinic, with patients flying in from all over the country and even from outside it. Couples traveled to Norfolk for two weeks to undergo what was then a state-of-the-art treatment of daily hormone-stimulating drugs, daily full-bladder ultrasound monitoring of egg follicle growth, egg retrievals performed in a hospital setting under general anesthesia, in vitro fertilization of the man's fresh sperm, and a three-day wait to see whether enough embryos survived and developed for the woman to undergo a "day-three" transfer of several embryos to her uterus through a catheter. As patients sat, day after day, in the clinic's waiting room, many discussions turned to the high cost of IVF and the almost universal lack of insurance. A chance meeting between a Maryland patient, where IVF was statutorily covered, and a Massachusetts patient, where it wasn't, provided the initial spark for what would become the "Massachusetts Infertility Mandate." Starting with five couples who were Jones Institute patients (including the author), a two-year, grassroots effort ultimately led by Resolve of the Bay State, a chapter of the national infertility organization RESOLVE, Inc., succeeded in enacting infertility insurance legislation in Massachusetts. That law, G.L. c. 175, § 47H, declared infertility a medical condition and required nondiscrimination against infertility treatment—including IVF—as and to the extent an individual met the legal definition of "infertile" and the treatment was not deemed "experimental." As recently as November 2010, the law was amended to add more protections. The 2010 amendment expanded the definition of "infertility" (initially defined in the law as "the condition of an individual who is unable to conceive or produce conception during a period of one year"). As amended, women over thirty-five now qualify for infertility insurance coverage after six months of trying to conceive; a pregnancy loss does not automatically "restart" the six-month or one-year clock; and the "presumably healthy" language that was being used to deny coverage to some insureds has been eliminated.[1]

Twenty years after its passage, and fresh from its updated provisions, the scope of the Massachusetts mandate remains among the broadest of the approximately 15 states that require some form of infertility coverage. In many respects, the Commonwealth's leading role in reproductive technology law stems from mandated insurance coverage coupled with developing cutting-edge medical programs within the state. Together, they have made Massachusetts fertile ground for this interdisciplinary field.

States that Require Some Form of Infertility Insurance Coverage[2]

Arkansas
California
Connecticut
Hawaii
Illinois
Louisiana
Maryland
Massachusetts
Montana
New Jersey
New York
Ohio
Rhode Island
Texas
West Virginia

Donor Gametes (Sperm and Eggs) and Family Building in Massachusetts

Both sperm and, more recently, egg donation for procreation have become a permanent part of the family-building landscape. Like all but a handful of states, Massachusetts has a sperm donor, but not an egg donor, statute. General Laws c. 46, § 4B states that "[a]ny child born to a married woman as a result of artificial insemination with the consent of her husband, shall be considered the legitimate child of the mother and such husband." Although this statute is legally adequate for a married couple using donor sperm, many couples find that a legal agreement as well as the husband's written consent are protections they, their donor, and their physicians want in place. Outside of Massachusetts, there are cases challenging the legal status of children born from donor sperm in a myriad of contexts, including denials of paternity by husbands claiming they did not consent to or know of, or were lied to about donor insemination; from donors claiming agreements or expectations that they had paternity rights; from women seeking alternatively sole parentage or financial support from men characterized as donors or fathers; and from estate claims that such children were or were not considered legitimate heirs.

Without an egg donor law in Massachusetts, medical programs typically require—and risk-averse patients typically want—a legal agreement between recipients and any egg donor—whether she is anonymous or known, and whether recruited by the recipient or from a third-party source. While legally untested, these agreements aim to clarify each party's legal status as a donor or parent, as well as document—among other issues—any payment provisions; assumptions of risk; under what, if any, circumstances there may be future contact among any of the parties and the child; the degree of shared medical information; and any restrictions on redonating unused embryos. Separate, independent legal representation for the donor is an important safeguard in the process.

While arguably the Massachusetts law on sperm donation should apply equally to egg donation under an equal rights analysis, some courts in other states have rejected such applicability, in part because artificial insemination and IVF are different medical procedures, so the strength of this analogy remains an open question. Written legal agreements, which provide a formal, memorialized record of intentions and agreed upon actions, taken together with comprehensive consent forms, are likely the best legal protections currently available. To date, Massachusetts has not been called to rule on any issues involving disputed parentage involving egg donation.

The future of egg donation will undoubtedly bring both medical and legal challenges and changes in practice. From a medical perspective, frozen eggs are quickly moving from the experimental phase into practice both for patients preserving their own eggs and for donors. Once widely available, frozen egg donation will once again transform applicable paradigms as donors and recipients will not have a contemporaneous relationship. From a legal perspective, regardless of fresh or frozen donations, there needs to be greater clarity over who is a parent or a donor; better health protections for donors, intended parents, and offspring; more uniform rules for compensation; and more uniform, reliable mechanisms for obtaining, storing, and sharing donor information for donor-conceived persons in the future.

Nontraditional Families, Same-Sex Marriage, and ART

Long before IVF and same-sex marriage became accepted practice in Massachusetts, same-sex couples were creating families and successfully seeking legal protections for them. Starting with *Adoption of Tammy* in 1993, the Supreme Judicial Court made it clear that a committed same-sex female couple could adopt a child together, including the biological child born to one of them.[3] The court in *Tammy* first made clear that state adoption statutes that required married couples to adopt together, G.L. c. 210, § 1, did not prohibit unmarried couples from adopting together. It then went one step further, reassuring biological parents who were coparenting with partners that they did not have to first relinquish their biological parentage rights in order to attain their adoptive parentage rights with their partners. *Tammy* marked a watershed moment in Massachusetts legal history—providing same-sex couples the first opportunity to protect themselves and their children as a family unit notwithstanding their inability to marry one another.

The Supreme Judicial Court's groundbreaking 2003 case recognizing same-sex marriage, *Goodridge v. Department of Public Health*, came amidst an explosion of ART treatments enabling same-sex male couples, as well as female couples, to have children.[4] The case provided the second significant legal means for Massachusetts same-sex couples to provide familial stability for themselves and their children within Massachusetts. With this new law, female same-sex couples could use artificial insemination or IVF and both be recognized as equal legal parents of the child to whom one of them gave birth. Male same-sex couples could work together with an egg donor to create an embryo, transfer it to a second woman as a gestational carrier, and upon birth be legally recognized as the only two legal parents of the resulting child due to their marital status and the state's Equal Rights Act. Before this, the only opportunity for same-sex male couples to have a biological child of one of them was through traditional surrogacy, a family-building method that is still fraught with legal vulnerability (and therefore seldom used) due to the traditional surrogate's legal status as a mother (see below).

The Supreme Judicial Court's groundbreaking 2003 case recognizing same-sex marriage, Goodridge v. Department of Public Health, *came amidst an explosion of ART treatments enabling same-sex male couples, as well as female couples, to have children.*

While same-sex families are an increasingly visible and legally recognized part of the fabric of American family life, many states lag behind Massachusetts in legal protections. Consequently, and somewhat ironically given the forward-thinking Massachusetts legislature and judiciary, even married same-sex couples routinely complete a postbirth adoption of their child much as they did after *Tammy* and prior to *Goodridge*. This ensures their family's legitimacy outside of Massachusetts.

Traditional Surrogacy and Gestational Carrier Surrogacy in Massachusetts

Surrogacy is as old as the Bible, but in modern times it entered the public's consciousness in a New Jersey case that became infamously known as the "Baby M" case.[5] Mary Beth Whitehead was recruited as a traditional surrogate to be artificially inseminated with sperm from William Stern. Stern and his wife were the intended parents of the resulting child. When Whitehead changed her mind and wanted to keep the child she was carrying, and to whom she was the biological mother, all parties headed to court. Debates over good parenting, biological ties, and defining motherhood raged beyond the New Jersey courts and into the national media. While the court delved into details of Ms. Whitehead's parenting ability, including whether she had, and properly used, educational toys in her home, little attention was given to the fact that she had never been carefully screened or informed of the psychological and emotional aspects of "traditional surrogacy." By the end of the litigation, the child was in the custody of the Sterns, Mary Beth Whitehead was a household name, and traditional surrogacy was being statutorily banned or regulated in many states, with some flatly outlawing it as illegal baby selling or finding that any such contracts violated existing adoption laws and protections for birth mothers or were unenforceable as against public policy. Despite, or perhaps because of, several efforts at legislation and conflicting views, Massachusetts did not follow suit and as of today, still has no statutes on surrogacy—traditional or otherwise. Instead, court decisions have played a major role in shaping the traditional and gestational surrogacy landscape in Massachusetts.

[In the absence of a surrogacy statute,] court decisions have played a major role in shaping the traditional and gestational surrogacy landscape in Massachusetts.

Before the advent of IVF, it was impossible for a woman to deliver a child without being that child's biological mother. Since traditional surrogacy required only artificial insemination, as it first came into use laws designed to protect birth mothers were seen as relatively analogous.

From both a medical and legal perspective, traditional surrogacy and gestational carrier surrogacy have little in common. A traditional surrogate, using technologies long predating the ARTs, is artificially inseminated with sperm that typically but not necessarily comes from the intended father. Artificial insemination often occurs with medical assistance but also can be done at home, hence the descriptive term "turkey baster" babies. Usually—but not always, the intended genetic father is married to a woman who cannot carry a child; and together the couple intend to be the rearing and legal parents. A traditional surrogate is thus both the genetic and gestational mother, and absent laws defining her otherwise, is presumably a birth mother and subject to state adoption laws.

In contrast to traditional surrogacy, gestational carrier surrogacy only became possible after IVF. It involves implanting an IVF embryo, typically but not necessarily created by the intended parents' sperm and eggs, into the uterus of a woman. Regardless of the source of the sperm and eggs, the pregnant woman is not the genetic mother of the child, and the applicability of older laws, adoption or otherwise, is less certain. Indeed, such arrangements in Massachusetts would ultimately be the first appropriate uses of the maternity statute noted above (G.L. c. 209C, § 21), since maternity could be proven via DNA or otherwise. The distinction between traditional surrogacy—which only needed to be qualified as "traditional" after the advent of gestational surrogacy—and gestational carrier surrogacy has critical significant implications for the law.

Defining motherhood when genetics, gestation, and intention can now be separated into two or three women has perplexed both courts and legislatures. Choice of language has often been determinative. To appreciate the developing law in Massachusetts in this field, it is critical to recognize that both traditional surrogacy and gestational surrogate carrier arrangements—in overlapping but distinct ways—challenge long-standing family law principles and presumptions. Massachusetts courts have weighed in on both traditional surrogacy and gestational carrier surrogacy arrangements. Three seminal cases—*R.R. v. M.H.* in 1998, deciding a traditional surrogacy case gone awry, and *Smith v. Brown* in 1999, a Supreme Judicial Court rescript opinion, together with *Culliton v. Beth Israel Deaconess Medical Center* in 2001, deciding legal parent-child status of children born to gestational carriers—have provided significant guideposts in this field.[6] (The author was the attorney of record in *Brown*, and filed amicus briefs in both *R.R.* and *Culliton*, for the purpose of explaining the significant medical distinctions between gestational and traditional surrogacy, thereby helping provide a factual basis to analyze, distinguish, and apply the law to these distinct situations more precisely.)

Gestational carrier arrangements in and outside of Massachusetts can require courts to

- define parentage in light of, or in contrast to, preexisting adoption and parentage laws (in the context of both disputed and agreed-to parentage and/or custody claims);
- determine the constitutionality of statutes intended to restrict or govern such arrangements;
- decide forum-shopping or jurisdictional disputes when multiple states (or countries) are involved; and
- assess liability for the myriad of professionals who help arrange these multiparty ways of making babies and families.

The Massachusetts appellate courts' first legal encounter with surrogacy was in, *R.R. v. M.H.*, a case involving a Massachusetts traditional surrogate and a Rhode Island couple.[7] In this case, much like the *Baby M* case, a married couple hired a woman to be a traditional surrogate. The agreement provided that the woman would relinquish physical custody of the child to the father or repay all funds she was to receive ($10,000). Despite a contract written under Rhode Island law, when the woman changed her mind midway through the pregnancy and sought to keep the child, the Massachusetts courts took jurisdiction and control. Many of the trial court's rulings were literally handed down during the surrogate's labor and delivery, by telephone, and under emergency conditions.

Ultimately, the case found its way to the Supreme Judicial Court, which issued a clear denunciation of paid, enforceable traditional surrogacy. Although the contract language assiduously avoided any reference to the surrogate relinquishing her parental rights, the Supreme Judicial Court was not swayed by that attempted distinction. It also rejected the contract's "choice-of-law" provision of Rhode Island, ruling that paid traditional surrogacy was "troubling," that under Massachusetts law a surrogate must have time to change her mind after the child's birth, and that eliminating payments other than "pregnancy-related expenses" (as permitted under adoption laws) was the only way to ensure against economic pressure on a woman to act as a surrogate. Ruling that a traditional surrogate is essentially a birth mother under Massachusetts adoption law, the Supreme Judicial Court then suggested that its concerns would be alleviated if a number of safeguards were in place, including eliminating payment; applying the mandatory four-day waiting period under the state's adoption laws; requiring that the surrogate be an adult with at least one living child and that her husband, if any, consent to the surrogacy in advance; and requiring that all parties subject themselves to some form of evaluation as to their "soundness of judgment and capacity." The court acknowledged the distinction between traditional and gestational surrogacy put forward in the amicus briefs, and the decision was a clear and predictable bright line, rejecting enforceable paid traditional surrogacy arrangements within Massachusetts. The decision also made clear that in traditional surrogate arrangements that did not go awry, a stepparent adoption would transfer maternity from the traditional surrogate/birth mother to the intended mother, so if everyone involved remained on the same legal page, parentage would ultimately be established through traditional adoption methods.

Following *R.R.*, few Massachusetts patients or professionals would consider entering into traditional surrogacy arrangements given the complete lack of prebirth legal protections that came with such a path. Although substantially less expensive than gestational surrogacy since IVF is not required, the significant legal vulnerabilities of traditional surrogacy were enough to deter most intended parents and virtually all physicians in Massachusetts. A small exception continues to this day of patients who are either confident in their choice of traditional surrogate (for example, a sister or close friend), or who are unfortunately naïve or ill-informed of the risks. For those traditional arrangements that go well, stepparent adoptions continue to be a clear protective path to parenthood after the child's birth. Sadly, there are continuing and unfortunately abundant examples of these arrangements falling apart despite the best of intentions and the highest of expectations of those entering into them. While many find their way into the glare of the national media, many more are settled quietly, if painfully. While preparing this text, at least four such cases anecdotally came to the author's attention—including two involving siblings who, while carrying a child, changed their mind about wanting to rear it. When traditional surrogacy goes awry, and the babies that were so desperately wanted are instead at the center of court battles, many families and relationships are permanently destroyed, regardless of the judicial decision and the child's ultimate placement.

In contrast to traditional surrogacy, gestational carrier surrogacy continues to thrive in Massachusetts and elsewhere. By substituting the newer, more expensive medical procedure of creating IVF embryos instead of artificial insemination, intended parents are able to create children who are biologically related to both of them and not to their gestational carrier. This newer process not only reduces the legal vulnerability of having a woman carry a child genetically related to her through artificial insemination, it also gave birth to new options to secure legal parentage for the parties.

Timeline of Key Developments

1983: *Taft v. Taft*, 388 Mass. 331: Holds that the constitutional right of privacy protects a wife from being forced by her husband to submit to surgery intended to help her carry a pregnancy to term.

1987: Massachusetts enacts a law mandating insurance coverage for the "diagnosis and treatment of infertility," which includes IVF. G.L. c. 175, § 47H.

1980 81 82 83 84 85 86 87 88 89 90 91 92 93 94 95

1981: Massachusetts' artificial insemination statute is passed. G.L. c. 46, § 4B.

The first known case in Massachusetts involved a client of the author's, a sister who had readily agreed to have her brother and sister-in-law's IVF embryo implanted and carry the child to term, but implored the author to avoid—in any way possible—her ever being considered the child's legal mother. As she bluntly put it, "I consider myself the aunt, I'm happy to be considered 'the little oven,' but having my name appear on a birth certificate with my brother as parents of this child is not something we—or our mother—ever want to see." With that challenge, we turned to the statutes to try to craft an alternative to what was then the standard procedure to secure parentage in any surrogacy arrangement—a postbirth stepparent adoption. Utilizing the artificial insemination and maternity statutes, we created a set of assented-to court pleadings under equity principles in the Probate and Family Court, petitioning for a "prebirth judicial declaration of legal parentage" for two genetic, married, intended parents whose child was being carried by another woman. The argument to the court was that if maternity could be defined by statute in the same way as paternity under Chapter 209C, then DNA should be available to establish maternity and override any presumption of maternity for a pregnant woman. Further, we argued that fairness required an analogous outcome for maternity given long-established legal principles that paternity of a child born to another man's wife could be legally determined through an agreed-upon voluntary acknowledgment of parentage. Novel, but legally supportable, the argument found a receptive ear in the Probate and Family Court, the "little oven" aunt never became a legal mother of the nephew she had so gladly carried to term, and no adoption was required. Several cases followed, with the Probate and Family Court readily granting such requests in gestational carrier cases, enabling these families to have legal certainty upon birth without having to wait for a postbirth adoption or accepting the legal fiction that the intended, genetic mother had no legal connection to the child while the gestational carrier was considered the child's legal mother—characterizations neither woman would want and that could leave the child vulnerable from a legal standpoint.

In 1999, a chain of legal circumstances led to appellate law being established in Massachusetts on gestational carrier arrangements. When the author brought what had

1998: *R.R. v. M.H.*, 426 Mass. 501: Holds that a traditional surrogacy contract that provides compensation to a surrogate in exchange for her relinquishment of the child is unenforceable.

2000: *A.Z. v. B.Z.*, 431 Mass. 150: Holds that an agreement and signed medical consent regarding a wife's use of frozen preembryos cannot be enforced against a husband who subsequently changes his mind, as it violates public policy to compel an individual to become a parent against his or her will.

Knoll v. Beth Israel Deaconess Medical Center, No. 00W-1343: The Suffolk County Probate and Family Court allows two women to be legally recognized as parents and named as a child's parents on the birth certificate, without the necessity of an adoption, where one intended mother contributed the eggs and the other gestated the baby.

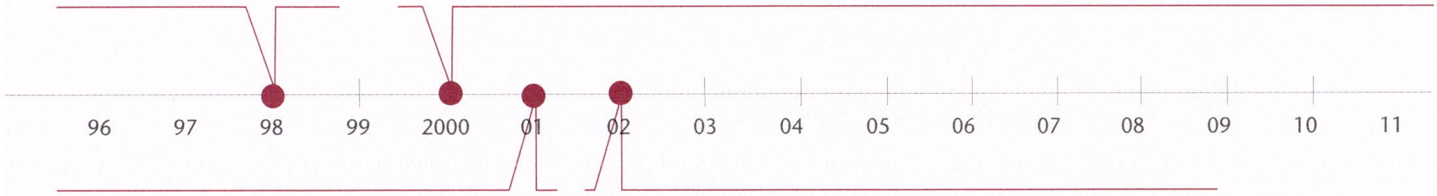

2001: *Culliton v. Beth Israel Deaconess Medical Center*, 435 Mass. 285: Holds that a prebirth order of legal parentage may be entered in cases of gestational surrogacy where the intended parents are the child's genetic parents and all parties are in agreement (without addressing the enforceability of the legal contract).

2002: *Woodward v. Commissioner of Social Security*, 435 Mass. 536: Holds that a posthumously conceived genetic child can inherit under the state's intestacy law if the decedent is the biological father, and agreed both to the posthumous conception and to the support of any resulting child.

become a relatively routine prebirth order equity case, a Probate and Family Court judge disagreed with the applicability of equity and instead ordered that the out-of-wedlock statutes be strictly applied. To do this, he created a legal fiction that the "mother" was the gestational carrier who was carrying another man's child, and ordered that statutory forms for acknowledgments by out-of-wedlock fathers be amended to apply to out-of-wedlock mothers. As then amended, all parties signed (the two women were sisters), and the court approved the order of maternity and paternity under this statutory protocol. The court "reported up" its decision on its own initiative, essentially asking the Supreme Judicial Court to rule on his legal analysis. The Supreme Judicial Court disapproved of the trial court's application of out-of-wedlock statutory schedule in a rescript (unsigned) opinion it called *Smith v. Brown*, above. The court opined that equity seemed the more logically applicable route to establish parentage in such cases. Given that the case involved sisters and had been impounded to protect their privacy, the Supreme Judicial Court waited to fully review and issue a formal opinion until a similar fact pattern presented itself without privacy protections having been invoked and in which it invited amicus briefs. Thus, in *Culliton v. Beth Israel Deaconess Medical Center*, the Supreme Judicial Court thoroughly reviewed the medical facts, legal issues, current law, and arguments in favor of establishing the legal parent-child relationship at the moment of birth. It ruled that at least where there was no dispute, and where the child born to a gestational carrier was the full genetic child of the intended parents, a prebirth order of parentage should issue to protect all involved, including the child, and insurance coverage should be provided for the child upon birth. The court declined to rule on the enforceability of legal agreements and noted that the Department of Public Health needed to be given notice of these cases from a public health standpoint.

Since *Brown* and *Culliton*, Massachusetts courts have continued to issue prebirth orders, and such orders have expanded to cover married couples (including same-sex married couples) who use donor gametes (egg or sperm). The Massachusetts judiciary's evolution on these legal protections is illustrated in two related cases involving the same growing family and the author. When the parties' first child was born, a probate judge denied their request for a prebirth order as to their child being carried by a gestational carrier because they had needed to use a donor egg. The trial court ruled that it was not persuaded that *Culliton* permitted such a ruling, since only one intended parent was a genetic parent, and instead required that the parties affirm their legal parental status through a postbirth stepparent adoption. Two years later, all of the same parties were back before the same judge, this time with the carrier carrying twins. By this time, the court was persuaded that it would be discriminatory not to treat children born through gestational surrogacy and a donor egg the same as it would treat those born from donor sperm without a carrier, in violation of the state's donor insemination statute, or with a carrier and a sperm donor, in violation of the Equal Rights Act, and so granted the requested prebirth order.

Massachusetts still has not been called on to rule on the issue of enforceability of such contracts, but presented with complex fact patterns, trial courts have demonstrated a continuing willingness both to be educated on the medical technologies and to sensitively interpret and apply the law. In the realm of legal clarity as to parent-child status and how to establish it, the Supreme Judicial Court has taken a clear leading role, and its decisions have been widely cited by other courts and jurisdictions.

IVF Embryo Disputes Under Massachusetts Law

An inevitable outcome of IVF and the ability to cryopreserve are frozen embryos. Once procreation can literally be frozen in time, cryopreserved embryos can and have become the center of heated legal disputes. Whether in the context of divorce and disputes over which former spouse can use or control the embryos, or issues over lost, mishandled, mixed-up, or abandoned embryos, the legal issues in this area are fraught with political and religious undertones. As a society, we have yet to come to a consensus on the status of the human embryo, so in any given court dispute, the disparate views of those involved are destined to play a role in the litigation, if only in judicial attempts to avoid resolving such views.

Regardless of varying religious perspectives on when life begins, under current, controlling constitutional law, until a fetus reaches the point of "viability," any rights it has are subservient to those of the woman who is carrying the fetus. IVF and cryopreservation preserve genetic material in an earlier state of development than a viable embryo, yet because an IVF embryo can be created and remain frozen outside a woman's body for an indefinite period of time, the technology has added complexity to the legal analysis regarding the constitutional rights of individuals to procreate or not to procreate within existing legal parameters. In 2000, Massachusetts once again was presented with what would become a groundbreaking ARTs case, this time involving a frozen embryo dispute between divorcing spouses. *A.Z. v. B.Z.* was a case brought by a divorced husband suing to stop his former wife and their IVF program from thawing and using any of their seven remaining frozen embryos following successful IVF treatment that had previously produced one daughter.[8] On file at the IVF program were seven separate consents signed by the ex-husband giving his then-wife the right to use the embryos in the event of a "separation." The ex-husband argued, however, that he signed some of the consents without reading them, or signed them before they were filled in completely, and that regardless, he no longer wanted his former wife to have another child from their embryos.

[In 2000,] the Supreme Judicial Court became the first high state court to wrestle with this difficult question of a change of mind involving procreative choices.

The facts of *A.Z. v. B.Z.* were different from prior frozen embryo divorce disputes in other states. In those cases, the couples' prior agreements had not involved procreation, but were agreements to discard or donate the embryos for research. Thus, the Supreme Judicial Court became the first high state court to wrestle with this difficult question of a change of mind involving procreative choices. The lower court had engaged in a lengthy—and legally interesting—analysis of contract law, citing multiple grounds on which it would not enforce any alleged agreement or consent signed by the couple. The Supreme Judicial Court affirmed the lower court's decision but was not persuaded by its reasoning. Instead, it ruled that "[a]s a matter of public policy, we conclude that forced procreation is not an area amenable to judicial enforcement." The court ruled that thawing and transferring a frozen embryo was the point at which procreation occurred and that such procreation could not be forced on an unwilling previously would-be parent despite having earlier created embryos for that purpose. Massachusetts thus became the first court to clearly reject, as a matter of public policy, the notion that prior agreements permitting one spouse to use or donate frozen embryos to another couple for procreation were enforceable against a subsequent change of mind and objection by the other.

Since *A.Z.*, virtually every court to consider the same question has cited *A.Z.* and has refused to enforce such agreements and allow frozen embryo use for procreation in the event of a subsequent change of mind.

Posthumous Reproduction Under Massachusetts Law

Becoming a parent after death, known as "posthumous reproduction" in legal terms, did not start with IVF or cryopreservation. It has always been possible for a child to have been conceived but not yet born before his or her father's death. Because of this, virtually every state has addressed this possibility with statutes that clarify for what time period and under what circumstances a deceased will be considered a father of a child born after his death. Frequently, time frames have been incorporated into law that were intended to cover any pregnancy initiated prior to death. What IVF and cryopreservation have fundamentally changed is the time frame in which a deceased can still biologically produce a child. As a consequence, laws that were passed with a roughly nine-month gestational time frame in mind do not adequately address children who may be posthumously conceived by either a surviving widow or girlfriend using previously cryopreserved and stored sperm or IVF embryos. The importance of the issue has most often arisen in the context of Social Security survivor benefits, a federal benefit that turns on state definitions of legitimacy and inheritance. Thus, only if a "child" is deemed a deceased's child under the applicable state law will he or she receive survivor benefits.

In *Woodward v. Commissioner of Social Security*, the Supreme Judicial Court became the first appellate court to rule on this question, in the context of a widow who had given birth to twins using her deceased husband's cryopreserved sperm.[9] The children were born two years after his death, and the court undertook a careful analysis of Massachusetts inheritance law. It ultimately concluded that there were three critical requirements that must be met for a determination of a parent-child relationship: proof that the child is the genetic child of the deceased; and proof that the deceased affirmatively consented to both posthumous reproduction and posthumous support of any resulting children. The court emphasized the "double consent" requirement because it said a man facing medical treatment that might leave him sterile might want to preserve his potential ability to have children later in life but not necessarily after death. Thus, the court's decision would seem to leave open the possibility of using a dead man's sperm to procreate without necessarily his being designated as the legal father but rather as a donor. The court added that even if all three requirements were met, there could be competing issues of timeliness or other heirs that could preclude inheritance, and that it would be necessary to give notice to interested parties if seeking a ruling on inheritance eligibility. Since *Woodward*, a number of state and federal courts have ruled on the issue and there is currently a split of opinion amongst the circuits. In late 2011, the U.S. Supreme Court accepted certiorari from a New Jersey case to address the issue.

A related set of legal issues, yet to be decided by an appellate court in Massachusetts, involve posthumous retrieval of sperm (or theoretically, eggs) from a deceased, and what legal requirements would be imposed on the ability of a surviving widow, girlfriend, mother, or other loved one, to retrieve gametes from a deceased in the hope of a future pregnancy and child. Trial courts have dealt with these issues sporadically in Massachusetts and elsewhere, and legal issues include both the questionable intent and appropriateness of retrieving the genetic material, who might use it if retrieved and stored, and what the legal status of any resulting child might be.

A particularly haunting example of the human dimensions that can be involved in such cases was reported in the July 2010 issue of the *New England Journal of Medicine*, the first reported case involving potential retrieval of eggs from a comatose woman. In that case, the family of a tragically brain-dead young woman at Massachusetts General Hospital agonized over whether to maintain her on life support in an effort to mature and retrieve eggs from her body prior to death. The sensitivity with which the medical team handled the matter, ultimately resulting in the family's reaching a consensus not to make such an attempt, and the looming ethical considerations involved, are chronicled in the article.[10]

Conclusion

The extraordinary medical advances of the past thirty years have literally remade the very concepts of family. Keeping pace to legally redefine and protect these newly possible families has demanded an ongoing transformation of both reproductive law and policy. Within the United States, Massachusetts has played both a prominent and prescient role in the development of these medical and legal advances, and it is likely to continue to do so for the foreseeable future. From redefining who can adopt and marry; to who can become parents through various means of assisted reproductive technologies, court orders, or following death; to equitable accessibility to infertility treatment, the legislature and courts of the Commonwealth have seemingly embraced the challenges of taking a leadership role in this arena. For the most part, these laws and court decisions have been thoughtful, forward thinking, sensitive to grappling with and understanding novel medical concepts, and—virtually always—protective of the resultant families these technologies create.

Massachusetts has played both a prominent and prescient role in the development of these medical and legal advances, and it is likely to continue to do so for the foreseeable future.

As we move further into the twenty-first century, advances in medical technologies undoubtedly will continue to create novel legal challenges for law and policy makers and by doing so continue to provide the Commonwealth with challenging opportunities to lead the way in shaping our future families.

NOTES

[1] G.L. c. 175, § 47H.

[2] *See* National Conference of State Legislatures website at http://www.ncsl.orgissues-research/health/insurance-coverage-for-infertility-laws.aspx.

[3] 416 Mass. 205 (1993).

[4] 440 Mass. 309 (2003).

[5] *In the Matter of Baby M*, 109 N.J. 396, *on remand*, 225 N.J. Super. 267 (1988).

[6] *R.R. v. M.H.*, 426 Mass. 501 (1998); *Smith v. Brown*, 430 Mass. 1005 (1999); *Culliton v. Beth Israel Deaconess Med. Ctr.*, 435 Mass. 285 (2001).

[7] 426 Mass. 501 (1998).

[8] 431 Mass. 150 (2000).

[9] 435 Mass. 536 (2002).

[10] D. Greer et al., "Case 21–2010—A Request for Retrieval of Oocytes from a 36-Year-Old Woman with Anoxic Brain Injury," 363 *New Eng. J. Med.* 276–83 (July 15, 2010).

CHAPTER 6

Public Pursuits: Government, Legal Aid, and Nonprofit Lawyers

Making a Difference in Public Life

CAROLYN STAFFORD STEIN

> *I like going home at night feeling that I have made a difference in someone's life.... I appreciate being able to do really good work on important matters, and still have a schedule that fits my family's needs.... I want to be doing work I care about.*

In a first-of-its-kind survey in 2009, the Women's Bar Association of Massachusetts quantified what had been apparent to even the most casual observer of the legal landscape: women are drawn to public service. Of current practitioners, 20 percent of women are in government or nonprofit settings in comparison to 9 percent of men.[1] Women lawyers are making their professional home in the government and nonprofit sectors in record numbers, and it is a trend that promises to continue. Women law students in Massachusetts, as across the country, consistently identify helping others and bringing about social change as important factors in their job choices.[2] Their early career decisions bear out these priorities: in the first ten years after graduation, women are considerably more likely than their male classmates to work in government, nonprofit, or other public interest law settings.[3] Nor is this embrace of public service a new phenomenon. From the time women started entering the profession in greater numbers in the 1960s and 1970s, they have been attracted to public service.

Government Service

The state and federal governments have provided women attorneys tremendous opportunities for public service, for advancement, and for leadership. In the courtroom, at the State House, and throughout the various state and federal agencies where the people's business is conducted, women attorneys have met with marked success. The ideal of a vigorous government that advances the common good has historic roots in Massachusetts. Embracing that ideal as their own—and finding government offices to be among the most welcoming of practice settings—women attorneys have flocked to government service.

REFLECTIONS AND INTERVIEWS

▲ Carolyn Stafford Stein is assistant director for alumni advising at Harvard Law School's Bernard Koteen Office of Public Interest Advising. A former assistant U.S. attorney, she graduated magna cum laude from Brown University and Harvard Law School and clerked for U.S. District Judge Robert E. Keeton.

IMAGE COURTESY OF HARVARD UNIVERSITY

OUR NEW ASSISTANT ATTORNEY GENERAL

Abounding Health and Vibrant Personality Make First Woman to Hold Job in Massachusetts Ideal Official—Daughter of First Woman to Argue Case Before a Jury—Brings Home Salad for Dinner—Assigned to Series of Big Cases

ASST ATTY GEN SCHOFIELD AND THE SCHOFIELD CHILDREN, PARKER (LEFT) AND ALBERT JR

Boston Globe headline, January 23, 1927

IMAGE SOURCE: *BOSTON GLOBE* ONLINE ARCHIVES

The Massachusetts Attorney General's Office has earned a reputation as a particularly hospitable environment for women. As in the government and the bar generally, women were a rarity in the 1960s and 1970s. But by the 1980s, especially in areas like consumer protection and environmental law, it was unremarkable to find women on staff or in supervisory positions. Today, fully half of all assistant attorneys general are women, and scores of women leaders in government and on the bench are alumnae of the office. Attorney General Martha Coakley, the first woman to hold the position, has led the office since her election in 2006.

Women attorneys have made their mark throughout other state and federal government agencies and departments as well. In education, environmental protection, and public finance, to name just a few, women attorneys are staffing and, in many instances, leading the office. At the highest levels of state service, women attorneys have been appointed by both Republican and Democratic governors as cabinet secretaries and undersecretaries. And because government service has given so many women significant courtroom experience and high-level responsibility, it has been a fertile ground for candidates for the bench. A considerable portion of the Commonwealth's state and federal women judges have served as government lawyers at some point in their careers.

Prosecutors and Defenders

Criminal practice, on both the government and the defense sides, is a field that has witnessed a dramatic transformation in the number and visibility of women practitioners. Few areas of the law held on to the boys' locker-room feel as long. Perhaps it was because of the sometimes graphic or even grisly nature of the subject matter; or perhaps it was just because most of the people one dealt with every day—police or other law enforcement, informants, the accused—were themselves overwhelmingly male. But the roles of both prosecutor and defender were traditionally considered fit more for men than for women.

In 1970, no district attorney's office in the Commonwealth listed a single woman assistant. But prosecution offers an opportunity to get into the courtroom matched by few areas of civil practice and a chance for meaningful public service. Attracted by these features, and likely a touch of contrariness, women did start making their way as prosecutors: up to 20 percent of assistant district attorneys by 1980 and more than a third of all ADAs by 1990.

First in the bigger, urban offices, but over time throughout the state, women joined the prosecution ranks in increasing numbers. A majority of today's assistant district attorneys in Massachusetts are women.

The U.S. Attorney's Office, home to federal prosecutors in Massachusetts, has seen a similarly dramatic rise in the number of women lawyers in recent years. A single female assistant U.S. attorney practiced in the otherwise all-male office in 1970. Forty years later, the office, including its civil division, is now some 40 percent women. Its leader, U.S. Attorney Carmen Ortiz, is the first woman to hold that post in Massachusetts. Appointed by President Obama in 2009, U.S. Attorney Ortiz had served as an assistant U.S. attorney for twelve years.

If female prosecutors were few and far between in the early days, women in the criminal defense bar were equally so. Practicing in a district attorney's office or another prosecution office at least meant working for the government, which women have traditionally found attractive. And being a prosecutor meant working on behalf of the victims of crime, a pursuit akin to other traditional female caretaking roles. But representing clients accused of serious, often violent, crimes? Visiting them in the courthouse lockup or the county jail? Butting heads with prosecutors and police who were almost exclusively men? Early women public defenders had the fortitude not only to tackle demanding work but to face the incredulity of everyone from court personnel to their own family members. Propelled by a commitment to serve the disadvantaged and to keep the government honest, these women took on the skeptics. An early handful of public defenders dedicated themselves to insuring that the promise of representation for all was a meaningful one. In so doing, they paved the way for today's considerable corps of women defenders.

Woman Among 7 New Assistant U. S. Attorneys

Seven Greater Boston lawyers, including a Watertown woman, have been appointed Assistant United States Attorneys for Massachusetts, according to an announcement yesterday by United States Attorney Anthony Julian. They will take office July 7.

Arleyne F. Hassett, 20, of 21 Elmwood av., is the first woman to be named to such a post here in 28 years.

▲ *Boston Globe* headline, June 25, 1953

IMAGE SOURCE: *BOSTON GLOBE* ONLINE ARCHIVES

In 2010, more than 60 percent of the lawyers at the Committee for Public Counsel Services were women. From the newest public defenders scrambling to juggle caseloads in multiple district courts in a single day to the most seasoned veterans handling serious felony cases, women have to a remarkable extent become the face of indigent criminal defense in Massachusetts.

The federal courts have seen parallel growth in the role of women defenders. The Federal Public Defender's Office for many years had a single woman attorney among its members. Today, women are as likely as men to serve in that office. Miriam Conrad, the first woman federal public defender in Massachusetts, oversees a staff that represents indigent defendants in the federal courts not only in Massachusetts but in New Hampshire and Rhode Island as well.

Legal Services and Nonprofits

The image of a legal services lawyer is the first that comes to mind for many when they think of a public interest lawyer. Legal services attorneys dedicate themselves to the representation of low-income clients who could not otherwise hope to afford an attorney. And more than any other area of public service practice, that image has long been, as often as not, of a woman. Working with the poor is characteristic of historically female occupations such as social work, and women attorneys found a place in legal services relatively early. But it was never an easy road. Women law students bound for legal services faced both the prejudice of classmates who believed the work unworthy and the prospect of low salaries with which to pay off law-school debt. Once practicing, women attorneys bore sizeable caseloads and sometimes overwhelming need on the part of their clients. But driven by a sense of social justice and a deep motivation to work on behalf of the disadvantaged, women have brought extraordinary energy and dedication to their work.

As legal services offices have expanded beyond their original focus on housing, family law, and government benefits, women have been at the forefront. Women have helped forge new practice specialties, for example, in consumer protection, bankruptcy, and predatory lending. Immigration, elder law, access for people with disabilities, and protecting the victims of domestic violence are all areas in which women have led the Commonwealth's legal services offices in aiding the most vulnerable populations.

Today, the prominence of women in legal services work is stunning.

Today, the prominence of women in legal services work is stunning. More than three-quarters of the attorneys at Greater Boston Legal Services, the state's largest legal services office, are women. In legal services organizations across the state, women practice at every level of seniority. Of course, while the personal rewards of fighting for those in need may be huge, the salaries for legal service work are not. The heavy representation of women in legal services, as in prosecution and public defense, demonstrates women's willingness to make significant financial sacrifices to pursue work they believe in.

Furthering a cause about which they are passionate has propelled other women to a wide range of nonprofit advocacy organizations outside of traditional legal services offices. Women advocates have challenged business-as-usual on issues from the environment, to education, to marriage equality. Sometimes making headlines, other times racking up smaller, less-public victories for their clients, women lawyers have made a difference. Bringing suit to prompt cleanup of contaminated waste, to insure that an economically disadvantaged neighborhood gets access to mass transit, to improve living conditions for incarcerated men and women, or to see that every vote counts, the women staffing and leading the state's public interest organizations have had an enormous impact.

Elected Office

Some women lawyers have answered the call to public service by running for office. The rough-and-tumble world of electoral politics does not appeal to all, male or female, but women have increasingly ventured in and made visible gains. But the success of women candidates, including women lawyers, has been mixed. Although the state legislature can boast a rise in the number of women representatives, for example, Massachusetts has not fared as well as its New England neighbors in electing a woman to the governor's office or the U.S. Senate.

Several of the greatest successes for women lawyers in elected office in Massachusetts have come in leading the offices where women have made such strides as rank-and-file attorneys. Elizabeth Scheibel became the Commonwealth's first woman district attorney in 1993 after serving as first assistant district attorney in the Northwestern District since 1988. First appointed to fill a vacancy, District Attorney Scheibel went on to stand for election four times before announcing that she would not seek a fifth elected term. Martha Coakley, elected to the first of her two terms as district attorney for the Commonwealth's largest county, Middlesex, in 1998, came to that position after serving more than ten years as an

Massachusetts Women Lawyers Go to Washington

Massachusetts has elected just four women to the United States Congress. All but the first, Edith Nourse Rogers, have been lawyers.

Margaret M. Heckler
8 terms; 1967–1983
Boston College Law School, 1936
IMAGE SOURCE: WOMENINCONGRESS.HOUSE.GOV

Louise Day Hicks
1 term; 1971–1973
Boston University School of Law, 1955
IMAGE SOURCE: WOMENINCONGRESS.HOUSE.GOV

Nicola S. (Niki) Tsongas
2007 to present
Boston University School of Law, 1988
IMAGE SOURCE: TSONGAS.HOUSE.GOV

assistant district attorney. When Martha Coakley won election as the Commonwealth's first woman attorney general in 2006, she became only the second woman lawyer in Massachusetts history to hold statewide office, following Shannon O'Brien's election as treasurer in 1998.

Women's election to legislative office in Massachusetts has climbed steadily in the last half century. Interestingly, however, and consistent with national trends, female elected officials in Massachusetts are less likely than their male colleagues to be lawyers. Here as elsewhere, women politicians have most often pursued other professions. Early women officeholders came largely from traditional female occupations such as teacher, homemaker, and secretary.[4] The 1965–66 state legislature, for example, included two women senators and seven women representatives. Of these nine women, four were secretaries or administrative staff members, two identified themselves as housewives, and the remainder listed volunteer positions, but no occupation. None had been to law school.

As the number of women officeholders started to climb in the 1980s, the number of women lawyers in office grew as well. By the 1989–90 term, for example, five of the forty Massachusetts state senators and thirty-one of the 159 state representatives were women. Of those women, three of the five senators and three of the thirty-one representatives were lawyers. Women continued to gain an increasing share of seats so that by the 2011–12 term, eleven of the forty state senators are women, six of whom are lawyers. On the House side, thirty-six of the 159 representatives are women, and eight of the thirty-six are lawyers. The representation of women lawyers among the ranks of elected officials has thus risen. Yet in Massachusetts, as across the country, male representatives continue to come in greater

Women Lawyers and Advocacy Campaigns: The Equal Rights Amendment

Lois H. Kanter

For me, working on the Equal Rights Amendment campaign was a defining moment. It was during my second year of law school at Harvard that I began working on the campaign. I worked as a legal researcher, along with other law students. Our research was vital to the campaign, as it formed the basis for speeches and helped give the public a real understanding of the ERA, away from the negative images the opposition was portraying. The law students involved in the campaign were not just legal researchers—a core group of law students organized and ran a fairly formal speaker's bureau that spoke at small-town gatherings across the state. We also published a basic legal text that was used by most proponents in their educational and campaign efforts (and it was later cited by the Supreme Judicial Court). It was a great campaign that was started by middle-class professionals as well as grassroots women from churches. Although, we had good support among men, the campaign leadership was nearly all female.

Lois H. Kanter

IMAGE COURTESY OF NORTHEASTERN UNIVERSITY SCHOOL OF LAW, PHOTO BY DAVID LEIFER

Ironically, the biggest opponents of the ERA were women. There was a very small group of anti-feminist women—certainly not a majority of women, but a very virulent group nonetheless—who opposed the state ERA. Some of these women believed the ERA would end traditional family life, legalize abortion and/or Medicaid funding for it, and legalize same-sex marriage. Their influence, bolstered by anti-ERA forces outside the state, was far stronger than their numbers would have indicated, and it was made to appear even stronger because the media gave both sides "equal time" despite the unequal numbers of proponents versus opponents. Despite the presence of anti-ERA sentiment expressed in the campaign, Massachusetts was one of the states to ratify the ERA. The time I spent working on the campaign was incredibly positive and rewarding.

Kanter is currently a clinical professor and director of the Domestic Violence Institute at Northeastern University School of Law.

Lois G. Pines

When I was elected to the Massachusetts House in 1972, I was one of eight women in the House. For me, helping to secure passage of the Massachusetts Equal Rights Amendment was an arduous and difficult four-year effort. Yet, at the same time it was an absolutely vital, pivotal, and critically important effort to impact the legal rights of girls and women in the Commonwealth at the time, as well as for future generations. During the four years following my election to the House, passage of the Massachusetts ERA was a top priority for me. It was not easy to get support for the amendment since it was not at that time a popular measure. Only seven legislators sponsored the Massachusetts ERA. Not a large number of legislators seemed to want to have their names attached to it since it was viewed as "avant garde" and "controversial." Many people did not support it because they either did not want women to have equal rights or were worried about the implications of mandating equal rights for women relating to many issues, including same-sex toilets, sexual preference, abortion, and women's property rights. Having encountered discrimination on the basis of sex in seeking admission to business school and law school and having practiced law and personally suffered discrimination in the awarding of stock options in a company for whom I was tax counsel, I wanted to change the laws in Massachusetts to ensure that my daughter and her generation would not be discriminated and would be able to make personal and career choices without regard to sex.

Lois G. Pines

IMAGE COURTESY OF CHRISTA KELLEHER

Pines served as a state representative from 1973 to 1978 and as a state senator from 1987 to 1998.

proportion from law and business, while women come in greater proportion from education and health care.[5]

Women have found federal office a challenging arena to break into in Massachusetts. Only a tiny fraction of the congressional delegation has been female, and no woman has been elected statewide to federal office. Among those who have been elected to the U.S. Congress, however, all but the first were lawyers. The legendary Edith Nourse Rogers, the longest-serving woman in the U.S. Congress and the first to serve from Massachusetts, represented her district from 1925 to 1960. Rogers, who was originally elected to fill the vacancy caused by the death of her husband, was not a lawyer. But all who have made it since then have been. Margaret Heckler, a pioneer who got her start in elective politics as the first woman to win a seat on the Governor's Council, served in the U.S. Congress from 1967 to 1983. Following her years in elected office, Margaret Heckler was appointed secretary of the U.S. Department of Health and Human Services and later the U.S. ambassador to Ireland under President Ronald Reagan. The next woman elected to the U.S. House of Representatives, Louise Day Hicks, was also an attorney. Elected in 1970, she served a single term. More than twenty years elapsed after Margaret Heckler's departure from Congress before lawyer Niki Tsongas was elected in 2007 as only the fourth woman to so serve from Massachusetts.

What difference does it make when women hold elective office? Women representatives are more likely, research shows, to advocate for legislation and programs intended to benefit women.[6] But more broadly, male and female legislators report that women legislators provide greater access to the legislature for other groups that have traditionally been shut out from the process, including racial and ethnic minorities and the economically disadvantaged.[7] And, as in so many other areas, the very presence of women begets more women. As young attorneys see women succeed in attaining high office, they will be emboldened to run themselves.

Why They Do It

> I always knew I wanted to be in public service, probably the government. I had my sight set on a career where I had a sense of purpose.
>
> I started out at a firm, but it was never a good fit. It took some looking to find the right public interest job. But once I did, everything I felt about being a lawyer changed. I sometimes can't believe there is a job where I can work on issues I care about all day.[8]

The pay is a fraction of what a lawyer might make in private practice, the offices less than posh, and the strains of having to handle too much work with too few resources a daily frustration. Why, then, are women lawyers so eager to work in public service? Eager enough that they are twice as likely as their male counterparts to do so? First and foremost, because they want to feel good about what they do every day.

Working for the greater good, making the world a better place, speaking on behalf of those who would not otherwise be heard, such are the words women use to describe why they practice public interest law. Working on issues that "matter" in some fundamental way to their community or the larger world is a powerful motivation for such women. Women in public interest practice report again and again that what drew them to their work and what keeps them going is the feeling that they are making a contribution to something bigger than themselves.

[W]hat keeps them going is the feeling that they are making a contribution to something bigger than themselves.

But an affinity for service is not the only reason women choose public interest practice. For some, of equal importance is the manageability of the day-to-day demands of their jobs. No description of why women elect to practice public interest law would be complete without recognition of the importance of work-life balance issues. The desire for a career that can work with the rest of a woman's life is for many a motivation almost as powerful as the drive to pursue work they believe in. For example, women surveyed by the MIT Workplace in 2007 who had moved from private practice to government or nonprofits consistently cited the desire for "better arrangements for combining work and time for families" as a reason for their move.[9] The prospect of such improved arrangements is, for many, what makes palatable the financial sacrifice that public service work often represents. On any given day, a public service lawyer's schedule may look just as crazy as—or crazier than—that of any private practitioner. An upcoming trial or legislative hearing can require anyone to work late into the night. But many attorneys in public service practice find that for the majority of their time, their schedule is more predictable and thus more amenable to child-care or other family responsibilities. Maternity leave and part-time schedules are also often more readily available, not merely as a matter of policy but of practice.

Women cite policies and practices that ease the strains of meeting family responsibilities while practicing law as a major plus of their government or nonprofit offices. Women also point to the strength in numbers: when a critical mass of attorneys in an office are using their maximum maternity benefits or working a part-time schedule, it creates an atmosphere that makes other women feel comfortable doing the same. Women who work a reduced schedule for years at a time, all the while continuing to handle significant work and to progress within the office, are not at all uncommon. Little wonder, therefore, that public interest practice not only attracts women, but keeps them.

A collegial and supportive work environment is another major draw, public service practitioners report. Working toward shared goals with dedicated coworkers creates a natural camaraderie that many women value. And the scarcity of resources in public service offices can, ironically, have benefits for workplace morale: with more worthy cases than the office could ever hope to handle, attorneys feel they are a needed and important part of the team. Experienced practitioners also enjoy the many opportunities to mentor student interns and young attorneys who share their public service aspirations.

Appreciation for work well done is another aspect of public interest settings that seems a priority for women practitioners. Lacking big salaries or bonuses to bestow, many government and other public service offices are liberal with nonmonetary rewards ranging from formal citations to daily informal recognition for strong effort. The institutional commitment to strive for advancement based solely on performance and merit is another critical attribute for many women.

The opportunity to do meaningful work in a setting that makes room for other aspects of a woman's life is not an easy one to find in the practice of law. But it is the promise of that winning combination that has led so many women lawyers in Massachusetts to enter public service.

Reflections and Interviews

Government Service

Navjeet Bal

Upon her appointment in 2008, Navjeet Bal became the first South Asian-American commissioner of the Massachusetts Department of Revenue. She is now in private practice at Nixon Peabody LLP.

I was appointed by Governor Deval Patrick and Secretary Leslie Kirwan to the position of Commissioner of Revenue for the Commonwealth in February 2008. I came to state government after practicing law in the public finance section of Mintz Levin for over seventeen years. It is interesting to note that I am the second woman to hold the DOR Commissioner's position in the Commonwealth's history, and the first DOR Commissioner to be named "Navjeet." I say that to remind people I am the first South Asian-American (and, indeed, the first person of color) to be appointed to my position. My professional experience as a woman and a lawyer of color in Boston are a reflection of the sea change that has taken place in the legal world here over the past twenty years.

My professional experience as a woman and a lawyer of color in Boston are a reflection of the sea change that has taken place in the legal world here over the past twenty years.

I am an immigrant to this country. I was born in Kenya, and lived in England, Ethiopia, and Zambia before moving here when I was eleven years old. I completed high school in upstate New York and graduated from Williams College in 1984. I then moved to Boston, and attended Northeastern University School of Law (class of 1989). There were very few attorneys of color at the major Boston law firms at that time, and, consequently, few role models for me to look to who could provide perspective and guidance on issues affecting minority lawyers. Law firm management and bar association leadership was dominated by white men and a few women, many of whom recognized the need for change and the need to be more inclusive of women and people of color.

Navjeet Bal

IMAGE COURTESY OF NIXON PEABODY LLP

Much has changed since then! There are now African-American, Hispanic, Asian-American, and South Asian-American lawyers throughout law firms, the courts, government agencies, and private corporations. The Boston area has become more cosmopolitan, and people are aware of our role in the global economy and the fundamental importance of having a global perspective in all of our industries, including within the legal profession. Law firms and other legal organizations have made a commitment to increasing the numbers of attorneys of color hired and then retained, and the results are borne out in the increasing numbers of attorneys of color throughout the area. Credit must also be given to area law schools which have made a concerted effort to increase the numbers of law students of color, thereby creating a healthy and diverse "pipeline" of future lawyers. Women lawyers and lawyers of color now hold prominent public elected positions, including Governor Deval Patrick, Attorney General Martha Coakley and State Auditor Suzanne Bump.

My own success mirrors the increasing prominence of lawyers of color in the city. I am hopeful that my position and experience can serve as a role model to younger attorneys and professionals—both men and women and of all colors! I am very fortunate to have been in the right city at the right time, and I take seriously my responsibility to mentor and provide leadership to others coming along after me.

Barbara Fischbein Berenson

Barbara Fischbein Berenson is a senior attorney at the Supreme Judicial Court.

If financial circumstances permit, working part-time is one "solution" to the dilemma of balancing children and work. But how does one define success for a part-time worker? Is it leaving work before the school day ends, having fulfilling work and a paycheck, or both? And what happens to a woman's career ambitions when she is only partially engaged in the legal life?

I made the choice to work part-time while my children were young, and worked at government jobs three days per week for thirteen years. In 2004, when my children were ten and thirteen, I returned to full-time work. My younger child is currently a senior in high school, so this seems a good time to evaluate the costs and benefits of the work-life balance I struck. As I look now through the rear-view mirror, I am pleased with my choices, although acutely aware of the career consequences.

I was married the summer before my last year at Harvard Law School. Perhaps because I married while still in school and knew I wanted children, I began to think about work-life balance even before I graduated. Applying for clerkships in Philadelphia (where my husband and I planned to spend at least one year), my top choice was federal judge Norma L. Shapiro, the first woman appointed to the Eastern District of Pennsylvania. Judge Shapiro had taken a nine-year leave of absence from a law firm while raising three sons to school age. I was delighted when she made me an offer, and recall thinking that maybe I would find a role model for "how to do it."

Barbara Fischbein Berenson

IMAGE COURTESY OF BARBARA FISCHBEIN BERENSON

My clerkship year was wonderful. At the end of the year, we returned to Boston (where we were both from), as my husband was offered a position with an exciting-sounding Cambridge-based start-up. Although I didn't fully realize it at the time, I lost a lot when I left Philadelphia. Judge Shapiro, it turns out, was for many years my only real mentor.

In Boston, I started at Hill & Barlow. While I always envisioned a career in public service and had acquired a master's degree from the Kennedy School of Government along with my law degree, I simply followed the well-trodden path from Harvard Law School to a clerkship to a law firm. Figuring out what I would do "when I grew up" was something I planned to postpone a few years.

I learned many useful skills at Hill & Barlow. I also witnessed firsthand the difficulties of balancing billable hours and family. There were many women associates, but those with a child (few seemed to remain when a second child was born) seemed to me to struggle hard—

and often unsuccessfully—to accommodate the demands of a child and those of the firm's partners. After trying without success to become pregnant, I decided to forego the salary and nice office for public service.

I applied for a job as an assistant district attorney in Middlesex County because I admired Scott Harshbarger; the job offered a chance to (as Scott always put it) "make a difference every day" and would give me the opportunity to get into court. I spent eighteen months trying cases before my first child was (finally!) born. I took a five-month maternity leave, loving every minute of that time. While it was clear I could be very content as a full-time mother, my professional identity was also important—as was the health insurance offered by the office, since my husband had become self-employed.

While it was clear I could be very content as a full-time mother, my professional identity was also important....

During my maternity leave, I asked Tom Reilly (who succeeded Harshbarger first as District Attorney and then as Attorney General) for the opportunity to return to work three days per week in the Appeals Bureau. I enjoyed research and writing, and appellate work seemed more compatible with a part-time schedule than trial work. Reilly and Appeals Bureau Chief Jim Sahakian agreed. The next eight years were a pleasure. I worked three days per week and took another lengthy leave when my second child was born. I regretted writing fewer briefs than my full-time colleagues and felt guilty that I was not with my children as much as full-time mothers. But, mostly, I was happy; I had interesting and important work, colleagues I liked, and delighted in every minute I spent with my children. I never tired of reading to and playing with them and took great pleasure in their love of books, board games, conversation, and learning. Meanwhile my husband's career path led to frequent travel and evenings and weekends spent working. Wanting my marriage to survive led me to accept this, if occasionally less than graciously.

By 1999, I was interested in a fresh challenge and accepted Tom Reilly's invitation to join him in the Attorney General's Office. I continued a 60 percent schedule, but now that my younger child was in kindergarten, I started working five short days each week. In 2002, when my kids were eight and eleven, I was again ready for something new, and I knew that the longer school day (plus after-school activities) meant that my children would be busy until the late afternoon nearly every day. However, I had no idea what I wanted to do. Painfully aware that eleven years of part-time work would almost certainly limit my options, I opted out in order to figure out how best to opt in.

I left my job and did some freelance appellate work while contemplating my next step: would it be a different law job; a career change, perhaps to becoming a high school history teacher; a Ph.D.? Teaching and graduate school were both appealing, but I had mixed feelings about starting over at a new career. Over a year went by while I consulted some, pondered lots, and continued to enjoy time with my children.

My indecision ended abruptly—and without real resolution—early in 2004 when I saw a *Lawyers Weekly* ad for a full-time senior attorney position at the Massachusetts Supreme Judicial Court. The job description sounded eclectic and engaging, so I applied. When I interviewed with Chief Justice Margaret Marshall, I was pleased, impressed, and relieved that my many years of part-time work did not seem to cause her any concern. She was satisfied by my statement that I was "ready" for full-time work at that moment in time. I did have doubts: I was nervous about giving up my daily school pick-ups and could not imagine dressing in "lawyer clothes" five days each week. But when I received an offer, I accepted. I was excited to work at the SJC and thought I would be happier if I had less time to ponder the "roads not taken." I surprised myself by adjusting quickly to a full-time schedule.

Seven years later, I remain at the SJC. The court wrestles with important legal and policy issues, and I have great colleagues, including—as is true in many other government jobs—many smart, nice, and hard-working mothers. Very happily, the court's commitment to civic education has allowed me to revive and apply my passion for American history. But I remain well aware of the consequences of my career path. At the court, I am a "staffer" rather than a leader. I don't know what the next stage of life will bring. I expect to cope with my empty-nest by ramping up my out-of-office commitments and seeing where, if anywhere, they may take me. Coediting this book, writing *Walking Tours of Civil War Boston: Hub of Abolitionism* (The Freedom Trail Foundation 2011), and planning other "projects" are steps in this direction.

Many young women lawyers ask me for guidance about choosing a part-time career path. My response generally begins with a short tirade about the meaning of "choice" in the context of work-family balance. Why, I ask, are women still making (most of) the hard choices? Why are so few men equal partners in child care? Hasn't anything changed during the past twenty years? And is it really a choice at all, when society and employers place the burden of balancing family and work on each individual woman's shoulders rather than tackling the issue through progressive policies? But after catching my breath, I offer the following guidance: If one can afford it financially, part-time work is an excellent compromise approach. But it is very much a compromise. Part-time work is more like treading water than swimming forward. At the same time, it's much more than sitting beside the pool. I'm the first to admit that, if there is a perfect solution, I haven't found it. Nonetheless, as I contemplate becoming an empty nester, I am glad that my regrets of lack of time pertain to my career rather than to my children.

Why are women still making (most of) the hard choices?

Prosecutors and Defenders

Miriam Conrad

Miriam Conrad began serving as Federal Public Defender for the Districts of Massachusetts, Rhode Island, and New Hampshire in 2005 after serving as an assistant federal public defender since 1992. She is the first woman to hold this position.

Miriam Conrad

IMAGE COURTESY OF MIRIAM CONRAD

I do not think of myself as a female criminal defense lawyer, and I hope others do not either.

My clients deserve the best possible defense. With a handful of exceptions, they don't seem to care if that defense is presented by a man or a woman. In fact, some have told me that they believe women are better defense lawyers because they do not belong to the "boys' club" and are less hesitant to ruffle feathers, less willing to go along. I don't think it's true. But it is a somewhat refreshing change from the ancient—and, I hope, discarded—belief that women are not tough enough to fight as hard as men.

I am well aware that it was not always so. My career path would not have been as smooth if it had begun twenty years earlier. I was privileged to clerk for the Honorable Rya W. Zobel, who went from being the first female partner in a big Boston firm to being the first

> My clients deserve the best possible defense. With a handful of exceptions, they don't seem to care if that defense is presented by a man or a woman.

female federal judge in Boston. As her law clerk, I was able to see firsthand the grace and intelligence that allowed her to break those barriers.

By the time I began my career as a public defender in 1988, there were many talented and respected female criminal defense lawyers in Boston. One of those who taught and inspired me was Stephanie Page, veteran trial lawyer at the Committee for Public Counsel Services. Another, whom I did not know well at the time but watched with admiration, was Nancy Gertner, a recently retired federal judge now teaching at Harvard Law School.

Law was my second career, and throughout law school I was far from sure that I wanted to commit to it. After college, I worked for about five years as a newspaper reporter. While I had tired of it, the work was lively and exciting, in a way that summer internships at law firms were not.

My doubts about becoming a lawyer vanished when I started my first job as a public defender. Here was the fast pace, fun, and camaraderie that I missed. And there was more: rather than spending a few hours exploring a subject, I could dig deeper. I could investigate a case thoroughly, develop and research legal issues, and form bonds with my clients. Plus, of course, there was the thrill of being in the courtroom.

I feel incredibly fortunate to have a job that I believe is valuable and that I continue to enjoy. I would be hard-pressed to say which is more important. I think I would not start each workday with enthusiasm if I didn't both believe in what I do and find it engaging.

Carmen M. Ortiz

Carmen Ortiz was confirmed by the U.S. Senate in 2009 as Massachusetts' first woman and first Hispanic U.S. attorney.

Please describe your family background and why you decided to become an attorney.

My parents came to the United States from Puerto Rico not speaking any English. I started grammar school in New York City, as a Spanish-only speaker, but quickly learned English. Early on, and I think it was from watching television—all of those crime shows!—that I developed the desire to be a lawyer.

My parents taught me that through hard work and education, I could be a success.... I could have a life they did not have. Thanks to the values and confidence that my parents instilled in me, I saw the fact that I was a Hispanic woman, of modest circumstances not as a hurdle—but rather as an opportunity to excel, break down barriers, and make a difference. It was that goal that brought me to a career in public service.

Carmen Ortiz

IMAGE SOURCE: U.S ATTORNEY'S OFFICE, DISTRICT OF MASSACHUSETTS WEBSITE

The questions and answers presented here are from a written interview with Carmen Ortiz by Barbara Berenson in October 2011.

I learned then that I had the passion for being on the front lines as a litigator….

Before being appointed United States attorney for Massachusetts, you worked both as a prosecutor and as a criminal defense attorney. What drew you to these jobs?

I first joined the Department of Justice in 1981 as a trial attorney. I learned then that I had the passion for being on the front lines as a litigator, representing the United States. I made my career decisions to work as an assistant district attorney and assistant United States attorney based on this passion. The primary reason I wanted to be a prosecutor was because I felt that there would be nothing more rewarding than applying the law in the right way to pursue justice for victims who had suffered terrible tragedies, while being in a position to ensure that defendants' rights were also protected. That has proven true, both as a state and federal prosecutor.

But I also enjoyed my work as a criminal defense attorney, representing people who had gotten into trouble and needed help. To this day, I see that career path as one of the most important that a lawyer can choose.

You also had some fascinating positions on the Harvard/Guatemala Criminal Justice Project and investigating allegations of sexual harassment against the New England Patriots as well as a stint in private practice. What drew you to these diverse undertakings?

In 1989, I had the opportunity to work on the Harvard/Guatemala Criminal Justice Project at Harvard Law School with Professor Philip Heymann, the Director of the Center for Criminal Justice (the Center). The Center had obtained a grant from the U.S. Agency for International Development to work with the judiciary of Guatemala to implement criminal justice reforms in that country. It was my experience as a prosecutor and fluency in Spanish that enabled me to get the job. When I started work at the Center, it was specifically to teach visiting judges from Guatemala about the U.S. criminal justice system. That short-term assignment developed into a challenging and rewarding endeavor that lasted for three years, when I assumed the role of training coordinator and program associate for the project. My responsibilities during the project included directing a pilot court program, which implemented judicial reforms throughout selected courts in Guatemala City and rural areas; designing and coordinating training programs for Guatemalan judges and prosecutors visiting the U.S.; conducting teaching sessions for criminal justice personnel in Guatemala; acting as liaison with senior policymakers in the Guatemalan justice system (including the president of the Supreme Court, the attorney general, and the minister of the interior); and writing training manuals in Spanish for instructors to use in Latin America to teach criminal investigative techniques.

While at the Center, in 1990, I worked on a short-term investigation involving allegations of sexual harassment by a female sports writer against several players of the New England Patriots. Professor Heymann was selected by then-Commissioner Paul Tagliabue of the National Football League to head the investigation as special counsel. The investigation lasted approximately two months and concluded with a final report that detailed our findings of facts supporting the allegations.

When I worked in private practice, I did so primarily to do civil litigation and vary my experiences from criminal prosecution. While at a small law firm, I did civil, criminal, and governmental agency litigation. A focus of my practice was employment law and conducting training seminars for corporate clients regarding issues of sexual harassment in the workplace.

How do you feel to be the first woman and the first Hispanic United States attorney in Massachusetts history?

I feel tremendous pride to have been given this opportunity, which is an opportunity of a lifetime. I believe that my professional and personal experiences—starting with my parents' example and encouragement—have led me to where I am today. I hope that I can serve as an inspiration to women and people of color who are in the process of navigating their own careers.

When the late Senator Edward Kennedy called me to tell me that I was his and Senator John Kerry's choice for U.S. attorney for Massachusetts, I was touched and honored at the confidence they had placed in me. Although I knew that the road to my confirmation would be long, I knew that I was on my way to achieving a dream of a lifetime.

While many different factors have propelled me into this position, being the first woman and first Hispanic U.S. attorney in Massachusetts is certainly not lost on me...and in fact, it has been and will continue to be, a source of strength and encouragement for me...and I hope for others as well.

What are some of the challenges you face and goals you have set as United States attorney?

Each and every day, federal prosecutors face some very difficult decisions. Defendants convicted in federal court generally receive very long sentences and are often ordered to serve them far away from the homes of their families and friends. One of the challenges that I face is determining what our priorities should be and how to expend our limited resources. As a United States attorney, I must ensure that the office focuses on the kinds of cases that the federal government should.

National security matters are our number one priority and do raise some very difficult issues. In these cases, we are charging individuals to prevent a potentially dangerous situation from occurring. While the violence may not have yet occurred, the plotting to do so has and we have to address that type of criminal conduct. These are never easy decisions.

I also think that one of the greatest challenges for me is granting immunity from prosecution to those individuals who may have broken the law. Sometimes these are individuals who have committed serious offenses, but immunity is granted in order to secure their assistance in an undercover investigation and/or testimony in the prosecution of someone who has committed an even more egregious offense.

Regarding initiatives, I have implemented the Civil Rights Enforcement Team (CRET), which is comprised of criminal and civil assistant U.S. attorneys and nonattorney staff members. The mission of the CRET is to invigorate and coordinate the efforts of the U.S. Attorney's Office in enforcing federal civil rights laws. The goal is to increase the number of enforcement actions generated by our office in both the criminal and civil contexts. To accomplish this goal and to increase our visibility among the affected communities in the District of Massachusetts, the CRET directs outreach efforts at such communities and maintains and/or establishes contacts with the appropriate state and local law enforcement agencies.

Community outreach is another very important goal. To a certain extent the U.S. Attorney's Office has always been engaged in our communities. But often this engagement was through assistant United States attorneys, teaching in schools, or speaking on panels. Many still do that important work. But it is my feeling that a prosecutor should be more than just an investigator and litigator. Prosecutors should be members of the communities they serve and should be out there explaining to and working with all kinds of people to inform them of who we are, the work that we do, and how we can help them. Our civil rights efforts are just one area where we reach out to affected communities—disability rights groups, veterans, GLBT organizations, and religious groups are just a few.

[I]t is my feeling that a prosecutor should be more than just an investigator and litigator.

We also have developed a robust gun and gang antiviolence effort, where we reach out to gang members and inner-city community residents; we work with groups of Somali young people who are having trouble with violence; in our National Security program we meet with businesses and train them to understand how their sensitive intellectual property can be stolen and compromised by those out to hurt interests of the United States; we work with inner-city schools to help young people understand the consequences of the choices that they make and how to keep them safe; we work with victims of violent crime to direct them to the services they need to recover from the trauma that has invaded their lives.

I also personally reach out to many communities across Massachusetts in an effort to let them know that we are here to help.

How have you balanced your personal and professional life?

There are ten principles that I've lived by, that have helped me to balance my personal and professional life. Some of these principles might seem as simply common sense, but whenever I talk about these principles of my life, people tell me that they identify with me and are inspired.

- **Dare to dream...to want it all.** Believe that you can have a very fulfilling career and a happy family life. If you want it to happen, you need to believe it can happen and do the things that are necessary to make it happen. I especially want to appeal to women...sometimes, especially in many strong ethnic cultures, you are raised to believe that you can't have it all...or that it would be impossible...women you stay home with the kids...but not so. I encourage you to do what you want.... To the men, you have challenges as well—certainly as men become more involved and engaged in their families as husbands and fathers.

- **Surround yourself with people who believe in you.** You need to have faith that you can accomplish what you set out to do...and have people around you who will encourage you because they believe in you. People who will support your career, your ambitions, and your dreams.

- **Be confident and when that confidence waivers—and it does in this business—lean on your family, friends, or colleagues who believe in you and will help you to battle and move forward.** You need confidence to take certain leaps of faith at different times in your life. When I first thought about applying for the position of United States

Attorney, I was reluctant. I did not think I would get it, I did not have complete confidence. But I listened to a few close friends and colleagues who convinced me that I had the necessary experience and, really, what did I have to lose? It is key that you take risks. I am so glad I listened to them!

▲ *U.S. Attorney Ortiz with the young women of GRLZ Radio.*

IMAGE COURTESY OF CARMEN ORTIZ

- **Prioritize.** Yes, your family needs to come first—but not at every moment. It is not always easy. Pick those family occasions that are a must, do everything to make way for them. Know when certain work matters are critical and can't be put aside, and distinguish those from ones that can. Seek to balance both. Sometimes there will be disappointment...but if you make every effort to explain and be there when it counts...despite any disappointments, your family will understand.

- **Never give up on what you want to achieve, despite life's hardships or setbacks.** I know how simple that sounds—but some of the setbacks that have occurred in my own life were so complicated that the simple notion of "don't give up" resonated when I needed it most.

  In 1992, my life was running on all cylinders and I thought that I had it all. I was a prosecutor trying serious felony cases in Middlesex County. I had a loving husband, Michael Morisi, whose law practice was doing quite well. I had two beautiful little girls—I thought my life was complete. I had it all. Then, after one phone call, it all changed. My husband was diagnosed with cancer and for the next seven years we all lived with his very aggressive and physically disabling disease. Then in 2000, Michael passed away and the center of my life was gone. But I knew I had two girls to raise and that they needed me. It was not easy. I struggled; I lost my zest for work—for fighting in the courtroom. But after some time, my energy and desire to get back to where I was returned. I was lucky to have my family, my wonderful friends and colleagues who got me through those dark days and to where I am today. Bottom line—setbacks will happen—don't let them define you.

- **Don't be afraid to ask for help.** I think that in our society, the demands and expectations of women, in particular, have increased exponentially in recent years. Many times, we are the ones who put the greatest pressures on ourselves. The solution is pretty simple, don't be afraid to ask for help. I have come to believe that asking for help is a sign of strength, not weakness. My own hesitancy. Had to overcome it.

- **Work hard—it's essential.** Make an impression—make your mark. It is critically important, especially for Hispanic women, to be twice as good. You want employers wanting you back, not happy to see you leave. Overcome stereotypes. Don't let others limit you.

- **Forge relationships, nurture them, stay in touch with your counterparts.** Over the years, it has been critically important to me to connect with the people I work with. When I moved on, they could speak about my work ethic, the quality of my work and more importantly, my demeanor as a person. It is so important to me to be known for loyalty, trust, and dedication.
- **Accept job disappointments with class and grace, and don't let them define you.** Don't turn bitter or cynical. Look for the silver lining. There usually is one.
- **Be nice...be pleasant.** Don't bring your work stress home and don't bring your home stress to work. People hate to be around people who whine or are ardent complainers...but everyone loves people who are a pleasure to be around!

Stephanie Page

Stephanie Page, now retired, was a public defender with the Committee for Public Counsel Services from 1978 to 2011.

Stephanie Page in court.

IMAGE COURTESY OF STEPHANIE PAGE

It was a different world back in 1978, especially as a young female public defender in the criminal courts of Suffolk County. Not so long ago, yet long enough that many of our younger lawyers can't imagine that any of our experiences were real. Feminism was a dirty word and a foreign concept to many we faced. There were very few role models for a female criminal defense trial lawyer who couldn't pick and choose her cases. The judges, clerks, court officers, and prosecutors really didn't know how to deal with us. As women we were expected to be seen and not heard. After all, we were not part of "the old boys club." It could get pretty rough-and-tumble.

Just to give you a flavor: I was often the only woman in a very crowded criminal courtroom. One of the clerks always opened "his" session with "Good morning to all male married private lawyers." A court officer made me show him my bar card every day for months before he allowed me to enter the well of "his" courtroom. My supervisor (male) was called up by the judge (male) during one of my first arraignments for a young man accused of a sexual assault to make sure it was all right for the facts to be read in front of me. Many a judge referred to the few of us at Mass Defenders as "girls." A number of us were referred to as "boy toys" because we represented

Stephanie Page and Janice Bassil in the Massachusetts Defender's office, circa 1980.

IMAGE COURTESY OF STEPHANIE PAGE

men accused of sex crimes. At a sentence appeal of a serious case, one of the judges (male) expressed disbelief that I had been the lawyer on the case. A court officer (male) filled up my trial file with condoms (that had been seized that morning from those in the lockup) so that when I appeared in the trial session they exploded, so to speak, when I was setting up. To this day I look before I sit down in court because a court officer once pulled a chair out from under me in the courtroom. I was banned from the courtroom for the rest of my career by an older judge because I had the temerity to object to his ruling. He chastised me as a girl who should learn what the proper rules were. I outlasted him.

I sent that judge the 1875 decision in the *Goodell* case that denied her admission into the bar:

> We cannot but think the common law wise in excluding women.... But it is public policy not to tempt women from their proper duties of their sex.... There are many employments in life not unfit for female character. The profession of law is surely not one of these. The peculiar qualities of womanhood, its gentle graces, its quick sensibility, its purity, its delicacy, its emotional impulses, its subordination of hard reason to sympathetic feeling, are surely not qualifications for forensic strife.... Discussions are habitually necessary in courts of justice, which are unfit for female ears.... Womanhood is moulded for gentler and better things.

In the Matter of the Motion to Admit Miss Lavinia Goodell to the Bar of this Court, 39 Wis. 232 (1875).

I learned to take advantage of this type of treatment hopefully to the benefit of my clients. I won a case I probably would not have but for the judge informing a jury that they were being released early so that the women could go home and get supper ready for their husbands. I won another case with a veteran prosecutor and judge who made it clear that in their minds I was not of any value in the courtroom. The women and I bonded in those moments. There were many of those.

Character building? Rites of passage? Sexism? All I know is that these experiences made me stronger, made me work and fight harder—and that they didn't happen to my male colleagues.

I was lucky enough to have started with the Massachusetts Defenders Committee at a time when they were not afraid to hire women. I started with Janice Bassil and Jay Carney. The best trial lawyers in the world were our teachers. I was fortunate to see, learn from, and later become friends with lawyers like Judith Lindahl (a real pioneer), Willie Davis, and John Prescott. It couldn't have been better. It was an atmosphere that was supportive and encouraged us to be as good as we could be. In retrospect, we were inventing a world that did not exist before—by just being us.

We have come a long way but the journey is not finished. History is Herstory—yes?

Legal Services and Nonprofits

Mary L. Bonauto

▲

Mary L. Bonauto

IMAGE COURTESY OF INFINITYPORTRAITDESIGN.COM

Mary L. Bonauto has served as the civil rights project director at Gay & Lesbian Advocates & Defenders (GLAD) since 1990.

How did you decide to become a lawyer?

I decided to become a lawyer when I was a teenager. It had a lot to do with being underdog identified, if you will.... [E]ven as a young person, it was not hard to discern vast inequalities and I wanted to do something to try to level the playing fields for people from all walks of life. My perspectives became more informed and nuanced with time, but there is no doubt that "the law" is a powerful structural force shaping what we value, and what is possible, and for whom.

Where do you think you got that sense of right and wrong and compelling justice?

Some day I will figure all that out. First of all, the real people I meet, talk to, and represent are the heart and soul of why we work to make "liberty and justice for all" a lived reality, and as soon as possible. Looking back, my parents taught my brothers and me about respect for others and the dignity and value of all persons—with no exceptions. I was also raised as a Catholic, and the social justice emphasis in Catholicism influenced me enormously. I attended public schools in a somewhat distressed area through high school, and I grew up knowing about people's struggles. And of course, like many people, I've experienced the sting of imposed otherness, both subtly and blatantly—whether because my last name ends in a vowel, or because my background and circumstances were different from others, or because I wasn't behaving properly "for a woman," or because of my sexual orientation. The upside of these experiences is that I learned how current societal norms can contort the basic values we share, such as living the Golden Rule and liberty and equality for all. My years of work at GLAD have only widened and deepened my perspectives on "justice for all." I should be clear, though, that I feel like my cup runneth over in terms of blessings. I am not complaining. The challenge is how to give back when I have been given so much.

How did you decide to go into law, as opposed to say, being a union organizer or taking another professional path?

There are many issues about which I am passionate beyond the work I do at GLAD, and law can be a tool in addressing many of them. I didn't know lawyers growing up...but I saw law as involving both big systems and big ideas and I was (and am) very interested in the role of law in establishing rules and norms by which we live.... I read about lawyers and historical conflicts. For example, in middle school, I became very taken with Abraham Lincoln, including how he evolved over time to recognize that slavery intolerably clashed with our basic constitutional values. Reading a biography of Justice Oliver Wendell Holmes, Jr. impressed upon me the necessity of our constitutional commitment to free speech in a diverse and sometimes disagreeable society. I came to understand the genius of the framers in

The questions and answers presented here are adapted from an interview with Mary L. Bonauto by Elizabeth A. Brown in February 2010.

setting forth enduring principles that would take shape in a dynamic and evolving society, rather than creating a rule book of eighteenth-century standards.

Did you have any role models when you were in law school or starting out who were female?

I have been lucky. I have learned from so many people over the years, starting with my immediate and extended families. Part of it was simply that they believed in me. Both of my parents are, and all of my grandparents were, hard-working people with outsized integrity and down-to-earth practicality. Others inspired me to do what I loved regardless of perceived practicality. One of my comparative literature professors at Hamilton College, Nancy Rabinowitz, nurtured my love of classical Greek and helped me to think critically *about everything.*

How does it feel to be compared to Thurgood Marshall?

Well, it was only for one issue, for marriage.

How does it feel? Honestly, absurd. What is great is the principles that I rely on in arguing that the constitutional commitment to liberty and equality applies to gay people, too; that there are no sexual orientation exceptions to the pledge of "equal justice under law." Generations of lawyers have relied on these promises to end the outsider status of groups of people or the stigma attending particular characteristics. Justice Marshall is clearly a lion among those lawyers, and of course I aspire to be a strategic thinker and emulate his many strengths. I appreciate the compliment, but the comparison just doesn't work.

Do you have a goal for your career, and how do you think about what you want to accomplish in your career?

I'm not ambitious—traditionally ambitious...about a career, per se.... [A]fter I went to law school, I wanted to jump into working directly with people right away, so I did not want to clerk (something I would now do differently). I took a job with a mid-sized law firm in Maine; I was their eighth lawyer. The firm's anchor partners had previously done civil rights work. They wanted me to make money, but they also let me loose to pursue my own interests. I signed up through the Volunteer Lawyers Project for pro bono work, but because it was the late 1980s, I found myself immersed in the AIDS crisis as well. Now that I look back on it, I can see that the work I did then was a model for what we do at GLAD. At that time, there was massive fear and discrimination...to the point that if you were suspected of being gay, some people would assume you had AIDS, and invariably, negative consequences would follow. I threw myself into helping individuals contest job discrimination when they were summarily fired for their presumed HIV status and also with end-of-life planning. And I worked on systemic

Mary Bonauto speaking with reporters outside the John Joseph Moakley Federal Courthouse following oral argument in Gill v. Office of Personnel Management, *May 6, 2010.*

IMAGE COURTESY OF INFINITYPORTRAITDESIGN.COM

◀

Mary Bonauto on City Hall Plaza on May 17, 2004, the date that same-sex couples began marrying in Massachusetts.

IMAGE COURTESY OF INFINITYPORTRAITDESIGN.COM

issues, helping state legislators craft insurance laws in light of the epidemic. It turned out that I was one of the few out lawyers in the entire State of Maine at that time. That meant business! I'm not saying that only a gay or lesbian lawyer could meet people's legal needs, but many people simply felt more comfortable with me at that point. I negotiated "moral turpitude" clauses out of employment contracts, helped young people emancipate themselves legally when their parents kicked them out of the house, and pressed the police to be more responsive to anti-gay violence.

But then…in November 1989, Governor Dukakis signed the…second law in the entire country, forbidding discrimination based on sexual orientation in employment, housing, public accommodations, and credit. And GLAD, where I work now, started advertising for a lawyer to enforce that law. I saw the ad…and I talked to my partner and said, "That's what I really want to do." She said to go for it. I applied, thinking GLAD would never hire me. I was…two years out of law school, and I assumed they would hire somebody with far more experience for such an important job. But in 1990, they hired me. At the time, I thought I would go do the job for two years, by the end of which I would be utterly exhausted and would then return to private practice. But after two years, I was just getting started. I'd barely scratched the surface of what I saw needed to be done. So I stayed. I accepted that job nearly twenty two years ago.

I have thought about my career in terms of the goal of eliminating that gap that exists between the law and the law as applied to gay people (and others) as opposed to achieving any particular position. I think a person's sexual orientation is and should be irrelevant to his or her rights, freedoms and opportunities; it's just another articulation of the pledge of "equal justice under law." Without a doubt, that gap has narrowed in the last twenty-plus years, and I'd like to stay at GLAD until…that gap no longer exists.

What are you proudest of in your life? I'll broaden it, rather than just your career. What are some of the things that you are proudest of having accomplished at this point in your existence?

I don't know if I would say proud, but I am just so grateful that I've been able to have my family that I have.

How old are your girls?

They were born in 2001.... I've been with my partner, Jennifer Wriggins, for twenty-two [now twenty-four] years, and we've been through a lot together....

Can you talk a little bit about balancing work and family?

As everyone knows, it is so difficult.

It is so difficult. Do you have any thoughts, do you have any advice, do you have any observations, having done it now for quite some time? Does it get any easier with time?

For all the joy in being a parent, it's still hard work. I have just come to accept that I am going to be extra tired for a number of years. Jenny and I both committed to being the best parents we can be and having a strong relationship with them. But inevitably, there are also just times when you are more pressured, you're on a deadline, and it is harder to be as present and as focused, and that can last for too long. It bothers me, but I also try to remember that overall, they have great lives, with lots of love and joy, and they know in their bones that they are deeply loved and respected by us. It helps enormously that GLAD has come to be an incredibly flexible employer, allowing me to work odd hours at times so I can chaperone an occasional school field trip or deal with the blizzard of appointments and activities. GLAD also understands that I will not be able to do everything I did before Jenny and I had children. That is hard for me to accept, but like all parents, you see that the constancy of children is change, and that means some things are possible now that were not when they were much younger.

Have you had any interest or opportunity in mentoring other women?

My philosophy is to give and not just get. The legal assistants at GLAD are usually recent college grads who are determined to go to law school. I try to add value to their experience with us by giving them challenging assignments, talking with them about why the assignment matters, and how to think both inside and outside the box when approaching a research project. We do the same with our summer clerks, and they always leave a clerkship with the tools to get a good next job. The truth of the matter is that we need every ounce of passion, commitment and intelligence these young people have to offer to help achieve our shared goals. The GLAD attorneys are colleagues in the best senses of the word. We respect each other and learn from each other. That is part of what makes GLAD a great place to work.

▲

Mary Bonauto on City Hall Plaza, May 17, 2004.

IMAGE COURTESY OF INFINITYPORTRAITDESIGN.COM

Can you talk about a case or two of which you are particularly proud?

On the one hand, the marriage cases are huge because being able to marry the person you love transforms your life. In point of fact, the *Goodridge v. Department of Public Health* [440 Mass. 309. (2003)] case from Massachusetts broke an historic barrier. Chief Justice Marshall and her colleagues are rightly hailed for the courage to live up to our constitutional commitments. Yet, paving the way also meant that many people had a share of grief that people in other states have not—the plaintiffs, the courts, the legislature, the governor, and the citizenry as a whole. I am so proud of and eternally grateful to all of those in Massachusetts who made that victory possible, and the many who made it secure when the legislature rejected a proposed constitutional amendment to reverse *Goodridge* in June 2007.

At the same time, I've worked on myriad cases that are consequential for the parties and also establish principles about how sexual orientation should not matter in terms of freedoms, rights and opportunities. I am thinking of cases involving blatant antigay discrimination in jobs, and in places of public accommodation, and how the legal process helped restore people's dignity and also reminded businesses to discard outdated attitudes about gay people. I'm thinking of cases where parents felt intense vulnerability about having no legal connection to their child, and how GLAD's cases were vehicles for moving the law closer to familial realities, by establishing joint adoptions, or joint guardianship or de facto parenthood. There are plenty of times when I've handled a case that that doesn't change life for everyone, but the effect is still profound....

How, if at all, do you think being female has affected the way you practice law? And I don't know...if it would be better to ask you...is there a way to separate being gay from being female?

There's me as a woman, and there's me as a lesbian.

First of all, I was always taught to be a "nice girl." I had to learn that being nice didn't mean I had to listen to another attorney berate or ridicule me or my legal position. All the same, it is no disservice to your client to press that client's interests in a pleasant manner and to extend basic courtesies to other counsel.

Second, I realize that for some people, dealing with me also means conjuring up their attitudes about gay people. For some, and increasingly, that's no big deal. But to this day, for others it means an automatic discounting of my legal analysis and credibility. Others believe they can simply intone the name of where I work—"Gay & Lesbian Advocates & Defenders"—and that affiliation is indictment enough. Being lesbian, gay, bisexual or transgender is still stigmatized, and it was that much more so when I started out. I recall making an oral argument early on during which a justice seemed hidden behind a redwell file on the bench and peered out over his papers to look at me. I'm not a mind reader, but you could just tell, this judge was spending more time thinking about who and what I was than about my legal argument. I still have experiences like that, but overall, there's been a sea change in attitudes.

Another thing which you now know from having now met me is that I'm five feet, two inches tall. And I don't have a very loud voice. It's easy for people to underestimate you in those circumstances, especially when you're female.... I think there was a period of time where I was underestimated by my opponents.... There's a way in which winning *Goodridge* blew my cover, so to speak.... And then I wasn't underestimated quite so much.

How did that change? How did people approach you differently? How did you sense that people interacted with you differently?

We've always had productive collaborations with private practice attorneys, and winning *Goodridge* brought more offers to partner with us. There is more respect that we know what we're talking about—about the law, about timing, about strategy. On a personal level, people project onto you. I recognize that it is an awesome gift and responsibility to be able to talk about the constitution's meaning for the lives of gay people and for same-sex relationships. But I am still the same person trying to get her work done so she could get home in time to have dinner with her kids....

So it sounds like there were times in your career where you felt like you sensed some disrespect. How do you deal with that? Because I think that's something that a lot of women in law face.

I don't have a grand strategy other than what we do at GLAD: maintain high standards about lawyering and how we interact with others, and try to let the rest roll off of your back. So essentially...that old saying—[a] woman has to work twice as hard to be thought of as half as good—that's been true for me as a woman, but it's also been true for us at GLAD. We care about getting things right, and it shows. What would be hard is to face disrespect among one's colleagues and that is not a problem we have at GLAD.

What do you love about your practice?

I work with a very talented and committed group of people, who have stratospherically high legal and ethical standards, who care deeply about people, and who are as respectful and supportive as they can be about their colleagues' family lives.... GLAD has been listed as one of the best law firms to work at in Massachusetts. I think it's because we do interesting and important work, and we're always facing new challenges and learning on the job. We're completely aligned with our clients in terms of our shared goals.... We will do what it takes to move forward, even though, as people often tell us, it looks impossible.... We even have fun. I'm at an intersection of law, politics, and policy where I can use the legal tools I have to...establish new precedents of fairness. It's extremely exciting. It's another example of how my cup runneth over.... I feel very fortunate.

I'm at an intersection of law, politics, and policy where I can use the legal tools I have to...establish new precedents of fairness.

Jacquelynne J. Bowman

Jacquelynne J. Bowman

IMAGE COURTESY OF THE RENTSCH FAMILY

Jacquelynne Bowman became executive director of Greater Boston Legal Services in 2011 after having served as the organization's deputy director since 2000.

My arrival in Massachusetts in the mid-Eighties was filled with anticipation and excitement about practicing in the midst of a diverse group of attorneys in the home of freedom, liberty, and justice for all. I had begun my practice as a legal services attorney in a small town in rural west Tennessee, where I was a novelty. There were only two other women attorneys who did not work for legal aid and only two other attorneys of color, both males. I was giddy thinking about the ability to be accepted as an attorney vigorously representing my client and not the secretary carrying the boss's briefcase or taking notes. Imagine, then, my surprise when I was told by Massachusetts court personnel that only

Jacquelynne Bowman with her family.

IMAGE COURTESY OF THE RENTSCH FAMILY

lawyers could see a particular file or use a particular table! Continue by picturing the young male attorney who struggled with what term to address me by in court: "As my brother, I mean sister or whatever...." Or the middle-aged counselor who spoke to me numerous times by telephone, presumably knowing my name, but upon in-person introduction immediately assumed that I was the social worker on the case, whose name bore no resemblance to my own. Now imagine that a few more years have gone by, three attorneys are appearing before a judge, all of whom have some level of friendship with him, perhaps mine being the most speculative, and the judge asking, "Anything more, counsel? Mr. Smith? Mr. Jones? Jacqui?"

Back in those earlier years in Massachusetts, I had multiple barriers to climb over as an African-American female attorney who worked for legal aid. I felt that, before the court and opposing counsel would take me or my client seriously, I had to look the part and be the best prepared. While any of these descriptors could be perceived as a handicap, clearly being different from most people's concept of an attorney was the big one. For a good number of years I spent much time and energy convincing the gatekeepers to justice that I had the credentials to be a member of the bar. I really do not remember when I no longer had to produce my bar card on a daily basis. I do recall being greeted by court officers as "the lady attorney" and having a sense that I had arrived.

Today, though, I take pride in the fact that there are many women attorneys of color who are playing very prominent roles in the judiciary, among court personnel, and presenting cases. Over the past twenty years, those of us who came in increasing larger numbers paved the way, so that nirvana I imagined in the eighties is almost real.

Mary M. (Meg) Connolly

Meg Connolly served as executive director of the Volunteer Lawyers Project of the Boston Bar Association from 1985 to 2009 and now works as a consultant to legal aid programs.

Meg Connolly

IMAGE COURTESY OF MEG CONNOLLY

In early 1971, about eight months after graduation from Boston College Law School, I attended my first annual dinner meeting of a county bar association. I was the only woman in attendance, except for the waitresses. During the reception hour, I was chatting with another young attorney, who inquired if I were the Mary Connolly who was the legal aid lawyer. When I confirmed that indeed I was, he commented, "Don't worry, some day you'll get a real job." His rather unpleasant remark captured the predicament of female public interest lawyers in 1970. We were unpopular in two instances: as women, we had no place at the bar, and as troublesome public interest lawyers, we were not part of the club.

For me, however, the legal aid position was the "real job." It was the job I went to law school to do, not the only work I could get. As a teenager, I was influenced by the lawyers of the civil rights movement, who were true heroes. They mounted a very sophisticated legal campaign to end segregation and risked their lives representing clients brave enough to try to register to vote. Thus inspired, in 1960 when I was fifteen, I announced to my parents, who were not college graduates, that I intended to be a lawyer. They didn't blink. No one told me that girls didn't go to law school. They just treated my aspiration as a normal one for a teenage daughter. Their attitude was the greatest gift they could give me.

No one told me that girls didn't go to law school. [My parents] just treated my aspiration as a normal one for a teenage daughter. Their attitude was the greatest gift they could give me.

While I was in college, the federally funded legal services program was created as part of the war on poverty. I then focused my goal on the new legal services effort. I would be a legal aid lawyer. During my second year at Boston College Law School, the BC Legal Assistance Bureau was created. This was an extracurricular clinical program with an office in Waltham. I was fortunate to be among the first group of students to work at the bureau, and the only woman in my class to do so. I also served as the bureau's second vice president. I was able to begin my career while still a law student.

The clinical work served me well as a new lawyer. Not only did I learn the rudiments of certain case types but, more importantly, I had many opportunities to appear in court. In the seventies and early eighties, it was very unusual to see a woman attorney in court. For instance, when I first appeared in one courtroom and took my seat inside the bar, a court officer came over to explain that those seats were reserved for lawyers.

When I graduated in 1970, approximately 5 percent of my classmates were women. Only eight years later, 30 percent of the graduating class was female. However, the impact of women on the profession took much longer. When I was regional counsel to the Office of Economic Opportunity from 1973 to 1975, I was the only woman out of the nine positions. When I served as deputy regional director for the newly-created Legal Services Corporation, I frequently met young women lawyers working in legal aid programs. These young women, often no more than ten years my junior, were suffering shock as practicing attorneys. They had attended law schools that were now generally co-ed institutions. The profession, however, was still overwhelmingly male-dominated, and the women had not yet developed skills necessary to function in a male environment. However, change continued at a rapid pace and legal aid programs now often have staff with a majority of women staff attorneys.

When immersed in representing the disenfranchised, one tends to concentrate on what still needs to be changed. However, writing this reflection has been an opportunity to acknowledge that an almost unimaginable revolution has occurred during the relatively brief period of my professional life.

Vickie L. Henry

IMAGE COURTESY OF INFINITYPORTRAITDESIGN.COM

Vickie L. Henry

Vickie Henry transitioned from private practice at Foley Hoag LLP to senior staff attorney at Gay & Lesbian Advocates & Defenders (GLAD) in 2011.

Contemplating this change felt quite a bit like jumping into the abyss. I had originally planned to work at a big firm for three years. I liked the work and the people much more than I anticipated, though, and three years became sixteen. My (now former) partners are an impressive and talented group of attorneys and I was proud of being an equity partner, especially given how few people attain that status—let alone out-lesbian attorneys. I certainly enjoyed the income of a partner at an Am Law 200 firm, as well as the resources, from technology to support staff. In short, I was not looking to leave when GLAD recruited me.

This potential change was huge, and my wife and I discussed it a long while. These discussions reminded me of a sermon at our church years earlier, entitled "The Abyss." When faced with an abyss, most people are dragged in kicking and screaming. Our minister posited instead that you jump in, because you just might find happiness in that great unknown. This is not how most lawyers are trained to think. As I was contemplating this life change, I told one of my soon-to-be colleagues that I was standing on the edge of the abyss, deciding whether to jump. He asked, "Does that mean we are in the abyss?" I responded, "Yes, but you look happy in there." My toes were now hanging over the edge. He replied, "We are. Jump in; we'll catch you." And so I jumped, and it is wonderful.

I always thought that when the book of my life is written, I want to have made an impact. I did as much as one could within the constraints of private practice. Now I have that chance on a daily basis.

As I shared the news of my career change, some people expressed admiration or even envy about my making this bold leap and that my family could leave the compensation of a big firm behind. In fact, this change was not the product of one decision. My family kept this career possibility open by making hundreds of frugal decisions over the years. I also logged twenty years of pro bono work with GLAD. Even in private practice, I always thought that when the book of my life is written, I want to have made an impact. I did as much as one could within the constraints of private practice. Now I have that chance on a daily basis.

Life in the abyss is fabulous so far. It is familiar and yet very different from my prior professional life. Some things are the same at a law firm and at a mission-driven organization such as GLAD. At both, the commitment to excellence is an organizational imperative. You also still need to "add value" for your client, though at a mission-driven organization, you also have to consider how your client's needs fit within the context of the organization's cause. Of course, you still have deadlines and conflicting client demands and the inevitable administrative responsibilities.

Ironically, the pull to work long hours, including nights and weekends, at a mission-driven organization is as strong or possibly stronger than in private practice. That may surprise some. At a firm, there are good business reasons to work hard—to make more money, because of client need, or to get an experience you want. At the mission-driven organization, the extra hours at some personal sacrifice are for the cause in which I so passionately believe.

The differences from private practice, though, are thrilling. At GLAD, my job is to fight for equality and to make the world a better place. I'm not trying to squeeze that work around fee-generating work. What a luxury! Civil rights work was my dream when I went to law school. Now I'm part of a fabulous team charged with envisioning and implementing paths to our community's goals.

Of course, at a nonprofit you have to do more with less because the economic resources are less. Looking on the bright side, this makes you think hard before committing dollars or time.

Vickie Henry speaking at GLAD's Summer Party Prelude in Provincetown, July 29, 2011.

IMAGE COURTESY OF INFINITYPORTRAITDESIGN.COM

Also, making money stretch further, whether it is the organization's funds or our family's lower income, can inspire creativity, which gives its own satisfaction. This is not just a mindset; it is a hard reality that there are some things the organization cannot pay for and so either you will pay for it yourself or you will find a different way. Although the pressure to change billing models has increased exponentially on private lawyers in the past few years, it is not the hard stop that the nonprofit's limited resources are.

In private practice, you want prospective clients to call you with new matters. At GLAD, however, I've learned to insist that potential new cases go through GLAD's intake process, even when the referring attorneys know me well. Once I hear of an injustice, it is difficult to say the organization cannot take on the challenge. Yet GLAD's core work is impact litigation, bringing cases and engaging in advocacy to address systemic injustices or achieve law reform. We have to select matters carefully, balancing needs and resources within that framework. That sometimes means we have to make tough calls and say no to matters that have real merit.

One aspect of the career change that is less comfortable but important is that part of my value to GLAD as a senior attorney is that I have a greater experience base and capacity to question how things are done or challenge the orthodoxy. Therefore I'm mindful of striking a balance between learning the ropes and questioning whether we should be using the ropes in a different way or using different ropes altogether.

In private practice and in the nonprofit sector, there is stress—just different, and I hope better, stress at GLAD. In the impact litigation that is GLAD's forte, if you make the wrong decision (e.g., about when, where, and what case to bring), you can set the movement back decades. The stress also stems from the breadth and complexity of the problems we are trying to solve. The legal obstacles and inequalities facing the lesbian, gay, bisexual, transgender, and queer (LGBTQ) and HIV+ communities run the gamut, affecting every stage of a person's life. At the senior end of our age spectrum, we have LGBTQ elderly who need assisted living or retirement homes where they can live safely and authentically without returning to the closet. We see people who paid into Social Security for decades but cannot get benefits for their spouse, though they desperately need and deserve them. As for LGBTQ youth, the

Mary Bonauto and Vickie Henry leading plaintiffs to the courthouse for oral argument in Gill v. Office of Personnel Management, *May 6, 2010.*

IMAGE COURTESY OF INFINITYPORTRAITDESIGN.COM

rejection and harassment that some face in both school settings and from their families lead to their disproportionate representation among homeless populations and in the child welfare system. That alone is heartbreaking, but it also means that discrimination because of their LGBTQ status is often only one of their problems. These examples are emblematic of the kinds of issues with which we wrestle.

The best part of this change is that my passion is my work and my work is my passion. Part of me sometimes thinks, "I cannot believe it is my job to work for equality full time." I feel blessed.

Welcome to the new job, same as the old job—except for when it is very different.

Carol Rose

Carol Rose joined the American Civil Liberties Union of Massachusetts as its executive director in 2003.

How did you decide to go to law school?

I had thought about law school off and on throughout college because I thought that it was interesting intellectual training. But I actually was a journalist first. I became a newspaper reporter for a number of years, both in this country and then based in Peshawar, Pakistan, reporting on Pakistan, Afghanistan, Northern India, Nepal, and the political situation in the Hindu Kush. In the course of doing that I became very interested in the work of the human rights lawyers that I met working in these countries, and it made me deeply appreciate the system of law and freedoms that we have in the United States. It reinforced for me that the rights that we have set forth in our Constitution and Bill of Rights are unique in many ways and that we in the United States are in the midst of a fascinating experiment in democracy. So I decided to come back to study and then practice in the United States legal system, in part so that then I might go abroad again someday to exchange best practices. I had to understand and master my own country's system of laws before I could have that kind of an exchange.

How long had you been a journalist when you went to law school?

About ten years.

▲

Carol Rose

IMAGE COURTESY OF CAROL ROSE, PHOTO BY MARILYN HUMPHRIES

What was the experience of law school like, coming from that professional world?

I had actually been abroad for three years without a visit home before I returned to the United States about a month before law school started. I was experiencing culture shock being back in the United States, but I was really excited about going to Harvard Law School because I thought, well, these are going to be some really incredibly smart people, and for the most part they were and it was terrific, academically. At the same time I had been away for so long that I knew what a luxury it was to sit in a classroom and listen and have an intellectual exchange with people. I never understood why students would skip classes. I felt that, "I'm paying for this so I have to get all of it." And so for me, law school was this kind of luxurious time of my life

The questions and answers presented here are adapted from an interview with Carol Rose by Elizabeth A. Brown in July 2010.

and I probably enjoyed law school more than most people because I'd been a working stiff for ten years.

Carol Rose addresses the ACLU of Massachusetts' annual Bill of Rights dinner in May 2011.

IMAGE COURTESY OF CAROL ROSE, PHOTO BY MARILYN HUMPHRIES

Did you experience any gender bias in law school that you remember?

Oh, sure. There's a tremendous amount of gender bias in law schools. The whole Socratic method of communicating, to the extent that it's still used, is incredibly patriarchal because there's a person in a position of authority demanding responses from people and then belittling them, critiquing them in a public setting. It takes a huge amount of ego resilience to thrive in that environment. I think that having been older, I was particularly appalled by it. I remember sitting in a classroom on the first or second day of law school, and I was called on by a professor who was a real bully. He asked me to state the facts and then to state the black letter law, so I answered the questions asked. Then he proceeded to say, "That's a ridiculous argument!" Well, he hadn't asked me to make an argument, he'd asked me to restate the black letter law. And he did this rant and then he stopped and he looked at me, and I said, "Are you quite finished?" *[Laughter]* And then I proceeded to say, "If you want to know what my theory would be, it would be the following," and I laid it out for him. He never called on me again. *[Laughter]* But I was, by then, thirty-three years old, and I had been living and working in war zones and poverty zones and dealing with grownups and being treated like a grownup, so I was unprepared for the infantilization that goes on in that teaching method. I don't know whether it's patriarchal or authoritarian or what, but had I been much younger, I would have had far fewer defenses and coping mechanisms to be able to survive in that kind of an environment. So much of the gender bias that I see has to do with the whole communication method and lack of process orientation. The good thing is that I actually had some law professors, many but not all of them women, who were great and created inclusive ways for everybody to participate and to learn in a collaborative environment. And those were the teachers who provided the most lasting skills to take into the world.

You practiced law at Hill & Barlow. How did you decide to go there?

I was looking for a few things. One was that I wanted to work in a place that had a good social justice docket that permitted associates to do law reform work in addition to their daily practice. So I was looking for a firm that encouraged that kind of civic engagement as part of their business model. They also had a really great parental leave policy and I was thinking about having a child.

After law school, did you clerk first before going to Hill & Barlow?

I clerked for Judge Patti Saris, who's a fabulous role model. It was a really great year. I was able to spend a lot of time in the courtroom because it was a trial court rather than appellate court. I was able to see the stories that people told and the colorful characters that show up in a courtroom. It was educational to watch Judge Saris manage her courtroom because she has such a nice touch. She has a lot of authority and command of the courtroom and yet she's got a really great style as a woman leader. Judge Saris gives her clerks a lot of time in the courtroom, so I was able to observe the different styles of lawyering, including how advocates should dress. For men figuring out how to dress in court is easy because they just wear their same suits and same hairdos, so they pretty much look alike, with some notable exceptions. But I would watch the women and some would come in suits and some would come in flowered dresses, others would wear peasant skirts and others mini-skirts. I tried to figure out the most effective way for a woman lawyer in a courtroom to dress. So I would watch them and I would think "she's effective" and "this one's not effective," "this works, this doesn't," and then I suddenly had the realization that what matters is that you figure out what your style is and go with it. The really good lawyers, male or female, are always the ones who are the most comfortable in their skin.

So after you clerked with Judge Saris, you went to Hill & Barlow?

I was in the litigation department, initially doing First Amendment work, and had some really great mentors. I then expanded my practice to be more of a sort of outside counsel for small companies that didn't have their own lawyers. So I started doing a lot of intellectual property and privacy work for small companies. So I was actually straddling the litigation and the corporate practices, providing a range of services. I ended up getting a good client base, most likely because I was older and was able to counsel people. It was scary, the first couple years of legal practice, because you don't know anything, so you spend time sounding authoritative and saying "let me get back to you on that" and then going and finding the answer and then calling them back. And then after a while the questions become the same and you don't have to look them up anymore and that's when you know you've become a lawyer. Even though now I'm doing public interest work, the training I got at the law firm was extraordinarily helpful because it taught me how to do the art and the craft of law.

Is that something you would recommend to other lawyers who are interested in public service work?

There's no one path. I would say the most important thing is don't feel as though you're selling out if you go to a law firm or that that means you have to stay at a law firm for your whole practice. For one thing, public interest law jobs are hard to get. I believe that a law firm, like a public interest organization, is a platform upon which you can do social justice work. So whether you're in-house counsel, at a law firm, or being paid as a staff attorney at a place like the ACLU, these are all platforms upon which you can direct resources to social justice work. And at a law firm you can access a lot of resources of the firm to do public interest work. So I think people need to understand they can do public interest work from a range of platforms and they needn't limit their vision.

What makes your job at the ACLU such a great fit for you?

My current job combines my expertise in law and journalism to create a model of integrated advocacy. Serving as the executive director also offers a unique opportunity to be a CEO and to try to put into practice policies that I used to say—when I was being supervised by others—"if I am ever the boss, I'll do things differently." Now I am the boss and I get to do that. I really enjoy the management aspect of the job. It's a third career for me; first, journalism, then law, and now managing an organization and staff. As such, it requires a broader definition of legal practice and advocacy, which I think is important if we are going to be effective agents of social change.

What do you like best about your job?

What I love best about my job is the mission and the advocacy. It's both challenging and fun to think creatively about ways to broaden our freedom and to make a difference. There is nothing better than actually seeing the impact that the work of the ACLU has on the lives of real people. Massachusetts has been first in the nation in a lot of things, from the abolitionist movement to equal marriage. That doesn't happen by accident. That happens because people make a decision to be involved. There's a tremendous amount of civic engagement in Massachusetts, which I think in part it comes from having a town-based government as opposed to county-based. It also comes from the fact that we have a wonderful state constitution—written by John Adams. So we have an extraordinary opportunity to take the experiment in democracy and pilot new avenues and new ways of expanding the horizons of liberty. We now face dramatic challenges to civil liberties and civil rights, whether from new technology or age-old inequalities in this country. And here again, Massachusetts is perfectly situated because we have high-tech and bio as our economic base, so there are people who understand and are making policy decisions about how we're going to deploy the technology. We can choose to deploy technology in ways that expand our freedom or we can deploy it in ways that limit freedom. But now is the time for the laws to catch up with the technology. The ACLU is an incredibly effective platform for working on cutting-edge issues around freedom, and the ACLU of Massachusetts is particularly well positioned to do so because of the unique aspects of Massachusetts that give us an opportunity to actually seize opportunities for social change. We are pushing the envelope of freedom and I think that's key to the human evolution process. That's the point, from my point of view, of law.

What I love best about my job is the mission and the advocacy. It's both challenging and fun to think creatively about ways to broaden our freedom and make a difference.

Were you the first woman executive director of the ACLU of Massachusetts?

That's an interesting question. I'm the third executive director of the ACLU. According to the official history, and we just had our ninetieth birthday this year, there have been three directors: Luther MacNair was the first executive director, paid, the second was John Roberts, and then I came after John. But when researching the history and going back to some of the archives, we discovered that Margaret Shurcliff had the title of "executive secretary" before Luther McNair, probably in an unpaid position. It seems to me that we should count Margaret Shurcliff as the first leader of the ACLU of Massachusetts.

When you first took on your position, or even now, do you feel like a woman executive director or do you just feel like an executive director?

I've been thinking a lot about women in management and in authority positions. We're finally to the age where there are enough women in positions of authority that we can begin to think about the differences between men and women leaders. I think of myself as a leader first and foremost but I'm not sure if everybody else does. And what I've had to come to terms with is that some people perceive me first as a woman, second as a leader. When managing an organization or being a public advocate, you also have to confront other people's stuff.

Carol Rose with her daughter Lily at the ACLU's Day of Action to Restore Law and Justice in Washington, D.C., in June 2007.

IMAGE COURTESY OF CAROL ROSE, PHOTO BY TOM HARRINGTON

Do you feel like being a woman affects the way you do your job?

Of course. It's fundamental to who I am and it's hard to know what's part of my gender and what's a part of my personality. You can never discount gender, race or class—these are aspects of ourselves that influence who we are and how we do our work.

In what ways?

I think perhaps women often have less of an assumption of power. I think men naturally assume they're going to be in the leadership position and [have] power and they take it for granted, and I actually think women don't. I think we realize that it's unusual still to be in a position of authority. So I think there's a consciousness about it. At the same time I don't let it get in the way at all. I'm comfortable with power. And while I don't think about it consciously most of the time, I'm aware that gender informs my management style, my thinking, and my whole approach. But leadership is more than gender, race or class: there are linear men and linear women and there are process-oriented men and process-oriented women. The key to good management is being able to manage each individual as a human being and not as a stereotype. So gender does and doesn't inform how I lead.

You can never discount gender, race or class—these are aspects of ourselves that influence who we are and how we do our work.

How do you balance work and family?

I have three kids, so it's really hard, but also tremendously fun. I would encourage both women and men, to, first of all, take advantage of any part-time opportunities that are available to you when your kids are young because it will make you happier and more balanced. Two, I would say don't confuse work and life, and always understand that life is more important than work. It's important to remember that many women and men don't have choices and to remember how hard it must be for them to have to call in and use a sick day when really their kid is sick and they have to lie. Or when they run out of sick days and their kid is sick and they have to lose their job, or whatever. At the ACLU, I'm the boss so I set my own hours. So while I have a big job, I may be doing it at four in the morning and ten o'clock at night, but then I get to go to the parent-teacher conference. I've had the ability and the luxury of being in a position to create flexibility for myself and also to offer the same flexibility to my employees. I run an office where my employees understand that their lives are as important or more important than the ACLU. After all, what's the point of fighting for freedom if you don't have it in your own life? So it's about living the principle not only in our advocacy but in the way we treat one another as equals and as grownups.

I run a very flat organization, it's not hierarchical, it's very collaborative. There's an expectation that whether it's your kids or your parents or your sore back, if you can't work effectively today then you need to take the time off until you can work effectively. The other thing I would just say is there isn't a single right answer on the work-life balance. It's influenced by a person's economic and personal situation. I am fortunate because my work is integral to my life. I talk to my kids about my work and they understand the work that I do. I expect them to do their school work and pursue their passions, just as I pursue my work and passions. We all have our work to do in the world—it's part of what gives shape and meaning to our lives. My children know that they're the most important thing in the world to me, but they also understand that my work is a part of who I am, and I have never been apologetic about it. I've never said I wish I didn't have to work, I always say I'm so lucky to have a job I love, and I hope my children will find passions so that they can find work they also love.

Can you talk about a case or experience that you are particularly proud of? Whether or not you won.

Well, the work is never done. Still, I am tremendously proud of the ACLU's role in defending free speech and challenging government secret surveillance of people who engage in political dissent, such as environmental activists and antiwar protestors. I'm also proud of the ACLU's leadership in ensuring that equal marriage rights won in the courts were not later overturned by ballot initiative. Finally, I'm proud of our on-going work to address racial disparities in the criminal justice system and to ensure that all people have equal protection and due process protections under the law. But more often than not, I focus on what remains to be done more than on our past accomplishments.

What do you wish you'd known when you were a young lawyer?

Not to be in a hurry; to be patient and to be open and to see every day as a learning day, to know that every day you go to the office and certainly every day you go to the courtroom is a day that matters. There is no wasted day; each one is a gift.

What advice would you offer other young women who want to follow in your footsteps?

Make your own footsteps! There's no right or wrong way, there's no magic formula, so figure out what your footsteps feel like, figure out what stride you have, and then go for it. And do it without fear. Never let fear get in the way of anything you do. When I was going overseas, I called my parents and told them that I had an opportunity to go and live in the tribal areas of Pakistan, which is a pretty scary place even back then. I asked: "Do you think it's going to be too dangerous?" And my father said, "Well, you face two potential dangers. One is the danger that you could go and that something bad could happen to you. The other danger is that you pass up this opportunity and instead live a life based on fear and regret. Which danger scares you the most?" And so I went and of course I didn't die and I ended up having a transformative life experience. So I think maybe my advice to young women—and men—would be make sure you never let your life be ruled by fear.

Elected Office

Andrea J. Cabral

IMAGE SOURCE: SUFFOLK COUNTY SHERIFF WEBSITE

Andrea J. Cabral

Andrea Cabral was sworn in as Suffolk County's first woman sheriff in November 2002. She was appointed to the position by Acting Governor Jane Swift and was later elected to her first full term in 2004.

When I started as a prosecutor in the Middlesex County District Attorney's Office, there were still male judges who thought female prosecutors ought not to wear pants in the courtroom. This was 1987. I could never quite figure out how pantyhose and a hemline made me more acceptable as an attorney, especially when no one thought there was anything wrong with certain male attorneys who regularly shuffled into court looking like unmade beds.

> I could never quite figure out how pantyhose and a hemline made me more acceptable as an attorney.

It may seem like a small thing and just a snapshot in time—far ahead of when women were not accepted to law schools and could not sit on juries, and far behind Supreme Judicial Court Chief Justice Margaret Marshall—but it made a significant impact on me. It was really about the perception of what a female lawyer should look like in what was then a very male-dominated profession. It didn't take long before I saw the direct connection between those expectations and ones that required sexual assault and domestic violence victims to look, act, and dress a certain way and judged them very harshly when they didn't. Since then, the most satisfying times of my career have been those spent fighting those kinds of expectations, the ones that exist solely to reassure those who define their own place in society by the limits they place on others.

When you're African-American, female, a lawyer, and have a "strong" personality, you encounter those expectations all the time, but it can be tough to tell if certain behavior is based on your race, gender, profession, or just you. I always assume it's my personality and wait for evidence that it's more than that. (I'm kidding. Of course it's never my personality.)

Sometimes it's not so tough. In 1992, I was working in the Attorney General's Office in what was then called the Torts Division. Plaintiff's counsel and I spoke about our case by phone in advance of the pretrial conference date.

Sheriff Cabral speaking with gang violence prevention activists.

IMAGE COURTESY OF ANDREA CABRAL

On the day of the pretrial conference, I arrived at the courthouse before he did. I was one of four people in the courtroom. The other three people were sitting together and appeared to be a mother, father, and daughter. They were all casually dressed. I had a case file and was wearing a suit (with pants, obviously, but a suit nonetheless).

I watched as this attorney poked his head into the courtroom three different times, about five minutes apart, scanned the room and retreated to the hallway. After the third time, I waited a few minutes and went after him. I found him about to call my office looking for me.

I introduced myself. "Were you in there?" he said. "I didn't see you." I smiled and said, "Maybe something was blocking your view."

Martha Coakley

Upon her election in 2006, Martha Coakley became Massachusetts' first woman attorney general.

After growing up in North Adams reading *Nancy Drew* and watching *Perry Mason*, perhaps it's no coincidence that after a few years as a civil litigator, I charted a career as a prosecutor on the state and federal levels.

I am fortunate to have been afforded many incredible opportunities as an attorney—investigating and trying complex cases, fighting for victims of violent crimes as district attorney, and working in the Attorney General's Office on landmark cases that affect the environment, civil rights, consumer protection, and public safety. But there will always be one experience that has shaped my commitment to, and understanding of, what it means to be a voice for justice for those who need it most.

Martha Coakley being administered the oath of office for her second term as attorney general by Supreme Judicial Court Chief Justice Roderick L. Ireland in 2011.

IMAGE COURTESY OF MARTHA COAKLEY

When I was tapped in the early 1990s to head the Middlesex District Attorney's Child Abuse Unit, I was hesitant. I had prosecuted motor vehicle cases, white-collar crimes, organized crime, and homicides, but I had little experience working with either the victims or the constructs of a child-abuse case. When I began the work, although almost 90 percent of the cases involved sexual abuse allegations, we also began to see an increase of referrals of cases of physical abuse.

The cases were totally different, as the sex-abuse cases depended largely upon the reliability of the victim, while the physical abuse cases often involved nonverbal children and were primarily medical diagnostic cases. The same haunting questions reverberated in each type of case, however: Who could or would do this to a child? And how could we successfully prove it, beyond a reasonable doubt, to a jury?

The defendants in sex cases often had a similarly dreary profile, except when they didn't. The public perception of what a sex offender "looked like" was continuously disproved when the alleged perpetrator in many cases was mom's boyfriend, or Uncle Jim, or a beloved coach, or even dad. Proving the unthinkable was particularly difficult, but trying to get it right was

Attorney General Coakley testifying in support of anti-human trafficking legislation at a State House hearing on May 18, 2011.

IMAGE COURTESY OF THE MASSACHUSETTS ATTORNEY GENERAL'S OFFICE

essential. The stress and heartbreak of the cases always took its toll on police, victim advocates, prosecutors, and yes, on the judges and juries.

These cases demanded both an emotional investment and the ability to emotionally detach to ensure objectivity. Careful, difficult charging decisions had to be made in what we hoped would prove to be in the best interest of the child. Trying these cases was high-wire courtroom drama: Would our young victim be able to answer the toughest questions, and be credible to the jury, when the corroborating evidence often was thin? When we knew a child had been physically abused, could we pinpoint who had acted or permitted the action that caused a swollen brain and retinal hemorrhaging?

The ability to work in a multidisciplinary fashion—interviewing and understanding children's cognitive development; deciding with parents and social workers whether prosecution made sense for a child; working with dedicated physicians to arrive at diagnoses of the injuries—was critical.

It was probably the most difficult and yet most exhilarating job I will ever have.

I learned that no two cases are ever alike and that, unfortunately, every wrong does not always have a remedy. I learned that it was vital to determine the right result, and then work as hard as possible to achieve it. I learned to constantly seek to improve how we did things through better prevention and reporting systems. Most importantly, I learned that every single case mattered: to the victim, to his or her family, and to the alleged perpetrator. The process, and the result at the end of that process, would change lives no matter what.

I was lucky enough to also learn that advocacy takes many different forms…and that in public service our skills and abilities, not just our emotions, will drive a result.

I was lucky enough to also learn that advocacy takes many different forms, in the courtroom and out, and that in public service our skills and abilities, not just our emotions, will drive a result. Our office's work now in addressing human trafficking has been informed by my work from twenty years ago in the Child Abuse Unit.

From my time serving on the board of the Women's Bar, at the beginning of my career and since, I feel extremely lucky to have been able to tackle significant challenges as an advocate for the public interest. But at the end of my career, whenever that may be, I'll know that one of the most difficult and yet most rewarding tasks was giving a voice to child victims in a justice system that was just beginning to hear them.

Cynthia Stone Creem

Cynthia Stone Creem was first elected senator for the First Middlesex and Norfolk District in 1998.

As a young girl growing up in Brookline, I always wanted to be an attorney. You could say that I inherited this desire from my parents, who were both lawyers. And, since many of their friends and colleagues were attorneys as well, our home was often full of lively discussions! However, Boston's legal community was quite different when I graduated from BU's School of Management and Boston University Law School in 1967. In fact, before being admitted to the bar, I was summoned to appear before the Board of Bar Overseers. With great trepidation, I made an effort to hide my fifth month of pregnancy under my coat when I appeared before this august group of men. They only had one question concerning my fitness for entrance to the bar: "Did I expect to have a family?" Dumbfounded, I replied, "Eventually, but not in the next two months." As shocking as this would be for women attorneys today, this accepted practice was mild compared to when my mother graduated law school in 1937, one of only five women in her BU Law school class.

I joined my parents' law firm, now Stone, Stone and Creem, specializing in domestic relations law, where my sister also practices today. And, I am proud that both my son and daughter have carried on the tradition by becoming attorneys themselves—even though as a young boy, when asked if he would become a lawyer, my son vehemently demurred, insisting, "Yuck, the law is for girls!"

My interest in politics began when I accompanied my father to a Democratic Convention. He had already run—unsuccessfully—for state representative. From an early age, he nourished my commitment to progressive values, civil liberties, and social justice, so that I, too, wanted to participate in public life. After first serving as a Newton alderman, including time as chair, in 1994 I was elected to the Governor's Council, which oversees judicial appointments in our state. Then, in 1998, I became a state senator, representing Brookline, Newton, and part of Wellesley.

I have been fortunate in law and in the Senate to work on concerns that are important to me and to my constituents. I have been privileged to work on larger issues, such as those that affect civil rights, education, and criminal justice, but I am particularly gratified when I can advocate for those issues that have a more personal impact on families and communities.

For example, when my community of Brookline was shocked by the fatal shootings that occurred at two local reproductive

Cynthia Stone Creem pictured in 2010 in the Senate chambers with her grandchildren.

IMAGE COURTESY OF CYNTHIA STONE CREEM

▲

Senator Creem speaking in her district with former Governor Michael Dukakis and supporters.

IMAGE COURTESY OF CYNTHIA STONE CREEM

health clinics, I was pleased to offer some measure of comfort by working to craft legislation to protect workers at women's health clinics throughout the state. Another time, I was approached by a young girl in my district with severe food allergies who was tired of being told she could not be accommodated at restaurants; it was gratifying to finally see signed into law my food allergy awareness legislation. And when my own daughter revealed to me that she had learned too late after the birth of my first grandchild about an option to bank umbilical cord blood, it led me to a deeper discussion about stem cell research and ultimately to the passage of legislation encouraging and supporting stem cell research here in Massachusetts.

Early in my Senate career, then-Senate President Tom Birmingham advised me to continue practicing law because he believed it would help me bring a broader perspective to my role as a legislator. I agree. Legislators who can bring their personal experiences from business, the legal system, and other areas of their lives are able to add examples and substance to debates, and I think this is particularly true for women legislators.

As an attorney and state senator, I see daily the impact that economic, health, educational, and social policy decisions have on individuals. And I often see divergent outcomes, often due to the past history of discrimination, and to contemporary cultural and political assumptions that continue to negatively impact opportunities for women. I believe that while much progress has been made, gender diversity in public office, in appointed positions, and in the legal profession is still insufficient to provide diverse and encompassing representation.

Over 20,000 men have served in the [Massachusetts] legislature in 230 years, and only 173 women.

The Massachusetts General Court is said to be the oldest continuously-operating legislative body in the United States. Yet, I was the twenty-first woman elected to the state Senate. Over 20,000 men have served in the legislature in 230 years, and only 173 women. Individually and collectively, women can bring unique perspectives to improve legislation and social policy. We must work to assure that the next generation improves on our progress in including these voices.

Elizabeth D. Scheibel

Elizabeth Scheibel was first appointed Northwestern District Attorney by Governor William Weld in 1993. She is the first woman to have served as a district attorney in Massachusetts.

In January 2011, I retired after thirty years of public service as a prosecutor—the years seemed to pass in the blink of an eye. Where had the time gone? I can remember my early days as a lawyer, fresh out of law school, with not a clue about what was in store for me. Now, after spending thirty years as a prosecutor, the last eighteen years as Northwestern District Attorney, it's exciting to wonder, again, what might be in store for me.

I dreamed of becoming a doctor, astronaut, FBI agent, and veterinarian, to name a few—but not a lawyer.

I never dreamed of being a lawyer. I dreamed of becoming a doctor, astronaut, FBI agent, and veterinarian, to name a few—but not a lawyer. I did not come from a family of lawyers, nor did I argue a lot as a child. I was, however, competitive and I did have a strong moral compass, or so my mother says. I stood up for others, even as a young child.

At Mount Holyoke College, I started out in pre-med, but, as is so often the case, I took a course that changed my life. It was an animal behavior course and I knew then that I had found my dream career. I changed my major, I studied animals—I even had an internship at the National Zoo studying marmoset monkeys. I alternated between wanting to go to veterinary and graduate school to study primates. A funny thing happened on the way to that dream career—I met a man, Paul Boudreau, who would become my future husband.

My dream career, as I thought I knew it, went out the window. Paul had just passed the Massachusetts bar and begun to practice law. As I've often said, the more I fell in love with him, the more I fell in love with the law! At the time, the closest veterinary school was too far away, while the closest graduate school for primates was in the South. I decided to apply to law school and was admitted to Western New England College School of Law, not coincidentally, a thirty-minute commute from my future husband.

I finished law school, took the Massachusetts bar and, on the day I learned I had passed the bar, my father learned that his cancer had spread. Later, I learned that he refused to let my mother tell me because he didn't want to ruin my day. He lived to see me begin work as an assistant district attorney in Hampden County, but he died eight months later, less than two months before I married Paul.

To say that I loved every minute of my career would be an exaggeration, but I did love most of it—particularly working with victims and survivors. I met the most extraordinary people who had gone through unimaginable horror and tragedy. Despite their personal suffering and loss, they continued to, as a

Elizabeth D. Scheibel

IMAGE COURTESY OF PETERSIMON.COM

friend used to say, "walk in the world, with their heads held high." They were, and continue to be, my inspiration.

I never planned to be district attorney; I never planned my career at all. Opportunity presented itself and I took advantage of it—if not with certitude, at least with determination. In 1993, I was appointed Northwestern District Attorney by Governor Bill Weld and became the first woman district attorney in Massachusetts. I was honored and pleased to receive the appointment. I realize that the stars were aligned, but I had also worked hard as an assistant district attorney in Hampden County for eight years from 1980 to 1988 (working my way up from District to Superior Court), and then as first assistant district attorney for the Northwestern District from 1988 to 1993.

After becoming district attorney, I was often mentioned as a role model for women. If true, I hope it was because I had worked hard to become an experienced and effective trial attorney—an advocate for murder victims, abused children, elders, domestic violence victims, and victims with disabilities. I was fortunate to run for office four times without opposition. I saw myself as an experienced prosecutor, not a politician. As such, I never felt the pressure to "put my finger up to see which way the wind was blowing." I established policies and implemented programs that I felt could make a real difference in the lives of children, elders, domestic violence victims, persons with disabilities, and many others in communities in my district and beyond.

At first, it was challenging to be the only woman district attorney in the Commonwealth and one of a small group around the country. Honestly, there were times I was treated differently because of my gender. The Northwestern district covers a large geographic area and, while it contains several cities, the majority is suburban and rural; its citizens are diverse. I had to earn my stripes with citizens who didn't know me and members of the law enforcement community that were skeptical about whether a woman could do what had always been a "man's job." To this day, I don't believe those attitudes reflected entrenched animosity but, rather, comfort levels and cultural values. The reality I've experienced is that women have to "work it" in our male-dominated world; how each woman does that is unique to her own personality and skill set. My approach was to continue to work hard, be a consensus builder, demonstrate loyalty to peers, and, when appropriate, relax and have fun with them. I believe that my peers respected and trusted me as an equal and I made lifelong friends.

I had to earn my stripes with citizens who didn't know me and members of the law enforcement community that were skeptical about whether a woman could do what had always been a "man's" job.

I had the great fortune to develop and implement communitywide education and outreach programs, as well as participate in statewide and national crime prevention initiatives. Those included our model efforts to address abuse and neglect against persons with disabilities, create effective domestic violence and teen dating violence prevention programs, and antibullying efforts. In addition, I had the extraordinary opportunity to travel to Japan with a domestic violence murder survivor to help educate members of her native country on domestic violence and its devastating effects.

By the end of my third term, I had decided that my fourth term would be my last, having served thirty years as a prosecutor. Candidly, I thought that my last year would be a quiet one, a time to slowly transition out of the 24/7 job of district attorney. However, it was anything but a quiet year. It started with a number of very high-profile cases, including the suicide of fifteen-year-old Phoebe Prince, who killed herself after having been relentlessly bullied. The resulting investigation into her death uncovered evidence of individual and institutional culpability of varying degrees. After a great deal of deliberation and review, charges were sought in connection with the acts of bullying. As it turned out, the case touched a nerve. It garnered national and international media attention and, I believe, helped provide a platform for a discussion of many important issues around bullying, including the national debate surrounding youth suicide, development of meaningful school policies, and the creation of legislation mandating training and responsiveness by authorities.

Serving as Northwestern District Attorney was a privilege. I had the opportunity to bring the office into the twenty-first century by using a multidisciplinary approach in reaching out to community stakeholders to address crime, create specialized units for the prosecution of cases involving victims with disabilities and elder and child victims, develop prevention and diversion programs for juveniles, and to work with law enforcement to develop best practices. Most importantly, I tried to instill in my staff recognition of the importance of integrity, compassion, and respect when representing the office.

Serving as Northwestern District Attorney was a privilege.

To every season there is an end. Serving as district attorney was all encompassing. I look forward to developing professionally in other areas, while continuing my work on behalf of our most vulnerable citizens. Most importantly, I look forward to spending more time with friends and family, particularly my husband of thirty years.

NOTES

1 Women's Bar Association of Massachusetts, *Where are We Now? A Report on the Occupational Status of Women Attorneys in Massachusetts* (2009).

2 Working Group on Student Experiences, *Study on Women's Experiences at Harvard Law School* 7 (Feb. 2004); Gita Z. Wilder, *Women in the Profession: Findings from the First Wave of the After the JD Study* 4, 28–29 (NALP Foundation 2007).

3 Wilder, *Women in the Profession: Findings from the First Wave of the After the JD Study* at 3, 7–8.

4 Marilyn Johnson & Kathy Stanwick, "Profile of Women Holding Office," Center for American Women and Politics, Eagleton Institute of Politics at Rutgers, xxviii (Feb. 1976).

5 Kira Sanbonmatsu, Susan J. Carroll & Debbie Walsh, *Poised to Run, Women's Pathways to the State Legislatures* 19–20 (Center for American Women and Politics, Eagleton Institute of Politics at Rutgers 2009).

6 *Women State Legislators: Past, Present and Future* 1–2, 9–11 (Center for American Women and Politics, Eagleton Institute of Politics at Rutgers 2001).

7 *Women State Legislators: Past, Present and Future* at 1–2, 9–11.

8 The observations of Harvard Law School alumnae speaking with advisors at the school's Bernard Koteen Office of Public Interest Advising.

9 Mona Harrington & Helen Hsi, *Women Lawyers and Obstacles to Leadership: A Report of MIT Workplace Center Surveys on Comparative Career Decisions and Attrition Rates of Women and Men in Massachusetts Law Firms* 5, 12–14 (MIT Workplace Center Spring 2007).

Challenging the Status Quo

Rape and Sexual Assault

Susan M. Finegan
Christine C. Gannon

Background

The crime of rape in the United States has its origins in English common law, which defined the offense as the "carnal knowledge of a woman forcibly and against her will."[1] Under the common law, women were the property of their fathers, and upon marriage, became the property of their husbands. The legal doctrine known as "coverture" declared a husband and wife one entity under the law, affording the husband the right of control while depriving the wife of any separate legal identity.[2] As a result, the crime of rape operated within this legal framework. Rape could be committed only by male perpetrators against female victims, and married men were exempt from rape charges against their wives entirely.[3] Indeed, rape itself was seen as a crime of theft—the unlawful deprivation of property from a husband or father—so criminal sanctions focused more on punishing the underlying thievery as opposed to the harm inflicted on the female victim.[4]

The United States eventually adopted the common-law definition of rape, which imposed a number of requirements for conviction that significantly distinguished the offense from other violent crimes. Most states, for example, required corroboration of a woman's claim. Fearful of convicting a defendant solely on the testimony of one woman, many courts required prosecutors to produce additional evidence, such as an eyewitness or physical injury, to support the victim's allegation.[5] Additionally, the law placed the burden of proving nonconsent on the female victim, and many states required that she resist a man's sexual advances to her utmost physical ability; only then would she be able to prove that the act was indeed against her will.[6] During rape trials, attorneys could introduce evidence about a victim's sexual history, and the victim's sexual reputation was frequently used to show a predisposition to consent as well as an overall lack of credibility.[7] It was therefore extremely difficult for prosecutors to secure rape convictions under the traditional common-law framework.

Susan M. Finegan is a litigation partner at Mintz, Levin, Cohn, Ferris, Glovsky and Popeo, P.C., currently serving as the firm's pro bono partner and chair of the Pro Bono Committee. From 2003–2006 she served as legal director of the Victim Rights Law Center.

IMAGE COURTESY OF MINTZ, LEVIN, COHN, FERRIS, GLOVSKY AND POPEO, P.C.

Christine C. Gannon is an associate at Ross Silverman LLP, where she practices business immigration law. Previously, she completed a year-long fellowship with the Victim Rights Law Center, representing rape and sexual assault survivors in a variety of civil legal settings.

IMAGE COURTESY OF CHRISTINE C. GANNON

By the 1960s and 1970s, feminist advocacy groups around the United States began challenging traditional rape laws and lobbying their legislatures for reform. Rape law reformists had two primary goals: symbolically, they sought to eliminate the patriarchal views underlying traditional rape laws in the name of women's sexual autonomy; and practically, they sought to increase reporting rates and secure more rape convictions within the criminal justice system.[8] By the 1980s, due in large part to this national reform movement, all fifty states and the District of Columbia had amended their rape laws to better reflect the modern social realities of sexual assault. Advocacy efforts prevailed in Massachusetts, and in 1974 the state legislature comprehensively redrafted its rape statute to restructure the crime and expand the scope of its protection.[9]

This statutory reform in Massachusetts coincided with an increase in women entering the legal profession. Female attorneys played an active role in applying the new sexual assault law and seeking further necessary changes. The following sections highlight some of the substantive legal developments in Massachusetts sexual assault law through the lens of the women attorneys who were on the forefront of these developments; many of whom continue to work for the betterment of victims in the Commonwealth today.

Criminal Legal Developments

Rape-Shield Statute

Once the Massachusetts legislature had redrafted and expanded the definition of rape, it turned its attention to the conduct of rape trials themselves; specifically, to the type of evidence that could be used against victims in court. Under the common law, evidence of the victim's sexual reputation in the community was admissible in court.[10] This was significant, as evidence of a victim's unchaste character could be used by a jury to evaluate whether or not the victim consented to the sexual act in question. The admissibility of reputation evidence thus reflected the common view that a chaste woman was more likely to have been raped, while an unchaste woman was more likely to have consented and lied about it at a later date.[11] The consequences of this antiquated rule were obvious and understandable: it tended to make victims more hesitant to come forward, as their sexual histories would be displayed in open court.

In 1977, the Massachusetts legislature responded to these concerns and enacted the Commonwealth's "rape-shield" statute.[12] The new law specifically prohibited the admission of a victim's sexual reputation in court and, in doing so, prevented defense counsel, except in limited circumstances, from eliciting evidence of a victim's sexual promiscuity as part of a general credibility attack.[13] The new rape-shield statute thus created an additional layer of protection for victims who chose to report to law enforcement, as their sexual reputation was no longer at issue during trial. The rape-shield statute did not, however, create an absolute bar to the admission of evidence pertaining to a victim's sexual history. To balance the victim's right to privacy with the defendant's right to a fair trial, the statute allowed evidence of the victim's past sexual history with the defendant and allowed evidence of the victim's past sexual conduct when it was alleged to be the cause of any physical feature or condition of the victim.[14]

The rape-shield statute sought to improve the treatment of women victims within the criminal justice system—a purpose one of the bill's sponsors, former State Representative Lois G. Pines, cared adamantly about. A 1960 graduate of Barnard College, Pines obtained her law degree from the University of Cincinnati School of Law in 1963. She had transferred to Cincinnati from Boston University School of Law due to her husband's stint in the U.S. Air Force, and upon enrollment, became the only female in her law-school class. She joined the Massachusetts legislature in 1972 as one of eight women in the 240-member House of Representatives. Having experienced gender discrimination in her own life, Pines began her political career with the firm agenda of advancing the equality of women in the Commonwealth. "After law school, I had worked as tax and corporate counsel at a major Boston corporation, at which I was the only female corporate officer," she recalls.[15] "The firm decided to issue stock options to its officers—of which I was one—and everyone received that benefit except for me. I didn't find out until after the fact."[16] Without an existing maternity leave option, Pines was also forced to take sick leave when she had her second child and returned to work only three weeks after giving birth. "I was very alert to the limitations imposed on women and the variety of obstacles we had to overcome," she says.[17] Motivated by her own experiences and the desire to improve the future for her daughter, Pines ran for office and was elected to the House of Representatives in 1972. There, she worked tirelessly on the Massachusetts Equal Rights Amendment and the Massachusetts Equal Credit Opportunity Act, which afforded women the right to obtain credit in their own names without the guarantee of their husbands. She was a founding member of the National Organization of Women in Boston and the Massachusetts Women's Political Caucus. "My goal," she says, "was to advance the opportunities for women."[18]

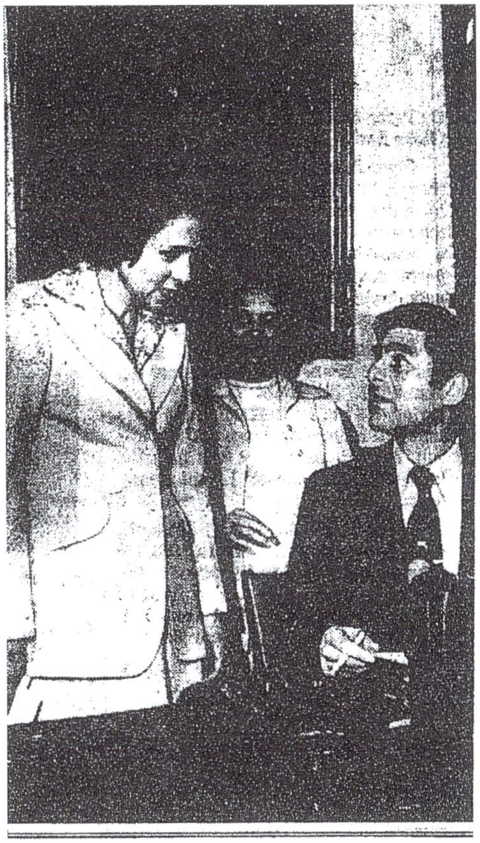

SIGNING CEREMONY — Gov. Dukakis has a word with Rep. Lois Pines of Newton at State House ceremony at which Dukakis signed rape testimony bill into law. Standing behind the governor is Rep. Marie Howe of Somerville. Measure disallows introduction of a rape victim's sexual history as testimony in trial of her alleged assailant. (Globe photo by Phil Preston)

An April 20, 1977, Boston Globe *photo of Representative Lois Pines and Governor Michael Dukakis at the rape-shield statute signing.*

IMAGE SOURCE: *BOSTON GLOBE* ONLINE ARCHIVES

The rape-shield legislation was yet another way for Pines to advocate for women's equality in the Commonwealth. "I felt very strongly that if you're going to court to face your attacker, you should not be undermined, and he should not be able to walk away, simply because you had had previous sexual relationships. That was not right."[19] The initial version of the rape-shield law prohibited the allowance of a rape victim's sexual history in its entirety, but the ultimate statute, which allowed evidence of the victim's past sexual history with the defendant, was the result of fervent negotiation. "I remember fighting extremely hard against efforts to water the statute down," Pines recalls.[20] "It essentially became a guys versus gals debate, where people would say, 'she wanted it, and now you're going to put me in jail?' There was a fear by the defense bar that the law would result in people being inappropriately charged with rape."[21] While the rape-shield law was ultimately an effort of compromise, Pines is proud of its overall impact. "The rape-shield law was one of many bills set on equalizing the status of women in Massachusetts. I am happy and proud to be part of an effort to move towards a set of laws where women were treated fairly."[22]

Marital Rape

A few years later, through the efforts of then-rookie prosecutor Diane Kottmyer, another longstanding barrier fell—that of the prohibition against criminalizing marital rape. For centuries, Massachusetts adhered to the principle that a man, as a matter of law, could not rape his wife.[23] This idea, frequently referred to as the "common law spousal exemption," can best be understood in light of other laws governing the legal status of married women at the time. Wives were the property of their husbands, so husbands could exercise ownership as they deemed appropriate; wives and husbands were one entity under the law, so wives relinquished any individual rights upon marriage; and wives, by entering into a marriage contract, agreed to sexual intercourse in perpetuity, with no ability to withdraw consent after taking their marriage vows.[24] Although the Supreme Judicial Court had nevertheless ruled in 1871 that a husband had no right to beat his wife,[25] over a century would pass before the same court reconsidered the issue of whether a husband had the right to engage in sexual relations with his wife against her will.

In 1979, Kottmyer joined the Essex County District Attorney's Office as a first-year prosecutor. A former civil litigation associate at the Boston firm currently known as Bingham McCutchen, Kottmyer entered the public sector with a desire to work on legal issues predominantly affecting women, having been one of the founders of the Women's Bar Association the year before. Her new position at the District Attorney's Office gave her that very opportunity, as she was hired to create and manage the first Sexual Assault Unit in Essex County, modeled after the state's first such unit in Norfolk County. A couple of months into her new post, Kottmyer received a call from a victim whose estranged husband had broken into her home, brutally attacked her, and raped her. The woman had filed a complaint for rape in the local court, but had been told by the clerk that she could only press for lesser charges because she was married to her assailant. Kottmyer met with the woman, researched the applicable law (complicated because there was little, if any, U.S. precedent, only English common law), and decided to move forward with the case—one of the first marital rape prosecutions in the country. During her first year at the DA's office, Kottmyer successfully fought off the defendant's motion to dismiss and won the rape case in front of a jury. After the defendant appealed his conviction, Kottmyer wrote the appellate brief and appeared before the Supreme Judicial Court in *Commonwealth v. Chretien*[26] to argue that marriage was not a defense to rape.

In *Chretien*, the court specifically adopted Kottmyer's arguments and ruled that the 1974 statutory amendments eliminated the common law spousal exemption in Massachusetts.[27] Marriage, therefore, was no longer a bar to a prosecution or conviction of rape. In reaching its decision, the court acknowledged the legislature's intent to expand the scope of protection to a larger group of victims.[28] The court also found support in the restraining order statute, G.L. c. 209A, recently enacted in 1978.[29] That law provided a variety of civil legal remedies for victims of abuse; it defined "abuse" as encompassing involuntary sexual relations between spouses and specified that proceedings under the statute would not prevent other civil or criminal remedies in the future. In light of these considerations, the court ruled that the legislature intended to criminalize sexual assault within marriage, thereby eliminating the spousal exemption altogether. Within her first few years as a criminal prosecutor, Diane Kottmyer had altered the landscape of rape law in Massachusetts. Reflecting back on the *Chretien* case, she notes that "[a]s with most street crimes, the prosecution of sexual assault cases is reactive. It is not often that a prosecution requiring a change in existing law presents itself with such strong facts and a credible victim."[30]

Within her first few years as a criminal prosecutor, Diane Kottmyer had altered the landscape of rape law in Massachusetts.

While the *Chretien* case represented a significant victory in Massachusetts rape law, Kottmyer acknowledges the challenges she faced in bringing the case forward. "There was negative feedback," she says, recalling one conversation with a former male colleague who could not understand why she would move forward with a marital rape charge.[31] "For some people, the thought of violence against women is so repulsive that they cannot accept that other people engage in activities like the defendant in *Chretien*. But, I do think my colleague believed that, no matter what the facts, prosecutors should not be invading the sexual relationship between spouses; and he was not alone in that belief."[32] Despite these challenges, Kottmyer never doubted her decision to prosecute the defendant. The facts of the case were chilling and the victim "so sympathetic."[33]

Fresh Complaint and First Complaint Doctrines

Under traditional common law, rape victims were required to raise a "hue and cry" and promptly complain of an assault to a third party in order for a criminal prosecution to move forward. This requirement stemmed from society's belief that a "true" rape victim would immediately cry out for help after an attack.[34] Unfortunately, this narrow view did not reflect the realities of sexual assault; most victims know their assailants, and the trauma associated with the assault often results in feelings of embarrassment, shock, and an overall loss of privacy. Victims may not immediately report due to fears of retaliation from the perpetrator or disbelief from their communities, and many are reluctant to relive their experience by discussing the intimate details of the assault with strangers. Under the common law, victims who delayed reporting were effectively precluded from seeking relief through the criminal justice system.

Massachusetts never expressly required a timely complaint for a criminal prosecution, but it did acknowledge that a report immediately following a sexual assault would make a claim more believable in the eyes of a jury.[35] Massachusetts therefore allowed evidence of a victim's complaint to be introduced at trial so long as the report was "freshly" made after the assault.[36] This rule, commonly referred to as the fresh complaint doctrine, allowed the prosecution to call as witnesses the persons to whom the victim freshly complained, and the witnesses could then tell the jury about the details of the complaint itself.[37] Its purpose was to bolster the credibility of the victim and counter the possibility that a jury may disbelieve her if it did not hear evidence that she had in fact made a prompt report.[38]

The fresh complaint doctrine was thus a useful tool in sexual assault prosecutions that were uniquely difficult to prove. Most cases did not involve weapons or actual physical wounds; most did not have eyewitnesses; and many involved conduct so appalling that juries were hesitant to accept them as humanly possible.[39] As these cases largely came down to the victim's word against the defendant's, the victim's credibility remained paramount, and evidence that she promptly reported to others could make her experience more believable to a jury.

By the early 1990s, however, the Supreme Judicial Court began to question the viability of the fresh complaint rule.[40] Its primary concern stemmed from the risk that a jury, after hearing multiple fresh complaint witnesses, may use the testimony to evaluate the truth of the complaint itself.[41] In addition, the court was troubled by the outmoded basis for the doctrine, as it reinforced the idea that a victim who immediately complained was more likely to have been assaulted, while a victim who delayed was more likely to have consented.[42] In 1991, the chief justice of the Supreme Judicial Court invited parties to argue the validity of the fresh complaint doctrine in its entirety, and an eager prosecutor soon accepted the challenge in Middlesex County.[43]

The case was assigned to Marguerite T. Grant, then a first-year assistant district attorney in the Middlesex appellate unit. A former civil litigator at the Boston firm Hill and Barlow, Grant had recently entered the public sector with a desire to make a difference in the lives of others. The case of *Commonwealth v. Licata*[44] gave her that chance, as this first assignment called on her to argue that a major doctrine in sexual assault law should not be eliminated. In preparation for the case, Grant read social science articles about common reactions to rape and studied the variety of emotions victims may feel in the aftermath of a sexual assault. "I thought it was important to bring this perspective to the Court, in addition to the law itself," she says, adding that she was "probably the most prepared for this case than any in [my] career."[45] Her efforts prevailed, and the court unanimously voted to keep the fresh complaint doctrine. The court remained troubled by the fact that the doctrine perpetuated the inaccurate assumption that a "true" victim would promptly report, but it acknowledged that juries still held this presumption. By upholding the fresh complaint doctrine, the court preserved a viable tool for victims who did in fact report to counter a jury's skepticism that may arise in its absence.

"It's an amazing experience to be able to change the law statewide, and the feeling of influencing the law is incredible."

—Marguerite Grant

Looking back years later, Grant describes the experience as "intoxicating," as she had the opportunity to respond to the concerns of the chief justice of the Supreme Judicial Court by insisting that the fresh complaint doctrine was vital to the plight of sexual assault survivors.[46] "After [the *Licata*] case, I became addicted to sexual assault appellate work," she says.[47] Noting that such appeals are particularly challenging due to the technical evidentiary issues involved, she nevertheless finds the work extremely rewarding. "It's an amazing experience to be able to change the law statewide, and the feeling of influencing the law is incredible."[48] In addition to effecting changes in the law, Grant's work also gives her an opportunity to work with the victims whose cases she argues on appeal. "It is often difficult to explain the appellate process to victims, and to explain how our system is very focused on defendants' rights," she says.[49] "However, the way I see it, there is a long line of victims helping each other, unwittingly, through their individual cases. Appeals are painful, but it can be beneficial to think that one victim's pain can be used to help so many others in the future."[50]

The fresh complaint doctrine remained in place for another thirteen years. In 2005, however, the Supreme Judicial Court again revisited the doctrine and decided the landmark case of *Commonwealth v. King*.[51] News that the Supreme Judicial Court was reconsidering the fresh complaint doctrine eventually reached Djuna E. Perkins, a civil litigator at the Boston firm Brody, Hardoon, Perkins and Kesten. Prior to joining Brody Hardoon, Perkins had served as chief of the Suffolk County District Attorney's Domestic Violence Unit, where she prosecuted both domestic violence and sexual assault cases. Drawn to the compelling nature of the cases at the district attorney's office, Perkins regularly worked with economically vulnerable women who depended on the legal system to escape the violence in their personal lives. When she heard that the Supreme Judicial Court again cast doubt on the fresh complaint rule, she thought: "They couldn't be more wrong."[52] As a prosecutor, she had seen that "juries, judges, and court personnel were full of ridiculous biases concerning rape and sexual assault," including the belief that a "true" victim would promptly report her attack.[53] As a result, she set to work with the Massachusetts domestic violence and sexual assault coalition, Jane Doe, Inc., and submitted an amicus brief for the *King* case, arguing that the fresh complaint doctrine should remain in place to support sexual assault victims during criminal trials. Perkins attended the oral argument at the Supreme Judicial Court, which she described as "incredibly rewarding."[54] "There were at least three times when a justice asked, 'But what about this idea in the Jane Doe brief?'"[55]

Ultimately, the court voted to change the fresh complaint rule to the first complaint rule and held that the prosecution may call as a witness only the first person the victim told about the assault.[56] The elimination of the "fresh" requirement was significant, as victims who delayed reporting were now able to present a corroborating witness in court, regardless of when the complaint was made.[57] While the court itself rejected the underlying assumption that a victim who reports is more credible than a victim who remains silent, it again acknowledged that many jurors may still harbor that misconception. As most sexual assault cases turned on the victim's credibility, the court concluded that a first complaint witness was a necessary tool for prosecutors to "counterbalance or address inaccurate assumptions regarding stereotypes about delayed reporting of a sexual assault or about sexual assault victims in general."[58] In ruling to preserve the essence of the doctrine, the court adopted many of Perkins' arguments against abolishing the rule in its entirety. Perkins notes that "[t]he Court acknowledged that rape myths do exist, and acknowledged the importance of counteracting those myths in the courtroom."[59] Looking back on the *King* case, Perkins describes the time as "one of those quintessential experiences you dream of in law school; most times, as a litigator, it feels like you don't have much control. Here, I felt like I had truly made an impact."[60]

While the elimination of the "freshness" requirement has allowed prosecutors to present a corroborating witness regardless of the complaint's timeframe, it has also restricted their ability to call multiple witnesses, as they are limited to the first person only. Assistant district attorneys have noted that in practice, the doctrine may actually preclude them from presenting their case in a logical way, as a victim's disclosure to the first person may be minimal, while her disclosure to a second person may contain more detail.[61] The *King* decision has also sparked extensive litigation in the appellate courts, as issues have arisen over what constitutes a full disclosure of a sexual assault and what happens when the first person told is actually adverse to the victim.[62] Ultimately, the first complaint doctrine remains a tool for prosecutors to corroborate a victim's story so a jury isn't left asking, "Why didn't she tell anyone?"[63]

The Role of the Prosecutor

Women attorneys in Massachusetts thus played a crucial role in developing the criminal law; working to expand the definition of sexual assault, enact the rape-shield statute, eliminate the spousal exemption, and permit the continued admission of first and fresh-complaint testimony. In addition to these broad-based changes, many female prosecutors have worked within the criminal justice system and have made a difference in the lives of the individual victims themselves on a case-by-case basis. In 1977, under the leadership of District Attorney Bill Delahunt, the Norfolk County District Attorney's Office established the first sexual assault unit in Massachusetts—the second of its kind in the nation. Delahunt transferred Sydney Hanlon, one of two female prosecutors in the District Attorney's Office, from her post as a first-year prosecutor in the Brookline District Court to the newly-created sexual assault unit. Once the unit was up and running, the cases followed, and soon Hanlon was swamped with prosecutions. Looking back, she notes that "[t]here were no training courses for this work" at the time.[64] To the extent there was training or mentorship, she was providing it to others in an informal way.

"Some members of the defense bar were uncomfortable with some women prosecutors,.... And some of the police weren't very accepting of women prosecuting their cases."

—Hon. Diane Kottmyer

Rookie prosecutor Diane Kottmyer benefited from Hanlon's guidance. In 1979, newly-elected Essex District Attorney Kevin Burke followed Norfolk County's lead and established a specialized sexual assault unit, hiring Kottmyer to oversee it. Kottmyer did not have any experience with criminal prosecutions, but, armed with the desire for trial work and an interest in addressing legal matters that primarily affected women, she enthusiastically accepted the position. "I grew up in Lawrence, so it was the fulfillment of a dream to be a D.A. in Essex County," she says.[65] Kottmyer's arrival made her the second female prosecutor in the county, joining fellow Assistant District Attorney Jane Haggerty (now a Superior Court judge). "Some members of the defense bar were uncomfortable with women prosecutors," she recalls.[66] "And some of the police weren't very accepting of women prosecuting their cases."[67] As a new assistant district attorney, Kottmyer worked particularly hard to learn the intricacies of trying sexual assault crimes. Echoing Hanlon's sentiments, she notes, "There were no programs or continuing legal education seminars on sexual assault back then."[68] She eventually met Hanlon, whom she describes as "extremely helpful," and from whom she learned the ropes of prosecuting sexual assault cases in Massachusetts.[69] Over many dinners at local restaurants, Hanlon taught Kottmyer what she knew about sexual assault prosecutions, even as the restaurant patrons seated around them slowly moved away from their table because of the graphic nature of their conversations.[70]

Now a Superior Court justice in Middlesex County, Kottmyer has presided over many sexual assault cases during her time on the bench. In this role, she has noticed a significant change in jury perceptions since her time as a prosecutor. "When I was trying these cases, there was a certain conventional wisdom about differences between male and female jurors in their approach to rape cases," she says.[71] "In cases in which the alleged victim dressed in a manner thought to be provocative or acted in a way that polite society didn't approve of, all jurors, but particularly women, tended to believe that she was at fault; in the vernacular, that she 'had asked for it.'"[72] As a prosecutor, Kottmyer thus preferred male jurors to females, as, at the time, "they were thought to be more sophisticated and to better understand the acceptable boundaries of male behavior."[73] Additionally, her current role as a judge has exposed her to the truly pervasive nature of sexual assault itself. "I've been involved in a number of voir-dire hearings where we ask potential jurors if they or anyone in their families has been a victim of sexual assault. We receive a large number of positive responses."[74] Noting this frequency, Kottmyer recognizes a shift from her days as a prosecutor, observing that people are now more aware of and open to communicating about sexual assault.[75]

While she found her time as a prosecutor very rewarding, Kottmyer acknowledges the many obstacles she faced, recalling one Essex County police department that routinely required women who reported a rape to take a lie-detector test before it would investigate the complaint. She was also shocked to learn that half of her caseload involved children. "That definitely takes a toll on you after a while," she says.[76] "With adult victims, one can explain the legal process, the concept of constitutional rights, and they understand. It is very difficult for a prosecutor to explain to young children the reason why they have to testify in court in front of the defendant and be cross-examined. They tend to think it isn't fair and that if people believed them, they would not have to testify."[77]

Assistant District Attorney Jane Mulqueen agrees with this perception, adding that "child abuse cases are particularly difficult because you never know what a child is going to say or do...you can prepare so much, but ultimately just hope for the best."[78] Mulqueen knows well the challenges of trying child sexual abuse cases, having spent over seventeen years at the Northwestern District Attorney's Office as a child abuse prosecutor. Despite the difficult nature of the work, Mulqueen remains driven. "[I]t's very rewarding to be a champion for a child who[m] no one else believed," she says.[79] In addition to prosecuting child abuse cases, she has also played a leadership role in the development of new overall approaches to support child victims throughout the criminal process. Working with her colleague, former District Attorney Elizabeth Scheibel, and others, Mulqueen helped develop one of the first District Attorney-based Child Advocacy Centers in Massachusetts, creating a successful multidisciplinary approach to the investigation and prosecution of child sexual assault. Such work has been instrumental in prosecuting these cases, according to Norfolk First Assistant District Attorney Jeanmarie Carroll. She notes: "We have made enormous strides with the establishment of Child Advocacy Centers and more comprehensive investigations. Before, a child would endure a number of interviews. Now, all the parties are present behind a glass window and we can work off of one videotaped interview. This is much more supportive for victims and their families."[80]

As a student at Northeastern University School of Law, Carroll always had a passion for issues that involved violence against women and children. This interest first led her to a co-op internship with the Attorney General's Office Criminal Bureau, where she worked with the bureau's head, Sydney Hanlon. With Hanlon's encouragement, Carroll completed her last law school co-op with the Norfolk County District Attorney's Office and stepped right in after graduation in 1988 as a first-year prosecutor. Carroll began her career specializing in sexual assault under the supervision of Marianne Hinkle and hasn't looked back. Now the chief of the sexual assault and domestic violence unit in Norfolk County and first assistant district attorney, Carroll acknowledges the poignant cases that have kept her in the field for all these years.[81] "Listening to survivors' stories is difficult and compelling at the same time. It teaches you amazing things about the human spirit. I am continually inspired."[82] At the end of the day, Carroll remains motivated by the plight of the survivors she serves. "I never cease to be amazed at the incredible models of strength and courage that the survivors with whom I have worked have been," she says.[83] "I believe in the justice system and want to make sure that the system works for everyone. In particular, I want to make sure that those who have experienced sexual and domestic abuse have a voice in the system. Simply put, I do this work because it matters."[84]

"I believe in the justice system.... I want to make sure that those who have experienced sexual and domestic abuse have a voice in the system. Simply put, I do this work because it matters."

—Jeanmarie Carroll

While Carroll remains passionate about her commitment to victims, she recognizes that sexual assault cases are very difficult to prosecute, especially where the majority of cases involve victims and defendants who know one another. "The attacker-on-the-street scenario is not very common," she explains, noting that sexual assault cases between acquaintances "impact juries differently."[85] "Many of these cases lack DNA evidence; if you don't have forensic evidence, the likelihood of conviction diminishes. Juries expect physical evidence and we need to explain why we don't have it.... We face a tremendous hurdle."[86] Mulqueen agrees, noting in the acquaintance scenario, the credibility of the witness is a crucial factor, and a victim's presentation in court can significantly affect a jury. "Juries start with a blank slate, but depending on what the defense offers, they can turn quickly...they can get hung up on things they shouldn't get hung up on."[87] Many victims, especially in acquaintance-rape cases, are therefore concerned with what juries may think of their actions; for example, meeting the defendant at a bar, wearing certain clothing, or entering a car voluntarily. As a prosecutor, Mulqueen addresses these issues head-on. "These are normal things that happen every day," she says.[88] "People across the country socialize and go to bars. No woman expects something like this to happen."[89]

1989 Gender Bias Study of the Court System in Massachusetts: Findings on Sexual Assault Cases

In 1986, Chief Justice Edward F. Hennessy of the Supreme Judicial Court appointed the Gender Bias Study Committee to investigate the extent of gender bias in the judiciary and make recommendations in support of the equal treatment of men and women within the court system. For three years, the committee studied the nature and consequence of gender bias within a variety of substantive legal settings—including family law, domestic violence, and juvenile justice—and within court administration itself. Specifically, the committee examined sexual assault cases by interviewing and surveying individual prosecutors, defense attorneys, police officers, victim-witness advocates, rape-crisis counselors, and judges to see if gender influenced the way these cases were handled compared to other violent crimes. In 1989, the committee published its findings in its official report, *Gender Bias Study of the Court System in Massachusetts*.[90] The following is a summary of the committee's major findings and recommendations pertaining to the treatment of sexual assault cases in the Commonwealth.[91]

In general, the report found that sexual assault cases were treated quite seriously by prosecutors. Case administration varied by county, as some had specialized sexual assault units while others did not, but on the whole, most respondents agreed that inexperienced prosecutors did not try major sexual assault cases. Based on interviews with rape-crisis counselors, however, the report recommended that prosecutors receive more training in the area of trauma so as to better understand victims' general fears of the court system. Additionally, the report found that judges were properly applying the rape-shield statute, but prosecutors and defense attorneys agreed that many of the issues in sexual assault trials indirectly involved victims' prior sexual conduct. Attorneys also felt that judges were more lenient with explorations into the character and emotional stability of sexual assault victims than with victims of other serious crimes.

Significantly, the report found that the majority of sexual assaults were committed by perpetrators who knew their victims, as only 18 percent of sexual assaults reported to rape-crisis centers between 1985 and 1987 involved strangers.[92] It concluded that, to some extent, sexual assault cases involving acquaintances were treated differently in the court system, even though most lawyers and judges were of the opinion that they should be treated similarly. For example, bail amounts were lower in acquaintance cases, as were sentences upon conviction.[93] However, the report acknowledged possible explanations for this discrepancy, as evidence showed that prosecutors tended to recommend lower sentences for sexual assault cases involving acquaintances than cases involving strangers.[94] Furthermore, both prosecutors and defenders observed that jurors expected more corroboration in sexual assault cases (such as medical proof or evidence of physical resistance) than other crimes, even though corroborating evidence was not legally necessary for a conviction. Similarly, the report found that jurors were less trusting of sexual assault victims than other crime victims, and were less likely to convict if the victim did not sustain any visible physical injury.

These various findings led the committee to ultimately conclude: "It is clear that the judicial system has become increasingly sensitive to the unique issues sexual assault cases

Continued ▶

present. It is equally clear that room for improvement remains."[95] Noting that the information collected depended largely on the perspective of the person interviewed, the report cautioned against accepting one particular view as conclusive of the truth. Despite this caveat, the report was clear in its ultimate recommendation that public education about sexual assault was essential. It encouraged lawyers to collaborate with rape-crisis centers to better understand one another's policies so they could eventually work together on educating the community about rape and sexual assault prevention.

REFLECTION

Wendy J. Murphy

Finding a Voice in the Room Without a Seat at the Table

When Debra Hagen called me in early 2001 to say she needed a "victims' rights" lawyer, she said she was told it had to be someone "outside the system." A man who had been convicted of raping her thirteen years earlier and was sentenced to prison had yet to serve a single day behind bars. Despite her many letters to the court and prosecutors, her attacker was still a free man. She wasn't sure what law was being violated, but she felt in her gut it was wrong and she wanted to know if there was anything I could do about it. I said yes but even without hearing the specifics, I knew it would get ugly.

By 2001, I'd already been practicing "outside the system" for almost a decade and had had mostly negative experiences because I was doing impact litigation for victims in ways that had never been done before. It wasn't that I liked being a contrarian. There were no rules explaining how a victim should seek redress when her rights were violated in a criminal case. So when I saw victims—mostly women and children—enduring abuses that a civilized legal system should not tolerate, I literally had to create motions from scratch and cite very old due process cases to construct a viable argument.

More recently, in 2009, the daughter of a woman named Ruby McDonough called me to say that her mother had been sexually abused by a male aide at the nursing home where Ruby lived. Only in her sixties, Ruby lived at the nursing home because

Wendy J. Murphy

IMAGE COURTESY OF WENDY J. MURPHY, PHOTO BY ELISE AMENDOLA

she became disabled as a result of a stroke ten years earlier. Her brain functioned well, but she developed expressive aphasia: she could answer "yes" and "no" questions and use gestures to indicate needs, but she could not speak or write to communicate. Using her limited skills, Ruby was able to report the sexual assault to her family, staff at the nursing home, and police. The man was arrested. During criminal proceedings, defense counsel requested that Ruby be subjected to a competency hearing. A court-appointed expert determined that Ruby was competent to testify but would need to communicate by answering "yes" and "no" questions and using gestures. The hearing proceeded without any such assistance, and defense counsel was allowed to ask questions that called for a narrative response. The court found Ruby incompetent to testify, primarily on the grounds that she was unable to narrate.

Not being an expert in the rights of persons with disabilities, I nonetheless recognized that Ruby had been the victim of discrimination and had been denied her rights under the Americans with Disabilities Act to reasonable accommodations that would have enabled her equal participation as a witness in a judicial proceeding. The case was scheduled for dismissal in a matter of weeks, so I filed an emergency petition with the Supreme Judicial Court. As with Debra Hagen's case, there was no existing mechanism by which Ruby could seek judicial review so I filed under G.L. c. 211, § 3, which allows people to seek redress when there is no other option. While the Supreme Judicial Court did not grant Ruby standing to appeal, the court addressed the merits and announced in a landmark decision new procedures to be followed when a witness with a disability needs accommodations to facilitate her equal participation in a criminal matter.

It remains troubling that almost all cases involving violations of third-party rights in criminal cases go unnoticed and unredressed. Things as important as women victims of violence suffering privacy violations rooted in gender discrimination in connection with pretrial matters are invisible because there is no systematic opportunity by which the interests of an individual victim, or women as a class, can object, be heard, and obtain judicial review to repair harmful and unconstitutional criminal common law doctrines.

To be sure, there would be little need for my work if there were better institutionalized protections against the strategic exploitation of things like sexism, privacy rights, and victims' disabilities. Until then, the willingness of courts to stretch the rights of the accused to include a one-way constitutional legal relationship between the defendant and victims will continue to provoke lawyers like me to inject ourselves into criminal proceedings and demand due process, even without an invitation or a welcome seat at the table of justice. A legal system that strives to promote civility should reward, or at least tolerate, uninvited efforts to inhibit the imposition of undue constitutional harm in the name of justice.

Civil Legal Developments

While the many efforts to improve Massachusetts rape law over the years have been focused on the criminal justice system, a number of women lawyers have dedicated their careers to civil legal advocacy in order to obtain remedies for sexual assault survivors that extend beyond the criminal-justice framework. Recognizing that a sexual assault can effectively destabilize a victim's fundamental needs—including her financial stability, safety, mental health, immigration status, housing, educational opportunities, and employment—women attorneys in Massachusetts have worked tirelessly to develop a civil legal response to sexual assault.

The Boston Area Rape Crisis Center and the Founding of the Victim Rights Law Center

The Boston Area Rape Crisis Center (BARCC) was established in 1973 as the first rape-crisis center in Massachusetts. Founded by a group of women advocates, BARCC offers a variety of comprehensive services to victims of rape and sexual assault, including medical and legal advocacy, crisis counseling, and housing and financial assistance.

In the late 1990s, Harvard Law student Susan H. Vickers arrived at BARCC as a volunteer rape-crisis hotline advocate. For three years, Vickers worked the hotline while attending law school and spoke to hundreds of rape survivors about their particular struggles in the aftermath of a sexual assault. After listening to their stories, Vickers realized that many survivors faced a number of legal issues that could not be addressed by the criminal justice system: those without immigration status were apprehensive about reporting for fear of deportation; those suffering from severe trauma could not attend work or school and were at risk of dropping out or losing their jobs; those who could no longer pay rent were at risk of becoming homeless; and those who feared for their safety were unsure if they even qualified for protection orders. Motivated by this need for civil legal services, Vickers founded the Victim Rights Law Center (VRLC) in 2000 as a division of BARCC. Stephanie DeCandia joined her as a staff attorney that same year. Kathryn Reardon, then a co-op student at Northeastern University School of Law, joined the team soon after and eventually became a full-time staff attorney upon graduation.

Through her practice, [Ilene Seidman] saw firsthand how domestic violence exacerbated this economic disparity, and much of her career has been devoted to serving clients struggling with both of these issues.

In 2001, Vickers also reached out to Ilene Seidman, then a clinical instructor at Harvard Law School, for practical training on direct legal services for sexual assault victims. Seidman was a key advisor and eventually became chair of the VRLC's board of directors. Now an associate dean, clinical professor of law, and associate director of clinical programs at Suffolk University Law School, Seidman began her career as a welfare-rights attorney with an express interest in the economic plight of low-income women. Through her practice, she saw firsthand how domestic violence exacerbated this economic disparity, and much of her career has been devoted to serving clients struggling with both of these issues. When Vickers contacted her, Seidman "didn't know much about sexual assault at all," but "I assumed I did because I knew a lot about domestic violence."[96] After working with sexual assault survivors, however, Seidman realized that sexual assault was remarkably different from domestic violence. "The sexual assault movement is where the domestic violence movement was thirty years ago," she explains.[97] "No one wants to talk about it, and it's deemed too personal for the legal realm because sex is involved. The victims are younger, and most cases involve acquaintances where drugs or alcohol are present. There is an incredible bias out there against young women who are not perfect."[98]

Through her work with the VRLC, Seidman came to understand that sexual assault had an equal, if not greater, economic impact on survivors than domestic violence. "People change their living habits when they are sexually assaulted," she says.[99] "They move, they change or lose their jobs, all of which have profound economic consequences."[100] These reasons, according to Seidman, highlight the importance of legal representation beyond the criminal justice system. "Even if we had a perfect criminal justice system, it wouldn't help victims with what they need in the *aftermath* of a sexual assault. Victims need to economically sustain themselves. As a result, lawyers need to assert legal remedies when they exist, and create new ones when they don't."[101]

Organized as an independent 501(c)(3) non-profit in 2003, the VRLC now serves approximately 400 clients a year throughout the Commonwealth of Massachusetts. Its dedicated staff attorneys and network of pro bono lawyers represent sexual assault victims in a variety of civil legal matters, including restraining and harassment prevention orders,

Stephanie DeCandia currently serves as the Boston Area Rape Crisis Center (BARCC)'s manager of system advocacy and policy development. She first arrived at BARCC in 1997 as a legal intern from Northeastern University School of Law. While BARCC did not have a formal legal program at that time, she stayed on for six months, working in part with the executive director, herself a lawyer, on developing training materials for volunteers to spot the legal issues facing rape survivors. DeCandia knew from the start that BARCC was where she belonged. "In law school, we can become so focused on the law itself, we lose sight of how it affects individual people. At BARCC, my legal work overlapped with that of counselors and social service providers, and I knew it was the right thing to be doing with my career."[104] She and a fellow BARCC legal intern from Boston University Law School tried to apply for fellowship grants to start a more formalized legal advocacy program at the center. While they did not receive the funding at the time, DeCandia was fortunate to rejoin BARCC a few years after law school to work with Susan Vickers and the Victim Rights Law Center (VRLC) division.

When Vickers established the VRLC as a stand-alone entity in 2003, DeCandia stayed on with BARCC to develop the center's formal legal advocacy program. "It's crucial to have a legal advocacy program at a rape-crisis center; to have a victim have access to a legal advocate and legal information as soon as possible after the first call to the hotline or visit to a hospital emergency room," she says.[105] "Together, they can go through a variety of legal options before they commence, and legal advocates can work with counselors so the survivor receives comprehensive, holistic services."[106] In addition to counseling individual clients, DeCandia works extensively with local community groups on sexual assault policy and prevention. Over the course of her career, she has noticed a dramatic improvement in the responses and feedback from these organizations. "For a long time, it was very difficult to get other providers to call an advocate from a rape-crisis center back. At BARCC, our goal is to work together with community groups. Now there is much more of an emphasis on coming together as we realize we have many similar goals."[107]

housing matters, college judicial hearings, immigration petitions, and employment negotiations. "This organization was premised on an innovative response to sexual assault and that is how we approach each representation," explains Colby Bruno, managing attorney at the VRLC.[102] "Since sexual assault laws are still developing, our lawyers are creatively working to keep victims on the job, in school, and in safe housing. At a time when victims feel powerless, our commitment to letting the victims choose their own course and dictate their own future helps them regain control of their lives after a sexual assault."[103] In addition to providing direct representation to clients in Massachusetts, the VRLC has become a national leader in training lawyers who work with sexual assault victims. For the past eight years, the U.S. Department of Justice's Office for Violence Against Women has enlisted the VRLC to provide national training and technical assistance to thousands of legal services attorneys who receive federal grant funds under its Legal Assistance for Victims program. The VRLC attorney-training manual, *Beyond the Criminal Justice System: Transforming Our Nation's Response to Rape: A Practical Guide to Representing Sexual Assault Victims*, is circulated to all grantees as a handbook for practitioners.

REFLECTION

Susan H. Vickers

After volunteering at a local rape-crisis center during three years of Harvard Law School, and after listening to hundreds of rape survivors talk about their struggles, it was clear to me that private civil attorneys could play a major role in helping to restore individual victims' lives. By listening to rape victims' stories, I heard what you would expect to hear: that rape creates profound psychological distress for victims in the weeks, months, and years after the assault. But I also learned that it was not just the rape itself, but the aftermath of it that had such a profound impact on the survivor. Many of the most debilitating problems related to rape, I learned, actually occur *after* the assault: on the job, in school, within public and private housing, with benefits administrators, and at the hands of many professionals. I came to see how numerous postassault variables played a major role in the course of victims' lives. I came to understand why rape victims drop out of school, lose their jobs, and become less economically productive and even homeless—and it is not often the direct result of the perpetrator—but a secondary result from actions taken by others after the perpetrator deals the first traumatic blow.

It is with these basic observations that I began to realize that the remedies in our civil legal system could offer many concrete solutions to rape victims' everyday postassault crises. Armed with this basic observation, a group of legal colleagues—Susan Estrich, Lois Kanter, Stephanie Lary, Karen O'Malley, Stephanie DeCandia, and Ilene Seidman—worked with me in founding the VRLC. Our goal was simple: to give legal voice to the basic, human needs of rape victims by providing direct legal representation to individual victims. While I am currently in private practice, I am heartened that this important work continues in Massachusetts and throughout the country.

REFLECTION

Krista Green Pratt

As a partner in the labor and employment section at the Boston firm Seyfarth Shaw, I was accustomed to managing a large caseload, but I always tried to devote meaningful time to pro bono work. One of my passions involves assisting rape and sexual assault survivors on a pro bono basis. For example, in 2005, I accepted a case from the Victim Rights Law Center involving a young rape victim whose family had been sued by the alleged rapist for defamation and other common law claims after the criminal charges against him were dismissed. Given the difficulty in prosecuting sexual assault cases, and the number of victims who never even come forward, I was concerned that a case like this would discourage even more victims from seeking help from the police following an assault. In defending the family, we argued that the sole—and improper—basis for the lawsuit was the victim's complaint to the police about the assaults. As a general rule, crime victims who file police reports are protected against suits based on that activity under the Massachusetts Anti-SLAPP statute (Strategic Litigation Against Public Participation), but in this particular case, the trial judge ruled that the statutory protections did not apply. Several years and hundreds of pro bono hours later, we represented the family before the Supreme Judicial Court. On June 25, 2009, the court found in favor of the victim and directed the trial court to dismiss the claims against the family. By reporting a crime to the police, the court concluded, the victim and her family had engaged in protected petitioning activity and were therefore immune from suit under the Anti-SLAPP statute. Through the combined efforts of our Seyfarth Shaw pro bono team and with this successful result, we hope that future victims may come forward without the threat of civil liability in the event the criminal charges do not proceed.

Krista Green Pratt

IMAGE COURTESY OF KRISTA GREEN PRATT

Civil Tort Remedies

In addition to the civil remedies offered by legal service agencies such as the Victim Rights Law Center, the private bar also plays an important role in assisting survivors of sexual assault. Djuna Perkins knows this well. A former prosecutor and current civil litigator at the Boston firm Brody, Hardoon, Perkins and Kesten, Perkins has represented numerous victims of rape and sexual assault in obtaining monetary compensation for their injuries not only from their perpetrators, but from other entities that have failed to protect them, such as employers, property owners, health-care facilities, and educational institutions. Having prosecuted many sexual assault cases in the past as a former assistant district attorney, Perkins understands the extreme emotional toll a criminal case may have on a victim. As a civil tort attorney, she offers options for crime victims beyond those provided by a criminal prosecution. "Survivors do not have to choose between seeking punishment for their perpetrators and obtaining financial compensation that will help them obtain whatever they need to rebuild their lives and regain control," she says.[108] "Many of my clients pursue both a criminal prosecution and a civil lawsuit. In a criminal prosecution, the focus is on the defendant, but in a civil lawsuit, the focus of the case is on making the victim whole. It can be an incredibly empowering experience for my clients."[109] Even when there is no criminal prosecution at all, Perkins says, "[c]ountless clients obtain justice through civil lawsuits."[110]

Perkins's clients have often endured incredible trauma. "My clients typically are experiencing feelings of shock, betrayal and self-blame, wondering, 'Why me?' For a significant number, this is not the first sexual assault of their lives, and they are asking, 'Why did this happen again?'"[111] Perkins's ability to work with survivors of crime has motivated her throughout her career, whether in the public or private sector. Describing her work at Brody Hardoon as "extremely compelling," she notes that the law is "fundamentally a service business."[112] "People go into it for a number of reasons, but the most important is to help people. I thought to myself, I can do that."[113]

Legislative Initiatives: 258E Harassment Prevention Orders

In addition to providing direct representation to individual sexual assault clients, women attorneys in Massachusetts have also focused on policy and legislative initiatives. In spring 2003, Helen Guyton, a first-year associate at Mintz, Levin, Cohn, Ferris, Glovsky and Popeo, took on her first pro bono case with a team from the firm. Guyton met "Jackie,"[114] a high-school senior who had been sexually assaulted in the eighth grade by two neighborhood boys. The assailants pled guilty under the youthful offender law and were expelled, but after completing probation, they returned frequently to taunt and harass Jackie at her high school. Jackie was a member of the cheerleading squad, and her assailants would appear at football games, sit directly behind her, and yell obscenities from the stands. They followed her in their cars, harassed her family members, and tormented her so much that she eventually quit cheerleading. All she wanted was to be safe, free from taunting and aggravation. She also wanted to attend her high school prom and graduation in peace. "After my initial meeting with [Jackie], I thought, 'let's get her a 209A restraining order,'" recalls Guyton, now an associate in Mintz Levin's Washington, DC, office.[115] "I thought if you were a victim of sexual assault, you could easily obtain a protective order."[116]

Guyton, however, was shocked to learn that Jackie did not qualify for a 209A domestic violence restraining order in Massachusetts because she didn't have a family, household, or dating relationship with her assailants. Like many victims of acquaintance sexual assault at the time, Jackie did not qualify for a criminally-enforceable restraining order due to this gap in the law. Dissatisfied with the status quo, Guyton pitched the idea of changing the law to her supervisor, Mintz Levin partner Susan Finegan, who agreed. In collaboration with the Boston Area Rape Crisis Center, the Victim Rights Law Center, Jane Doe, Inc., and other advocacy groups such as Feel Safe Again, Inc., Guyton drafted proposed legislation and testified before executive and judicial committees with Finegan and Layla D'Emilia, then

Governor Deval Patrick signs An Act Relative to Harassment Prevention Orders into law on February 9, 2010.

IMAGE COURTESY OF GOVERNOR DEVAL PATRICK'S OFFICE, PHOTO BY EUGENA OSSI

director of public policy at Jane Doe, Inc., about the need for non-intimate-partner sexual assault protective orders. Fellow Mintz Levin attorney Elissa Flynn-Poppey soon came on board and redrafted the legislation, working with the legislature to develop a group of stakeholders that included the defense bar, district attorneys, victim-witness advocates, and members of the court. "It was a great experience to have all the stakeholders work together to craft legislation to protect victims," she says.[117] "It was gratifying to see the defense bar become our biggest advocate on the passage of the legislation."[118] State Representative Cory Atkins, the bill's primary sponsor, credits Mintz Levin and the pivotal role the firm played in its passage. "This desperately needed legislation took over ten years to pass. The tireless assistance from Mintz Levin—including bringing together all the stakeholders in the year before final passage—helped those of us in the legislature push it over the top."[119]

On February 9, 2010, several years after Guyton first met Jackie, Governor Deval Patrick signed into law Senate Bill 2212, An Act Relative to Harassment Prevention Orders. The law, codified at G.L. c. 258E, enables victims of harassment, stalking, and or sexual assault to obtain civil protective orders against their assailants, regardless of their relationship. A court may order a perpetrator to stop abusing, harassing, and/or contacting a victim and mandate that the perpetrator stay away from the victim's person, home, and workplace. Additionally, a court may order a perpetrator to pay a victim's out-of-pocket expenses suffered as a result of the harassment, stalking, or sexual assault, such as medical expenses, loss of earnings, and reasonable attorney fees. Perpetrators who violate the order can be punished by a fine up to $5,000, imprisonment for no more than two-and-a-half years, or both.

The new 258E harassment prevention law therefore fills a critical gap left by the 209A restraining order legislation. Significantly, the new law provides sexual assault victims like Jackie with the security of a criminally-enforceable protective order, regardless of their

Governor Deval Patrick speaking on the occasion of the February 9, 2010, enactment of the new Chapter 258E. Also pictured from left to right are: Senator Harriette Chandler, Attorney General Martha Coakley, Lieutenant Governor Tim Murray, and First Lady Diane Patrick.

IMAGE COURTESY OF GOVERNOR DEVAL PATRICK'S OFFICE, PHOTO BY EUGENA OSSI

relationship to the perpetrator. Victims assaulted by friends, coworkers, neighbors, classmates, landlords, or teachers may now petition a court for protection. This result, according to Guyton, was very much worth the wait. "The signing ceremony was an amazing experience," she says.[120] "Knowing you worked so hard on something for so long, and seeing it finally become a reality is a very special thing."[121] Finegan agrees, noting that at the signing ceremony, "the room was filled with so many people who had been instrumental in getting the law passed."[122] After the bill signing, Finegan represented some of the first sexual assault victims to avail themselves of the new law, a feeling she describes as "overwhelming."[123] "To know that these women could now be helped, when weeks before, there was no remedy, was heartwarming. As a lawyer, it doesn't get much better than that."[124]

NOTES

1 4 William Blackstone, Commentaries *210. The first statutory prohibition against rape in Massachusetts was passed in 1642. See *Commonwealth v. Burke*, 105 Mass. 376, 380 (1870) (citing 2 Mass. Col. Rec. 21).

2 *See generally* Claudia Zaher, "When a Woman's Marital Status Determined Her Legal Status: A Research Guide on the Common Law Doctrine of Coverture," 94 *Law Libr. J.* 459 (2002).

3 In this chapter, "victims" are often referred to in the feminine, as the vast majority of sexual assault cases involve female victims and male perpetrators. However, when appropriate, the substantive content is meant to apply similarly to male victims, and/or to victims who are the same gender as the perpetrators.

4 *See generally* Alexandra Wald, "What's Rightfully Ours: Toward a Property Theory of Rape," 30 *Colum. J.L. & Soc. Probs.* 459 (1997). When a man raped an unmarried woman, he was punished for depriving her father of the value of her virginity, as it then became more difficult for the father to find a future husband for his daughter. When a man raped a married woman who was not his wife, he was punished for stealing the property of the victim's husband. When a man raped his own wife, however, he was immune from punishment, as he was merely exercising ownership over his own property. *See also* "To Have and To Hold: The Marital Rape Exemption and the Fourteenth Amendment," 99 *Harv. L. Rev.* 1255, 1257 (1986) ("Rape of an unmarried woman rendered her unmarriageable because her value to future husbands was destroyed....").

5 Massachusetts, unlike many other jurisdictions, did not have an express corroboration requirement. Faith H. Biggs, "Rape Law in Massachusetts: Our Puritan Forbearers and Other Cultural Remnants," 22 *New Eng. L. Rev.* 89, 105 (1987). It did, however, place a high value on corroboration evidence. Faith H. Biggs, "Rape Law in Massachusetts: Our Puritan Forbearers and Other Cultural Remnants," 22 *New Eng. L. Rev.* at 105.

6 *See* Cassia Spohn & Julie Horney, *Rape Law Reform: A Grassroots Revolution and Its Impact* 23 (James Alan Fox & Joseph Weis eds., Plenum Press 1992) (citing *Brown v. State*, 106 N.W. 536, 538 (Wis. 1906)). In *Brown*, the Wisconsin Supreme Court stated that "there must be the most vehement exercise of every physical means or faculty within the woman's power to resist the penetration of her person, and this must be shown to persist until the offense is consummated." *Brown v. State*, 106 N.W. at 538. Massachusetts, however, did not require a woman to use all physical means necessary to resist an assault; rather, the state required that nonconsent be "honest and real," and such a determination was left to the discretion of the jury. *Commonwealth v. McDonald*, 110 Mass. 405, 406 (1872); Faith H. Biggs, "Rape Law in Massachusetts: Our Puritan Forbearers and Other Cultural Remnants," 22 *New Eng. L. Rev.* at 102–03.

7 Michelle J. Anderson, "From Chastity Requirement to Sexuality License: Sexual Consent and a New Rape Shield Law," 70 *Geo. Wash. L. Rev.* 51, 52–53 (2002) ("A chaste woman was considered more likely to have resisted the defendant's sexual advances and to have lodged a legitimate claim of rape. By contrast, an unchaste woman was considered more likely to have succumbed willingly to the defendant's sexual advances and to have lied about it later.").

8 Walter R. Mebane, Jr. and Stacy Futter, "The Effects of Rape Law Reform on Rape Case Processing," 16 *Berkeley Women's L.J.* 72, 73 (2001).

9 Faith H. Biggs, "Rape Law in Massachusetts: Our Puritan Forebearers and Other Cultural Remnants," 22 *New Eng. L. Rev.* at 96–98 (chronicling changes to Massachusetts rape statute). Specifically, the new statute replaced "female" with "person" to make the definitions of perpetrator and victim gender-neutral; added "unnatural" sexual intercourse to contemplate acts beyond penile vaginal penetration; and included "threat of bodily injury" to acknowledge other forms of coercion besides physical force, such as verbal threats. Faith H. Biggs, "Rape Law in Massachusetts: Our Puritan Forebearers and Other Cultural Remnants," 22 *New Eng. L. Rev.* at 96–98.

10 *Commonwealth v. Kendall*, 113 Mass. 210, 210 (1873), *superseded by statute*, G.L. c. 233, § 21B (1977), *as recognized in Commonwealth v. Harris*, 443 Mass. 714 (2005).

11 Michelle J. Anderson, "From Chastity Requirement to Sexuality License: Sexual Consent and a New Rape Shield Law," 70 *Geo. Wash. L. Rev.* at 52–53.

12 G.L. c. 233, § 21B (amended 2011).

13 *See Commonwealth v. Fitzgerald*, 412 Mass. 516, 523 (1992) (articulating purpose of rape-shield statute).

14 In addition to the two exceptions highlighted in the statute, Massachusetts courts have also held that a victim's past sexual history is admissible when it is being used to show her bias or motive to lie, or when it is necessary for a defendant to put on a complete defense. *Commonwealth v. Joyce*, 382 Mass. 222 (1981); *Commonwealth v. Cardoza*, 29 Mass. App. Ct. 645 (1990). This evidence is permissible, though, only after a

hearing is conducted outside the presence of a jury and a judge determines it is appropriate. G.L. c. 233, § 21B (amended 2011).

15 Interview with Lois Pines (Nov. 19, 2010).

16 Interview with Lois Pines (Nov. 19, 2010).

17 Interview with Lois Pines (Nov. 19, 2010).

18 Interview with Lois Pines (Nov. 19, 2010).

19 Interview with Lois Pines (Nov. 19, 2010).

20 Interview with Lois Pines (Nov. 19, 2010).

21 Interview with Lois Pines (Nov. 19, 2010).

22 Interview with Lois Pines (Nov. 19, 2010).

23 *See Commonwealth v. Fogerty*, 74 Mass. 489, 491 (1857). "Of course, it would always be competent for a party indicted to show, in defence of a charge of rape alleged to be actually committed by himself, that the woman on whom it was charged to have been committed was his wife."

24 *See* Morgan Lee Woolley, "Marital Rape: A Unique Blend of Domestic Violence and Non-Marital Rape Issues," 18 *Hastings Women's L.J.* at 276–77 (outlining various legal justifications for spousal exemption); "To Have and To Hold: The Marital Rape Exemption and the Fourteenth Amendment," 99 *Harv. L. Rev.* at 1255–57 (explaining theories of implied consent, coverture, and property ownership as basis for spousal exemption).

25 *Commonwealth v. McAfee*, 108 Mass. 458, 461 (1871).

26 *Commonwealth v. Chretien*, 383 Mass. 123 (1981).

27 *Commonwealth v. Chretien*, 383 Mass. at 130.

28 *Commonwealth v. Chretien*, 383 Mass. at 130.

29 *Commonwealth v. Chretien*, 383 Mass. at 131–32.

30 Interview with Hon. Diane Kottmyer (Nov. 15, 2010).

31 Interview with Hon. Diane Kottmyer (Nov. 15, 2010).

32 Interview with Hon. Diane Kottmyer (Nov. 15, 2010).

33 Interview with Hon. Diane Kottmyer (Nov. 15, 2010).

34 *See* Michelle J. Anderson, "The Legacy of the Prompt Complaint Requirement, Corroboration Requirement, and Cautionary Instructions on Campus Sexual Assault," 84 *B.U. L. Rev.* 945, 955 (2004) (articulating rationale for hue and cry principle).

35 Faith H. Biggs, "Rape Law in Massachusetts: Our Puritan Forebearers and Other Cultural Remnants," 22 *New Eng. L. Rev.* at 105 (citing *Commonwealth v. Cleary*, 172 Mass. 175, 176 (1898) ("[T]he party ravished might give evidence upon oath, the value of which would be affected by corroborative facts, he [Lord Hale] recurred to the matter of fresh complaint, and said that, if she 'presently discovered the offense, made pursuit after the offender,' etc., 'these and the like are concurring evidences, to give greater probability to her testimony.'")).

36 There was no absolute timeframe as to what made a complaint sufficiently "fresh;" rather, a judge determined whether the complaint was reasonably prompt in light of the surrounding circumstances. The "freshness" of the complaint was specific to each individual case. *See, e.g., Commonwealth v. Kruah*, 47 Mass. App. Ct. 341, 346–47 (1999) (testimony about complaint made fifteen months after assault was sufficiently "fresh" when defendant held position of high respect in Liberian community and elders warned victim she would bring them shame if she reported); *Commonwealth v. Dion*, 30 Mass. App. Ct. 406, 413–14 (1991) (testimony about complaint made eighteen months after assault not sufficiently "fresh" because there was no evidence that the defendant threatened or intimidated the victim after the assault).

37 While many other states follow the "fresh complaint" doctrine, Massachusetts is the rare state that allows the witness to testify about the *details* of what the victim said during the complaint. *Commonwealth v. Licata*, 412 Mass. 654, 657 (1992) (overruled on other grounds).

38 Fresh complaint testimony could only be used to corroborate the victim's testimony; it could not be used to establish the truth of the complaint itself. *Commonwealth v. Licata*, 412 Mass. at 657.

39 *Brief for Jane Doe, Inc., et al. as Amici Curiae Supporting Respondent* at 11–12, *Commonwealth v. King*, 445 Mass. 217 (2005) (SJC–09417).

40 *Commonwealth v. Lavalley*, 410 Mass. 641, 646 (1991); *Commonwealth v. Licata*, 412 Mass. at 656–58.

41 *Commonwealth v. Lavalley*, 410 Mass. at 646.

42 *Commonwealth v. Lavalley*, 410 Mass. at 646 n.7; *Commonwealth v. Licata*, 412 Mass. at 657–58.

43 *Commonwealth v. Lavalley*, 410 Mass. at 646 ("We therefore invite parties in the future to give the court an opportunity to reassess the rule which allows the Commonwealth to introduce the details of the a fresh complaint for corroborative purposes during its case-in-chief.").

44 *Commonwealth v. Licata*, 412 Mass. 654 (1992).

45 Interview with Assistant District Attorney Marguerite Grant (Oct. 19, 2010).

46 Interview with Assistant District Attorney Marguerite Grant (Oct. 19, 2010).

47 Interview with Assistant District Attorney Marguerite Grant (Oct. 19, 2010).

48 Interview with Assistant District Attorney Marguerite Grant (Oct. 19, 2010).

49 Interview with Assistant District Attorney Marguerite Grant (Oct. 19, 2010).

50 Interview with Assistant District Attorney Marguerite Grant (Oct. 19, 2010).

51 *Commonwealth v. King*, 445 Mass. 217 (2005).

52 Interview with Djuna Perkins (Oct. 28, 2010).

53 Interview with Djuna Perkins (Oct. 28, 2010).

54 Interview with Djuna Perkins (Oct. 28, 2010).

55 Interview with Djuna Perkins (Oct. 28, 2010).

56 *Commonwealth v. King*, 445 Mass. at 241–43.

57 The new rule also addressed the court's concern that a jury would hear multiple fresh-complaint witnesses and impermissibly use that testimony to determine the truth of the victim's complaint. *Commonwealth v. King*, 445 Mass. at 242–43.

58 *Commonwealth v. King*, 445 Mass. at 240.

59 Interview with Djuna Perkins (Oct. 28, 2010).

60 Interview with Djuna Perkins (Oct. 28, 2010).

61 Interview with Assistant District Attorney Jane Mulqueen (Oct. 14, 2010).

62 Interview with Assistant District Attorney Jane Mulqueen (Oct. 14, 2010). In 2011, the Supreme Judicial Court considered the vitality of the first complaint doctrine for the first time since its adoption six years prior in *Commonwealth v. King*. In *Commonwealth v. Aviles*, 461 Mass 60 (2011), the court affirmed the continued need for the doctrine, but modified the scope of review for future appeals based on the admission of first complaint testimony. Significantly, it changed the appellate standard of review from the prejudicial error standard (when the defendant objected to the admission of first complaint evidence) and the miscarriage of justice standard (when the defendant raised no objection) to a uniform abuse of discretion standard. *Commonwealth v. Aviles*, 461 Mass. at 71–73. Noting that many factual intricacies give rise to a first complaint analysis, the court adopted the abuse of discretion standard to give trial judges greater flexibility to address factual scenarios that were unanticipated by the doctrine's original rubric. *Commonwealth v. Aviles*, 461 Mass. at 72–73.

63 Interview with Assistant District Attorney Jane Mulqueen (Oct. 14, 2010).

64 Interview with Hon. Sydney Hanlon (Nov. 10, 2010).

65 Interview with Hon. Diane Kottmyer (Nov. 15, 2010).

66 Interview with Hon. Diane Kottmyer (Nov. 15, 2010).

67 Interview with Hon. Diane Kottmyer (Nov. 15, 2010).

68 Interview with Hon. Diane Kottmyer (Nov. 15, 2010).

69 Interview with Hon. Diane Kottmyer (Nov. 15, 2010).

70 Interview with Hon. Diane Kottmyer (Nov. 15, 2010).

71 Interview with Hon. Diane Kottmyer (Nov. 15, 2010).

72 Interview with Hon. Diane Kottmyer (Nov. 15, 2010).

73 Interview with Hon. Diane Kottmyer (Nov. 15, 2010).

74 Interview with Hon. Diane Kottmyer (Nov. 15, 2010).

75 Interview with Hon. Diane Kottmyer (Nov. 15, 2010).

76 Interview with Hon. Diane Kottmyer (Nov. 15, 2010).

77 Interview with Hon. Diane Kottmyer (Nov. 15, 2010).

78 Interview with Assistant District Attorney Jane Mulqueen (Oct. 14, 2010).

79 Interview with Assistant District Attorney Jane Mulqueen (Oct. 14, 2010).

80 Interview with First Assistant District Attorney Jeanmarie Carroll (Oct. 20, 2010).

81 Interview with First Assistant District Attorney Jeanmarie Carroll (Oct. 20, 2010).

82 Interview with First Assistant District Attorney Jeanmarie Carroll (Oct. 20, 2010).

83 Interview with First Assistant District Attorney Jeanmarie Carroll (Oct. 20, 2010).

84 Interview with First Assistant District Attorney Jeanmarie Carroll (Oct. 20, 2010).

85 Interview with First Assistant District Attorney Jeanmarie Carroll (Oct. 20, 2010).

86 Interview with First Assistant District Attorney Jeanmarie Carroll (Oct. 20, 2010).

87 Interview with Assistant District Attorney Jane Mulqueen (Oct. 14, 2010).

88 Interview with Assistant District Attorney Jane Mulqueen (Oct. 14, 2010).

89 Interview with Assistant District Attorney Jane Mulqueen (Oct. 14, 2010).

90 The 1989 report is published in two segments in two different law reviews. The "Introduction," "Domestic Violence and Sexual Assault," and "Gender Bias in Courthouse Interactions" sections may be found at 23 *Suffolk U.L. Rev.* 576 (1989). The "Executive Summary," "Family Law," and "Civil Damage Awards" sections may be found at 24 *New Eng. L. Rev.* 745 (1990). A copy of the original report in its entirety is available through the administrative office of the Trial Court, 2 Center Plaza, 9th Floor, Boston, MA, 02108. Additionally, in 1994, the Gender Bias Study Committee published *Five Years Towards Gender Equality: Reflections on the Work of the Committee for Gender Equality of the Massachusetts Supreme Judicial Court 1989–1994*. The work consists of a series of essays written by committee members and their colleagues as they reflect, five years later, on their personal efforts to make gender equality in the courts a reality. This publication is also available through the administrative office of the Trial Court.

91 *See generally Report of the Gender Bias Study of the Supreme Judicial Court, Commonwealth of Massachusetts* 98–110 (1989).

92 *Report of the Gender Bias Study of the Supreme Judicial Court, Commonwealth of Massachusetts* at 100 (referencing 1985–87 survey by the Massachusetts Department of Public Health).

93 While bail amounts were much lower in sexual assault cases where the parties knew one another, the report concluded that on the whole, bail was just as effective in preventing a defendant's default as in other similar violent crimes. *Report of the Gender Bias Study of the Supreme Judicial Court, Commonwealth of Massachusetts* at 102.

94 The report also noted that these lower recommendations could be the result of victims' requests, as a majority of both prosecutors and defenders indicated that victims in acquaintance sexual assault cases tended to recommend lower sentences. *Report of the Gender Bias Study of the Supreme Judicial Court, Commonwealth of Massachusetts* at 106.

95 *Report of the Gender Bias Study of the Supreme Judicial Court, Commonwealth of Massachusetts* at 108.

96 Interview with Ilene Seidman (Oct. 6, 2010).

97 Interview with Ilene Seidman (Oct. 6, 2010).

98 Interview with Ilene Seidman (Oct. 6, 2010).

99 Interview with Ilene Seidman (Oct. 25, 2010).

100 Interview with Ilene Seidman (Oct. 25, 2010).

101 Interview with Ilene Seidman (Oct. 6, 2010).

102 Interview with Colby Bruno (Oct. 15, 2010).

103 Interview with Colby Bruno (Oct. 15, 2010).

104 Interview with Stephanie DeCandia (Sept. 21, 2010).

105 Interview with Stephanie DeCandia (Sept. 21, 2010).

106 Interview with Stephanie DeCandia (Sept. 21, 2010).

107 Interview with Stephanie DeCandia (Sept. 21, 2010).

108 Interview with Djuna Perkins (Oct. 28, 2010).

109 Interview with Djuna Perkins (Oct. 28, 2010).

110 Interview with Djuna Perkins (Oct. 28, 2010).

111 Interview with Djuna Perkins (Oct. 28, 2010).

112 Interview with Djuna Perkins (Oct. 28, 2010).

113 Interview with Djuna Perkins (Oct. 28, 2010).

114 This name has been changed to protect the client's privacy.

115 Interview with Helen Guyton (Aug. 20, 2010).

116 Interview with Helen Guyton (Aug. 20, 2010).

117 Interview with Elissa Flynn-Poppey (Nov. 22, 2010).

118 Interview with Elissa Flynn-Poppey (Nov. 22, 2010). *See* Elissa Flynn-Poppey and Stefanie Giuliano Abhar, "Chapter 258E Harassment Prevention Orders—Balancing the Rights of Victims and Defendants," 94 *Mass. L. Rev.* 1, 23 (Sept. 2011). This article describes the goals and legislative history of "An Act to Prevent Harassment," which was signed into law by Governor Deval Patrick on February 9, 2010. The article also addresses who is able to seek relief under G.L. c. 258E, and how the law differs from G.L. c. 209A.

119 Interview with State Representative Cory Atkins (Mar. 3, 2011).

120 Interview with Helen Guyton (Aug. 20, 2010).

121 Interview with Helen Guyton (Aug. 20, 2010).

122 Interview with Susan M. Finegan (Nov. 12, 2010).

123 Interview with Susan M. Finegan (Nov. 12, 2010).

124 Interview with Susan M. Finegan (Nov. 12, 2010).

CHAPTER 7

Building a Legal Community: Bar Leaders

A Brief History

Bar associations have a deep-rooted history in the Massachusetts legal community.[1] The Suffolk County Bar Association, forerunner of the Boston Bar Association, was founded in 1770 and counted John Adams as its first secretary. Initially, bar associations generally operated by invitation only and served as a way to regulate the profession by establishing minimum educational requirements and standards for admission to practice. Such regulation, however, was also aimed at excluding persons deemed "unwanted" on the basis of their class, race, ethnicity, religion, or gender.

As women began to enter the legal profession they took matters into their own hands by forming their own association, the Massachusetts Association of Women Lawyers, in 1905. Within the next decade, male bar associations began to move towards greater inclusiveness. The Massachusetts Bar Association included an African-American member at its founding in 1910 and admitted its first woman member in 1913. The Boston Bar Association followed with its first woman member in 1916.

The influx of women into the legal profession during the 1970s changed bar associations. In 1978, the Women's Bar Association of Massachusetts was founded with an explicitly activist mission: to work for the professional advancement of women lawyers and to advocate for the broader interests of women in society. In the late 1980s, both the

Bar Association "Firsts"

1770	The **Suffolk County Bar Association,** forerunner of the **Boston Bar Association,** is founded
1905	The **Massachusetts Association of Women Lawyers** is founded
1910	The **Massachusetts Bar Association** is founded
1913	The **Massachusetts Bar Association** admits its **first woman member,** Mary A. Mahan
1916	The **Boston Bar Association** admits its **first woman member,** Clara Power
1978	The **Women's Bar Association of Massachusetts** is founded
1981	**(Hon.) Barbara A. Dortch-Okara** becomes the first woman president of the Massachusetts Black Lawyers Association
1985	**Judith A. Cross** is elected first woman president of the Hampden County Bar Association
1986	**Alice E. Richmond** is elected first woman president of the Massachusetts Bar Association
1987	**Gene D. Dahmen** is elected first woman president of the Boston Bar Association

Snapshots from the First Decades

The Massachusetts Bar Association, at its annual meeting in December 1913, admitted its first woman member: Mary A. Mahan. After her name was read with that of the other thirty-four members favorably acted upon by the membership committee, Hollis R. Bailey, rose to comment:

> I hope that this will not interfere with our banquets and prevent smoking. We are taking a step which we must consider as a precedent, and which we should consider in this light. I have no objection to make, but I merely wanted to call attention to it. The question of women members has been brought before the American Bar Association but the members have dodged it.

Boston Evening Transcript, Dec. 23, 1913.

Law Notes.

VOLUME VIII.

APRIL, 1904, TO MARCH, 1905.

PROF. WHEELER OF YALE LAW SCHOOL DEAD.—Albert S. Wheeler, professor of Roman law in the Yale Law School for the last twenty-eight years, died in New Haven, January 30, aged seventy years.

WOMEN LAWYERS HOLD ANNUAL DINNER.—The Massachusetts Association of Women Lawyers, the only organization of its kind in the United States, held its annual dinner in Boston on January 28, at Young's Hotel.

DEATH OF LAWYER WHO SAW LINCOLN ASSASSINATED.—Col. James Watson, for many years a leading attorney of Columbus, Ohio, died there January 28, of paresis. He witnessed the assassination of President Lincoln in Ford's Theatre, Washington, in April, 1865.

LAWYER SHOT BY JEALOUS EDITOR.—Harvey F. Schultze, a well-known lawyer of Storm Lake, Iowa, was shot on January 21, by Albert Smith, publisher of a local newspaper, and was seriously wounded. The trouble is said to have arisen from an attempt on the part of Schultze to poach on Smith's domestic preserves.

▶

The "News of the Profession" section of the April 1904 to March 1905 volume of Law Notes *(published by Edward Thompson Law Company, Law Publishers) reported on the Massachusetts Association of Women Lawyers' first annual dinner.*

IMAGE SOURCE: GOOGLE BOOKS

BAR ASSOCIATION ADMITS MISS POWER

First Woman Member of Boston Organization.

Also First Allowed to Practice in United States Supreme Court.

Feminism advanced another step in Massachusetts yesterday when the Boston Bar Association, by a vote of 34 to 16, determined to admit a woman to membership, the first admitted to any local bar association.

The woman is Miss Clara L. Power, who has been second assistant register of probate for Suffolk County since the Legislature, in 1908, created that position and provided that it might be held by a woman. This distinction is supplementary to that [illegible] when, in 1899,

MISS CLARA LOUISE POWER.

she was the first woman authorized to practice before the United States Supreme Court.

▲

Noting that Clara Power's admission to the Boston Bar Association had been "long sought," the Daily Globe *reported on January 9, 1916, that she had previously been rejected by the executive committee, but now the question of her admission had come before the members in general meeting.*

IMAGE SOURCE: *BOSTON GLOBE* ONLINE ARCHIVES

SUFFRAGIST AND ANTI.

Officers of Massachusetts Association of Women Lawyers Take Opposite Sides On Question of Rates.

MRS MARY A. MAHAN, PRESIDENT, AND MISS MONICA FOLEY, SECRETARY.

On April 26, 1914, the Boston Daily Globe *reported on the strikingly different positions on women's right to vote taken by the Massachusetts Association of Women Lawyers' newly-elected secretary and president. The president, Mary A. Mahan, was a suffragist while the secretary, Monica Foley, was an anti-suffragist. The* Globe *commented: [O]ne would say offhand that a woman lawyer would be fairly likely to be a suffragist." Foley, however, believed "that suffrage ought to be given to women when a majority of them want it." She did not believe the majority of women wanted to vote in 1914.*

IMAGE SOURCE: *BOSTON GLOBE* ONLINE ARCHIVES

BAY STATE WOMEN LAWYERS ENTERTAIN LEADER IN PROFESSION FROM OREGON

Miss Grace E. Smith, Assistant Attorney General of That State, Guest at Luncheon of Massachusetts Association

Front Row, Left to Right—Sadie Sipner Schulman, Marjorie Hurd, Evelyn Sawyer, Miss Smith, Mrs R. W. Walton, Harriet Weiler. Rear Row—Viola C. Smith, Angela C. O'Brien, Mary E. Hyde, Harriet G. Smith, Greta C. Coleman (president), Emma Fall Schofield, Bertha R. Kiernan.

WOMEN LAWYERS AND GRACE ELIZABETH SMITH, THEIR GUEST.

In July 1925, the Massachusetts Association of Women Lawyers hosted Oregon Assistant Attorney General Grace E. Smith at a luncheon at the Women's Republican Club, 46 Beacon Street in Boston. The July 3, 1925, edition of the Boston Daily Globe *reported that the guest of honor spoke about the fact that "although there is a great field open to women, she has to show expert ability, whereas ability in a man is taken for granted, almost invariably."*

IMAGE SOURCE:
BOSTON GLOBE ONLINE ARCHIVES

Massachusetts Bar Association and the Boston Bar Association elected their first women presidents.

This chapter features the reflections of women who have had key leadership roles in the Commonwealth's bar associations.

Reflections

Elaine M. Epstein

Women's Bar Association of Massachusetts President, 1978–1980
Massachusetts Bar Association President, 1992–1993

The Thrill of Change: The Not So Early Years

In my experience, the rearview mirror often makes objects appear smaller—softening past realities. We tend to look back on women's progress at the bar and in its organizations as a logical, noncontroversial march forward—culminating in women readily assuming leadership positions and bringing into question the continued need for separate women's bar associations. But in fact, the history of the Women's Bar Association in Massachusetts and the involvement of women attorneys in other bar associations are in many ways closely linked to the history of women's legal rights.

The miniscule number of women attorneys in Massachusetts for the greater part of the first century (yes, century!) following Lelia Robinson's admission to the bar in 1882 was mirrored in the lack of women attorneys active in bar associations. One need only look at various associations' group portraits right through the early 1970s for confirmation. Even as modestly increasing numbers of women gained admission to the bar in the 1950s and 1960s, their options were limited—searching titles, probating estates, or being relegated to "administrative," i.e., largely nonlegal, work. Assignments of research and writing work in a wider array of practice areas pushed the outer limits. I have always admired the pluck of these women, and their resolve in establishing their own bar association in 1905: the Massachusetts Association of Women Lawyers (MAWL). Its role and purpose were constrained by the times. Formed as an educational association, MAWL could not (and never has) taken positions on political issues. Yet, particularly in those early decades of women at the bar, MAWL no doubt provided a much-needed forum for women attorneys to come together on their own terms, find informal "mentoring," and, I venture a guess, get some good tips on navigating an inhospitable environment. Surely the male bar associations could not

Elaine M. Epstein

IMAGE COURTESY OF ELAINE M. EPSTEIN

have been much more welcoming than the experience of "Ladies' Days" at law school. Assailing these all-male bastions likely did not look like any fun.

I came of age—legally speaking—in the mid-1970s, years that saw the great march of women into law schools. The 1960s had produced a small and stalwart group of women lawyers inured to being in the very small minority—tolerated but without much say. But the ethos of the day had raised expectations all around. Surely the Great Society could not fail to include women in leadership roles—or so some of us thought. Yet, the gut-wrenching years of the Vietnam War saw hardly a surge in women in such roles in the law or elsewhere.

A 1980s photo of (Hon.) Bernadette L. Sabra and (Hon.) Dyanne Polatin (Klein) proudly displaying their WBA T-shirts sporting the logo: "Passing the Bar.... Doesn't mean you're past the barriers."

IMAGE COURTESY OF SANDRA SHAPIRO/ KAREN NEVINS

The need for an Equal Rights Amendment to the Constitution seemed all too evident. Originally drafted in 1923, it was reintroduced and approved by both the U.S. House and Senate in 1972, with widespread bipartisan support. Optimism flowed. But passage required ratification by thirty-eight states—a task that proved to be the amendment's undoing. As the battle lines formed in state legislatures in the following years, its chances sank as it became a minefield of conservative ideology and caricature. Alarms were raised: bathrooms would be unisex, women would be drafted, and protections for women would come to an end. Despite optimistic steps such as an executive order that prohibited federal contractors from discriminating in hiring women, it became discouragingly clear that women's rights were not something one even had to be embarrassed about opposing. By the late 1970s, the federal Equal Rights Amendment was in deep trouble, although Massachusetts had ratified its own version in 1976.

These were the years and events that sent women to law school and into politics in droves. They came armed with a new set of expectations, tempered by a firm grip on reality. Change was certainly not going to be brought about by petitioning almost uniformly male legislatures or awaiting changes in public attitudes. Women simply had to do it themselves—go to law school, get elected, change the laws, change the world. Most legislatures were dominated not only by men but by men who were attorneys. The path was clear. The Women's Political Caucus had been founded in 1971 with an explicit goal of changing the composition of those bodies, both federal and state.

What does this history have to do with women and bar associations in Massachusetts? In fact, a great deal. I offer my own saga as an example. Born in 1947, I headed south to college in 1964 as a young seventeen-year-old. The women's college at Tulane (Newcomb) had all of the earmarks of the day: separate male and female facilities, strict curfews, a dress code (skirts to class and dinner), and sororities segregated by religion—then grappling with integration. Returning north after two years with a bit of understanding of what the civil rights

Sandra Shapiro, WBA president from 1985–1986, speaking at the WBA's annual meeting.

IMAGE COURTESY OF SANDRA SHAPIRO/KAREN NEVINS

movement was about, I graduated in the bellwether year of 1968, went on to graduate school, and found the antiwar movement consuming whatever political interests I had.

By 1971, armed with a master's degree in sociology, I landed in Kansas City, Missouri, and began my search for a "real" job—not clerical, thank you—in which I was well served by my longstanding refusal to learn to type. I talked my way into a management training program intended for "minorities," convincing them that hiring women was the next big step—probably denying some superbly qualified minority candidate the opportunity to build a career at a place I left two years later. That same year, I saw a flyer for an organizational meeting for the local Women's Political Caucus. The election of women and passage of the Equal Rights Amendment became my focus. Missouri was supposed to be one of the "swing" states that would put the amendment over the top. We printed a "countdown calendar" and plotted lobbying strategies—all wildly unsuccessful. Getting an eyeful of the Missouri legislature (and its legislator-attorneys) convinced me, and others, that action (i.e., returning to law school, seeking political office, or both) was what was needed. In 1973 I took my LSAT in Houston, where I was a delegate from Missouri to the first national meeting of the National Women's Political Caucus. It was headquartered at the now-defunct Rice Hotel, which had to alter its longstanding policy of not paging women—so unladylike!

By the fall of 1973, I was in Boston at Northeastern School of Law—in its first class composed half of women. I graduated in 1976, joined the Massachusetts Bar Association, but bypassed MAWL, which my impatient activist eyes saw as a bit tame. (I later acquired a much greater appreciation of its pioneering role and support of the advancement of women attorneys.) I settled into a small practice in Brockton, where a number of women attorneys regularly had lunch together. We all became involved in the Plymouth County Bar Association. In fact, the local bar associations presented a clear path for acceptance with "the guys" in a social setting. With all the challenges presented to women appearing in court in those years, I found the county bar wonderfully welcoming, and it still holds a special place in my heart. I set out with a mentor (male) to run educational programs and ultimately sat on its board—even though still a kid, legally speaking.

In 1978, one of my women lunch partners gave me a call. She had received notice of an organizational meeting for a new Women's Bar Association and, knowing my predilections, thought I might be interested. I was, and showed up at a meeting in the Old Friend's Meeting House in Boston.

What I learned was intriguing. A small group of women attorneys had been meeting for some time to address issues of women in the practice of law, in bar associations, the fate of the Equal Rights Amendment, and other women's legal issues of the time. Passage of the federal amendment was still possible. MAWL could not and would not take a stand. The other bar associations viewed this as rather outside their bailiwick. The "founding mothers" (principally Pat McGovern, Charlotte Perretta, Wendy Gershengorn, Diane Kottmyer, Elizabeth Cremens, Mindy Milburg, Ellen Janos, and others) knew something new was needed. I plunged in and served as the copresident pro tem with Wendy Gershengorn while we organized, then as its first president (although I was really part of the "second wave"). I glibly told a *Boston Globe* reporter that the mainstream bar associations were "old-boy networks" and "too damn conservative," thinking I was "off the record," but causing a not-so-pleasant stir. But the Women's Bar Association was off and running, no matter the verbal miscues of its then spokeswoman.

I glibly told a Boston Globe *reporter that the mainstream bar associations were "old-boy networks" and "too damn conservative," thinking I was "off the record," but causing a not-so-pleasant stir.*

In the early years, the WBA set about taking positions on and influencing legislation impacting women, presenting programs, and pressing for women's appointment to positions of importance, from the judiciary to the myriad of appointed boards. We also began working closely with the Massachusetts Bar Association, forwarding lists of women suitable for appointment to section councils and for nominations everywhere the MBA had a say. With $4,000 in our bank account and a budget that allocated $200 to each committee, we were slim on resources but long on goals. Not much escaped our eyes. In 1979, I wrote to then MBA President Wayne Budd expressing our concern that the MBA-sponsored disability insurance excluded maternity leave, based on "stereotypical assumptions" that reduced the value of these policies to the "increasing number of women attorneys in the Commonwealth." A similar letter followed to BBA President Jack Curtin, albeit with no reference to any offending BBA insurance policy. By 1985, we broadened our scope when Pat McGovern—then in the state senate—miraculously obtained funding for the first gender bias committee, established

A meeting of the 1985-1986 WBA board of directors at the offices of Foley, Hoag & Eliot. From left to right are: (Hon.) Margaret S. Fearey, Sandra Shapiro, Martha Coakley, and Jamie Ann Sabino.

IMAGE COURTESY OF SANDRA SHAPIRO/KAREN NEVINS

The WBA's 1985–1986 board of directors. Seated left to right: (Hon.) Margaret H. Marshall, (Hon.) Margaret S. Fearey, Mary K. Ryan, Martha Coakley, Sandra Shapiro, Jamie Ann Sabino, and (Hon.) Patti Saris. Standing left to right: Sarah Wald, (Hon.) Dyanne Polatin (Klein), Gilda Tuoni (Russell), Barbara R. Arnwine, Elaine M. Epstein, (Hon.) Judith Dilday, Carolynn N. Fischel, Penny Billings, Dianne Wilkerson, Judith Miles, Harriet Onello, Susan Crockin, (Hon.) Margot Botsford, and Toni G. Wolfman.

IMAGE COURTESY OF SANDRA SHAPIRO/KAREN NEVINS

The inclusion of women was not just a goal in and of itself. It expanded the focus of the issues bar associations were willing to tackle.

under the auspices of the Supreme Judicial Court. The resulting study and its implementation had enormous impact on the treatment of women at all levels in the courts, ending what often felt like a fraternity initiation ritual for many. By 1992, the WBA formed its own foundation to fund projects of importance to women, including the Framingham Project (for incarcerated women), Women's Lunch Place Project (for homeless women), and Family Law Project (for battered women).

At the outset, the WBA asked for a seat on the MBA Board of Delegates, while leaving MAWL's seat on the board intact. As WBA president, I began attending these meetings, beginning a long period of involvement with the MBA. While women were, by that time, participating in the MBA and other bar associations in increasing numbers, no woman had yet served as president of the MBA, the BBA, or, indeed, other bar associations in my recollection. I heard stories of qualified women who were passed over in previous years but was confident that bar association leadership was now committed to making this happen. I leapt at the chance to serve on the MBA nominating committee when offered—knowing my friend Alice Richmond was a logical choice for this "first." She was selected without controversy and served from 1986 to 1987. The BBA followed with Gene Dahmen serving as president from 1987 to 1988.

Having segued into involvement in the MBA via the WBA, I was the direct beneficiary of the years the WBA had spent clamoring for more involvement of women in all aspects of law. This now included bar associations, and by the time I became the second woman president of the MBA (1992–93), my gender was no big deal. Indeed, a few years earlier, I had run a contested election opposing an "all Boston" slate of MBA officers—running against another woman. Margaret Marshall had been president of the BBA in 1991–92 and by the time Sandra Lynch did so the following year, both the MBA and the BBA were headed by women. Numerous county bar associations either had or soon would have women presidents. The diversity issue in bar associations shifted to concerns that the involvement of attorneys of color in bar associations had not kept pace with that of women.

What difference has it all made? An enormous one, in my view. The inclusion of women was not just a goal in and of itself. It expanded the focus of the issues bar associations were willing to tackle. Once untouchable issues of advancement, bias, and equal treatment became staples of bar association support. The MBA's financial support of the WBA's Judicial Consent for Minors Referral Panel (organized to recruit and train attorneys to represent minors required to seek judicial consent for abortions) stands as a classic example of a strictly women's issue first receiving this kind of "crossover" support. And the WBA always remained free to tackle tougher issues, participating in amicus briefs in landmark cases on sexual discrimination and harassment, and opposing restrictions on Medicaid funding for abortions. The combined prodding of the WBA on a number of important issues and the number of women at the table through bar associations brought many "women's" issues into the mainstream of bar concern.

This shifted the balance on numerous issues of importance to women and played a leading role in creating change in the courts. The gender bias committee started its work at a time when women attorneys, litigants, court personnel, and even judges did not receive the respect that is de rigueur today. Continued change in women attorneys' roles at law firms, on boards, and in the public sector will no doubt depend, at least in part, on the urging of those same associations. And a host of once-forgotten women, e.g., incarcerated women, are served by the bar foundations that now routinely fund "women's" causes.

I hesitate to wax eloquent about the importance of bar associations. As I always tell new presidents, you have to keep a sense of perspective and humor: it's only a bar association and you're not the leader of the free world! But the work of bar associations does matter—often big-time—and the increased role of women attorneys over the last several decades has made for huge strides in areas we now take for granted. And, in my view, bar association involvement has simply been a lot of fun. It gets you out of the office, expands the range of folks you know, forces you to stretch your thinking, and often keeps your ego in check. After all these years, I still recommend it, particularly to women!

Mary K. Ryan

Women's Bar Association of Massachusetts President, 1984–1985
Boston Bar Association President, 1997–1998

Tales of a Bar Junkie

When I joined the Boston College Law School Class of 1977, I was part of the first large wave of women who chose law school rather than business school when those previously closed doorways to professional opportunities and power opened wide in the 1970s. I had grown up as the youngest of five children (and the only girl) in the Irish Catholic enclave of South Boston. Only a few of my relatives had gone to college; one of them, my uncle Thomas ("Bobby") Linehan, was a city councilor and then a District Court judge. But my parents somehow managed to get all five of us through college. When it came to me, the career paths for college-educated women were to become a teacher or a nurse. My mother desperately wanted me to be a teacher, and would have settled for nursing, but I had neither the interest nor the aptitude for either calling.

So my becoming the lawyer in the family was rather a surprise to me (and even more so to my family, particularly Uncle Bobby). I spent the first three years of my career as a law clerk, where there were as many women clerks as men, if far fewer women judges. I had the extraordinary opportunity to clerk at the Supreme Judicial Court for Justice Ruth Abrams, a great mentor not just to me but to many other women. I learned from Justice Abrams and her colleagues about the challenges that they had faced, which seemed so historic and removed. After BC Law, where approximately one-third of the class were women, and my clerkships, I (and many others) had been lulled into thinking women had already gained a strong footing in the profession. We soon learned, in the words of the slogan that graced the WBA T-shirts, that "Passing the Bar.... doesn't mean you're past the barriers." While I may not have expected when I started practice that so many challenges remained for women who wanted to achieve full equality with men in the profession, I can't say I was unprepared. After all, I had grown up in male-dominated South Boston with four older brothers, so in many ways I was well equipped to deal with the predominance of men in my work environment and in the courts.

Unlike some of the other women in this book, I was neither a "first" nor even a founder of the WBA. I was a law clerk when I attended the first open meeting of the WBA in the auditorium of what was then the First National Bank building at 100 Federal Street in the late 1970s. It was clear to me that individual women like me couldn't do what the concerted effort of the WBA—and later, many other bar groups—could and would do to advance the profession's recognition that a new day had come and old ways had to change if the women joining the profession in great numbers were to flourish in their legal careers. I was so impressed by the "founding mothers" that a year later when I met Carol Kenner through one of my Nutter colleagues, and she asked me to help with a WBA project, I couldn't say yes fast enough. That first WBA project was to survey law firms and government agencies about their maternity/paternity and part-time work policies. In the early 1980s there were only a handful of firms that had formal policies, so one of the WBA's responses was to draft a model policy.

Mary K. Ryan speaking at the WBA's annual meeting in 1985 at the Parker House in Boston.

IMAGE COURTESY OF SANDRA SHAPIRO/ KAREN NEVINS

Another major effort by the WBA grew out of the fact that our complaints and frustration about the lack of women on the bench, in appointed positions with the state and federal government, and in the leadership of the then-mainstream bar associations, were met with the constant refrain that there were no qualified women. The WBA Appointments Committee, still an active WBA committee, was formed in response, and we were always ready with a list of qualified women candidates to give to anyone who tried to use that dated excuse.

The issues we dealt with thirty years ago seemed daunting at the time, even if I can look back now and smile at some of them. For example, in the 1980s the courts were hardly accustomed to women litigators. On the lighter side, it seemed like we debated endlessly among ourselves about whether we could wear pants in the courtroom, which reminded me of Justice Abrams' similar stories of the dilemma she and her peers faced on whether they had to wear hats and gloves to court, as was the norm elsewhere in society in their day. Then there was the simple problem of how to address women lawyers, which involved some comic moments. The first time I appeared in a suburban District Court, my male opposing counsel and I approached the bench. The judge, predictably a male, stared at us for a long moment, looked me in the eye and proceeded to address us both as "gentlemen." Later, I realized that he hesitated because he simply had no idea what to call me, since the gender-neutral term of "counsel" was not yet in use, or at least not in his court. How many times did something like this happen? Sometime later, in another case, after argument in federal District Court on a summary judgment motion, my cocounsel asked me how I knew the judge. When I said I didn't, he explained that he assumed I did because the judge called me by my first name while calling him "Mr." On another occasion, I was representing the lead defendant in a construction case with numerous parties. We all appeared in court for a status conference. Looming down from the bench, the judge asked "the gentlemen" to approach. One of other lawyers graciously pointed me out to the judge and explained I was one of the lead counsel in the case. Without skipping a beat, he said "I know, and if she doesn't like it, she can report me to the Gender Bias Committee."

(Hon.) Margaret H. Marshall, Toni G. Wolfman, and Judith Miles at the WBA's annual meeting in March 1985.

IMAGE COURTESY OF SANDRA SHAPIRO/ KAREN NEVINS

I didn't have to "report" him to the Gender Bias Committee, since I was on it. The work of the Gender Bias Committee addressed the more serious and substantive consequences of gender bias in the legal system for all the women affected—as judges, court staff, lawyers, and litigants. The Gender Bias Committee was one of many projects instituted by the leadership of the WBA with the collaboration of the courts, particularly the women judges, and a strong assist from Pat McGovern, then chair of the Senate Ways and Means Committee and a founding member of the WBA—a great example of the blossoming "old girls" network. That project, among many others, epitomized the WBA's commitment not just to women lawyers but to all women whose lives are impacted by the legal system.

This is what got me started as a "bar junkie." Several times a month, morning, noon, or night, I tell my office colleagues that I am off to the bar. Though I try to say "bar meeting," most of the time, I think they always know what I mean: I am either off to my home away from home at 16 Beacon Street, the Boston Bar Association, or to any number of other locales—some near, some far—for a meeting of some bar association board or committee, or some other meeting of a group of lawyers. I have been involved, at almost every level, in many bars and legal groups, including not only the WBA, but also the BBA, the MBA, the Real Estate Bar Association, the American Bar Association, and various court and legal services committees. I am still involved in bar work, and I am not alone. Why do I—and many other lawyers—spend time on bar work? For me, there are three main reasons.

One reason is the opportunity for service to the profession and the legal system. To put it less grandly, bar work gives me a chance to help accomplish things I care about but that I (or any other individual) could not do on my own. This was a lesson I learned from my early and indelible experiences with the WBA. I have had the same experience many times since, though I can only mention a few of those experiences

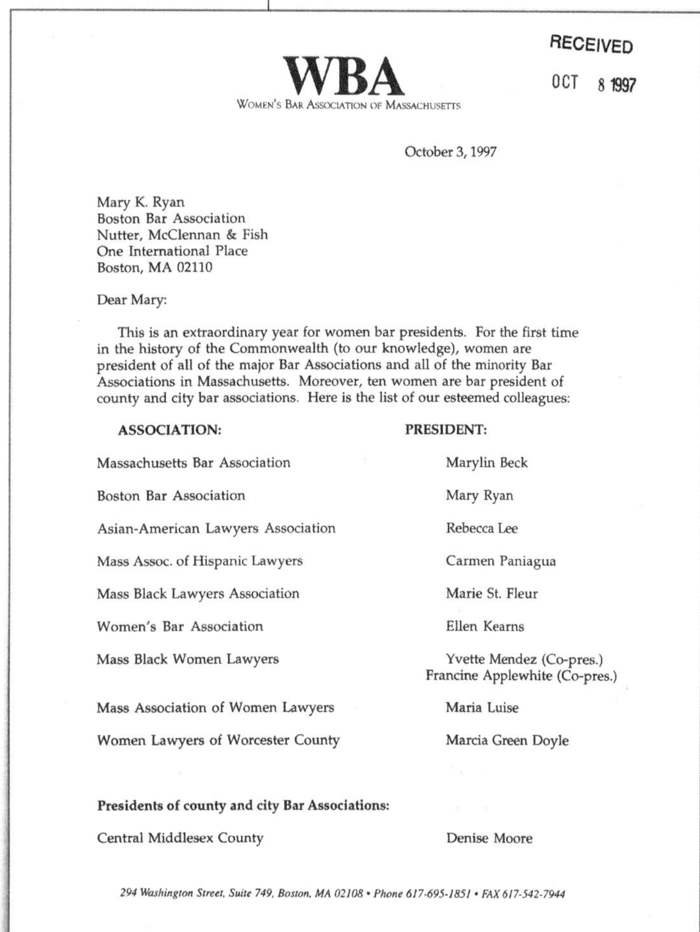

RECEIVED

OCT 8 1997

WBA

WOMEN'S BAR ASSOCIATION OF MASSACHUSETTS

October 3, 1997

Mary K. Ryan
Boston Bar Association
Nutter, McClennan & Fish
One International Place
Boston, MA 02110

Dear Mary:

This is an extraordinary year for women bar presidents. For the first time in the history of the Commonwealth (to our knowledge), women are president of all of the major Bar Associations and all of the minority Bar Associations in Massachusetts. Moreover, ten women are bar president of county and city bar associations. Here is the list of our esteemed colleagues:

ASSOCIATION:	PRESIDENT:
Massachusetts Bar Association	Marylin Beck
Boston Bar Association	Mary Ryan
Asian-American Lawyers Association	Rebecca Lee
Mass Assoc. of Hispanic Lawyers	Carmen Paniagua
Mass Black Lawyers Association	Marie St. Fleur
Women's Bar Association	Ellen Kearns
Mass Black Women Lawyers	Yvette Mendez (Co-pres.) Francine Applewhite (Co-pres.)
Mass Association of Women Lawyers	Maria Luise
Women Lawyers of Worcester County	Marcia Green Doyle

Presidents of county and city Bar Associations:

Central Middlesex County	Denise Moore

294 Washington Street, Suite 749, Boston, MA 02108 • Phone 617-695-1851 • FAX 617-542-7944

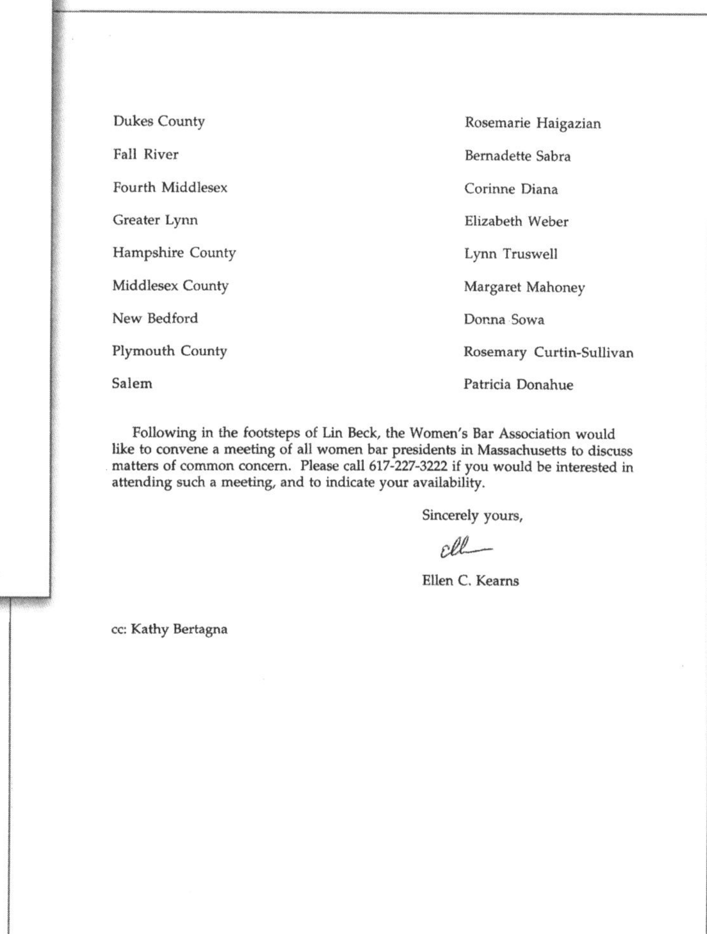

Dukes County	Rosemarie Haigazian
Fall River	Bernadette Sabra
Fourth Middlesex	Corinne Diana
Greater Lynn	Elizabeth Weber
Hampshire County	Lynn Truswell
Middlesex County	Margaret Mahoney
New Bedford	Donna Sowa
Plymouth County	Rosemary Curtin-Sullivan
Salem	Patricia Donahue

Following in the footsteps of Lin Beck, the Women's Bar Association would like to convene a meeting of all women bar presidents in Massachusetts to discuss matters of common concern. Please call 617-227-3222 if you would be interested in attending such a meeting, and to indicate your availability.

Sincerely yours,

Ellen C. Kearns

cc: Kathy Bertagna

▲

Letter from WBA President Ellen C. Kearns to BBA President Mary Ryan on October 3, 1997, identifying the many women then serving as bar association presidents.

IMAGES COURTESY OF MARY K. RYAN

here. I have great memories of my first leadership involvement with the BBA, after I had been president of the WBA and gained some reputation among the bar. Thanks again to personal outreach, this time from Dick Renehan, then president of the BBA, I chaired the BBA's committee for the celebration of the bicentennial of the Bill of Rights in the mid-1980s, which started the BBA Law Day in the Schools, a program that continues to this day. The legislative reform effort I did the most work on was the ongoing effort to reform spousal share legislation, largely spurred by the WBA. (Formerly known as "dower," spousal share refers to the right to receive a share of the probate estate in the event one spouse, traditionally the working husband, tries to disinherit the other, traditionally the stay-at-home wife.)

My interest in advancing women's rights soon led me to what has become a lifelong avocation to increase access to justice for all those affected by the legal system, particularly those unable to afford a lawyer. Under my leadership as president in 1997–1998, the BBA issued a groundbreaking study on unrepresented litigants in the Massachusetts courts, the first such effort by any bar association in the United States; the study played an important role in many of the reforms that help pro se litigants today. In addition to leading the BBA campaign to increase pro bono efforts, I had the opportunity to serve on the committee that recommended adoption of Rule 6.1 of the Massachusetts Rules of Professional Conduct, which urges each lawyer to perform at least twenty-five hours of pro bono legal service to help the poor in our community. I went on to chair the SJC's standing committee on pro bono legal services for over a decade. Currently, I am working with a dedicated committee, convened by the BBA but composed of lawyers from across the state, to advance "Civil Gideon," the campaign to recognize a right to counsel in civil cases involving basic human rights, such as shelter, sustenance, safety, health, and child custody, when legal representation is essential to protect those rights. From my work at the ABA on access-to-justice issues, I have learned so much about the issues we face in Massachusetts. Any one of us would make little progress toward goals such as these by ourselves, but when working as part of the organized bar, the sky is the limit.

Any one of us would make little progress toward goals such as these by ourselves, but when working as part of the organized bar, the sky is the limit.

A second reason is the opportunity to improve professionally. Providing excellent legal work to our clients is at the core of a good legal practice. Staying current and learning the best practices are essential. Every bar association offers substantive law committees dedicated to making its members the best lawyers they can be. Attending or teaching a CLE program run by the bar or by MCLE makes better lawyers. The same is true for the countless lunch programs that take place day after day. I think, for example, of the BBA Environmental Law Section or the REBA Environmental Committee and know how much they have helped me become a better lawyer.

The third reason is collegiality. Writing this brief piece has made me smile when I think of the people I have worked with on bar projects over the past thirty years. I have been inspired by the leadership and wisdom of so many of the colleagues I have worked with. Some have become personal friends, some trusted professional colleagues, some referral sources. My "bar" friends have helped me through some of the most difficult moments of my career. All have helped me in small ways and big, and made my life richer. Volunteer bar work, while usually enjoyable, is not always easy when there are difficult issues to be dealt with, but working with good people makes meeting challenges possible and worthwhile.

I truly consider myself privileged to have been a part of this era, but without bar work, my career would not have been nearly as satisfying, rewarding, or enjoyable.

Alice E. Richmond

First Woman President of the Massachusetts Bar Association, 1986–1987
First Woman Treasurer of the American Bar Association, 2008–2010

My Life as a First: An Abbreviated Version

I was about 10 years old when I became a serious baseball fan. Since I lived just outside New York City, I was, of course, a Yankees fan, cutting out stories about my favorite players from the newspapers and carefully pasting them into notebooks. I begged my Dad to take me to Yankee Stadium where, lo and behold, I saw a young boy not much older than I, handing balls to the home plate umpire and disappearing into the Yankee dugout. Fabulous, I thought to myself. That's something I want to do. So I wrote a letter to Yankee announcer, Mel Allen, the only name I knew in the Yankee organization (this being well before the Internet Age) and asked how to apply to be a ball boy. I still have Mel Allen's response, thanking me for my interest in the Yankees and not so gently informing me that only boys could be ball boys. I think my determination to be the "first girl" to be or do something started there and, I confess, has continued to this day.

The September 1, 1986 issue of Massachusetts Lawyers Weekly *announcing Alice Richmond as the MBA's new president.*

IMAGE SOURCE: *MASSACHUSETTS LAWYERS WEEKLY*, SEPT. 1, 1986

MASSACHUSETTS Lawyers weekly

Vol. 14, No. 50 Cite this Page 14 M.L.W. 1917 September 1, 1986 Boston, Mass. $3 per copy $140 per year

The Week's Important Opinions

Attorneys - Fees - Disability Benefits Claim

Where, following a court award of contested disability benefits, the Social Security Administration calculates attorney's fees by (1) offsetting the award of past disability benefits by the amount of other benefits received by the claimant, and then (2) taking a percentage of that net figure, this method is permissible and will be upheld, the U.S. District Court rules. (14 MLW 1922) .... page 6

Practice, Criminal - Guilty Plea - Mental Retardation - Substituted Judgment

Where a criminal defendant is found incompetent by reason of mental retardation and there is medical evidence that he will never become competent to stand trial, he cannot offer to enter a plea of guilty through his guardian on an agreed upon plea bargain, decides the SJC. (14 MLW 1928) .... page 12

Richmond At Helm Of MBA

Boston attorney Alice E. Richmond takes over the reins of the Massachusetts Bar Association this week with money matters—membership dues, legal malpractice insurance, and financial services for the association—high on her agenda.

Richmond, a 40-year-old trial attorney, quickly rose through the ranks of the 17,000-member association to become the first woman president of the MBA.

She will serve in that office during some heady—and troubled—times for her organization and her profession. Having just completed a year-long celebration of its 75th anniversary, the MBA is embarking on its next quarter-century with membership at an all-time high. But Richmond and the MBA's board of delegates face a number of thorny issues as well, including the financial well-being of the association. In addition, Richmond takes office at a time when the legal profession is being attacked on both the state and national levels and finds itself fending off raids on the tort system and criticism of its members' professionalism.

During a recent interview in her downtown law office, Richmond made it clear that she would not step into this arena gingerly. She suggested that her administration will be an aggressive one, especially as it tackles money-related problems for the bar.

Alice E. Richmond

Salting Away Money

According to Richmond, the MBA's expenses have increased with the "rapid

(See page 32)

High Court Opines On Linkage

In the latest development in the city of Boston's "linkage" case, the Massachusetts Supreme Judicial Court has suggested that linkage arrangements do not unconstitutionally corrupt the zoning process by influencing the city's zoning board with promises of extra revenue.

Judge Herbert P. Wilkins wrote for the court: "The fact that a particular decision by a municipal agency will benefit the municipality, by providing employment or reasonably priced housing to its residents or by generating additional revenue for it in one way or other, does not invalidate that decision as a matter of law." However, the court said that, in other circumstances, the existence of "a potentially distracting, irrelevant influence on a public agency's decision-making process may cast doubt on the fairness of the process and warrant careful judicial scrutiny."

The court left open the related question of whether the city's zoning board had the authority to enact the linkage provision in the first place.

It was about the same time that I decided to become a lawyer, though I cannot remember whether the two events were related. There were not many women lawyers, but I knew one: the wife of my father's best friend from law school. Although very smart, she did not practice and was home with her three young children. My own mother was also very smart, and I loved the way both women would dominate conversations about politics and current events. It frankly never occurred to me that they were in any way unusual. My parents were amazing people, well ahead of

Alice Richmond and Governor Michael Dukakis during a bill signing.

IMAGE COURTESY OF ALICE E. RICHMOND

their time. It was their view that their two daughters could do or be anything, and it was never mentioned that "girls" were limited to any particular role or occupation. It took me decades to understand that their views were not widely shared, and by that time I was a practicing lawyer and my older sister was a board-certified neurosurgeon with a Ph.D. in neurobiology and electron microscopy.

I knew from the beginning that I wanted to be a trial lawyer because, in my view, that was where the action was. As one of two women law clerks on the Massachusetts Superior Court (having turned down a job with CBS News), I interviewed at Boston's major firms. I was a graduate of Harvard Law School with good credentials and a prestigious clerkship. You can imagine my surprise when, after I mentioned that I really, really wanted to be a trial lawyer, there were suddenly no jobs. Estate planning, OK. In some places, probate or domestic relations (i.e., divorce), OK. But civil or criminal trial practice? Not possible.

I went to talk with my boss, Chief Justice Walter McLaughlin, a steadfast mentor and, later, friend. "How about the public sector?" he said after listening to my job-hunting woes. "Defense or prosecution?" There were, of course, no visible women in either role at the time. "Prosecution," I said. "If I make a mistake as a defense lawyer, someone goes to jail." This seemed to satisfy the Chief, who made one telephone call to Garrett Byrne, then the Suffolk County District Attorney, and, within weeks, I reported to the Misdemeanor Session to begin my life as an assistant district attorney. "Here's the file," said the senior ADA. "The trial starts at two. We've never seen a girl try a case."

"Here's the file," said the senior ADA. "The trial starts at two. We've never seen a girl try a case."

I cannot remember if I won or lost that particular case, but I can report, immodestly, that I won much more often than I lost. At the time I arrived in the DA's office, there was one other woman ADA, who handled drug cases; there were no women on the felony trial list. By legend, I appear to be the first woman to have tried a murder case in the history of the Commonwealth; I am certain that I was the first to try a gang-rape case. For most of the time I was trying cases, there were no other women ADAs trying felonies in Suffolk, and only one in the other counties. I was an object of curiosity and there was usually a gallery of courthouse onlookers resembling Olympic swimming judges ready to raise the low score for a missed performance. I had no role models, and my now lifelong habit of wearing heels as high as my knees will support is a result of wanting to be at eye level with my adversaries in the courtroom. Through it all, there were many ADAs who were nothing but supportive, as

▲

Alice Richmond speaking at an event while president of the MBA.

IMAGE COURTESY OF ALICE E. RICHMOND

well as a legion of court officers and assistant clerks who regarded it as their personal mission to make sure I ate and got home safely.

It is said that District Attorney Garrett Byrne was the model for one of the major characters in *The Last Hurrah*, not necessarily a feminist-friendly group. I can, however, say without qualification that Garrett Byrne gave me every opportunity to succeed and, in fact, supported my becoming a Special Assistant Attorney General to try the *Blaikie* murder case, then a nationally publicized trial that became the subject of a bestseller by a *Time* magazine writer. After the case mistried amid public comment about the wisdom of giving such an important prosecution to a "girl," Attorney General Frank Bellotti insisted that I try it again. By the time that happened, I was an Assistant Professor at New England School of Law. The case was eventually won in the courtroom where Lizzie Borden was acquitted.

Around this time it occurred to me that I should join a bar association. The Boston Bar Association was having a "brown bag" lunch meeting on a criminal law topic, so I went. It was one of the most uncomfortable experiences of my life. I smiled and tried to make conversation, but no one said a word to me. I was the only woman in the room. "This isn't going to work," I thought, and would probably have remained a nonjoiner if not for the fact that someone said I should try the Massachusetts Bar Association. I did. Livingston Hall, one of my Harvard Law School professors and past MBA president, was working on the new ABA Juvenile Justice Standards, and he asked me to work with him. That led to my becoming active in the MBA Criminal Justice Section, and from that to the ABA House of Delegates as the newly mandated "young lawyer" representative. I became a member of the MBA Board of Delegates, and although there were several women who appeared likely to move into the leadership track to become the MBA's first woman president, none did. I thought then, and think now, that several of them would have been very good bar presidents, but resistance to the idea of a woman president was very strong and evidently shared throughout the United States. As I became an officer, it was clear to me that I would not become the first woman MBA president without help from my (male) friends. Two past MBA presidents—Roy Hammer, then my law partner, and Richard K. Donahue, a legendary figure who had been President John F. Kennedy's political appointments secretary in the White House—were instrumental in convincing others that I was up to the task. (Of course, by the time I was nominated, I was pregnant, but that's another story.) At the time, only Illinois and the District of Columbia had had women bar association presidents, so I was not only the first in Massachusetts, I was one of the first in the country.

I followed my term as MBA president by serving three years as the first woman president of the Massachusetts Bar Foundation. I was also the first (and, for twenty-five years, the only) woman Massachusetts Bar Examiner and, eventually, one of the first two women elected to the American College of Trial Lawyers from Massachusetts. Most recently, I served, as Justice Ruth Ginsburg noted in August 2010, as the first woman Treasurer of the American Bar Association. Although I was flattered and honored by Justice Ginsburg's reference, the interests of full disclosure require me to report that I was a student of hers when she was a Visiting Professor at Harvard Law School. (She was not offered a permanent position because the law school faculty deemed her not aggressive or scholarly enough.) I will be forever grateful that I had the opportunity to learn from this incredibly wise and patient woman.

I am sure that there are several other "first woman" designations that I have either forgotten or never knew. I do know that ever since I was a young girl, when I hear that there has never been a "female" something, it's like waving a red flag in front of a bull. If I can break that barrier and be the first, I will. It hasn't been easy and, yes, I might have done things differently, but here's my reasoning: once that barrier is broken and there is a "first," then the next woman and the one after that and the one after that can achieve and perform (or not) depending on their individual qualities and not on the accident of gender. I compare it to those great words of Martin Luther King, who looked forward to the time when children would be judged by the content of their character and not by the color of their skin. The same is true for gender, and I am grateful that I had the chance to participate in a process where gender is now irrelevant in selecting leaders of the organized bar. There are even girl ball boys. Now that's a first I wish I could have accomplished, although only for the Red Sox.

I do know that ever since I was a young girl, whenever I've heard that there has never been a "female" something, it's been like waving a red flag in front of a bull. If I can break that barrier and be the first, I will.

Gene D. Dahmen

First Woman President of the Boston Bar Association, 1987–1988

Thrust into the Forefront

My mother was a college May Queen and the Sweetheart of Sigma Chi. She was also a pioneer in the health care field. Having achieved neither of the first two distinctions, and with no aptitude for science, I had to find another path to success. Something completely different. I had been in all-female institutions for much of my education, so Harvard Business School, my father's alma mater, sounded quite appealing. In the early 1960s, though, only the Harvard-Radcliffe Business Program for Women was available. That didn't suit my purposes, and law school seemed the next best thing. Thus, off I went to the University of Virginia, not having the faintest idea whether I wanted to be a lawyer. It was part dream-come-true (so many men!) and part worst nightmare (only three women—and I was the only one in my section of 125). But I quickly decided that my choice was a good one. I loved the school, I loved my classmates and professors (for the most part), and I loved the law. When I got my diploma at graduation, I also got a kiss from the dean. Imagine that today! And, importantly, I began to develop a social conscience.

Then came Boston. Why Boston, when my classmates were going to places like Richmond and Atlanta? I was proud of being Southern, but ambivalent too, growing up as I

▶ *Gene D. Dahmen presenting an award to the Honorable Richard L. Banks of the Roxbury District Court at the BBA annual dinner dance in 1987.*

IMAGE COURTESY OF GENE D. DAHMEN

did in the 1950s and 1960s. I thought I could make more of a difference in another part of the country, especially the North. Boston seemed more hospitable than New York, and it was closer than San Francisco. Besides, as my very-Virginia grandmother always reminded me, Jamestown was founded before Plymouth, and that endowed me with a certain superiority. Only in her mind, I suppose, since finding a job proved difficult. I was never clear whether the problem was my being Southern or being a woman—probably both. Once employed, what little overt discrimination I experienced in my professional life came while I was an associate in my first law firm (where, for example, women were not allowed to go to the firm outings because male bonding might be disrupted). Almost as bad was being turned away from the dining room at Locke-Ober!

I joined the BBA in the early 1970s, knowing that this was a place where I could give voice to my growing interest in social justice and public service.

I was attracted to the Boston Bar Association early in my career because people I had quickly come to admire were involved there—people like John Brooks, Sumner Babcock, Ed Barshak, Haskell Cohn, and a host of young activists and civil rights advocates. I joined the BBA in the early 1970s, knowing that this was a place where I could give voice to my growing interest in social justice and public service. Affirmative action was beginning to take hold, and as one of a small number of women lawyers on the scene in the early 1970s, I soon found myself on the BBA Council. These were heady days when public interest projects such as the Lawyers Committee for Civil Rights Under Law, Legal Advocacy and Resource Center, Inc., and Volunteer Lawyers Project were in their infancies, and challenging issues of desegregation, housing, and civil rights were high on the agenda. I was excited to be part of it all.

After my time on the council, I remained involved in the BBA in various ways. Then came the momentous day in 1985 when I casually mentioned to then executive director Sue Malone that I had started violin lessons and thought it would be fun to play music with other lawyers. Without my knowledge, and certainly without my consent, Sue posted a notice in *Lawyers Weekly* saying that the BBA was starting an orchestra, and that anyone interested should call me. And they *did* call. Dragooned though I was, I am happy to say that the BBA Orchestra exists to this day, having nothing to do with the law, of course, other than giving talented colleagues a chance to relieve stress and blow off steam. This was such an eccentric activity for the BBA, coming at a time when women in leadership positions were needed, that I was thrust into the forefront and somehow found myself nominated to be vice president. I was so obscure that president-elect David Rideout had no idea who I was when I was nominated. It was not an auspicious beginning.

In the two years before I became president, we worked hard on a long-range plan for the BBA that began to set the course toward more involvement with the City of Boston. To my great satisfaction, David also focused much attention on improving the status of women in the profession. In my presidential year (1987–88), we celebrated the bicentennial of the Constitution. As the sixty-fourth successor to the BBA's founder, John Adams, and the first woman president in 222 years, I thought of myself as "Abigail's revenge," fulfilling her promise to John as the Constitution was being drafted that "if particular care and attention is not paid to the ladies, we are determined to foment a rebellion, and will not hold ourselves bound by any laws in which we have no voice or representation." How we wish her name were on our courthouse.

Almost every bar president will say that his or her year in office was a uniquely rewarding experience. It was certainly true for me. I was scared to death, of course, and although I got a little training at the American Bar Association's "Charm School" for incoming bar presidents, it barely began to prepare me for the challenges (and joys) of the job. My primary goal that year was to expand and diversify our membership, with a special outreach to minority lawyers. We established a taskforce on which all minority bar associations were represented, and I believe we did some very good groundwork during that year, which has been ongoing ever since. We were honored to have Dennis Archer (then chief justice of the Michigan Supreme Court, later mayor of Detroit and president of the ABA) speak at a special luncheon sponsored by the BBA and the minority bar associations. Perhaps the recognition for which I am most grateful came from the Asian American Lawyers Association of Massachusetts, Massachusetts Association of Hispanic Attorneys, Massachusetts Black Lawyers Association, and Massachusetts Black Women Attorneys, who presented me with a plaque at the end of the year in appreciation for my "outstanding leadership and courage in promoting equal opportunities for minorities in the legal profession." Another special delight was working with Ned Hines as president-elect. We had been friends for many years, and all who knew and remember Ned will understand why the partnership with him was such a gift.

From left to right: James C. Hamilton, Sue U. Malone, Gene Dahmen, and the Honorable Dennis W. Archer at a luncheon sponsored by the BBA and the minority bar associations during Dahmen's presidency.

IMAGE COURTESY OF GENE D. DAHMEN

Gene Dahmen, Hon. Dennis W. Archer, and Mayor Raymond L. Flynn at a luncheon sponsored by the BBA and the minority bar associations.

IMAGE COURTESY OF GENE D. DAHMEN

How did I achieve any kind of work-life balance that year (or any year, for that matter)? It starts with forgiving colleagues, a wonderful assistant (who has been with me thirty-two years), a supportive spouse, somewhat tolerant children (who referred to themselves as "bar orphans"), a remarkable nanny, and nineteen au pairs (including a Bengali plasma physics student, an Irish nun, a Peruvian computer programmer, a French-horn player, two pianists, and a Dutch artist). And working in environments that honor and respect the importance of public service work and a healthy life outside the office has been a huge factor. I have been very lucky in that respect.

My BBA presidency opened the door to many other opportunities, including continuing service on the Boston Bar Foundation and "first woman" leadership positions at MCLE, the University of Virginia School of Law, and other organizations. I was an early beneficiary of the women's movement, and in many ways my path was easier than that of those who followed me. Those who have stood on my shoulders—and now there are many—have brought huge distinction to the bar in ways I could never have imagined. I am honored to be associated with these women and with all those who have traveled our road by whatever means.

Gina Walcott

Massachusetts Black Lawyers Association President, 1999–2000

Standing in the Shadow of Greatness: Reflections from a Grateful Beneficiary

I am standing at the podium of the Sheraton Boston Hotel's grand ballroom, facing the more than 800 attendees of the 2010 Massachusetts Black Lawyers Association (MBLA) Annual Gala. It is a long-awaited and magical moment for me, as I am charged with discussing the life and works of someone I had the good fortune to be able to call friend and mentor: the late, great Judge Reginald Lindsay of the U.S. District Court for the District of Massachusetts. I am honored to be a part of the MBLA's tribute to this man who was both a remarkable human being and a distinguished jurist, and in whose name we are unveiling the first-ever Reginald Lindsay Scholarship to a deserving law student. I welcome the opportunity to publicly declare just how profound an effect he had on my career and, indeed, my life.

As I prepare to begin my remarks, I am reminded yet again of the myriad ways in which Judge Lindsay enhanced my professional experience as a law student and as a lawyer. This reflection, in turn, reminds me of those who have guided, encouraged, supported, and otherwise walked beside me at every critical juncture in my professional and educational development. When it really mattered, these individuals selflessly offered up their hard-won wisdom in the form of candid advice, prescient introductions, cautionary tales, practice tips, and unwavering motivation. It is their selflessness—like Judge Lindsay's—that cloaks and inspires me.

As I conclude my remarks, I pay homage to Judge Lindsay through our shared appreciation for "all things Shakespeare" by reciting a particularly apt passage from *Twelfth Night*: "Be not afraid of greatness: Some are born great, some achieve greatness, and some have greatness thrust upon 'em." Judge Lindsay is one such example of "greatness," as are the other selfless individuals in my life who have taken time out of their busy lives to mentor and help me in my educational and professional journeys.

I have always been acutely aware that any progress made by me in the educational and professional arenas resulted, in part, from the sacrifices of pioneering women and people of color who paved the way for others like me. This deep awareness was ingrained in me as a child by my parents, who cautioned against wasted opportunities and "blessings" as they recounted tales of their own difficult and very poor upbringings in the segregated South and in a non-English–speaking region of Central America. My parents worked hard to see to it that we would all receive top-notch educations, largely influenced by their own limited educational prospects as children and their inability to complete high school. They believed that it was fine to accept help from others on the way to achieving our goals, but that it was not enough to "accept the good" and then simply rest on our laurels without somehow demonstrating that we were worthy beneficiaries of such kindnesses. Rather, it was incumbent on us to show our gratitude by doing something to improve the lives of others in like manner. Bottom line: Accept the good, but remember to pay it forward.

My earliest mentoring relationships were all educational in nature. The first significant mentoring relationship was with my

Gina Walcott with Judge Reginald Lindsay at her swearing-in ceremony for the U.S. Attorney's Office.

IMAGE COURTESY OF GINA WALCOTT

second-grade teacher, Ms. Fanning, who took a special interest in my educational advancement, encouraging my mother to apply to local private schools with first-rate reputations. Ms. Fanning walked my mother through the complex school and financial aid application process, even helping her navigate the competing deadlines and understand the bevy of paperwork associated with these applications. Ultimately, it was Ms. Fanning who helped my mother select Buckingham Browne & Nichols School (BB&N) after evaluating and comparing my acceptances.

Another significant mentoring experience occurred while I was a senior at BB&N high school and involved Mrs. Williams, the mother of a classmate, who knew of my interest in English literature generally, and in William Shakespeare's writings specifically. Mrs. Williams was also passionate about Shakespeare's works and had been an English major in college, so she took it upon herself to assist in my college application process, even researching and advising me of New England schools reputed to have excellent English departments. Mrs. Williams was unaware of this, but her intervention was both timely and critical because the person who should have been performing this function—my high school guidance counselor—spent the majority of our sessions discouraging, rather than encouraging, me from pursuing my areas of interest and overall educational goals. Without Mrs. Williams' positive influence, encouragement, and attention, coupled with the faith, strength, conviction, and unwavering support of my family, I am certain my life would have turned out very differently and I would have missed out on a myriad of wonderful opportunities and experiences. Ultimately, I attended Mrs. Williams' alma mater, Wellesley College, from which I graduated as president of the college's Shakespeare Society with a dual major in English and Black Studies. While not legal in nature, these early mentoring relationships set the standard and laid the groundwork for all future mentoring expectations and experiences.

My first significant legal mentoring relationship took place when contemplating whether to pursue a law degree. Once again turning to educational contacts, I called upon a former BB&N parent, the Honorable Geraldine Hines of the Massachusetts Superior Court, who was, quite literally, the only attorney then known to my family. Judge Hines was a founder and principal of the Law Offices of Burnham, Hines & Dilday, the state's first Black woman–owned and –operated law firm. She was instrumental in assisting me with decisions related to my law school selection, application, and acceptance processes. Throughout law school, in my subsequent legal positions, and even now, Judge Hines has always been there for me as a source of support, counsel, and guidance. She was my first attorney mentor, and she introduced me to many other women and people of color in the Massachusetts legal community, some of whom later served as mentors to me in varying capacities.

Gina Walcott presenting Judge Lindsay with an award during her time as president of the MBLA. Also pictured is Tonomey Coleman.

IMAGE COURTESY OF GINA WALCOTT

Throughout high school and college, I was always active—whether in a leadership capacity or as a volunteer—in organizations directed toward providing support to women, people of color, LGBTQ, economically challenged, and other historically underrepresented populations. Law school was no different. While a student at Boston University School of Law, I was very active in a number of student associations and groups created to support women, people of color, victims of domestic violence, and indigent clients. This was my first introduction to the importance and utility of affinity law student associations, and later of affinity and mainstream bar association involvement. Indeed, it was during a Black Law Students Association (BLSA) program in my first year of law school that I was introduced to the MBLA. This introduction came in the form of a posted flyer concerning an upcoming MBLA program featuring Judge Reginald Lindsay as the keynote speaker. Until that point, I was unaware of the existence or purpose of bar associations of any sort.

Curious and with no competing obligations, I decided to attend the publicized MBLA program, which proved to be one of the best career-related decisions I have ever made. When I entered the event, there stood Judge Lindsay, majestically commanding the audience and waxing poetic about a "phoenix rising," which immediately appealed to the English major in me. His words resonated with me, so I sent him a card telling him how much I enjoyed his remarks, and thought nothing more of it until I received a call from his clerk inviting me to meet with the judge. I had no way of knowing that this single MBLA event would prove to be "the gift that keeps on giving." For instance, I had no idea that it would lead to my first time meeting a judge and visiting a courthouse. Nor did I know that my attendance would result in numerous valuable contacts with people such as Judge Joyce London Ford, Judge Antoinette E. M. Leoney, Judge Judith Nelson Dilday, Judge Annette Ford, former State Representative Marie St. Fleur, former MCAD Commissioner Charles Walker, and attorney Steven Wright, to name a few. Many of these legal giants would later serve as mentors, references, valuable contacts, supportive colleagues, and dear friends, and would introduce me to other valuable bar associations such as the Boston Bar Association (BBA), the Massachusetts Bar Association (MBA), and the Women's Bar Association (WBA), all of which have proven invaluable in my professional development.

Women Presidents of the Massachusetts Black Lawyers Association

(Hon.) Barbara A. Dortch-Okara	1981–1982
Marie St. Fleur	1997–1998
Gina Walcott	1999–2000
Angela C. McConney	2006–2007
Nikiki T. Bogle	2007–2008

I was similarly unaware that, years later, the MBLA's guest speaker that evening—Judge Lindsay—would preside over my own swearing-in ceremony when I began working as an assistant U.S. attorney. Finally, I could not have known at that time that I would later have the privilege of leading that same sponsoring organization—the MBLA—as its president. After this initial introduction to the MBLA, I continued to make that organization a part of my law-student and professional life. This helped with the sense of isolation and unease I sometimes felt as one of very few people of color at law school, and later as an attorney practicing in Massachusetts.

The people I've met through my bar association affiliations have proven invaluable. While I was a law student, the bar associations held back-to-school welcome and orientation events, a variety of programs on job-search skills and practice tips, law school and bar exam relief events, and the like. Bar association members answered questions about their own occupations, even allowing me to "shadow" them at the office in order to get a true feel for what their practice entailed. I was also able to vent to them concerning my fear of the bar exam, the inequity of grading on a "bell curve," or my fear of an upcoming moot court or mock trial presentation. These successful role models reminded me that at one point they, too, may have struggled with a federal tax course, or were uncertain about what they wanted to ultimately do with their degree. We were able to discuss what role, if any, race and gender played in their classes and practices. They were forthcoming with resource information about other helpful, partnering organizations, such as the Boston Lawyers Group. They were there to talk, listen, provide support, and periodically remind me that I would successfully complete my law-school experience, just as they did, and would one day be able to practice. And so it finally did come to pass.

Meanwhile, another valuable mentoring relationship cultivated during law school took place during my second year, while taking a professional responsibility course for the Civil Practice Clinic. That mentor was Scott Harshbarger, the state's attorney general at the time. I had no idea when I signed up for his course that he would play a pivotal role in my career, serving as professor, mentor, and ultimately employer, culminating with my being hired as an assistant attorney general.

Prior to taking Professor Harshbarger's class, I had never heard of public interest law or any government attorney positions, apart from the assistant district attorneys seen in reruns of old *Perry Mason* episodes. After the course ended, I continued to inquire about public sector work. Taking notice of that interest, one of my civil rights professors invited me to serve with him as a volunteer on the attorney general's Hate Crimes Task Force. This volunteer opportunity further familiarized me with that office and its many divisions and bureaus, and my work on the task force showcased some of my research, writing, and communication capabilities. As the task force drew to a close, I was certain that I wanted to work for the attorney general's office, and I hoped that my work would positively influence my application for employment.

I continue to benefit from camaraderie, support, and encouragement from the members of the local, state, and affinity bar associations.

Thankfully, I did receive an offer from that office and I served as an assistant attorney general for the six years following my graduation from law school. I found out after I began working there that many of my task force colleagues had put their personal and professional capital behind my application, for which I was grateful.

As an attorney, I continue to benefit from camaraderie, support, and encouragement from the members of the local, state, and affinity bar associations. As a young lawyer, these associations gave me a platform to try my hand at making presentations, creating programming, and, over time, chairing committees and overseeing initiatives. This led to leadership posts, such as my current role as chair of the WBA Women of Color Committee and my former role as president of the MBLA. As executive director of Lawyers Concerned for Lawyers, Inc., I was able to use that varied skill set and leverage my contacts within the

Greater Boston legal community to build and diversify the organization and increase its relevancy.

Although I am blessed with the ability to perform in a demanding profession, that alone is not enough. I credit any success of mine to two factors: my family's legacy of a hard-driving work ethic, and the efforts of those who selflessly bestowed their care and counsel at the most critical junctures of my educational and professional life.

That they would choose to share their "greatness" with me without an eye toward personal gain or benefit inspires me to do likewise and live by their "pay it forward" philosophy. This has resulted in my acting as mentor, guide, and source of support for others, especially those who constitute the future of our profession. I take great pride in this act of "giving back" and consider it an unspoken obligation of anyone who has ever been on the receiving end of such gifts.

Kathy B. Weinman

Boston Bar Association President, 2008–2009

A Year at the Bar: Advancing Justice Through Our Collective Efforts

As a law student I vowed never to join the American Bar Association. At that time, I thought that bar associations were just lawyers helping lawyers and ignoring—if not opposing—the concerns of the public at large. It was more than a little ironic, then, that decades later I agreed to serve as president of the Boston Bar Association. My earlier views had been wrong.

Active in the BBA for about ten years, including stints as a Criminal Law Section cochair, council member, and officer, I watched other presidents use their terms to further the BBA's mission "to advance the highest standards of excellence for the legal profession, to facilitate access to justice, and to serve the community at large." A few examples important to me: Under the leadership of Renée Landers and Joe Kociubes, the BBA supported equal marriage rights in *Goodridge v. Department of Public Health* and its aftermath. Jack Cinquegrana launched a new effort to achieve greater racial and ethnic diversity in the legal profession. And

Kathy B. Weinman speaking at a BBA event.

IMAGE COURTESY OF BOSTON BAR ASSOCIATION

The BBA presidents dinner in 2008.[2]

IMAGE COURTESY OF KATHY B. WEINMAN

The women who had occupied [the BBA presidency} before me...were my inspiration and supporters.

Tony Doniger's Civil Gideon task force, led by former BBA president Mary Ryan, developed pilot programs to evaluate the impact of appointing counsel for indigent litigants in civil cases that affect their fundamental interests, such as tenant eviction matters. As some of my predecessors emphasized, serving as president of the association was an opportunity to give back.

In some ways, my BBA presidency came at a perfect time. I had devoted the previous twenty years mostly to helping build a law firm, developing a white-collar practice, and raising a family. The day I shared my plans for the upcoming term with the BBA Council was the same day we sent our youngest daughter off to college for her freshman year. With the support of my partners at Collora LLP (then Dwyer & Collora), I looked forward to committing a large part of the year to helping strengthen the BBA and to advancing issues of concern to our community. The women who had occupied that position before me—Chief Justice Margaret Marshall, Chief Judge Sandra Lynch, Gene Dahmen, Mary Ryan, Joan Lukey, Lauren Stiller Rikleen, Renée Landers, and the late, great Ellen Carpenter—were my inspiration and supporters. Many said it would be the best year of my legal career.

They were right. The initial goals for the year were ambitious: In addition to plans to build out new conference and office space at the BBA, turn the diversity task force's recommendations into action, and develop a strategic plan for the BBA, we opened the term by launching a task force to recommend criminal justice reforms that would reduce the risk of wrongful convictions. This issue was personally important to me. As a criminal defense attorney, I had seen enough and read enough to convince me that certain changes—such as reducing bias in witness identifications and providing access to DNA testing—could improve accuracy in the results of our criminal justice system.

But approximately two weeks after I assumed office on September 1, 2008, Lehman Brothers filed for bankruptcy and the United States plunged into the worst economic crisis since the Great Depression. Lawyers, clients, and the courts were not immune from the effects—and, therefore, neither was the BBA. Although, luckily, our own stability was not threatened, we needed to do what we could to help those in our community who were not faring as well. The demand for legal aid for the growing number of indigent people was escalating, but the funding for legal services dropped precipitously, resulting in an unprecedented decline in the availability of legal representation. Similarly, the budget for our state courts—and, therefore, access to justice for our citizens—was threatened at every stage of the process. Although I am somewhat reserved by nature, I was privileged to be able to lend my voice to advocate on their behalf.

Women Presidents of the Boston Bar Association

Gene D. Dahmen	1987–1988
(Hon.) Margaret H. Marshall	1991–1992
(Hon.) Sandra L. Lynch	1992–1993
Mary K. Ryan	1997–1998
Lauren Stiller Rikleen	1998–1999
Joan A. Lukey	2000–2001
Renée M. Landers	2003–2004
M. Ellen Carpenter	2004–2005
Kathy B. Weinman	2008–2009
Lisa C. Goodheart	2011–2012

Perhaps the best part of being president of the BBA was that I didn't have to do anything on my own. I called on hundreds of lawyers to volunteer their time and energy and, remarkably, virtually all of them agreed. They cochaired sections and committees, served on task forces, and gathered at the State House to speak out for our issues. Collaboration advanced our work and made it rewarding for all of us. I was struck then—and remain awed today—by the generous and committed legal community of which we are a part. It was an honor to lead as BBA president for that one-year term.

Jane Taubner Barney

Massachusetts Association of Women Lawyers President, 2009–2010

Professional Relationships and "Sisterly Support"

The Massachusetts Association of Women Lawyers (MAWL) was founded in 1905, when there were only nineteen women attorneys in Boston. Its mission was "to exchange ideas and offer 'sisterly' support" to its members. This mission has evolved over the years but its spirit is still "to further justice, to promote professional excellence and the advancement of women lawyers [and] to support the civic, educational and social interests of the profession...." We accomplish this by sponsoring educational workshops in different practice areas, the judicial nominating process, and other topics of interest to our members; by

The Massachusetts Association of Women Lawyers was founded in 1905, when there were only nineteen women attorneys in Boston. Its mission was "to exchange ideas and offer 'sisterly' support" to its members.

celebrating the achievements of our members; and by hosting our two signature events, the Annual Holiday Toast and the Annual Business Meeting and Banquet.

▲

Jane Taubner Barney speaking at MAWL's annual banquet in 2009.

IMAGE COURTESY OF JANE TAUBNER BARNEY

The Holiday Toast is traditionally held in December at the College Club in Boston, which is always beautifully decorated for the holidays. There, we honor an individual or group from the court system not ordinarily recognized, such as the victim/witness advocates, providers of lawyer-for-the-day programs, and court security. On that special evening we also present the Carol DiMaiti Scholarship Award to a deserving law school student. Our Annual Banquet in June is the setting for the introduction of our incoming president, officers, and board members, and it is where we present our Distinguished Jurist Award to a member of the bench. In addition, the MAWL Scholarship Foundation awards scholarships to law students at this event.

I would like to say that I initially joined MAWL because it is the oldest women's bar association in Massachusetts and has a rich history of education and support of women in the law—but, in actuality, MAWL was one of a number of bar associations that I joined shortly after I was sworn in as a member of the bar and opened my own law practice. It seemed to be one of the best ways to get involved in the legal community, to meet more-seasoned attorneys, and to obtain practical education concerning the practice of law. I met many solo and small-firm practitioners among MAWL's members (both women and men), many of whom shared the same areas of practice that I had at the time, domestic relations and housing court matters. Many of the educational workshops MAWL offered interested me as a small-firm practitioner. As my career evolved, I left private practice to work in the financial services industry, using my legal background to assist individuals and business owners with financial, tax, estate, and investment planning. Through my involvement in MAWL, I was able to continue to network with the attorneys I already knew and those I would continue to meet at workshops and events.

My active involvement and eventual leadership role in MAWL was a more conscious decision, made after belonging to the organization for a number of years. As I attended MAWL events and workshops, I met and became friendly with a number of women on MAWL's board of directors. One of the board members invited me to assist on a project to revise the organization's bylaws. When she learned of my interest in becoming more involved, I was nominated and elected to the board in 1998. After serving on the board for a few years, an officer position became vacant and I was nominated to the position of assistant treasurer, which I accepted in 2001. Shame on me for being out of town for the first planning meeting, where it was announced that the treasurer was unable to serve. In my absence I was appointed treasurer! Historically, the officers move up through each position, eventually serving as president; however, I became pregnant with my first child during my term as treasurer and declined to move up. I was invited to continue as a member of the board and after serving in a variety of positions, eventually became president in 2009.

At the time, I was working as a financial advisor at TFC Financial Management, a fee-based financial planning and investment firm. Fortunately for me, my firm and our board of directors were both very supportive of my nomination. The most difficult part of serving as president was the time commitment, but our board worked very well together and I learned

Jane Taubner Barney with her daughter Juliette presenting an award to Patrice Provitha for the Victim Witness Advocates of the Middlesex District Attorney's Office. Patricia Blackburn stands in background.

IMAGE COURTESY OF JANE TAUBNER BARNEY

to delegate responsibility. I thoroughly enjoyed my term as president.

Looking back, the professional relationships I developed through my association with MAWL have helped advance my career by bringing referrals to me for prospective clients and by enabling me to confidently provide referrals to MAWL members for legal work that my clients require. I feel fortunate to consider many of the members of MAWL to be my friends. As a working mother, I have enjoyed much support and encouragement from other members, so many of whom are also working mothers with children of all ages. I was even able to bring my daughter, Juliette, to an occasional board meeting when I was unable to find a babysitter. You could say she has grown up in MAWL—she has attended our Annual Holiday Toast each year since she was two, and in 2009, at age seven, she assisted me in presenting the awards we bestowed upon the victim/witness advocates we recognized. I think the founders of this vibrant organization would agree that the "sisterly support" they envisioned is still present today in the Massachusetts Association of Women Lawyers.

Valerie A. Yarashus

Massachusetts Bar Association President, 2009–2010
Massachusetts Academy of Trial Attorneys President, 2002–2003

Working Together To Do More

The core mission of both bar associations for which I have served as president (the Massachusetts Bar Association and the Massachusetts Academy of Trial Attorneys) is helping to secure "justice for all." It is a theme that, to me, means we need to envision the common good as including all of us, in a way that is broader than we might otherwise be tempted to think. I have always believed that the unique function women trial lawyers can play in that mission is rooted in the struggle of generations of women to achieve justice for themselves in their communities, in the legal profession, and, even more specifically, in the

As a woman trial lawyer and a bar leader, I believe that by serving and sharing together, we can do far more than any of us can do alone.

courtroom. It is particularly true that we need the involvement of women (and men) who have acquired the kind of life experience and insights that come only from raising a family and practicing law at the same time. Trial lawyers have their own special role in preserving our justice system and in making it truly accessible to all. As a woman trial lawyer and a bar leader, I believe that by serving and sharing together, we can do far more than any of us can do alone.

Keeping in mind the importance of this mission has helped me to balance my personal and professional lives during the ten years I served in senior leadership positions of these bar associations, because I see it as a natural extension of the work I am trying to accomplish in order to benefit the next generation, which, of course, includes my own children.

My years as an MBA officer have also been woven together with the story of adopting two baby boys. At the time I submitted my papers to the nominating committee, I had two girls by birth—Sarah (then age nine) and Rachel (then six). When I was younger, I had always wanted a large family, but after two children I felt content with my family life as it was. In December 2004, when I was driving home from an MBA meeting (on the same day I had decided to run for an officer's position), I received a call from my mother, who lived in Maryland. She told me that one of our teenage relatives was pregnant and that she wanted to know if I would adopt the baby. My first reaction, without hesitation, was to scream "yes." I quickly remembered that I would need to talk with my husband before giving a final answer.

Ultimately, that adoption did not work out, but in the process I realized that I wanted more children. I took some time to reflect on the reasons I was so excited about the prospect of adoption; I thought about my vision of "family" and realized that it was more inclusive than I had been envisioning. After speaking with a domestic adoption agency and doing some research, I learned that there were many more African-American babies available for adoption than there were prospective families at that time. Instantly, I knew that this was what I wanted to do. I thought about all of my beliefs about diversity, the nature of family, and the positive (and negative) directions of our society in dealing with people of color. Just before Labor Day in 2005 (the month I began my term as an MBA officer), I contacted the adoption agency and indicated that I had an approved homestudy (necessary for adoption)

Valerie A. Yarashus with her family in September 2009 at the Massachusetts Bar Association President's Reception.

IMAGE COURTESY OF VALERIE A. YARASHUS

Women Presidents of the Massachusetts Bar Association

Alice E. Richmond	1986–1987
Elaine M. Epstein	1992–1993
Kay H. Hodge	1994–1995
Marylin A. Beck	1997–1998
Carol A.G. DiMento	2001–2002
Kathleen M. O'Donnell	2004–2005
Valerie A. Yarashus	2009–2010
Denise Squillante	2010–2011

completed and that I was interested in adopting an African-American baby boy at birth. Within a week, I was matched with a birth mother from Texas, and on September 26, Daniel was born.

The following November, we placed an application for a second African-American baby boy, and on the day before Thanksgiving, in 2006 (a few months into my second term as an officer), we learned that we were chosen by a birth mother who was in labor at a hospital in Kansas City, Missouri. Benjamin was born later that day. The first week after his birth was very frightening because he was born with severe medical issues. Although it sounded to some people like a situation to avoid, my overriding thought was, "If we can't do it, who can?" We already knew that we were loving, experienced parents and we had the family support and resources to handle a baby with medical issues. So we traveled to Kansas City and spent the first eight weeks of his life living at the Ronald McDonald house next to Children's Mercy Hospital on a tag-team schedule. My husband and I alternated every other week so that Ben was never alone in the hospital and one of us was always with the other three children back in Massachusetts. Saturday was our "swap day" when we would switch, with our airplanes usually in the air at the same time. Finally, after eight weeks on a ventilator, Ben was growing stronger and was finally cleared for air travel. The bar association work went on uninterrupted and I was able to keep up with everything that was time sensitive.

The time away from our other children was difficult, but they understood that we had a commitment to each of them and were able to see it in a larger context. After I returned home, Sarah (then eleven) told me that adopting her brothers was the best thing we'd ever done together as a family. Rachel feels the same way, and I agree wholeheartedly. Occasionally, someone who doesn't have any experience with adoption will remark to me about how fortunate the boys are to have such a great, loving home. Anyone with experience in adoption will know that my sons have already been more of a blessing to me than I could ever be to them. It is also absolutely clear to me that the love I feel for each of my children is exactly the same, although they came into my life in different ways.

A few years ago, I separated from my husband and divorced on an amicable basis (also during my term as an officer at the MBA, but not in any way because of it). He continues to live in the same town and we share parenting responsibilities. I completed my term as president of the MBA in 2010 when my children were ages fifteen, eleven, five, and three—high school to preschool. I feel incredibly fortunate to have been able to balance a successful

Valerie Yarashus presenting Chief Justice Margaret H. Marshall with the MBA's Edward F. Hennessey Award in October 2009.

IMAGE COURTESY OF VALERIE A. YARASHUS

career as a trial lawyer, a mother, and a bar leader. Whenever possible, I try to bring the kids to bar events and let them know how I have chosen to spend my time to try to contribute to the larger community. I have always believed that an important part of role modeling is to show our children that we love our profession and that we find meaning in life through helping others. Although I aspire to be the best trial lawyer I can be, I have never been a workaholic, and I believe that I am able to represent my clients better because of it. I think that this is true both because I have time for creativity that I would not experience if I were burned out and because I have a full and satisfying life that allows me to put things in perspective when I need to connect with jurors (or anyone else in the legal profession). Fortunately, the work I do as a plaintiff's personal injury trial lawyer is judged on results, not billable time, and so I have found that, throughout my bar leadership, I have been able to provide better representation to clients because of my bar association experience and the professional relationships I formed during that time. I look back on the thousands of hours I have devoted to service in the bar and hope it has made a difference. Although I am looking forward to many more evenings at home, I feel that the example I have given to all four of my children—finding meaning in life by contributing to larger issues and helping others through our profession—is one of the most important values that I can pass on to them, and ultimately to the next generation.

I feel that the example I have given to all four of my children—finding meaning in life by contributing to larger issues and helping others through our profession—is one of the most important values that I can pass on to them, and ultimately to the next generation.

Valerie Yarashus, her daughters, and Denise Squillante. When outgoing MBA President Yarashus handed the gavel to incoming President Squillante, it was the first time in the association's history that the presidency was passed from one woman to another.

IMAGE COURTESY OF VALERIE A. YARASHUS

Hon. Barbara M. Hyland

Hampden County Bar Association President, 2010–2011

A Sense of Community

In the 1980s, I was teaching grade school children and attending law school in the evening. In an incoming law school class of 100 at Western New England College School of Law, there were fewer than twenty-five women. This was my first introduction to competing academically in an outnumbered environment. However, I am pleased to say my male and female law school colleagues were supportive of each other. The law school experience instilled in me a sense of community. What struck me most was that I did not have one woman law school professor in my first or second years of law school. Was this the way it was going to be?

Women Presidents of the Hampden County Bar Association since its 1864 founding

Judith A. Cross	1985–1986
(Hon.) Patricia M. Dunbar	1996–1997
Carol Kantany Casartello	2000–2001
Mary J. Kennedy	2003–2004
(Hon.) Barbara M. Hyland	2010–2011

I graduated from law school in 1983 and entered the legal profession in western Massachusetts. I was in search of the same sense of community I had felt in law school. I think it was more difficult for the male lawyers in practice over twenty years than for me. I came from a law school cocoon of encouraging friends and colleagues. That was my expectation, and I found that it was right and wrong at the same time. I didn't understand what the expectations would be of a well-established male bar. I could count on one hand the number of woman lawyers in Holyoke.

I was also in search of mentors. I was luckier than most in finding both male and female mentors, lawyers who would spend their valuable time with me. That is what I recall most: a welcoming and supportive local bar. I had found my community. I did encounter more than one "older" male practitioner who would call me "dear" or "honey," and I was at first offended, then amused. I recall an attempt to defuse this by once saying, "Although you are old enough to be my grandfather, I am not your granddaughter." Remarkably, I received a quick apology and then a quick denial that there was any way he could be old enough to be my grandfather! Perhaps not. He later said he would be proud to have a granddaughter who entered the legal profession.

In 1983, Judge Ann M. Gibbons, then a District Court judge, started a dinner group for woman lawyers. We met regularly in Holyoke, Northampton, and Springfield. There are about five of us who still get together several times each year for dinner. Two of these women are my best friends. Judge Gibbons, now retired, remains my mentor and close friend. These women supported me, encouraged me, befriended me, and answered my questions, giving me yet another community. I hope I can one day be a mentor and friend to other young lawyers starting in my profession.

Hon. Barbara M. Hyland

IMAGE COURTESY OF HAMPDEN COUNTY BAR ASSOCIATION

I was only the fifth woman to become president of the Hampden County Bar Association in its almost 150-year existence.

Where else do you go to be supported, encouraged, and feel part of a special community? I went to my local bar associations. I was encouraged to join the Holyoke Bar Association and the Hampden County Bar Association in my first year of practice. Both are voluntary bar associations. I owe a debt to the people who encouraged this membership.

These local bar associations give you an immediate network. What is more important than community? I was recruited to participate in the Hampden County Bar Association as a board member five years ago. I found my name on the ballot for election. At my first meeting I was elected treasurer. I spent three years as treasurer, one year as president-elect, and one year as president. I was only the fifth woman to become president of the Hampden County Bar Association in its almost 150-year existence. Three of us sat together the evening I was sworn in as president. The biggest change, though, is the fact that I began my participation as a board member on the leadership track. This is thanks to the men and women of the bar association. Interestingly, of the four western Massachusetts counties, three had women bar association presidents the year I was elected.

The bar association resulted in my greater commitment to the legal community of which I was a part. I participated in many activities and committees. Two are most significant. The first is the Probate and Family Court bench bar committee, and the second is the New Lawyers Section. I had been practicing over twenty years when I became a board member—certainly not a new lawyer, though I remembered what it was like to be a new lawyer. I find this group to be the best of the bar association. What is more important than a start in the profession that I love and admire? The New Lawyers Section members give me a new reason to commit to my community. The energy, the dynamic, the support—it's community at its best. I enjoy every opportunity to participate with the new lawyers. Maybe that is also the reason I so enjoyed my time as chair of the Probate and Family Court Bench Bar Committee. This is a much smaller community of Probate and Family Court practitioners. It was the support of this special community that led to my application for a judicial position in that same court. I was sworn in as an associate justice of the Probate and Family Court on January 28, 2011. I have found yet another supportive and encouraging legal community.

NOTES

1 The introduction to this chapter was adapted in part from *Legal Chowder: Lawyering and Judging in Massachusetts* (MCLE, Inc. 1st ed. 2002).

2 Front row, seated (L to R): Joel M. Reck, Richard W. Renehan, William F. Looney, Jr., Edward J. Barshak, Kathy B. Weinman, Joan A. Lukey, and Raymond H. Young. Middle row (L to R): Lisa C. Goodheart, Joseph L. Kociubes, Richard A. Soden, James J. Marcellino, Donald R. Frederico, Mary K. Ryan, Hon. Edward P. Leibensperger, Lena G. Goldberg, Lauren Stiller Rikleen, Hon. Margaret H. Marshall, Gene D. Dahmen. Back Row (L to R): James. D. Smeallie, Richard M. Page, Jr., Jack Cinquegrana, Edward I. Masterman, Gary A. Spiess, Tony Doniger, Tom Dwyer, Wm. Shaw McDermott, Michael Keating, Jack Regan, and Sandra L. Jesse.

Conclusion

This book celebrates the achievements of women judges and lawyers of the past 130 years. It is both sobering and vital to remember that Lelia J. Robinson was not admitted to the Massachusetts bar until 1882, and that her initial attempt to join the bar was actually thwarted by the Supreme Judicial Court. The all-women Portia Law School opened in 1908, and in 1929, nearly 30 percent of all women law students in the nation attended Portia. The Massachusetts Association of Women Lawyers was established in 1905, Massachusetts women gained suffrage in 1920, and the first two women judges in Massachusetts were appointed in 1930. Harvard Law School, the last all-male law school in the state, accepted its first women in 1950, the same year women were finally permitted to serve as jurors. For decades, women remained a small minority in the legal profession—in 1959, only twelve women were admitted to the Massachusetts bar—and in 1960, women constituted less than 4 percent of the nation's lawyers. Progress was slow.

With the inspiration of the women's rights movement, the legal profession and the law have been transformed over the last fifty years. Today, half of new lawyers are women. In Massachusetts, women constitute a majority of all assistant district attorneys, assistant attorneys general, public defenders, and legal services attorneys. As of the writing of this book, Boston University, Harvard, Northeastern, Suffolk, and University of Massachusetts law schools all have female deans. The Massachusetts attorney general, United States attorney, and federal defender are women. The number of women judges in Massachusetts state courts has exploded, from 13 in 1977 to 144 in 2012. Seven women have been appointed to the Massachusetts Supreme Judicial Court since 1977 when Justice Ruth I. Abrams was appointed, and Margaret H. Marshall served as chief justice of that court from 1999 to 2010. Women are a force on the federal bench as well. Rya W. Zobel became the first federal District Court judge in Massachusetts in 1979, and Sandra L. Lynch became the first woman chief judge of the U.S. Court of Appeals for the First Circuit in 2008.

While progress has been slower and harder for minority women, there has been considerable progress on that front too. In 2009, Carmen M. Ortiz became the first woman and the first Hispanic United States attorney in Massachusetts. In 2010, O. Rogeriee Thompson became the first African-American woman to serve on the U.S. Court of Appeals for the First Circuit and Denise Jefferson Casper became the first on the U.S. District Court for the District of Massachusetts. In 2011, Fernande R.V. Duffly became the first Asian American (and first Asian-American woman) appointed to the Supreme Judicial Court.

As chronicled in this book, women lawyers in Massachusetts have used their skills in both the political and legal arenas to transform our substantive law in many areas, including employment discrimination, marriage and divorce, child custody, reproductive rights and technology, domestic violence, and sexual assault.

These strides must be considered, though, in light of the slower progress of women in the private bar, particularly at the partnership level in large firms. Although women constitute half of new associates at large firms, they lag behind in achieving an equity stake and even further behind in assuming leadership roles. Simply placing sufficient numbers of women in the law firm "pipeline" has not fixed the imbalance. The relative paucity of women in the private sector at senior levels and the preponderance of women in the nonprofit and public sectors raises important questions. As then-dean of Harvard Law School (now associate justice of the United States Supreme Court) Elena Kagan noted in 2006, "[i]t is intriguing to consider whether women see public interest work not only as more personally fulfilling but also as more open to them—more likely to provide opportunities for advancement and recognition, more prone to generate mutually appreciative relationships, more flexible regarding leave-taking and reentry."

Many of the personal reflections contained in this book discuss the struggles, trade-offs, and acrobatics involved in scaling the "maternal wall." From the days of the earliest women lawyers, professional advancement has often been limited by the personal choices women must make in order to balance career and caretaking. Women lawyers with young children confront particularly daunting demands: some have opted out of the profession at least temporarily; some have chosen to work part-time; some have changed jobs; some juggle day-by-day.

This book celebrates the tremendous progress of women lawyers, even as we acknowledge that progress has been uneven and imperfect. Perplexing questions and difficult challenges remain. We hope that future generations of women lawyers will remember the many women on whose shoulders they stand and draw inspiration, courage, and confidence from their many struggles and successes.

PATTI B. SARIS
MARGOT BOTSFORD
BARBARA F. BERENSON

JUNE 30, 2012

Table of Authorities

Page numbers containing "f," "n," or "t" refer to figures, notes, or tables, respectively.

CASES

FEDERAL

MASSACHUSETTS

Index

Page numbers containing "f," or "t" refer to figures or tables, respectively.

D